Two week loan

Please return on or before the last
date stamped below.
Charges are made for late return.

INFORMATION SERVICES PO BOX 430, CARDIFF CF10 3XT

Cavendish
Publishing
Limited

London • Sydney • Portland, Oregon

CORPORATE AND PERSONAL INSOLVENCY LAW

Second Edition

Fiona Tolmie

School of Law, Kingston University

Cavendish
Publishing
Limited

London • Sydney • Portland, Oregon

Second edition first published in Great Britain 2003 by
Cavendish Publishing Limited, The Glass House,
Wharton Street, London WC1X 9PX, United Kingdom
Telephone: + 44 (0)20 7278 8000   Facsimile: + 44 (0)20 7278 8080
Email: info@cavendishpublishing.com
Website: www.cavendishpublishing.com

Published in the United States by Cavendish Publishing
c/o International Specialized Book Services,
5824 NE Hassalo Street, Portland,
Oregon 97213-3644, USA

Published in Australia by Cavendish Publishing (Australia) Pty Ltd
3/303 Barrenjoey Road, Newport, NSW 2106, Australia

© Tolmie, Fiona	2003
First edition	1998
Second edition	2003

The first edition of this book was first published by Sweet & Maxwell Ltd as
Introduction to Corporate and Personal Insolvency Law.

British Library Cataloguing in Publication Data
Tolmie, Fiona M
Corporate and personal insolvency law – 2nd ed
1 Bankruptcy – England 2 Bankruptcy – Wales
I Title II Introduction to individual and corporate insolvency law
346.4'2'078

Library of Congress Cataloguing in Publication Data
Data available

ISBN 1-85941-772-8

1 3 5 7 9 10 8 6 4 2

Printed and bound in Great Britain

Dedicated to Andrew, Isabel and Tom

PREFACE

This is the second edition of a work first published in 1998; such has been the pace of change in the last five years that many portions of it have had to be almost entirely rewritten. There have been, or are about to be, major developments affecting most sections of this book. The changes have been caused both by statute (including the Welfare Reform and Pensions Act 1999, the Insolvency Act 2000, the European Council Regulation on Insolvency Proceedings 2000, the Limited Liability Partnerships Act 2000 and the Enterprise Act 2002) and as a result of the considerable volume of case law (particularly *Re Brumark*). As a consequence, changes have been made or are planned to company administration orders, voluntary arrangements and bankruptcy; administrative receivership is on its way to being abolished. Changes have also been made both to the assets which are available to creditors in a bankruptcy and to the order of distribution in both bankruptcy and liquidation. There have been major developments in the areas of disqualification of directors, funding of litigation by officeholders and cross-border insolvency within Europe. The impact of the human rights legislation has been felt in a number of areas of insolvency law. The Department of Trade and Industry has indicated a wish to address the issue of over-indebtedness more generally; this has prompted an expansion in the relevant areas of this text.

There is yet more change on the way; detailed implementation of the provisions of the Enterprise Act 2002 will happen over the next couple of years as well as new company legislation (which is likely to include radical change in relation to the registration of security over personalty), amendments to the Transfer of Undertakings Regulations and changes to civil enforcement procedures. Reform of the county court administration procedure and consequential reform of bankruptcy is possible. Although the law referred to in the text was up to date as at Easter 2003, things are likely to have moved on even by the time the book reaches the bookshops. Readers are recommended to bear in mind the need to consult the websites of the Insolvency Service (www.insolvency.gov.uk) and the newly-named Department of Constitutional Affairs (www.lcd.gov.uk) and to look at recent case law. Relevant articles are particularly likely to be found in the Insolvency Lawyer, Insolvency Intelligence, Tolley's Insolvency Law and Practice, the Company Lawyer and the Journal of Business Law; the sprawling nature of insolvency law means, however, that material might also be found in almost any legal journal.

The aim of this book remains to provide a book on both corporate and personal insolvency within the price range of students. The intention is to provide a basic framework of knowledge of the current legal rules (which will also be useful for those meeting the area in practice) and an introduction to the underlying issues, with signposts to sources of additional material; as with the first edition, it is not designed to provide my students with an escape from wider and deeper research, rather to facilitate it. Insolvency law is a particularly appropriate topic of study for students on cross-disciplinary law and business courses and for that reason, this book does not assume much prior knowledge of property law and attempts to provide an introduction to the necessary concepts.

Fiona Tolmie
School of Law, Kingston University
July 2003

CONTENTS

PART IV: MAINTAINING PUBLIC CONFIDENCE

PART V: THE CREDITORS' BATTLE FOR THE ASSETS

PART VI: AN INTRODUCTION TO ISSUES OF CROSS-BORDER INSOLVENCY

TABLE OF CASES

CHAPTER 1

INTRODUCTION

1 INTRODUCTION TO INSOLVENCY LAW

Insolvency can be defined broadly as the inability to meet one's debts either because of a lack of available cash at the relevant time[1] or, more fundamentally, because total liabilities exceed the assets which can be made available to meet them. Insolvency is something which will have to be dealt with by any society which recognises the use of credit; as soon as society provides the ability to commit to the future performance of an obligation, it provides the chance that performance will not be possible at that future time. Even if society could prevent the voluntary incurring of future obligations, there would still be imposed obligations such as tort damages and tax which some might find impossible to meet.

As the Cork Committee[2] recognised: 'the roots of insolvency law are embedded deep in our legal, social and economic history. It has always been recognised that the topic is one which touches on most aspects of commercial law, in the sense that there is always a risk that all mercantile contracts may at one time or another fall to be investigated by the Bankruptcy Courts.'[3]

The Cork Report further observed[4] that 'the law of insolvency takes the form of a compact to which there are three parties: the debtor, his creditors and society'. Any system which is to cope with the consequences of an insolvency has to bear in mind the interests of these three parties. The debtor is concerned to be relieved from the harassment of his or her creditors and to be able to make a fresh start, preferably without having to undergo the rigours of a formal insolvency regime. The creditors want to recoup as much as possible of what they are owed and will be concerned about the division between themselves of the available assets. This question of the distribution of the insolvent's assets clearly raises fundamental issues of priority as between the various creditors and also, in the case of an individual insolvent, of the conflict between the debtor's dependants and creditors. Society as a whole is concerned that commercial morality should be maintained; the system should not favour the debtor to such an extent that there is no incentive for debtors to meet their obligations. Insolvency law has always had to grapple with the question of the extent to which those unable to pay their debts should be treated as culpable or as merely unfortunate.

The balance between the interests of these three parties is a fundamental issue of policy. Where the insolvent is an individual, it is clear that rehabilitation of the debtor must be an aim of the law, although there is scope for debate about the extent to which the creditors must lose out in order to leave the debtor with sufficient assets to achieve that aim. In the case of a corporate debtor, there is not the same unarguable need to

---

1   This is often referred to as a cashflow or liquidity problem.
2   Report of the Review Committee on Insolvency Law and Practice, 1982, Cmnd 8558, hereinafter 'the Cork Report'. See Chapter 2 for an explanation of the importance of this Report in shaping current insolvency legislation.
3   At para 30.
4   At para 192.

achieve a rescue of either the legal person or the business entity; this is demonstrated by a comparison of the differing degrees to which the 'rescue culture' has become embedded in insolvency laws throughout the world. In the United States, for example, the balance is in favour of the debtor at the expense of the creditors, whereas in the UK, the converse has traditionally been the case.

The Cork Committee stated[5] the following extensive list of the aims of a good modern insolvency law:

(a) to recognise that the world in which we live and the creation of wealth depend upon a system founded on credit[6] and that such a system requires, as a correlative, an insolvency procedure to cope with its casualties;

(b) to diagnose and treat an imminent insolvency at an early rather than a late stage;[7]

(c) to relieve and protect where necessary the insolvent, and in particular the individual insolvent, from any harassment and undue demands by his creditors,[8] whilst taking into consideration the rights which the insolvent (and, where an individual, his family)[9] should legitimately continue to enjoy; at the same time, to have regard to the rights of creditors whose own position may be at risk because of the insolvency;

(d) to prevent conflicts between individual creditors;[10]

(e) to realise the assets of the insolvent which should properly be taken to satisfy his debts, with the minimum of delay and expense;[11]

(f) to distribute the proceeds of the realisations amongst the creditors in a fair and equitable manner, returning any surplus to the debtor;[12]

(g) to ensure that the processes of realisation and distribution are administered in an honest and competent manner;[13]

(h) to ascertain the causes of the insolvent's failure and, if and so far as his conduct or, in the case of a company, the conduct of its officers or agents, merits criticism or punishment, to decide what measures, if any, require to be taken against him or his associates, or such officers or agents;[14]

(i) to recognise that the effects of insolvency are not limited to the private interests of the insolvent and his creditors, but that other interests of society or other

---

5   At para 198.

6   This is considered further in Chapter 3 below.

7   Part II of this text is concerned with 'rescue' procedures.

8   See Chapters 8 (relating to county court administration) and 9 (on individual voluntary arrangements) for the circumstances in which a debtor may be protected from creditors in the course of a 'rescue'. See Chapter 25 for the stay on proceedings brought about by a liquidation or bankruptcy.

9   See Chapter 27 on the bankrupt's home, income and pension.

10 See Part V generally on the battle between the creditors.

11 See Chapters 26–29.

12 See Chapter 34.

13 See Chapter 20 on the control of the insolvency system.

14 See Chapter 21 on investigation of the insolvent, Chapter 22 on sanctions in bankruptcy and Chapter 23 on preventing the abuse of limited liability.

groups in society are vitally affected by the insolvency and its outcome, and to ensure that these public interests are recognised and safeguarded;[15]

(j)   to provide means for the preservation of viable commercial enterprises capable of making a useful contribution to the economic life of the country;[16]

(k)   to devise a framework of law for the governing of insolvency matters which commands universal respect and observance, and yet is sufficiently flexible to adapt to and deal with the rapidly changing conditions of our modern world;

(l)   to ensure due recognition and respect abroad for English insolvency proceedings.[17]

There are those who would argue that such an ambitious list is doomed to failure and that insolvency law should restrict itself to dealing with the distribution of the assets of an insolvent. This is a debate which has largely taken place between American academics,[18] with Professor Jackson[19] as a leading proponent of the more restrictive view and Professor Warren[20] advancing the case of those with other interests. Professor Jackson, who sees the purpose of insolvency law as debt collection, argues that the purpose of insolvency law is the co-ordination of the claims of creditors in order to enhance the value of the debtor's assets for all claimants. He says that insolvency law should guarantee the claimants in total at least as much as they would in total have received by individual enforcement of their claims; this has been described as the 'common pool' philosophy. Professor Warren, on the other hand, advances the case for consideration of wider interests including those of employees, suppliers, customers, neighbours and government. She argues that the purpose of insolvency law is to provide a forum in which all interests can be heard. Professor Goode summarises and considers the debate from this side of Atlantic in the second edition of his *Principles of Corporate Insolvency;*[21] he finds Professor Warren convincing and Professor Jackson's arguments ultimately unpersuasive.

If insolvency law is to be concerned with all aspects of over-indebtedness rather than being narrowly focused on debt collection against those whose liabilities exceed their assets, then it could be argued that a further aim of providing discouragement to unreasonable or irresponsible risk-taking by both users and providers of credit should be added to the list set out by the Cork Committee. The stated aims of diagnosing and treating an imminent insolvency at an early rather than a late stage and ascertaining whether culpable behaviour has led to the insolvency (aims (b) and (h)) go some way in this direction, but are still in the 'cure' rather than the 'prevention' zone. It could perhaps be argued that such matters are the concern of those areas of the law relating to consumer credit, financial services and company law. Alternatively, this may simply

---

15   See Part IV generally.

16   See Part II generally.

17   See Chapter 35.

18   In recent years, more has been written on this side of the Atlantic. See, for example, Finch (1997) (see also Finch, 2002, Chapter 2); Keay (2001a); Mokal (2002).

19   Jackson, 1986; Jackson (1982); Baird and Jackson (1984); Baird and Jackson (1988); Jackson (1985).

20   Warren (1987) and see Professor Baird's reply: Baird (1987).

21   Goode, 1997, p 35 *et seq.* For another synopsis and discussion see Flessner, Chapter 2, in Ziegel, 1994. Some of the seminal US literature is conveniently collected in Bhandari and Weiss, 1996.

imprisonment put it beyond the debtor's ability to earn and the system was a drain on public expense, despite the supposed duty of the creditor to contribute to the cost of the debtor's imprisonment. In 1813, a Court for the Relief of Insolvent Debtors was established to provide a permanent way of addressing the problem. This introduced insolvency as a concept separate from bankruptcy and available to non-traders who, provided their debts were below a certain level, could petition the court for 'protection from process'. The court could make an interim order protecting the insolvent from legal process and from imprisonment at the suit of a creditor; a final order could be made where, on investigation, the court was satisfied that the insolvency had not arisen from fraud, breach of trust or from becoming indebted without reasonable assurance of being able to repay. This order would probably involve the vesting of the debtor's property in a trustee as well as provision for payment of the remaining debts from after-acquired income or earnings. The problem with this approach[18] was that requiring debtors to meet debts from subsequent income deprived them of any incentive to earn and could not be seen as rehabilitative.

In 1861, the bankruptcy laws were extended to cover non-traders and the Court for the Relief of Insolvent Debtors and the insolvency laws were abolished. These two parallel systems were about to be replaced by a different pair since, with the introduction of the limited liability company, many traders would in future incorporate their businesses. Whereas bankruptcy law was previously the system which dealt with insolvent businesses, that would become the concern of corporate insolvency law and bankruptcy law would deal largely with the non-trading insolvents previously excluded from its provisions.

One of the major issues of dispute during the 19th century was the question of who should control the insolvency process.

Parliament's first attempt at a thorough investigation of insolvency was a Select Committee set up in 1817–18. At this time, creditors had virtually full control over the administration of bankrupt estates since the commissioners in bankruptcy (who sat in conditions of extreme chaos) would appoint one or more creditors as assignees of the assets, theoretically under their supervision. Abuses of the system by both creditors and debtors were frequent.

In 1831, Brougham's Bankruptcy Act introduced the concept of official assignees; these were officers attached to the London Bankruptcy Court who would administer the estates. Both the new court and the system of official assignees gave rise to widespread dissatisfaction. The Court was abolished in 1847, the jurisdiction being transferred to the Chancery Court, and in 1869, control of the assets was transferred from the official assignees to the creditors at the insistence of the commercial community, who thought this would be a cheaper system. The principle of decision-making by a majority of the creditors had been introduced in 1844 and it soon became apparent that it was too easy for a minority of creditors and their advisors to manipulate the proceedings in their own interests through the use of proxies. The creditor-managed system was a particular failure in the case of small bankruptcies where the prospect of realisation was insufficient to engage the interest of the creditors. There was also disquiet at the absence of inquiry into the affairs of debtors who arranged a liquidation of their assets with the consent of their creditors; they obtained a full discharge without any judicial inquiry into their finances.

---

18   As a Royal Commission in 1840 pointed out.

The basis of the modern system was introduced by Joseph Chamberlain, the President of the Board of Trade, in the Bankruptcy Act 1883. He declared that the law had both to provide for the administration of the estates of those who were bankrupt and to act as a disincentive to behaviour leading to insolvency. There was a requirement for thorough and independent investigation into the causes of insolvency in the public interest rather than leaving matters in the hands of the creditors. Official Receivers, acting under the direction of the Board of Trade, were introduced. The system was intended to be self-financing through fees on bankruptcy petitions, a percentage payable on the assets collected and the interest on amounts collected in the course of the bankruptcy, which were to be paid into the Bank of England.

The provisions of the Bankruptcy Act 1883 lasted, in effect, for over a century until the passage of the Insolvency Act 1986. The Bankruptcy Act 1914 was mainly a measure of consolidation and tidying up. In 1908, the Muir Mackenzie Committee had reported general satisfaction with bankruptcy law and procedure, a view repeated by the Blagden Committee in 1955.

3   HISTORY OF CORPORATE INSOLVENCY

Bankruptcy law had developed well in advance of the introduction of the limited liability company. The Companies Acts contained their own provisions for the winding up of insolvent companies and, whilst the rules borrowed to an extent from the bankruptcy legislation, the two systems developed in parallel.

The Companies Act 1862 laid down the foundation on which subsequent legislation in relation to company winding up has been based. This provided for the possibilities of voluntary liquidation, winding up by court and winding up under the supervision of the court. The court with jurisdiction was the Chancery Court. The Companies (Winding Up) Act 1890 extended the 1883 bankruptcy innovation of the Official Receiver's investigatory role to companies. Together with the Directors Liability Act 1890, this was a package of legislation aimed at fraudulent and dishonest company promoters and directors. Complaints about malpractice by promoters and directors of companies remained (and remain) a constant theme of discussion of insolvency law. There were amendments to various aspects of corporate insolvency law in the Companies Acts of 1908, 1929 (which introduced the concept of the creditors voluntary liquidation) and 1947/1948.

Two separate branches of insolvency law had emerged; company liquidation and individual bankruptcy were generally dealt with by different courts and under different sets of procedural rules. The rules of bankruptcy law and corporate insolvency law were similar, but there were various differences of substance.

4   INSOLVENCY ACT 1986[19] AND SUBSEQUENT LEGISLATION

In 1973, on the UK's accession to the European Community, it became necessary to consider the EC Draft Bankruptcy Convention; in the course of its report, an advisory committee set up under the chairmanship of Kenneth Cork pointed to the need for

19   See Fletcher (1989); Carruthers and Halliday, 1998, pp 106–43.

revision of a number of areas of national insolvency law. The Justice Report on Bankruptcy in 1975 noted a number of problems highlighted by the recession of the early 1970s which led to small measures of reform in the Insolvency Act 1976; public examination was dispensed with in some cases and discharge made easier.

A further committee under the chairmanship of Sir Kenneth Cork was appointed in 1977 to review the law and practice relating to insolvency, to examine the possibility of harmonising and integrating the existing procedures, to suggest less formal procedures as alternatives to bankruptcy and liquidation and to make recommendations. The full, lengthy report was published in 1982. The Cork Committee identified a need for extensive change[20] in order to restore respect for the law of insolvency and to ensure that the solutions provided to situations of insolvency were as fair and equitable as could reasonably be achieved. In particular, they saw a need to simplify and modernise the existing law which they described as 'cumbersome, complex, archaic and over-technical' with a view to harmonising and integrating where possible the law and practice relating to companies and to individuals. They saw a need for the law to encourage, wherever possible, the continuation of businesses as a going concern with consequent preservation of jobs for at least some of the employees. In the case of an individual debtor, they considered it important to increase the possibility of claims being met out of future wages and income. They were concerned to improve the standard of administration of insolvent estates, to prevent abuse and to encourage the ordinary unsecured creditor to take a more active interest in the proceedings. They were concerned to increase the amount available for the ordinary creditors and to allay the prevalent dissatisfaction with the current distribution of the assets. They recommended relaxing the excessive severity of the law towards the individual insolvent, particularly where incompetent rather than dishonest, but increasing the severity of the law towards the director of the failed company who had acted irresponsibly. They observed that it was unfortunate that their terms of reference did not include a review of the general law of credit and security and remedies for debt enforcement.

After an initial slow response, the government, prompted by public dissatisfaction with insolvency law as it was seen to be operating during the recession of the early 1980s, brought forward legislation which incorporated some, but by no means all, of the suggestions of the Cork Report. The first attempt at legislation was the Insolvency Act 1985, but this never came into force since it was immediately superseded. The Insolvency Act 1986 and the Company Directors Disqualification Act 1986 together consolidated the Insolvency Act 1985 and sections of the Companies Act 1985 relating to company liquidation and receivership.

Debate about insolvency law, particularly about its role as part of the 'rescue culture', has continued intermittently throughout the 1990s[21] and the Insolvency Act 2000 has made a number of amendments to both the Insolvency Act 1986 and the Company Directors Disqualification Act 1986. The recently enacted Enterprise Act 2002 will, when it comes fully into force, make further radical amendments to the Insolvency Act 1986. The legislation is becoming ever less user-friendly with increasing amounts of the 'meat' of insolvency law to be found in the schedules to the

---

20   For a summary of their recommendations, see Chapter 52 of the Cork Report.
21   See Chapter 7.

Insolvency Act 1986 and in subordinate legislation, chiefly the Insolvency Rules 1986 as amended.

5   SUMMARY OF CURRENT INSOLVENCY REGIMES

(a) Personal insolvency processes

A bankruptcy order may be made in respect of an insolvent individual and will lead to the vesting of most of the bankrupt's assets in a trustee in bankruptcy for distribution amongst the bankrupt's creditors. During the period for which he or she is an undischarged bankrupt, the individual will be subject to certain legal disabilities and the background to the bankruptcy will be investigated. This process is fully explained in Chapter 15.

An individual may be able to avoid bankruptcy by entering into an individual voluntary arrangement, fully explained in Chapter 9, under which the individual may be released from some of the debts or given longer to pay or a combination of both. If the requisite majority of creditors agree, a minority of creditors can be bound by the agreement against their will. Another way of obtaining protection from creditors and avoiding bankruptcy is by obtaining a county court administration order, explained in Chapter 8. The Lord Chancellor's Department is currently carrying out research into the possibility of incorporating the current bankruptcy and county court administration processes within one unified structure; a report is expected in autumn 2003.

(b) Corporate insolvency processes

An insolvent company may decide to put itself into voluntary liquidation or may be ordered by the court to go into compulsory winding up. The terms 'liquidation' and 'winding up' are synonymous and are used interchangeably in this text. Voluntary liquidation is explained in Chapter 16 and compulsory liquidation in Chapter 17. In either case, a liquidator will be appointed with the responsibility to realise the company's assets and distribute them between the creditors. The conduct of those responsible for running the company's affairs in the period leading to the insolvency will be investigated. At the end of the liquidation process, the company is dissolved and ceases to exist. It is also possible, as explained in Chapter 19, for defunct companies to be struck off the register of companies without undergoing a formal liquidation procedure.

A company may be able to avoid a liquidation by entering into a company voluntary arrangement or by obtaining a company administration order giving it a moratorium against creditors whilst it attempts to put its finances in order. A small company can now obtain a moratorium by activating the process of negotiating a company voluntary arrangement. Company voluntary arrangements are explained in Chapter 9 and company administration orders in Chapter 10.

Administrative receivership is not strictly an insolvency process but a method whereby an individual corporate creditor has been able to enforce a floating charge over the whole undertaking. It is, however, subject to the insolvency legislation in some respects. As a result of the Enterprise Act 2002, administrative receiverships will eventually become a thing of the past. Chapter 6 contains a broad outline of administrative receivership.

6   STATISTICAL INFORMATION FOR 1999–2001

The statistics for county court administration orders are derived from the Judicial Statistics.[22] All other statistics are provided by the Insolvency Service.[23]

	1999	2000	2001
Personal insolvency procedures			
Bankruptcy orders	21,611	21,550	23,477
Individual voluntary arrangements	7,195	7,978	6,298
County court administration orders	8,720	7,916	7,548
Total personal insolvency proceedings	37,526	37,444	37,323
Corporate insolvency procedures			
Compulsory liquidations	5,209	4,925	4,675
Creditors' voluntary liquidations	9,071	9,392	10,297
Receiverships	1,618	1,595	1,914
Company administrations	440	438	698
Company voluntary arrangements	475	557	597
Total corporate insolvency proceedings	16,813	16,907	18,181

---

22   Available at www.lcd.gov.uk in the 'Judges and QCs' section.
23   Available at www.insolvency.gov.uk.

CHAPTER 3

THE CREDITORS

1 INTRODUCTION

This chapter examines the role of credit in society and identifies the main categories of contractual creditors in relation to both individual and business debtors. It goes on to provide a brief introduction to the mechanics of credit provision and then considers the ways in which a creditor can seek to enhance his or her chances of repayment by taking security. It must also be remembered that in any insolvency, there may also be amounts owing to non-contractual creditors; in particular, there may be unpaid tax and other duties, criminal penalties and civil damages.

2 THE ROLE OF CREDIT IN SOCIETY[1]

Credit was described as 'the lifeblood of the modern industrialised economy' and 'the cornerstone of the trading community' by the Cork Report.[2] The credit industry enables those who have money lying idle to make it available, in return for payment, to those who have a need for it. Businesses have always sought to raise capital in order to finance the production of the goods or services which will earn them profits; the ability to borrow that capital enables the business to grow faster than if it were solely dependent on the input from the owners' resources. As the scale of production increased with the Industrial Revolution, so did the need for capital. The 19th century saw great developments in the means by which such finance could be supplied;[3] this included an increase in the financing of commerce and industry by way of loans secured on the assets of the business.

Credit may be provided on a long term basis (by a fixed-term loan, for example) but much credit is provided on a short term basis, often as an integral part of a transaction of supply whereby the goods or services are supplied in advance of the requirement to pay for them. A business will hope to be able to obtain its supplies on credit so that it does not have to pay for them before being able to collect payment from its customers for the goods or services for which it has used the supplies. Many suppliers find themselves providing credit without their consent when their customers fail to pay them within the agreed period. The Late Payment of Commercial Debts (Interest) Act 1998,[4] which gives businesses a statutory right to claim interest from other businesses for the late payment of commercial debt and the right to claim a sum in debt recovery costs for each overdue bill, is intended to address this problem. In many cases, however, customers are likely to continue to

---

1 See, generally, the Crowther Report, 1971; Berthoud and Kempson, 1992; Ramsey, 1986; Howell *et al*, 1993.

2 At para 10.

3 See the description in Chapter 4 of the development of the limited liability company.

4 As amended in 2002 to implement EU Directive 2000/35/EC. See the website (www.payontime.co.uk) of the Better Payment Practice Group which was formed in 1997 as a partnership between the public and private sectors with the aim of improving the payment culture of the UK business community and reducing the incidence of late payment of commercial debt. See also Singleton (2002).

3 WHO ARE THE CREDITORS?

(a) Creditors of individuals

Credit industry membership of the Department of Trade and Industry Task Force on Overindebtedness gives a good indication of the main types of provider of credit to consumers: amongst the members are the British Bankers' Association,[14] the Council of Mortgage Lenders (whose members undertake around 98% of UK residential mortgage lending),[15] the Finance and Leasing Association (which describes[16] its members as providing asset finance to business, consumer credit, point of sale, credit card and instalment finance) and the Consumer Credit Association (representing providers of home credit).[17]

In 1995, bank loans formed 56% of total consumer credit, excluding mortgage borrowing, and bank credit card lending had risen from nearly 12% of consumer credit in 1981 to 21%. Credit card expenditure in 1995 amounted to £41.2 billion; there were nearly 30 million credit cards in issue at the end of that year and £15,920 million was outstanding on credit cards (out of a total outstanding consumer credit figure of £62,559 million). At the end of 2001, the figure outstanding on credit cards was £42,802 million (out of a total £98,355 million)[18] and in 2002,[19] it appeared that the most common form of consumer credit commitment (excluding mortgages) was credit cards, with goods bought on credit from mail order catalogues and cash loans being nearly as common. Hire-purchase and credit sale agreements were only slightly less common. Overdrafts and store cards were the least common forms. Mail order, overdrafts and store cards tended to involve low levels of credit whereas hire-purchase and loans tended to involve relatively high amounts of credit.

Unlike the position in some countries, credit unions have only a very small share (0.3%) of the UK credit market.[20] Credit unions are co-operative organisations which encourage their members to save regularly and enable them to borrow at lower interest rates than those which would be charged by other financial institutions. Membership is restricted to those who meet the common bond (for example, living in the same place, working for the same employer) on the basis that the members will know each other and will be able to exert moral pressure to ensure that loans are repaid. They are largely run by unpaid volunteers and provide a service to people who may have no dealings with the commercial banking sector.

The government is also a lender albeit to a relatively small proportion of the population. In *Lending Support: Modernising the Government's Use of Loans*, published by

---

14 Whose website can be found at www.bba.org.uk. The concomitant to the expansion of consumer credit has been the extension of the business of the banks from their traditional role of lending to commerce and industry into the personal lending market.

15 Their website (www.cml.org.uk) is a good source of further information.

16 On its website, www.fla.org.uk.

17 The Association describes (on its website, www.ccauk.org) home credit as providing for lower income consumers who require small cash loans or consumer goods on credit. Repayments are typically collected on a weekly basis from the customer's home.

18 Social Trends, 1997; Kempson, 2002.

19 Kempson, 2002.

20 See Ryder (2001a), (2001b); HM Treasury, 1999. The website of the Association of British Credit Unions may be found at www.abcul.org.

the Performance and Innovation Unit in March 2002,[21] it was noted that the government's use of loans has gradually increased over the last 15 years. Notable examples of recent loans schemes include the Social Fund in 1988 and student loans in 1990.

(b) Creditors of businesses[22]

Credit will often be provided on a long term basis by banks and other institutional lenders, but businesses will also seek to obtain a delay in the time at which they need to make payments of a revenue nature. Short term creditors are likely to include employees, who will usually be paid in arrears, and suppliers, who will often supply on credit terms either by way of a simple credit sale or through conditional sale, leasing or hire-purchase arrangements. Other commonly encountered creditors are landlords and utility suppliers. Customers who make pre-payments also supply credit to firms. The government may also be a creditor, perhaps because it has supplied finance from the Enterprise Fund or because there are direct or indirect tax payments owing.

Borrowing by small and medium-sized companies is dominated by banks, although the use of overdrafts seems to be declining and smaller businesses seem to be relying less on external funding. Hire-purchase and leasing firms are also often approached. Factoring, venture capitalists and trade customers play a fairly small part in the provision of credit to these companies.

4 MECHANISMS FOR THE PROVISION OF CREDIT AND THE TAKING OF SECURITY[23]

(a) Introduction

There are two basic mechanisms of credit provision recognised by the law: sales credit and loan credit.

Sales credit arises where the creditor leaves the price for goods or services outstanding but charges more (either expressly to the debtor or by raising the price of the goods to all customers) to cover the risk. The seller will also consider that the risk of default is offset by the greater volume of sales. Some forms of sales credit leave the seller with a proprietary claim to the goods being sold until payment has been received in full.

Loan credit consists of the lending of a sum of money in return for an agreement to return the money and to pay interest on the loan. Creditors are putting their money

---

21 Available at www.cabinet-office.gov.uk/innovation/2002/loans/report/default.htm. This report contains a considerable amount of interesting material on the government's use of lending and on credit and debt generally.

22 For a thorough survey of patterns and methods of corporate borrowing, see Finch, 2002, Chapter 3 and the materials referred to therein. Summaries of the ESRC Centre for Business Research, Cambridge papers are available from their website at www.cbr.cam.ac.uk. There is also useful information on the Bank of England website at www.bankofengland.co.uk and on the Small Business Service website, www.sbs.gov.uk.

23 See, generally, Goode, 1988 and 1995, Parts IV and V.

charge can exist only in equity[33] or by statute. A charge may be fixed, in which case it will attach to specific assets with which the chargor cannot then deal without the consent of the chargee, or floating,[34] in which case the chargee can continue to deal with the charged assets as if they were free of the charge until the charge crystallises. A floating charge will hover over a class of assets until it crystallises, at which point it will attach to the assets which the class contains at that time. Once a charge attaches to a specific asset, the chargor cannot dispose of the asset free of the charge without the chargee's consent. The provisions of the Bills of Sale legislation, which require specific details of all assets caught by the security, make it impossible for an individual to give a floating charge. The Bills of Sale legislation does not apply to companies who are, therefore, able to give valid floating security over the entirety of their undertaking. The only individuals able to give floating security are farmers who can give agricultural charges.[35]

Most forms of mortgage or charge require registration in order to bind third parties to whom the secured property may be transferred.[36] A number of different public registers are maintained for this purpose; for example, there are registers for mortgages and charges over land, ships and aircraft, for bills of sale and for charges granted by companies.

(b) Personal security: the guarantee[37]

A guarantee is an undertaking to answer for the default of another either by way of personal commitment or by the provision of real security or both. A guarantee is typically a unilateral contract under which the guarantor promises to provide the guarantee if the bank provides the credit but where the bank makes no promise to do so. A guarantee must be evidenced in writing.[38]

A guarantor can only be sued if the principal debtor defaults and the guarantor's obligation is enforceable only to the same extent as that of the debtor.[39] A guarantor will be discharged by an event which extinguishes the principal debtor's liability. In the absence of clear words to the contrary, the guarantor will be liable to the damages for which the principal debtor would be liable on failure to pay.[40]

A guarantor has an implied contractual right to be indemnified by a debtor at whose request the guarantee has been given. A guarantor who discharges the debt he or she has guaranteed is entitled to be subrogated to the creditor's rights against the debtor, including the right to enforce security. If the guarantor's rights against the

---

33 Since it requires neither conveyance nor assignment, it can only be given validity by the equitable notion that that which is agreed to be done shall be treated as having been done.

34 See Chapter 29 for a discussion of the case law on the distinction between fixed and floating charges.

35 Under the Agricultural Credits Act 1928.

36 The Law Commission (Consultation Paper No 164) has recommended a switch to a system of notice filing. See Chapter 29 below.

37 See Goode, 1995, Chapter 30.

38 This is one of the few remaining provisions of the Statute of Frauds 1677, s 4. If it secures a regulated agreement under the Consumer Credit Act 1974, it must actually be in writing.

39 This may be contrasted with an indemnity which is a primary obligation with an existence independent of the contract between the lender and the principal debtor.

40 *Moschi v Lep Air Services Ltd* [1973] AC 331.

debtor are adversely affected by the creditor's conduct, the guarantor will usually be discharged from his or her obligations.

Lenders will frequently seek a guarantee of the borrower's obligations from a third party. Groups of companies often provide cross-guarantees of each other's indebtedness. Directors of small companies may be asked to guarantee the company's obligations.

6 THE DISTINCTION BETWEEN A SECURED LOAN AND SALE CREDIT[41]

Sale credit has always been regarded by the law as distinct from loan credit and has been the subject of different common law rules. For example, until the passing of the Consumer Credit Act 1974, which equates the two forms of credit with regard to transactions below a certain limit entered into by individuals, the legislation regulating money lending did not apply to forms of sale credit. A major consequence of this distinct treatment is that retention of title under sale credit is not regarded as a security interest for the purposes of registration.[42] It is also possible to raise finance whilst strictly avoiding becoming party to a loan; one such means available to businesses is factoring or invoice discounting. This involves selling the amounts owing from customers to a finance house in return for an immediate cash payment from which is deducted an administration charge. The discount is so calculated that the effect is the same as if the finance house had made the business an interest-bearing loan. In some cases, the finance house also collects the amounts owing, but it is also possible that the business may collect as agent for the finance house and the customer may not have any knowledge of the arrangement. In some cases, the finance house will bear the risk of bad debts, but in others the business will retain the risk.

There are situations in which someone in need of credit may be restricted, by statute or otherwise, from taking a loan; this restriction would not prevent the achievement of the same end through the mechanism of sale credit.[43] Businesses may also seek to structure their acquisition of finance in the way most favourable to their accounting records; increasingly, however, accountants are being required to have regard to the economic rather than the legal substance of transactions.

The courts have frequently been faced with the need to decide whether or not a particular transaction is a loan with security, generally in connection with the question of whether registration was necessary for the validity of the transaction. The Court of

---

41 See, generally, Diamond, 1988. Amongst the many articles on this topic and the need for reform are Goode (1984); Diamond (1989); Lawson (1989); Bridge (1992a); Ziegel (1995); Berg (2003).

42 This will change if the recommendations of the Law Commission Consultation Paper No 164 (2002) are accepted; see below.

43 See, for example, the background to the case of *Darlington BC v Wiltshier Northern* [1995] 3 All ER 895, where the council needed finance to build a recreation centre but was subject to government borrowing restrictions. Instead of lending the authority the money needed to pay the builders, the bank contracted with the builders and subsequently sold the benefit of the contract to the council.

Appeal in *Welsh Development Agency v Export Finance Co Ltd*[44] held that the court must look at the legal substance of a transaction and not at the labels which the parties have chosen to put on it. The court is not, however, to look beyond the legal form of the transaction to its economic effect. The court may decide that the transaction is not what it purports to be because it is a sham intended to mask the true agreement of the parties. Where the agreement is not a sham, it may still fail to fall into the legal category into which the parties have sought to put it because its provisions are inconsistent with the legal nature of such a transaction.

The courts have found it difficult to arrive at any precise distinction between transactions of sale and transactions by way of security. Romer LJ set out what he regarded as the essential differences between a sale and a mortgage or charge in *Re George Inglefield Ltd*.[45] Firstly, in a transaction of sale, the vendor is not entitled to get back the subject matter of the sale by returning to the purchaser the money which has passed between them. A mortgagor, on the other hand, is entitled until foreclosure to get back the subject matter of the mortgage by returning the money. Secondly, if the mortgagee sells the subject matter of the mortgage for a sum more than sufficient to repay him or her, he or she must account to the mortgagor, whereas a purchaser may keep the profit on a sub-sale. Thirdly, if mortgagees sell the property for less than the amount needed to repay them, they may still claim the balance from the mortgagor, whereas if purchasers resell for less than they paid, they cannot recoup the loss from the vendor. A transaction need not, however, bear all three indicia to fall into a particular category. Dillon LJ in *Welsh Development Agency v Export Finance Co Ltd* said that: 'In my judgment there is no one clear touchstone by which it can necessarily and inevitably be said that a document which is not a sham and which is expressed as an agreement for sale must necessarily, as a matter of law, amount to no more than the creation of a mortgage or charge on the property expressed to be sold.'

The agreement in the *Welsh Development* case is an example of the type of transaction which sits very close to the borderline between sale and security. A company whose business involved the sale of computer disks to overseas buyers raised finance by selling the disks to Export Finance Co ('Exfinco') before selling them, as agent for Exfinco, to the overseas buyers. Exfinco would pay the company 90% of the price payable by the overseas buyer, less a discount fixed at the time of the transaction, which was to be adjusted later by reference to the time which it took all overseas buyers to pay what they owed. The agreement also provided that on giving three months' notice, the company would be liable to pay to Exfinco a sum equal to all amounts owed by overseas buyers and thereupon all rights in the goods and the debts of the overseas buyers would be relinquished in favour of the company. The company had also given a floating charge over all its assets to the Welsh Development Agency who claimed that Exfinco's interest in the disks only amounted to a charge, which was void for non-registration, to secure the money it had advanced to the company. They argued that the discount was really an interest payment and that there was a right of redemption. The Court of Appeal held that none of the features which the Welsh Development Agency relied on was necessarily inconsistent with a contract of sale, although they would more usually be found in a contract to lend money. At the same

---

44 [1992] BCC 270. See also *Orion Finance Ltd v Crown Financial Management Ltd* [1996] 2 BCLC 78. *Lavin v Johnson* [2002] EWCA Civ 1138 is a recent Court of Appeal decision on a similar point.
45 [1933] Ch 1.

time, it was plainly intended that Exfinco would have the rights and remedies of a seller of goods against the overseas buyers, should it find it necessary to exercise them. The description of the transaction as a sale, although not conclusive, could not be ignored.

There is considerable criticism of the artificiality of the distinctions which the courts are forced to make and which would in most cases be unnecessary if the legal consequences of the transactions were determined by their purpose rather than by their form. The Law Commission has now recommended[46] that English law move away from the current system of registration of charges over property other than land to a system of notice filing along the lines of that contained in Art 9 of the Uniform Commercial Code in the United States and that this should be extended to include quasi-security devices such as retention of title. This would reduce considerably the circumstances in which there would be any need to identify whether or not a given transaction included the giving of true security or not.

---

46   Law Commission Consultation Paper No 164 (2002). See McCormack (2002).

(c) Sole traders

Sole trader is the term used for an individual who is in business by him or herself. He or she will be personally liable, without limit, for the liabilities of that business. Research into reasons for business failure is considered at the end of this chapter.

(d) Guarantors of insolvent companies

Individuals who have guaranteed the liabilities of an insolvent company will have unlimited liability to the extent of the amount guaranteed. A survey by the Society of Practitioners of Insolvency published in July 1997 found that 14% of the non-business individual insolvencies considered by the survey had resulted from the giving of guarantees.[13]

3 PARTNERSHIPS[14]

Partnership is the relationship between two or more persons carrying on business in common with a view to profit.[15] The relationship between the partners is governed by contract and agency law, codified to a great extent in the Partnership Act 1890. In England and Wales, a partnership is not a separate legal entity although procedural rules allow litigation to be brought by and against the partners in the firm name. Property brought into the partnership stock or acquired on account of the firm or for the purposes and in the course of the partnership business will be partnership property to be held and applied by the partners exclusively for the purposes of the partnership and in accordance with the partnership agreement.[16] The issue of whether particular property is partnership property or the property of an individual partner will be of great importance as between the creditors of the firm and the creditors of the individual partners in the event of insolvency.

In most cases, partners will be jointly liable without limit for the debts of the partnership.[17] A joint obligation is one owed by two or more persons together so that anyone bringing a claim to enforce the obligation must sue them all. Where the obligation is joint and several, the claimant may choose to sue them all together or one or more of them individually; partners are severally as well as jointly liable for loss or injury caused to a third party by wrongful acts or omissions of the firm or by its misapplication of funds.[18]

Section 17 of the Partnership Act 1890 provides that a person who is admitted as a partner into an existing firm does not thereby become liable to the creditors of the firm for anything done before he or she became a partner and that a partner who leaves the firm does not thereby cease to be liable for partnership debts or obligations incurred

---

13 In the 9th Survey of Personal Insolvency (relating to 1999), the figure was 5%.
14 See, generally, Morse, 2001.
15 A partnership has no separate legal personality, although the rules of civil procedure sometimes allow the firm to be treated as a separate person.
16 Partnership Act 1890, s 20(1).
17 Partnership Act 1890, ss 5–18 set out the circumstances in which partners will become liable to persons dealing with the firm. These rules are based on normal agency principles.
18 Partnership Act 1890, s 12.

before his or her retirement, unless there is an agreement to the contrary between the retiring partner, the newly constituted firm and the creditors. A retiring partner will continue to incur liability for the debts of the partnership to those who have not been notified of the retirement; those who have previously dealt with the business should be given actual notice but a notice in the London Gazette will be treated as sufficient notice to those who have not previously dealt with the firm. It is common for retiring partners to be given an indemnity by the continuing partners against continuing liability, but an agreement which does not involve the creditors will only protect the ex-partners if the continuing partners remain solvent.

It is possible for one partner to go bankrupt in relation to his or her personal affairs without the partnership business being treated as insolvent, although the bankruptcy will be treated as dissolving the partnership unless there has been agreement to the contrary.[19] Equally, the partnership business may be incapable of meeting its debts but some or all of the partners may still be solvent.

The current law relating to insolvent partnerships is contained in the Insolvent Partnerships Order 1994 made under s 420 of the Insolvency Act 1986. Since 1986, it has been possible for a partnership to be wound up as if it were a company; this has led to partners becoming liable to many of the sanctions available against directors.

The Limited Partnerships Act 1907 made it possible for partners not involved in the management of the business to enjoy limited liability, but this provision was little used because it was usually preferable to set up a limited liability company.[20] The Limited Partnerships Act 1907 did not, in any event, assist those who wished to be active in the management of the business. Many professional bodies did not permit their members to operate through limited liability companies until relatively recently; some still do not. Many existing professional partnerships did not wish to incur the tax costs and loss of privacy involved in incorporation but became increasingly outspoken about what they perceived as the unfair exposure of their businesses to limited liability. These complaints may have been met by the Limited Liability Partnerships Act 2000, which creates a new form of legal entity with (unlike a partnership) legal personality.[21] An LLP may be formed by 'two or more persons associated for carrying on a lawful business with a view to profit'; one or more of the persons may be corporate bodies. Creditors will contract with the LLP and individual members of the LLP will have no contractual liability to creditors. Internally, the LLP closely resembles a conventional partnership. Relations between the partners are regulated by agreement between the partners, or where there is no agreement, default provisions largely based upon the 1890 Act apply. Partners will be taxed individually as now, and the creation of an LLP is intended to be tax neutral.

The regulatory provisions of an LLP resemble a company and include a requirement for accounts to be made public. An annual return must be filed, with audited accounts, and many of the provisions of the Companies Acts apply (although protection for minorities is excluded). Much of the insolvency legislation applies, as do the provisions on director disqualification. Although it was expected that this new

---

19   Partnership Act 1890, s 33.
20   See the next section of this chapter.
21   Finch and Freedman (2002).

insolvent liquidation will be liable for the further loss caused to creditors.[28] Under the Company Directors Disqualification Act 1986, directors whose conduct in relation to an insolvent company shows them to be unfit to be concerned in the management of a company will be disqualified for a period of years from being a director.[29] The legislation employs the concept of the 'shadow director'[30] to prevent those who are in fact running a company from insulating themselves from exposure to these risks by not formally holding the office of director. A shadow director is a person in accordance with whose directions or instructions the directors of the company are accustomed to act (but so that a person is not deemed a shadow director by reason only that the directors act on advice given in a professional capacity).[31] In *Secretary of State v Deverell*,[32] the Court of Appeal held that the concept was intended to identify those, other than professional advisers, with real influence in the affairs of the company; although a shadow director will frequently 'lurk in the shadows', this is not essential.

A *de facto* director is someone who holds him or herself out as a director without having been properly appointed.[33] In *Re Richborough Furniture Ltd*,[34] the court held that in order to be a *de facto* director, the alleged director had either to be the sole acting director or to be acting on an equal footing with the *de jure* directors; in that case, although the defendant had considerable responsibility and was viewed by a number of creditors as a director, he was not a signatory to the company bank account as were the *de jure* directors and should not be treated as a *de facto* director. In *Re Kaytech International plc*,[35] the Court of Appeal held that in deciding whether an individual was a *de facto* director of a company the crucial question was whether he or she had assumed the status and functions of a company director so as to make him or herself responsible as if he were a *de jure* director. In this case, the individual had been deeply and openly involved in the company's affairs from the outset, and although he had done his best to avoid being seen to act as a director, using his office as *de jure* secretary and his professional status as camouflage, on some very important occasions, he openly acted as a director. Accordingly, he was a *de facto* director of the company and therefore a director for the purposes of s 6 of the Company Directors Disqualification Act 1986. In relation to another defendant in that case, the Court of Appeal observed that an honest but thoroughly unreasonable belief that he was not a director could not be a defence;[36] Robert Walker LJ said that the law should give no encouragement to the notion that if a man takes on so many directorships that he cannot remember them, he is thereby released from the heavy responsibility which he has undertaken.

---

28 See Chapter 31.
29 See Chapter 23.
30 Insolvency Act 1986, s 251; Company Directors Disqualification Act 1986, s 22(5).
31 Company Directors Disqualification Act 1986, s 22(5); Insolvency Act 1986, s 251.
32 [2001] Ch 340. This was apparently the first case in which the interpretation of the definition was crucial to the outcome of the case. It has since been applied in *Secretary of State and Industry v Becker* [2002] EWHC 2200.
33 See *Re Hydrodan (Corby) Ltd* [1994] 2 BCLC 180 for Millett J's discussion of the distinction between a *de facto* and a shadow director.
34 [1996] 1 BCLC 507.
35 [1999] BCC 390.
36 See also *Re Promwalk Services* [2002] All ER (D) 134 (Dec).

6   REASONS FOR BUSINESS FAILURE

Various studies have been undertaken into the reasons for the financial failure of businesses and some academic writers have produced formulae designed to identify those businesses at risk of insolvency.[37]

Other less scientific approaches to this question are perhaps easier to comprehend. There seems to be a consensus[38] that most failures are the result of bad management, although in a small minority of cases, the business has been the victim of bad luck such that even the most competent of management could not have survived (clearly, competent management will succeed in riding out unforeseen events which completely defeat less competently managed businesses). Another frequent problem is inadequate or inappropriate initial capitalisation of the business. The Cork Committee observed[39] that in all insolvencies of substance, a crucial element contributing to the collapse is the wilful, or at least grossly negligent, failure of the insolvent to have kept proper books of account, or a refusal to inspect them or to believe what they reveal or what he or she is told about them. Proper accounting systems will provide for accurate cashflow forecasts and project projections, adequate provision for contingencies, accurate and up-to-date costing systems, proper systems of credit control and checks against theft and other fraud.[40] Lingard identified three areas as being of particular importance; inefficient production (which includes technical problems, inefficient procedures, poor labour relations, poor stock control and overstaffing), lack of skilful marketing and absence of stringent financial control. Argenti also focused on the lack of adequate accounting information whilst also identifying structural defects (such as one-man rule, an unbalanced top team, a lack of management depth and a weak finance function). Swords notes that the R3 surveys shifted over the 10 year period from 1991 from regarding loss of markets as the main cause of failure to attributing most failures to poor management; management failure encompasses failures in strategic and change management as well as failures in financial control. Swords also observed that the conclusion in the 9th Survey was that it appeared in many cases that management was failing either to acquire the necessary skills to lead the business or to understand the need for the business to change; he also noted that, anecdotally, insolvency practitioners reported a concern that managers in larger firms, where the money at risk was not their own, appeared less concerned about external factors and the need to react to change in the business than those who both owned and ran the business.

The 11th Survey of Company Insolvency published by R3 in 2002 in relation to insolvencies in 2001 is the first to be based on all insolvencies registered at Companies House during the survey period. The survey noted that the vast majority of insolvent

---

37   See Cooke and Hicks (1993); Hamilton *et al* (1997); Day and Taylor (2001) (and references cited therein).

38   See Argenti, 1976; Lingard, 1989, Chapter 1. The 10th Annual Survey of R3, the Association of Business Recovery Professionals, published in 2001 included a summary by Dominic Swords of the surveys from the previous 10 years; it should be noted that the basis of the surveys during this period was those insolvencies in which licensed insolvency practitioners were involved and, therefore, excluded from consideration the asset-poor compulsory liquidations managed by the Official Receiver.

39   At para 217.

40   Research carried out by Day and Taylor (see Day and Taylor (2001)) identified a lack of commitment to the provision of good quality accounting information.

companies had a turnover of less than £1 million and observed that small companies of this sort were more likely to be reliant on a single customer and were prone to suffer from the 'domino effect' if that customer got into financial difficulty.[41] The Survey also noted that one in three insolvent companies were less than three years old and more than two-thirds were less than six years old. Being small and recently formed are clearly risk factors.

---

41 The 10th Survey had also noted the additional vulnerability of small firms with the risk of a single product, lack of diversification and lack of access to funds.

CHAPTER 5

ENFORCEMENT OF DEBT OUTSIDE INSOLVENCY

1 INTRODUCTION

The creditors of a debtor who has not yet been made formally insolvent will take individual action to recover the outstanding amounts; each creditor is entitled to attempt to obtain all of what is owing, even though this would leave insufficient to cover the other debts.

The rights of the creditor may be personal (*in personam*) against the debtor or, in some circumstances, real (*in rem*) against the assets in the possession of the debtor. Real rights may arise from contract or by operation of law; an example of the latter is the ancient common law remedy of distress over goods on the debtor's premises which can be exercised by the landlord to recover arrears of rent. Some creditors have other self-help measures available which may assist them in persuading their debtor to pay; utility companies, for example, may be able to disconnect supplies, which is likely to persuade any debtor who can do so to meet arrears.

A creditor who cannot persuade the debtor to pay[1] may take court action to obtain judgment for the debt.[2] Only a small minority of civil claims for debt are defended. In most cases, the creditor will obtain judgment by default. Over half of all default judgments do not, however, result in payment to the creditor.[3] It is clearly pointless (and a waste of resources for both the creditor and the court system) for a creditor to take court action against a debtor who is in arrears because of inability to pay; ideally, creditors should be able to distinguish those who are unable to pay from those who are just unwilling to do so. Research carried out recently[4] for the Lord Chancellor's Department into the approach of creditors to individual debtors in arrears identified creditors as falling into three groups: those adopting a holistic approach to arrears management, those adopting a hard business approach and those who adopt a standard set of procedures. Those using a holistic approach have systems which enable them to discover the circumstances of the people who fall into arrears and the reasons for this; they are well placed to distinguish those with the ability to pay from those who cannot pay and aim only to take the former to court. The main concern of those adopting the hard business approach was seen as ensuring that any arrears are recovered at minimum cost; they tend to work to the letter rather than the spirit of their industry code of practice and often view money advisers as an obstacle to the process. They, together with those who use a standard set of procedures, are poorly placed to distinguish those who are refusing to pay from those who are unable to pay. A suggested method of addressing this is that all creditors should be covered by codes

---

1 The persuasion will often come from commercial debt collection agencies to whom the debts have been passed. Harassment of debtors is a criminal offence punishable by a fine. The Credit Services Association (www.csa-uk.com) is the trade association of such agencies; its code of conduct, agreed with the OFT, can be found on its website.

2 Ford, 1991, p 89 argues that the judicial debt recovery process is too weighted in favour of the creditor.

3 See Baldwin, 2003.

4 Dominy and Kempson, 2003, at www.lcd.gov.uk/research/2003.

of practice which reflect the holistic approach and that they should be required to state in pre-action protocols that they have complied with the code of practice in bringing the case to court.

Creditors embarking on litigation against debtors whom they judge to have assets available may seek to obtain one of the various procedural securities available to prevent debtors from rendering those assets unavailable; these include an order for the payment into court of money and the appointment of a receiver of property by the court. Alternatively, but less securely due to giving a purely personal right against the debtor, the creditor may seek what used to be called a Mareva injunction (now a 'freezing injunction') freezing the assets of the debtor; this is appropriate where the creditor fears the removal of the assets from the jurisdiction.

Creditors who have obtained a judgment against a debtor will need to take further steps to enforce the judgment if the debtor still does not pay. During the review of the enforcement system which has recently been undertaken by the Lord Chancellor's Department,[5] it was suggested[6] that at least £600 million a year is lost to creditors through unpaid civil judgment debts; this was based on statistics suggesting that at least half a million judgments had remained unpaid in 1998. The Review acknowledged that many debts will remain unenforceable, however effective the system, because the debtor does not have the means to pay and suggested that the greatest improvement to the situation would probably be achieved by looking beyond the enforcement system to try and cut down the amount of unenforceable debt coming through the court system. It was, however, apparent that the enforcement process itself was not particularly effective, difficult to understand and prone to excessive delay and would benefit from revision. The Review recognised a need to balance allowing those who have established a legitimate claim to pursue satisfaction of that claim, through a system that is both straightforward and effective, with protection of the interests of those debtors who do not have the means to pay and the prevention of oppressive pursuit of debts. The next section of this chapter considers briefly the various processes whereby a creditor can seek to enforce a judgment debt, together with the proposals for reform contained in the White Paper on Effective Enforcement.

---

5   The Review began in March 1998. After a series of consultation exercises, a report on the first phase of the Review was published in July 2000; this contained 40 proposals for reform, some of which were implemented by secondary legislative changes, delivered through the Civil Procedure Rules, which came into effect in March 2002. A Green Paper, *Towards Effective Enforcement: A Single Piece of Bailiff Law and a Regulatory Structure for Enforcement* was published in May 2002 (following a research paper by Professor J Beatson which had been published in June 2000). The White Paper *Effective Enforcement: Improved Methods of Recovery for Civil Court Debt and Commercial Rent and a Single Regulatory Regime for Warrant Enforcement Agents* was published in March 2003. All the documentation is available from the Lord Chancellor's Department website at www.lcd.gov.uk/enforcement.

6   In the report of the first phase in July 2000.

2 ENFORCEMENT OF A JUDGMENT DEBT AGAINST A SOLVENT DEBTOR

(a) Introduction and statistics

The court may make an order allowing the judgment debtor to pay by instalments. If the debtor still refuses to pay pursuant to the judgment, the creditor may then proceed to enforce judgment in one of a number of ways.

The judicial statistics for county court enforcement processes[7] for 2000 and 2001 are as follows:

	2000	2001
County court warrants of execution issued	470,270	394,611
Attachment of earnings orders to secure payment of judgment debt: applications	81,309	77,876
Attachment of earnings orders to secure payment of judgment debt: issued	35,545	42,011
Third Party Debt Order summonses issued	3,174	4,139
Applications for charging orders	16,357	22,098

(b) Obtaining information

The debtor may be called before the court for an oral examination as to his or her means, thus allowing the creditor to inquire into the debtor's financial position and choose the most effective method of enforcing the judgment.[8] A standard list of questions will be asked,[9] but the creditor can ask for additional questions to be asked. A debtor who wilfully fails to co-operate with the process risks imprisonment for contempt. A central conclusion of the Enforcement Review was that there needed to be improvement of the information available on which to base informed and responsible decisions about enforcement and it was recognised that this requires that information can be sought from third parties as well as from the debtor. Chapter 3 of the White Paper contains proposals for the introduction of a Data Disclosure Order. This would be an order of the court, applied for by or, in some circumstances, on behalf of the creditor by completion of the relevant paperwork and the payment of the appropriate fee. The application could be made either on obtaining a default judgment or after subsequent unsuccessful attempts at enforcement. The order would enable the creditor to obtain, via the court service, information from relevant third parties[10] about the debtor in order to assist with identifying the most appropriate enforcement method.

---

7   Available from the Lord Chancellor's Department website, www.lcd.gov.uk in the 'Judges and QCs' section.
8   See CPR, Part 71, Form N316. N316A, in the case of a company debtor, is used to apply for an order to seek information.
9   See Court Form EX140 for an individual, EX141 in the case of the officer of a company.
10 The White Paper addresses Data Protection Act considerations and the European Convention on Human Rights, Art 8 at paras 275–76. The likely third parties are government agencies, banks, building societies and employers.

(c) Taking control of goods

The most commonly used method of enforcement is taking control of goods of the debtor (either individual or corporate) with a view to realising their value by sale and thereby obtaining payment, which is currently referred to as 'execution' and will be renamed 'taking legal control of goods'. Frequently, the threat of execution will be sufficient to produce payment. This process takes place pursuant to a writ of *fieri facias* (fi fa) in the High Court or warrant of execution in the county court;[11] the High Court procedure has generally been seen as more effective. In the county courts, the debtor is sent a letter advising that the creditor has authorised the bailiffs to act. This may well result in payment but, if not, the bailiffs will visit the premises with a view to taking money and/or levying on goods. Goods will be taken into the control of the bailiff with a view to subsequent sale if payment is not forthcoming. In the High Court, the Sheriff's Officer does not usually send a letter prior to making a visit to the premises. The Sheriff's Officer can negotiate an instalment arrangement, with the agreement of the creditor, without further reference to the court, whereas a county court bailiff can accept an informal instalment arrangement lasting for only a short time and a more permanent arrangement requires the court's sanction. Certain goods in the categories which are often described as 'tools of the trade' and 'domestic chattels' are exempt from seizure under s 15 of the Courts and Legal Services Act 1990. Where goods are seized which the debtor claims should be exempt, or which a third party claims to own, the court may be called upon to decide, in an interpleader procedure, whether the seizure is valid. It will often be the case that there are no goods worth seizing on the premises or that goods apparently belonging to the debtor are discovered to belong to a third party.

Chapter 2 of the White Paper on Effective Enforcement sets out recommendations[12] for the regulation of enforcement agents and for a single piece of legislation to govern the actions of enforcement agents when taking legal control of goods. This will be implemented by primary legislation supported by secondary legislation and a code of practice.[13] The legislation will have a particular emphasis on ensuring that there is time for the debtor (or third party) to apply to court to prevent sale of goods; a consistent list of goods that will be exempt from all types of legal control; ensuring proportionality between the size of the debt and the sale of goods; and a clear statement on the systems available to address any wrongful actions by the creditor or the debtor. There should be three types of legal control of goods: by agreement (formerly walking possession); by securing goods on the premises; and by

---

11   County court judgments over £600 may be transferred to the High Court for enforcement; judgments over £5,000 must be so transferred. See Millett LJ in *Re a Debtor (No 340 of 1992)* [1996] 2 All ER 211 for recent consideration of execution against chattels under the writ of fi fa.

12   Drawing on recommendations made by Professor J Beatson's *Independent Review of Bailiff Law: A Report to the Lord Chancellor* (Beatson, 2000) and the Green Paper, *Towards Effective Enforcement* (LCD, 2002a). Responses to the Green Paper indicated overwhelming support for increased regulation, and a majority in support of establishing a statutory executive non-departmental public body to regulate private and public enforcement agents; the recommendation of the White Paper is that this task should be given to the Security Industry Authority.

13   The code of practice is expected to build on the *National Standards for Enforcement Agents* (LCD, 2002b) which was widely endorsed by trade associations in the private sector, by bodies representing enforcement agents within the public sector, and also by representatives of the major creditors who make use of their services.

removal from the premises. The proposal in the report of the first phase of the Enforcement Review for the unification of the rules relating to county court warrants and High Court writs received overwhelming support. The White Paper recommends that there should be one standard form requesting execution and that this should be based on the current county court request, written in plain English so as to remove the Latin phrases presently used in the High Court. The proposed standardisation, based on the current county court procedure, would render obsolete the need to transfer enforcement between courts.

(d) Attachment of earnings

The second most popular[14] method of enforcement is the attachment of earnings order,[15] which will be appropriate where an individual judgment debtor has regular employment but no substantial assets; it cannot be used where the debtor is self-employed and cannot be used at the same time as a warrant of execution. Debtors will have to submit a statement of means and will be told that it is possible to apply for a suspended order under which, provided they makes regular payments, their employers will not be contacted.[16] The court will determine both a normal deduction rate and a protected earnings rate, the latter being a minimum sum necessary to provide for the debtor and his or her dependants below which the debtor's earnings may not be reduced by the order. The order will be addressed to the debtor's employer and requires them on penalty of a fine to take all reasonable steps to ensure that the appropriate deduction is made from the debtor's wages and paid to the court.[17] Where more than one attachment of earnings order is in existence, the orders are consolidated and payment is made by the employers to the court service for proportionate distribution between judgment creditors.[18] Under s 15 of the Attachment of Earnings Act 1971, the debtor is required to notify the court of any new employer and give details of earnings from that employment. Section 23 of the Act makes it an offence to fail to comply with s 15, punishable by a fine or up to 14 days' imprisonment; the White Paper on Effective Enforcement noted that the sanction appears, however, to be little used and in any case to have little effect.

The White Paper on Effective Enforcement[19] recognises a need for substantial overhaul of the attachment of earnings system, which it says is prone to delay and is too dependent on information being obtained from the debtor in order to set the rate of deductions from the debtor's salary. It is proposed to introduce a system of fixed deductions set according to standard tables with a process for reviewing individual circumstances if a debtor so requests. An agreement by the court that reduced payments should be made would lead to the suspension of the order provided that the debtor keeps up with the payments; failure to do so would result in the reinstatement of the order at the standard rate of deduction. The White Paper

---

14 Second by some distance with only about one-tenth as many applications for an attachment of earnings order as warrants for execution.

15 See Attachment of Earnings Act 1971 and CCR Ord 27.

16 In the county court in 2001, 30,461 of the 42,011 orders made were suspended.

17 The employer is entitled to deduct £1 per period from the employee's pay as an administration charge.

18 The court service takes a percentage of the money received towards the administrative costs.

19 Chapter 4, paras 317–66.

recognised that the facility of having the order suspended was open to abuse, but concluded that it should be retained as a necessary safeguard for debtors in that it enabled them to protect their privacy in the workplace; there was also recognition that it was not unknown for employers, particularly those without sophisticated payroll systems, to dismiss employees against whom orders had been made. It is proposed that a system, using Inland Revenue records, will be introduced to track debtors who change jobs and fail to comply with the obligation to tell the court.

(e) Third party debt orders

A third party debt order (the new name for a garnishee order)[20] will be the appropriate enforcement method (against both individual and corporate debtors) where the creditor knows that a judgment debtor has debts owing to him or her which could instead be paid to the creditor. The order is a method of securing payment by freezing and seizing money owed or payable by a third party to the debtor. The most common form of debt attached in this way is money standing to the credit of a debtor in a bank account. The judgment creditor makes an application,[21] which may be without notice to avoid alerting the debtor and giving him or her a chance to empty the account. The application must give details of the bank and branch at which the account is held and, to prevent 'fishing expeditions', must provide evidence to substantiate his or her belief that the debtor has such an account. The judgment creditor is also required to state if he or she knows or believes that anyone other than the judgment debtor has any claim to the money owed by the third party. The application will be dealt with by a judge without a hearing who may make an interim third party debt order (which used to be known as a garnishee order nisi). Once this order is served, the third party must not make any payment that reduces the sum owed to the judgment debtor to less than the amount specified in the order. A bank or building society served with an interim third party debt order is now expressly required to carry out a search to identify all the accounts held with it by that debtor and to inform the court and the judgment creditor of the search results within seven days. Following service of the interim order, a hearing takes place which both the third party and the judgment debtor may attend to object to the court making a final third party debt order (which used to be called a garnishee order absolute). At that hearing, the court may make the order final, ordering the third party to pay over the amount specified in the order to the judgment creditor. There are arrangements under which it is possible for a debtor who has been prevented by an interim order from withdrawing from a bank or building society account to apply for a payment towards meeting ordinary living expenses where he or she would otherwise be in hardship.

Third party debt orders are infrequently used compared with other enforcement procedures. Two major problems are the fact that the order only applies to any funds in an account at the moment it is applied, so that timing is crucial, and that the

---

20 The Effective Enforcement Review first phase report recorded some disagreement between consultees about a new name for the procedure but said that they were of the view 'that the term "garnishee" is so obscure that almost anything would be an improvement'. The change was made by the Civil Procedure (Amendment No 4) Rules 2001 (SI 2001/2792). The provisions relating to third party debt orders are contained in CPR, Part 72.

21 Using Form N349.

procedure cannot be used against accounts held in joint names.[22] The Enforcement Review recognised the problems caused by the fact that the order only attaches to the funds in an account at the time it is applied and the report of the first phase of the Review said that the Lord Chancellor's Department was exploring with the banks whether a system could be devised under which the order could be applied over a number of days, without incurring excessive costs or imposing excessive practical difficulties on the banks. The first phase report also recommended that joint accounts should be attachable subject to a limit of 50% of the funds being taken (in the case of two account holders) and provision for the other joint holder to be able raise objections; it is not considered right that a debtor should be able to avoid paying a debt by the simple expedient of putting money into a joint account. The proposal was not, however, carried through to the White Paper in the light of a number of difficulties connected with defining the accounts which should be caught by such a proposal and a number of other operational difficulties.[23]

(f) Charging orders

The final method of enforcement to be considered is the charging order,[24] which is available against individuals and companies. A charging order allows the imposition of a charge on any immovable property (particularly land, but also shares) owned by a judgment debtor so as to provide security for payment of the judgment debt. In the first instance an interim order will be made on the application without notice of the creditor, possibly accompanied by an injunction restraining dealings with the land. At a subsequent hearing, the court will decide whether to make the order final or discharge it. Section 1(5) of the Charging Orders Act 1979 provides that the court should consider all the circumstances of the case and, in particular, any evidence before it as to the personal circumstances of the debtor and as to whether any other creditor of the debtor would be likely to be unduly prejudiced by the making of the order. The court will take into account the possibility of jeopardising an arrangement between debtor and creditors generally.[25] The charging order creates an equitable interest in favour of the creditor and registration against the property is an essential feature of the system. If the debtor owns the entire equitable interest, the order will be made against the legal estate and the creditor can register the order against that estate by a notice in relation to registered land or as a land charge in relation to unregistered land. The order will then bind even a purchaser of the legal estate and it will be difficult to sell the land without first obtaining a discharge of the order. Otherwise, the charging order can only be made against part of the equitable interest and the creditor may seek some protection in the case of registered land by registering a caution against dealings. A caution gives the cautioner a chance to object to any proposed dealing with the land, but does not bind the land and is only effective in practice because of the reluctance of buyers to proceed unless proper arrangements are made for the discharge of the charging order. Under s 3(4) of the Charging Orders Act 1979, 'a charge imposed by a charging order shall have the like effect and shall be

---

22   *Hirschon v Evans* [1938] 3 All ER 491, CA held that a joint account cannot be attached.
23   The various problems are described in some detail at paras 409–30 of the White Paper.
24   See the Charging Orders Act 1979 and CPR, Part 73. See Gray, 2000, para 6.21 (and references cited therein).
25   *Rainbow v Moorgate Properties Ltd* [1975] 2 All ER 821.

enforceable in the same courts and in the same manner as an equitable charge created by the debtor under his hand'.

Creditors who wish to enforce the charge must apply for an order for sale as if they were mortgagees of the land; the court has wide powers under s 36(2) of the Administration of Justice Act 1970 and s 15 of the Trusts of Land and Appointment of Trustees Act 1996 (if the charging order is against a share in jointly owned land) to adjourn the proceedings or stay or suspend its order if it seems likely that the debtor will pay the secured debt within a reasonable time.[25a] The White Paper observes that the possibility of an order for sale prevents debtors living in expensive property, who have run up large debts, from avoiding payment of the debts whilst remaining comfortably accommodated. It also notes that many creditors say that, although they obtain charging orders, they wait for the voluntary sale of the property and never apply for orders for sale either because they do not wish to be seen to turn debtors out of their homes or because they regard orders for sale as being too difficult to obtain.

The White Paper recommends[26] some minor changes to the charging order procedure to help it run more smoothly. It also suggests that charging orders should be made available in cases in which the debtor is paying the debt by instalments and is not in arrears, to close a loophole which allows debtors with large debts paying small instalments to benefit from the sale of a property without paying off the debt; orders for sale would not be made unless the debtor did actually fall into arrears and safeguards should be put in place to ensure that the existence of the charging order does not prevent a debtor from being able to move house when necessary.

3 DISTRESS FOR RENT[27]

This is a self-help remedy[28] entitling landlords in certain circumstances to seize property found on the premises and to recoup any arrears of rent from the proceeds of sale. Landlords see distress as an easier remedy than forfeiture of the lease, a right which is qualified by the court's discretion to grant relief and which also carries the risk that the landlord may be left with empty premises and no rent. Distress may also be used as a bargaining ploy to achieve payment of the arrears of surrender of the lease.

The right to distrain arises as soon as the tenant is in arrears with the rent. The process of distraint is governed by complex and often obscure ancient rules, including, for example, a prohibition on the levy of distress on Sundays or between sunset and

---

25a The Court of Appeal in *Owo-Samson v Barclays Bank* [2003] EWCA Civ 714 suggested that CPR 73.10 imports no such wide discretion. This appears to conflict with the views in the White Paper.

26 Chapter 4, paras 367–408.

27 See Gray, 2000, p 1294 *et seq*; Law Commission, *Distress for Rent*, Working Paper No 97, May 1986; Law Commission, *Landlord and Tenant: Distress for Rent*, Law Com No 194, 4 February 1991; Clarke (1992). Remedies referred to as distress exist under statute for the recovery of rates, taxes and certain fines imposed by magistrates' courts.

28 Leave of the court will be required in some circumstances (protected or statutory tenancies under the Rent Act 1977 or assured tenancies within the Housing Act 1988, protected occupancy or statutory tenancy within the Rent (Agriculture) Act 1976) and corporate landlords will have to use a certificated bailiff who will have to comply with additional rules.

sunrise. Distress consists of entry (not by force)[29] onto the demised premises, seizure (by identifying the goods to be taken) and impounding (by transferring them to the landlord's control). Goods may be transferred to the physical control of the landlord or the landlord may take walking possession of the goods by leaving them in the tenant's possession on the tenant undertaking not to disturb or dispose of them. The landlord will generally have the power to sell the goods after five days from the time of impounding.

Any goods may be seized apart from those in the category of privileged goods under common law or statute; it can be difficult to determine which goods fall into this category. Goods immune from distress include clothes and bedding to a value of £100, tools of trade to a value of £150, perishable foods, tenant's fixtures, the property of lodgers and things in actual use. Where the goods of a third party have been seized, the true owner may reclaim his or her property by serving a statutory declaration under the Law of Distress Amendment Act 1908. Anyone with a prior claim to the goods at the time of the levy will be protected; the exception is that the landlord will have priority in respect of arrears of rent for up to 12 months over an execution creditor.

The Law Commission has recommended the abolition of distress: 'We see distress for rent as wrong in principle because it offers an extra-judicial debt enforcement remedy in circumstances which are, because of its intrinsic nature, the way in which it arises and the manner of its exercise, unjust to the debtors, to other creditors and to third parties.' The response to the Law Commission Report was overwhelmingly from landlords rather than tenants and most of them were in favour of retaining distress for commercial properties, seeing it as a quick and effective remedy for recovery of rent arrears. In the vast majority of cases, distress for rent actions do not result in goods being removed and sold. It has been argued that it enables landlords to let to 'marginal' business tenants (who would otherwise be denied properties because of their credit rating). It has also been suggested that, whereas residential tenants will usually pay their rent if they are able to do so, in commercial tenancies, delay in paying rent may be deliberate as a method of easing cashflow rather than obtaining a short term loan.

The White Paper on Effective Enforcement[30] proposes the abolition of distress for rent as a remedy in the residential sector, and the introduction of a modified procedure (to be called Commercial Rent Arrears Recovery) for the commercial sector for the recovery rental arrears above a specified minimum level in respect of commercial premises only.[31] Restrictions would be placed on who could carry out the procedure and the enforcement agents would be subject to the new regulations and legislation described above in relation to warrants of execution. There would be a requirement that notice be given to a tenant and that tenants would be given the ability to apply to court to challenge the existence of the debt and to seek an injunction to stop the process. Certain goods, including all third party goods, would be exempt from the process and a safeguard would be introduced to ensure that the goods seized

29 There is a lack of clarity around the issue of what is actually permitted.
30 Chapter 2, at para 207 onwards. See also LCD, 2001.
31 Responses to consultation were contained in the report CP(R) 13/01 *Distress for Rent – Responses to Consultation*, published by the LCD in May 2002 and available on the LCD website – www.lcd.gov.uk/consult/distress/distresp.htm.

were commensurate in value with the amount of rent arrears and costs due. Notice would also have to be given ahead of any sale of goods. Consideration was given in the earlier consultation document[32] to the impact of the European Convention on Human Rights (particularly Arts 6, 8 and 14 and Art 1 of the First Protocol) and the Lord Chancellor's Department considers that the proposals will be in compliance with the Convention.

The Lord Chancellor's Department has expressed the view that, even with additional safeguards, distress for rent would not be an appropriate or proportionate way to collect rent arrears in a residential property (or a commercial property with inhabited living quarters attached) and that it should be abolished. Evidence suggests that it is currently rarely if ever used in the residential context.

4 ENFORCEMENT OF SECURITY[33]

(a) Introduction

A creditor may have security rights either because he or she has entered into a contract to that effect[34] or because of some principle of law. The main categories of real rights arising by operation of law which may avoid the creditor having to take personal action against the debtor are[35] the lien,[36] the statutory charge, non-contractual rights of set-off and the equitable right to trace. Receivership as a method of enforcing a mortgage or charge is considered in greater detail in Chapter 6. As was seen in Chapter 3, some forms of sale credit provide the creditor with 'quasi-security' rights, in that the creditor retains proprietary rights over the property supplied on credit.

(b) The remedies of a mortgagee[37]

A mortgagee[38] may have the right to go into possession of the property, the right to appoint a receiver of the income of the property, the right to sell the property and the right to foreclose (which is exercised very rarely).

A mortgagee who goes into possession becomes subject to strict liabilities which, where the mortgagee's concern is to obtain the income from the property, make going into possession a less attractive option than appointing a receiver of the income. The right to possession will usually only be exercised in order to obtain vacant possession by a mortgagee intending to exercise a right to sell the property. The High Court has an equitable jurisdiction to stay possession proceedings[39] which is exercised

---

32 LCD, 2001, para 8. See also Beatson, 2000.
33 See, generally, Goode, 1988.
34 See Chapter 3.
35 See Goode, 1995, p 668 *et seq*.
36 Including the statutory lien conferred by the Sale of Goods Act 1979, s 41 on the unpaid seller of goods.
37 See Gray, 2000, Chapter 11.
38 Including a holder of a mortgage by way of legal charge.
39 A court order is not necessary to go into possession if this can be done without committing a breach of the peace or making a violent entry unless the right is restricted by statute. See also *Ropaigealach v Barclays Bank plc* [2000] 1 QB 263 (CA).

sparingly.[40] Statutory relief is provided by s 36 of the Administration of Justice Act 1970 in respect of 'dwelling houses' where there appears to be a realistic possibility that the mortgagor may remedy his or her default within a reasonable period of time.[41] One of the main difficulties is that defendants often fail to communicate with the court or attend the hearing, thus depriving the court of the ability to exercise its discretionary powers.

A mortgagee must take reasonable care to obtain the proper market value for the property, although the timing of the sale is entirely a matter for the mortgagee.[42]

(c) Charge

Documents conferring charges will usually confer an express right on the chargee to possession and sale of the encumbered property in the event of default. Such powers will often be conferred impliedly or by statute[43] but, in the absence of an express provision, an equitable chargee will need court consent for possession and, unless the charge was under seal, to sell or appoint a receiver. A chargee of land by way of legal mortgage has the same rights and remedies as a legal mortgagee.[44]

(d) Pledge

A pledgee will have a right to sell the pledged goods.

(e) Contractual lien

A lienee has the right to detain the goods until the debt is paid. There may also be a contractual right of sale in which case the security will be tantamount to a pledge except that the lienee will have been in possession of the goods before the security rights came into existence.

---

40 *Birmingham Citizens Permanent Building Society v Caunt* [1962] Ch 883.
41 The standard length of a reasonable period is between two and four years, but in *Cheltenham and Gloucester Building Society v Norgan* [1996] 1 WLR 343, it was held that a reasonable period could be the full term of the mortgage providing there was sufficient equity to protect the lender's eventual entitlement to repayment in full and a reasonable prospect of the borrower being able to pay off the arrears in full by that time as well.
42 *Cuckmere Brick Co Ltd v Mutual Finance Ltd* [1971] 2 All ER 633; *Palk v Mortgage Services Funding plc* [1993] 2 All ER 481; AIB *Finance v Debtors* [1997] 4 All ER 677; *Freeguard v Royal Bank of Scotland plc* [2002] EWHC 2509 (Ch).
43 See the Law of Property Act 1925, s 109 where the charge is contained in a deed.
44 Law of Property Act 1925, s 87(1).

CHAPTER 6

RECEIVERSHIP[1]

1 INTRODUCTION

If insolvency law is taken to be concerned with the collective process of realising and distributing assets amongst the creditors of an insolvent, then receivership strictly has no place in a study of it. This is because the essence of a receivership is that it is a mechanism by which individual secured creditors enforce their security against debtors; historically, no collective considerations arose. It is theoretically possible for a company which has been in receivership to return to financial health and avoid liquidation. More frequently, a receiver appointed to enforce a floating charge over the whole undertaking (known since 1986 as an administrative receiver) will have achieved the sale of those parts of the business which were financially healthy and have left a corporate shell to be liquidated.[2] Receiverships, however, have been so bound up with the development and operation of collective insolvency regimes, and with the development of the rules of property law which tend to be relevant in an insolvency, that it is very difficult to study insolvency law without at least a basic grasp of the nature of receivership.

The Enterprise Act 2002 will bring about radical change in relation to administrative receivership. Once s 250 of the Enterprise Act 2002 comes into force (expected to be September 2003), it will no longer be possible, except in a few specific instances, to appoint an administrative receiver to realise a floating charge created on or after a date to be appointed by secondary legislation. Holders of floating charges will instead have to appoint an administrator.[3] Administrative receivers will continue to be appointed for some time in relation to existing charges. Fixed charges and floating charges over less than the whole undertaking will continue to be enforceable by non-administrative receivers. An understanding of the state of the law in relation to administrative receivership during the period immediately before the passage of the Enterprise Act 2002 is necessary for an understanding of the context in which the reforms have taken place; the aim has been to preserve what have been seen as the best features of receivership whilst addressing the problems to which it has given rise.

2 THE HISTORY OF RECEIVERSHIP[4]

Receivership as a method of enforcing a security originated with the court appointment, at the request of a mortgagee, of a receiver to collect the income from mortgaged property and apply it towards payment of the mortgage interest. Over the years, the practice developed of the mortgage deed incorporating a power for the mortgagee to appoint the receiver, as agent of the mortgagor, directly. This enabled the mortgagee to avoid both the risk of incurring potential liability imposed on a

---

1   See generally Lightman and Moss, 2000.
2   For an exception, see *Gomba Holdings UK Ltd v Minories Finance Ltd* [1989] 1 All ER 261.
3   See Chapter 10 below.
4   See McCormack (2000).

(b) Distinction between administrative and Law of Property Act receiver

In many ways, the position of an administrative receiver does not differ from that of a Law of Property Act receiver or receiver of part only of the property. For example, any receiver appointed under a charge which was floating when created will have first to pay those who would be preferential creditors in a liquidation out of the assets subject to the charge[13] and a liquidator may apply to the court to fix the remuneration of a receiver of any type.[14] In summary, the differences are as follows:

(a) A debenture holder with the power to appoint an administrative receiver has the power to veto a company administration order. This has given rise to the so called 'lightweight floating charge' which is not required for the additional assets it secures but in order to protect the lender's rights from being damaged by an administration. An administrative receiver must vacate office if an administration order is made, whereas an ordinary receiver may remain in office.[15]

(b) An administrative receiver must be a qualified insolvency practitioner. This requirement does not apply to other types of receiver in respect of whom the only limitation is that they may not be bodies corporate[16] or undischarged bankrupts.[17]

(c) An administrative receiver has obligations to investigate the background to the receivership,[18] report to the creditors, usually within three months of his or her appointment,[19] and to report to the Insolvency Service if he or she considers that the conduct of a director requires a disqualification order.[20] Other receivers have no investigatory function and their duty to provide information is restricted to ensuring that all the letters and other documentation of the company state that a receiver has been appointed[21] and accounts of the receiver's receipts and payments must be delivered to the registrar of companies.[22]

(d) An administrative receiver has an extensive range of powers conferred by statute, including the power to apply for an order to dispose of property charged to another creditor,[23] whereas other receivers have the powers conferred by the debenture under which they were appointed.

(e) An administrative receiver's liability on adopted contracts of employment is restricted to qualifying liabilities.[24]

---

13 Insolvency Act 1986, s 40.
14 Insolvency Act 1986, s 36.
15 The moratorium brought into effect by the order will, however, prevent further enforcement of the security without leave.
16 Insolvency Act 1986, s 30.
17 Insolvency Act 1986, s 31.
18 Insolvency Act 1986, ss 46,47.
19 Insolvency Act 1986, s 48.
20 Company Directors Disqualification Act 1986, s 7(3)(d).
21 Insolvency Act 1986, s 39.
22 Insolvency Act 1986, s 38.
23 Insolvency Act 1986, s 43.
24 The liability of other receivers is governed by the Insolvency Act 1986, s 37, which was not amended by the Insolvency Act 1994 when it amended the Insolvency Act 1986, s 44.

(f) An administrative receiver can only be removed by court order if he or she refuses to resign.

4 APPOINTMENT AND POWERS OF AN ADMINISTRATIVE RECEIVER

In order for the appointment of an administrative receiver to be valid, the following conditions need to be fulfilled: there should be no administration order in force, the security under which the appointment is made must be valid, the obligations secured by the debenture must arise from a valid contract, the power to appoint the receiver must have become exercisable under the terms of the debenture, the appointment must have been made in the manner authorised by the debenture and the person appointed must be qualified to act.

The appointment of the receiver crystallises floating charges which have not already crystallised. It also suspends the directors' powers as regards both assets comprised in the security and the conduct of the business in so far as it falls within the sphere of the receiver; given the width of the receiver's powers, this effectively deprives the directors of a role.[25] The appointment will terminate any contracts of employment which are incompatible with the administrative receiver's powers but does not affect other contracts of employment.[26] Other contracts are not affected by the appointment, since the receiver will be appointed as agent for the company.[27] This agency lasts unless and until the company goes into liquidation.

The source of the receiver's powers is the debenture under which he or she is appointed, but the Insolvency Act 1986 provides[28] that the powers conferred by the debenture are deemed to include those listed in Sched 1 to the Act in so far as not inconsistent with the provisions of the debenture. Schedule 1 contains 23 powers covering virtually every aspect of the management of the business and of the assets comprised in the security. The powers which are exercisable in relation to the assets covered by the security will survive a liquidation of the company, but the personal powers given to the receiver to manage the business cease if the company goes into liquidation.

The court has the power[29] to allow the receiver to dispose of property which is subject to a security in favour of a creditor ranking ahead of or equally with the debenture holder as if it were not subject to the security if it considers that this would be likely to promote a more advantageous realisation of the company's assets than would otherwise be effected. The net proceeds of the sale, plus the amount by which those proceeds fall short of the value determined by the court as the net amount which would be realised by a sale on the open market, is to be applied in meeting the liabilities secured by the displaced security. This means that any deficiency caused by

---

25 See *Newhart Developments Ltd v Co-operative Commercial Bank* [1978] QB 814 and *Gomba Holdings UK Ltd v Homan* [1986] 3 All ER 94 for a discussion of their residual powers.

26 *Griffiths v Secretary of State for Social Services* [1974] QB 468.

27 Insolvency Act 1986, s 44, which merely gives statutory effect to what would anyway be the position under most debentures. In the case of a Law of Property Act receiver, the agency derives from the Law of Property Act 1925, s 109(2).

28 Insolvency Act 1986, s 44.

29 Insolvency Act 1986, s 43.

the manner of disposal comes out of the assets available to the debenture holder and is payable to the secured creditor in priority to other claims.

As an office-holder under the Insolvency Act 1986, an administrative receiver is given power to take possession of documents and to insist on co-operation from officers and employees of the company.[30]

5 DUTIES OF AN ADMINISTRATIVE RECEIVER

Historically, the receiver's main duty has been to the debenture holder and there have been only very limited duties owed to other parties. Although the receiver is appointed as agent of the company, it is an unusual form of agency which does not impose the usual duties of agent towards principal upon the receiver. The primary obligation is to act *bona fide* to realise the assets of the company in the interest of the debenture holder.

During the period of expansion of the ambit of the duty of care in negligence, several cases[31] held that a receiver would owe a tortious duty of care to the company, subsequent encumbrancers and guarantors of the debt. The duty would be to use care when selling assets so as to obtain the best price possible. The Privy Council adopted a more restrictive view of the duties of the receiver in *Downsview Nominees Ltd v First City Corp*[32] and held that, although on a sale of the assets there would be an equitable duty to take reasonable care to obtain a proper price, in relation to dealing with the assets the duty owed by the receiver to other encumbrancers and to the company was merely a duty of good faith in equity. More recently, however, the Court of Appeal in *Medforth v Blake*[33] has held that a receiver does owe an equitable duty of care in managing the mortgaged property. Scott VC summarised the duties owed by a receiver in the following seven propositions:

(a) A receiver managing mortgaged property owes duty to the mortgagor and anyone else with an interest in the equity of redemption.

(b) The duties include, but are not necessarily confined to, a duty of good faith.

(c) The extent and scope of any duty additional to that of good faith will depend on the facts and circumstances of the particular case.

(d) In exercising his or her powers of management the primary duty of the receiver is to try and bring about a situation in which interest on the secured debt can be paid and the debt itself repaid.

(e) Subject to that primary duty, the receiver owes a duty to manage the property with due diligence.

---

30 Insolvency Act 1986, ss 234, 235, 236, which are considered in more detail in Part IV.

31 *Standard Chartered Bank Ltd v Walker* [1982] 1 WLR 1410; *Cuckmere Brick Co Ltd v Mutual Finance Ltd* [1971] Ch 949; *American Express v Hurley* [1986] BCLC 52. In New Zealand, Canada and Australia, statutory duties have been placed on receivers to act in a reasonable manner.

32 [1993] AC 295. See Berg (1993). For earlier decisions taking the same restrictive view of the equitable source of the obligations, see *Parker-Tweedale v Dunbar Bank plc* [1991] Ch 12 and *China and South Sea Bank Ltd v Tan Soon Gin* [1990] 1 AC 536.

33 [1999] 3 All ER 97. See Bulman and Fitzsimmons (1999); Frisby (2000a); Sealy (2000).

(f) Due diligence does not oblige the receiver to continue to carry on a business on the mortgaged premises previously carried on by the mortgagor.

(g) If the receiver does carry on a business on the mortgaged premises, due diligence requires reasonable steps to be taken in order to try to do so profitably.

It has been pointed out[34] that there is considerable scope for uncertainty and future litigation as a result of this judgment. Subsequent cases[35] have not shown the imposition of a more onerous standard of behaviour on receivers. In particular, it is clear that the decision as to when to exercise a power of sale remains with the receiver and that, in deciding when to exercise that power, the interests of the mortgagee will be the main priority.

There are also various statutory duties owed by the receiver. Duties owed to the public at large are notification of appointment,[36] a duty to investigate the affairs of the company and submit a report to the Registrar of Companies and the creditors[37] and a duty to report anyone whom he or she thinks should be disqualified from acting as a director.[38]

There is also a duty to those who would be preferential creditors on a liquidation to pay them ahead of the chargeholder. Section 40 of the Insolvency Act 1986 provides as follows:

(1) The following applies, in the case of a company, where a receiver is appointed on behalf of the holders of any debentures of the company secured by a charge which, as created, was a floating charge.

(2) If the company is not at the time in the course of being wound up, its preferential debts[39] ... shall be paid out of the assets coming to the hands of the receiver in priority to any claims for principal or interest in respect of the debentures.

(3) Payments made under this section shall be recouped, as far as may be, out of the assets of the company available for payment of general creditors.

There has been some debate as to the situation where an administrative receiver is appointed under a debenture to which there was a prior ranking floating charge. In *Griffiths v Yorkshire Bank plc*,[40] Morritt J held that the wording of s 40 of the Insolvency Act 1986 led to the conclusion that the preferential creditors only ranked in priority over a charge which was created as a floating charge and in respect of which a receiver had been appointed. The same point arose subsequently in *Re H&K Medway Ltd*[41] and Neuberger J reached a different conclusion. The company had granted a floating charge to Ford Credit Europe plc over certain vehicles and their proceeds of sale. Subsequently, it granted a charge in favour of National Westminster Bank plc and then another to 3i plc. The 3i charge subjected the company's vehicle stock to a floating charge. It was agreed between the three creditors that the Ford charge would have

---

34 Finch, 2002, p 250 *et seq*.

35 *Meftah v Lloyds TSB Bank Plc (No 2)* [2001] 2 All ER (Comm) 741 (Ch D); *Silven Properties Ltd v Royal Bank of Scotland Plc* [2002] EWHC 1976; *Worwood v Leisure Merchandising* [2002] 1 BCLC 249; *Lloyds Bank v Cassidy* [2002] BPIR 1006; *Cohen v TSB Bank plc* [2002] BPIR 243.

36 Insolvency Act 1986, s 46.

37 Insolvency Act 1986, ss 47, 48.

38 Company Directors Disqualification Act 1986, s 7(3)(d).

39 See Chapter 34 below.

40 [1994] 1 WLR 1427.

41 [1997] 2 All ER 321.

priority over the 3i charge in respect of the vehicles. Shortly before 4 January 1995, the company ceased trading, which crystallised the floating charges. On 4 January 1995, 3i appointed administrative receivers under its charge. The court had to decide whether or not the preferential creditors had priority over Ford. The preferential creditors argued that the expression 'the debentures' at the end of s 40(2) of the Insolvency Act 1986 was a reference back to 'any debentures of the company secured by a charge which, as created, was a floating charge' in s 40(1) of the Insolvency Act 1986. Ford argued that 'the debentures' in s 40(2) was limited to those debentures under which 'a receiver [had been] appointed' so that Ford would have priority over the creditors. Neuberger J preferred the argument of the preferential creditors and held that they had priority to all the holders of floating charges over a company's assets and not just that under which the receivers were appointed. He was influenced in part by the fact that the consequence of adopting the other interpretation would be that well advised chargees would always be able to avoid s 40 of the Insolvency Act 1986 by requiring the borrower to execute a second floating charge in favour of a nominee with a view to any receiver then being appointed under the second charge.

6 LIABILITY OF AN ADMINISTRATIVE RECEIVER

The administrative receiver will be the agent of the company unless and until it goes into liquidation and, as such, will be able to bind the company to contracts. The receiver is not obliged to fulfil or to permit the company to fulfil existing contracts and will incur no personal liability by repudiating a contract in the name of the company even where this exposes the company to liability.[42]

Section 44 of the Insolvency Act 1986[43] provides that the administrative receiver will be personally liable on any contract entered into by him or her in the carrying out of his or her functions unless the contract provides otherwise and, to the extent of any qualifying liability, on any contract of employment adopted by him in the carrying out of these functions. He or she will not be taken to have adopted a contract by reason of anything done in the first 14 days of the appointment.

---

42 *Airlines Airspares Ltd v Handley Page Ltd* [1970] Ch 193.
43 As amended by Insolvency Act 1994. These amendments followed the furore caused by the Court of Appeal decision in *Powdrill v Watson* [1994] 2 All ER 513, which is discussed in Chapter 12 below.

PART II
AVOIDING BANKRUPTCY
OR LIQUIDATION:
THE 'RESCUE CULTURE'

which they were affected varied widely. The extent to which there was judicial involvement in the process also varied. Most of the procedures replaced the existing management but some, most notably the United States, had debtor-in-possession[33] regimes.

Chapter 11 of the United States Bankruptcy Code 1978 provides a mechanism for reaching agreement among the relevant parties for the reorganisation of a company which may or may not be insolvent.[34] An automatic stay comes into effect once a petition has been filed in the US Bankruptcy Court commencing a case under the Code. The secured creditor will be able to lift the stay against him or her unless the court finds that he or she is 'adequately protected'; this will be the case if it is clear that the creditor has adequate security which will keep its value or where the debtor agrees to make periodic payments to offset any decline in value. Post-petition financing is often enabled by the provision of super-priority for such financing. The management of the debtor company remains in office, but will have to provide the court with constant information and cannot take actions outside the normal course of its business without court consent which creditors will have the opportunity to oppose. As debtor-in-possession, the management will negotiate with creditors, working through the creditors' committee if one has been appointed, for approval to a plan of reorganisation. Every class of creditor must approve the plan unless the court can override the objection of an opposing class; this is referred to as the 'cramdown' of creditors. Secured creditors may be forced to agree if they receive at least the value of their security. Unsecured creditors cannot be overridden unless claimants below them in priority receive nothing. The different views on the question of the debtor-in-possession in the United States probably reflect to some extent cultural differences of attitude to entrepreneurial risk-taking. The historical legacy in the UK is an attitude that allowing a business to get into a state of insolvency is culpable whereas in the United States there has been greater acceptance of the view that a growing economy requires risk-taking which will inevitably lead to instances of insolvency.[35] The views expressed in the White Paper *Insolvency: A Second Chance* reflect a move towards the US view.[36]

The Canadian Bankruptcy and Insolvency Act of 1992[37] introduced new commercial reorganisation provisions which bring secured creditors within the scope of a stay. Secured creditors have to give notice of any intention to enforce security so that the company can seek commercial reorganisation and obtain a stay preventing enforcement. The commercial reorganisation process is initiated by the filing of a notice of intention to make a proposal which brings about an automatic stay of proceedings against both secured and unsecured creditors for an initial period of 30 days, renewable for up to six months. The Act includes a provision preventing the termination of contracts as against the company during the restructuring period as well as the automatic stay. The court does not have to become involved until creditors have approved the proposal by the requisite majority. There are sharp differences

---

33   The term used where the pre-insolvency management remains in office.
34   One prevalent criticism of the procedure is its use for non-insolvency purposes such as forcing the compromise of litigation or avoiding onerous employment contracts.
35   See Westbrook in Rajak, 1993, Chapter 11; Ziegel, 1994; Carruthers and Halliday, 1998.
36   Attributed to a visit to the US by Peter Mandelson, the then Secretary of State for Trade and Industry.
37   Ogilvie (1994).

between this procedure and the US Chapter 11 procedure. This process does not provide for a debtor-in-possession; a trustee takes over management and there is no possibility of overriding the rights of a particular class of claimant in the restructuring. These new provisions do not repeal the extensively used[38] Companies' Creditors Arrangement Act 1985 which provides for a debtor-in-possession arrangement leading to a restructuring which can affect secured and unsecured creditors. This Act gives the court very wide discretion to impose a stay which the courts have interpreted as being intended to restrain conduct which would impair the ability of the debtor company to stay in business during the negotiation period, maintain the status quo as amongst the creditors and restrain conduct which would seriously impair the debtor's ability to concentrate its efforts on negotiating compromise or arrangement. Each class of creditors must approve the plan by a three-quarters majority. Courts have prohibited suppliers and other parties contracting with the debtor for termination of contracts without court approval; suppliers have normally been required to continue to supply throughout the reorganisation on normal market terms without enjoying super-priority.

Australian and English insolvency law have a common heritage, but Australia has diverged in a number of ways. The Australian Corporate Law Reform Act 1992 introduced a new voluntary administration regime which may be invoked by any company which is insolvent or likely to become so and does not involve an application to court. The object is to maximise the possibility of saving the company or its business or to provide a better rate of return to creditors than under a liquidation. The appointment of the administrator brings about a stay of enforcement against the company and its property. Fully secured creditors will be caught by the stay unless they elect within 14 days to enforce their security. The administrator controls the affairs of the debtor and has to decide whether to recommend a deed of company arrangement, the termination of the administration or liquidation. The creditors decide which of the options is to be accepted. The court has a general, supervisory role.

French and German provisions display very different attitudes to the priorities to be adopted by insolvency law. France introduced a *'redressement judiciaire'*[39] procedure in 1986 with an emphasis on saving businesses and employment;[40] following criticism, particularly by creditors who felt their rights were being eroded, reform of the system took place in 1994 and the court no longer has to consider rescue where all business activity has ceased or where rescue is manifestly impossible. Where a debtor goes into *redressement judiciaire*, there will be a period of observation lasting at least six months, during which the business of the debtor is scrutinised and a stay will affect all creditors. A court appointed administrator and a representative of the creditors will manage the business under the supervision of the court. The administrator has the power to demand that third parties perform their contractual obligations, irrespective

---

38 Including the Olympia and York reconstruction which involved both a UK administration and Canadian CCCA proceedings.

39 See de Dree in Rajak, 1993, Chapter 18.

40 The objectives of the procedure are stated to be the reorganisation of the debtor, the continuation of the activity of the debtor and of the employment of its workforce and the repayment of debts to the creditors; at one time there was an argument that this was an ordered hierarchy of objectives, but the view now prevails that the objectives are of equal importance.

of breaches by the debtor, provided the administrator pays the required consideration; contracts in France may not validly contain provisions for termination on the grounds of the insolvency of the other party. The administrator will make a report to the court at the end of the observation period. The court will decide either to permit the debtor to reorganise its business or sell it to a third party or wind up the business. The court will only agree to reorganisation or sale if there is a serious chance that the business will survive. The court will consider the interests of all parties before making a decision and if the proposed reorganisation includes redundancies it must hear representatives of the workers. Creditors must agree to any reduction of their claims before the plan will take effect.

Germany[41] enacted a new insolvency law in 1994 (after long discussions about reform which began in 1978), which came into effect at the beginning of 1999 and replaces bankruptcy law which dates back to 1877. The new law is based on the principle that the role of insolvency law is to organise collective action in such a way that the value of the debtor's assets will be maximised so that all benefit. The proceedings will be unified, in that the same procedure may result in liquidation or in reorganisation, and creditor driven in that it is for the creditors to decide which outcome best suits them. Creditors will decide whether or not the debtor will remain in possession. Action by secured and unsecured creditors will be stayed. Interference with pre-bankruptcy entitlements, particularly security interests, is to be kept to a minimum and there will be no preferential creditors in bankruptcy. Secured creditors will be entitled to regular interest payments despite the stay as a disincentive to junior creditors to delay proceedings. The plan may be confirmed by the court only when each dissenting claimant receives the full cash equivalent of its claim as that claim would be realised in a liquidation. In addition, the class or debtor must be treated fairly and adequately as against all other classes.

Comparisons with other systems are interesting but, as the Insolvency Service has cautioned,[42] it is unwise to extrapolate from what happens in other countries into discussions for reform here. This is partly because of the absence of reliable data, partly because of the complex relationship between insolvency law and the wider economy and partly because of the impact of different cultural settings in which the various laws are operating.

---

41 Burger and Schelberg (1995).
42 Insolvency Service, 2000, para 34.

CHAPTER 8

RESCUE OUTSIDE THE INSOLVENCY LEGISLATION

1 INTRODUCTION

This chapter looks at methods, other than those contained in the Insolvency Acts, of avoiding liquidation or bankruptcy. It starts by considering the processes which may lead to an informal resolution of debt problems. Whether the debtor is a low-income individual in debt to his landlord and electricity supplier or a multi-national enterprise owing millions of pounds to dozens of banks, the basic need is the identical one of agreeing a rescheduling of obligations in order to remove the threats posed by indebtedness. Any agreement to reschedule debts arrived at by the parties will only be binding on them if the principles of contract law so provide so this chapter considers some of the relevant points of contract law. The final two sections of the chapter explain two formal processes whose history pre-dates the Insolvency Act 1986; these are the county court administration order for individuals and the scheme of arrangement under s 425 of the Companies Act 1985.

2 ASSISTANCE FOR CONSUMER DEBTORS[1]

Consumer debtors in financial difficulty have a number of possible alternatives.[2] It may be possible to negotiate with the creditors a way of paying off the arrears or they may be able to get funding to pay off the arrears from friends, family or refinancing.[3] Some debtors may be able to claim on a payment protection insurance policy if their difficulties are due to redundancy or ill health.[4]

Many consumer debtors may need to seek assistance in dealing with their debt problems; if they cannot afford to pay for the advice of professionals, they may be able to seek the assistance of debt-counsellors or other advice agencies. There is also increasing pressure on the creditors themselves to provide assistance. The DTI Task Force on Tackling Overindebtedness observed in its second report[5] that the aim of responsible lenders and borrowers should be to avoid credit turning into debt as much as possible. Lenders were recommended to review their systems to ensure that they do all they can to identify at an early stage those customers who might be in financial difficulty and to take appropriate action in such cases. The Task Force report

---

1   See Kempson, 1995. See also Berthoud and Kempson, 1992; Ford, 1991.
2   See Kempson, 2002 ('the 2002 research'). The research was carried out by MORI and analysed by Elaine Kempson.
3   The 2002 research suggests that about half of those who fall into arrears manage to renegotiate with all their creditors. About a quarter had been lent or given money by family or friends. 15% of households surveyed had borrowed money in the previous year to pay off creditors or make ends meet.
4   The 2002 research suggests that this only makes a small contribution to tackling the problem of arrears.
5   In January 2003. The Task Force was set up, following a conference hosted by the Minister for Consumer Affairs, in October 2000 to explore the causes and effects of overindebtedness and look at ways of achieving more responsible lending and borrowing. Its first report was published in July 2001.

also stressed that consumers facing debt problems should receive clear and helpful information about contacting the creditor, receive a positive response when they make contact and should be treated fairly and sympathetically; it commented that there were indications from Citizens Advice Bureau debt clients that customers with multiple debt problems are not always treated sympathetically when they approach their creditors. The government response[6] supported the recommendations of the Task Force.

Accountants, solicitors and banks[7] have traditionally been the source of debt advice but there has been considerable growth in recent years in the provision of debt counselling and debt management services in the commercial sector. Commercial debt management companies charge a fee[8] for providing debt advice, rescheduling payments, negotiating with creditors and distributing payments on a customer's behalf. Many consumers have been drawn to their services due to high profile advertising and ease of access. In December 2001, after receiving a considerable volume of complaints about the activities of many such businesses, the Office of Fair Trading published guidance as to the minimum standards to be expected from them. Companies were warned that they could lose their consumer credit licence, which they need to operate, if they do not comply with the guidance. The guidance includes requirements that advertisements and marketing must be accurate, clear and not misleading, that consumers be given adequate information before entering an agreement and that any reference to 'savings' on repayments must make it equally clear that debt rescheduling will usually lead to an increase in the size of the sum to be repaid and potentially affect the consumer's credit record. There should be no cold calling by personal visit. A realistic assessment of the customer's financial circumstances must be made before advice is given, including verification of income and regular outgoings and any advice must be in the best interests of consumers. Companies must inform clients of the outcome of negotiations with creditors, as well as any developments with creditors such as the issue of default notices or the threat of legal action. Payments from consumers should normally be passed on to creditors within five working days of receipt of cleared funds. The content of the guidance gives a clear indication of the type of malpractice which exists in this field.

It is recognised that there is a need for the provision of debt advice services within the voluntary sector.[9] The Cork Committee referred both to the recommendation of the Payne Committee[10] that a debt counselling service be established and to the Money Advice Centres set up by the National Association of Citizens Advice Bureaux. The Cork Report observed[11] that 'we believe that the development of either of these services would reduce the time spent by county court staff in advising debtors and would assist in sorting out debtors' muddles at an earlier stage'. More recently, the

---

6   By the Minister for Competition, Consumers and Markets, Melanie Johnson, on 30 January 2003. See www.dti.gov.uk/ccp/topics1/overindebtedness.htm#second.

7   Further consideration of bank involvement is left to the next section of this chapter.

8   According to an article in *The Guardian* ('So, who should you turn to?', 21 September 2002), customers typically pay charges equal to 15–25% of their total debt. The debt management firm may also take the entire first month payment as an upfront fee.

9   See, eg, the websites of the National Association of Citizens Advice Bureaux (www.nacab.org.uk), the Money Advice Trust (www.moneyadvicetrust.org) and the Consumer Credit Counselling Service (www.ccss.co.uk).

10   Cmnd 3909, 1969.

11   At para 349.

DTI Task Force on Overindebtedness said in its July 2001 report that it was essential that all consumers have the option of free, independent money advice and that the existing range of free advice services had difficulty in meeting the demand for their services. The Task Force recommended that the DTI in partnership with the Money Advice Trust, providers of free money advice and all credit grantors should continue to develop a national infrastructure that would result in the ready availability of free debt advice throughout the UK. The Money Advice Trust in its 2000–01 report referred to there being some 2,750 advice agencies across the UK offering money advice; many are general agencies offering money advice alongside a range of other support. Many have very stretched resources and clients may have to wait some time for appointments. The Money Advice Trust has been successful in increasing the volume of contribution provided by the credit industry to free money advice services.

Various forms of money advice service have been developed by the voluntary sector; one-to-one debt counselling, telephone helplines and the provision of self-help packs are the main forms. Debt counselling tends to involve those with multiple debts whose arrears have reached a serious state and who are facing court proceedings, repossession of their homes, disconnection of fuel or water supply or a business failure. The objective of this form of money advice is to help debtors maximise their income and minimise their expenses and to assist in negotiating with creditors. This will usually be time-consuming and very demanding of money advice resources. This form of counselling is particularly successful in averting imminently threatened crises such as homelessness and in increasing income by identifying benefits to which the debtor is entitled. Although most debtors seem to feel relief at finding help, not all of them retain an adequate commitment to the repayment schedule. It is not clear that debt counselling achieves its re-educative aims, since many of those who have sought debt counselling have come to rely on the counsellor to help with future difficulties.

Telephone helplines and the provision of self-help packs are less resource demanding methods[12] and seemed to appeal to those at a less serious level of indebtedness and who are, therefore, more likely to make a full financial recovery as a result of the assistance. Both these methods usually involve giving debtors advice designed to enable them to take control of their budgets and give them confidence in dealing with creditors. This method will not assist those with numeracy and literacy problems who will need face-to-face advice. A survey of National Debtline users showed that three-quarters had eventually been able to make affordable arrangements to repay what they owed. National Debtline was originally founded at the Birmingham Settlement in 1987 as Housing Debtline, to prevent homelessness caused by mortgage and rent arrears, but grew to serve the whole country; it has recently been used as a base for a much larger operation run by the Money Advice Trust as a result of a successful bid in 2001 for government and private sector funding for an 18 month pilot. The pilot, together with two smaller pilots in Fife and Cornwall, has been designed to test the feasibility and cost-effectiveness of meeting a significant proportion of the demand for debt advice by telephone and the potential for dealing with disbursements to creditors, together with the assessment of the requirement for face to face activities.[13]

---

12 The Money Advice Trust estimated that a telephone counselling session in 2000–01 cost on average £28 to £63 to provide, whereas a face-to-face consultation could cost up to £500.

13 Early data apparently shows encouraging results.

There are organisations within the voluntary sector[14] whose function is to manage debt repayments and whose services are provided free to debtors. These agencies are typically funded by donations from the creditors. The debtor will provide the organisation with details of their financial affairs and creditors and the organisation will then reach agreement with the creditors to reduce the regular repayments. The debtor then pays the new total amount to the organisation which will distribute it to the creditors. Some critics of such agencies argue that they do not always give the debtor the most comprehensive advice about alternatives (such as bankruptcy) to rescheduling.

The research carried out in 2002[15] suggests that the free money advice services, despite working to near capacity, still only assist about 20% of households facing arrears. The survey found that twice as many people in financial difficulty had refinanced existing commitments as had sought advice from any source at all. Demand for money advice outstrips supply but should probably be even greater. It is quite clear that money advice does assist debtors, but the Policy Studies Institute survey in 1989 identified a reluctance to seek assistance with debt problems. Nearly 60% of those surveyed who had been identified as having had a problem debt in the preceding year had not discussed it with anyone, even family or friends. Only a third had taken formal advice from a money adviser, solicitor, bank manager or accountant. Those who sought advice came disproportionately from amongst owner-occupiers rather than tenants, particularly council tenants. A feeling that financial difficulty was a personal matter to be sorted out in private was the most frequent reason given for failure to seek advice.

3   BANK RESCUE

(a) Introduction

Borrowers, particularly businesses, with bank loans will find that the bank or banks will become involved in trying to find a solution. Even where the bank is adequately secured, it will feel that a successful rescue will keep it a customer and source of future income; banks are also conscious of the risk to their reputations of being seen to react over-harshly. Justice observed in its 1994 report[16] that there were signs in the more economically significant cases that rescue operations are increasingly being conducted by the banks and the commercial community outside the confines of the insolvency system. Bank-led business rescues are often referred to as 'company workouts' and may involve the introduction of an expert 'company doctor' as a replacement for or in addition to the management of the company.[17] The British Bankers' Association publishes two voluntary codes: the Banking Code, to be followed by banks in their relations with personal customers, and the Business Banking Code. These, together with their Guidance notes, set out possible procedures for dealing with over-

---

14   For example, Consumer Credit Counselling Service (which recovered £41.2 million in 2001 and set up more than 11,000 debt management plans) and Payplan.

15   See note 2 above.

16   Justice, 1994.

17   See Godfrey (2002).

indebtedness.[18] Large companies with finance provided by a number of banks may find themselves the subject of the London Approach, a set of guidelines developed by the Bank of England for co-ordinating multi-bank rescues.

(b) Personal customers

The fifth version of the Banking Code was published in January 2001. This provides that subscribers to the Code will consider cases of financial difficulty 'sympathetically and positively' and will try to help overcome the difficulties by developing a plan to deal with the difficulties. The Guidance provides that subscribers to the Code will consider customers to be in financial difficulty when income is insufficient to cover reasonable living expenses and meet financial commitments as they become due. When it becomes clear to the subscriber that the customer needs specialist assistance, the customer should be referred promptly to specialist teams, who deal with customers in financial difficulties, where these exist. In some cases, referral to a debt recovery unit may also be necessary. The Code suggests that customers in difficulty should obtain help from debt counselling organisations, states that subscribers to the Code will inform customers where they can get free money advice and will undertake to liaise with such organisations where customers so request. The British Banking Association and the Money Advice Trust have devised a Common Financial Statement to be used by money advisers when submitting information to subscribers to the Code.

The Guidance notes describe in some detail the approach which will be taken by subscribers to the Code in developing debt management plans for customers. If the customer has assets which could reasonably be expected to be sold to reduce outstanding debts, the subscriber may request that the customer and, if appropriate, their adviser, considers this option. Thereafter, the subscriber should acknowledge that income may only be available to repay 'non-priority' debts once provision has been made for any 'priority' debts. A debt will be considered 'priority' where the customer's failure to pay could lead directly to the loss of one or more of the following: the customer's home (for example, rent, mortgage, secured loans), their liberty (for example, council tax, child support maintenance, income tax, court fines), their utility supplies for example, water, gas, electricity), or their essential goods or services (for example, a cooker, a fridge, or the means to travel to work). In general, subscribers should then be prepared to accept an offer of repayment which is based on the principle of equitable distribution of available income, in line with the amount outstanding to each creditor. When a customer is in receipt of an income and/or there are credit balances on accounts held with the subscriber, the subscriber will, as part of a repayment plan, leave the customer with sufficient money for reasonable day-to-day expenses, taking into account individual circumstances. Token offers may be accepted where the customer has demonstrated they have no surplus income available for their 'non-priority' creditors and there is a realistic prospect of the customer's circumstances improving. Subscribers may consider agreeing with their customers in financial difficulty appropriate concessions, relating to charges and interest payable by the customer. The nature of any concessions will need to be assessed on a case-by-case

18   The Codes and the Guidance notes are available on the British Bankers' Association website: www.bba.org.uk. Other members of the credit industry have their own codes of practice (for example, the code of practice of the Finance and Leasing Association).

basis, taking account of the seriousness of the customer's situation. Where the subscriber considers the customer's personal and financial circumstances to be exceptional and unlikely to improve, the subscriber may, among other options, consider writing off or not pursuing part or all of the customer's debts. Agreements between subscribers and customers in financial difficulty may be subject to regular review. Any review period will be agreed with the customer or their adviser, and subscribers should seek to revise contributions only at the end of the review period or if a customer's personal circumstances change. Customers and/or his or her advisers will be expected to inform the subscriber when the customer's personal situation changes.

(c) Company 'workouts'

There is a separate Business Banking Code, based closely on the personal Banking Code, whose most recent edition was published in March 2003. This is supported by the British Bankers' Association's Statement of Principles which was originally published in 1997[19] and is intended to inform relationships between banks and customers with borrowing facilities; the approach should also be applied in relation to the provision of merchant services. The Business Banking Code closely resembles the general Banking Code in approach in that it focuses on the development of a debt management plan and stresses the possible involvement of debt counselling and business support organisations. The Code states that 'We will do all we can to help you overcome your difficulties. With your co-operation, we will develop a plan with you for dealing with your financial difficulties and we will tell you, in writing, what we have agreed'; the Guidance notes emphasise that 'the solution has to be based on the needs of both subscriber and customer. For the avoidance of doubt, this paragraph does not require an institution to "help" a customer by simply writing off a debt or agreeing to an inappropriate repayment programme'.

The Statement of Principles contains a detailed explanation of the circumstances in which the lender is likely to become concerned about the existence of problems and the consequences of this. There is also a detailed explanation of what will happen if the lender suggests an independent review of the business. The Principles state that lenders will support a rescue proposition if they believe it will succeed; that where the business makes the necessary changes early enough to preserve the underlying business, the lender will not usually start action for the recovery of the borrowing; that if the lender does not believe the rescue proposal will succeed, the reasons will be explained and the business and their advisers helped to consider other options and that any decision to appoint an administrative receiver will be confirmed within the bank at a senior level.

It may prove possible to avoid receivership or a formal insolvency regime by considering a sale of the business as a going concern, a refinancing or a gradual run down. A main advantage to be derived from this approach is that it avoids giving harmful publicity to the difficulties being faced by the business.

---

19   Revised in 2000.

(d) The London Approach[20]

This is a set of guidelines developed by the Bank of England and the major banks designed to assist with the informal rescue of companies[21] where a number of lenders are involved. The Bank of England is available to provide mediation assistance in resolving disputes amongst the lenders involved. There are no formal sanctions for breach of the guidelines other than the disapproval of the Bank of England.

The basic premise is that no one lender will seek to do better out of the situation than any other lender. It involves the lenders agreeing to freeze[22] their proportion of the company's indebtedness and any security at its existing level and to provide short term finance whilst a plan is considered. One bank is appointed as 'lead banker' to investigate the situation, produce a report as a matter of urgency and co-ordinate rescue plans with the assistance of a steering committee. An inter-creditor debt rescheduling agreement will then be drawn up.

The plan may sometimes involve the lenders entering into a 'debt-equity' swap under which they exchange some of the unpaid debt for shares, usually special preference shares giving the lenders priority as to dividends and repayment and sometimes containing an option to convert to ordinary shares.

The London Approach was first devised during the 1970s at a time when the banks were predominant amongst the providers of finance. The increasing numbers[23] and diverse nature[24] of those with a financial stake in companies has made it more difficult for the banks to remain in control of a rescue operation. Commentators point to the increasing problems, and expense, in operating it given the increased involvement of foreign banks, amongst whom the Bank of England has less influence. The development of a secondary market in debt has both increased the number of creditors in any particular case and made it difficult to know who they are; additionally there is the problem that where debt is viewed as a commodity there is less incentive to secure the long term existence of the borrower. The problem with any system which does not allow for the overriding of a minority creditor is that such a creditor is then in a strong position to bargain for the other creditors to buy out his or her blocking interest at an enhanced price.

4 CONTRACTUAL ARRANGEMENTS

A debtor has always been able to make arrangements with his or her creditors for the settlement of his or her debts entirely independently of any court proceedings. It is possible to arrange with an individual creditor that the creditor will accept less or will accept what is owing later. Contract law students all encounter the problems the

---

20 See Floyd (1995). See the information on the Bank of England website at www.bankofengland.co.uk.

21 Such informal corporate rescue operations are often referred to as company workouts; the company working its way out of difficulty. The Bank of England has been involved in more than 160 cases since 1989.

22 Often referred to as implementing 'a standstill'.

23 The rescue of Heron International, for example, involved 82 banks.

24 Amongst those who may be interested parties are bondholders, insurance companies and other institutional shareholders and purchasers of debt from the original holders of it.

courts have had in finding sufficient consideration to support a promise by the creditor to accept less than the amount owing in full settlement; the rule in *Pinnels's Case*[25] provides that a promise to accept part of what is owing in settlement of the full sum is not enforceable although consideration can be found if the debtor agrees to pay in a different form, at a different place or at an earlier time than that originally agreed. This principle was upheld by the Court of Appeal in *Re Selectmove Ltd*,[26] despite arguments that changing views of consideration should lead the courts to accept that the creditor does derive a benefit from such an arrangement, in that some payment is received, whereas in absence of the arrangement, the creditor might receive nothing.[27] Selectmove Ltd was fighting a petition by the Inland Revenue to have it put into compulsory liquidation; it claimed that it had entered into an agreement with the Revenue to pay off the debt in instalments.[28] The Court of Appeal held that no such agreement had been reached but that even if there had been, it would not have been contractually binding.[29]

This problem of a lack of apparent consideration ought logically to arise in relation to an arrangement (usually called a composition) between the debtor and all his or her creditors under which each agrees to accept a stated percentage of his or her debt in full satisfaction of what is owing. The creditors have clearly provided consideration and will be bound *inter se*, but it is not obvious what consideration has been provided by the debtor. The courts have, however, been prepared to uphold such arrangements, probably for pragmatic reasons of commercial convenience but purportedly on the basis that it would be a fraud upon all the parties concerned for one creditor to deny the existence of the agreement.[30] There will be no problem with consideration where a deed is used to record the agreement.

An agreement between the debtor and his or her creditors can, of course, only bind those who are party to the agreement. Any creditor who has not agreed to be party to such an arrangement will not be bound by it and will be able to take action against the debtor.

5   DEEDS OF ARRANGEMENT

Deeds of arrangement[31] between insolvent debtors and their creditors became a source of disquiet during the 19th century since they were often the occasion of fraud

---

25   (1602) 5 Co Rep 117a, upheld by the House of Lords in *Foakes v Beer* (1884) 9 App Cas 605.
26   [1995] 2 All ER 531.
27   An argument which Lord Blackburn had produced in *Foakes v Beer* when he had pointed out that 'all men of business, whether merchants or tradesmen, do every day recognise and act on the ground that prompt payment of a part of their demand may be more beneficial to them than it would be to insist on their rights and enforce payment of the whole'.
28   The Inland Revenue does frequently make such agreements. An article in *The Observer* on 15 October 1996 on the charity Taxaid which provides advice about tax debts compared the number of people against whom the Revenue took action in the year to April 1996 (2,217 made bankrupt, 400 judgment executions) with the number of tax debts queries dealt with by the CAB in the same period (87,000).
29   The court also held that promissory estoppel would not be relevant since the company had not behaved in such a way as to merit the assistance of equity.
30   *Wood v Robarts* (1818) 1 Stakr 417; *Cook v Lister* (1863) 13 CBNS 543; *Couldery v Bartrum* (1881) 19 Ch D 394; *Hirachand Punamchand v Temple* [1911] 2 KB 330.
31   The definition of which includes certain instruments not under seal.

against the majority of creditors. These arrangements usually contemplated that the debtor give up virtually the whole of his or her assets to a trustee for the benefit of creditors in return for a release from their claims. Unscrupulous persons frequently induced insolvent debtors to execute deeds of arrangement in their favour and then failed to make proper distribution to the creditors out of the property. The Deeds of Arrangement Act 1887 was intended to ensure adequate publicity for these arrangements and better protection for creditors. The Deeds of Arrangement Act 1914 introduced an element of court and Board of Trade control; if the deed was not registered within seven days of execution it was automatically void. Deeds of arrangement became very popular for a while after 1914 but by the time of the Cork Report their use had dramatically declined. One problem was the ability of any dissenting creditor to destroy the protection achieved by the agreement with the other creditors. Another problem was that entry into a deed of arrangement was an act of bankruptcy available as the basis of a petition for bankruptcy for the following three months; a successful petition for bankruptcy would lead to the setting aside of the deed so the trustee under the deed would not be able to collect or distribute the estate safely within the three month period. The Deeds of Arrangement Act 1914 has not been repealed, as was recommended by the Cork Committee, but deeds of arrangement are now very rarely encountered.

6 COUNTY COURT ADMINISTRATION

(a) Current position[32]

Section 112 of the County Courts Act 1984 provides that where a debtor is unable to pay forthwith the amount of a judgment obtained against him and alleges that his or her whole indebtedness[33] is less than the county court limit of £5,000, the county court has a discretion on his or her application to make an order providing for the administration of his or her estate. Any county court has jurisdiction, not just those with insolvency jurisdiction. The request for an administration order must state[34] whether the debtor proposes to pay creditors in full or how much he or she proposes to pay and the amount of the monthly instalments. It must be accompanied by a list of his or her creditors. Creditors will be given notice of the hearing and will be able to object to the inclusion of any debt in the list of debts or to the proposals.

An administration order may provide for the payment of the debts by instalments either in full or to such extent as appears practicable to the court under the circumstances and subject to any conditions as to future earnings or income which the court thinks just. The court may vary or subject the order to periodical review. Once an order has been made, creditors will be unable to pursue:

> any remedy against the person or property of the debtor in respect of any debt: (a) of which the debtor notified the appropriate court before the administration order was made; or (b) which has been scheduled to the order, except with leave of the appropriate court and on such terms as that court may impose.[35]

---

32 County Courts Act 1984, Part VI; County Court Rules 1981, Ord 39.
33 'Indebtedness' is not defined.
34 Forms N92 and N93.
35 County Courts Act 1984, s 114.

This has raised an issue[36] in relation to mortgage lenders whose borrowers are in arrears. In most cases they will be able to show that mortgage repayment default has led to the entire outstanding loan becoming repayable at once so that the total indebtedness is too great for an administration order to be possible. Where this argument does not work, it would appear that they might be caught by the freeze since there is no saving of the rights of secured creditors.

Whilst an administration order is in force those creditors whose existence has been notified to the court by the debtor will not be able to present a bankruptcy petition against the debtor without leave of the court;[37] the exception to this is that a creditor owed more than £1,500 may do so within 28 days of being notified of the order. Additionally, execution may be levied if the assets exceed £50 and the creditor requests it.[38] Section 116 of the County Courts Act 1984 preserves the right to distrain for rent for six months up to the date of the order (but not for any rent after the date of levy of distress).

The court takes a fee of not more than 10% of the total amount of the debts in relation to the implementation of an administration order.[39] The debtor will be required to make a single regular payment to the court of an agreed amount. Regular payments are then made to creditors by the court according to the terms of the order. The money paid in is applied first in payment of the fees. There is no concept of preferential creditors.

The order will be discharged automatically when the scheduled creditors have been paid as provided for in the order and costs met.[40] The order may be revoked if the debtor fails without reasonable cause to comply with it.[41] The court may suspend the order or vary it if the debtor is unable to comply for a good reason.

Where a debtor has sought to take advantage of the administration order and has failed to comply with it, the insolvency legislation allows the imposition of some of the disabilities of the undischarged bankrupt on the debtor.[42] The debtor may be prevented from obtaining credit or carrying on business without, in either case, disclosing that an order has been made and may be prevented from acting as a director or being involved directly or indirectly in the promotion, formation or management of a company.[43] These restrictions may last for up to two years.

(b) History[44] and proposed reform

The administration order procedure was introduced by the 1883 Bankruptcy Act which gave the county courts the power to administer the estates of judgment debtors whose whole indebtedness was less than £50. This vested a loose discretion in the judge to arrange for the relief of the small debtor by reasonable composition; the court

---

36   See Harper (1997).
37   County Courts Act 1984, s 112(4).
38   County Courts Act 1984, s 115(1) as amended by the Insolvency Act 1985, s 220(3)(4).
39   County Courts Act 1984, s 117(1).
40   County Courts Act 1984, s 117(2).
41   County Court Rules, Ord 39.
42   Insolvency Act 1986, s 429.
43   Company Directors Disqualification Act 1986, s 12.
44   See the Cork Report, paras 68–73.

was enjoined to take into consideration the circumstances in which the indebtedness had been incurred and whether there had been any fraud, idleness, improvidence, gambling or intemperance. An inquiry in 1887 found that the system was not working well since the cases were too small to support the expense of the machinery.

The procedure was re-enacted in the 1914 Act and transferred into the legislation governing the county courts in the County Courts Act 1934. At that time, it was subject to a £50 ceiling which was only raised in 1965 to £300 and then in 1977 to £2,000. As long ago as the Muir Mackenzie Committee in 1908, it was recommended that a debtor should be entitled to apply for an order even where there was no outstanding judgment against him or her, but this has yet to be implemented.

Amendments contained in the Courts and Legal Services Act 1990[45] which have not been brought into force would improve the position in some respects. The range of people entitled to apply for such an order would be extended to include debtors against whom there was no outstanding judgment and the creditor under a judgment. The court would also be able make an order of its own volition or on the application of a creditor. The upper limit on indebtedness would also go. An order would not last longer than three years; the proposed time limit is intended to help persuade creditors that an administration order is not necessarily a worse option than a bankruptcy.

A further unimplemented section of the Courts and Legal Services Act 1990[46] would allow a county court to make a restriction order where it could otherwise make an administration order. A restriction order would provide for a stay of enforcement in that no creditor specified in the order would have any remedy against the debtor or his or her property in respect of debts specified except with the leave of the court.

The amendments to the County Courts Act 1984 were originally delayed in order to allow for provision to be made for the expected increase in the number of applications for administration orders. The problem of the lack of definition of the debts which are covered by an administration order was then raised and gave rise to a need for further consideration; possible amendment of the administration order was included within the scope of the review of civil enforcement processes undertaken by the Lord Chancellor's Department. The White Paper published in March 2003[47] contained a statement that whilst there are some aspects of s 13 of the Courts and Legal Services Act 1990 that would be welcome, its implementation in its current form would be unworkable and is therefore not a viable option; the Lord Chancellor's Department would publish a paper on options for change later in 2003. The White Paper observed that research carried out by the Lord Chancellor's Department in 2001 had shown that administration orders in their current form have not been successful in meeting their objectives.

The White Paper envisaged the possibility of administration orders being replaced by a reformed personal insolvency regime.[48] Any new scheme would, however, have to be workable for both debtors and creditors and affordable for the state; the White Paper pointed out the cost implication in providing relief for those with no ability to pay and stated that research was being carried out in order to identify the potential costs of reform. Other possibilities would be to do nothing (which would mean a

---

45   Section 13 amending the County Courts Act 1984, s 112.
46   Section 13(5) inserting s 112A into the County Courts Act 1984.
47   LCD, 2003.
48   This was also envisaged by DTI, 2001, para 5.12.

dwindling number of debtors taking advantage of administration orders), increase the financial limit of indebtedness from the current limit of £5,000 or implement a revised court-based system that would address some of the current problems.

7 SCHEMES OF ARRANGEMENT[49]

A scheme of arrangement under s 425 of the Companies Act 1985 enables a company, whether or not it is insolvent, to enter into a compromise or arrangement with any class of its creditors or members and may be used to restructure the capital of companies in financial difficulties. It may be used as an alternative to liquidation (possibly coupled with an administration order)[50] or within a liquidation as a means of reaching a compromise with creditors. Recently it has been used by provisional liquidators of distressed insurance companies as a quasi-administration process (until recently insurance companies did not have access to an administration order procedure).

Approval of the scheme requires, firstly, the consent of each of the various classes of members and creditors affected and, secondly, the sanction of the court. Consent of a class requires a majority of three-quarters in value of those present and voting either in person or by proxy. Once approved, the scheme is binding on all the relevant classes of creditors and members and on the company.[51]

The s 425 procedure is initiated by an application to the court for an order summoning a meeting of the relevant class of creditors (which may include contingent creditors)[52] or members affected by the scheme. The application may be made by the company or any creditor, member, liquidator or administrator of it. The application should be supported by an affidavit which explains the need for the proposed scheme and sufficient information to enable the court to determine whether the meetings ought to be summoned. It is for the applicant to identify the composition of the class meetings to be summoned. A class will consist of those persons whose rights are not so dissimilar as to make it impossible for them to consult together with a view to their common interest.[53] Where a class has no interest in the arrangement because of the insolvency of the company, it is unnecessary to summon a meeting of that class.[54]

In order for the court to sanction the scheme,[55] it has, firstly, to be satisfied that there is strict compliance with the statute, including the obligations to disclose the

---

49   See Rajak, 1993, Chapter 20; Milman (2001b).

50   See, for example, *Re Polly Peck International plc* [1996] BCC 486, discussed in Chapter 25.

51   This contrasts with the company voluntary arrangement provisions under which only those creditors who had notice of the meeting and were entitled to vote will be bound.

52   *Re Midland Coal* [1895] 1 Ch 267, a case on the 1870 provision which was the precursor of the Companies Act 1985, s 425. It only applied to insolvent companies and logic required that claims be valued as if being proved in a liquidation.

53   *Sovereign Life Assurance Co v Dodd* [1892] 2 QB 573 and *Re Hellenic and General Trust Ltd* [1976] 1 WLR 123 are amongst the substantial body of case law on this point. Recent case law includes *Re Equitable Life Assurance Society* [2002] 2 BCLC 510; *Re Hawk Insurance Co Ltd* [2001] 2 BCLC 480; *Re BTR plc* [2000] 1 BCLC 740; *Re Osiris Insurance Ltd* [1999] 1 BCLC 182.

54   *Re Tea Corp* [1904] 1 Ch 12; *Re BCH plc (No 3)* [1992] 1 WLR 672; *Re MCC plc (No 2)* [1994] 1 BCLC 1 (contractually subordinated creditors excluded).

55   See *Re Anglo-Continental Supply Co Ltd* [1922] 2 Ch 723 at 736 for a statement of these requirements.

terms of the arrangement[56] and to convene separate meetings of the different categories of creditors, and that the scheme is a compromise or arrangement within the section. The court also has to be satisfied that the class was fairly represented at the class meeting and that the majority were exercising their power *bona fide*. Finally, the court must be satisfied that the terms of the arrangement are such that an intelligent and honest member of the class acting in respect of his or her own interest might normally approve of the arrangement.[57] Once the court has approved the scheme, it may use the wide powers given to it by s 427 of the Companies Act 1985 to assist in the implementation of the scheme;[58] these powers include the ability to transfer property and dissolve a company without winding it up.

The Cork Committee identified[59] a number of problems with this procedure. The absence of a moratorium causes difficulty, particularly given the delay and complexity involved in applying to court and summoning the various meetings. A minimum period of eight weeks will be necessary to get the scheme in place. It can be difficult to identify the relevant classes correctly and there is always the risk that if the classes have been incorrectly defined the scheme will not be sanctioned.

The Insolvency Service Review Group in its Report on Company Rescue and Business Reconstruction Mechanisms considered[60] the s 425 scheme of arrangement. It described such schemes as complex and, because of the absence of a moratorium, difficult to organise, demanding of expensive legal resource and generally the preserve of larger companies. It did, however, say that there were suggestions that a s 425 procedure augmented by a moratorium and 'monitoring' of directors on behalf of the creditors could assist with 'London Approach' situations and recommended liaison with the Company Law Review[61] to ensure full consideration of the possibility.

---

56 Contained in the Companies Act 1985, s 426.

57 *Re Dorman Long & Co* [1934] Ch 635.

58 *Re Anglo American Insurance Co Ltd* [2001] 1 BCLC 755; *Re Allied Domecq plc* [2000] BCC 582.

59 At paras 404–18.

60 At para 43.

61 The Company Law Review visited the issue of s 245 schemes of arrangement in CLRSG, 2000 and in CLRSG, 2001, Chapter 13.

CHAPTER 9

INDIVIDUAL AND COMPANY VOLUNTARY ARRANGEMENTS

1 INTRODUCTION

The introduction by the Insolvency Act 1986 of the individual voluntary arrangement ('IVA') and the company voluntary arrangement ('CVA') followed the recommendation of the Cork Committee that it should be possible to make an effective collective agreement with creditors even where a minority of creditors dissent from the arrangement. The Committee recommended that the individual voluntary arrangement should replace the Deeds of Arrangement Act 1914, which it considered unsatisfactory in a number of respects,[1] and also provide a more satisfactory alternative to bankruptcy than was then provided by the possibility of a composition or arrangement being arrived at pursuant to a receiving order against a debtor.[2] The Committee also felt that something less complex and speedier than the s 425 of the Company Act 1985 scheme of arrangement was needed for companies. This different ancestry of the two forms of voluntary arrangement is reflected in the fact that an individual has to be insolvent or nearly so in order to obtain approval to a voluntary arrangement, whereas there is no such requirement for a company; insolvency would previously have been required for a receiving order but not for a company scheme of arrangement.

The Cork Committee felt that court involvement could be replaced to an extent by that of an insolvency practitioner given the new controls as to who would be eligible to act as such.[3] It will be seen that there is a need to involve a licensed insolvency practitioner or other authorised person[4] at an early stage in any attempt to achieve a voluntary arrangement. The intention was always that the insolvency practitioner should exercise professional independent judgment in considering whether the process for seeking approval should be pursued;[5] the Insolvency Act 2000 reinforces this by requiring an express statement from the insolvency practitioner of the likelihood of success in obtaining approval. The only process which has to involve a court decision is the IVA with interim order; in relation to the other versions of a voluntary arrangement, the only requirement is for the filing of prescribed documentation with the court, although it will be possible for the court subsequently to be asked to decide whether an arrangement which has obtained approval should be set aside.

---

1 The Deeds of Arrangement Act 1914 has not in fact been repealed but has fallen into almost total disuse. See Chapter 8 above.

2 The receiving order was the first stage in the bankruptcy process; if a composition or scheme of arrangement could be achieved (unusual because of the onerous requirements which had to be met) the receiving order would be rescinded, otherwise it would lead to the making of a bankruptcy order.

3 See Chapter 20.

4 Insolvency Act 1986, new s 389A (introduced by the Insolvency Act 2000, s 4(4)) provides for the Secretary of State to recognise a body for the purposes of authorising persons to act as nominees or supervisors in voluntary arrangements.

5 See www.insolvency.gov.uk/information/dearip/dearipmill/chapter24.htm for the somewhat exasperated comments of the Insolvency Service in this respect.

whichever of the Official Receiver, trustee in bankruptcy and bankrupt is not making the proposal.

(b) IVA with no protective interim order

In *Fletcher v Vooght*,[17] it was held that an IVA which had not commenced with an application for an interim order was invalid; this problem was addressed by s 3 of and Sched 3 to the Insolvency Act 2000, which enables the procedure to be started without an application for an interim order.

Section 256A of the Insolvency Act 1986 provides that, where a debtor intends to make a proposal for an individual voluntary arrangement but an interim order has not been made and no application for one is pending, the debtor shall submit to the nominee the terms of the proposed arrangement and a statement of his or her affairs. If the nominee is of the opinion that the debtor is an undischarged bankrupt or is able to petition for his or her own bankruptcy, the nominee shall, within 14 days (or such longer period allowed by the court) of receiving the documents from the debtor, submit a report to the court stating whether he or she thinks there is a reasonable prospect of the arrangement being approved and whether a meeting of the debtor's creditors should be summoned to consider the proposal and, if so, giving details of time and place for the meeting.

The nominee will then proceed to call the meeting as outlined above in relation to the procedure commenced by an interim order.

(c) Fast-track individual voluntary arrangement for undischarged bankrupt

Section 263A of the Insolvency Act 1986, introduced by s 264 of and Sched 22 to the Enterprise Act 2002, will make a fast-track to an IVA possible where the debtor is an undischarged bankrupt, the Official Receiver is specified in the proposal as the nominee in relation to the voluntary arrangement[18] and no application is made for an interim order. The debtor will submit to the Official Receiver a statement of the proposed arrangement together with a statement of his or her affairs and, if the Official Receiver thinks that the arrangement has a reasonable prospect of being approved and implemented, he or she may make arrangements for inviting creditors to decide whether to approve it.

(d) CVA without moratorium

This procedure is similar to that for an IVA without interim order. Unlike the procedure accompanied by the protection of a moratorium, this form of CVA (the form originally introduced in 1986) is available to all companies. Since the interests of members as well as creditors may be affected, there will need to be two meetings summoned to consider a CVA proposal.

---

17   [2000] BPIR 435.
18   See Chapter 7 for the thinking behind the introduction of the ability of the Official Receiver to act as a nominee and supervisor of an IVA.

Section 1 of the Insolvency Act 1986 provides that the directors of a company, other than one in liquidation or administration, may propose[19] a voluntary arrangement to the company and its creditors. This must be either a composition in satisfaction of its debts or a scheme of arrangement of its affairs.[20] The proposal must explain why the directors think an arrangement is desirable and why the creditors may be expected to concur in it. It must include a statement of the company's assets, any other assets to be made available, the liabilities and how it is proposed to deal with them. There is no requirement that the company be insolvent or unable to pay its debts. A liquidator or administrator may also propose a voluntary arrangement. The proposal must provide for a qualified insolvency practitioner ('the nominee') to act as supervisor of the arrangement.

The proposal and a statement of the company's affairs[21] must be submitted to the intended nominee, unless the nominee is already liquidator or administrator of the company. The nominee then has 28 days[22] in which to submit a report to the court stating whether he or she thinks the proposed arrangement has a reasonable prospect of being approved and implemented[23] and whether meetings of the company and of its creditors should be summoned to consider the proposal and, if so, details of the proposed meetings.

If the nominee fails to submit the report, the court may, on the application of the person intending to make the proposal, order his or her replacement by another qualified insolvency practitioner.[24] A nominee who has reported that the proposal should be considered should, unless the court directs otherwise, summon the meetings for the time, date and place proposed in the report.

A nominee who is already liquidator or administrator does not have to submit a report to the court and may summon the meetings to consider the proposal as he or she thinks fit, giving at least 14 days' notice.[25]

(e) CVA with moratorium

Section 1 of and Sched 1 to the Insolvency Act 2000 amend the Insolvency Act 1986 to enable the directors of eligible companies to obtain an initial moratorium for the company where they propose a company voluntary arrangement. Section 1A of the Insolvency Act 1986 provides that where the directors of an eligible company intend to make a proposal for a voluntary arrangement, they may take steps in accordance with Sched A1 to the Insolvency Act 1986 to obtain a moratorium.

A company is eligible for a moratorium if it met the qualifying conditions set out in para 3(2) of Sched A1 to the Insolvency Act 1986 in the year ending with the date of

---

19 Insolvency Rules 1986, r 1.3 sets out the items which must be included in a proposal.
20 See the Court of Appeal discussion of the meaning of 'composition or scheme of arrangement' in *Commissioners of Inland Revenue v Adam & Partners Ltd* [2000] 1 BCLC 222.
21 Whose contents are prescribed by the Insolvency Rules 1986, r 1.5. The nominee may request further information.
22 Insolvency Act 1986, s 2. The court may extend the 28 day period.
23 This requirement was inserted into the Insolvency Act 1986, s 2(2) by the Insolvency Act 2000.
24 Or by a person authorised to act as a nominee: Insolvency Act 1986, s 2(4).
25 Insolvency Rules 1986, r 1.11.

(c) CVA

Meetings of creditors and of members must be held within 28 days of a moratorium taking effect if there is one and not less than 14 and not more than 28 days after the nominee files his or her report with the court in other cases. The meetings may be held on separate days, but not more than seven days apart.[70] Those summoned to the meetings must be sent a copy of the proposal, a summary of the statement of affairs and the nominee's comments on the proposal.[71] Notice of the creditors' meeting must be sent to all creditors of the company of whose claims and addresses the nominee is aware.[72] The meetings will decide whether to approve the proposed arrangement with or without modification.[73] The meetings may not approve any proposal or modification which affects the rights of a secured creditor to enforce a security or affects the priority of payment of preferential debts unless the creditor affected consents.[74] Where the meetings disagree, the creditors' meeting will prevail, but members will have the right to apply to court within 28 days of the later of the two meetings.[75] It is an offence for an officer of a company to seek to obtain a moratorium or an extension to a moratorium or approval to a proposed voluntary arrangement by making a false representation or committing a fraudulent act.[76]

The voting rights and the requisite majorities applicable to the meetings are set out in the Insolvency Rules 1986.[77] Members vote in accordance with the rights attaching to their shares and a resolution at a members' meeting requires a majority of more than one-half of those present in person or by proxy and voting on the resolution.[78] The requisite majority at the creditors' meeting in respect of a resolution to approve the proposal or any modification of it is a majority in excess of three-quarters in value of the creditors present in person or by proxy and voting on the resolution. Other resolutions at the creditors' meeting require a majority in excess of one-half. Any resolution of the creditors will be invalid if those voting against it include more than half in value of the creditors entitled to vote who are not connected with the company.

Every creditor who was given notice of the meeting is entitled to vote at it and votes are calculated, in a case where there is no moratorium, according to the amount of the creditor's debt at the date of the meeting or, where relevant, at the start of the liquidation or administration. In a case with a moratorium, votes will be calculated according to the amount of the debt at the beginning of the moratorium, deducting any amounts repaid since then. Creditors may not vote in respect of secured claims to the extent of their security.

The position in relation to unliquidated and uncertain claims has already been dealt with above in the context of an IVA.

---

70   Insolvency Rules 1986, r 1.13 as amended.
71   Insolvency Rules 1986, r 1.9.
72   Insolvency Rules 1986, r 1.9.
73   Insolvency Act 1986, s 4.
74   Insolvency Act 1986, s 4(3), (4).
75   Insolvency Act 1986, s 4A.
76   Insolvency Act 1986, s 6A, Sched A1, para 42.
77   Insolvency Rules 1986, rr 1.17–1.20.
78   See the Insolvency Rules 1986, rr 1.17–1.20 for voting rights and majorities.

5   CONSEQUENCES OF APPROVAL OF A VOLUNTARY ARRANGEMENT

(a) Approval under fast-track process[79]

Where the Official Receiver reports to the court that a proposed voluntary arrangement has been approved, the arrangement will take effect and bind the debtor and every person who was a creditor in respect of a bankruptcy debt of the debtor and of whose claim and address the Official Receiver was aware. The court shall annul the bankruptcy order in respect of the debtor on an application made by the Official Receiver once the period has elapsed in which a successful challenge to the arrangement is possible.

(b) Approval by meeting[80]

Where the meeting approves the proposal, the arrangement will take effect as if made by the debtor at the meeting. An approved arrangement binds all those who would have been entitled to vote at the meeting if they had had notice of it. Unknown creditors who subsequently appear will be entitled to claim the amount they would have received under the arrangement.[81] The arrangement must contain provisions for dealing with the claim of any person who is bound by the arrangement but did not receive notice of the meeting. The amendment binding unknown and unnotified creditors into an arrangement has dealt with the problems addressed by a series of cases[82] relating to creditors who had not been given notice of the meeting.

Where an IVA is approved, any pending bankruptcy petition will be dismissed unless the court orders otherwise.[83] It will delay making any order for 28 days from receiving the report of the meeting to give time for a challenge to the arrangement to be made under s 262. The interim order remains in effect for 28 days after the report to the court, but will then cease to have effect unless the court extends it in connection with a s 262 application challenging the arrangement.[84] The arrangement has to be notified to the Insolvency Service,[85] which maintains a register open to public inspection,[86] but this is the only publicity given to it.

In relation to a CVA where the company is in administration or liquidation, the court may stay the winding up or discharge the administration or give directions with respect to its conduct which will facilitate the implementation of the voluntary arrangement. No such order will be made until 28 days after the chairman of the

---

79   Insolvency Act 1986, s 263D introduced by the Enterprise Act 2002, Sched 22.
80   Insolvency Act 1986, ss 5 and 260 as amended by the Insolvency Act 2000.
81   Insolvency Act 1986, 260(2)(b), (2A). In *Oakley Smith v Greenberg* [2002] EWCA Civ 1217, the Court of Appeal held that a creditor wrongfully excluded from voting at the meeting would only be able to enforce claims to the same extent as the voluntary arrangement creditors.
82   *Re a Debtor (No 64 of 1992)* [1994] 2 All ER 177; *Beverley Group v McClue* [1995] BCC 751; and *Re Bielecki* (1995) unreported, 19 October.
83   Insolvency Act 1986, s 260(5).
84   Insolvency Act 1986, s 260(4).
85   Insolvency Rules 1986, r 5.24.
86   Insolvency Rules 1986, r 5.23.

meeting has reported the approval to the court[87] to give time for a challenge to the arrangement to be made under s 6 of the Insolvency Act 1986.

(c) Effect of voluntary arrangement on third parties

The question arises as to the effect of a voluntary arrangement on solvent third party co-debtors and guarantors. This issue has arisen particularly frequently in the leasehold context in which a landlord often has rights against third parties, particularly guarantors, in respect of the tenant's defaults. The tenant debtor will be concerned to prevent claims both by the landlord and by any third party who has had to meet a claim by the landlord arising out of the tenant's default and is seeking to enforce an indemnity against the tenant. Questions have also arisen as to the right of the third parties to prevent the creditor from claiming against them.

After several cases at first instance,[88] the issue came before the Court of Appeal in *Johnson v Davies*,[89] which concerned the effect of an IVA on a solvent third party co-debtor of the IVA debtor. The Court held that a term in a voluntary arrangement could, as a matter of principle, have the effect of releasing a jointly liable co-debtor and that whether it actually did so depended on whether, as a matter of construction, having regard to the surrounding circumstances and taking into account also any terms which could properly be implied, it constituted an absolute release in relation to all the joint debtors. In this particular case, the wording of the voluntary arrangement construed as a whole was inconsistent with any intention to effect an immediate or absolute release of the debts. It was necessary in order to give efficacy to the arrangements to imply a term that the creditors would take no steps to enforce their debts against the debtor whilst he was in compliance with the voluntary arrangement, but no such term was necessary in the case of co-debtors. It followed that the co-debtors were not released from their liability, which could be enforced against them. Chadwick LJ observed that in a case in which the wording of the arrangement was appropriate to release co-debtors or sureties, a creditor prejudiced by the decision of the majority to approve such proposals would be able to apply to the court for the approval of the meeting to be revoked.

In his judgment in *Lloyds Bank plc v Ellicott and Another*,[90] Chadwick LJ reiterated the principles established by *Johnson v Davies* and went on to make the point that the solvent co-debtor would be entitled to an indemnity from the debtor protected by the voluntary arrangement were she not herself bound by the arrangement. In the *Ellicott* case, the third party co-debtor was not a party to the voluntary arrangement and would be able to claim an indemnity; this could not now happen since, as a contingent creditor, she will now always be so bound as a result of the amendment to ss 5 and 260 of the Insolvency Act 1986.[91]

---

87   The chairman must report the result of the meetings to the court within four days: Insolvency Act 1986, s 4(6) and the Insolvency Rules 1986, r 1.24.

88   *R A Securities v Mercantile Credit Co* [1995] 3 All ER 581; *Burford Midland Properties Ltd v Marley Extrusions* [1994] BCC 604; *Mytre Investments Ltd v Reynolds* [1995] 3 All ER 588; *March Estates v Gunmark Ltd* [1996] 32 EG 75.

89   [1998] 2 All ER 649.

90   [2002] EWCA Civ 1333.

91   The co-debtor wife in *Ellicott* would now have to challenge the IVA on the basis that she had not been given notice of the proposal.

In *Greene King plc v Stanley and Others*,[92] the Court of Appeal considered a situation involving a third party surety as distinct from a third party joint debtor and held that the same principles applied. In this case, the elderly parents of a debtor who had entered an IVA had given a charge over their home by way of surety for a loan made to the debtor by the appellants; when agreeing to the IVA, the appellants had made clear in correspondence that they reserved the right to rely on the charge and, subsequently, they purported to do so. The Court refused to accept the argument of the respondents that in the absence of a provision in the contract of surety entitling him or her to do so, a creditor cannot reserve his or her rights against the surety on the release of the principal debtor. Earlier authority[93] provided clear support for the proposition that one of the qualifications to the general rule that the release of the principal debtor discharges the surety is where there is a reservation of the creditor's rights against the surety at the time of discharging the debt. The surety's right to sue the principal debtor remains unaffected by the release of the principal debtor, since in accepting the release subject to the reservation the principal debtor impliedly consents to the surety's rights against him or her remaining on foot notwithstanding the release. Accordingly, the IVA had not had the effect of releasing the parents from their obligations under the charge.[94]

The principles identified by the Court of Appeal were applied in *Koutrouzas v Lombard Natwest Factors Ltd*,[95] a case in which a creditor prevented by an IVA from enforcing a guarantee against one of two co-guarantors sought to enforce it against the defendant solvent co-debtor. Field J held that although it was obviously contemplated that the creditors should stay their hand whilst the IVA was being implemented, it was plain that if the IVA failed, the creditors were to be able to rely on the pre-IVA against the debtor. In the absence of words expressly declaring that the creditors' rights were there and then being extinguished, a court should not seek an interpretation that goes any wider than is necessary to give effect to the plain intention of the parties and that meant that the IVA should be construed as suspending the creditor's rights pending implementation of its terms rather than effecting an immediate release of those rights. The IVA did not therefore have the effect of extinguishing the guarantee and the creditors were therefore able to enforce it against the solvent co-guarantor.

(d) Effect on claimant with an unliquidated claim

In *Alman v Approach Housing Ltd*,[96] it was held that a claimant in respect of an unliquidated claim on which a nominal value has been placed for voting purposes will not be prevented from pursuing the claim unless the voluntary arrangement makes it clear that this is the effect of the arrangement. Where there is no express provision to this effect, the implication of a term into the arrangement would at least

---

92 [2001] EWCA Civ 1966.
93 *Kearsley v Cole* (1846) 16 M&W 128; *Bateson v Gosling* [1871] LR CP 9; and *Cole v Lynn* [1942] 1 KB 142 (CA).
94 The Court went on to avoid the charge under the principle in *Royal Bank of Scotland v Etridge* [1998] 4 All ER 705.
95 [2002] EWHC 1084 (QB).
96 [2001] 1 BCLC 530.

require that the arrangement provided some machinery for the determination of such disputed claims.

6   CHALLENGE TO A VOLUNTARY ARRANGEMENT

There are two methods of challenging a voluntary arrangement, either indirectly by petitioning for a bankruptcy or liquidation order,[97] or directly under the provisions considered below.

The voluntary arrangement may be challenged[98] within 28 days of the approval of the arrangement being reported to the court on the grounds that it unfairly prejudiced the interests of a creditor or that there has been some material irregularity in relation to the meeting. Those with standing to present such a challenge are, in the case of an IVA, the debtor, any person entitled to vote at the meeting, the nominee, the trustee in bankruptcy and the Official Receiver and, in the case of a CVA, anyone entitled to vote at either meeting, the nominee or a liquidator or administrator of the company. The court has power to revoke or suspend any approval or give directions for calling a further meeting and may continue or renew the interim order for this purpose.[99]

Hoffmann J has said[100] that 'unfair prejudice' means unfairness brought about by the terms of the voluntary arrangement itself with respect to the relationships between the creditors themselves.[101] In *Re a Debtor (No 101 of 1999),*[102] the court held that the existence of differential treatment in a voluntary arrangement which was not assented to by a creditor who considered that he was less favourably treated was not by itself sufficient to prove unfair prejudice under s 262 of the Insolvency Act 1986, since in deciding whether the interests of a creditor were unfairly prejudiced, the court had to consider all the circumstances of the case. Equally, it has been held[103] that on an application under s 262, the fact that all creditors were treated by the arrangement in the same way was not necessarily conclusive of the absence of unfair prejudice; in that case, it was held unfairly prejudicial that a creditor was prevented by the arrangement from pursuing a claim which would be met in full by the debtor's insurers. In *Re a Debtor,*[104] it was held that the special position of a wife with a matrimonial debt could result in unfair prejudice not only to the wife, but also to the other creditors, if, for example, she were able to frustrate a voluntary arrangement against their wishes or force them to accept a voluntary arrangement. To avoid the possibility of a claim of unfair prejudice, the special position of a wife with a matrimonial debt had to be recognised in the voluntary arrangement, unless she and the other creditors were in

---

97   Under s 276(1) in the case of bankruptcy; see Chapter 15.

98   Under the Insolvency Act 1986, s 262, or s 263F in the case of an IVA, or s 6, Sched A1, para 38 in the case of a CVA. In the case of a creditor not given notice of the meeting, the application may be made within 28 days of him or her becoming aware that the meeting has taken place.

99   In the case of a fast-track IVA, the only power is to revoke the IVA.

100 *Re a Debtor* [1992] 1 WLR 226.

101 This was approved by the Court of Appeal in *Somji v Cadbury Schweppes plc* [2001] 1 WLR 615, in which it was held that a secret deal between some of the creditors was grounds for setting the arrangement aside and making a bankruptcy order instead but that it was unlikely to amount to unfair prejudice within s 262.

102 [2000] 1 BCLC 54.

103 *Sea Voyager Maritime Inc and Others v Bielecki* [1999] 1 All ER 628.

104 [1999] 1 FLR 926.

agreement. The facts of the case were that the husband obtained an agreement for an IVA shortly after the making of a lump sum order against him in family proceedings. Under the IVA, the wife was compelled to accept a dividend in satisfaction of her matrimonial debt and her lump sum order would not survive discharge of the IVA. She claimed that the debts of the other creditors were fabricated (her debt was just less than 25% of the overall debt) and that the IVA had been approved as a result of her husband's fraud. It was held that, in the particular circumstances of the case, she should not be bound by the IVA, because it unfairly prejudiced her in that it over-rode her entitlement under the lump sum order in a way that a bankruptcy order could not have done.

Material irregularities include approving an arrangement wrongly affecting a secured creditor.[105] In *Re a Debtor (No 87 of 1993) (No 2)*,[106] the court held that material irregularities could extend to matters other than the conduct or convening of the meeting. In that case, the debtor's failure to disclose all his assets and liabilities in his statement of affairs was held to amount to a material irregularity. This would also be grounds for presenting a bankruptcy petition in respect of the debtor, but the court held that it was not illogical to have two remedies in respect of the failure, since there might be cases in which a creditor felt that bankruptcy of the debtor would not improve his or her position. In *Lombard North Central plc v Brook*,[107] the chairman refused to admit a claim on the basis that it was based on a contractual provision which would be void as being a penalty; the court held that this view was mistaken, that the refusal to allow the creditor to vote was therefore an irregularity and, since it had affected the outcome, it was material.

7   IMPLEMENTATION AND VARIATION OF THE ARRANGEMENT

The nominee becomes the supervisor of the arrangement with the responsibility of overseeing its implementation; he or she may apply to the court for directions if necessary.[108] Assets included in the proposal and any income promised by the debtor will be transferred to the supervisor. Supervisors of an arrangement are to be treated as trustees of the assets in their hands.[109]

It may become necessary to make alterations to the voluntary arrangement and an arrangement may include a power to vary it.[110] In *Horrocks and Another v Broome*,[111] Hart J envisaged the possibility of a clause being so repugnant to the nature of the IVA in which it is contained that it could be struck down as void and of no effect. He also commented on the potential for such clauses to produce unpredictable results for those bound by the arrangements and said that it would be appropriate to challenge a

---

105 *Peck v Craighead* [1995] BCC 525.

106 [1996] BCC 80.

107 [1999] BPIR 701.

108 Insolvency Act 1986, s 263(4).

109 *Re Leisure Study Group Ltd* [1994] 2 BCLC 65.

110 The standard conditions for IVAs recently produced by the Association of Business Recovery Professionals does include a variation clause.

111 [1999] BPIR 66.

clause with potentially unfair consequences at the time of its approval. In *Raja v Rubin*,[112] it was held that the omission of an express power of variation in the voluntary arrangement itself did not preclude the debtor and those creditors who had an interest in the arrangement from agreeing to vary its terms, provided that the rights of another person bound by the arrangement were not adversely affected. Such a consensual variation did not have statutory force as part of the original arrangement, but had force in contract. Thus, the variation could not affect the rights and obligations of any person who was not a party to it, and such a person could properly seek the intervention of the court under s 263(3) of the Insolvency Act 1986 if he or she could show an interest which was adversely affected by the alteration.

Where it appears to a supervisor[113] that an officer of a company or an individual debtor has committed any criminal offence in connection with the voluntary arrangement, the matter must be reported to the Secretary of State[114] and the supervisor must provide such information and reasonable assistance as is required in connection with considering and bringing a prosecution.

Anyone dissatisfied by the conduct of the supervisor may apply to the court.[115] The supervisor has to report to the creditors, the court and the Insolvency Service every 12 months on the progress of the arrangement and within 28 days of its completion.[116]

8   CONSEQUENCES OF A FAILED VOLUNTARY ARRANGEMENT

The supervisor of an IVA or any person bound by it is entitled to present a petition for the bankruptcy of the debtor[117] on the grounds[118] that the debtor has failed to comply with his or her obligations under the arrangement or that false or misleading information was given by the debtor to the creditors when they were considering the proposal or that the debtor has failed to comply with the reasonable requirements of the supervisor. The supervisor of a CVA has *locus standi* to petition for the winding up or administration of a company.[119]

The issue arises of the consequences for the voluntary arrangement of the subsequent liquidation or bankruptcy of the debtor; the Court of Appeal considered this for the first time in *Re NT Gallagher & Son Ltd*.[120] This was a case of a CVA followed by a creditors' voluntary liquidation, but the court made it clear that its conclusions would also apply to an IVA. Previously, there had been a number of first instance decisions which had made very fine distinctions depending on the type of

---

112 [1999] 3 All ER 73.
113 Or, at an earlier stage in the proceedings, to a nominee.
114 Insolvency Act 1986, ss 7A, 262B
115 Insolvency Act 1986, ss 7(3), 263(3), Sched A1, para 39(3).
116 Insolvency Rules 1986, rr 5.26, 5.29.
117 Insolvency Act 1986, s 264(1)(c).
118 Insolvency Act 1986, s 276.
119 Insolvency Act 1986, s 7(4).
120 *Re NT Gallagher & Son Ltd (in Liquidation); Shierson and Another v Tomlinson and Another* [2002] 3 All ER 474.

liquidation or the identity of the petitioner for the bankruptcy order. These distinctions were based on inferences drawn from r 4.21A of the Insolvency Rules 1986[121] and from s 276(2) of the Insolvency Act 1986,[122] which provide for the expenses of a voluntary arrangement to be a first charge on the assets of a company which subsequently goes into compulsory liquidation and of an individual against whom a bankruptcy order is made on the petition of a supervisor of an IVA. It had been argued that these provisions should be taken to mean that the voluntary arrangement in such circumstances would have come to an end; the Court of Appeal held that these were consistent with such a result, but did not have the effect of bringing about that result and that there was, in fact, no statutory provision dealing with the issue. The Court went on to hold that the effect of the liquidation of the company or the bankruptcy of the debtor on a trust created by the voluntary arrangement will depend on the provisions of the arrangement. If the arrangement makes express provision for the situation, effect will be given to this. If there is no provision, the trust will continue notwithstanding the liquidation, bankruptcy or failure and will take effect according to its terms.[123] The creditors under the voluntary arrangement will be able to prove in the liquidation or bankruptcy for so much of their voluntary arrangement debt as remains after payment of what they have recovered under the trust. The voluntary arrangement itself will have been a binding settlement of any greater amount which they had been owed before they entered into the voluntary arrangement[124] so that the pre-IVA debts cannot be revived.

9   THE EXPERIENCE OF INDIVIDUAL VOLUNTARY ARRANGEMENTS IN OPERATION

Unlike company voluntary arrangements whose use is recognised to have been hampered by the lack of a moratorium, individual voluntary arrangements have been seen as a success story. They have grown from accounting for 5% of formal personal insolvencies in 1987 to 25% in 2002 (see the statistics at the end of Chapter 2).

The Loughborough University Banking Centre has carried out a considerable amount of research over the years into the operation of individual voluntary arrangements.[125] It carried out a study in 1989 of 100 IVA proposals followed by a 1992 follow-up survey of 78 of the proposals which had been accepted. About 33% of accepted arrangements subsequently met trouble, of which over two-thirds eventually failed. Some recurrent factors in the failure were identified; these included circumstances beyond the debtor's control such as redundancy and divorce but were often attributable to non-co-operation by the debtor in providing appropriate information in the preparation of the IVA or lack of will to continue to meet the agreed

---

121 In relation to CVAs.

122 In relation to IVAs.

123 *Re Bradley-Hole (a Bankrupt)* [1995] 2 BCLC 163; *Re Excalibur Airways Ltd* [1998] 1 BCLC 436; *Wellesby v Breleg* [2000] 2 BCLC 576; and *Re Kudos Glass Ltd* [2001] 1 BCLC 390 applied. *Davis v Martin-Sklan* [1995] 2 BCLC 483 and *Re Arthur Rathbone (Kitchens) Ltd* [1997] 2 BCLC 280 doubted.

124 See *Re McKeen* [1995] BCC 412 in relation to the effect of a voluntary arrangement on the pre-existing debts.

125 Pond (1989); Pond (1993); Pond (1995); Evans and Pond (1995); Pond (2002).

payments. IVAs which provided for payment of income by the debtor over an extended period were the most likely to fail. The survey found that the costs associated with the IVAs were demonstrably lower than would have been the case in a bankruptcy. Dividends for unsecured creditors were higher than would have been the case in bankruptcy. Arrangements which only involved the transfer of assets produced a higher dividend than would have been the case in a bankruptcy because of the lower costs involved. Arrangements which involved subsequent payments from the income of the debtor produced a much higher level of dividend than a bankruptcy where they succeeded but such arrangements were much more likely to fail than asset only arrangements.

More recent research[126] established that IVAs accounted for 82% of those formal personal insolvencies with assets and a dividend forecast. Dividends have been shown by the R3 surveys to be 17% higher for IVAs than for bankruptcies, although the time taken to produce this dividend was five years rather than the three years of bankruptcy. It would appear, not surprisingly, that creditor recoveries are greatest where the debtor is honest and the insolvency practitioner is diligent; the combination of a less diligent insolvency practitioner and a less than honest debtor tends to be fatal for the success of the IVA. Pond suggests that those IVAs where the creditors have insisted on the inclusion of more onerous provisions than originally suggested by the debtor are more likely to fail; in such cases, the creditors might have been better advised to reject the proposal completely and go for bankruptcy from the start. From the debtor's point of view, the stigma of an IVA may not be so much less than that of a bankruptcy; credit reference agencies tend to view both processes in the same light.

---

126 Pond (2002).

CHAPTER 10

COMPANY ADMINISTRATION ORDERS

1 INTRODUCTION

Company administration orders were introduced by the Insolvency Act 1986 on the recommendation of the Cork Committee, which saw them as a way of making the advantages of the receivership mechanism available in those circumstances in which receivers were not or could not be appointed. Essentially, the idea behind the administration order is to give a company facing insolvency a breathing space from the pressures of creditors to see if a means can be found of effecting a rescue. The Cork Committee recommended such a moratorium in the case of both administration and administrative receiverships, but the then government[1] only accepted the proposal in relation to administration: 'The Government believes that only a court-appointed official, the administrator, whose duty will be to act in the interests of all creditors and shareholders, should enjoy such temporary protection.'

Administration is not necessarily used with a view to rescuing the company. An administration may also allow a more effective realisation of the assets than would be available in a liquidation because of the difficulty a liquidator has in permitting a company to continue trading.[2] As seen in Chapter 6 above, the result of the Enterprise Act 2002[3] is that administration will replace administrative receivership in most cases and will become the mechanism for the enforcement of floating security over substantially the whole undertaking. The Enterprise Act 2002 makes radical changes to the administration order to enable it to fulfil the functions of an administrative receiver whilst, at the same time, taking into account as far as possible the interests of all the creditors.

Section 248 of the Enterprise Act 2002 replaces Part II of the Insolvency Act 1986 with a new s 8 of the Insolvency Act 1986, which states that 'Schedule B1 to this Act (which makes provision about the administration of companies) shall have effect'. Schedule 16 to the Enterprise Act 2002 contains Sched B1, which is to be inserted into the Insolvency Act 1986 after Sched A1; all paragraph references in this chapter are to paragraphs of that Schedule. Section 249 of the Enterprise Act 2002 disapplies these provisions in relation to water and sewerage undertakers, railways, air traffic services, public-private partnership agreements and building societies.

Paragraph 1 of Schedule B1 to the Insolvency Act 1986 provides that a company is 'in administration' while the appointment of an administrator has effect and that an administrator is a person appointed under the Schedule to manage the company's affairs, business and property. During the administration, the company is protected from its creditors. The administrator takes control of the company's property, manages its affairs and draws up proposals to achieve the purposes of the administration.

---

1   *A Revised Framework for Insolvency Law,* Cmnd 9175.
2   See Brown (1998).
3   These provisions are expected to come into force in September 2003.

The next section of this chapter explains the precise mechanisms by which administration may come about and then goes on to consider the nature of the moratorium on the exercise of rights against a company in administration. The chapter will then go on to consider the process of the administration, the hierarchy of purposes for which it should be conducted and the position of the administrator. The final sections consider the ending of an administration and the issue of meeting the expenses of the administration.

2   ROUTES INTO ADMINISTRATION

Under the original provisions, a court order was always required before a company could go into administration. Supporters of administrative receivership argued that one of its main beneficial features was the speed with which a company could be put into administrative receivership out of court. The Enterprise Act 2002 retains the ability of a holder of a floating charge over the whole undertaking to take such speedy out-of-court action and extends the possibility to the company itself and its directors. The three routes into administration are, therefore, a court order under para 11 of Sched B1, appointment under para 14 by the holder of a qualifying floating charge or appointment under para 22 by the company or its directors. The administrator is an officer of the court, whether or not he or she has been appointed by the court.[4]

(a) Appointment of administrator out of court by the holder of a qualifying floating charge

The holder of a qualifying floating charge or charges (or forms of security including at least one qualifying floating charge) relating to the whole or substantially the whole of the company's property may appoint an administrator under para 14. A floating charge will be a qualifying floating charge if created by an instrument which states that para 14 applies to the charge or purports to empower the holder of the charge to appoint either an administrator or an administrative receiver of the company. Paragraph 14 is so drafted as to allow instigation of an administration by holders of so called 'lightweight' floating charges which were originally developed purely for the purpose of conferring the veto of administration provided by the original s 9 of the Insolvency Act 1986 rather than in order to provide any additional real security.[5]

A person may not appoint an administrator under para 14 unless at least two business days' written notice has been given to the holder of any prior qualifying floating charge or such holder has consented in writing to the appointment. A person who appoints an administrator under para 14 shall file with the court a notice of appointment which must include a statutory declaration that the person is the holder of a qualifying floating charge in respect of the company's property, that each floating charge relied on in making the appointment was enforceable on the date of the

---

4   Insolvency Act 1986, Sched B1, para 5. It is presumably hoped that this will enable recognition of the administration procedure by overseas jurisdictions without the need for a court order. See Dawson (1996) for a discussion of the consequences of being an officer of the court.

5   Vinelott J held in *Re Croftbell* [1990] BCC 781 that this device worked. See Oditah (1991).

appointment and that the appointment is in accordance with Schedule B1; it will be an offence to make a statement in the statutory declaration which is false and which is not reasonably believed to be true. The notice of appointment must also be accompanied by a statement by the administrator that he or she consents to the appointment, that in his or her opinion the purpose of the administration is reasonably likely to be achieved and giving such other information and opinions as may be prescribed. The administration does not begin until the required documentation is filed.

(b) Appointment of administrator out of court by the company or directors

Both a company and the directors of a company[6] may appoint an administrator under para 22. A para 22 appointment may not take place during the period of 12 months from a previous administration made either under para 22 or as a result of an application made by the company or its directors.[7] A para 22 appointment cannot be made either within 12 months of the end of a moratorium under Sched A1 which has not resulted in a CVA or within 12 months of the premature ending of a CVA made in pursuance to a moratorium.[8] Paragraph 25 prevents the appointment of an administrator by a company or by its directors if a petition for winding up or administration has been presented and not disposed of or if an administrative receiver is in office. A person proposing to make a para 22 appointment must give at least five business days' written notice to anyone entitled to appoint an administrative receiver or an administrator under para 14; the appointment cannot be made until the period of notice has expired or each person to whom notice has been given has consented in writing. A copy of the notice must also be filed with the court and must be accompanied by a statutory declaration that the company is or is likely to become unable to pay its debts, that the company is not in liquidation and that, so far as the person making the statement is able to ascertain, the appointment is not prevented by paras 23 to 25. A person appointing an administrator of a company under para 22 must file with the court a notice of the appointment including a statutory declaration by the person making the appointment that the person is entitled to make a para 22 appointment, that the appointment is in accordance with the Schedule and that, so far as the person making the statement is able to ascertain, the statements made and information given in the statutory declaration filed with the notice of intention to appoint remain accurate. The notice of appointment must be accompanied by a statement by the administrator that he or she consents to the appointment, that in his or her opinion the purpose of the administration is reasonably likely to be achieved and giving such other information and opinions as may be prescribed. The administration does not begin until the notice of appointment is correctly filed; if, before this happens, a para 14 administration takes effect, the para 22 appointment shall not take effect.

---

6   Insolvency Act 1986, Sched B1, para 105 provides that any reference to something being done by the directors of a company includes a reference to the same thing being done by a majority of the directors to a company.

7   Insolvency Act 1986, Sched B1, para 24.

8   Insolvency Act 1986, Sched B1, para 24.

(c) Court order

Those who may make an application for such an order are[9] one or more of: the company, the directors of the company, one or more creditors[10] of the company and the justices' chief executive for a magistrates' court in relation to a fine imposed on the company. The applicant must as soon as reasonably practicable after making the application notify any person who has been or is or may be entitled to appoint an administrative receiver of the company or who may be entitled to appoint an administrator under para 14.[11] An administration application may not be withdrawn without the permission of the court.

The court may make an administration order in relation to a company only if satisfied that the company is or is likely to become unable to pay its debts and that the administration order is reasonably likely to achieve the purpose of administration.[12] The original requirement in s 8 of the Insolvency Act 1986 was for an order to be 'likely to achieve one or more' of the specified purposes of administration and there was a certain amount of litigation about the meaning of this. In *Re Consumer and Industrial Press*,[13] an early decision on the section, Peter Gibson J took the view that the court had to be satisfied that it was more probable than not that the order would achieve its purpose. Hoffmann J refused to follow this restrictive view in *Re Harris Simmons Ltd*[14] and said, referring to the explanation in the Cork Report of when it was envisaged that an administration order would be made, that the question was whether there was a 'real prospect' that one of the purposes would be achieved. This view was followed by Vinelott J in *Re Primlaks*[15] and is now generally accepted.[16] In *Re SCL Services*[17] Peter Gibson J, in using the 'reasonable prospect' test, held that only purposes which passed the test could be included in the order. Professor Milman suggested[18] that 'the real significance of the "reasonable prospect" test lay in its symbolic offering of support by the courts for the administration order process'. The addition of the word 'reasonably' to the reinstatement of the requirements in para 11 of Sched B1 is presumably intended to reinforce the interpretation which the courts have reached of the original provision.

There has recently been court consideration of what is meant by 'is or is unlikely to become unable to pay its debts'. In *Re Colt Telecom Group plc*,[19] the petitioners, who held about £75 million face value of notes issued by the company, claimed that, despite net assets of £997 million being shown in the latest balance sheet, the company was or was likely to become insolvent on the basis of a dramatic fall in the company's

---

9   Insolvency Act 1986, Sched B1, para 12(1).
10   Including contingent and prospective creditors.
11   Insolvency Act 1986, Sched B1, para 12(2).
12   Insolvency Act 1986, Sched B1, para 11. The statutory declarations and administrators' statements required under paras 11 and 22 perform the same function.
13   [1988] BCLC 177.
14   [1989] 1 WLR 368.
15   [1989] BCLC 734.
16   *Re Land and Property Trust Co* [1991] BCC 446 is an example of a case in which it was held there was no reasonable prospect of success. Costs were awarded against the directors personally.
17   [1990] BCLC 98.
18   See Rajak, 1993, p 373.
19   [2002] EWHC 2815 (Ch).

share price and on its substantial operating losses and negative cashflows. The court held, dismissing the petition (and holding that on the evidence the company was not in any event insolvent on either the cashflow or the balance sheet basis), that it was not enough merely to show a 'real prospect' of insolvency as opposed to insolvency being more likely than not. Parliament could not have intended that companies should be exposed to that kind of hostile proceeding where it was more likely than not that the company was not insolvent. However, the court did not think insolvency was proved on the 'real prospect' test either. That was not to say insolvency was impossible; in a sense, anything might happen to the company or many other companies in the business. But that was not the same thing as a real prospect of insolvency. Even on the lesser test, the 'real prospect' had to be tangible.

On hearing the application, the court may[20] make the order sought, dismiss the application, adjourn the hearing conditionally or unconditionally, make an interim order, treat the application as a winding up petition and make any order which the court could make under s 125, or make any other order which the court thinks appropriate. An interim order may restrict the exercise of a power of the directors or the company and make provision conferring a discretion on the court or on a person qualified to act as an insolvency practitioner in relation to the company. Where there is an administrative receiver of the company, the court must dismiss the application unless the person by or on behalf of whom the receiver was appointed consents to the making of the administration order or the court thinks the security by virtue of which the receiver was appointed would be liable to be released, discharged or avoided under ss 238, 239 or 245 of the Insolvency Act 1986.[21]

Paragraph 13 retains the wide discretion given to the court originally by s 9(4) of the Insolvency Act 1986 as to whether or not to make the order and cases under that section will remain relevant. In *Re Arrows (No 3)*,[22] the court refused to make an administration order on the ground that a compulsory liquidation was appropriate; the administration had been opposed by a majority in value of the creditors and there were serious matters requiring thorough investigation. Less weight will be given to the interests of the secured creditors than to those of the unsecured creditors, since the former have less to lose from the administration.[23] In *Re West Park Golf and Country Club*,[24] the court held that it was an abuse of process to present a petition, as a means of applying commercial pressure, in circumstances where there were no reasonable grounds for believing that the petition would be granted. In *Re Dianoor Jewels Ltd*,[25] it was held that, although the purpose of one of the directors of a company in petitioning for an administration order might well have been to frustrate his wife's ancillary proceedings claim, it was appropriate, given that the company was in fact insolvent, for the company to be put into administration to protect its creditors.

On an application by the holder of a qualifying floating charge, the court may make an administration order regardless of the state of solvency of the company provided it is satisfied that the applicant would be able to appoint an administrator

---

20 Insolvency Act 1986, Sched B1, para 13.
21 Insolvency Act 1986, Sched B1, para 39.
22 [1992] BCC 131.
23 *Re Consumer & Industrial Press* [1988] BCLC 177; *Re Imperial Motors* [1990] BCLC 29.
24 [1997] 1 BCLC 20.
25 [2001] 1 BCLC 450.

under para 14.[26] If an application is made by someone other than the holder of a qualifying floating charge and the holder of a qualifying charge asks for the appointment of a specified person as administrator, the court will normally grant the request. Paragraph 37 enables a court to make an administration order on the application of a holder of a qualifying floating charge who is only prevented from making a para 14 appointment by the fact that the company is in compulsory liquidation; if an administration order is made, the court shall discharge the winding up order. Paragraph 38 enables the liquidator of a company to make an administration application in similar manner to para 37.

3 THE MORATORIUM

Paragraph 42 provides that where a company is in administration, it is not possible for a resolution to be passed to wind the company up nor for a winding up order to be made other than pursuant to s 124A of the Insolvency Act 1986 (in the public interest) or under s 367 of the Financial Services and Markets Act 2000. Paragraph 43 contains an extensive moratorium protecting a company in administration from its creditors unless either the administrator or the court agrees to an exception. No step may be taken to enforce security over the company's property or to repossess goods in the company's possession under a hire-purchase agreement.[27] The exercise of a right of forfeiture by peaceable re-entry by a landlord in relation to premises let to the company is prohibited, as is the institution or continuation of legal process (including legal proceedings, execution and distress) against the company or property of the company.

An interim moratorium will be brought into effect under para 44 by the presentation of an administration application or by the filing of a notice of intention to appoint an administrator under para 14 or para 22. The interim moratorium will continue throughout the period before the court considers the application or, in relation to a notice, for five days from filing unless the appointment of an administrator is made earlier than this. During an interim moratorium a winding up petition may be presented or an administrative receiver or an administrator under para 14 appointed but otherwise the moratorium contained in para 43 will apply.

The moratorium contained in para 43 re-enacts in almost identical terms s 11(c) and (d) of the Insolvency Act 1986, which gave rise to considerable litigation to determine the precise scope of the moratorium and the circumstances in which a court would (and, therefore, an administrator should) give leave for an exception to be made. Most of the phrases used in the sub-sections (and now used in para 43) have been subject to judicial scrutiny and it is notable that the courts have frequently referred to the legislative policy behind the legislation. The court in *Barclays Mercantile Business Finance v SIBEC*[28] made the point that the rights of creditors are not substantively affected; the moratorium prevents enforcement and is designed to

---

26 In a situation with cross-border implications, the administrator may need to have been appointed by the court in order to be recognised within certain other jurisdictions.

27 Which by para 111 includes a conditional sale agreement, a chattel leasing agreement and a retention of title agreement.

28 [1992] 1 WLR 1253.

enable the administrator to control the assets free from interference by creditors.[29] In *Re Maxwell Fleet and Facilities Management Ltd (in Administration)*,[30] it was held that an administration order does not stop time running for limitation purposes.

In *Bristol Airport plc v Powdrill*,[31] the Court of Appeal had to consider the meaning of 'other steps', 'security' and 'the company's property'. The issue here was whether an airport authority could exercise its statutory right of detention[32] against aircraft leased to a company in administration. The court held that the taking of a step involved preventing the administrator from doing something with respect to the assets covered by the security which he or she would otherwise be entitled to do[33] and included the retaking of property. The court went on to hold that 'the company's property' included property held by the company under a lease; it looked to s 436 of the Insolvency Act 1986 and was also influenced by the fact that equipment leasing is commonplace as a method of corporate finance. The court also held that 'security' included a statutory lien. In *London Flight Centre (Stansted) Ltd v Osprey Aviation Ltd*,[34] the court held that the moratorium also extends to a contractual lien.[35]

The meaning of 'enforcement of security' has exercised the courts on a number of occasions. It has been held that, in relation to a possessory security, passivity does not constitute enforcement; something more such as failure to deliver up the property after a request by the administrator would be required for there to be enforcement.[36] It is no longer necessary to consider whether a landlord's right of forfeiture is a security right so as to fall within the moratorium since the amendment to the Insolvency Act 1986 introduced by the Insolvency Act 2000 has been re-enacted in para 43, which makes it clear that such a right is within the moratorium.[37]

In *Re Atlantic Computers*,[38] the Court of Appeal had to decide, firstly, whether administrators could continue to receive rents on computers which had been sub-let to customers without handing over the rents to the lessors of the computers and, secondly, whether the owners could repossess the computers from the customers. In answer to the first point, the court held that it was not improper for the administrators to continue to use the computers.[39] The Court of Appeal held that goods sub-let by a company were still 'in the company's possession' as between the company and the lessor and, therefore, leave was required before the lessors could repossess them; the court went on to give leave for reasons explained below.

---

29 See Prentice, Oditah and Segal in Ziegel, 1994, Chapter 5.

30 [1999] 2 BCLC 721.

31 [1990] Ch 744.

32 Under the Civil Aviation Act 1982, s 88.

33 On this basis, s 11 would not stop the service of a demand in respect of an on-demand loan or of a notice rescinding a contract.

34 (2002) unreported, 2 July (ChD).

35 But not, according to Jacob J in *Osborne Clarke v Carter* (unreported, noted by Unwin (2003)), liens over title deeds (which survive the appointment of an administrator under the Insolvency Act 1986, s 246(3)).

36 *Re Sabre International Products Ltd* [1991] BCLC 470, which concerned the right of carriers to detain goods.

37 *Re Lomax Leisure* [1999] 3 All ER 22 had held, following *Razzaq v Pala* [1997] EGCS 75 and *Ezekiel v Orakpo* [1977] 1 QB 260, that it was not.

38 [1990] BCC 859.

39 And there was no room for the application of the expenses principle from liquidation (as to which, see Chapter 34, below).

Goods will still be held 'under a hire-purchase agreement' where the agreement provides for its determination on the presentation of an administration petition.[40]

Paragraph 43(6) of Sched B1 to the Insolvency Act 1986 provides that 'no legal process (including legal proceedings, execution, distress and diligence) may be instituted or continued against the company or property of the company'. This has replaced s 11(3)(d), which provided that 'no other proceedings and no execution or other legal process may be commenced or continued and no distress may be levied'. The new wording reinforces the view of the Court of Appeal in *Bristol Airport plc v Powdrill*[41] that 'proceedings' meant legal proceedings or quasi-legal proceedings such as arbitration rather than some act of a more general nature. In *Re Railtrack plc*,[42] Lord Woolf observed that the moratorium would cover a wide category of legal or quasi-legal proceedings but that such proceedings would have to be *against* the company or its property. The decision in *Re Barrow Borough Transport Ltd*[43] (that an application for an out of time registration under s 404 of the Companies Act 1985 was not prevented by the moratorium) was based on the view that although such an application was 'proceedings', it was not proceedings against the company or its property.[44] In *Air Ecosse Ltd v CAA*,[45] the Inner House of the Court of Session, holding that an application for the removal of the company's civil aviation licence was not within the moratorium, said that 'other proceedings' were limited to those by creditors against the company; this view has not been followed on several occasions. It has been held that industrial tribunal applications are caught by the moratorium,[46] as is the adjudication process referred to in s 108 of the Housing Grants, Construction and Regeneration Act 1996.[47] In *Biosource Technologies Inc v Axis Genetics plc*,[48] Ferris J held that an action by a competitor company for revocation of a patent licence fell within the ambit of the moratorium. In *Re Railtrack plc*,[49] the Court of Appeal held (reversing Sir Andrew Morritt VC) that determinations by the Rail Regulator of applications by train operators for access to the railtrack, although having many of the qualities of procedure associated with legal proceedings, did not fall within the ambit of the moratorium and that, although the judgment in *Air Ecosse* had been doubted in part, it was equally unlikely that Parliament would have intended to limit the regulatory powers conferred on the Civil Aviation Authority.

In *Environment Agency v Clark*,[50] the Court of Appeal held that a prosecution of a company in administration for failure to comply with the conditions attached to a waste disposal licence fell within the ambit of the moratorium since 'other

---

40   *Re David Meek Plant Hire Ltd* [1994] 1 BCLC 680.
41   [1990] 2 All ER 493 at 506–07.
42   [2002] 4 All ER 435.
43   [1990] Ch 227.
44   *Re Bristol Airport* [1990] Ch 744, holding that the exercise of statutory lien or rights under contract was not proceedings.
45   (1987) 3 BCC 492.
46   *Powdrill v Watson* [1995] 2 All ER 65; *Carr v British International Helicopters* [1993] BCC 855. Leave to bring the action will usually be given, but further leave would be needed to enforce any order made by the tribunal.
47   *A Straume (UK) Ltd v Bradlor Developments Ltd* [2000] BCC 333.
48   [1999] 1 BCLC 286.
49   [2002] 4 All ER 435. See Simmons (2003).
50   [2000] 3 WLR 1304. See Abbott (2001).

proceedings' included criminal as well as civil proceedings.[51] Scott Baker J observed that:

> the ambit of criminal offences that may be committed by corporations is very wide, ranging from very grave, eg manslaughter, at one end of the scale to the quite trivial at the other. Sometimes, the fact that a company is in administration will be of little or no significance when weighed against the public interest in proceeding with the prosecution. But in others the interests of the creditors, for example, may be the critical consideration. There may be a very good reason for not proceeding with a prosecution during the administration, as the consequence may be to tip the company into irretrievable insolvency. Also, as was pointed out in argument, refusal of leave is not necessarily permanent; the court could entertain a further application. The court dealing with the administration is, in my judgment, particularly well placed to weigh up the arguments for and against granting leave. When the public interest so dictates, leave to pursue criminal proceedings ought readily to be given, but that will not be every case.

The Court went on, however, to decide that in this case, the judge at first instance had been in error in refusing leave. He should not have regarded the interests of the creditors of the company as trumping all other considerations and had failed to take into account the extent of the pollution of the environment and detriment to the amenities of the locality caused by the breach of the licence over a long period. Scott Baker J also pointed out that in the event of conviction, there is a statutory obligation[52] on the court fixing the amount of any fine to take account of all the circumstances, including the financial circumstances of the company.

In *Re Atlantic Computer Systems plc*,[53] the Court of Appeal laid down some general guidelines to assist administrators in deciding whether or not to give consent. They hoped, by so doing, to reduce the number of applications being made to court for consent. The guidelines in summary were:

(a) the onus was on the party seeking leave to make out a case;

(b) if granting leave would be unlikely to impede the achievement of the purpose of the administration, leave should normally be given;

(c) in other cases, the court must carry out a balancing exercise, weighing the legitimate interests of the secured creditor against those of the company's other creditors;

(d) an administration for the benefit of unsecured creditors should not be conducted at the expense of those who have proprietary rights;

(e) it will normally be a sufficient ground for the granting of leave that a refusal would cause significant loss to the applicant but, if substantially greater loss would be caused to others by the grant of leave, that may outweigh the loss caused to the applicant by a refusal;

---

51 In *Re Railtrack plc (in Railway Administration)* [2002] 3 All ER 140, which arose in the context of a railway administration order under the Railways Act 1993, the court considered some of the case law on the Insolvency Act 1986, s 11 in concluding that a determination by the Rail Regulator of an application by a train operator for access to the railtrack was 'proceedings' and therefore caught by the moratorium in the railway administration.

52 Criminal Justice Act 1991, s 18(3).

53 [1990] BCC 859.

(f) in assessing what loss would accrue, the court will consider the financial position of the company; if relevant, its ability to pay rental arrears and continuing rentals; the administrator's proposals; the period for which the administration order has already been in force and is expected to remain in force; the effect on the administration if leave is given; the effect on the applicant if leave is refused; the end result sought to be achieved by the administration; the prospects of that result being achieved; the history of the administration so far; and the probability of the suggested consequences.

The conduct of the creditor is also relevant. It can be seen from *Bristol Airport plc v Powdrill*[54] that leave will not normally be granted where the creditor has been benefiting from administration. It is more likely that a creditor will get leave if he or she has made it clear from the start that he or she is opposed to the administration and wishes to enforce his or her security.

The company in administration in *Re Atlantic Computers*[55] was in the business of leasing computers, a substantial number of which it held under hire-purchase agreements. Two suppliers sought leave to repossess the stock and the Court of Appeal held that leave should be granted, despite the fact that this would make it more difficult for the administrators. A failure to grant leave would cause significant loss to the lessors since the computers were a wasting asset. The court said that the starting point in the balancing act was the protection of the security holder and that it would not be fair to leave the secured creditors in the weak bargaining position of not being able to rely on proprietary rights as a bargaining counter. Administration should not be used for redistributional purposes and should not be conducted for the benefit of unsecured creditors at the expense of those with proprietary claims.

At the start of an administration, any administrative receiver shall vacate office and any receiver of part of the company's property shall vacate office if the administrator so requires. The remuneration of any such administrative or other receiver shall be charged on and paid out of any property of the company which was in the custody or under the control of the receiver immediately before vacating office.

4   PURPOSES OF ADMINISTRATION

The Enterprise Act 2002 has substantially revised the provisions relating to the purpose of an administration. The original s 8(3) of the Insolvency Act 1986 provided that there were four possible purposes for which an administration order could be made and each order had to specify the purpose(s) relevant to it. The four possible purposes were:

(a) the survival of the company and the whole or any part of its undertaking as a going concern;

(b) the approval of a company voluntary arrangement;

(c) the sanctioning of a scheme of arrangement under s 425 of the Companies Act 1985; and

---

54   [1990] Ch 744.
55   [1990] BCC 859.

(d) a more advantageous realisation of the company's assets than would be effected on a winding up.

It was possible for an administrator to go back to the court for approval of a change to the purposes for which the administration order was being pursued.

The result of the Enterprise Act 2002 is that there is a hierarchy of possible purposes which applies in every case. Paragraph 3 of Sched B1 provides that the administrator of a company must perform his functions with the objective of:

(a) rescuing the company as a going concern,[56] or

(b) achieving a better result for the company's creditors as a whole than would be likely if the company were wound up (without first being in administration), or

(c) realising property in order to make a distribution to one or more secured or preferential creditors.

The paragraph goes on to provide that the administrator must perform his functions in the interests of the creditors as a whole and in pursuance of objective (a) unless he or she thinks that it is not reasonably practicable to achieve that objective, or that the objective specified in (b) would achieve a better result for the creditors as a whole. An administrator may only pursue objective (c) if he or she thinks it not reasonably practicable to achieve either (a) or (b) and he or she does not unnecessarily harm the interests of the creditors of the company as a whole. Litigation is likely to be necessary before it becomes entirely clear how this hierarchy of purposes will work in practice.

5   PROCESS OF ADMINISTRATION

An administrator must publish his or her appointment as prescribed by para 46; this includes a requirement to notify the company and every creditor of whom he or she is aware. The administrator must obtain a statement of the affairs of the company from one or more of a list of persons set out in para 47; in most cases, this will mean officers and employees of the company. A statement of affairs must be provided within 11 days of the request for it unless either the administrator or the court extends the period. The administrator must make a statement setting out proposals for achieving the purpose of the administration and send a copy of the statement to the registrar of companies and the members and creditors of the company within eight weeks of the start of the administration;[57] in relation to the members, it will be sufficient to publish a notice informing them how they can obtain a copy. Each copy sent to a creditor must be accompanied by an invitation to an initial creditors' meeting set for a date within 10 weeks of the start of the administration.[58] Under para 52, a meeting need not be held if the administrator states that the company has sufficient property to enable each creditor to be paid in full, or insufficient property to enable a distribution to be made to unsecured creditors other than from the ring-fenced portion of the assets subject to a floating charge, or that neither of the objectives specified in para 3(1)(a) and (b) can be achieved. The decision not to call a meeting may be overridden by creditors whose

---

56   There was considerable debate as the Enterprise Bill went through Parliament as to whether the purpose should be the rescue of the company or of the business.

57   Insolvency Act 1986, Sched B1, para 49.

58   Insolvency Act 1986, Sched B1, para 51.

debts amount to at least 10% of the total; such a percentage of creditors may require the calling of a creditors meeting at any time during the administration.

Paragraph 73 provides that an administrator's proposals may not include any action which affects the right of a secured creditor to enforce security, would result in a preferential debt of the company being paid otherwise than in priority to its non-preferential debts or would result in one preferential creditor of the company being paid a smaller proportion of his or her debt than another. An affected creditor may, however, consent to his or her rights being affected and para 73 does not apply to a proposal for a voluntary arrangement or a scheme of arrangement.

At the initial creditors' meeting, the administrator's proposals may be approved without modification or with modification to which the administrator consents.[59] The administrator shall then report the decision of the meeting to the court and the registrar of companies. If the administrator subsequently wishes to make substantial revision to the approved modifications, another meeting of creditors must be called in accordance with para 54. The court has wide discretionary powers under para 55 where an administrator has to report a failure by a creditors meeting to approve proposals.

A creditors' meeting may establish a committee of creditors.[60] Anything which is required or permitted to be done by a meeting of creditors may be done by correspondence[61] instead, under para 58.

6   POWERS AND RESPONSIBILITIES OF THE ADMINISTRATOR[62]

The administrator takes custody or control of all the property to which he or she thinks the company is entitled.[63] Paragraph 59 provides that the administrator of a company may do anything necessary or expedient for the management of the affairs, business and property of the company..The administrator has the powers specified in Sched 1 of the Insolvency Act 1986. The administrator may remove or appoint directors, call meetings of members or creditors and apply to the court for directions. A person who deals with the administrator of a company in good faith and for value need not inquire whether the administrator is acting within his powers. An act of an administrator will be valid in spite of a defect in his appointment or qualification.[64] A company in administration or an officer of a company in administration may not exercise a management power without the consent of the administrator. The directors will be under an obligation to co-operate with the administrator.[65]

Subject to any directions given by the court, the administrator has a duty to manage the company in accordance with any proposals approved by the creditors,

---

59   Insolvency Act 1986, Sched B1, para 53.
60   Insolvency Act 1986, Sched B1, para 57.
61   Insolvency Act 1986, Sched B1, para 111 provides that this includes correspondence by telephonic or electronic means.
62   Insolvency Act 1986, Sched B1, paras 59–73.
63   Insolvency Act 1986, Sched B1, para 67.
64   Insolvency Act 1986, Sched B1, para 104.
65   Insolvency Act 1986, ss 235, 236. Failure to co-operate might also be grounds for a disqualification order on the grounds of unfitness: see the Company Directors Disqualification Act 1986, s 6 and Sched 1.

any revision of those proposals which the administrator does not consider to be substantial and any revision of the proposals approved by the creditors. Once the creditors have approved proposals, the court may only give directions which are consistent with those proposals or are required to reflect a change in circumstances since the approval or which the court thinks desirable because of a misunderstanding about approved proposals.

The case law shows a distinct reluctance on the part of the courts to become involved in the day-to-day management of an administration. In *Re T & D Industries plc (in Administration)*,[66] the issue arose as to the power of the administrator to dispose of company assets before the creditors have had a chance to approve proposals. Neuberger J held, in relation to the similarly worded original provisions of the Insolvency Act 1986,[67] that an administrator could dispose of company assets without the leave of the court unless the administration order provided otherwise. A conclusion to the contrary, requiring the administrators to apply for directions whenever they wished to do something, would involve administrators in potential delay and expense and would be inconsistent with the policy of the administration system which was meant to be a more flexible, cheaper and comparatively informal alternative to liquidation. Moreover, it was questionable whether, in the majority of cases, there would be any real benefit for anyone in requiring administrators to apply for directions since such an application would normally be made without notice, and the court would almost always conclude that the answer was either obviously favourable or that the decision was a commercial or administrative one for the administrator. Thus, obtaining a direction from the court would normally be a waste of time and money unless such a direction ensured that the administrator was thereafter free from any liability to anyone, including the creditors, which would be a surprising result, not least because those who might have a claim against the administrator, deriving from the course he proposed, would normally not appear or be able to make representations. The administrator should, however, put his or her proposals to the creditors as quickly as possible and, in many circumstances, even where it was not possible to call formal creditors' meetings, it would be possible to obtain and take into account the view of creditors.

In *Re CE King Ltd (in Administration)*,[68] the court showed a similar disinclination to become involved in the management of an administration, holding that the court would not interfere with a commercial decision of administrators unless they were proposing to take a course which was based on a wrong application of the law and/or was conspicuously unfair to a particular creditor or contractor of the company when the court could and, in an appropriate case, should be prepared to do so, but the course the court should take would depend on the precise facts and circumstances of the case.

Schedule B1 to the Insolvency Act 1986 includes an express requirement that the administrator must perform his or her functions as quickly and efficiently as is reasonably practicable.[69]

---

66 [2000] 1 All ER 333.
67 The court was considering the Insolvency Act 1986, s 17(2). Similar provisions are to be found in the Insolvency Act 1986, Sched B1, para 68.
68 [2000] 2 BCLC 297.
69 Insolvency Act 1986, Sched B1, para 4.

The administrator may deal with or dispose of any property subject to a floating charge as if it were not subject to a floating charge;[70] if such property is disposed of, the holder of the floating charge shall have the same priority in respect of the proceeds of sale (or other property acquired in return for the disposed of property). Paragraph 71 allows the court to enable the administrator to dispose of property subject to a security other than a floating charge as if it were not subject to the security if it thinks that such disposal would be likely to promote the purpose of administration. The net proceeds of sale must be applied towards discharging the sums secured by the security together with any additional money required to produce the amount determined by the court as the net proceeds which would be realised on a sale of the property at market value. Paragraph 72 allows the court, where it thinks it will be likely to promote the purpose of the administration, to enable the administrator to dispose of goods in the possession of the company under a hire-purchase agreement as if all the rights of the owner under the agreement were vested in the company. The same rules about the proceeds of sale apply as under para 71.

Paragraph 65 provides that the administrator has the power to make a distribution to a creditor of the company. Section 175 of the Insolvency Act 1986 shall apply in the same way as it does to a liquidation. Court permission will be needed for a distribution to a creditor who is neither secured nor preferential. The provisions of para 65 are new and address the problem that creditors who would have enjoyed the status of preferential creditors where an administration is followed by compulsory liquidation are likely to object to a voluntary liquidation, which will deprive them of this status, taking place instead.[71] The new provisions will allow the administrator to make a distribution to such creditors in the course of the administration.

7 CHALLENGE TO THE ADMINISTRATOR

Paragraph 74 restates the provisions of s 27 of the Insolvency Act 1986 in that it provides for a creditor or a member of a company in administration to be able to apply to the court claiming either that the administrator is acting or has acted so as unfairly to harm the interests of the applicant (whether alone or in common with some or all other members or creditors) or that the administrator proposes to act in such a way. Paragraph 74(2) adds a new provision to the effect that a creditor or member of a company in administration may apply to the court claiming that the administrator is not performing his or her functions as quickly or as efficiently as is reasonably practicable. The court has a very wide discretion as to its response to such an application, but may not make any order which would impede or prevent the implementation of an approved voluntary arrangement, approved compromise or arrangement sanctioned under s 425 of the Companies Act 1985 or proposals (or revisions) approved under para 53 or para 54 more than 28 days previously.

---

70 Insolvency Act 1986, Sched B1, para 70.
71 This is because of the provisions of the Insolvency Act 1986, s 387(3) which determines the relevant date for preferential status in a liquidation. See, for example, *Re Powerstore* [1998] 1 All ER 121 and *Re UCT (UK) Ltd* [2001] 2 All ER 186. See Brown (1998).

Re Charnley Davies Ltd[72] was an application under s 27 of the Insolvency Act 1986 brought by creditors who complained that the administrator had negligently failed to get the best price available for the assets. Millett J found that the evidence did not support the claim of negligence and went on to say that, in any event, a sale at a negligent undervalue would not, *per se*, fall within the section. He said that 'an allegation that the acts complained of are unlawful or infringe the petitioners' legal rights is not a necessary averment in a section 27 petition. In my judgement, it is not a sufficient averment either'. He went on to say that a complaint that the administrator was showing insufficient regard for the interests of the creditors would be appropriate under s 27, but that if the whole gist of the complaint lay in the unlawfulness of the conduct, it could be adequately redressed by the remedy provided by the law for that wrong. In the case of professional negligence by the administrator, the appropriate remedy would be to have the administration order discharged and the company put into liquidation so that the liquidator could pursue the former administrator under s 212 of the Insolvency Act 1986.[73]

Paragraph 75 provides for the court to consider an allegation of misfeasance against an administrator during the course of the administration. This provision, which is new, parallels the misfeasance provisions which apply in a liquidation under s 212 of the Insolvency Act 1986.

8   REPLACING AN ADMINISTRATOR

Paragraph 87 provides for the resignation in prescribed circumstances of an administrator; under the original provisions, the circumstances were ill health, or because he or she intends to cease acting as an insolvency practitioner, or because of a conflict of interest or change in personal circumstances which precludes or makes impracticable his or her continuation as administrator, or on other grounds with the leave of the court. An administrator may be removed by court order under para 88 and must, under para 89, vacate office on ceasing to be qualified to act as an insolvency practitioner. A vacancy in the office of administrator will be dealt with under paras 90 to 95. Paragraph 98 provides for the discharge from liability of an administrator.

9   THE END OF THE ADMINISTRATION

Paragraph 81 allows a creditor of the company to apply to the court for the appointment of an administrator to cease to have effect; the application must allege an improper motive on the part of the applicant for the administration order where the administrator was appointed by court. If the administrator was appointed under para 14 or para 22, the application must allege an improper motive on the part of the person who appointed the administrator.

---

72   [1990] BCC 605.
73   As to which, see Chapter 31.

An administration will automatically end one year after it takes effect[74] unless it has been extended by the court. The administration can be extended by up to six months, once only, without going to court with the consent of all the secured creditors and in excess of 50% of the company's unsecured creditors, disregarding any creditor who does not respond to an invitation to give or withhold consent. If the administrator has already made a statement that there will be nothing for the unsecured creditors (apart from the ring-fenced assets), then the required consent is that of secured creditors and in excess of 50% of the preferential creditors.

The administrator may apply to the court for the administration to be ended; such an application must be made if the administrator thinks the purpose of the administration cannot be achieved or that the company should not have entered administration. An application must also be made if required by a creditors' meeting or, where the administration was commenced by court order, when the administrator thinks that the purpose of administration has been sufficiently achieved.

If the administrator was appointed under para 14 or para 22, the administration may be brought to an end by filing a notice under para 80 with the court and the registrar of companies.

Paragraph 82 provides for the ending of an administration as a consequence of a successful petition to wind up the company under s 124A of the Insolvency Act 1986 (public interest) or on a petition by the Financial Services Authority. Paragraph 83 provides for the moving of the company from administration to creditors' voluntary liquidation, once secured creditors have been provided for, in order to make a distribution to the unsecured creditors. If there is no possibility of a distribution to creditors, the company may move from administration to dissolution under para 84.

10 THE EXPENSES OF THE ADMINISTRATION

Where a person ceases to be an administrator, his or her remuneration and expenses shall be charged on and payable out of property of which he or she had custody or control immediately before cessation and will be payable in priority to any floating charge.[75] In *Spring Valley Properties Ltd v Harris*,[76] the court held that s 19(5) of the Insolvency Act 1986 offered no assistance to the landlord of property which had been rented by a company in administration, as it only afforded priority in respect of claims arising under new contracts made by the administrator, not, as in this case, in respect of claims under a subsisting contract. The fact that the court might have required the administrator to pay rent as a condition of permitting him to remain in occupation was irrelevant as the landlord had made no such application to re-enter and the court could not make a retrospective order to that effect several years after the event.

Sums payable in respect of wages or salary[77] under contracts of employment adopted by the administrator and debts and liabilities arising out of contracts entered into by the administrator (or any predecessor as administrator) will be payable in

---

74   Insolvency Act 1986, Sched B1, para 76.
75   Insolvency Act 1986, Sched B1, para 99.
76   [2001] BPIR 709.
77   As defined in the Insolvency Act 1986, Sched B1, para 99(6).

priority to the remuneration and expenses.[78] Nothing done in the first 14 days of the administration shall be taken to amount to or contribute to the adoption of a contract. This super-priority given to contractual obligations incurred by the administrator in relation to contracts which he or she has adopted has chiefly been an issue in relation to liability on contracts of employment and is explained, in Chapter 12, in the context of the consideration of the position of the employee in the rescue culture.

---

78 See *Re a Company (No 005174 of 1999)* [2000] 1 WLR 502 for a case on the predecessor to this provision.

CHAPTER 11

PARTNERSHIP RESCUE[1]

1 INTRODUCTION

The possibility of partnership rescue was introduced into insolvency law by the Insolvent Partnerships Order 1994[2] ('IPO'). A partnership voluntary arrangement ('PVA') and partnership administration procedure were introduced which are similar to the corporate procedures contained in the Insolvency Act 1986.

The IPO provides appropriate interpretations for the partnership context of the corporate terminology used in the Insolvency Act 1986. References to companies are to be construed as references to insolvent partnerships and all references to the registrar of companies are to be ignored. An 'officer of the company' will be a member of a partnership or a person who has management or control of the partnership business. Article 3(4) provides that 'other expressions appropriate to companies shall be construed, in relation to an insolvent partnership, as references to the corresponding person, officers, documents or organs (as the case may be) appropriate to a partnership.'

In most cases, any solvent partners will be expected by the creditors to make contributions to the rescue package. Where the partners, as well as the partnership business, are insolvent, a successful rescue will require individual voluntary arrangements to be interlinked with the partnership rescue package.

2 PARTNERSHIP VOLUNTARY ARRANGEMENTS[3]

Article 4 provides that the provisions of Part I of the Insolvency Act 1986 (the company voluntary arrangement provisions) shall apply in relation to an insolvent partnership as modified in Sched 1 to the IPO. Article 5 provides that where winding up and bankruptcy orders are made against an insolvent partnership and an insolvent member of that partnership in his capacity as such, Part I of the Insolvency Act 1986 applies to corporate members and Part VIII (individual voluntary arrangements) to individual members of that partnership, with the modification that references to the creditors of the company or of the debtor include references to the creditors of the partnership.

This procedure follows the structure of the company voluntary arrangement.[4] A PVA with the benefit of a moratorium has been introduced in the same circumstances

---

1   This chapter does not refer to limited liability partnerships. Section 14 of the Limited Liability Partnerships Act 2000 provides for the corporate insolvency provisions of the Insolvency Act 1986 as amended by regulation to be made available to such partnerships. The necessary modifications are to be found in the Limited Liability Partnerships Regulations 2001 (SI 2001/1090), reg 5 and Sched 3.

2   SI 1994/2421.

3   The Order was amended by the Insolvent Partnerships (Amendment)(No 2) Order 2002 (SI 2002/2708) to reflect the amendments to voluntary arrangements contained in the Insolvency Act 2002.

4   See Chapter 10.

as for a CVA. Partners are given the roles played by both directors and shareholders in a CVA so that, in addition to making the proposal for the arrangement they also have to hold a members' meeting to consider the proposal.

Individual partners may also seek to enter into interlocking IVAs in order to lock in their own personal creditors as well as the creditors of the firm.

3   PARTNERSHIP ADMINISTRATION ORDERS[5]

Article 6 provides that the provisions of Part II (company administration orders) of the Insolvency Act 1986 shall apply in relation to an insolvent partnership as modified in Sched 2 to the IPO. An agricultural charge holder,[6] who may be granted a floating charge over partnership assets, is given the same veto as those entitled to appoint administrative receivers are given in relation to company administrations. There is no other floating charge possible over partnership assets. Article 6 extends the application in connection with an administration order of certain other parts of the Insolvency Act 1986, including s 212 which provides a remedy for misfeasance or breach of duty against insolvency practitioners and members of the partnership and the provisions of the Act relating to preferences and transactions at an undervalue, to insolvent partnerships.

Partnership administration brings a moratorium on creditors' actions against the partnership but not against the partners individually; for this they would have to propose IVAs and apply for interim orders. An agricultural receiver, in common with any other receiver,[7] will only have to leave office if requested to do so by the administrator. The power of the administrator to deal with charged property under s 15 of the Insolvency Act 1986 permits the administrator to dispose of property which is subject to a charge which, as created, was floating as if it were not subject to a charge unless an agricultural receiver has been appointed under it. The administrator will need a court order to dispose of property subject to any other form of security.

Section 14 of the Insolvency Act 1986 is amended in relation to insolvent partnerships[8] to provide that the administrator may prevent any person from taking part in the management of the partnership business and may appoint any person to be a manager of that business. Section 14(6) as modified provides that an officer of the partnership shall not, unless he or she otherwise consents, be personally liable for the debts and obligations of the partnership incurred during the period of the administration order.

The Insolvency Service published a consultation document[9] at the end of January 2003 with a view to bringing the provisions of the IPO into line with the amendments to company administration orders made by the Enterprise Act 2002. Following

---

5   *Re Kyrris* [1998] BPIR 103; *Re HS Smith & Sons* (1999) *The Times,* 6 January; *Barclays Bank v Davidson* (2000) unreported, 8 February (CA); *Re West Park Golf & Country Club* [1997] 1 BCLC 20.

6   Under the Agricultural Credits Act 1928.

7   But unlike an administrative receiver in respect of a company in administration.

8   By IPO, Sched 2, para. 8.

9   Available from the consultation register on the Insolvency Service website at www.insolvency.gov.uk.

consultation, it is intended that the reforms will be extended to insolvent partnerships by an amendment to the IPO 1994 to come into force three months after it is made. It is proposed that the nature and purpose of administration will remain the same for partnerships as for companies with the primary objective being the rescue of the partnership and as much of its business as possible. It is proposed that the out-of-court route for the appointment of an administrator will be extended to partnerships by allowing one or more of the partners to appoint an administrator in the same way that a director will be able to appoint an administrator through the out-of-court route. The ability of the holder of a qualifying floating charge to appoint an administrator will be extended to the holder of a qualifying agricultural floating charge. It is envisaged that the processes and time-scales for administration, as set out in the Enterprise Act 2002, will apply equally to a partnership business that goes into administration, as will the functions of the administrator and the challenges to his or her conduct. It is proposed that the administrator of a partnership will have the power to make distributions to secured and preferential creditors, and to unsecured creditors with the permission of the court. When there is a surplus of assets, it is proposed that the administrator will be able to end his or her appointment by way of a notice to the court and each of the creditors and the partnership will enter into a Partnership Voluntary Arrangement with the former administrator acting as the trustee. Alternatively, the administrator would be able to apply to the court for a winding up order to be made against the partnership in order that dividends can be made to unsecured creditors. If there are no realisations to distribute to unsecured creditors, then the administrator will be obliged to dissolve the partnership.

CHAPTER 12

THE PLACE OF THE EMPLOYEE
IN THE RESCUE CULTURE[1]

1 INTRODUCTION

A major difficulty faced by the law is the balancing of the legitimate interests of those involved in an insolvent business. It has to be decided how the inevitable losses should be shared between the providers of capital, trade creditors, workforce and customers and, in particular, what emphasis should be placed on the preservation of jobs. The question of priority of claims against a business which is being liquidated is considered in Chapter 34. Where the insolvency practitioner is attempting to rescue a business, two specific questions may arise; firstly, the extent to which continuing to employ the workforce during an insolvency gives rise to liability and, secondly, the extent to which the rights of the workforce reduce the value to a purchaser of the business as a going concern. The first question is dealt with by the insolvency legislation, but the provisions relating to the second, although clearly affecting distributional rights within an insolvency, are to be found within the ambit of employment law.

2 LIABILITY FOR CONTINUING TO EMPLOY THE WORKFORCE

(a) Introduction

This issue is relevant both to the question of whether an administrative receiver will decide to shut down the business subject to the charge or attempt to keep trading and sell it as a going concern and to the question of whether an administration is a viable proposition. It is obvious that keeping the business going and retaining the workforce will involve meeting the ongoing entitlements of the employees to salary. The controversial question has been that of the extent to which their continued employment bestows on the employees priority over other creditors and gives them claims against the insolvency practitioner with regard to payments due to them on termination, which would have been ordinary unsecured claims in a liquidation. It has been argued that any such favourable treatment, whilst apparently beneficial to the employees, would in fact result in the closure of businesses and the loss of jobs which might otherwise have been rescued.

(b) Consequence of immediate dismissal by insolvency practitioner

When an insolvency practitioner taking control of an insolvent business immediately dismisses the employees, they are likely to have a number of claims against the employer. There will be contractual claims for wrongful dismissal because they have

---

1   See Villiers (1999); Armstrong and Cerfontaine (2000) on the extent to which employees should be protected by company and insolvency law, with the example of the French concept of corporate governance recognising employees as participants.

not been given the notice of dismissal to which their contract entitles them[2] and claims under the employment protection legislation. The employment protection legislation will enable those with sufficient accrued service to claim redundancy payments and, possibly, unfair dismissal compensation, although where the entire workforce is dismissed, the latter claim is unlikely to be successful. Partial dismissal of the workforce might entitle those dismissed to claim that they had been unfairly selected for dismissal. Where a sufficient number of employees are made redundant at the same time, there will be an obligation on the employer to consult and failure to comply with this obligation may lead to the making of a protective award.[3]

These claims will all be unsecured ordinary claims against the employer,[4] although some of the payments will be guaranteed by the National Insurance Fund[5] which will be subrogated to the claims against the employer.

(c) Effect on employees of administration

The appointment of an administrator has no effect upon the contracts of the employees since s 14(5) of the Insolvency Act 1986[6] deems him or her to act as the agent of the company. The administrator has the power to dismiss employees but the moratorium will prevent any proceedings being taken against the company without the consent of the administrator or the court during the administration.[7] Section 19 of the Insolvency Act 1986[8] provides that sums payable under new contracts entered into by an administrator and certain obligations to those whose contracts of employment have been adopted[9] by the administrator are to be paid out of the company's assets in priority to the administrator's own fees and expenses. The obligations arising under adopted contracts which acquire priority are wages, salaries and pension contributions arising during the administration. The administrator will not be taken to have adopted a contract of employment by reason of anything done or not done in the first 14 days after his or her appointment. Administrators will therefore be unwilling to retain the services of employees unless confident that there will be sufficient assets remaining to meet the costs of the administration after paying the employees.

(d) Effect on employees of administrative receivership

It was decided by the case of *Griffiths v Secretary of State for Social Services*[10] that the appointment of a receiver as agent of the company by debenture holders did not automatically terminate the contracts of employment. The court held that contracts

---

2   There may also be contractual claims for arrears of pay and accrued holiday pay.
3   See below.
4   See Chapter 34.
5   See Chapter 33.
6   Insolvency Act 1986, Sched B1, para 69 when brought into force under the Enterprise Act 2002.
7   As seen above in Chapter 10, leave would usually be given to obtain, but not to enforce, a decision.
8   As amended by the Insolvency Act 1994. This will be replaced by the Insolvency Act 1986, Sched B1, para 99 as a result of the Enterprise Act 2002.
9   This concept is discussed below in the context of dismissal by the insolvency practitioner. See *Re Antal International Ltd* [2003] All ER (D) 56 (May).
10   [1974] 1 QB 468.

would only be terminated by a concurrent sale of the business,[11] or if the receiver entered into new contracts, or if the contract was inconsistent with the existence of a receiver. In some circumstances, the role of a managing director might be inconsistent with that of a receiver; this was an argument raised in the *Griffiths* case, although on the facts, this particular managing director had not been dismissed. If a company in receivership goes into liquidation, the receiver's agency comes to an end[12] and a compulsory liquidation is said to bring the contracts of employment to an end.[13] It seems therefore that if an administrative receiver continues to trade after the company goes into liquidation, he or she must be trading and employing those working in the undertaking as principal.

Section 44 of the Insolvency Act 1986[14] provides that administrative receivers will be personally liable for any new contracts which they make and will be liable for wages, salaries and pension contributions arising during the receivership of those whose contracts of employment they have adopted.[15] This is an amendment to the common law position under which the receiver, as agent of the company, would incur no personal liability. Since 1947, receivers have been statutorily personally liable on new contracts of any type entered into by them unless such liability is specifically excluded by the contract. The Insolvency Act 1986 imposed liability on them in relation to adopted contracts of employment, which has since been restricted by the Insolvency Act 1994 to the obligations arising during the currency of the employment. The receiver will not be taken to have adopted the contract of any employee dismissed within 14 days of the start of the receivership. An administrative receiver will be entitled to an indemnity out of the company's assets in respect of this personal liability but if the assets prove insufficient the loss will fall on the receiver. Receivers will therefore only retain the services of employees where they are confident that funds will be available to meet these obligations without putting themselves or their debenture holders at risk.

(e) Dismissal during an administration or administrative receivership

An employee dismissed in the course of an administrative receivership or administration is likely to be redundant, will have a wrongful dismissal claim if dismissed without the correct notice and may have an unfair dismissal claim. The employee may be able to claim some of these payments from the National Insurance Fund[16] which will be subrogated to the employee's rights. If liability for these termination payments were to be treated in the same way as liability for obligations arising during the currency of the employment, the insolvency practitioner would have to weigh up in the first 14 days whether the risk to the rescue operation and of a potential personal large bill on later dismissal required the immediate dismissal of any employees whom the business might subsequently seek to dismiss. Sections 19 and 44

---

11 This has since been altered by the Transfer of Undertakings Regulations, explained below.
12 Insolvency Act 1986, s 44, which enacts the common law rule in *Gaskell v Gosling* [1897] AC 575.
13 See Chapter 17.
14 As amended by the Insolvency Act 1994.
15 This concept is discussed below in the context of dismissal by the insolvency practitioner.
16 See Chapter 33.

of the Insolvency Act 1986[17] as amended now make it quite clear that claims for termination payments are claims against the company and do not affect the insolvency practitioner. The history of this area of insolvency law has been described as an example of 'the British system of law making at its worst'.[18]

Until 1986, the position was that an administrative receiver could only have any liability on a contract of employment if he or she had entered into the contract. For example, in Re Mack Trucks,[19] the receiver expressly terminated the old contracts because he erroneously thought this was the effect of the company going into receivership and entered into new contracts of employment on the same terms in November 1964. The company ceased trading in July 1965 and it was held that the receiver could be sued for the wrongful dismissals since he was personally liable on the new contracts. That the receiver had no liability on continuing contracts was demonstrated by Nicoll v Cutts,[20] in which the plaintiff managing director, who had been on sick leave since the start of the receivership, was dismissed by the receivers some weeks after the start of the receivership; the Court of Appeal held that he had no claim against the receivers since they had not entered into a contract with him. This case prompted an amendment to the insolvency legislation then going through Parliament, which imposed liability on receivers in respect of contracts adopted by them. The same terminology was used in relation to the new provisions on administration in which priority over the administrator's costs was given to claims arising under 'adopted' employment contracts.

No definition was provided by the legislation of the circumstances in which a contract would be adopted. Receivers and administrators took to sending letters to the workforce informing them that they would continue to be employed, but that their contracts were not being adopted. The efficacy of this practice was upheld by Harman J in the unreported case of Re Specialised Mouldings,[21] a judgment on which insolvency practitioners placed great reliance.[22] In Powdrill v Watson,[23] however, it was held at first instance by the Court of Appeal and by the House of Lords that letters of this type do not work and that the contract of any employee whose services are retained after the 14 day grace period will be taken to be impliedly adopted. This case concerned claims brought by employees dismissed by a company in administration in respect of salary, including pension contribution, in lieu of the notice to which they were entitled under their contracts and arrears of holiday pay. They also brought unfair dismissal claims but Evans-Lombe J held that the right not to be unfairly dismissed arose under the employment protection legislation and not under the contract of employment so that unfair dismissal rights did not fall into the category of liabilities given priority by s 19 of the Insolvency Act 1986 and there was no appeal from this decision. The House of Lords heard the case jointly with two cases on the same point in relation to

---

17 Insolvency Act 1986, Sched B1, paras 69, 99 when brought into force under the Enterprise Act 2002.
18 Pollard (1995).
19 [1967] 1 All ER 977.
20 [1985] BCLC 322.
21 3 February 1987 (ChD).
22 Unwisely as it transpired and as several commentators had warned might prove to be the case. See, for example, Goode, 1997, p 101 et seq.
23 [1994] 2 All ER 513 (CA); [1995] 2 All ER 65 (HL).

administrative receivership: *Re Leyland DAF Ltd and Re Ferranti International plc*.[24] Lord Browne-Wilkinson, delivering the judgment of the House of Lords, expressed his sympathy for the position of receivers and administrators and recognised the difficulty of having to decide within 14 days whether to close down the business, dismiss the employees and sell on a break-up basis or to continue the business, keep on the employees and try to sell it as a going concern. His Lordship adopted a basis of statutory interpretation which was as generous as possible to the insolvency practitioners in that he held that if the words of the legislation had a meaning which was consistent with the presumed intention not to frustrate the rescue culture and produce unworkable results, that construction should be adopted. Otherwise, the literal meaning of the provisions could only be rejected if they produced an absurd result. He then proceeded to reject the first instance decision of Lightman J in *Re Leyland DAF*[25] that s 44 of the Insolvency Act 1986 imposed liability on a receiver for all sums claimed under an adopted contract on the basis that it was most improbable that Parliament had intended such a discrepancy between those dismissed in the first 14 days and those kept on and that such a construction would make the position of the receiver almost impossible; to interpret the section in this way would be absurd. The interpretation of s 44 must be that it was subject to the same limitation as applied to an administrator's liability under s 19 of the Insolvency Act 1986 and that liability would only relate to debts in respect of the period of office of the receiver. He felt constrained to decide that adoption connoted some conduct by the insolvency practitioner which amounted to an election to treat the continued contract of employment with the company as giving rise to a separate liability in the administration or receivership and that it was not possible to adopt part only of a contract. The outcome was that, in addition to the liability to pay the employees during the currency of their employment during the insolvency, there would also be an obligation to pay wages during the contractual notice period including pension contributions, or damages in lieu thereof, and holiday pay referable to the employment since the appointment of the officeholder.

Within less than two months[26] of the Court of Appeal decision in *Powdrill v Watson*,[27] the Insolvency Act 1994 had been enacted to amend the offending provisions of the Insolvency Act 1986 and restrict the potential liability of administrative receivers[28] and administrators to claims arising from the currency of the employment, which the insolvency practitioners had always been quite happy to meet. The government refused, however, to make the legislation retrospective[29] beyond the date when the proposed amendment to the law had been announced to Parliament; it only applies, therefore, to contracts adopted on or after 15 March 1994.

---

24 [1994] 4 All ER 300. See Fletcher (1995).

25 [1994] 4 All ER 300.

26 Lord Browne-Wilkinson described this as 'almost unprecedented speed'. Several businesses which went into receivership immediately after the judgment were shut down which might previously have been allowed to continue trading; this highlighted the need for immediate action to keep 'the rescue culture' afloat.

27 [1994] 2 All ER 513.

28 But not of Law of Property Act receivers who are subject, under the Insolvency Act 1986, s 37, to liability identical to that under the unamended version of s 44.

29 The lobbying power of the banks and the insolvency practitioners with respect to a situation which they were powerless to do anything about was insufficient to overcome the usual antipathy to retrospective legislation as being contrary to the rules of natural justice.

There have been reports of at least some large claims having been brought in respect of the period between 1986 and 1994, although the limitation rules will have prevented those affected in the early days from bringing actions and the principle of mitigation of loss will have cut down other potential claims. Those who will have benefited from the *Powdrill v Watson* decision are employees whose contractual entitlement to notice moneys exceeded the amount of notice money guaranteed by the National Insurance Fund,[30] either because they were contractually entitled to a longer period of notice than that provided by the employment protection legislation, or because their weekly salary exceeded the National Insurance Fund ceiling. This has been argued to be particularly unfair since these employees are the most likely to have been responsible for any mismanagement leading to the collapse of the business.

(f) Consultation about collective redundancies

Section 188 of the Trade Union and Labour Relations (Consolidation) Act 1992,[31] re-enacting s 99 of the Employment Protection Act 1975 which was passed to implement EC Directive 75/29[32] on Collective Redundancies, gives employees the right to have their representatives consulted about proposed collective redundancies. An employer proposing to dismiss as redundant 20 or more employees at one establishment within a period of 90 days or less is obliged to consult the appropriate representatives of employees who are affected by the proposed dismissals or may be affected by measures taken in connection with those dismissals. Where the proposal is to dismiss at least 100 employees, the consultation shall begin at least 90 days before the first dismissal; in other circumstances, the consultation period is at least 30 days. Appropriate representatives are either representatives of an independent trade union recognised by the employer or, if there is no such recognised union, elected employee representatives. If the employees are not represented and have been given a genuine opportunity to elect representatives, the employer may discharge its obligations by giving the information set out in s 188(4) of the Trade Union and Labour Relations (Consolidation) Act 1992 to each affected employee.

In the event of a failure to consult, a 'protective award' may be sought[33] from an employment tribunal by the representatives who have not been consulted or, where there are no representatives, by the employees themselves. A protective award is an order that the employees be paid remuneration beginning with the date on which the first dismissal takes place for such period as the tribunal determines to be just and equitable in all the circumstances, having regard to the seriousness of the default, but

---

30   See Chapter 33.
31   As amended by the Collective Redundancies and TUPE Amendment Regulations 1995 and 1999 (SI 1995/2587 and SI 1999/1925). The 1995 amendments were necessary to deal with the failure of the original UK provisions to comply with the Directive in relation to employees without a recognised union: see *Commission v United Kingdom* [1994] ICR 692.
32   As amended by Directive 92/56.
33   Under the Trade Union and Labour Relations (Consolidation) Act 1992, s 189.

not exceeding the length of the appropriate consultation period.[34] If the employer fails to pay the protected award, individual employees are then able to enforce it.[35]

There is a defence[36] which provides that if there are 'special circumstances which render it not reasonably practicable' for the employer to comply with the provisions, 'the employer shall take all such steps towards compliance with that requirement as are reasonably practicable in those circumstances' which may mean no steps at all. The Collective Redundancies Directive contains no 'special circumstances' defence, but it does not apply to 'workers affected by the termination of an establishment's activities where that is the result of judicial decision'. This fails to take account of the fundamentally different nature of UK insolvency procedures which do not necessarily involve the court. According to the Court of Appeal in *Clarks of Hove Ltd v Bakers Union*,[37] the correct approach to the defence provided by the UK legislation is to ask, firstly, were there special circumstances; secondly, if so, did they render compliance not reasonably practicable and, thirdly, had the employer taken such steps as were reasonably practicable? The court then went on to hold that, whilst a sudden disaster leading to the closure of the business might be special circumstances, there was nothing special about a gradual run-down of the company. This was followed in *GMB v Messrs Rankin & Harrison*[38] and in *Re Hartlebury Printers Ltd*.[39] The latter case was one in which the directors, and subsequently administrators, had failed to consult the trades unions over dismissals which were held to have occurred when the administration was superseded by a liquidation. It was held, however, that the administrators, and directors before them, did not actually 'propose' to make redundancies although they were aware of the financial difficulties and realised that redundancies might become necessary; the redundancies occurred because of the decision of the court. Morritt J rejected the argument that administrators were not subject to the consultation provisions.

There are similar rights provided to employees on the transfer of a business.[40] The transferring employer must give information to representatives of all those affected by the transfer and consult in relation to all those employees in respect of whom he or she envisages that measures will be taken. Failure to comply may lead to a complaint[41] by the representatives or, if there are none, by the employees to the employment tribunal which may award appropriate compensation not exceeding four weeks' pay.

---

34 Trade Union and Labour Relations (Consolidation) Act 1992, s 190 contains further details of the calculation of the award which is subject to a statutory maximum weekly amount of, currently, £260.
35 Under the Trade Union and Labour Relations (Consolidation) Act 1992, s 192. Protective awards will be preferential debts and guaranteed by the National Insurance Fund.
36 Trade Union and Labour Relations (Consolidation) Act 1992, s 188(7).
37 [1978] ICR 366.
38 [1992] IRLR 514 (Scottish EAT case on receivership).
39 [1992] ICR 559. The case was actually an application under the Insolvency Act 1986, s 130(2) (see Chapter 25 below) for leave to commence proceedings and was heard in the Chancery Division.
40 Transfer of Undertakings (Protection of Employment) Regulations 1981, reg 10 as amended by the 1995 Amendment Regulations, see note 29 above.
41 Under TUPE, reg 11.

3 EMPLOYEES' RIGHTS ON THE SALE OF THE BUSINESS

(a) The pre-1981 position

Prior to 1981, a receiver was able to sell the business as a going concern divested of any accrued liability to its employees. The employees would be made redundant by the insolvency practitioner prior to the transfer of the business and the transferee would offer employment to such of the workforce as were wanted under new contracts. The employees would be paid redundancy payments whether or not they were going to be re-engaged and those who were re-employed would begin their employment with the transferee without any accrued rights.

(b) The Transfer of Undertakings Regulations[42]

Since the Transfer of Undertakings (Protection of Employment) Regulations 1981 ('TUPE') were enacted to implement EC Directive 77/187 on Business Transfers (the Acquired Rights Directive), and particularly since the House of Lords' interpretation of them in *Litster v Forth Dry Dock*,[43] it has been difficult to sell a business without transferring the liabilities of the seller to the transferee.

TUPE applies to a 'transfer from one person to another of an undertaking'[44] situated in the UK. There has been considerable conflicting case law[45] on what constitutes the transfer of an undertaking as distinct from a sale of tangible or intangible assets. In the context of the discussion of attempted rescue, this is unlikely to be an issue.

Regulation 5 provides for an automatic transfer of the contracts of employment and acquired rights of those employed in the business 'immediately before the transfer'. The transferee employer is treated as having been responsible for anything done by the transferor in relation to the contract and takes over the terms of the contract under which the employee has been employed except for rights in relation to occupational pension schemes.[46] The employee's accrued continuous service is transferred. Continuous service is relevant both for determining entitlement to bring claims under the employment protection legislation and to the calculation of amounts to be paid where the claim is successful. It is now clear that non-contractual liabilities, such as sex discrimination claims and tortious liability for personal injury, are capable of being transferred and the Court of Appeal held in *Bernadone v Pall Mall Services*

---

42 See Pollard (1996); Frisby (2000b).
43 [1989] 2 WLR 634.
44 TUPE, reg 3.
45 See *Sinclair v Argyll Training Ltd* [2000] IRLR 630 (EAT) and *ADI (UK) Ltd v Willer* [2001] IRLR 542 (CA) for a survey and attempts to reconcile the case law. Article 1 of the amended directive provides a definition (an organised grouping of assets with the objective of pursuing an economic activity) which is likely to be incorporated into the revision of TUPE proposed for 2003.
46 TUPE, reg 7. This is in accordance with the Directive: *Adams v Lancashire CC* [1997] IRLR 436. In *Hagen v ICI* [2002] IRLR 31, it was held that reg 7 extended to tortious liability for misrepresentation about pension rights. The government proposed in its 2001 consultation on TUPE that pension rights should be included in the future in order to address the anomaly that personal pension rights under contract will transfer whereas occupational pension scheme rights are currently exempt (see Ingram (2002)).

Group[47] that the employer's insurance protection will also transfer along with the liability to the employee.

In *Kerry Foods Ltd v Creber*,[48] the Employment Appeal Tribunal held (distinguishing the earlier case of *Angus Jowett Ltd v NUTGW*)[49] that a transferor's liability for a protective award under s 188 of the Trade Union and Labour Relations (Consolidation) Act 1992 in respect of failure to consult on collective redundancies would pass to the transferee. The Employment Appeal Tribunal in Scotland subsequently held, however, in *Transport & General Workers' Union v McKinnon, JR Haulage Ltd*[50] that liability under TUPE for failure to consult the employees about a transfer should not transfer, since there should be an incentive for the transferor to comply with the consultation obligations.

The term 'immediately before' is not defined in TUPE and there was considerable controversy as to whether the practice of dismissing employees before completion of the sale prevented their being employed in the business 'immediately before' so that they did not transfer with it. In *Secretary of State v Spence*,[51] the Court of Appeal held that reg 5 only applied to employees employed by the transferor at the moment of the transfer, so that dismissal only hours previously would be fatal to their continuity; even those re-engaged by the transferee would be entitled to redundancy payments and their new employer would inherit no obligations in relation to them. *Spence* provided certainty at the expense of rendering TUPE more or less a dead letter. This potentially major gap in the protection intended to be provided by TUPE was rectified by the House of Lords in *Litster v Forth Dry Dock*.[52] Their Lordships, following *Pickstone v Freemans*,[53] gave a purposive interpretation of TUPE and said that Art 4 of the Directive required that reg 5(3) be read as if there were inserted after the words 'immediately before the transfer' the words 'or would have been so employed if he had not been unfairly dismissed in the circumstances described in regulation 8(1).' Regulation 8(1) provides that dismissals in connection with the transfer of the business will be automatically unfair and reg 8(2) goes on to provide that if 'an economic, technical or organisational reason entailing changes in the workforce of either the transferor or the transferee before or after a relevant transfer' (an 'ETO reason') is the reason or principal reason for dismissing an employee, then the dismissal is not automatically unfair (although it might still be unfair by an application of the normal rules relating to unfair dismissal). It has been held that the *Litster* principle applies only where the dismissal is or is principally in connection with the transfer of the undertaking[54] and does not apply where the dismissal is for or principally for an ETO reason within reg 8(2). In the latter case, if the relevant employee has been effectively dismissed by the transferor at such a time that he or she cannot be said to fall within reg 5(3) on its ordinary meaning (and not its meaning as

---

47 [2000] 3 All ER 544 (see Sargeant (2000)).
48 [2000] ICR 556.
49 [1985] ICR 646.
50 [2001] ICR 1281.
51 [1987] QB 179.
52 [1989] 2 WLR 634.
53 [1989] AC 66.
54 There are conflicting cases on whether a dismissal can be in connection with a transfer when there is no definitely identified transferee: see, for example, *Harrison Bowden v Bowden* [1994] ICR 186; *Ibex Trading v Walton* [1994] IRLR 564; *Michael Peters Ltd v Farnfield* [1995] IRLR 190.

extended by the *Litster* principle), any liability to the employee falls upon the transferor and not upon the transferee. In *Re Maxwell Fleet and Facilities Management (No 2)*,[55] it was held that the *Litster* principle should also be applied to any attempt to take advantage of the 'hive-down' provisions of reg 4 to avoid what would otherwise be the effects of TUPE.[56]

The extent to which a finding that the dismissal was for an ETO reason prevents the dismissal from being automatically unfair has also given rise to some confusion in the case law. The Employment Appeal Tribunal (EAT) considered the state of the case law in *Thompson v SCS Consulting Ltd*.[57] The employee in question had been dismissed by a receiver 11 hours before the transfer of the business. The agreement provided that before the sale and purchase agreement took effect, the receiver would dismiss the employees not on a list of those required by the transferee 'at the request of the purchaser as a precondition to the purchaser entering into this agreement on the grounds that they are not required for the operation of the business and that it would not be economically viable for the business to continue if the dismissed employees remained in the employ of the vendors'.[58] The employment tribunal had held that the employee was not 'employed immediately before the transfer' unless the *Litster* principle applied and that, since the business was over-staffed and could only be made viable if the workforce was reduced, the dismissal was for an 'economic, technical or organisational reason entailing changes in the workforce'.[59] The employment tribunal had found that if the purchaser had not been on the scene, the receiver would have dismissed all the employees. On that view, the dismissal of the applicant could properly be seen as taking place not in order to secure a sale or to enhance the sale price or at the behest of the transferee, but for an ETO reason. The EAT said that, whatever the correct approach to the interrelationship between regs 8(1) and 8(2), if the tribunal concludes that the reason or principal reason is an ETO reason, reg 8(2) applies, reg 8(1) is excluded, and the extended construction of reg 5(3) in *Litster* does not apply. The EAT observed that, however beneficial it might be if the potential liability for unfair dismissal and any liability for other claims in a case of dismissal for an ETO reason were to fall on the transferee, in the situation in this case, the law was to the contrary effect. In its 2001 consultation paper on amendments to TUPE, the government recognised the confusion on the case law in this area and proposed making it clear that economic, technical or organisational reasons entailing changes in the workforce (ETO reasons) are a subset of reasons connected with the

---

55 [2000] 2 All ER 860.

56 This is apparently the only reported case on reg 4, which says that where there is a transfer to a wholly owned subsidiary of a company, the transfer shall be deemed not to take place until immediately before the business (or the shareholding in the company) is sold on. The provision does not appear in the Directive and it seems likely that it will be taken out of the proposed amended version of TUPE.

57 [2001] IRLR 801.

58 In *Longden & Paisley v Ferrari Ltd and Kennedy International* [1994] IRLR 157, it had been held that an indication by a potential transferee that he would want to retain specified employees did not amount to a request to dismiss the others.

59 Citing *Whitehouse v Blatchford* [1999] IRLR 492, where Beldam LJ said that 'an ETO reason must be connected with the future conduct of the business as a going concern'.

transfer; it was noted that any other position would render the ETO exception essentially redundant, as it would be clear that the Directive could have no effect on changes completed unconnected to the transfer.

Where the dismissal is held to be in connection with the transfer, employees who have been employed in an insolvent business immediately before its transfer will be able to bring their claims against the solvent transferee instead of against the insolvent transferor and can be sure that the claims will be met in full. The transferee will insist on an adjustment to the price to take account of this potential liability and the insolvency practitioner will recover less for distribution amongst the other creditors. Where the value of the business falls below the amount the insolvency practitioner could obtain by selling the assets on a break-up basis, the business will be closed since there is a duty to maximise realisations. There is therefore a risk that more jobs will be lost than if the Regulations did not apply.[60] According to evidence given by the Society of Practitioners of Insolvency to the House of Lords Select Committee on the European Communities[61] the effect is: 'that the transfer of undertakings legislation is an impediment to the rescue of businesses in the context of formal insolvency and therefore has the opposite from its intended effect of preserving employment and employees' rights.' On this basis, it has been argued that the Regulations should not apply to transfers of insolvent businesses.[62]

(c) Applicability of the Acquired Rights Directive to insolvency

There was no specific mention in the original Directive of insolvency. In the English language version, Art 1(1) provided that the Directive applied to the transfer of an undertaking 'as a result of a legal transfer or merger'. The other language versions of the Directive, however, with the possible exception of the Danish version, were drafted more restrictively to refer to contractual transfers. In the *Abels* case,[63] the European Court of Justice considered the argument that transfers by insolvent transferors are not, at least in some Member States, considered to be genuinely consensual and therefore fall outside the Directive.

The Court, having held that it was not possible to determine the question as a matter of interpretation and that it was necessary to consider the purpose of the Directive, held that the Directive was intended to safeguard workers' rights when an undertaking was transferred. The argument that insolvency was an exception to the directive was *prima facie* tenable as 'insolvency law is characterised by special procedures intended to weigh up the various interests involved, in particular those of the various classes of creditors; consequently, in all member states there are specific rules which may derogate, at least partially, from other provisions of a general nature including provisions of social law'. Whether this was intended in the case of this Directive depended upon whether the protection of employees would be furthered by

---

60 There is some evidence that this happened in Germany. See Schumacher (1994).

61 Session 1995–96, 5th report.

62 See Collins (1989); Floyd (1989); Davies (1989); Sargeant (2002a); Hardy (2003). Armour and Deakin (2000), however, said efficiency arguments for and against *Litster* are finely balanced.

63 *Abels v The Administrative Board of the Bedrijfsvereniging voor de Metaalindustrie en de Electrotechnische Industrie* [1987] 2 CMLR 406.

PART III
BANKRUPTCY AND
LIQUIDATION PROCEDURES

CHAPTER 13

·INTRODUCTION TO PART III

This part of the text deals with the formal regimes applicable to an insolvent debtor incapable of rescue. It explains the procedures by which such regimes are initiated, the conduct of the regimes and the consequences for the insolvent of being subject to such regimes.[1] The mere fact of being in a state of insolvency does not have any legal consequences until either the debtor or a creditor relies on that state to invoke one of the formal regimes provided by the insolvency legislation.

Since the routes into compulsory liquidation and bankruptcy frequently commence with the service of a statutory demand by a creditor, Chapter 14 begins this Part by looking at the rules relating to such demands before moving on to explain the processes whereby a bankruptcy or liquidation can be brought about. A full explanation of those responsible for the administration of the processes of bankruptcy and liquidation can be found in Chapter 20, in Part IV of this text.

The regime relevant to an insolvent individual is bankruptcy, which is considered in Chapter 15. Individual insolvency law has to make provision not just for the distribution of the assets of the insolvent to the creditors but also for the continued existence and eventual discharge from bankruptcy of the insolvent. As explained in Chapter 7, the question of the consequences of a bankruptcy order can also be seen as a 'rescue culture' issue as well as in the context of measures for maintaining public confidence in insolvency law as a bolster of commercial morality, considered in Part IV of this text.

Insolvent companies may be wound up (or put into liquidation; the terms are synonymous) either voluntarily on the resolution of the members, as explained in Chapter 16, or compulsorily by order of the court, as explained in Chapter 17. Liquidation will result in the termination of the existence of the company; once this process is underway, it is clear that the rescue of the company is no longer possible. The rescue of some part of the business might still be feasible, but it is difficult to keep the business trading once the company is being wound up. The majority of liquidations are voluntary; in many cases, this will suit all the interested parties since a winding up ordered by the court will swallow up more of the available assets, the liquidator will have less freedom of action and there will be a greater degree of investigation into the background to the insolvency than is the case in a voluntary liquidation. The rules governing all types of liquidation, even of solvent companies, are to be found in the Insolvency Act 1986, which removes a number of the previous procedural distinctions between the processes of bankruptcy and liquidation. Individual and corporate insolvency law are, however, still distinct and are dealt with in separate parts of the Act, although this is an improvement on the previous position under which the corporate provisions were contained in the Companies Acts and the individual provisions in the Bankruptcy Act.

---

1   The consequences for the creditors are considered in Part V. Further consequences for bankrupts and those connected with companies in liquidation whose conduct is considered culpable are dealt with in Part IV.

It is possible for a company's life to be terminated without it undergoing a formal liquidation process. Section 652 of the Companies Act 1985 has long given the Registrar of Companies the power to strike off the register any company which he or she has reasonable cause to believe is defunct, usually on the basis of failure to comply with filing requirements. Sections 625A–625F of the Companies Act 1985 now allow the directors of a defunct private company to apply for the company to be struck off the register at the expiration of three months from the publication by the Registrar in the Gazette of an advertisement inviting any person to show cause why this should not happen.

The rules relating to insolvent partnerships (other than limited liability partnerships) are currently to be found in the Insolvent Partnerships Order 1994 and are explained in Chapter 18. Partnership insolvency law has been largely assimilated into corporate insolvency law but has the additional complication that the partners are likely to have individual liabilities in addition to their liability for the partnership debts.

CHAPTER 14

THE STATUTORY DEMAND

1 INTRODUCTION

The statutory demand procedure was first introduced as a method for creditors to establish evidence of their corporate debtors' inability to pay. The Insolvency Act 1986 implemented the recommendation of the Cork Committee that the statutory demand procedure be extended to individuals to replace the ancient and complex procedure under which the creditor of an individual could present a petition to the court within three months of the debtor having committed an 'act of bankruptcy'.[1] 'Acts of bankruptcy' comprised a list of events thought to be indications of the debtor's inability to meet his or her liabilities which had been added to in a piecemeal fashion over the years and still included such arcane provisions as 'with intent to defeat or delay his creditors he does any of the following things, namely, departs out of England, or being out of England remains out of England, or departs from his dwellinghouse, or otherwise absents himself, or begins to keep house'.[2] The most commonly relied on act of bankruptcy was the debtor's failure to comply with a 'bankruptcy notice' requiring him or her to pay a judgment debt due to a creditor.

The provisions relating to companies and individuals are still not identical. In particular, a statutory demand served on a company can only relate to a debt which is currently payable, whereas a statutory demand served on an individual may relate either to a debt which is currently payable or to one which is not yet due. Unless the petitioner can show unsatisfied judgment process, a statutory demand will have to be served before a creditor can petition to have a debtor declared bankrupt. In the case of a debtor company, however, the statutory demand is only one method open to the creditor who has complete freedom as to how he or she seeks to persuade the court that the debtor is unable to pay his or her debts.[3]

One issue with which the courts have had to grapple is the extent to which a creditor should be permitted to use a statutory demand to apply pressure on a probably solvent debtor to pay.

2 SERVICE OF A STATUTORY DEMAND[4]

A statutory demand is a document requiring the debtor to pay the debt or to secure or compound for it to the creditor's satisfaction if the debt is payable immediately. In the case of an individual debtor not under an immediate obligation to pay, the demand

---

1   The complexities were compounded by the relation back of the bankruptcy to the earliest act of bankruptcy proved to have been committed within the three months preceding the presentation of the bankruptcy petition.

2   This was s 1(d) of the repealed Bankruptcy Act 1914.

3   See Chapter 17. See comments of Robert Walker LJ in *Garrow v Society of Lloyds* [2000] Lloyd's Rep IR 38.

4   In the case of a company, see the Insolvency Act 1986, s 123(1)(a) and the Insolvency Rules 1986, rr 4.4–4.6. For bankruptcy, see the Insolvency Act 1986, s 268 and the Insolvency Rules 1986, rr 6.1–6.5.

will require the debtor to establish to the satisfaction of the creditor that there is a reasonable prospect that the debtor will be able to pay when the debt does fall due.

There are various prescribed forms of statutory demand; the precise form depends on whether the debtor is an individual or a company, on whether or not the debt is a judgment debt and whether it is payable immediately or at some time in the future. A statutory demand must explain that the potential consequence of the demand, if not complied with, is that proceedings for winding up or bankruptcy, whichever is appropriate, may be instituted. The demand must give details of the time within which it must be complied with and how the debtor can enter into negotiations with a view to securing or compounding for the debt to the creditor's satisfaction.

A creditor must, where practicable, effect personal service of the statutory demand on an individual debtor.[5] If personal service is not possible, it may be effected by other means such as first class post or insertion through a letterbox. Where the post is used, service is taken to have been effected on the seventh day after posting. Advertisement may be used by way of substituted service where the demand is in respect of a judgment debt, the debtor is keeping out of the way with a view to avoiding service and there is no real prospect of the debt being recovered by execution or other process.[6]

A demand served on a company must be shown to have been delivered at the company's registered office.[7]

3   CHALLENGE TO A STATUTORY DEMAND

(a) Introduction

The statutory demand is intended as a method of establishing the insolvency of the debtor. It should not therefore be used as a method of obtaining payment of a debt in circumstances where the debtor has a reason other than insolvency for failing to pay. The courts have shown concern for the problems faced by creditors in extracting payment from recalcitrant debtors and a mere desire to delay payment has not been treated as such a reason. At the same time, the courts are alive to the potential for abuse by creditors of the system.[8] It is difficult, however, to prevent abuse of the system where a debtor responds to an improper statutory demand without involving the courts. Justice observed[9] that there was disturbing evidence that statutory demands were being used as a means of intimidating debtors who might have a genuine defence to the claim into paying the amount claimed in the belief that the demand emanated from the court and without realising that it could be challenged. They suggested that it might be desirable for there to be a more stringent test to be satisfied before a statutory demand could be issued in respect of debts other than judgment debts.

---

5   Insolvency Rules 1986, r 6.3.
6   *Practice Note* [1987] 1 WLR 82 and 85.
7   *Re a Company* [1985] BCLC 37.
8   This is a problem which also arises in the context of petitions for compulsory liquidation presented on the basis of evidence other than a statutory demand; see Chapter 17.
9   Justice, 1994, para 4.14 *et seq*.

The procedural aspects of challenging a statutory demand differ between individual and corporate debtors. The previous bankruptcy law provisions under which a bankruptcy notice could be challenged are reflected to an extent in the Insolvency Rules, although the courts have refused to take the previous over-technical approach to the content of a statutory demand where it is clear that the debtor has not been prejudiced by defects in the drafting.

(b) Individual debtor

The Insolvency Rules 1986[10] set out the circumstances under which an application may be made to set aside a statutory demand served on an individual debtor. The application has to be made within 18 days and stops the time for compliance with the demand from running unless and until the application is dismissed. If the court is satisfied that the application is without merit, then it may be dismissed without a hearing or notice to the creditor. There are four grounds for setting a demand aside: first, that the debtor appears to have a counterclaim, set-off or cross-demand at least equal to the amount specified in the demand;[11] secondly, that the debt is disputed on grounds which appear to the court to be substantial; thirdly, that the creditor appears to be secured for at least the amount of the debt; and, finally, that the court is satisfied on other grounds that the demand ought to be set aside.

The Court of Appeal had occasion to consider the provisions dealing with the setting aside of statutory demands in *Re a Debtor (No 1 of Lancaster 1987)*.[12] The debtor challenged the demand on the grounds that the wrong form had been used and, at a later stage in proceedings, that the amount of the debt was incorrectly stated. Warner J, whose decision to dismiss the application was upheld by the Court of Appeal, said that it was not appropriate to follow the old law applicable to bankruptcy notices which placed supreme importance on strict adherence to technicalities. Defects in the statutory demand should only cause it to be set aside where they had positively misled the debtor, not, as under the old law, where they might reasonably have misled him. Nicholls LJ pointed out that the purpose of the statutory demand was to activate a presumption of inability to pay and that the residual discretion to set the demand aside should only be used where circumstances would make it unjust for the demand to give rise to that presumption. He then observed that 'there may be cases where the terms of the statutory demand are so confusing or misleading that, having regard to all the circumstances, justice requires that the demand should not be allowed to stand. There will be other cases where, despite such defects in the contents of the statutory demand, those defects have not prejudiced and will not prejudice the debtor in any way and to set aside the demand in such a case would serve no useful purpose'.[13] This case fell into the latter category since, although the amount of the debt was incorrectly stated, the debtor had clearly not been confused by it since he did not raise the issue until a late stage in the proceedings and had originally relied on the technical

---

10 Insolvency Rules 1986, rr 6.4–6.5.
11 *AIB Finance v Debtors* [1997] 4 All ER 677 illustrates the need for the counterclaim to be at least equal to the debt specified in the statutory demand.
12 [1989] 1 WLR 271 (first instance decision of Warner J reported at [1988] 1 WLR 419).
13 The test was applied in *Re a Debtor (No 51 of 1991)* [1992] 1 WLR 1294 and in the cases mentioned in the next note.

defect that the wrong form had been used. Nicholls LJ did warn creditors and their advisors not to take the decision as an invitation to draft demands in a slipshod manner.

Re a Debtor (No 1 of Lancaster of 1987) is also authority for the proposition that it will not necessarily be fatal to the statutory demand that the extent of the indebtedness has been overstated. Where part of the amount claimed is disputed, the debtor will have to pay the undisputed element before applying to the court to have the demand set aside in respect of the disputed balance.[14]

Where a statutory demand is based on a judgment debt, the court should not go behind the judgment on an application to set aside the statutory demand nor inquire into the validity of the debt nor, as a general rule, adjourn the application to await the result of an application to set aside the judgment.[15] When the debtor:

(a) claims to have a counterclaim, set-off or cross-demand (whether or not he or she could have raised it in the action in which the judgment or order was obtained) which equals or exceeds the amount of the debt or debts specified in the statutory demand; or

(b) disputes the debt (not being a debt subject to a judgment or order),

the court will normally set aside the statutory demand if, in its opinion, on the evidence there is a genuine triable issue.[16] The Court of Appeal in *Platts v Western Trust & Savings Ltd*[17] held that in a case in which the statutory demand was challenged on the basis that the creditor was fully secured, the court hearing the application had a wide discretion as to how to deal with the matter.[18]

If the application to set the demand aside succeeds, the court may make a penalty order for costs against the creditor and the creditor's advisors. The court may review, rescind or vary[19] an order made on an application to set aside a statutory demand. In *Re a Debtor (No 32 of 1991)*,[20] Millett J held that this was a jurisdiction which should be rarely exercised since it allowed what amounted to a renewed application to set aside a demand after the period limited for making such an application. The question for the court is whether the order ought to remain in force in the light of changed circumstances or fresh evidence, whether or not such evidence might have been available at the time of the hearing. The decision of the court may also be the subject of an appeal.[21] It has been held that the hearing of an application to set aside a statutory demand is not a hearing 'on the merits' and therefore the principles

---

14 *Re a Debtor (No 490 of 1991) v Printline (Offset) Ltd* [1992] 1 WLR 507; *Re a Debtor (No 657 of 1991)* [1993] BCLC 181.

15 *Practice Direction* [1987] 1 WLR 119; *Re a Debtor (No 657 of 1991)* [1993] BCLC 181.

16 *Practice Direction* [1987] 1 WLR 119. Applied in *Garrow v Society of Lloyds* [2000] Lloyd's Rep IR 38. See also *Re a Debtor (No 87 of 1999), Debtor v Johnson* [2000] BPIR 589; (2000) *The Times*, 14 February.

17 [1993] 22 LS Gaz R 38.

18 See also *Liveras v A Debtor (No 620 of 1997)* [1999] BPIR 89.

19 Under the Insolvency Act 1986, s 375(1).

20 [1993] 1 WLR 314.

21 Insolvency Act 1986, s 375(2). See Chapter 5 above.

contained in *Ladd v Marshall*[22] about the introduction of new evidence at the appeal stage do not apply.[23] The decision as to whether or not to allow new evidence in such a case will be a matter of discretion for the appeal court.

(c) Corporate debtor

There is no specific provision in the Insolvency Rules permitting a company to challenge a statutory demand, but where a company disputes a statutory demand which has been served on it and the creditor refuses to withdraw it, the company may apply for an injunction to restrain the issue of a winding up petition.[24] This procedure was used, for example, in *Cannon Screen Entertainment Ltd v Handmade Films (Distribution) Ltd*,[25] in which the creditor had served a statutory demand in respect of a debt which transpired to be disputed. Warner J said that there was nothing improper in a creditor who has no notice of a substantial defence to his claim taking a short cut and serving a statutory demand rather than pursuing the normal course of issuing a writ against the debtor, but that the creditor took such a course of action at his own risk as to costs if it should turn out that there was a defence to the claim.

In *Cornhill Insurance plc v Improvement Services Ltd*,[26] the plaintiff insurance company sought an injunction to restrain the defendants from presenting a petition for winding up on the basis of a statutory demand which had been served on them. Cornhill claimed that such a petition would constitute an abuse of the process of the court since it was clear that they were solvent. Harman J refused the injunction on the basis that persistent non-payment of a debt suggested insolvency[27] and that Cornhill had its own remedy in that it could make payment.

Hoffmann J made it clear in *Re a Company (No 0012209 of 1991)*[28] that a statutory demand should not be used as a method of debt collection against a solvent company where the debt is disputed in good faith. An injunction restraining the issue of a winding up petition in such circumstances was granted and the petitioner was ordered to pay the applicant's costs on an indemnity basis to make it clear that abuse of the petition procedure in this way was a high risk strategy. The judge said:

> It does seem to me that a tendency has developed, possibly since the decision in *Cornhill Insurance plc v Improvement Services Ltd*[29] to present petitions against solvent companies as a way of putting pressure upon them to make payments of money which is *bona fide* disputed rather than to invoke the procedures which the rules provide for summary judgment. I do not for a moment wish to detract from anything which was said in the *Cornhill Insurance* case ... It was, however, a somewhat unusual case in which it was quite clear that the company in question had no grounds at all for

---

22 [1954] 1 WLR 1489.
23 *Salvidge v Hussein* [1999] BPIR 410 considered the conflicting first instance decisions on whether *Ladd v Marshall* applied generally to appeals against dismissals of applications to aside statutory demands and concluded that it did not.
24 See Chapter 17 below for applications to strike out a petition for winding up.
25 [1989] 5 BCC 207.
26 [1986] BCLC 26.
27 Relying on observations of Ungoed-Thomas J in *Mann v Goldstein* [1968] 2 All ER 769 at 773.
28 [1992] 2 All ER 797.
29 [1986] 1 WLR 114.

its refusal. ... if, as in this case, it appears that the defence has a prospect of success and the company is solvent, then I think that the court should give the company the benefit of the doubt and not do anything which would encourage the use of the Companies Court as an alternative to the RSC Ord 14 procedure.

CHAPTER 15

THE PROCESS OF BANKRUPTCY

1 INTRODUCTION

This chapter explains how a debtor may be declared bankrupt, the consequences of the bankruptcy order for the bankrupt and the duration of the bankruptcy. It also explains the role of the Official Receiver[1] and the appointment of the trustee in bankruptcy and the duties, powers and potential liability of the trustee. The law relating to the investigation of the background to the bankruptcy is considered in Part IV and the rules governing the collection, realisation and distribution of the assets are considered in Part V.

The Enterprise Act 2002 will bring about some radical changes to bankruptcy law once the provisions are brought into force; the amendments, expected to take effect during 2003–04, are outlined in the relevant sections of this chapter.

2 COURT JURISDICTION

Jurisdiction in individual insolvency is exercised throughout England and Wales by the High Court, where it will be dealt with by a registrar in bankruptcy, and those of the county courts which exercise an insolvency jurisdiction.[2] The county court has the powers of the High Court in this respect. Jurisdiction is allocated to a particular court on the basis of the debtor's geographical connection with it and the High Court exercises insolvency jurisdiction in relation to the London Insolvency District, those cases in which the debtor does not appear to have a connection with any other court and in certain cases brought by the government.[3]

Every court having jurisdiction in individual insolvency matters may review, rescind or vary any order which it has made.[4] Appeal lies from decisions by the county court or from a registrar in bankruptcy of the High Court to a single judge of the High Court.[5] The procedure normally relating to appeals to the Court of Appeal will apply to such an appeal.[6] Leave may be given, either by the judge or by the Court of Appeal, to appeal to the Court of Appeal. An appeal may be taken to the House of Lords where a point of law of general public interest arises.

1   See also Chapter 20.
2   Insolvency Act 1986, s 373.
3   Insolvency Rules 1986, rr 6.9, 6.40.
4   Insolvency Act 1986, s 375(1) in bankruptcy; Insolvency Rules 1986, r 7.47 in liquidation.
5   Insolvency Act 1986, s 375(2) in bankruptcy; Insolvency Rules 1986, r 7.47(2) in winding up.
6   Insolvency Rules 1986, r 7.49.

3 INITIATING BANKRUPTCY

(a) Who may be made bankrupt?

Section 265 of the Insolvency Act 1986 provides that a bankruptcy petition can only be presented by a creditor or the debtor where the debtor is either domiciled in England or Wales, personally present in England or Wales on the day on which the petition is presented or, during the previous three years, has either been resident or carried on business in England and Wales.[7]

(b) Who may petition for a bankruptcy order?[8]

The bankruptcy procedure may be initiated either by an unpaid creditor[9] or creditors together or by a debtor who considers that bankruptcy is the only way out of financial difficulty. Where an individual voluntary arrangement is in existence, the supervisor and those bound by the arrangement also have standing to petition. The majority of petitions are presented by creditors, but the percentage of petitions which result in bankruptcy orders is much larger in the case of petitions presented by debtors than those presented by creditors since bankruptcy petitions presented by creditors often result in payment of the debt and withdrawal of the petition. The Justice report[10] said that bankruptcy orders were being sought by far too many debtors because of the absence of a suitable alternative.

	2000		2001	
	Debtors' *petitions*	*Creditors'* *petitions*	*Debtors'* *petitions*	*Creditors'* *petitions*
County court	12,170	7,296	14,285	6,947
High Court	587	9,924	699	8,624
Total	12,757	17,220	14,984	15,571

In 2001, the High Court made 697 bankruptcy orders on debtors' petitions and 4,380 bankruptcy orders on creditors' petitions.

(c) The debtor's petition

The sole ground for a debtor's petition is that the debtor is unable to pay his or her debts.[11] The petition has to be accompanied by a statement of the debtor's affairs containing prescribed particulars[12] including details of the debtor's creditors and

---

7   See Chapter 35 for bankruptcies with a cross-border element. See *North v Skipton Building Society* (2002) unreported, 7 June for a recent case in which a bankruptcy order was annulled after the court decided that the bankrupt was not within the Insolvency Act 1986, s 265.
8   Insolvency Act 1986, s 264.
9   Insolvency Act 1986, s 383(1) defines a creditor as a person to whom a bankruptcy debt (defined in the Insolvency Act 1986, s 382) is owed.
10   Justice, 1994.
11   Insolvency Act 1986, s 272.
12   See Insolvency Rules 1986, rr 6.41, 6.68.

liabilities and assets. The debtor will also have to meet the court fee of, currently, £120 and a £250 deposit on account of the Official Receiver's costs, although the court fee may be waived in cases of undue financial hardship. In *R v Lord Chancellor ex p Lightfoot*,[13] the Court of Appeal held that the requirement to pay the Official Receiver's deposit did not impede the debtor's constitutional right of access to the court, since the deposit was not a fee for access but one towards the cost of services provided by others for the debtor's benefit. Article 6(1) of the European Convention on Human Rights did not apply either, since that only applied where there was a dispute whose outcome would decide rights and obligations and in this case there was no dispute. Simon Brown LJ observed that 'it is not difficult to recognise the hardship and worry that many will suffer through their financial exclusion from the undoubted benefits of this rehabilitation scheme and, in the more compassionate times in which we now live, it may be hoped that the competing interests will be considered anew and perhaps a fresh balance struck'. Attempts were made during the passage of the Enterprise Bill through Parliament[14] to remove or reduce the deposit payable but the government maintained that it was not appropriate that the entire cost of the bankruptcy should be met by either the creditors or the taxpayer. A similarly unsuccessful attempt was made to have the costs reduced where a couple are simultaneously declaring themselves both bankrupt.

Inability to pay debts means inability to meet payments currently due; this was demonstrated by *Re a Debtor (No 17 of 1966)*,[15] an example of an attempted abuse of the insolvency legislation by a debtor. The debtor had been ordered to pay £2,400 damages as a result of an incident in which he had shot the judgment creditor in the eye. The damages were to be paid by weekly instalments of just over £1. The debtor presented a petition for his own bankruptcy, accompanied by a statement of affairs showing that he owed £2,400 in damages, £34 for clothes and £8 in respect of a moped. His assets were shown as £10 cash and the moped valued at £10. He was adjudicated bankrupt. His victim successfully applied for annulment of the order. The court held that only the instalments of the damages currently payable should be taken into account in deciding whether the debtor was able to pay his debts and that the debtor could pay these: 'a man is not unable to pay his debts because at some future time he will have to pay a debt which he would be unable to meet if it were presently payable.'[16]

A debtor's petition may lead to the court ordering an investigation into the possibility of setting up an individual voluntary arrangement rather than the making of a bankruptcy order.[17] This is possible where the unsecured liabilities which would be bankruptcy debts are less than the small bankruptcies level (currently £20,000), the value of the debtor's estate in a bankruptcy would be at least £2,000 and the debtor has not been adjudged bankrupt or entered into a composition with his or her creditors or scheme of affairs in the previous five years. If the court considers it appropriate to investigate the possibility of the debtor entering into an individual voluntary arrangement, it will appoint an insolvency practitioner to investigate and to

---

13 [1999] 4 All ER 583.

14 A clause suggested by the National Association of Citizens Advice Bureaux was discussed at committee stage in the House of Commons on 14 May 2002.

15 [1967] 1 All ER 668. The relevant legislation was the Bankruptcy Act 1914, s 6.

16 *Per* Goff LJ.

17 Insolvency Act 1986, s 273.

make a report to the court. The report may lead to the making of an interim order[18] and the calling of a meeting of creditors to consider the proposal. The approval of the proposal by the creditors will cause the deemed dismissal of the bankruptcy petition, unless the court orders otherwise.[19]

Prior to the Enterprise Act 2002, the court had the power[20] in any case in which a bankruptcy order was made, the liabilities were below the small bankruptcies level and the bankrupt had not been adjudged bankrupt within the previous five years, nor made a composition with his or her creditors, or entered into a scheme of arrangement to issue a certificate for the summary administration of the bankrupt's estate. This had the consequence that the bankruptcy remained under the control of the Official Receiver rather than a private sector insolvency practitioner, would probably end in two rather than three years and would involve less investigation than would otherwise be the case. This provision will be rendered redundant by the general reduction in the discharge period and is to be repealed.

(d) Petition in connection with default under an IVA

Section 264 of the Insolvency Act 1986 gives the supervisor of an IVA[21] or any person bound by it standing to petition to have the debtor made bankrupt. The grounds for such a petition[22] are that the debtor has failed to comply with his or her obligations under the arrangement or has given false or misleading information in the process of having the IVA approved or has failed to comply with the reasonable requirements of the supervisor in connection with the arrangement.

(e) Creditor's petition

A petition may be presented by a single creditor or by several creditors jointly on the basis of a liquidated and unsecured debt or debts which at least equal the bankruptcy level, which is currently £750, and which the debtor appears either unable to pay or, where the debt is not currently payable, to have no reasonable prospect of being able to pay.[23] There is no requirement in the Insolvency Act 1986 that a petition be based on a debt which is provable in the bankruptcy,[24] but the Court of Appeal held in *Levy v Legal Services Commission*[25] that it would not usually be appropriate to make a bankruptcy order in such circumstances.[26] In determining whether there is a

---

18   See Chapter 9.
19   Insolvency Act 1986, s 260(5).
20   Under the Insolvency Act 1986, s 275.
21   See Chapter 9.
22   Insolvency Act 1986, s 276.
23   Insolvency Act 1986, s 267. It is not an abuse of process to have other reasons for a petition as well as the wish to recover a dividend: *Hicks v Gulliver* [2002] BPIR 518.
24   See Chapter 34 for an explanation of which debts will be provable.
25   [2001] 1 All ER 895.
26   The debt in question was an obligation arising under an order made in family proceedings. The Court held (disapproving of *dicta* in *Russell v Russell* [1999] 2 FCR 137) that the fact that the debtor may have so misconducted his affairs that it may be said that he or she (in effect) deserves to be made bankrupt cannot justify the making of a bankruptcy order on a petition based on a non-provable debt. The only conceivable situation would be one in which a supporting creditor with a provable debt obtained a change of carriage order (see below).

reasonable prospect of the debtor being able to pay when the debt falls due, it is to be assumed that the prospect given by the facts and other matters known to the creditor at the time he or she entered into the transaction resulting in the debt was a reasonable prospect.[27] A creditor may petition in respect of a secured debt[28] if willing to give up the security or in respect of that part of the debt which will not be covered by the security.[29] Where a secured creditor gives up a security, the security passes to the trustee in bankruptcy for realisation for the benefit of all the creditors; the security is not destroyed and, therefore, any subordinate security over the property is not accelerated.[30]

Section 268 of the Insolvency Act 1986 provides that inability to pay a debt is to be established only by reference either to unsatisfied execution of a judgment debt in favour of a petitioning creditor[31] or to non-compliance with a statutory demand[32] and by no other means.[33] No petition may be presented if there is an application outstanding to have the statutory demand set aside.[34] In *Re a Debtor (No 340 of 1992)*,[35] the petition was presented on the basis of unsatisfied execution of judgment in that the sheriff was unable to obtain access to the debtor's premises. Millett LJ held that the wording of s 268 of the Insolvency Act 1986 contemplated that an execution would actually have taken place and that it was not possible to present a petition on the basis of inability to obtain access to effect execution.[36] The petition had, therefore, to be dismissed. The petitioner in that case would have been able to proceed by way of the statutory demand route, although that would have caused a delay of three weeks.[37]

There is provision[38] for presentation of a petition after the service of a statutory demand before the three week period for compliance has expired, if there is a serious possibility that the debtor's property or its value will be significantly diminished during that period.[39] The bankruptcy order may not be made until at least three weeks have elapsed since the service of any statutory demand, but once a petition has been presented, the court may appoint an interim receiver to take immediate

27 Insolvency Act 1986, s 271(4).
28 Insolvency Act 1986, s 383 provides that a debt is secured to the extent that the person to whom the debt is owed holds any security for the debt (whether a mortgage, charge, lien or other security) over any property of the person by whom the debt is owed.
29 Insolvency Act 1986, s 269.
30 *Cracknell v Jackson* (1877) 6 Ch D 735.
31 See Chapter 5.
32 See Chapter 14.
33 Unlike the grounds for compulsory liquidation of a company where inability to pay debts may be established by reference to any evidence. See the comments of Peter Gibson J in *TSB Bank plc v Platts* [1998] 2 BCLC 1.
34 Insolvency Act 1986, s 267(2)(d). An informal letter asking that the statutory demand be set aside which did not comply with the appropriate formalities prescribed by the Insolvency Rules did not prevent presentation of a petition: *Ariyo v Sovereign Leasing plc* (1997) *The Times*, 4 August.
35 [1996] 2 All ER 211 (CA).
36 Jacob J in *Re a Debtor (No 78 of 2000), Skarzynski v Chalford Property Company Ltd* [2001] BPIR 673 said that it was not necessary to be over-technical about compliance with the procedural requirements of an execution which had actually taken place.
37 It is apparent that the petitioner wanted to obtain a bankruptcy order before the passing of two years since the debtor had transferred property to his wife. See Chapter 30 for the relevance of this.
38 Insolvency Act 1986, s 270.
39 See *Re a Debtor (No 22 of 1993)* [1994] 2 All ER 105.

possession of the debtor's property.[40] The person applying for the appointment of an interim receiver will have to deposit or secure for such sum as the court directs to cover the expenses of the interim receivership; if a bankruptcy order is subsequently made, the sum will, provided there are sufficient funds, be repaid out of the bankrupt's estate.

In most cases, the court will not hear the bankruptcy petition until at least 14 days after it has been served on the debtor.[41] The debtor must give at least seven days' notice of an intention to oppose the petition at the hearing. In addition to the petitioning creditor and the debtor, the supervisor of any voluntary arrangement in force for the debtor and any creditor who has given the requisite notice[42] may be heard by the court.

A bankruptcy petition is viewed as a class action brought on behalf of all the creditors with the consequences that once a petition has been presented it may only be withdrawn with the leave of the court at the hearing of the petition.[43] Other creditors may be substituted[44] for the original petitioning creditor and the court will take into account the interests of all the creditors in deciding whether or not to make the order. The court has a general power to dismiss a bankruptcy petition or stay proceedings, on such terms as it thinks fit, where it thinks it appropriate to do so.[45] In Re Williams[46] it was held that the court should not grant repeated adjournments of bankruptcy proceedings on the basis that the debtor had indicated that he would eventually (but not within a reasonable time) be able to repay what was owing by instalments.

The debt must be outstanding at the time of the petition,[47] but a debtor cannot ensure the avoidance of bankruptcy simply by paying the amount owed to the petitioning creditor since the court may substitute[48] another creditor for the petitioning creditor. Substitution requires that the petitioning creditor is unable, or does not wish, to pursue the petition and that the substituted creditor would have been able to present a bankruptcy petition on the date when the petition was presented because he or she could show either an unsatisfied execution or an unsatisfied statutory demand at that time. Where a payment is made to the first petitioner and a bankruptcy order is made after the substitution of another petitioner, the payment will be a void disposition within s 284 of the Insolvency Act 1986.[49]

It is possible for a creditor who could not have presented a bankruptcy petition at the same time as the petitioner to apply for a 'change of carriage' order enabling the creditor to take control of the proceedings without being substituted as the petitioner;[50] the court may make such an order if satisfied that the petitioning creditor

---

40 Insolvency Act 1986, s 286. This will either be the Official Receiver or may be an insolvency practitioner previously appointed under the Insolvency Act 1986, s 273 to consider the possibility of an IVA.
41 Insolvency Rules 1986, r 6.18.
42 Insolvency Rules 1986, r 6.23.
43 Insolvency Rules 1986, r 6.32.
44 Insolvency Rules 1986, r 6.30.
45 Insolvency Act 1986, s 266.
46 (1997) The Times, 16 July.
47 Re Patel [1986] 1 WLR 221.
48 Insolvency Rules 1986, r 6.30.
49 See Chapter 30.
50 Insolvency Rules 1986, r 6.31.

does not propose to pursue proceedings diligently or at all. It was held in *Re Purvis*[51] that where the debt in respect of which the petition was presented has been paid, a change of carriage order is not possible, since s 271 of the Insolvency Act 1986 provides that the court cannot make a bankruptcy order where, if the petition was based on a debt currently payable, the debt has been paid, secured or compounded for. Chadwick J held that s 271 overrides the provisions of r 6.31 of the Insolvency Rules 1986 despite the fact that this appears to give the court power to make a change of carriage order unless the payment has been made by someone other than the debtor or with the approval of the court.[52] The Court of Appeal in *Smith v Ian Simpson & Co*[53] held, by a majority, that s 271(1) did not in fact preclude the court from making a bankruptcy order where the petition debt had been paid out of the debtor's own property. They construed the section as being confined to circumstances where the payment was not liable to be avoided in the event of a bankruptcy order; this was a highly purposive interpretation made on the basis that otherwise r 6.31 and, in circumstances where the debtor paid before the hearing, r 6.30 would be pointless and also that it would be inconsistent both with s 284(1) of the Insolvency Act and with the whole scheme and policy of the Insolvency Act 1986 to allow the debtor to bring the petition to an end by paying the petition debt in the face of supporting creditors who sought a bankruptcy order.

The court may refuse to make a bankruptcy order if it is satisfied that the debtor is able to pay all his or her debts (taking into account contingent and prospective liabilities) or is satisfied that the petitioner has unreasonably refused an offer by the debtor to secure or compound for a debt in respect of which the petition is presented.[54] *Re a Debtor (No 32 of 1993)*[55] shows that it will be rare for the petitioner's refusal of the debtor's offer to be unreasonable. It was held that before it could be said that the refusal was unreasonable, the court had to be satisfied that no reasonable hypothetical creditor in the position of the petitioning creditor and in the light of the actual history as disclosed to the court would have refused the offer and that the refusal was therefore beyond the range of possible reasonable actions in the circumstances. The court held that a reasonable creditor might well wish for the full investigation that a bankruptcy would occasion even if there was little to be gained financially by the creditor.[56] In *IRC v A Debtor*,[57] Robert Walker J said that, first, the test must be objective and relate to matters bearing objectively on the debtor-creditor relationship and, secondly, creditors were entitled to have regard to their own interests and were not required to show patience or generosity.

---

51 [1997] 3 All ER 663.
52 Such approval validating the payment for the purposes of the Insolvency Act 1986, s 284 (see Chapter 30). The purpose behind r 6.31 seems to be an attempt to prevent a creditor from using the presentation of a bankruptcy petition as a means of exerting pressure on the debtor to pay him at the expense of other creditors in that if the bankruptcy order were to be made at the behest of another creditor the payment would be invalidated by the Insolvency Act 1986, s 284.
53 [2001] Ch 239. See also *Levy v Legal Services Commission* [2001] 1 All ER 895.
54 Insolvency Act 1986, s 271.
55 [1995] 1 All ER 628.
56 In *Ex p Travel and General Insurance* [1990] 3 All ER 984, it was held that a refusal to vote in favour of a proposal for an IVA is not within the Insolvency Act 1986, s 271, since a proposal of an IVA is not to be regarded as an offer to each creditor individually.
57 [1995] BCC 971.

In *Eberhardt & Co Ltd v Mair*,[58] Evans-Lombe J held that since the bankruptcy court has a duty to ensure that it does not make an order in circumstances which would cause injustice, it was not bound by any previous decision arising in connection with any judgment on the debt or an application to set aside a statutory demand; it could reconsider afresh the question of whether the debt was due. The Court of Appeal in *Turner v Royal Bank of Scotland*[59] pointed out that Evans-Lombe J did not appear to have had cited to him *Brillouett v Hachette Magazines Ltd*.[60] In that case, Vinelott J had said that it would only be in rare cases, such as a change of legislation as a result of which the debt had become unenforceable, where it can be said that a debt not paid, secured or compounded for, which has been claimed in a statutory demand and which there has been an unsuccessful attempt to set aside, is not payable at the date of the petition. The Court of Appeal said that Vinelott J had stated the position correctly when he said that the debtor could not go back and re-argue the very grounds on which he had unsuccessfully sought to set the statutory demand aside.

(f) Notification of bankruptcy petition

The court will forthwith send notice to the Chief Land Registrar of the filing of a petition for bankruptcy. This will be registered in the register of pending actions.[61]

(g) Notification of bankruptcy order

The making of the bankruptcy order will be advertised by the Official Receiver in a local newspaper and in the London Gazette.[62] The Insolvency Service's Bankruptcy Public Search Room in Birmingham contains public records of all bankruptcies taken from the official notification to the Gazette.

(h) Appeal against bankruptcy order

There are two ways in which the decision of a bankruptcy court can be revisited.[63] The court which made the bankruptcy order may be asked to review or rescind the order.[64] An application must be based on a change in circumstances since the order was made or on the discovery of further evidence which it would not be possible to adduce on appeal. In *Fitch v Official Receiver*,[65] the Court of Appeal held that a change of mind by the petitioning creditor would amount to changed circumstances and since the change of mind had happened since the making of the bankruptcy order, it could

---

58 [1995] 3 All ER 963.
59 (2000) unreported, 30 June.
60 Delivered on 24 June 1991 and now reported at [1996] BPIR 519.
61 Insolvency Rules 1986, rr 6.13, 6.43.
62 Insolvency Rules 1986, rr 6.34, 6.46.
63 See *Hoare v IRC* [2002] EWHC 775 (Ch); *Re RSM Engineering* [1999] 2 BCLC 485; *RBS v Farley* [1996] BPIR 638.
64 Insolvency Act 1986, s 375(1). See the comments of Chadwick LJ in *Mond v Hammond Suddards* [2000] Ch 40 as to the history of the power to review and the circumstances in which it should be used.
65 [1996] 1 WLR 242.

not be raised on appeal. It is also possible to appeal in the normal way against the decision of the court to make or refuse a bankruptcy petition.

4   CONDUCT OF THE BANKRUPTCY

(a) Official Receiver's role

The Official Receiver[66] performs a caretaking role in relation to the bankrupt's estate under s 287 of the Insolvency Act 1986 until a trustee in bankruptcy is appointed. This is restricted to protecting the property, but he or she is entitled to sell or otherwise dispose of any perishable goods comprised in the estate and any other goods so comprised the value of which is otherwise likely to diminish. The Official Receiver must not incur expense at this stage without the sanction of the court. The Official Receiver will be protected from liability in respect of any loss or damage resulting from seizure or disposal of assets which are subsequently determined not to form part of the bankrupt's estate provided he or she had reasonable grounds for believing that he or she was entitled to do so.

Whether the Official Receiver becomes trustee in bankruptcy or is replaced by a private sector insolvency practitioner, he or she retains investigatory obligations in relation to the bankruptcy which are explained in Part IV below.[67]

If, at any stage in the bankruptcy, a vacancy arises in the office of trustee in bankruptcy, the Official Receiver will be the trustee until the vacancy is filled.[68] Where the Official Receiver administers the estate, the costs will be charged on the Official Receiver's scale[69] as a percentage on both realisations and distributions; in the case of a small bankruptcy with realisations of between £10,000 and £20,000, the Official Receiver's costs will amount to about 40% of the assets.

(b) The function of the trustee in bankruptcy

Section 305 of the Insolvency Act 1986 provides that the function of the trustee is to get in, realise and distribute the bankrupt's estate in accordance with the provisions of the Act.[70] This is considered in detail in Part V below.

(c) Appointment of the trustee in bankruptcy[71]

Where the bankruptcy order has followed an insolvency practitioner's report that an IVA is not feasible, the court may if it thinks fit appoint that insolvency practitioner as trustee in bankruptcy.[72] If there is an IVA already in existence, the court may appoint

---

66   See Chapter 20.
67   See Chapter 21.
68   Insolvency Act 1986, s 300.
69   Insolvency Fees Order 1986 (as amended).
70   If not also the Official Receiver, he or she will have a duty to co-operate with the Official Receiver in the investigatory aspects of the bankruptcy; see Chapter 21.
71   See Chapter 20 for qualification to act as a trustee in bankruptcy.
72   Insolvency Act 1986, s 297(4).

the supervisor as trustee in bankruptcy.[73] In either of these cases, the trustee must give notice of his or her appointment, stating whether he or she proposes to call a meeting of the creditors for the purpose of establishing a creditors' committee and, if not, stating the power of the creditors to require that one be called.

In all other cases, s 293 of the Insolvency Act 1986 provides that the Official Receiver must decide in the first 12 weeks of the bankruptcy whether to summon a general meeting of the bankrupt's creditors for the purpose of appointing a trustee of the bankrupt's estate. The Official Receiver will be assisted in coming to this decision by the statement of the bankrupt's affairs and the other information which he or she is entitled to in relation to the bankrupt's affairs.[74] If he or she decides within the 12 week period not to summon such a meeting, notice[75] of this decision must be given to the court and to every known creditor of the bankrupt and, as from the giving to the court of the notice, the Official Receiver is the trustee in bankruptcy.[76] The Official Receiver's decision as to whether or not a private sector insolvency practitioner should become the trustee in bankruptcy will depend upon the assets available in the bankrupt's assets; where these are insufficient to meet the costs of a private sector appointment, the Official Receiver will be the trustee in bankruptcy.

The Official Receiver may be compelled, under s 294 of the Insolvency Act 1986, to summon a meeting of the creditors to appoint a private sector insolvency practitioner as trustee; this will require the concurrence with the request for the meeting of not less than one-quarter in value of the bankrupt's creditors, including the creditor making the request. If a meeting is called and fails to appoint a trustee, the Official Receiver has to decide whether to refer the need for an appointment to the Secretary of State for Trade and Industry who may decide to make an appointment.[77] If the Official Receiver decides to make no reference or if no appointment is made, the Official Receiver will give notice of this to the court and will become trustee at that time. Where the Official Receiver has become trustee, he or she may at any time ask the Secretary of State to appoint an insolvency practitioner instead.[78]

(d) Appointment of a creditors' committee

Provision is made[79] for the appointment of a committee of creditors to oversee the conduct of the bankruptcy. Where the Official Receiver is trustee, the committee cannot operate, but its functions will be vested in the Secretary of State.[80]

---

73 Insolvency Act 1986, s 297(5). This would not be possible where there was a potential conflict of interest between the IVA creditors and the bankruptcy creditors.
74 See Chapter 21.
75 Insolvency Act 1986, s 293(2).
76 Insolvency Act 1986, s 293(3).
77 Insolvency Act 1986, s 295.
78 Insolvency Act 1986, s 296.
79 Insolvency Act 1986, s 301. See Chapter 20, which deals with the control of the insolvency system.
80 Insolvency Act 1986, s 302.

(e) Powers of the trustee in bankruptcy[81]

The trustee in bankruptcy has the powers conferred by s 314 of the Insolvency Act 1986 which are particularised in Sched 5 to the Act. Part 1 of the Schedule lists the powers which may be exercised with the permission of the creditors' committee or the court. Part 2 lists the powers for the exercise of which the trustee does not need such permission and Part 3 lists the powers which may be exercised ancillary to any of the powers in Parts 1 or 2. The Part 2 general powers include the power to sell property comprised in the bankrupt's estate, to give receipts for money which discharge the payer from responsibility and to pursue debts comprised in the estate. The Part 1 powers requiring sanction include the power to continue the bankrupt's business for its beneficial winding up, the power to litigate as claimant or defendant in relation to the bankrupt estate, the power to raise money by granting security over the property in the bankrupt's estate, the power to accept postponed payment for property in the estate, the power to exercise rights, options or powers comprised in the estate and the power to enter settlements of claims. The trustee is also given the power,[82] with the sanction of the creditors or the court, to appoint the bankrupt to assist in the managing of the estate or the carrying on of a business for the benefit of the creditors.

(f) Ceasing to be trustee in bankruptcy[83]

The trustee will vacate office if the bankruptcy order is annulled or when the administration of the estate is complete and a final meeting of the creditors has been held.[84] A trustee in bankruptcy must vacate office if he or she ceases to be qualified to act as such and may also resign on grounds of ill health or where there is some conflict of interest or change of personal circumstances which precludes or makes impracticable the further discharge by him or her of the duties of a trustee.[85] A trustee appointed by the Secretary of State may also be removed by the Secretary of State.[86] In other circumstances, a trustee in bankruptcy may be removed from office only by an order of the court[87] or by a general meeting of the bankrupt's creditors summoned for that purpose in accordance with the rules.[88]

A trustee on ceasing to hold office will be given his or her release from all liability in respects of acts and omissions in the administration of the estate and otherwise in relation to his or her conduct as a trustee at the time prescribed by s 299 of the Insolvency Act 1986. Nothing will prevent the court from imposing liability under s 304[89] of the Insolvency Act 1986 on a trustee who has been guilty of the misapplication of property or of misfeasance or breach of fiduciary or other duty in the carrying out of his or her functions. The trustee is given protection[90] from claims

---

81   The power to disclaim onerous property is considered in Chapter 26.
82   Insolvency Act 1986, s 314(2).
83   See generally the Insolvency Act 1986, s 298.
84   Under the Insolvency Act 1986, s 331.
85   Insolvency Act 1986, s 298(7); Insolvency Rules 1986, rr 6.126–6.128.
86   Insolvency Act 1986, s 298(5); Insolvency Rules 1986, r 6.133.
87   Insolvency Rules 1986, r 6.132.
88   Insolvency Act 1986, s 298; Insolvency Rules, rr 6.129–6.131.
89   See Chapter 20.
90   By the Insolvency Act 1986, s 304(3).

of those whose property has been wrongfully seized or disposed of provided that he or she reasonably believed at the time in an entitlement so to act unless any damage was caused by his or her negligence.

5 CONSEQUENCES OF BEING AN UNDISCHARGED BANKRUPT

(a) Loss of property

As explained in Part V below,[91] the bankrupt will be under an obligation to hand over most of his or her property to the trustee in bankruptcy for distribution to the creditors.

(b) Freedom from harassment by creditors

The creditors of the bankrupt lose the right to take individual action against the bankrupt and his or her assets, as explained below.[92]

(c) Investigation, possible criminal liability and personal disabilities

The bankrupt will be under an obligation to co-operate with the Official Receiver's investigation into the background to the bankruptcy.[93] There are a number of criminal offences which can only be committed by undischarged bankrupts. These are explained below[94] and it will be seen that some of the offences arise from the pre-bankruptcy actions of the bankrupt whereas others are committed during the currency of the bankruptcy. An undischarged bankrupt is subject to a number of personal disabilities which are considered in Chapter 22, below. Once the relevant provisions of the Enterprise Act 2002 come into force, a bankruptcy restriction order may be made against a bankrupt; this is also considered in Chapter 22.

6 CEASING TO BE BANKRUPT

(a) Discharge from bankruptcy

Section 278 of the Insolvency Act 1986 provides that the bankruptcy of an individual commences with the day on which the bankruptcy order is made and continues until the individual is discharged. It used to be the case that a bankrupt had to apply for his or her discharge and large numbers of bankrupts never did so.[95] Automatic discharge from bankruptcy was first introduced in 1976. Under the current provisions, the bankruptcy will usually expire automatically either at the end of two years, in the case

---

91 See Chapter 27 in particular.
92 See Chapter 25.
93 See Chapter 21.
94 In Chapter 22.
95 Particularly since public examination of the bankrupt was at that time a necessary prerequisite to obtaining discharge.

of a summary administration, or at the end of three years in other cases. The period of a bankruptcy which will end automatically may be extended[96] if the court is satisfied on the application of the Official Receiver that the bankrupt has failed or is failing to meet his or her obligations under the Insolvency Act 1986. In such a case, the court may order that the period of two or three years shall cease to run for such period, or until the fulfilment of such conditions, as may be specified in the order. Section 256 of the Enterprise Act 2002 will reduce the normal period of bankruptcy to one year or, if earlier, until the time when the Official Receiver files a notice with the court stating that investigation of the conduct and affairs of the bankrupt is unnecessary or concluded.

Where the individual has previously been an undischarged bankrupt within the 15 years before the bankruptcy order, a court order will be required to bring the bankruptcy to an end.[97] An application for such an order may not be made until five years after the commencement of the bankruptcy and the court may refuse to grant it or may grant it with or without conditions. At the hearing of such an application, the Official Receiver, trustee in bankruptcy and creditors may appear, make representations and put to the bankrupt such questions as the court allows. The Official Receiver will make a report to the court which has usually carried great weight with the court in making its decision. Conditions imposed by the court may relate to the time at which the discharge is to take effect or to what is to happen to after-acquired property of the discharged bankrupt.

The Cork Committee said[98] that the written evidence presented to it was fairly evenly balanced between those, mainly practitioners, who supported the new automatic procedure and those who did not. The latter were mainly creditors and some individuals who had themselves been bankrupt. The Committee suggested that in more serious cases, there should be an automatic review of whether discharge should be granted rather than an automatic discharge. In the consultation document *Bankruptcy: A Fresh Start*,[99] the Insolvency Service envisaged that bankruptcy would in effect become a period in which the great majority of individuals could 'sort out their finances and their futures in the expectation of early rehabilitation'.

Discharge has no effect on the distribution of the assets which vested in the trustee in bankruptcy during the bankruptcy nor on the right of any creditor to prove in the bankruptcy.[100] The discharged bankrupt is, however, released from most bankruptcy debts. The exceptions are fines and debts which were incurred in respect of, or forbearance in respect of which was secured by means of, any fraud or fraudulent breach of trust to which the bankrupt was a party.[101] The bankrupt will not be discharged from bankruptcy debts consisting of liability for damages for personal

---

96 Under the Insolvency Act 1986, s 279. In *Jacobs v Official Receiver* [1999] 1 WLR 619, it was held that an interim suspension order could be made in a case where the bankrupt challenged the Official Receiver's request for a suspension of discharge.

97 Insolvency Act 1986, ss 279(1), 280; Insolvency Rules 1986, rr 6.217, 6.218.

98 Paragraph 607.

99 Paragraph 7.4.

100 Insolvency Act 1986, s 281. The discharged bankrupt remains under an obligation to co-operate with the trustee in the performance of his duties: Insolvency Act 1986, ss 333, 366.

101 See *Woodland-Ferrari v UCL Group Retirement Benefits Scheme* [2002] 3 All ER 670.

injury or arising under an order made in family or domestic proceedings[102] unless and to the extent ordered by the court.[103] Discharge does not affect the right of any secured creditor of the bankrupt to enforce his or her security for the payment of a debt from which the bankrupt is released. Discharge only releases the bankrupt; it does not affect the liability of any guarantor or anyone else with liability for the released debts.

(b) Annulment of bankruptcy order

The court may annul a bankruptcy order under s 282 of the Insolvency Act 1986 if it appears that, on any grounds existing at the time the order was made, the order ought not to have been made.[104] The order may also be annulled if the bankruptcy debts and the expenses of the bankruptcy have all been either paid or secured for to the satisfaction of the court since the making of the order. A bankruptcy may be annulled even if the bankrupt has been discharged from the bankruptcy. The other circumstance in which a bankruptcy order may be annulled[105] is where a bankrupt has entered into an individual voluntary arrangement. Transactions carried out by or under the authority of the Official Receiver, the trustee in bankruptcy or the court before the annulment under either section will be valid, but any of the bankrupt's estate vested in the trustee at the time of the annulment shall revert to the bankrupt unless the court orders that it shall vest in another person.[106] Any time when a person was a bankrupt by virtue of an order that was subsequently annulled will be disregarded in establishing entitlement to be discharged from a subsequent bankruptcy. Annulment has the effect that the bankruptcy order is regarded as never having been made.[107]

---

102 Or maintenance proceedings under the Child Support Act 1991.

103 Insolvency Act 1986, s 281(6) provides that discharge does not release the bankrupt from such other bankruptcy debts, not being debts provable in his bankruptcy, as are prescribed.

104 Any person affected by a bankruptcy order and who claims it should not have been made apply under s 282: *Forder v Forder* [2002] EWCA Civ 1527.

105 Under the Insolvency Act 1986, s 261.

106 This enables the court to order the vesting of property in the supervisor of an IVA.

107 Insolvency Act 1986, s 282(4) preserves the validity of any acts done by the Official Receiver or the trustee before the annulment.

CHAPTER 16

VOLUNTARY LIQUIDATION

1 INTRODUCTION

A voluntary liquidation is set in motion by a resolution of the members of the company. It may be either a members' voluntary liquidation or a creditors' voluntary liquidation; in the case of an insolvent company, it will have to be a creditors' voluntary liquidation. The distinction is that in a creditors' voluntary liquidation, the creditors have ultimate control over the conduct of the liquidation.

2 COMMENCEMENT OF THE WINDING UP

(a) Resolution of the members

A company may be wound up voluntarily in the three circumstances outlined in s 84 of the Insolvency Act 1986. The relevant provision in the context of insolvency is s 84(1)(c) of the Insolvency Act 1986, which provides that a company may be wound up voluntarily if the company resolves by extraordinary resolution of its members to the effect that it cannot by reason of its liabilities continue its business and that it is advisable to wind up. A company may be wound up voluntarily in any circumstances by special resolution of its members under s 84(1)(b) of the Insolvency Act 1986. The distinction between an extraordinary and a special resolution is that the former only requires 14 days' notice of the meeting at which the resolution is to be passed, whereas a special resolution requires 21 days' notice. Both types of resolution require a three-quarters majority of those members voting.[1]

A voluntary winding up is deemed to commence at the time of the passing of the resolution by the company. The company must then within 14 days give notice of the resolution by advertisement in the Gazette.[2] The Registrar of Companies must be notified within 15 days after the passing of the resolution.[3]

(b) Inability to swear statutory declaration of solvency

Where the directors cannot swear a statutory declaration of solvency under s 89 of the Insolvency Act 1986 within the five weeks before the winding up resolution, a voluntary liquidation will have to be a creditors' voluntary liquidation. The directors will only be able to swear such a declaration if they think that the company will be able to pay its debts in full, together with interest, within 12 months from the commencement of the winding up;[4] it is a criminal offence to make such a declaration without reasonable grounds for believing it.

---

1 Companies Act 1985, s 378.
2 Insolvency Act 1986, s 85(1).
3 Companies Act 1985, s 380(1) and (4).
4 See *Re Corbenstoke Ltd (No 2)* (1989) 5 BCC 767.

(c) Creditors' meeting

Where the winding up is to be a creditors' voluntary winding up, a meeting of the creditors must be called under s 98 of the Insolvency Act 1986 to be held not later than 14 days after the day of the company meeting. Creditors must be given at least seven days' notice of the meeting and the notice must either give the name and address of the insolvency practitioner to whom they can apply free of charge for such information about the company's affairs as they may reasonably require. Alternatively, creditors may be given details of a place in the relevant locality where on the two business days before the meeting, a list of the names and addresses of the company's creditors will be available for inspection. The directors must prepare a statement of the affairs of the company to be laid before the meeting and one of their number must preside at the meeting.[5]

(d) Consequences of going into voluntary liquidation

The company ceases from the commencement of the winding up to carry on its business except so far as may be required for its beneficial winding up.[6] The directors lose most of their powers with the appointment of a liquidator.[7] The corporate state and powers of the company continue until the company is dissolved.[8] Any transfer of shares made without the sanction of the liquidator or alteration in the status of the company's members after the commencement of the liquidation is void.[9] All business documentation must contain a statement that the company is being wound up.[10]

(e) Conversion from members' to creditors' voluntary liquidation

If a winding up commences as a members' voluntary winding up but the liquidator forms the view that payment of all debts will not be possible, a meeting of creditors must be summoned[11] for a date within a month of the liquidator coming to that conclusion. The liquidation will be converted to a creditors' voluntary winding up as from the day of the creditors' meeting, which will be treated as a meeting called under s 98 of the Insolvency Act 1986.

3 CONTROL OF THE WINDING UP

(a) Appointment of liquidator[12]

In most cases, the creditors will choose the liquidator. Both the creditors and the members at their respective meetings may nominate a person to be liquidator. The

---

5   Insolvency Act 1986, s 99.
6   Insolvency Act 1986, s 87(1).
7   Insolvency Act 1986, ss 114, 103.
8   Insolvency Act 1986, s 87(2).
9   Insolvency Act 1986, s 88.
10 Insolvency Act 1986, s 188.
11 Insolvency Act 1986, s 95. See, for example, *AMF International Ltd* [1996] 1 WLR 77.
12 Insolvency Act 1986, s 100.

liquidator will be the person nominated by the creditors or, where no person has been so nominated, the person nominated by the members. If the two meetings nominate different liquidators, any director, member or creditor of the company may within seven days of the creditors' nomination apply to the court for a decision as to who should be liquidator. The court may order that either nominee be the sole liquidator or that both be joint liquidators or that some other person be liquidator.

A liquidator nominated by the company meeting will be unable,[13] without the sanction of the court, to exercise any powers during the period before the holding of the creditors' meeting; the exception to this is that the liquidator will be able to take custody of the company's property, to dispose of perishable goods and other goods the value of which is likely to diminish if they are not immediately disposed of and to do all such other things as may be necessary for the protection of the corporate assets. These restrictions are intended to prevent the dissipation of corporate assets by a liquidator friendly to those in control of the company; this practice is referred to as Centrebinding, since it was held in the case of *Re Centrebind*[14] that, under the then law, the acts of a liquidator subsequently displaced by the creditors were valid.

If a vacancy occurs in the office of a liquidator, other than a liquidator appointed by, or by the direction of the court, the creditors may fill the vacancy.[15] If, for any reason, there is no liquidator acting, the court may appoint a liquidator.[16] The liquidator must publish notice of his or her appointment in the Gazette within 14 days of the appointment and also notify the registrar of companies.[17]

(b) Ceasing to be liquidator[18]

The court may, on cause shown, remove a liquidator and appoint another.[19] A liquidator may also be removed from office by a general meeting of the company's creditors summoned for that purpose in accordance with the Insolvency Rules 1986;[20] if the liquidator was appointed by the court such a meeting will only be summoned if requested by at least half in value of the creditors, otherwise the meeting must be called if requested by at least 25% in value of the creditors. The liquidator must vacate office if he or she ceases to be qualified to act as an insolvency practitioner and may resign because of ill health or where some conflict of interest or other circumstance makes it impracticable to continue to act; resignation requires the calling of a creditors' meeting and notice to the registrar of companies.[21] The liquidator will also vacate office after the liquidation is complete.

---

13 Insolvency Act 1986, s 166.
14 [1966] 3 All ER 889.
15 Insolvency Act 1986, s 104.
16 Insolvency Act 1986, s 108.
17 Insolvency Act 1986, s 109.
18 See, generally, Insolvency Act 1986, s 171; Insolvency Rules 1986, rr 4.108–4.123.
19 Insolvency Act 1986, s 108(2). See Chapter 20.
20 Insolvency Act 1986, s 171(2)(b).
21 The courts have shown themselves willing to order the removal of an insolvency practitioner where this avoids the need for calling a large number of creditors' meetings: *Bullard v Taplin* [1996] BCC 973; *Re Sankey Furniture* [1995] 2 BCLC 594; *Re Alt Landscapes* (1998) unreported, 15 December.

A liquidator who has ceased to hold office will be released from potential liability in connection with the liquidation at the time prescribed in s 173 of the Insolvency Act 1986. Nothing will prevent the exercise of the court's powers under s 212 of the Insolvency Act 1986 in relation to a liquidator guilty of breach of fiduciary or other duty or of misapplying company property.

(c) Liquidation committee[22]

The creditors may elect a liquidation committee of not more than five persons to exercise the functions conferred on it by the insolvency legislation. If such a committee is appointed, the company may appoint up to five members to sit on the committee. The creditors may resolve to object to some or all of the members appointed by the company in which case those members may not act unless the court directs that they may. On an application to the court, the court may appoint substitutes to act as members of the committee.

(d) Cessation of directors' powers

Once the company is in liquidation, the powers of the directors are limited to calling the creditors' meeting, drawing up the statement of affairs and protecting the assets of the company unless the court allows them to do something else.[23] On the appointment of a liquidator, all the powers of the directors cease, except so far as the liquidation committee (or, if there is no such committee, the creditors) sanction their continuance.[24]

(e) Function and powers of the liquidator

The liquidator will proceed to wind up the company's affairs in accordance with the provisions of the Insolvency Act 1986.[25]

Section 165 of the Insolvency Act 1986 sets out the powers of a liquidator in a voluntary liquidation, partly by reference to Sched 4 to the Act. The liquidator is to pay the company's debts and adjust the rights of the contributories amongst themselves.[26] The liquidator may call meetings of the company. He or she may exercise the powers specified in Part II of Sched 4 without any further permission;[27] these allow the liquidator to institute and defend legal proceedings[28] and to carry on the business of the company so far as necessary for its beneficial winding up. Part III of Sched 4 contains a list of powers which any liquidator has; these include the power to sell the company's property, the power to appoint agents to do any business the liquidator is unable to do him or herself and a general power to do all such other

---

22 Insolvency Act 1986, ss 101, 102.
23 Insolvency Act 1986, s 114.
24 Insolvency Act 1986, s 103.
25 Insolvency Act 1986, s 107. See Part V below.
26 As to contributories, see Chapter 31.
27 A liquidator in a compulsory liquidation will need permission to exercise these powers.
28 Enterprise Act 2002, s 262 will require sanction for proceedings brought in the liquidator's own name (including actions under the Insolvency Act 1986, ss 339, 340 and 423).

things as may be necessary for winding up the company and distributing its assets. Part I of Sched 4 lists the powers which the liquidator can only exercise with the consent of the court, the liquidation committee or, where there is no committee, a meeting of the creditors; these are the power to pay any class of creditors in full and the power to enter compromises with those claiming against the company or against whom the company has a claim. Where the whole or part of the company's business or property is proposed to be transferred to another company, s 110 of the Insolvency Act 1986 gives the liquidator the power to accept shares or other interests in the transferee company instead of cash for distribution amongst the members of the transferor company provided, in the case of a creditors' voluntary liquidation, that the court or the liquidation committee consents.[29]

The liquidator, any contributory or any creditor may apply to the court to determine questions arising in the course of the liquidation or to exercise any of the powers which the court would have if the company were being wound up by the court.[30] Where the liquidation takes longer than one year, the liquidator has to call meetings of the members and of the creditors at the end of the first year from the commencement of the liquidation, and of each succeeding year, or at the first convenient date within three months from the end of the year or such longer period as the Secretary of State may allow.[31] At these meetings, the liquidator presents an account of his or her acts and dealings and of the conduct of the winding up during the preceding year.

4 STAY OF THE WINDING UP

Once a resolution for voluntary liquidation has been passed, it is not possible to rescind it. An application may be made to the court under s 112 of the Insolvency Act 1986[32] to exercise the power which it has to stay a compulsory liquidation.[33]

5 END OF THE WINDING UP

As soon as the company's affairs are fully wound up, the liquidator will make up an account of the winding up, showing how it has been conducted and the disposition of the company's property, and will lay this account before meetings of the company and of the creditors.[34] The liquidator will then send to the registrar of companies a copy of the account and a return of the holdings of the meetings. The company will be deemed to be dissolved under s 210 of the Insolvency Act 1986 three months after registration of this return unless the court makes an order deferring dissolution.

---

29 Which is not likely unless all the creditors have been paid in full.
30 Insolvency Act 1986, s 112.
31 Insolvency Act 1986, s 105.
32 Which allows the court to exercise in a voluntary liquidation any power which it could exercise in a compulsory liquidation.
33 Under the Insolvency Act 1986, s 147.
34 Insolvency Act 1986, s 106.

CHAPTER 17

COMPULSORY LIQUIDATION

1 INTRODUCTION

This chapter considers the circumstances in which the court will order that an insolvent company be wound up, the consequences of the winding up order and the rules governing the conduct of the liquidation.

2 OBTAINING A WINDING UP ORDER

(a) Introduction

Obtaining a winding up order involves the presentation of a petition by one of the categories of eligible petitioner asking that the court make a winding up order and appoint a liquidator. The High Court has jurisdiction[1] to wind up any company registered in England and Wales. If the company in question has a paid up share capital which does not exceed £120,000, then the county court has concurrent jurisdiction. Companies whose registered offices are in London will have to be wound up by the High Court since there is no county court jurisdiction in the London insolvency district.

(b) Eligibility to petition

Those eligible to petition for a winding up order under the Insolvency Act 1986 are:[2]

(a) the company, which may by special resolution resolve to seek a winding up order, although it would more normally resolve to go into voluntary liquidation;

(b) the directors all acting together;[3]

---

1   See the Insolvency Act 1986, s 117 as to jurisdiction. Insolvency Act 1986, s 118 deals with the situation where proceedings have been started in the wrong court. Insolvency Act 1986, s 119 provides for the county court to refer questions by case stated to the High Court.

2   See generally the Insolvency Act 1986, s 124. There are additional rules allowing regulators to petition for the winding up of insurance companies, banks, investment businesses and charities. Under the Financial Services and Markets Act 2000 (FSMA 2000), s 367(1), the Financial Services Authority may ask the court to compulsorily wind up any company or partnership which is or has been an authorised person or an appointed representative or is carrying on or has carried on a regulated activity without authorisation in contravention of the general prohibition on this in the FSMA 2000. On such a petition, the court may wind up the body if it is unable to pay its debts or if the court 'is of the opinion that it is just and equitable that it should be wound up'. See Finch (2002).

3   *Re Instrumentation Electrical Services Ltd* [1988] BCLC 550. The normal powers delegated to the directors of managing the business on a majority basis do not give them authority to present a petition for winding up: *Re Emmadart* [1979] Ch 540.

(c) any creditor or creditors, including those with contingent or prospective claims.[4] Creditors may petition in respect of both legally and equitably assigned debts.[5] A person claiming to be a creditor on the basis of a debt which is *bona fide* disputed by the company is not a creditor and the company will be able to have the petition struck out.[6] In practice, the vast majority of petitions are presented by creditors;

(d) any contributory.[7] A shareholder must have held the shares for at least six of the 18 months before the presentation of the petition unless either the company is a public or unlimited company and the number of members has fallen below two[8] or the shares devolved on the shareholder through the death of a former holder. A contributory will only be permitted to bring a petition if he or she can show some financial interest in a liquidation;[9] this means that either there must be some outstanding liability on the shares,[10] or that the company must be solvent, or that on liquidation, resultant investigation may swell the funds and make a surplus possible;

(e) the Official Receiver where the company is already in voluntary liquidation. The court will not make a winding up order on the petition unless it is satisfied that the voluntary winding up cannot be continued with due regard to the interests of the creditors or contributories;[11]

(f) administrators and administrative receivers have the power both to present and defend winding up petitions;[12]

(g) the Secretary of State may petition on the just and equitable ground if it appears, as a result of various forms of statutory investigation,[13] expedient in the public interest that the company should be wound up.

---

4   In practice, they will have to be owed at least £750 before the court will agree to grant the order.

5   Insolvency Act 1986, s 123(1)(a). See *Re Steel Wing Co* [1921] 1 Ch 349; it was held in this case that although equitable assignees of part of a debt could petition for winding up, they did not have standing to serve a statutory demand and would have to find another method of establishing inability to pay.

6   *Re a Company (No 0012209 of 1991)* [1992] BCLC 865.

7   This broadly means the past and present members of the company. See the Insolvency Act 1986, ss 74, 79.

8   In which case, after six months, the member becomes personally liable for the company's debts: Companies Act 1985, s 24 as amended by the Companies (Single Member Private Companies) Regulations 1992 (SI 1992/1699).

9   *Re Rica Gold Washing Co* (1879) 11 Ch D 36.

10 Either because the shares were issued partly paid or the company is unlimited or limited by guarantee.

11 See below.

12 Insolvency Act 1986, Sched 1, para 21.

13 See the Insolvency Act 1986, s 124A. This provision permits the state to trigger a winding up where it is in the general interest to do this perhaps because a firm was prejudicing the interests of a large number of consumer creditors, but where none of the creditors possessed a debt of sufficient size to justify the cost of proceedings (see discussion in the Cork Report, paras 1745–51). See Finch (2002); Campbell (2001); Keay (1999).

(c) Grounds for petition

There are seven permissible grounds on which a petition may be based; the only one relevant to insolvency law[14] is s 122(f) of the Insolvency Act 1986, that 'the company is unable to pay its debts'.

Section 123 of the Insolvency Act 1986 defines the situations in which a company in England or Wales will be deemed unable to pay its debts. The first is where the company has been served with a statutory demand[15] by a creditor to whom the company is indebted in a sum exceeding £750 and the company has for three weeks thereafter neglected to pay the sum or to secure or compound for it to the reasonable satisfaction of the creditor. It would appear not to be possible for creditors with debts smaller than £750 to band together to serve a statutory demand. In *Re London and Paris Banking Corporation*[16] it was held that neglecting to pay means omitting to pay without reasonable excuse so that refusal to pay where the existence of the debt is disputed on substantial grounds does not give rise to a ground for a winding up order. In *Re Tweeds Garages*,[17] it was held that if there is no dispute as to the fact of the indebtedness but there is a dispute as to the amount, then, provided the undisputed balance exceeds £750, a statutory demand can be served for that amount. Where there is a genuine dispute as to the company's liability to pay the creditor, the court will usually dismiss the petition and the creditor will have to sue the company for the debt to establish the right to base a petition on it.[18]

Section 123(1)(e) provides that a company will be deemed unable to pay its debts if it is proved to the satisfaction of the court that the company is unable to pay its debts as they fall due. This provides an alternative, not available in bankruptcy, to the statutory demand route and creditors who are satisfied that they have the evidence to establish the company's insolvency may dispense with the three week period required by the statutory demand; in *Taylors Industrial Flooring v M&H Plant Hire (Manchester) Ltd*,[19] the Court of Appeal made it clear that there is no obligation to proceed via the statutory demand route and held that, if a debt is due from a company and is not disputed, failure to pay is evidence of an inability on the part of the company to pay its debts. Dillon LJ observed that 'The practice for a long time has been that the vast majority of creditors who seek to petition for the winding up of companies do not serve statutory demands.'

Both sub-ss 123(1)(a) and (e) of the Insolvency Act 1986 refer to non-payment of debts. This is a cashflow test of insolvency since the concept of a debt is narrower than that of a liability; a debt is a liquidated demand presently due and a company is not to be treated as unable to pay its debts because at some future time it will have to pay a debt which it would be unable to meet if it was presently payable.[20] Since 1907, the court has also been able to look to the balance sheet test which is currently contained

---

14 Although, somewhat oddly, all the provisions relating to the winding up of solvent companies are also contained in the Insolvency Act 1986.
15 See Chapter 14.
16 (1874) LR 19 Eq 444.
17 [1962] Ch 406.
18 See below in relation to applications to strike out the petition.
19 [1990] BCLC 216.
20 *Re European Life Assurance Society* (1869) LR 9 Eq 122.

in s 123(2) of the Insolvency Act 1986. This provides that a company is also deemed unable to pay its debts if it is proved to the satisfaction of the court that the value of the company's assets is less than the amount of its liabilities, taking into account its contingent and prospective liabilities. In *Winter v IRC*,[21] Lord Reid defined a contingent liability as one which, by reason of something done by the person bound, will necessarily arise or come into being if one or more of certain events occur or do not occur.[22] He said that the term could not be extended to include everything that a prudent businessman would think it proper to provide against. In *Re Byblos Bank*,[23] the court held that in comparing the company's assets with its future liabilities, it was not appropriate to take into account assets which it hoped to acquire.[24]

The company's inability to pay its debts may also be established by showing that execution or other process issued on a judgment, decree or order of any court in favour of a creditor of the company has been returned unsatisfied in whole or in part.

(d) Advertisement of the petition[25]

A creditor's petition must be advertised once in the London Gazette, at least seven business days before the day appointed for the hearing and not less than seven days after service of the petition on the company, unless the court otherwise directs.[26] The court may direct that the advertisement may be placed in a specified newspaper instead of the Gazette if it is not reasonably practicable to place it there. The advertisement serves the purpose of informing creditors and other interested parties, as well as notifying the public generally. If the petition is not duly advertised, the court may dismiss it.[27] The court may also dismiss a petition which has been advertised too early; the seven day gap between service of the petition on the company and its advertisement is intended to give the company a chance to apply to the court for the petition to be struck out before the damage of an advertisement is done.[28] In *Re Roselmar Properties Ltd*,[29] the court declined to strike out a petition which had been advertised too early on the grounds that the company was already in voluntary liquidation and, therefore, the advertisement could have done no harm. A similar situation arose in *Secretary of State for Trade & Industry v North West Holdings*,[30] which concerned an application to strike out a petition on the basis that press notices had been released by the Department of Trade and Industry on the day on which the

---

21 [1961] 3 All ER 855.

22 See also *Customs and Excise Commissioners v Broomco (1984) Ltd* (2000) unreported, 30 March.

23 [1987] BCLC 232.

24 Although this might be relevant in deciding whether or not to exercise the discretion to make the winding up order.

25 For details of the procedure involved in presentation and service of the petition, see the Insolvency Rules 1986, rr 4.7–4.19.

26 Insolvency Rules 1986, r 4.11.

27 *Practice Direction* [1996] 1 WLR 1255 stresses that this is a mandatory provision designed to ensure that a compulsory liquidation is a class remedy made available to all creditors, not just a way of applying pressure on a debtor company to pay. The court will only rarely dispense with the need for an advertisement. See *Applied Data Base Ltd v Secretary of State for Trade and Industry* [1995] 1 BCLC 272.

28 *Re Signland Ltd* [1982] 2 All ER 609; *Woolwich plc v Barnes* (2000) unreported, 1 March (CA).

29 (1986) 2 BCC 157.

30 [1999] 1 BCLC 425.

petition was served; the Court of Appeal refused since provisional liquidators had previously been appointed in respect of the company and the matter was therefore already in the public domain. There has been some disagreement as to whether notifying third parties individually before the end of the seven day gap justifies the court in dismissing the petition.[31]

(e) Application to strike out the petition

It may be possible for the company to apply for the petition to be struck out before the date on which it is due to be heard on the ground that the company has a defence to the petitioner's claim. The court may order the petitioner to refrain from advertising the petition before the striking out motion has been heard. The court may treat as an abuse of the process of the court a petition which is presented upon the basis of a debt which is *bona fide* disputed on substantial grounds.[32] Hoffmann J explained in *Re RA Foulds Ltd*[33] that this was because the presentation of a winding up petition puts very great pressure on the company and it is not right for that pressure to be used in order to induce the company to abandon a fairly arguable defence to the claim. He went on to express his doubts about the effect of the court being required to strike out such a petition without regard to the question of whether the company was in fact solvent and held that, since the creditor in that case had clearly had *locus standi* as a creditor at the time of presentation (in that the debtor had subsequently paid the undisputed part of the debt), he could exercise his discretion more widely in deciding whether the petition should be allowed to go on to advertisement and hearing. The evidence suggested that there might be other creditors who would seek to support the petition. In the belatedly reported 1981 case of *Re Claybridge Shipping Co SA*,[34] the Court of Appeal held that dismissing petitions where there was a disputed debt was only a rule of practice and that it was possible for the court to determine the issue in the course of the winding up proceedings where appropriate and possible without undue inconvenience. This was something the court might do where the likely result of striking out the petition would be to deprive the petitioner of a remedy altogether.[35] In *Re a Company (No 006685 of 1996)*,[36] it was held that the true rule was that the court would not allow a winding up petition to be used for the purpose of deciding a dispute as to a debt which was raised *bona fide* on substantial grounds. In this case, the dispute now said to exist was not founded on any substantial grounds; it was one of those cases in which an unwilling debtor was raising a cloud of objections in order to claim that a dispute of fact existed which could not be determined without cross-examination so that the petition could not be allowed to proceed. The company's evidence could not be believed and the petition should be allowed to proceed.

---

31 See *Re a Company (No 001127 of 1992)* [1992] BCC 477; *Re Bill Hennessey Associates* [1992] BCC 386; *SN Group plc v Barclays Bank plc* [1993] BCC 506. In *Re Doreen Boards Ltd* [1996] 1 BCLC 501, a contributory's petition was struck out as an abuse of process on the basis of publicity which she had given to the petition before the time provided by the Rules which had caused the bank to freeze the company's account.
32 *Mann v Goldstein* [1968] 1 WLR 1091.
33 (1986) 2 BCC 99, 269 at 99, 273.
34 [1997] 1 BCLC 572.
35 See also *Re Boston Timber Fabrications Ltd* [1984] BCLC 328.
36 [1997] 1 BCLC 639.

In *Re a Company (No 3079 of 1990)*,[37] Ferris J said:

The test which I ought to apply is the test which appears from *Stonegate Securities v Gregory*[38] and *Mann v Goldstein*, that is to say that if I can see now that the petition, if and when it comes on for substantive hearing, is bound to be dismissed because the *locus standi* of the petitioners is disputed, then it will be appropriate to strike-out the petitions and not to leave them on file with a view to their coming back before the court at some future time, when the result will inevitably be the one that I have indicated. Of course if I am not satisfied that that is inevitably the result then the test is not satisfied and I ought not to strike-out.

In *Re Bayoil SA; Seawind Tankers Corp v Bayoil SA*,[39] it was held that the court had a greater discretion where the petitioner is clearly a creditor (and therefore has standing to petition) but the company is asking for the petition to be stayed or dismissed on the basis of the existence of a cross-claim of a greater amount; the petition will, however, still be dismissed where there is a genuine cross-claim except in special circumstances.[40] In this case, the cross-claim was genuine and serious, it was one which the company had been unable to litigate, and it exceeded the amount of the petitioner's debt and there were no circumstances which should be treated as special and the petition should have been dismissed. In *Montgomery v Wanda Modes Ltd*,[41] Park J held[42] that a company was not precluded from relying on a cross-claim as a ground for opposing a winding up petition by the fact that it could reasonably have litigated the cross-claim before the winding up petition was presented. In principle there was nothing objectionable in a company which had refrained from pursuing a claim which it believed it had against another party, later deciding to pursue the cross-claim if the other party threatened it with winding up proceedings for non-payment of a debt, since it would be undesirable if companies were penalised for refraining from litigating an issue or if parties were encouraged to litigate possible claims sooner rather than later.

It has been held that a petition will not be stayed or dismissed merely because the company clearly could pay the petitioner's debt where the company has persistently failed to do so: *Cornhill Insurance plc v Improvement Services Ltd*.[43] As seen above,[44] however, in *Re a Company (No 0012209 of 1991)*,[45] the court warned that creditors should not be tempted to use insolvency procedures to pressurise debtors where there is a *bona fide* dispute about the existence of the debt.

It is not appropriate to stay a petition for more than a short time since any eventual winding up will be deemed to have commenced at the time of presentation

---

37 [1991] BCLC 235. See also *Greenacre Publishing Group Ltd v The Manson Group* (1998) *The Times*, 17 December.
38 [1980] Ch 576.
39 [1999] 1 All ER 374.
40 *Re Portman Provincial Cinemas Ltd* (1964) 108 SJ 581 (CA); *Re LHF Wools Ltd* [1969] 3 All ER 882. See also *Re Euro Hotel (Belgravia) Ltd* [1975] 3 All ER 1075, in which Megarry J held that where an undisputed debt was overtopped by a disputed cross-claim, the court would have a discretion as to whether or not to strike it out.
41 [2002] 1 BCLC 289.
42 Doubting *dicta* of Nourse LJ in *Bayoil* and following Rimer J in *Re a Debtor (No 87 of 1999)* [2000] BPIR 589.
43 [1986] 1 WLR 114.
44 See Chapter 14.
45 [1992] 2 All ER 797. See also *Re a Company* [1983] 1 BCLC 98.

of the petition, the company would have to trade with the petition hanging over it and the other creditors would be prevented from presenting their own petitions.[46] Where there is some matter which needs to be resolved before the right to pursue the petition can be established, the appropriate course will normally be to dismiss the petition.

(f) Withdrawal of petition

The court can allow the petitioner to withdraw the petition up to five days before the hearing date if it has not been advertised and no notices in support or opposing the petition have been received and the company consents (on such terms as to costs as the parties may agree).[47] The court may substitute as petitioner any creditor or contributory who in its opinion would have a right to present a petition and who is desirous of prosecuting it.[48]

(g) Consequences of presentation of petition

Once a petition has been presented, an application may be made to the court by the company or by any creditor or contributory to restrain any action or proceeding pending against the company from further proceeding.[49] The court may appoint a provisional liquidator; the Official Receiver or any other fit person may be appointed.[50] The court will establish the functions and powers of the provisional liquidator; in practice, these will be confined to taking possession of the company's assets and preserving and protecting them.

If a winding up order is made, the liquidation will be deemed to have commenced at the time of presentation of the petition.[51] Any attachment, sequestration, distress or execution put in force against the company after commencement of the winding up will be void.[52] Any disposition of the company's property or transfer of shares or alteration in status of the members after the commencement of the winding up will be void unless the court orders otherwise;[53] it is therefore difficult for a company against whom a petition has been served and advertised to continue trading normally.

(h) Court's powers on hearing the petition

Those who wish to appear on the hearing of the petition will only be able to do so with the leave of the court unless they have given notice of intention to appear either in support of the petition or in opposition to it in accordance with the Insolvency Rules.[54]

---

46 *Re Boston Timber Fabrications Ltd* [1984] BCLC 328.
47 Insolvency Rules 1986, r 4.15.
48 Insolvency Rules 1986, r 4.19.
49 Insolvency Act 1986, s 126. See Chapter 25.
50 Insolvency Act 1986, s 135. See *Re Namco Ltd* [2003] All ER (D) 118 (Apr).
51 Insolvency Act 1986, s 129.
52 See Chapter 25.
53 Insolvency Act 1986, s 127. See Chapter 30.
54 Insolvency Rules 1986, r 4.16. See *Re Piccadilly Property Management Ltd* [1999] 2 BCLC 145 for a discussion of the entitlement of creditors to be heard by the court.

The court may make a winding up order, dismiss the petition, adjourn the hearing or make an interim order or any other order that it thinks fit, but the court may not refuse to make a winding up order on the ground only that there are no assets available for distribution;[55] this ensures that those in control of companies cannot avoid the investigation pursuant on a winding up order by disposing of all the company's assets. In *Bell Group Finance (Pty) Ltd v Bell Group (UK) Holdings Ltd*,[56] Chadwick J held that bringing about investigation of an insolvent company's affairs where there was a prospect of benefit to creditors justified making an order notwithstanding the lack of immediate prospect of assets for distribution.

A petition for winding up invokes a class right and the court will take into account the wishes of other creditors and contributories and may in its discretion decline to make a winding up order even where the petitioner makes out a valid ground.[57] In *Re Demaglass Holdings Ltd*,[58] the company went into administrative receivership between the service of a statutory demand by a trade creditor and the service of a winding up petition based on it. The receivers applied for a six month adjournment to enable them to dispose of the company's stock more advantageously but the petitioner was anxious that the receivers should be replaced by liquidators. Neuberger J held[59] that a creditor who had not been paid was entitled to a winding up order virtually as of right in the absence of a good reason as to why the order should not be made. Where some creditors were in favour and others were against the order being made, the order would be made if the majority of creditors supported the petition and would only be refused if the majority were against it.[60] When considering the views of the creditors on the question of whether to wind up a company, the court would not rely on mathematical niceties in exercising its discretion; it would give little, if any, weight to the views of the secured creditors[61] because they were protected in any event at least to the value of their security, and to that extent they had no interest in whether the company was wound up or not; on the other hand, the court would have greater regard to the views of independent creditors as opposed to creditors connected with the company. The mere fact that the majority of creditors opposed the making of a winding up order was not by itself sufficient reason for the court to refuse to make a winding up order; instead, the court had to be satisfied that the opposing majority had good reason for refusing to wind up the company.[62] Where the court was satisfied that the opposing majority's opposition to the making of a winding up order was justified but the petitioning creditor's desire to have a winding up order made was also justified, it had to carry out a balancing exercise. Although such a balancing exercise depended on the facts of each case, the court would have regard to whether there were any other procedures by which the petitioner or the opposers could be

---

55 Insolvency Act 1986, s 125.

56 [1996] 1 BCLC 304.

57 See, for example, *Re Pleatfine Ltd* [1983] BCLC 102; *Re Esal (Commodities)* [1985] BCLC 450; *Re Crigglestone Coal Co Ltd* [1906] 2 Ch 327; *Re Lines Bros Ltd* [1983] Ch 1.

58 [2001] 2 BCLC 633.

59 Relying on *dicta* of Lord Cranworth in *Bowes v Directors of Hope Life Insurance and Guarantee Co* (1865) 11 HL Cas 389 at 402.

60 See *dicta* of Brightman J in *Re Southard & Co Ltd* [1979] 1 WLR 546 at 550; [1979] 1 All ER 582 at 585–86, and Hoffmann J in *Re Palmer Marine Surveys Ltd* [1986] BCLC 106 at 110.

61 *Bell Group Finance Ltd v Bell Group Holdings Ltd* [1996] 1 BCLC 304.

62 The requirement of there being good reasons is emphasised by the decision of the Court of Appeal in *Re P&J Macrae Ltd* [1961] 1 WLR 229; [1961] 1 All ER 302.

adequately protected and would also have regard to the principle that ordinarily it was the duty of the court to direct a winding up.

The court may refuse to make a winding up order where it finds that the petitioner is motivated by some reason other than recovery of the amount owing. Unsuccessful petitioners might find themselves not just penalised in costs but also facing a malicious prosecution claim in tort.[63]

(i) Rescission[64] or stay of the order

Any court which has the jurisdiction to wind up a company also has the power to review, rescind or vary any order made in the exercise of that jurisdiction.[65] Any application for the rescission of a winding up order must be made within seven days from the date of the order, although the court has the power to extend the time limit in appropriate circumstances.[66] Only a party able to appear on the petition to wind up the company has *locus standi* to apply to rescind the winding up order.[67]

The court may at any time, on the application of the liquidator or the Official Receiver or any creditor or contributory, make an order that the winding up be stayed either altogether or for a limited time, on such terms and conditions as the court thinks fit. The court may permit the directors to resume the management of the company. Liquidations have been stayed where the company has paid or settled all the claims of the creditors and provided for the liquidator's remuneration and expenses.[68]

3 PETITION IN RESPECT OF A COMPANY IN VOLUNTARY LIQUIDATION

The voluntary winding up of a company does not bar the right of any creditor or contributory to have it wound up by the court.[69] The court should not make an order unless it is satisfied that the voluntary winding up cannot be continued with due regard to the interests of the creditors and contributories.[70] Creditors are only likely to seek conversion of the liquidation into a more expensive compulsory one where they are dissatisfied with the progress of the voluntary liquidation or feel that additional investigation is necessary. In *Re Inside Sport Ltd*,[71] it was suggested that where the real dispute was as to the identity of the liquidator, it might be more appropriate to apply to the court under s 171 of the Insolvency Act 1986 to replace the liquidator.

---

63 See Keay (2001b) (and cases cited therein).
64 *Re Dollar Land (Feltham) Ltd* [1995] 2 BCLC 370.
65 Insolvency Rules 1986, r 7.47.
66 *Re Virgo Systems* (1989) 5 BCC 833.
67 *Re Mid East Trading* [1997] 3 All ER 481.
68 *Re South Barrule Slate Quarry Co* (1869) LR 8 Eq 688; *Re Lowston Ltd* [1991] BCLC 570; *Re Calgary and Edmonton Land Co Ltd* [1975] 1 All ER 1046.
69 Insolvency Act 1986, s 116.
70 Insolvency Act 1986, s 124(5).
71 [1999] 1 BCLC 302.

The general rule is that the court will follow the wishes of the majority in value of the creditors. In *Re JD Swain*,[72] Harman J said that where a liquidation in progress was supported by the majority of creditors, it was necessary for a petitioner to show some reason why the majority of the class should not prevail over the minority. The cases show that the court will give greater weight to the wishes of independent creditors than to creditors who also happen to be connected with the company.

Re Hewitt Brannan[73] is an example of a case in which a petition was presented by the Official Receiver. The company had been in voluntary liquidation for six years during which time a substantial sum had been collected by receivers appointed on behalf of certain secured creditors. Once the secured creditors had been paid off, the receiver handed a substantial balance over to the liquidator who paid himself generously out of it. The liquidation continued to proceed slowly and eventually the Official Receiver petitioned for a compulsory winding up. The petition was opposed actively by 10% of the creditors and not actively supported by any of them. The liquidator had just offered a dividend of 38.6 pence in the pound which they preferred to the delay and extra cost of a compulsory liquidation. Harman J granted the compulsory winding up order, saying that the liquidator had shown a deplorable attitude and needed investigation; winding up by the court was in the public interest and the conduct of the creditors in failing to keep the liquidator up to the mark counted against them. In *Re Pinstripe Farming Co Ltd*,[74] it was held that the liquidator in the voluntary winding up may appear but should confine him or herself to pointing out relevant facts and should not adopt a partisan view in favour of or against the petition.

In *Re Zirceram Ltd (in Liquidation), J Paterson Brodie & Son (a Firm) and Another v Zirceram Ltd (in Liquidation)*,[75] the court said that regard should be had to the general principles of fairness and commercial morality, and the exercise of discretion should not leave substantial independent creditors with a strong legitimate sense of grievance. Fairness and commercial morality might require that an independent creditor should be able to insist on the company's affairs being scrutinised within a compulsory liquidation; the petition may be granted so that there can be an investigation which is not only independent, but seen to be independent. Inter-group transactions might require special scrutiny if they operate to the prejudice of creditors and the court may take account of the fact that an opposing creditor is not an independent creditor, but an associated company. Even if there is no criticism of the liquidator appointed in the voluntary winding up, the fact that associated supporting creditors have gone to great lengths to install and maintain him or her in office may be a disqualification in the eyes of the creditors and the petitioning creditors may view with cynicism any investigation undertaken by a liquidator chosen by the very persons whose conduct is under investigation.

72   [1965] 1 WLR 909.
73   [1990] BCC 354.
74   [1996] 2 BCLC 295.
75   [2000] 1 BCLC 751.

4 CONSEQUENCES OF A WINDING UP ORDER

The liquidation will be deemed to have commenced at the time of presentation of the petition unless the company was already in voluntary liquidation in which case the commencement of the liquidation will be the date of the resolution for voluntary liquidation.[76] The registrar of companies[77] and the Official Receiver[78] must be notified forthwith.

No action or proceeding can be started or proceeded with against the company without the consent of the court.[79]

A compulsory winding up order is always said to bring contracts of employment and agency[80] to an end automatically. *Chapman's Case*[81] is always taken as authority for the proposition in relation to employees although the issue in that case was when the notice of termination (whose existence was assumed in that case) was given and not whether a winding up necessarily involves termination of employment. *Re English Joint Stock Bank ex p Harding*[82] did not assume that a court order for winding up terminates contracts, but in *Macdowell's Case*,[83] Chitty J held that a winding up order operated as a dismissal, apparently on the basis that *Chapman's Case* had been universally accepted as based on this proposition. The Privy Council in *Commercial Finance Co Ltd v Ramsingh-Mahabar*[84] has recently accepted the view, although it is not apparent that any obligation universal to every employer is necessarily rendered incapable of performance as a result of a winding up order if the company continues to trade and retain employees through the agency of the liquidator.

The powers of directors cease forthwith on the appointment of a liquidator.[85]

5 CONTROL OF THE LIQUIDATION

(a) The role of the Official Receiver

Section 136 of the Insolvency Act 1986 provides that the Official Receiver will be the liquidator of the company unless and until replaced by another liquidator and will be the liquidator during any vacancy. The Official Receiver also has the investigatory duties explained below.[86]

---

76 Insolvency Act 1986, s 129.
77 Insolvency Act 1986, s 130(1).
78 Insolvency Rules 1986, r 4.20.
79 Insolvency Act 1986, s 130(2).
80 *Gosling v Gaskell* [1897] AC 575.
81 (1866) LR 1 Eq 346.
82 (1867) LR 3 Eq 341.
83 (1886) 32 Ch D 366.
84 [1994] 1 WLR 1297.
85 *Fowler v Broad's Patent Night Light Co* [1893] 1 Ch 724.
86 See Chapter 21.

(b) Appointment of a liquidator

The Official Receiver must decide within 12 weeks of the winding up order being made whether or not to summon meetings of the company's creditors and of the company's contributories for the purpose of choosing a person to be liquidator in his or her place.[87] If he or she decides not to call such meetings, notice of that decision must be given to the court and to the creditors and contributories. Any notice to the creditors must explain that one-quarter in value of the creditors may require the Official Receiver to summon a meeting. Section 139 of the Insolvency Act 1986 provides that the liquidator will be the person nominated by the meeting of the creditors or, where no person has been so nominated, the person nominated by the contributories. In the case of different persons being nominated, any contributory or creditor may, within seven days after the date on which the nomination was made by the creditors, apply to the court for an order either appointing the person nominated as liquidator by the contributories to be liquidator instead of, or jointly with, the person nominated by the creditors or appointing some other person to be liquidator instead of the person nominated by the creditors.

If the winding up order is made immediately upon the discharge of an administration order or at a time when there is a supervisor of a voluntary arrangement approved in relation to the company, the court may appoint as liquidator the person who was the administrator or is the supervisor instead of the Official Receiver.

The Official Receiver may at any time, including where meetings have been held which have not resulted in the appointment of a liquidator, ask the Secretary of State to appoint a liquidator in his or her place.[88]

(c) Liquidation committee

Meetings of creditors and contributories may establish a liquidation committee[89] where the liquidator is not the Official Receiver.[90] A liquidator who is not the Official Receiver must call such meetings if requested to do so by one-tenth in value of the company's creditors. Where only one of the meetings decides to establish a committee, a committee will be established unless the court orders otherwise.

(d) Function and powers of the liquidator

Section 143 of the Insolvency Act 1986 provides that the functions of the liquidator of a company which is being wound up by the court are to secure that the assets of the company are got in, realised and distributed to the company's creditors and, if there is a surplus, to the persons entitled to it.[91] Where the liquidator is not the Official

---

87   Insolvency Act 1986, s 136(5).
88   Insolvency Act 1986, s 137.
89   Insolvency Act 1986, s 141.
90   Where the Official Receiver is the liquidator, the functions of the committee are vested in the Secretary of State.
91   See Part V below.

Receiver, the liquidator also has a duty to co-operate with the Official Receiver in the performance of his or her functions.

The liquidator may, with the sanction of the court or the liquidation committee, exercise any of the powers specified in Parts I and II of Sched 4 to the Act and, without needing any sanction, exercise any of the general powers specified in Part III of that Schedule.[92] The liquidator has an obligation to notify any liquidation committee where he or she disposes of property of the company to a person connected with the company or employs a solicitor. The liquidator has the power to summon general meetings of creditors and contributories and may apply to the court for directions in relation to any matter arising in the winding up.

(e) Ceasing to be liquidator[93]

The liquidator may be removed from office only by order of the court or by a meeting of the creditors summoned for that purpose. A liquidator appointed by the Secretary of State may be removed by the Secretary of State. A liquidator may resign in the prescribed circumstances by giving notice to the court;[94] the liquidator must resign where he or she ceases to be qualified to act. A liquidator also vacates office on the giving of notice to the court and to the registrar of companies that the final meeting has been held.

The liquidator will be released from potential liability in connection with the liquidation at the time specified by s 174 of the Insolvency Act 1986. Nothing will release a liquidator from potential liability under s 212 of the Insolvency Act 1986 for misuse of company property or breach of duty.

6 END OF THE LIQUIDATION

Section 202 of the Insolvency Act 1986 allows the Official Receiver to apply to the registrar of companies for the early dissolution of the company where he or she is liquidator and it appears that the realisable assets of the company are insufficient to cover the expenses of the winding up and that the affairs of the company do not require any further investigation. At least 28 days' notice of intention to make this application must be given to the creditors, the contributories and any administrative receiver, all of whom have the right to apply to the Secretary of State for directions enabling the winding up to proceed.[95]

In other cases, where it appears to the liquidator, not being the Official Receiver, that the winding up of the company is for practical purposes complete, he or she shall summon a final general meeting of the creditors which will receive the report of the winding up and determine whether the liquidator should have his or her release.[96] The company will be dissolved three months after notice of the holding of the final

---

92 Insolvency Act 1986, s 167. See Chapter 16 for discussion of the content of Sched 4.
93 Insolvency Act 1986, ss 172, 174. See also Chapter 16, note 21.
94 Insolvency Rules 1986, rr 4.108–4.112.
95 Insolvency Act 1986, s 203. There is a right to appeal to the court from the decision of the Secretary of State.
96 Insolvency Act 1986, s 146.

meeting is given to the registrar of companies.[97] Where the Official Receiver has been the liquidator, the company will be dissolved three months after the registrar receives notice from him or her that the winding up is complete.[98]

---

97   Insolvency Act 1986, s 205.
98   Insolvency Act 1986, s 205.

CHAPTER 18

WINDING UP INSOLVENT PARTNERSHIPS[1]

1 INTRODUCTION

Since 1986, it has been possible for the court to make an order putting an insolvent partnership into liquidation under Part V of the Insolvency Act 1986 as if it were an unregistered company.[2] The relevant provisions are currently contained in the Insolvent Partnerships Order 1994,[3] which 'translates' the corporate terminology used in the Insolvency Act 1986 into the appropriate references for the partnership context.[4] Where a firm is wound up as an unregistered company, each present and former partner liable to contribute is classified as a contributory, as is anyone who has been held out as a partner. Each contributory will be liable to contribute up to the extent of their assets.

If the partners can between them meet the claims of the creditors, any insufficiency in partnership assets will fall on the partners and will be borne between them in accordance with the terms of the partnership. It will frequently happen that when the partnership business becomes insolvent, at least some of the individual members of the partnership will be unable to bear their share of the loss and will themselves become insolvent; a partner may be an individual or a company so the relevant regime may be either bankruptcy or liquidation. The question then arises as to how the estate of an insolvent partner should be distributed as between his or her private creditors and the creditors of the firm or his or her solvent partners, who will have had to pay more than their share of the business losses to make up for the shortfall.

The Insolvent Partnerships Order 1994 makes provision for the presentation by creditors of a petition against the partnership alone[5] and also for the simultaneous presentation of petitions against the partnership and one or more of the partners in their capacity as such.[6] It is also possible[7] for all the members to present a joint petition for the bankruptcy of each of them in his or her capacity as a member of the partnership and the winding up of the partnership business without the partnership being wound up as an unregistered company. Article 19 of the Order permits

---

1   This chapter does not refer to limited liability partnerships. Section 14 of the Limited Liability Partnerships Act 2000 provides for the corporate insolvency provisions of Insolvency Act 1986 as amended by regulations to be made available to such partnerships. The necessary modifications are to be found in the Limited Liability Partnerships Regulations 2001, SI 2001/1090, reg 5 and Sched 3.

2   Insolvency Act 1986, s 220 as modified by Sched 3 to the Insolvent Partnerships Order 1994. Before 1986, it would be necessary to make all the partners bankrupt. It is still open to creditors to take action against one or more of the partners individually without proceeding against the partnership: *Schooler v Customs and Excise Commissioners* [1995] 2 BCLC 610.

3   SI 1994/2421 made under the Insolvency Act 1986, s 420. This has been amended by the Insolvent Partnerships (Amendment) Order 2002 to reflect the EC Regulation (see Chapter 35).

4   See Insolvent Partnership Order 1994, Arts 2, 3 and Chapter 11 above.

5   Insolvent Partnerships Order 1994, Art 7.

6   Insolvent Partnerships Order 1994, Art 8.

7   Under the Insolvent Partnerships Order 1994, Art 11.

proceedings to be commenced against an individual partner for a partnership debt without petitioning against the partnership or against any other partner. The court is, however, given a general power by Art 14[8] of the Insolvent Partnerships Order 1994 to make orders as to the future conduct of the insolvency proceedings where a petition for winding up or bankruptcy has been presented against any person and the court's attention is drawn to the fact that the person is a member of an insolvent partnership. Any such order may apply the provisions of the Insolvent Partnerships Order 1994 to the future conduct of the insolvency proceedings and may include provisions as to the administration of the joint estate of the partnership and how it and the separate estate of any member are to be administered. It is likely that in any situation where an insolvent partnership is being wound up and bankruptcy or compulsory liquidation orders are made against individual partners that the provisions of Art 8 of the Insolvent Partnerships Order 1994 will be applied in order to achieve a fair distribution of the assets amongst the various creditors.

The law on insolvent partnerships is enacted in a somewhat complex way by modifying the relevant provisions of the Insolvency Act 1986. The position is somewhat better than under the previous regulations in that the Insolvent Partnerships Order 1994 does set out the modified provisions in its schedules. A considerable amount of cross-referencing still has to take place. In this account of the various regimes provided under the Insolvent Partnerships Order, the introduction to each regime explains[9] which provisions of the Insolvency Act 1986 apply, which have been modified and in which schedule the modified provisions are to be found. It should be noted that s 229 of the Insolvency Act 1986 provides that the provisions of Part V of the Act with respect to insolvent partnerships are in addition to and not in restriction of any provisions in Part IV with respect to winding up companies by the court; that the court or liquidator may exercise any powers or do any act in the case of insolvent partnerships which might be exercised or done in winding up companies registered under the Companies Acts.

2 WINDING UP OF INSOLVENT PARTNERSHIP ON PETITION OF CREDITOR

(a) Introduction

Article 7 of the Insolvent Partnerships Order 1994 provides for the presentation of a petition for winding up an insolvent partnership where no petition is presented by the petitioner against a member or former member of the partnership in his or her capacity as such. The provisions of Part V of the Insolvency Act 1986 will apply to the winding up as modified by the Insolvent Partnerships Order 1994 so that the modified provisions are as set out in Sched 3 to the Order; the provisions modified by Sched 3 are ss 117, 131, 133, 220 to 223, 234 and Sched 4 to the Insolvency Act 1986. Sections 73(1), 74(2)(a) to (d) and (3), 75 to 78, 83, 122, 123, 202, 203, 205 and 250 of the Insolvency Act 1986 will not apply.

---

8   Which amends the Insolvency Act 1986, ss 168, 303.
9   As does the Insolvent Partnerships Order itself.

(b) Jurisdiction

The courts will have jurisdiction if the partnership has a principal place of business in England and Wales or if the debt on which the petition is based arises from business carried on by the insolvent partnership within the three years before presentation of the petition at a place of business within England and Wales, even if that is not the principal place of the partnership's business.[10]

(c) Eligibility to petition

Creditors and the Secretary of State and certain insolvency practitioners may present a petition against the partnership under Art 7.[11] The insolvency practitioners with *locus standi* are the liquidator or administrator of a corporate member or of a former corporate member, the administrator of the partnership, the trustee of an individual member or former member's estate or the supervisor of voluntary arrangement approved in relation to a corporate or individual member or the partnership.

(d) Grounds for petition

The grounds for winding up a partnership as an unregistered company are the following:[12]

(a) the partnership is dissolved or has ceased to carry on business or is carrying on business only for the purpose of winding up its affairs;

(b) the partnership is unable to pay its debts;

(c) the court is of the opinion that it is just and equitable that the company should be wound up.

Inability to pay debts will be shown by any of the following:[13]

(a) failure of the partnership to comply with a statutory demand[14] in respect of a sum exceeding £750;

(b) the bringing of an action or other proceeding against one or more partners personally in respect of a partnership debt of which notice has been given to the partnership and in respect of which the partnership has taken no action for three weeks to pay, secure or compound for the claim or procured a stay of the action or indemnified the defendant against liability from the action;

(c) execution or other process issued on a judgment against the partnership is returned unsatisfied;

---

10 Insolvency Act 1986, s 221 as modified by the Insolvent Partnerships Order 1994, Sched 3. There are specific provisions relating to partnerships with principal places of business in either Scotland or Northern Ireland.

11 Insolvency Act 1986, s 221(A) (as modified).

12 Insolvency Act 1986, s 221(7); Insolvent Partnerships Order 1994, Sched 3.

13 Insolvency Act 1986, ss 222, 223 (both as modified by the Insolvent Partnerships Order 1994, Sched 3) and s 224.

14 Insolvency Act 1986, s 222(2); Insolvent Partnerships Order 1994, Sched 3 sets out the requirements for service of the demand.

(d) it is proved to the satisfaction of the court that the value of the partnership's assets is less than the amount of its liabilities taking into account its contingent and prospective liabilities.

If a petitioning insolvency practitioner can satisfy the court that a bankruptcy or winding up order has been made against the member of whom the petitioner is trustee or liquidator on the grounds of that member's inability to pay a joint debt, the order shall be rebuttable proof that the partnership is unable to pay its debts.

(c) Conduct of the insolvency

The winding up of the partnership will be conducted as if it were a compulsory winding up of a company.[15]

Where the petition has been presented by an insolvency practitioner who is already trustee or liquidator of a member, the court may appoint that practitioner as provisional liquidator of the partnership under s 135 of the Insolvency Act 1986.[16] Such an insolvency practitioner may also be appointed as liquidator by the court on the making of a winding up order, in which case the Official Receiver will not become liquidator.[17]

3 WINDING UP OF PARTNERSHIP ON MEMBER'S PETITION

(a) Introduction

Article 9 of the Insolvent Partnerships Order 1994 is the appropriate article where a member petitions for the winding up of an insolvent partnership whilst not petitioning for the insolvency of any member of the partnership. Part V of the Insolvency Act 1986 will govern the winding up with modifications to ss 117, 131, 133, 234 and Sched 4 of the Insolvency Act 1986 set out in Part II of Sched 3 to the Insolvent Partnerships Order 1994 and with the modifications to ss 117 and 221 of the Insolvency Act 1986 set out in Sched 5 to the Insolvent Partnerships Order 1994. Sections 73(1), 74(2)(a) to (d) and (3), 75 to 78, 83, 122, 123, 124(2) and (3), 202, 203, 205 and 250 of the Insolvency Act 1986 will not apply.

(b) Jurisdiction

The court has jurisdiction where the partnership has, or has had within the previous three years, a principal place of business in England or Wales.

---

15 See Chapters 17 and 21.
16 Insolvency Act 1986, s 221A(4) as modified.
17 Insolvency Act 1986, s 221A(5) as modified.

(c) *Locus standi* and grounds for petition

Any member of a partnership which consists of not less than eight members may petition under Art 9.[18] The grounds for petitioning are[19] that:

(a) the partnership is dissolved, or has ceased to carry on business, or is carrying on business only for the purpose of winding up its affairs, or

(b) the partnership is unable to pay its debts;[20] or

(c) the court is of the opinion that it is just and equitable that the partnership should be wound up.

Any member of any sized partnership may petition[21] with the leave of the court if the court is satisfied that the member has served a demand on the partnership in respect of a joint debt exceeding £750 due from the partnership, but paid by the member other than out of partnership property, which the partnership has for three weeks failed to pay and the member has obtained a judgment, decree or order of the court for reimbursement which all reasonable steps have failed to enforce.

(d) Conduct of the liquidation

The winding up of the partnership will be conducted in the same way as a winding up under Art 7 of the Insolvent Partnerships Order 1994.

4   WINDING UP OF PARTNERSHIP AND CONCURRENT INSOLVENCY OF PARTNERS ON PETITION OF CREDITOR

(a) Introduction

Article 8 of the Insolvent Partnerships Order 1994 provides for the presentation by a creditor of petitions both for the winding up of an insolvent partnership and at the same time for the bankruptcy or liquidation of one or more members or former members of the partnership in their capacity as such.[22] Article 7, explained above, will be the relevant article if petitions are presented against the partners in their individual capacities.

Under Art 8, the provisions of Part V of the Insolvency Act 1986, apart from ss 223 and 224, will apply (as modified by Sched 4 to the Insolvent Partnerships Order 1994)[23] to the winding up of the partnership. Corporate partners against whom a petition has been concurrently presented may be wound up under Parts IV, VI, VII and XII to XIX of the Insolvency Act 1986 as modified by Sched 4 to the Insolvent Partnerships Order 1994. Individual members against whom concurrent petitions

---

18 Insolvency Act 1986, s 221A(1); Insolvent Partnerships Order 1994, Sched 5.

19 Insolvency Act 1986, s 221(7); Insolvent Partnerships Order 1994, Sched 5.

20 As established under the Insolvency Act 1986, ss 222 to 224.

21 Insolvency Act 1986, s 221A; Insolvent Partnerships Order 1994, Sched 5.

22 See, for example, *Residuary Milk Marketing Board v SC & J Gunningham* (2000) unreported, 2 November (CA).

23 Insolvent Partnerships Order 1994, Sched 4, para 1 lists more than 50 provisions of the Insolvency Act 1986 which it modifies.

have been presented will be subject to the bankruptcy provisions of Part IX (other than ss 269, 270, 287 and 297) and Parts X to XIX, as modified by Sched 4 to the Insolvent Partnerships Order 1994. A member of a partnership against whom an insolvency order is made under Art 8 will not be treated as a contributory[24] under the Insolvency Act 1986 unless the contrary intention appears.

Jurisdiction in respect of Art 8 of the Insolvent Partnerships Order 1994 is the same as under Art 7, explained above.

(b) Eligibility and grounds to petition

Creditors to whom the partnership and its members are indebted in respect of a liquidated sum payable immediately may petition on the grounds that the partnership is unable to pay its debts. An insolvent partnership will be deemed unable to pay its debts where a statutory demand in respect of a debt in excess of £750 has been served on the partnership and on any one or more members or former members liable to pay the sum due and the partnership and its members have for three weeks neglected to pay the sum or to secure or compound for it to the creditor's satisfaction.[25] This is the only basis on which the petitioner can establish inability to pay debts. Sections 122, 123, 267 and 268 of the Insolvency Act 1986 are amended[26] so that the only basis for the concurrent petitions against the members of the partnership is inability to pay partnership debts exceeding £750, such inability to be established by the statutory demand route.

The petition to wind up the partnership will be heard first and the court will not make orders in respect of the members until either an order has been made to wind up the partnership or the petition to do so has been dismissed.[27] The court has the power to make any order that it thinks fit on the hearing of the petition against the partnership and the order may contain directions as to the future conduct of any insolvency proceedings in existence against any insolvent member in respect of whom an insolvency order has already been made.[28] When a winding up order has been made against the partnership, the court may make orders against the members in respect of whom concurrent petitions have been presented. If no such orders are made within 28 days of the order against the partnership, the winding up of the partnership will be treated as taking place under Art 7. If the petition against the partnership has been dismissed, proceedings under any order made against a member will take place without the modifications made by the Insolvent Partnerships Order 1994.

(e) Conduct of concurrent insolvencies of partnership and members

The winding up of the partnership and of any corporate partner will be conducted as if it were a compulsory liquidation of a company[29] and the bankruptcy of any

---

24   Insolvency Act 1986, s 221(7); Insolvent Partnerships Order 1994, Sched 4.
25   Insolvency Act 1986, s 222; Insolvent Partnerships Order 1994, Sched 4.
26   By Insolvent Partnerships Order 1994, Sched 4, Part II.
27   Insolvency Act 1986, ss 124(6) and 125A; Insolvent Partnerships Order, Sched 4.
28   Insolvency Act 1986, s125(2); Insolvent Partnerships Order 1994, Sched 4.
29   See Chapter 17.

individual member will be conducted in accordance with the usual rules,[30] in both cases as modified by Sched 4 to the Insolvent Partnerships Order 1994.

The Official Receiver will become the responsible insolvency practitioner in respect of both the partnership and any member in respect of whom an order has been made unless and until he or she is replaced by an insolvency practitioner either chosen by a combined meeting of the creditors of the partnership and the creditors of an insolvent member or appointed by the Secretary of State in like manner to a compulsory liquidation of a company.[31] The Official Receiver will have to call a meeting to appoint a private sector insolvency practitioner if required to do so by one-quarter in value of the partnership creditors or by one-quarter in value of the creditors of an insolvent partner.[32] Any combined meeting of creditors will be conducted as if it were a meeting of a single set of creditors.[33] The meeting may also appoint a committee which will act as liquidation committee of the partnership and for any insolvent corporate partner and as creditors' committee for any insolvent individual partner.[34]

The responsible insolvency practitioner can become trustee of any member who is subsequently made bankrupt in respect of a partnership debt.

If the responsible insolvency practitioner feels there is likely to be a conflict of interest between the various estates, he or she may call separate meetings of creditors to ascertain their wishes. The insolvency practitioner may also be requested to summon a meeting at any time by one-tenth in value of the creditors or contributories. He or she may apply to the court for directions.[35] The court may decide to appoint additional insolvency practitioners either to act jointly with or to replace the existing practitioner.

(f) Collection and distribution of the assets

The Insolvent Partnerships Order 1994 makes some amendments, in the case of an Art 8 insolvency, to the provisions of the Insolvency Act which deal with the collection and distribution of the assets.[36] The insolvency practitioner will keep distinct accounts of the joint estate of the partnership of the separate estate of each member of that partnership against whom an insolvency order has been made.

The definition of exempt property in the bankruptcy of an individual partner is amended[37] so that any assets which are partnership property fall into the estate.

Provision is made for the payment of the expenses in relation to the various estates.[38] Joint expenses will firstly be applied against joint assets. Expenses of the individual estates will firstly be applied against the separate assets. If there is a shortfall in the joint estate, the unpaid balance will be apportioned equally between the separate estates of the insolvent partners and rank *pari passu* with those expenses.

---

30 See Chapter 15.
31 Insolvency Act 1986, ss 136, 136A, 137, 137A; Insolvent Partnerships Order 1994, Sched 4.
32 Insolvency Act 1986, ss 136, 136A, 137, 137A; Insolvent Partnerships Order 1994, Sched 4.
33 Insolvency Act 1986, s 139; Insolvent Partnerships Order 1994, Sched 4.
34 Insolvency Act 1986, ss 141, 141A; Insolvent Partnerships Order 1994, Sched 4.
35 Insolvency Act 1986, s 230A; Insolvent Partnerships Order 1994, Sched 4.
36 See generally Part V below.
37 Insolvency Act 1986, s 283; Insolvent Partnerships Order 1994, Sched 4.
38 Insolvent Partnerships Order 1994, Sched 4, s 175.

If there is a shortfall in any of the separate estates, the unpaid balance will form part of the expenses to be paid out of the joint estate. Any balance remaining will be apportioned equally between the other estates and will continue to be apportioned equally until the balance has been paid. If the creditors' committee agree or if the court gives leave, the responsible insolvency practitioner may pay any expenses incurred for any separate estate as part of the expenses to be paid out of the joint estate, or pay out of any separate estate any part of the expenses incurred for the joint estate which affects that separate estate.

An insolvency practitioner appointed under Art 8 of the Insolvent Partnerships Order 1994 will deal first with the expenses of the various estates and then with the claims of the joint estate creditors. Any shortfall will then be proved for in the individual insolvencies. The Cork Committee recognised[39] that it was correct in principle that the separate creditors should have no resort to the joint estate until the joint estate creditors were paid in full, since a partner would not be entitled to receive any share of the firm's assets until the firm's debts were paid and there was no reason why his private creditors should be in a better position. A distribution from the individual estate will be paid up to the joint estate and then distributed to the joint estate creditors. The aggregate amount of the shortfall is claimable against each individual estate, but the rule against double proof means that the liquidator cannot recover more than once on behalf of the joint estate.

The priority of debts in both joint and separate estates is that expenses will be paid first, then preferential debts followed by ordinary debts and then interest on joint debts (other than postponed debts), followed by postponed debts and then, finally, interest on postponed debts. Where there is a shortfall in the joint estate, the debts will be a claim on the estate of each insolvent partner against whom an order has been made under Art 8. The claims will rank equally with debts of the same category in the separate insolvencies. This abrogates the previous rule that where there was any joint estate, the joint estate creditors were postponed to the separate estate.

Schedule 4, s 175C(2) contains the common law rule[40] that a partner cannot prove against either the joint estate or the separate estate of his or her bankrupt co-partner in competition with the firm's creditors who are in fact his or her own creditors; he or she will have to wait until the partnership liabilities have all been discharged. If all the joint creditors have been paid and the separate estate of the co-partner is clearly insolvent, the rule does not apply. There are exceptions in the case of fraud and where debts have arisen in the ordinary course of a separate business. A partner who has incurred personal liability in reliance on an indemnity from his or her partners will find that his or her claim is subordinated to the claims of joint estate creditors until they have been paid out in full.

(g) End of the insolvencies

When it appears to the insolvency practitioner, not being the Official Receiver, that the winding up of the partnership or any corporate member or the administration of the estate of any individual member is for practical purposes complete, he or she must summon a final general meeting of the relevant creditors, which may be a combined

39   Paragraph 1689.
40   *Ex p Collinge* (1863) 4 De G&J 533.

meeting, to receive the report and to determine whether the practitioner should be released from potential liability.[41]

5 WINDING UP OF PARTNERSHIP AND INSOLVENCY OF ALL MEMBERS ON MEMBER'S PETITION

(a) Introduction

Article 10 is the relevant article where a member of a partnership presents a petition against the partnership and against all its members in their capacity as such. Many of the provisions are the same as apply under Art 8 where a petition has been presented by a creditor against the partnership and some of the partners, but the provisions as to eligibility to petition and grounds for petition are different.

The partnership may be wound up as an unregistered company under Part V of the Insolvency Act 1986. Sections 220, 225 and 227–29 of the Insolvency Act 1986 will apply modified as set out in Part II of Sched 4 to the Insolvent Partnerships Order 1994. Sections 117, 124, 125, 221, 264, 265, 271 and 272 of the Insolvency Act 1986 will apply modified as set out in Sched 6 to the Insolvent Partnerships Order 1994. Sections 73(1), 74(2)(a) to (d) and (3), 75 to 78, 83, 124(2) and (3), 154, 202, 203, 205, 222, 223, 224 and 250 of the Insolvency Act 1986 will not apply.

The winding up of any corporate members of the partnership will be governed by Parts IV, VI, VII and Parts XII to XIX of the Insolvency Act 1986. The bankruptcy of individual members will be governed by Part IX (other than ss 273, 274, 287 and 297) and Parts X to XIX. Those of these provisions which are modified by the Insolvent Partnerships Order 1994 are set out in Sched 4 to the Order, with the exception of the provisions on summary administration which will apply as set out in Sched 7 to the Order. Unless the contrary intention appears, members against whom an order has been made will not be treated as contributories for the purposes of the Insolvency Act 1986.[42]

Jurisdiction is the same as under Art 9 of the Insolvent Partnerships Order 1994, explained above.

(b) *Locus standi* and grounds for petition[43]

A member can present a petition if the partnership is unable to pay its debts and if petitions are presented at the same time by that partner for insolvency orders against every partner of the partnership (including him or herself) and each partner is willing for an insolvency order to be made against him or her and the petition against him or her contains a statement to this effect. The court may allow the petitioner to leave out some partners where it considers it impracticable to present petitions against them. The court will have the same powers on hearing the petitions as under Art 8 of the Insolvent Partnerships Order 1994, explained above.

---

41 Insolvency Act 1986, ss 146, 331; Insolvent Partnerships Order 1994, Sched 4.
42 Insolvency Act 1986, s 221(7); Insolvent Partnerships Order 1994, Sched 6.
43 Insolvency Act 1986, s 124; Insolvent Partnerships Order 1994, Sched 6.

(c) Conduct of the insolvencies

The conduct of the insolvencies and the rules as to priority of expenses and debts will be as apply under Art 8 of the Insolvent Partnerships Order 1994, explained above. The court may issue a certificate for summary administration if the total of the partnership debts and the separate debts of the member is less than £20,000 and the member concerned has neither been adjudged bankrupt nor made a composition with creditors in satisfaction of his or her debts nor a scheme of arrangement of his or her affairs within the five years before the presentation of the joint petition.

6 JOINT BANKRUPTCY PETITION BY ALL MEMBERS

(a) Introduction

Under Art 11 of the Insolvent Partnerships Order 1994, the court can make orders for the bankruptcy of all the members and the winding up of the business, but not as a registered company, on the joint petition of all the members. Parts IX (other than ss 273, 274 and 287) and X to XIX of the Insolvency Act 1986 will apply in so far as they relate to the insolvency of individuals where a bankruptcy petition is presented by a debtor and modified as set out in Sched 7 to the Insolvent Partnerships Order 1994. The provisions which Sched 7 modifies are ss 264 to 266, 272, 275, 283, 284, 290, 292 to 301, 305, 312, 328, 331 and 387. The Company Directors Disqualification Act 1986 will not be applicable in this situation.

For there to be jurisdiction under this Article, the partnership must have or have had within the previous three years a principal place of business in England and Wales.

(b) Grounds and eligibility to petition[44]

A joint bankruptcy petition may be presented under Art 11 of the Insolvent Partnerships Order 1994 by all the partners, in their capacity as such, provided that they are all individuals and that none of them is a limited partner. The court may allow the presentation of a petition by some only of the members of the partnership where it is satisfied that it would be impracticable to require presentation by all the members. The only ground for presentation of the petition is that the partnership is unable to pay its debts and the petition shall be accompanied by a statement of affairs of each member and of the partnership.

The court may issue a certificate for summary administration if the total of the partnership debts and the separate debts of the member is less than £20,000 and the member concerned has neither been adjudged bankrupt nor made a composition with creditors in satisfaction of his or her debts nor a scheme of arrangement of his or her affairs within the five years before the presentation of the joint petition.

---

44 Insolvency Act 1986, ss 264, 265, 266 and 272; Insolvent Partnerships Order 1994, Sched 7.

(c) Conduct of the bankruptcies

The Official Receiver will be appointed as trustee of the estates of the members and of the partnership until a replacement trustee is appointed. The provisions which apply to the conduct of a partnership winding up and concurrent insolvencies of members under Art 8 of the Insolvent Partnership Order 1994[45] also apply, appropriately modified, in this situation.

7 PERSONAL CONSEQUENCES FOR INDIVIDUAL PARTNERS

A partner of an insolvent partnership will be deemed to be an officer or director for the purposes of the Insolvency Act 1986 and the Company Directors Disqualification Act 1986 and may face liability for criminal offences, civil liability for wrongful and fraudulent trading[46] and disqualification under the Company Directors Disqualification Act 1986.[47]

Schedule 8 to the Insolvent Partnerships Order 1994[48] contains the modifications of the Company Directors Disqualification Act 1986. Disqualification orders may be made against those who are or have been officers of partnerships which have become insolvent. Officers of partnerships are those who are members of the partnership and those who have management or control of the partnership business. In many cases, the partners will be disqualified because they are undischarged bankrupts, but a longer period of disqualification could be imposed under s 6 of the Company Directors Disqualification Act 1986.

---

45 Explained in section 3(e)–(g) above.
46 These provisions will be of no consequence to a partner whose liability is anyway unlimited.
47 Except under the Insolvent Partnerships Order 1994, Art 11.
48 As amended by the Insolvent Partnerships (Amendment) Order 2001 to reflect the amendments to the Company Directors Disqualification Act 1986 in the Insolvency Act 2000.

PART IV
MAINTAINING PUBLIC
CONFIDENCE

CHAPTER 19

INTRODUCTION TO PART IV

This Part focuses on what the Cork Committee described as one of the main aims of insolvency law: the maintenance of public confidence in the system as being one under which those to whom credit is extended should not be lightly released from their obligation to pay. The Cork Committee observed[1] that 'it is a basic objective of the law to support the maintenance of commercial morality and encourage the fulfilment of financial obligations. Insolvency must not be an easy solution for those who can bear with equanimity the stigma of their own failure or their responsibility for the failure of a company under their management'. Later in the Cork Report,[2] the Committee observed that society requires to be satisfied in respect of four distinct matters: first, whether or not fault or blame attaches to the conduct of the insolvent; secondly, if it does, that the insolvent will be suitably punished; thirdly, that the insolvent's opportunity to repeat such conduct in the future should be controlled whilst at the same time allowing re-establishment of legitimate trading activities; finally, whether and to what extent the responsibility for the insolvency is attributable to someone other than the insolvent.

A fundamental requirement of public confidence in the system is the integrity and competence of those charged with the implementation of the insolvency procedures. There has been considerable debate in the course of the history of insolvency law about who should control the process of collection and distribution of the assets in order to prevent abuse by debtors, creditors or by those in control of the assets. The issue of the financing of the insolvency system is pivotal to the area of public confidence both as regards the question of how and to what extent public sector involvement should be funded and also because any perception that private sector insolvency practitioners are making unjustified profits will be a major factor in public dissatisfaction with the system. Chapter 20 considers who controls the insolvency system and looks, in particular, at the licensing and control of trustees in bankruptcy, liquidators, administrators and administrative receivers. The final section of the chapter deals with the question of cost.

Insolvency does not necessarily involve criminal liability, but it does indicate a state of affairs which requires public explanation and inquiry. The Cork Committee said:[3] 'If the basic objectives of the law are to be achieved, it is essential that proper investigation will be made in every case in which it is warranted. Justice and fairness to those whose conduct is liable to be investigated, and the proper constraints on public expenditure, alike require that no investigation will be undertaken unless it is warranted.' At one time, all bankrupts had to undergo a public examination before they could obtain their discharge but this is now seen as unnecessarily draconian. Chapter 21 explains the extent to which the insolvency legislation provides for the investigation of those who, or whose companies, become insolvent. Increasingly, litigation in this area has involved a consideration of the provisions of the European Convention on Human Rights.

---

1   Paragraph 191.
2   At para 1735.
3   At para 194.

An evaluation of whether the consequences of bankruptcy provide a sufficient sanction to maintain public confidence in the system depends in part on the view taken of the extent to which being unable to pay is a culpable state. A tension between the feeling that being unable to pay one's debts is always a state of affairs which should be punished and the recognition that the debtor has sometimes merely been unlucky has existed throughout the history of insolvency law. There is a difficult balance to be struck between the measures required to support commercial morality and the objectives of insolvency law considered in Part II in relation to the rescue culture and rehabilitation. Support for the rescue culture is currently in the ascendancy together with the recognition that some risk-taking is an inevitable aspect of a growing economy and that failure on occasions is a necessary concomitant. The recent White Paper on Enterprise, Skills and Innovation[4] said:

> Entrepreneurship involves balancing potential risks with possible reward. For many business people, success comes only after numerous attempts. We should not deal with business failure in a way which creates a barrier to future success.[5] An entrepreneurial economy needs to support responsible risk taking. Insolvency law must be updated so that it strikes the right balance. It must deal proportionately with financial failure, whilst assuring creditors that it is handled efficiently and effectively. The law currently makes no distinction between someone whose bankruptcy comes about as a result of their fraud, and someone who fails because they have, for example, guaranteed a company's bank overdraft.

The perennial problem has been that of sorting the deserving from the undeserving without employing unacceptably expensive procedures to do so. Chapter 22 explains the provisions which, together with the loss of property explained in Chapter 27, currently provide the deterrent effect of bankruptcy; the amendments to bankruptcy law contained in the Enterprise Act 2002 are the latest attempt at balancing rehabilitation for the unfortunate with adequate sanctions for those who are guilty of abusing the system.

The existence of limited liability increases the potential for abuse of the system. Prevention of abuse of this privilege requires investigation into the conduct of those responsible for the insolvent company and the incorporation into the law of measures designed to deter them from allowing their companies to become insolvent. The various criminal offences which may be committed in connection with corporate insolvency are considered in Chapter 23, together with the provisions of the Company Directors Disqualification Act 1986 which, whilst having an undeniably penal effect, are not strictly part of the criminal law. The measures relating to fraudulent and wrongful trading, considered in Chapter 31, also impose a sanction on directors who allow a company to continue to incur obligations which it will be unable to meet. These aspects of insolvency law have provided the dynamic for modernisation of the standards of care and skill to be expected from directors. The proposed codification of directors duties contained in the White Paper *Modernising Company Law* includes a statement of the duty of care and skill based on that contained in the wrongful trading provisions. The concern of the government not to deter entrepreneurial risk-taking is

---

4　DTI, 2001, paras 5.9 and 5.10.
5　The Global Entrepreneurship Monitor 2001 showed that in the UK, 31.5% of the population said that the fear of failure would prevent them from starting a business, whereas the level in the United States was only 21% (see www.gemconsortium.org).

evidenced by the refusal in the White Paper to accept the final recommendation of the Company Law Review Steering Group that the statutory statement of directors' duties place a duty on the directors of companies in financial difficulty to have regard to the interests of creditors: 'Directors would need to take a finely balanced judgment, and fears of personal liability might lead to excessive caution. This would run counter to the "rescue culture" which the government is trying to promote.'[6]

The Cork Committee recognised that there was particular concern about the prevalence of what are referred to as 'phoenix companies'. These arise where the owners of a business allow the limited liability company through which it has been trading to become insolvent and then transfer the assets of the business to a new company trading under a name which leads customers to think that they are still dealing with the same entity. The liabilities of the old company are not transferred; the 'phoenix company' rises from the ashes of the insolvent company, having shed its debts. The new company may well meet the same fate as the old and it has not been uncommon for the process to be repeated by the same people on a number of occasions. Section 216 of the Insolvency Act 1986, which is also explained in Chapter 23, is intended to prevent this happening.

The final section of Chapter 23 contains an evaluation of the provisions intended to prevent the abuse of limited liability from which it will be seen that there is still perceived to be a problem. There has been an improvement in the rate at which the authorities obtain sanctions against wrongdoers, but it is not clear that the law works adequately to prevent culpable behaviour occurring in the first place. It is noteworthy that there are no qualification requirements to become a director, so control over dishonest and incompetent directors can only be exercised after the event.[7] A survey by the Institute of Directors in 1990 indicated that fewer than 10% of directors had received any training as such and that fewer than a quarter possessed any professional or managerial qualifications.[8] It could be argued that it might it be better to impose qualifications on directors, in the same way that auditors and insolvency practitioners have to be qualified, rather than disqualifying them after the event as currently happens.[9]

A final problem to note is that a majority of the companies removed from the register do not go through any formal proceedings. Companies House statistics for England and Wales for 2001–02 show that in that year, 149,200 were struck off the register and dissolved[10] and that only 14,900 were formally wound up. Whilst employees, creditors and other interested parties are given the opportunity to object, there is some suspicion[11] that the procedure is enabling directors to bring the life of an insolvent company to end without formal investigation.

6   Paragraph 3.11 of the White Paper *Modernising Company Law*.
7   See Finch (1992) at 210, noting that the prospective company director does not have to cross a threshold of minimal competence. Hoffmann (1997); Sealy (2001); Walters (2001b).
8   See Finch (1992).
9   See Hicks (1988).
10 See Chapter 13 for an explanation of the Companies Act 1985, ss 652, 652A.
11 Hicks (2001) at 445.

CHAPTER 20

CONTROL OF THE INSOLVENCY SYSTEM

1 INTRODUCTION

The Cork Committee observed that 'the success of any insolvency system is very largely dependent upon those who administer it'[1] and that 'while the method of control over the administration of bankruptcy varies from country to country, in almost all bankruptcy systems creditors were originally given the primary responsibility for administering the process. In country after country, however, this had led to scandal and abuse, and exclusive control has been progressively removed from creditors and varying degrees of official control have been introduced as it has been increasingly accepted that the public interest is involved in the proper administration of the bankruptcy system'.[2]

In England and Wales, creditors were given control of the system by the Bankruptcy Act 1869[3] as a consequence of persuasive argument by the commercial community that since the estates were being administered primarily for the benefit of the creditors, they were the persons best calculated to look after their own interests. The reality turned out to be very different and the overwhelming indifference of the vast majority of those owed small amounts or who stood to gain nothing from the bankruptcy meant that there was little control exercised. In many cases, bankrupts and their advisers found it possible to take control of the administration of the bankruptcy in their own interests to the prejudice of the majority of creditors.

In consequence, official control was re-introduced by the Bankruptcy Act 1883 with the introduction of a public official to be known as the Official Receiver, under the control of the Board of Trade which had overall responsibility for bankruptcy law. These functions of the Board of Trade now rest with the Insolvency Service, an Executive Agency of the Department of Trade and Industry whose role is considered in the next section of this chapter. The intention in 1883 was that the Official Receiver would carry out an impartial and independent examination into the causes of each bankruptcy and the conduct of each bankrupt. The cost was to be met from a fee levied on each petition, a small percentage on the assets collected and interest on amounts collected which would be paid into an account at the Bank of England. The Official Receiver's role was subsequently extended to compulsory liquidations in 1890. Nearly a century later, a Department of Trade and Industry consultation document published in July 1980 suggested that there should no longer be official involvement in personal insolvencies, but this suggestion met with a hostile reaction from the insolvency profession and from the Cork Committee and was not pursued.[4] The Cork Report considered the practice in several other countries and noted that in two countries, Scotland and Germany, where all bankruptcy work was then undertaken by the private sector, there were a substantial number of cases which

---

1   Paragraph 732.
2   Paragraph 702.
3   See Chapter 2 on the history of insolvency law.
4   See Carruthers and Halliday, 1998.

could not be dealt with because of the lack of assets to meet the costs.[5] The current role of the Official Receiver is considered in greater detail later in this chapter.

In addition to arguing forcefully for the retention of the public sector Official Receiver in bankruptcy cases, the Cork Committee expressed concern about the lack of control over who could be appointed as liquidator in a voluntary liquidation or as receiver and manager to enforce a floating charge over the undertaking of a company. Whilst the appointment of trustees in bankruptcy and liquidators in compulsory liquidations was subject to control by the courts and the Department of Trade and Industry, anyone could be appointed as a voluntary liquidator or receiver. Evidence was presented to the Cork Committee of abusive practices such as the sale of the assets of the company to those previously connected with it at prices prejudicial to the creditors. It was also felt that directors of companies in voluntary liquidation were not being properly investigated. The Cork Report recommended subjecting all insolvency practitioners to proper regulation, through the medium of their membership of appropriate professional bodies, in order to maintain standards both of competence and of integrity and these recommendations were given effect in the Insolvency Act 1986, as explained in more detail below. This mechanism was used so that, whilst ultimate responsibility for the authorisation and monitoring process would rest with the Secretary of State, the operational burden of regulation should not rest with the Department of Trade and Industry.

The system of regulation of insolvency practitioners was reviewed between 1996 and 1998 by the Insolvency Regulation Working Party which included representatives of the recognised professional bodies and members of the Insolvency Service;[6] the terms of reference of the Working Party were 'to review the current state of regulation in the insolvency profession and, in the light of that review, to consider whether there are ways in which, in the public interest and in the interest of all those affected by insolvency proceedings, such regulation could be made more efficient and effective'. The Working Party was composed of members of the authorising bodies and there are those who would argue that its Report cannot, therefore, conclusively rebut the suggestion that the regulation of insolvency practitioners contains too much self-regulation. As a result of the Report, the Insolvency Practices Council was established with a remit to examine the standards and practices of insolvency practitioners and to make recommendations for change where necessary to the Joint Insolvency Committee, the main body concerned with standard-setting for the insolvency profession. The current role of these bodies and the issue of standard setting generally is dealt with in more detail later in this chapter.

The introduction of regulation of insolvency practitioners in 1986 was linked to a lessening of court involvement in certain areas of insolvency practice; it has been seen,[7] for example, that there is no need for a court to be actively involved in a company voluntary arrangement. As will be explained below, the conduct of insolvency practitioners is controlled partly by monitoring by the regulating professional bodies, partly by the creditors in any particular insolvency and,

---

5   Although the focus of this chapter is public interest in investigation and control, there is a
    link here with the public interest in encouraging the rescue culture considered in Chapter 7.
6   It published a consultation document *Insolvency Practitioner Regulation – Ten Years On* in 1998
    and *A Review of Insolvency Practitioner Regulation* in 1999. See Finch (1998); Finch (1999b).
7   In Chapter 9.

ultimately, by the court. There is less external control of those insolvencies administered by the Official Receivers than those conducted by the private sector.

Much of the debate and difficulty in this area revolves around the question of balancing the need for adequate control of the system with the costs involved in so doing, the final issue considered later in this chapter. Questions of the required level and nature of the control cannot be divorced from issues of how that control is to be financed. Even once consensus is achieved as to the extent of control, there is still scope for debate about the most cost-effective means of achieving it. The involvement of the private sector gives rise to additional difficulties, in particular the issue of the extent of the profit which private sector insolvency practitioners should make from their work. The profit motive also gives rise to potential for malpractice, particularly in relation to conflict of interest, which does not arise in relation to the work carried out in the public sector. The ultimate difficulty in addressing dissatisfaction with the working of the system is that, given the nature of insolvency, many of those who come into contact with it are inevitably going to feel unhappy with the financial outcome.

2 THE INSOLVENCY SERVICE[8]

Overall responsibility for the administration of insolvency law in English and Wales lies with the Department of Trade and Industry. This has been delegated to the Insolvency Service, which is an executive agency under the direction of the Inspector General of Insolvency. The Insolvency Service describes itself[9] as existing 'to ensure that financial failure is dealt with fairly and effectively, encouraging enterprise and deterring fraud and misconduct'. In 2001–02, it employed an average of 1,375 staff in London and the regions, the majority being employed in Official Receiver operations. The Service deals with five operational areas: policy, Official Receiver operations, enforcement (dealing with reports of possible criminality and of unfit conduct), insolvency practitioner regulation and banking services for users of the Insolvency Services Account. It has also recently taken over responsibility for the Redundancy Payments Offices and maintains registers of voluntary arrangements and disqualification orders. The functions of the Insolvency Service in relation to Official Receivers, insolvency practitioner regulation and banking services are considered in more detail later in this chapter and the enforcement work of the Service is considered in the remaining chapters of Part IV. The work of the Redundancy Payments Offices is considered in Chapter 33.

The DTI Quinquennial Review of the Insolvency Service in 2000 concluded that, with the possible exception of banking, the main functions of the Insolvency Service were essential and would not happen without public sector involvement and/or funding. The Review concluded[10] that the Service was well-managed, responsive and

---

8   For more detailed information on the Insolvency Service, see the Quinquennial Review of the Insolvency Service undertaken by the DTI in 2000 (www.dti.gov.uk/inssweb) and the Insolvency Service Annual Reports available on the Insolvency Service website (www.insolvency.gov.uk). For a somewhat jaundiced private sector view of the Insolvency Service, see Floyd (1999) and the following article of response from the Insolvency Service.

9   Annual Report 2001–02.

10   Review Stage 2 Executive Summary April 2001 (www.dti.gov.uk/inssweb_execsum.pdf).

had improved its performance significantly over the previous five years, but that it was being constrained by its financial regime and by an outdated IT system.[11] As explained below, the Enterprise Act 2002 will bring about changes in the financial regime. The Insolvency Service has a published procedure for dealing with complaints about its work; in 2001–02, in which it took on 26,500 new cases, it received 595 complaints of which 174 (mainly relating to the quality of the service provided) were found to be justified in whole or part. 97 of the unjustified complaints were complaints about the insolvency legislation itself. In its 2001–02 Report the Insolvency Service announced that it planned to introduce an independent external adjudicator to deal with complaints which remain unresolved in the internal process; this task has been taken on by the Adjudicator's Office, which was originally set up in 1993 to deal with taxpayers' complaints about the Inland Revenue.

3   OFFICIAL RECEIVERS[12]

The Official Receiver is not a single person. The functions of the Official Receiver are carried out by a number of people appointed to the office of Official Receiver by the Secretary of State for Trade and Industry. At the time of the Quinquennial Review in 2000, there were 43 Official Receivers managing 33 offices in England and Wales. These people are generally individuals who have, until their appointment, been civil servants within the Insolvency Service and who, although they continue by law to act at and under the direction of the Secretary of State, cease on appointment to be civil servants in the proper sense of servants of the Crown employed in the business of government: *Re Minotaur Data Systems, Official Receiver v Brunt*.[13] Every person holding the office of Official Receiver is attached either to the High Court or to one or more specific county courts having an insolvency jurisdiction and will exercise the functions of the Official Receiver in relation to bankruptcies and liquidations falling within the jurisdiction of that court. The Official Receiver has the status of officer of the court in relation to which he or she exercises the functions of the office.[14]

Each Official Receiver is empowered to bring proceedings, including disqualification proceedings, in his or her own name, and each is accorded by law a right of audience before the court to which he or she is attached. In *Mond v Hyde*,[15] the Court of Appeal held that the getting in of a bankrupt's estate for the purpose of being distributed to the creditors is part of the bankruptcy proceedings, and therefore the Official Receiver in bankruptcy, as an officer of the court, is immune from suit in respect of statements made by him or her as such, even if made negligently.

As has been seen,[16] the Official Receiver will serve as trustee in bankruptcy or liquidator in compulsory liquidations where no private sector insolvency practitioner has been appointed; these will be insolvencies where the assets are insufficient to bear the cost of a private sector appointment. In every case of bankruptcy and compulsory

---

11   See Chapter 10 of the Annual Report 2001–02 for the IT plans of the Insolvency Service.
12   See the Insolvency Act 1986, ss 399–401.
13   [1999] 3 All ER 122, in which it was held that an Official Receiver will be a litigant in person. See also Beldam LJ in *Mond v Hyde* [1999] 2 WLR 499 at 515–16.
14   Insolvency Act 1986, s 400(2).
15   [1998] 3 All ER 833.
16   In Chapters 15 and 17.

liquidation, the Official Receiver carries out an initial examination to establish the extent of the assets; cases where assets are sufficient to cover costs are passed on to private sector insolvency practitioners. The Official Receiver will remain in charge in about 75% of cases.[17] Under s 264 of the Enterprise Act 2002, Official Receivers will be given the power to act as nominees and supervisors in relation to post-bankruptcy individual voluntary arrangements. The Official Receiver also has an investigatory function to perform in relation to bankruptcies[18] and compulsory liquidations. Where possible criminal liability is identified, the Official Receivers will pass the cases to DTI solicitors, the Serious Fraud Office or another prosecuting agency. In 2000, Official Receivers submitted 906 reports to the DTI regarding possible criminal offences and assisted police and other prosecuting authorities in a further 209 criminal investigations.[19]

It can be seen that Official Receivers have responsibility both for ensuring the administration of insolvent estates and for investigating the background to the insolvencies. The White Paper of 1984 on insolvency reform envisaged that the Official Receivers should be able to concentrate strongly on their investigative duties. In 1994, Justice reported that the increased caseload of the Insolvency Service had been such that the resources available to undertake these investigatory functions had fallen, comparatively speaking, to a very low level. Consideration was given by the government in the mid-1990s to the privatisation of the role of Official Receiver and various tenders were considered, but it was eventually decided that it would not be cost-effective to proceed. In the 2000 Quinquennial Review, it was recognised that, although the case administration work clearly could be contracted out (as shown by the model used in Scotland), it would not be sensible to re-run the tendering exercise with each Review; what was important was that the Insolvency Service benchmarked itself against the best in the private sector and set up arrangements to test and improve its performance continuously. Some selective use of agents could, however, help with handling fluctuations in workload and it would be possible to contract out some of the investigatory work, subject to ultimate control by Insolvency Service staff.

4   INSOLVENCY PRACTITIONERS

(a) Requirement of qualification

The Insolvency Act 1986 prohibits unqualified persons from acting as insolvency practitioners[20] and requires that holders of the office of liquidator, administrator and administrative receiver be qualified insolvency practitioners.[21] The Act defines acting as an insolvency practitioner[22] in relation to a company as acting as a liquidator, provisional liquidator, administrator, administrative receiver or nominee or supervisor of a voluntary arrangement. In relation to an individual, a person acts as

---

17   DTI, 2000, para 9.13.
18   Currently there is no requirement to investigate in the case of a summary administration, but once the individual insolvency provisions of the Enterprise Act 2002 come into force, the obligation will extend to all bankruptcies.
19   DTI statistics.
20   Insolvency Act 1986, s 389.
21   Insolvency Act 1986, s 230.
22   Insolvency Act 1986, s 388.

an insolvency practitioner by acting as a trustee in bankruptcy, interim receiver of property, a trustee under a deed of arrangement, administrator of the insolvent estate of a deceased individual or nominee or supervisor of an individual voluntary arrangement. Section 389A of the Insolvency Act 1986[23] makes it possible for individuals to be recognised as qualified to act as nominees or supervisors of voluntary arrangements only. Official Receivers do not act as insolvency practitioners for the purposes of requiring qualification. Any other person who acts as an insolvency practitioner at a time when not qualified to do so is liable to imprisonment, a fine or both.[24]

Insolvency practitioners must be individuals; companies cannot be qualified to act as insolvency practitioners.[25] Undischarged bankrupts, persons subject to disqualification orders under the Companies Directors Disqualification Act 1986 and 'patients' within the mental health legislation are all disqualified from acting as insolvency practitioners. Qualification to act as an insolvency practitioner requires authorisation to act either by virtue of membership of a recognised professional body which has granted authorisation or by virtue of an authorisation granted by the Secretary of State in response to a direct application to the Insolvency Service.[26] Seven professional bodies have been recognised as able to grant authorisation;[27] a member of any of these bodies may be licensed to act as an insolvency practitioner by complying with their rules. In 2000, there were a total of 1,863 authorised insolvency practitioners, of whom 789 were authorised by the Institute of Chartered Accountants in England and Wales and 350 by the Insolvency Practitioners Association. The Law Society of England authorised 199 and 128 were directly authorised by the Secretary of State.

The authorising body must consider whether applicants are fit and proper persons to act as insolvency practitioners and meet educational, training and experience requirements. The Insolvency Practitioners Regulations 1990[28] lay down the requirements which will be applied by the Insolvency Service. The recognised bodies are required to have 'acceptable' rules and the Regulations clearly provide a guideline as to what is acceptable; a body which departed markedly from these rules would be likely to find its status as a recognised body at risk. Authorisation to act as an insolvency practitioner will only be given to those who have reached a certain educational standard, which will include examination on insolvency law, and have had a certain amount of practical experience. Matters specified in the Insolvency Practitioners Regulations 1990 as relevant to the question of whether an applicant is a fit and proper person to be an insolvency practitioner include the honesty, integrity and competence of the individual. Where applicants have previously been insolvency practitioners, it will be relevant to consider whether they have been guilty of any

---

23 Inserted by the Insolvency Act 2000, s 4.
24 Insolvency Act 1986, s 389.
25 Insolvency Act 1986, s 390(1).
26 Insolvency Act 1986, s 390.
27 Insolvency Act 1986, s 391; Insolvency Practitioners (Recognised Professional Bodies) Order 1986 (SI 1986/1764). The recognised bodies are the Chartered Association of Certified Accountants, the Insolvency Practitioners Association, the Institute of Chartered Accountants in England and Wales (and the equivalent bodies in Ireland and Scotland), the Law Society and the Law Society of Scotland.
28 SI 1990/439.

contraventions of insolvency law, whether they have adequate systems of control and accounting records and whether they have allowed themselves to get into positions of conflict of interest.

Authorisation will only be given for three years at a time and in order to renew the licence, the insolvency practitioner will have to show that he or she has maintained his or her level of practical involvement by having been appointed as officeholder in at least one case or having acquired at least 500 hours of higher insolvency work experience in the previous three years. Any person whose authorisation is withdrawn or refused by the Secretary of State may refer his or her case to the Insolvency Practitioners Tribunal (and, on appeal therefrom, to the High Court) under s 396 of the Insolvency Act 1986. Decisions of the recognised bodies are subject to judicial review by the High Court.

(b) Insurance

Insolvency practitioners, before being qualified to act as such, must furnish security for the proper performance of their functions by each depositing with the recognised body which authorised them (or the Secretary of State) a bond issued by an insurance company by which it makes itself jointly and severally liable with them for the proper performance of their duties.[29] Each bond must be for a general sum of £250,000 and for additional specific sums in accordance with the prescribed limits applicable to particular cases in which he or she is to act. The amount of the required cover in relation to any specific appointment is calculated by reference to the value of the assets of the insolvent with a minimum of £5,000 and a maximum of £5,000,000.

5   CONTROL OF INSOLVENCY PRACTITIONERS

(a) Conflict of interest

The issue of conflict of interest[30] arises in relation to whether an insolvency practitioner should accept an appointment and also in relation to his or her conduct of cases. Any insolvency practitioner who becomes involved in a situation of conflict of interest will be putting his or her licence at risk. It is clear that insolvency practitioners should be, and be seen to be, independent and not subject to any conflicts of interest in their administration of the insolvent estate and investigation of the background to the insolvency. The Insolvency Rules contain express provisions enabling insolvency practitioners to resign on the ground of conflict of interest. There is considerable guidance provided by the code of conduct issued for practitioners licensed by the Secretary of State, which emphasises the need for practitioners to avoid relationships and commitments which might affect, or appear to affect, their objectivity. If there is a conflict of interest, the insolvency practitioner should refuse the appointment and if he or she might appear to have a conflict of interest, this should be disclosed to interested parties so that they can decide whether or not the appointment should go ahead. Insolvency practitioners should not accept appointment where they have previously

---

29   Insolvency Act 1986, s 390; Insolvency Practitioners Regulations 1990.
30   See generally Anderson in Clarke (ed), 1991, Chapter 1.

held office in relation to a company as director, auditor or administrative receiver since they might subsequently find themselves in the position of having to investigate their previous actions. The case of *Re Corbenstoke Ltd (No 2)*[31] was a particularly striking example of a liquidator in a position of conflict of interest since the liquidator had been a director of the company being wound up to whom he owed money and was the trustee in bankruptcy of an individual with a claim against the company.[32]

There has been considerable controversy[33] as to whether insolvency practitioners should accept an appointment following on from monitoring or advisory work in relation to the insolvent business carried out as investigating accountants by themselves or their firms. In 1999, an unsuccessful Private Member's Bill attempted to prohibit this practice. On the one hand, there is clearly potential for cost-saving if an administrative receiver or administrator already has a good working knowledge of the business but, on the other, there will always be the suspicion that the advice leading to the need for the appointment might not have been entirely independent. In its report in May 2000, *A Review of Company Rescue and Business Reconstruction Mechanisms*, the Review Group acknowledged[34] that there was a very real issue of the perception of conflict of interest in this situation although they felt that, on the basis of empirical research,[35] there was no evidence of a problem in reality. The Group recommended that this issue should be addressed by way of the Code published by the British Bankers' Association. This Code now provides[36] that, if the reasons are given by the debtor why a member of a firm which has undertaken an independent review of the business's finances should not be appointed as administrative receiver, the bank will appoint an alternative insolvency practitioner unless there are exceptional circumstances.

One situation which could cause difficulty is that of the insolvency of a group of companies where it would be impractical in many cases to appoint more than one firm of insolvency practitioners. The Insolvent Partnerships Order 1994 expects that there will be a single practitioner where a partnership is being wound up and there are bankruptcy petitions against insolvent members, but that the practitioner can apply for directions if a conflict arises. In *Re Esal (Commodities)*,[37] where a company in liquidation had members of the liquidator's firm as either liquidator or directors of several of its subsidiaries, Dillon LJ remarked that the possible conflicts of interest 'do not in practice give rise to any serious difficulty because they are well-known to the experienced insolvency practitioners'. *Re P Turner (Wilsden) Ltd*[38] is an example of a case where the court decided that conflict of interest meant that separate liquidators were necessary; this case involved two companies in liquidation, only one of which was solvent, owned by the same two shareholders where there was a possibility that the solvent company had prospered by milking the insolvent company of its assets.

---

31   (1989) 5 BCC 767.
32   The court ordered his removal under the Insolvency Act 1986, s 172(2): see Chapter 17.
33   See McCormack (2000) at p 243. Finch (2002) at p 160.
34   At para 121.
35   Katz and Mumford (1999).
36   British Bankers' Association, 2001, para 3.5.
37   (1988) 4 BCC 475.
38   [1987] BCLC 149.

(b) Monitoring

Insolvency practitioners are subject to a regime of inspection which is the responsibility of their authorising body. Insolvency practitioners are required to keep records of prescribed information in respect of each insolvency in relation to which they act and to produce the record on request to the body which authorised them [39] The monitoring regime is designed to ensure that these requirements are met, that reports relating to the possibility of disqualification of directors are submitted as required and, generally, that the practitioner continues to be a fit and proper person to be licensed. The disciplinary response to breach varies with the gravity of the breach but could lead to the withdrawal of a licence. The Joint Insolvency Monitoring Unit (JIMU) came into being in 1994 to monitor insolvency practitioners as agent for the larger recognised professional bodies in carrying out their obligations to monitor their appointees and report on the monitoring to the Insolvency Service. The Insolvency Practitioner Unit of the Insolvency Service makes regular monitoring visits to the Recognised Professional Bodies and their monitoring agents and to insolvency practitioners authorised by the Secretary of State. The Insolvency Regulation Working Party recommended that the Secretary of State should cease to be involved in the licensing of insolvency practitioners and concentrate on regulation of the regulators.

The Insolvency Service and the Recognised Professional Bodies have agreed a set of principles for monitoring of insolvency practitioners.[40] This envisages that each practitioner should normally be visited every three years, but that the period may be extended to a maximum of six years if satisfactory risk assessment measures are employed. Targeted interim visits should be made if an authorising body becomes aware of concerns about a practitioner's activities. Steps should be taken to check satisfactory levels of compliance with all relevant aspects of insolvency law and practice, including the insurance bonding requirements. Checks on professional competence should include a review of the systems and controls employed to ensure proper conduct of work, a check on the ability of the practitioner to carry out the work undertaken, a check on the level of control exercised by practitioners when officeholders and checks on the financial systems employed and procedures for dealing with complaints. Checks should also be carried out as to whether work is being carried out in timely fashion and into any undue influences to which the practitioner is exposed, including financial, emotional, professional or those exerted by significant work providers. A written report should normally be provided to the practitioner and the authorising body within 30 working days of the visit, although any serious matter for concern shall be reported as soon as possible. Reports should be sufficiently detailed to assist the authorising body to make an objective assessment of the conduct and performance of practitioners and to ascertain whether they are and continue to be fit and proper.

(c) Withdrawal of licence

Those aggrieved by the actions of an insolvency practitioner may put the renewal of his or her licence in jeopardy by complaining to the practitioner's professional body or

---

39 Insolvency Practitioners Regulations 1990, rr 16, 17, Sched 3.
40 See www.insolvency.gov.uk/information.

to the Department of Trade. Withdrawal of authorisation during the currency of the licence may be effected by the Secretary of State[41] on the grounds either that the holder is no longer a fit and proper person or that he or she has failed to comply with the obligations imposed on insolvency practitioners or has furnished false, inaccurate or misleading information in purporting to comply with those obligations.

(d) Creditors and creditors' committees

The creditors as a body are given certain powers by the legislation in relation to the conduct of the insolvency. The power of any particular creditor will be in proportion to the amount owed to him or her since this is how voting rights at a meeting of the creditors will be calculated. A creditor will need to prove his or her debt[42] before being entitled to vote. A meeting may be requisitioned by one-tenth in value of the creditors, although a court has the power to block such a requisition where there is no evidence that it will assist in the proper operation of the process of the liquidation or bankruptcy and to justice between all those interested in the assets: *Hamilton v Law Debenture Trustees Ltd*.[43]

The creditors will usually determine the identity of the liquidator in a voluntary liquidation.[44] They may determine the identity of the liquidator in a court liquidation[45] and of the trustee in a bankruptcy,[46] although this might require a sufficient percentage of them being willing to override the Official Receiver's decision not to summon a meeting of creditors to make an appointment. In each case, the creditors also have the power to remove the officeholder.[47] The creditors' meeting may refuse to release the liquidator from liability, in which case he or she will need to apply to the Secretary of State for release from liability in relation to the insolvency. The creditors as a body may bring an administration to an end.[48] Any creditor owed a sufficient amount will be in a position to present a petition for compulsory liquidation in respect of a company in administrative receivership with a view to the liquidator taking steps with respect to any malpractice by the receiver.

As has been seen,[49] supervising committees may be established in liquidations and bankruptcies unless the Official Receiver is acting as liquidator or trustee and in administrations and administrative receiverships. Any creditor other than a fully secured creditor will be eligible to be elected on to the committees. These are intended to monitor the conduct of insolvency practitioners and, to the extent that a liquidator or trustee in bankruptcy requires permission to exercise some powers, to exercise

---

41 Under the Insolvency Act 1986, s 393(4). The rules of the recognised bodies contain similar provisions.
42 See Chapter 25.
43 [2001] EWHC Ch 402.
44 See Chapter 16.
45 See Chapter 17.
46 See Chapter 15.
47 Insolvency Act 1986, ss 171(2)(b), 172(2), 298.
48 Insolvency Act 1986, s 18(2)(b).
49 In Chapters 15 (creditors' committee in bankruptcy), 16 (liquidation committee in voluntary liquidation) and 17 (liquidation committee in compulsory liquidation).

some control over the conduct of the insolvency.[50] They must be kept informed of the progress of the insolvency and may request information, although the insolvency practitioner may refuse to comply with the request where he or she considers it frivolous or unreasonable or that the cost of complying would be excessive or would not be covered by the assets. In *Re BCCI (No 3)*,[51] the court held that it had a residual discretion to direct a liquidator or trustee not to follow the wishes of a committee where special circumstances so warranted. Where there is a committee, it will be responsible for deciding the remuneration of administrators, liquidators and trustees in bankruptcy.[52] Where there is no creditors' committee, its powers and functions will be usually be exercisable by the Secretary of State, acting through the Official Receiver.[53]

The major problem with creditor control of insolvency is that creditors are often not interested in becoming involved, particularly if they are only owed relatively small sums or it is clear that there will be no assets left for the ordinary creditors. It has been argued that committees tend to be dominated by banks whose interests tend to be in a speedy resolution of the insolvency rather than the maximisation of assets for the benefit of all the creditors.

(e) Court control over officeholders

The court has the power to remove liquidators,[54] trustees in bankruptcy,[55] administrative receivers,[56] administrators[57] and the supervisors of voluntary arrangements.[58] In *Re Keypak Homecare Ltd*,[59] an application to remove a voluntary liquidator, Millett J held that an order for removal did not require that the liquidator had been guilty of personal misconduct; it was sufficient that he had failed to carry out his duties with sufficient vigour. In *AMP Enterprises v Hoffman*, Neuberger J, refusing an application for the removal of the liquidators, said that a court should be slow to grant such a request merely because the conduct of the liquidator had been less than ideal in one or two respects because this would encourage applications from creditors who for whatever reason were dissatisfied with the choice of liquidator.

---

50 For the powers of the liquidator, see Chapters 16 and 17. For the trustee in bankruptcy, see Chapter 15.

51 [1993] BCLC 1490.

52 Insolvency Rules 1986, r 2.47 (administrator), r 4.127 (liquidation), r 6.138 (bankruptcy). If there is no committee, the remuneration is decided by the creditors as a body. If not fixed by the creditors, an administrator's fees will be fixed by the court and those of a liquidator or trustee will be in accordance with the Official Receiver's scale. A receiver's fees will be fixed by the debenture holder; the liquidator may apply under the Insolvency Act, s 36 for the court to adjust the remuneration.

53 Insolvency Act 1986, ss 141(5) (compulsory liquidation), 302 (bankruptcy).

54 Insolvency Act 1986, ss 172 (compulsory liquidation), 108 (voluntary liquidations).

55 Insolvency Act 1986, s 298.

56 Insolvency Act 1986, s 45. This is the only method of removing an administrative receiver; this is intended to prevent the placing of undue pressure on the receiver to follow a particular course of action by the debenture holder.

57 Insolvency Act 1986, s 19(1).

58 Insolvency Act 1986, ss 7(5), 263(5).

59 [1987] BCLC 409.

Any person who is 'aggrieved'[60] by an act or decision of the liquidator or 'dissatisfied' by the conduct of the trustee in bankruptcy may apply to the court which may confirm, reverse or modify an act or decision and make such order as it thinks just.[61] The term 'aggrieved' previously applied to bankruptcy as well. In *Port v Auger*,[62] Harman J refused to decide whether 'dissatisfied' is wider than 'aggrieved', but said 'a person can only be dissatisfied if he can show that he has some substantial interest which has been adversely affected by whatever is complained of'. In *Engel v Peri*,[63] Ferris J held that where it is the bankrupt seeking to complain, it would usually but not invariably be necessary that there will be a surplus. In *Mahomed and Another v Morris*,[64] the Court of Appeal held that the class of persons who could apply under s 168(5) of the Insolvency Act 1986 was limited to creditors and contributories and others who were directly affected by the exercise of a power given specifically to liquidators, and who would not otherwise have any right to challenge the exercise of that power. An outsider to the liquidation, such as a person denied an opportunity to buy an asset of the company from the liquidators or a surety whose subrogation rights did not depend on the company being in liquidation, could not properly apply under s 168(5).

The court will not readily interfere in the administration of an insolvency; in *Re a Debtor (No 400 of 1940)*,[65] the court said that administration in bankruptcy would be impossible if the trustee must answer at every step for the exercise of his or her powers and discretions in the management and distribution of the property. The court will intervene only if the insolvency practitioner proposes to act illegally or in breach of his or her duties[66] or wholly unreasonably, or has already done so. In *Re Hans Place Ltd*,[67] the court said that it would not interfere with the exercise of a discretionary power unless the insolvency practitioner has been guilty of fraud or bad faith or his or her decision was perverse. The Court of Appeal in *Re Edennote Ltd*[68] confirmed that, fraud and bad faith apart, the court will only interfere with the act of a liquidator if he or she had done something so utterly unreasonable and absurd that no reasonable person would have done it; Nourse LJ went on to hold that a reasonable liquidator was a properly advised liquidator and that since the liquidator in this case had failed

---

60 Nourse LJ in *Re Edennote Ltd* [1996] 2 BCLC 389 said it was 'neither necessary nor desirable to attempt a classification of those who may be aggrieved', but that it must include the unsecured creditors of an insolvent company.

61 Insolvency Act 1986, ss 168(5), 112(1) (liquidations), 303(1) (bankruptcy). In a liquidation, any creditor or contributory may apply to the court with respect to the exercise or proposed exercise of the liquidator's powers: Insolvency Act 1986, s 167(3).

62 [1994] 3 All ER 200. The meaning of 'dissatisfied' was also considered in *Re Dennis Michael Cook* [1999] BPIR 881. In *Osborn v Cole* [1999] BPIR 251, the court held that the slight change in terminology from 'aggrieved' to 'dissatisfied' made no difference.

63 [2002] EWHC 799 (Ch).

64 [2000] 2 BCLC 536.

65 [1949] 1 All ER 510.

66 In *Re Armstrong Whitworth Securities Co Ltd* [1947] Ch 673, for example, a liquidator had admitted an inflated claim for proof and the court gave directions for the future distribution of the assets so as to correct the error.

67 [1993] BCLC 768. Previous influential cases in this area include *Re Peters ex p Lloyd* (1882) 47 LT 64; *Re a Debtor (No 400 of 1940)* [1949] 1 All ER 510; *Leon v York-o-matic* [1966] 3 All ER 272.

68 [1996] 2 BCLC 389.

to take advice[69] which would have caused him to act differently, his act[70] could be set aside.

It will be seen[71] that creditors or members of the company who are aggrieved by the actions of an administrator may apply to the court under s 27 of the Insolvency Act 1986.[72] Where an administrator or administrative receiver is in breach of duty, the appropriate course of action will be for the company to be put into liquidation and action taken under s 212 of the Insolvency Act 1986.[73] An action may be brought under s 212 against a liquidator, administrator or administrative receiver of a company in liquidation for misapplication of property of the company or breach of fiduciary or other duty in relation to the company. The equivalent section in case of a trustee in bankruptcy is s 304 of the Insolvency Act 1986. In either case, the application may be made by the Official Receiver, Secretary of State or creditor. In the case of a bankruptcy, an application may be brought by the bankrupt himself and, in the case of a liquidation, by a contributory. If the insolvency practitioner has been given his or her release, an application may only be brought with the leave of the court. The court may order the insolvency practitioner to restore or account for the property or to pay a sum by way of compensation.

In addition to the duties laid on the insolvency practitioner by the legislation, the practitioner will also be under common law duties of care and good faith to the company.[74] Liquidators in compulsory[75] windings up, trustees in bankruptcy and administrators are considered to be officers of the court and therefore subject to the rule in *ex p James, Re Condon*[76] that an officer of the court must act honourably and may not, therefore, always be entitled to insist on his or her strict legal rights.

(f) The need for an ombudsman?

The Justice report in 1994 viewed the introduction of qualification requirements for insolvency practitioners as the 'most spectacular' of the achievements of the 1986 legislation. It observed that, although there had been some lapses in the required standards of independence and objectivity, the situation was generally a great improvement on the previous unregulated position. It did however note that it was very difficult to challenge the conduct of an insolvency practitioner. It adverted to the

---

69 Although rather oddly, the court then decided not to uphold Vinelott J's removal of the liquidator on the basis that he had acted honestly and on advice.

70 Of selling a cause of action (see Chapter 32).

71 In Chapter 10.

72 Or the Insolvency Act 1986, Sched B1, para 74, once the Enterprise Act 2002 brings it into force. This will also allow creditors or members to complain that an administrator is not performing his functions as quickly or efficiently as reasonably practicable.

73 See Chapter 31 on the Insolvency Act 1986, s 212. Once the Insolvency Act 1986, Sched B1 is in force, misfeasance proceedings will be able to be brought against a current or former administrator during the currency of the administration.

74 *Pulsford v Devenish* [1903] 2 Ch 625; *Re Home and Colonial Insurance Co Ltd* [1930] 1 Ch 102; *Re Windsor Steam Coal Co (1901) Ltd* [1929] 1 Ch 151; *Re AMF International Ltd (No 2)* [1996] 2 BCLC 9.

75 But not voluntary.

76 (1874) 9 Ch App 609. See Dawson (1996).

Cork Committee proposal, which had not been accepted, that an Insolvency Ombudsman should be appointed and argued[77] that the need for such an appointment had increased. The Insolvency Regulation Working Party gave further consideration to this suggestion, but concluded that it would be unlikely to bring practical benefit. They had found persuasive the arguments of many consultees that it was inappropriate to have an ombudsman scheme in a situation where there was no clear customer or client relationship and where the process could not easily be re-opened once completed. The likelihood was that an ombudsman would be swamped by complaints from those unhappy with the many judgmental decisions which had to be made by insolvency practitioners.

6 STANDARD-SETTING FOR THE INSOLVENCY PROFESSION

(a) Association of Business Recovery Professionals

The Society of Practitioners of Insolvency ('SPI') was established after the reforms introduced by the Insolvency Act 1986 as a representative body for practitioners and has since become a service organisation for the profession in the standard-setting field. This function is performed by its Technical Committee which acts as the draftsmen of general Statements of Insolvency Practice (SIPs) which are then adopted by the professional bodies as standards against which the conduct of members in their activities as insolvency practitioners can be judged. SPI was recently renamed R3, the Association of Business Recovery Professionals, as an indication of its association with the rescue culture.

(b) Joint Insolvency Committee

The Insolvency Regulation Working Party considered whether the existence of a variety of authorising bodies posed problems in that it might give rise to a fragmentation of the insolvency profession, inconsistency in regulatory rules, differences in complaints procedures or an undesirable temptation to authorising bodies to compete for entrants. It discovered a substantial body of opinion which felt that the variety of regulatory bodies reflected the fact that insolvency practice draws its membership from a variety of professional backgrounds. There was also evidence that concentrating regulation in a single body might increase the costs of regulation since these costs were currently lost to an extent amongst the other activities of the bodies. The Working Party did recommend that further initiatives should be taken to encourage joint or co-operative activities in relation to regulation; the result was the establishing of the Joint Insolvency Committee ('JIC') as a major forum for discussion of issues of concern to the profession with representatives from each of the Recognised Professional Bodies and from the Insolvency Service. The Association of Business Recovery Professionals and the Insolvency Service, Northern Ireland have observer status. JIC has assumed responsibility for the work previously undertaken by other joint committees such as the Insolvency Licensing Forum, the Best Practice Liaison Committee and the Joint Ethics Committee. It is particularly concerned with

---

77 Justice, 1994, para 5.19.

professional and ethical standard-setting and with achieving consistency across the profession. JIC met for the first time in December 1999 and during its first year of existence, it revised the procedure for promulgating Standards of Insolvency Practice, commissioned new guidance on the subject of creditors' committees, reviewed insolvency ethical guidance to ensure that all insolvency practitioners work to the same code and worked with insurers to develop cover for the costs of cases transfers and investigations where an insolvency practitioner loses his or her authorisation.

(c) The Insolvency Practices Council

The Insolvency Regulation Working Party observed in its final report[78] that it had been made aware of the unpopular image of insolvency practice which probably reflected the fact that the insolvency processes deal with the apportionment of loss and are therefore likely to provoke discontent. The report considered that professional and ethical standard-setting was the element of regulation which could most practically be influenced by some external input to reflect public interest concerns. On the recommendation of the Working Party, an Insolvency Practices Council was established in 2000[79] with a majority of lay members and a minority of representatives from the insolvency area. The role of this body is to put proposals to the professional bodies about areas of concern and also to consider whether standards, once adopted, were observed and enforced.

The Insolvency Practices Council made three recommendations for change in its first annual report: that debtors considering entering an IVA should be given a written explanation of all the possible options and the relative advantages and disadvantages of each; that the Joint Insolvency Committee should consider setting a standard of best practice to ensure that insolvency practitioners keep debtors and creditors informed of what is happening and that they respond to correspondence in a timely fashion; and that steps should be taken to reduce uncertainty and uneven practice in relation to the equity in family homes. All three of these recommendations have been implemented in one form or another.[80] In the 2001 Annual Report, four further recommendations were made. The first was that any insolvency practitioner whose IVAs show a high rate of failure at an early stage should be the subject of an investigation by his or her authorising body; the Joint Insolvency Committee should also look at the possible conflict of interest where the supervisor of a failed IVA is subsequently appointed as trustee in bankruptcy. The Recognised Professional Bodies have responded that they do not currently have the relevant information to be able to identify those insolvency practitioners with a high rate of failure. The second recommendation was that the monitoring units of all the Recognised Professional Bodies needed to be properly and effectively resourced and that urgent consideration should be given to simplifying and speeding up the regulatory processes; the Insolvency Service should cease to licence insolvency practitioners directly, since this was inconsistent with a role of regulating the regulators. The jointly agreed principles of monitoring explained above address this recommendation. Finally, insolvency practitioners should give a clear indication

---

78 Paragraph 1.8.
79 Harrison (2002).
80 See Insolvency Practices Council Annual Report 2002, available at www.insolvency practices.org.uk.

in writing in advance of the likely costs and charges, especially in relation to IVAs; this has been met to a large extent by Statement of Insolvency Practice 9. In its 2002 Annual Report, the Insolvency Practice Council observed that it continued to think that some reduction in the number of authorising bodies would be desirable, but in the absence of such reduction, greater co-operation and harmonisation between the various RPBs was to be encouraged, particularly in relation to complaints handling. They welcomed the announcement of the setting-up of a joint complaints contact number by the Insolvency Practitioners Association, Institute of Chartered Accountants in England and Wales and Association of Chartered Certified Accountants, together with the Insolvency Service.

7 COST OF THE SYSTEM

(a) Insolvency Service

The issue of the cost of maintaining the public interest aspect of insolvency law has been a central focus throughout the development of modern insolvency law. The bankruptcy reports of the Board of Trade in the latter half of the last century were noticeably concerned to show how economically the insolvency department of the Board operated in its supervision of bankruptcy law, presumably in response to the earlier arguments of the commercial community that official control introduced unnecessary expense; this is mirrored in the concern of contemporary Annual Reports with the unit costs of case administration. The introduction of the Official Receiver in 1883 was not intended to be a burden on the public purse; the cost was to be met by a fee levied on each petition, a small percentage on the assets collected and interest on amounts collected which would be paid into an account at the Bank of England.

The current position is that the Insolvency Service is funded out of general taxation on an annual basis from the moneys voted by Parliament to the DTI. It both incurs expenses and generates income. The income is derived from fees for case administration, costs recovered from disqualified directors and investment income earned from funds held in the Insolvency Services Account. The investment income is paid directly to the Treasury Consolidated Fund and the other income is paid to the DTI. In 2001–02, total expenditure was £81.8 million and total income of £91.7 million was generated, including £39.4 million from investment income. The level of investment income arises because the Insolvency Services Account has not paid a commercial rate of interest to its depositors.

The existence of the Insolvency Services Account is a matter of some controversy. The DTI 2000 Quinquennial Review noted that, as well as the funding aspects, the requirement that insolvency practitioners should pay assets from insolvent estates into the Insolvency Services Account was originally intended to safeguard clients' funds in the aftermath of several 19th century financial scandals and that, with the regulation and bonding of insolvency practitioners, there now seemed no justification for the requirement on regulatory grounds. It has certainly been felt by many for some time that failure to pay a commercial rate of interest deprives creditors of amounts to which they have a legitimate claim. The Cork Committee recommended[81] that the Insolvency Services Account should be abolished and that other methods of funding the Insolvency Service should be found; they suggested that if it was not acceptable for the costs to come out of general taxation, a levy on the registration of new companies could be considered.

The Enterprise Act 2002 will result in considerable change to the financial regime of the Insolvency Service, intended to take place in 2004. There will be a simplification of the fee structure and the Insolvency Service will move to full cost recovery for its chargeable services. This will enable any increased level of fees generated by an increase in the rate of insolvencies to be used in resourcing the administration of those insolvencies. There will be an increase in the rate of interest paid on funds deposited in the Insolvency Services Account with the intention of abolishing the financial support given by creditors to the public interest work carried out by the Insolvency Service and enabling a fairer return to creditors. There will cease to be a transfer of funds from the Insolvency Services Account to the Consolidated Fund. Liquidators in voluntary liquidations will no longer be required to use the Insolvency Services Account.

(b) The Official Receiver's scale

Where the Official Receiver acts as officeholder, fees are currently charged on the Official Receiver's scale prescribed by regs 33–36 of and Sched 2 to the Insolvency Regulations 1994. Where the Official Receiver is liquidator or trustee in bankruptcy the fees will be a percentage of the receipts or realisations plus a percentage of the value of the assets distributed. The percentage is fixed on a sliding scale in each case, the realisation scale being such that the maximum of 20% is chargeable on the first £5,000 and the minimum of 5% is applicable on the excess above £100,000. The distribution scale is half the realisation scale. In cases other than acting as liquidator or trustee in bankruptcy, the Official Receiver's fee is calculated by reference to an hourly rate.

(c) Insolvency practitioners' charges

The fees charged by private sector liquidators, trustees in bankruptcy and administrators are subject to agreement by the creditors (if not in committee, then in general meeting), who also have to right to appeal against the level of the remuneration provided that 25% in value of the creditors join in the appeal.[82] The fees will be fixed either as a percentage of the value of property dealt with or by reference to the time given by the insolvency practitioner and his or her staff in attending to the insolvency. The creditors will decide which of these two methods should be used and, if it is the former, the percentage to be applied.[83] In making this decision, the creditors

---

81 See Chapter 17 of the Cork Report generally.

82 Insolvency Rules 1986, rr 2.47–2.50 (administration), 4.127–4.131 (liquidation), 6.138–6.142 (bankruptcy).

83 The latter is generally preferred by insolvency practitioners. Lightman J (1996) remarked on the need to discount unproductive and valueless expenditure of time. See also *Re Tony Rowse NMC Ltd* [1996] 2 BCLC 225.

should take into account the degree of complexity of the case, the extent to which the practitioner is subject to any exceptional responsibility, the effectiveness with which the duties appear to have been carried out and the value and the nature of the assets with which the practitioner has had to deal.

Throughout the history of insolvency law, there has been concern at the possibility of those involved in administering insolvent estates making an undue profit for themselves at the expense of the creditors. More generally, a recurring theme has been the need to balance the benefits to be derived from the insolvency system with the costs of obtaining them. For instance, the Justice report[84] remarked on the improvements to the system brought about by the licensing of insolvency practitioners, but went on to observe that 'these improvements have, however, been obtained at a price, in the shape of additional costs and expenses which have by and large fallen upon the insolvent estate to the ultimate financial detriment of the general body of creditors.'

The level of insolvency practitioners' charges has been the subject of considerable controversy. There has been adverse comment from a number of quarters both on the level of remuneration charged and on the extent of the expenses incurred by officeholders. The House of Commons Social Security Select Committee inquiry into the Maxwell affair concluded in July 1993 that the accountants and their legal advisers were on the whole too expensive, too slow and too unaccountable. Ferris J commented unfavourably in July 1997[85] on the fact that all but £40,000 of the £1.67 million personal estate of the late Robert Maxwell had been swallowed up in fees; the following day, a judge in Luxembourg reduced by a million pounds the fees of nearly £3 million claimed by the liquidators of BCCI. Lightman J, commenting extra-judicially,[86] referred to the perceived[87] unacceptably high level of costs as being a matter of concern and suggested that the main problem was a lack of monitoring in practice, particularly in relation to receiverships.

In *MGN plc v Maxwell*,[88] Ferris J made a number of general observations about the level of costs incurred by officeholders in managing insolvent estates. He said that there was a perception that insolvency practitioners and their lawyers were subject to little or ineffective control. If this were true, it should be addressed and, if it was not, there was a need for a clear exposition of the controls and procedures. The judge pointed out that officeholders were in a fiduciary position and had an obligation to account for the way in which they exercised their powers and dealt with the property under their control. Officeholders should therefore both consider whether they should incur expenditure out of the insolvent estate and be able to produce evidence that such consideration has taken place. This approach was supported by Lightman J, again speaking extra-judicially,[89] who suggested that the onus should be very much

---

84 Justice, 1994.

85 *MGN plc v Maxwell* (1997) *The Times*, 15 July. Ferris J observed that 'I cannot escape saying that I find [the charges] profoundly shocking ... the receivership will have produced substantial rewards for the receivers and their lawyers and nothing at all for the creditors of the estate'.

86 Lightman (1996). For the other side of the debate, see (1995) 11 IL&P 161. See also (1997) 13 IL&P 141.

87 He observed that he was in no better position than the public to judge whether the costs were in fact excessive or justly earned.

88 (1997) *The Times*, 15 July.

89 At the Institute of Advanced Legal Studies on 11 December 1997.

on officeholders to show that they had considered carefully whether to incur costs, particularly in relation to litigation.[90] Amongst his suggestions were that officeholders should consider mediation as an alternative to litigation, should attempt to sell any causes of action in the insolvent estate rather than pursue the litigation themselves, should limit the risk of costs by entering into contingency agreements so far as possible, should negotiate market rates of payment for advisers, should ensure thorough advice on the percentage chance of success before going ahead with litigation and should attempt to keep the costs of litigation down by co-operation with the other side.

In 1998, Ferris J was asked to chair a working party convened by the Vice Chancellor to consider the determination of the remuneration of officeholders by the court; the court will always be responsible for fixing the remuneration of any receiver appointed by the court and of provisional liquidators and may be asked to fix the remuneration of officeholders in other disputed cases. The Report of the working party[91] made it clear that its recommendations should be seen as having more general application whenever and by whoever remuneration was to be determined and said that it was important that there should be predictability and transparency in the system. The Report recommended that r 4.30 of the Insolvency Rules 1986 on the remuneration of provisional liquidators should be more generally applied; complexity, exceptional responsibility, effectiveness and assets have to be taken into account in addition to the time spent on the work. Where remuneration is based on time spent, officeholders should focus on explaining what has been done as well as why rather than simply listing the number of hours worked. The Report suggested the introduction of an Insolvency Practitioners' Scale, more widely acceptable than the Official Receiver's Scale, which could allow charging on a fixed percentage basis in straightforward cases. The Report also said that there was a need to be able to justify hourly charge rates used by comparison with current market rates. There was a public interest in having the work carried out with care and skill and not necessarily as cheaply as possible. The principles of the Ferris report were applied recently by Ferris J in *Re Independent Insurance Company Ltd*.[92]

Following on from the Ferris Report, a new Statement of Insolvency Practice (SIP 9) was agreed at the end of 2002 by the insolvency profession. This sets out the precise rules which apply in each type of insolvency, provides a set of explanatory notes on remuneration of officeholders for creditors in each type of insolvency and includes a suggested format for the provision of information by insolvency practitioners to creditors. The Insolvency Practices Council has welcomed the new SIP, although it has expressed reservations about whether it sufficiently addresses the issue of value for money.

---

90 See Chapter 32 for more detail on the funding of litigation.
91 Available at www.lcd.gov.uk/civil/ferris.htm.
92 [2003] All ER (D) 219.

CHAPTER 21

INVESTIGATION OF THE INSOLVENT

1 INTRODUCTION

The Cork Committee saw the investigative processes of insolvency law as the means by which the demands of commercial morality could be met. It said:

> Creditors and debtors alike must know that in the event of insolvency proceedings taking place there is a risk that an investigation, fully and competently carried out, will take place with a view to uncovering assets concealed from creditors, to ascertaining the validity of creditors' claims and to exposing the circumstances surrounding the debtor's failure. Anything less would, we believe, be unacceptable in a trading community such as our own and would be bound to lead to a lowering of business standards and an erosion of confidence in our insolvency law.[1]

The current structure of investigation in bankruptcy and compulsory liquidation is based on that introduced by the Bankruptcy Act 1883, which was designed to ensure that an impartial and independent examination should be undertaken into the causes of each bankruptcy as well as into the conduct of each bankrupt. Powers to gather information[2] and obligations to take notice of criminal activity are provided in the case of all collective insolvency regimes, with the exception of individual and company voluntary arrangements, but the extent to which there is an obligation on anyone actively to investigate varies.

The aims of the investigatory provisions are to punish wrongdoing and to deter others from engaging in behaviour prejudicial to creditors as well as to assist in the discovery of the assets. The legislation provides the court with powers to assist the insolvency practitioner in discovering the true state of the insolvent's affairs. There is, however, a balance to be struck between the needs of the investigatory processes and the need to avoid oppressive and unreasonable behaviour on the part of the investigators;[3] this is an issue which has given rise to a considerable amount of case law in recent years, particularly in the light of the provisions of the European Convention on Human Rights.

2 EXTENT OF THE OBLIGATION TO INVESTIGATE

(a) Bankruptcy

The Official Receiver has a duty[4] to investigate the conduct and affairs of every bankrupt and, if she or he thinks fit, to make a report to the court unless he or she thinks an investigation unnecessary.

---

1   At para 238.
2   Given to liquidators, administrators and administrative receivers who are referred to collectively as 'officeholders'.
3   Campbell (2000).
4   Insolvency Act 1986, s 289 as amended by the Enterprise Act 2002, s 258.

(b) Corporate insolvency

There are varying degrees of scrutiny into the conduct of those involved in a company which has become insolvent depending upon the insolvency regime to which it has become subject.

On a compulsory winding up, the Official Receiver has a duty[5] to investigate the causes of failure and the promotion, formation, business, dealings and affairs of the company and to make such report to the court as he thinks fit. Where the liquidator is someone other than the Official Receiver, the liquidator has an obligation to furnish the Official Receiver with such information, assistance and documents as the Official Receiver reasonably requires for the purposes of carrying out the investigation. There is[6] an obligation on the liquidator to notify the Official Receiver where it appears that a criminal offence has been committed by any past or present officer or member of the company. The court may, on the application of a person interested in the winding up or of its own motion, direct the liquidator to refer the matter to the Secretary of State.[7]

In the case of a voluntary liquidation there is no mandatory requirement of investigation. The liquidator will wish to investigate the whereabouts of assets which might be available for the creditors and may ask the court[8] to exercise all or any of the powers which it might exercise in a compulsory winding up, including those which assist with the investigatory process. There is an obligation[9] on the liquidator to notify the Secretary of State[10] where it appears that a criminal offence has been committed by any past or present officer or member of the company. The court may, on the application of any person interested in the winding up or of its own motion, direct the liquidator to make such a report.[11]

The directors of an insolvent company will, therefore, face a lesser degree of investigation if the company decides to go into voluntary liquidation rather then being put into compulsory liquidation by a creditor. Since the introduction of the requirement that a liquidator in a voluntary liquidation be a qualified insolvency practitioner, it is less likely that a court will feel the necessity to make a winding up order for compulsory liquidation in respect of a company already in voluntary liquidation in order to achieve an adequate investigation.

Creditors of companies in administrative receivership will be able to seek a compulsory winding up order where they feel that further investigation and punishment is required. Creditors of a company in administration will, if sufficient of them agree, be able to seek a discharge of the administration order and a winding up order to enable further investigation and punishment.

---

5   Insolvency Act 1986, s 132.
6   Under the Insolvency Act 1986, s 218(3).
7   Insolvency Act 1986, s 218(1) as amended by the Insolvency Act 2000, s 10(2). Notification would be via the Prosecution Unit of the Insolvency Service.
8   Insolvency Act 1986, s 112.
9   Under the Insolvency Act 1986, s 218.
10   Via the Prosecution Unit of the Insolvency Service.
11   Insolvency Act 1986, s 218(6).

Section 7 of the Company Directors Disqualification Act 1986 places an obligation on officeholders in all forms of corporate insolvency to make a report to the Secretary of State where it appears that a disqualification order should be made under s 6 of that Act.[12]

3 OBLIGATION ON THE INSOLVENT TO SUPPLY INFORMATION

(a) Bankruptcy

All bankrupts have an obligation to supply the Official Receiver with information. Those made bankrupt on their own petition will have submitted a statement of affairs[13] with the petition. A person made bankrupt on a creditor's petition is required,[14] unless released from the obligation by the Official Receiver, to provide a statement of affairs within 21 days of the bankruptcy order unless the court or Official Receiver allows longer. In either case, the statement, verified by affidavit, must give details of the assets and liabilities of the bankrupt. The Official Receiver may employ someone at the expense of the estate to assist in the preparing the information.

Bankrupts have a duty[15] to hand over to the Official Receiver all[16] books, papers and other records of which they have possession or control and which relate to their estate and affairs. They also have a duty to give the Official Receiver such information as is reasonably requested.[17] The Official Receiver can require that accounts relating to three years prior to the bankruptcy be submitted and the court can order submission of accounts for earlier years.[18] The court may, on the application of the Official Receiver or the trustee in bankruptcy, order that the bankrupt's mail be re-directed for up to three months.[19] In *Foxley v United Kingdom*,[20] the European Court of Human Rights held that, whilst the interception of correspondence was capable of breaching Art 8 of the European Convention as interference by a public authority with the right to respect for correspondence, an order under s 371 of the Insolvency Act 1986 would not in principle be a breach, since it would be granted in accordance with the law and in furtherance of the protection of the 'rights of others' (the creditors) for the purposes of para 2 of Art 8.[21] Interference with correspondence from the bankrupt's legal advisers would be a breach, since such correspondence was privileged and its interception went beyond what was necessary to trace the assets.

---

12 See Chapter 23.
13 Insolvency Act 1986, s 272 and Insolvency Rules 1986, rr 6.41, 6.68. The statement will contain the particulars required by Form 6.28.
14 Insolvency Act 1986, s 288 and Insolvency Rules 1986, rr 6.58–6.63.
15 Insolvency Act 1986, s 291.
16 Including any which would be privileged from disclosure in any proceedings.
17 Insolvency Act 1986, s 291(4). In *Official Receiver v Cummings-John* [2000] BPIR 320, the bankrupt was imprisoned for 20 months for, amongst other things, breach of s 291.
18 Insolvency Rules 1986, rr 6.64–6.65, 6.69–6.71.
19 Insolvency Act 1986, s 371.
20 (Application No 33274/96) (2000) *The Times*, 4 July.
21 On the facts of this case, there had been a breach since the interception had continued after the expiry of the order.

In addition to the provision of documentary information, the bankrupt may have to answer questions in person. The bankrupt may be required to attend on the Official Receiver at such times as the Official Receiver may reasonably require in order to assist with the provision of information.[22]

Section 333 of the Insolvency Act 1986 also provides that bankrupts shall give to the trustee such information as to their affairs, attend on the trustee at such times and do all such other things as the trustee may reasonably require. In *Morris v Murjani*,[23] the Court of Appeal held that the provision gave the court jurisdiction to issue an injunction preventing the bankrupt from leaving the country since any departure might deprive the trustee of information to which he or she was entitled. The trustee in bankruptcy, where not the Official Receiver, has an obligation[24] to furnish the Official Receiver with such information, assistance and documents as the Official Receiver may reasonably require.

(b) Corporate insolvency

Where the court has made a winding up order or appointed a provisional liquidator, the Official Receiver may require some or all of the persons specified to provide him or her with a statement in the prescribed form as to the affairs of the company.[25] This must be done within 21 days unless the Official Receiver extends the time available. Those who may be asked to submit the statement are those who are or have been officers of the company (or were officers or employees of a company which was an officer of the insolvent company in the year before liquidation); those who have taken part in the formation of the company during the year before the liquidation; and those who are in the company's employment, or have been within the year before the liquidation, and whom the Official Receiver thinks can give the information required. If any of these people fail without reasonable excuse to comply with the request, they will be liable to a fine and, for continued contravention, a daily default fine.

In the case of a voluntary liquidation, a statement of affairs will have to be presented to the creditors[26] as part of the process of going into liquidation.

Where an administration order has been made, the administrator is under an obligation[27] to require a statement of affairs in the manner which would be required if the company had gone into compulsory liquidation.[28] There is a similar obligation placed on an administrative receiver.[29]

---

22   Insolvency Act 1986, s 291(4).
23   [1996] BCC 278
24   Insolvency Act 1986, s 305.
25   Insolvency Act 1986, s 131 and Insolvency Rules 1986, rr 4.32–4.38 deal generally with the statement of affairs. Insolvency Act 1986, s 131(2) sets out the required contents.
26   Insolvency Act 1986, s 99.
27   Insolvency Act 1986, s 22; Insolvency Rules 1986, rr 2.11–2.16; Insolvency Act 1986, Sched B1, para 47.
28   See above.
29   Insolvency Act 1986, s 47; Insolvency Rules 1986, rr 3.3–3.7.

4   COURT ASSISTANCE IN INVESTIGATION

(a) Bankruptcy

Section 366 of the Insolvency Act 1986 gives the court various powers with which to support the investigation of the bankrupt. The court may on application by the Official Receiver or the trustee in bankruptcy summon before it the bankrupt, the bankrupt's spouse and anyone else thought to be in possession of property comprised in the bankrupt's estate or to be indebted to the bankrupt or otherwise able to give information. Anyone who fails to appear without reasonable excuse or who appears likely to abscond to avoid appearing may be arrested in order that he or she may be brought before the court. These are essentially private proceedings and the court may exclude others from the hearing; those summoned to appear may be examined on oath about the bankrupt and his or her dealings, affairs and property.[30]

Section 366 of the Insolvency Act 1986 also gives the court the power to request those whom it can summon before it[31] to provide evidence on affidavit. They may also be asked to produce any documents[32] in their possession or control which relate to the bankrupt or his or her dealings, affairs or property and, if they fail to do so, the court may issue a warrant authorising seizure of the documents. Inland Revenue officials may also be requested[33] by the court to produce documents submitted by the bankrupt, assessments made by the Inland Revenue in relation to the bankrupt and any correspondence between the Inland Revenue and the bankrupt.

(b) Corporate insolvency[34]

Section 234[35] of the Insolvency Act 1986 allows the court to require anyone with possession of or control over tangible[36] property, books, papers or records to which the company appears to be entitled to hand them over to the officeholder. The section can be used to determine ownership disputes,[37] but cannot form the basis of a claim for damages in conversion.[38]

Section 235 of the Insolvency Act 1986 imposes an obligation on specified persons to give to the officeholder such information as may reasonably be required and to attend for interview at such times as may reasonably be required. The specified persons are those who are or have been officers of the company; those who have taken part in the formation of the company at any time within a year before the insolvency; those who are employed by the company, or were employed in the year before the

---

30   Insolvency Act 1986, s 367(4).
31   Other than the bankrupt and bankrupt's spouse or former spouse, who need not be included in the section since the Official Receiver already has adequate powers to obtain information and documents from them.
32   In *Re Ouvaroff (a Bankrupt)* [1997] BPIR 712, the court held that the powers of a trustee in bankruptcy under s 366 did not override the right of a third party to assert legal professional privilege as a ground for refusing to deliver up documents.
33   Insolvency Act 1986, s 369.
34   See Marshall (1997).
35   Pearson (2002).
36   See *Welsh Development Agency v Export Finance* [1992] BCC 270.
37   *Re London Iron & Steel* [1990] BCLC 372.
38   *Smith (Administrator of Cosslet (Contractors) Ltd) v Bridgend CBC* [2002] 1 AC 336.

insolvency, and whom the officeholder thinks capable of giving information; those who are, or were within the year before the insolvency, officers or employees of another company which is, or was within that year, an officer of the insolvent company; and, in the case of a company being wound up by the court, anyone who has acted as administrator, administrative receiver or liquidator of the company.

Section 235 of the Insolvency Act 1986 enables information to be obtained on a quick and informal basis which nonetheless overrides any duty of confidentiality. The officeholder will often proceed on the basis that any information obtained will only be used for the purpose of administration of the insolvency.[39] Failure to comply with s 235 without reasonable excuse is a criminal offence leading to a fine and, for continued contravention, to a daily default fine.[40] The officeholder may enforce the obligations contained in s 235 by application to the court.[41] The Court of Appeal has held[42] that such an application would entitle the officeholder to seek interim relief such as an Anton Piller or freezing injunction. Alternatively, failure to comply with obligations under s 235 of the Insolvency Act 1986 may lead to a successful application under s 236 of the Insolvency Act 1986 for a formal examination.

Under s 236 of the Insolvency Act 1986, the court may, on the application of the officeholder,[43] summon specified persons before it to be examined on oath or order them to submit an affidavit to the court, in either case as to their dealings with the company. They may also be required to produce any books, papers or other records in their possession or under their control relating to the company and its affairs. Those who are subject to this section[44] are the officers of the company, those known or suspected to have in their possession any property of the company or supposed to be indebted to the company and those whom the court thinks capable of giving information concerning the promotion, formation, business, dealings, affairs or property of the company.[45] The court may order the arrest of those who fail to appear without reasonable excuse or appear likely to abscond. The court may also order the seizure of books, papers, records, money or goods in their possession. An examination under s 236 of the Insolvency Act 1986 takes place before a registrar or judge and both the officeholder and the respondent are entitled to be represented. The procedure can be lengthy and expensive. Examinees are entitled to be given advance notice of the topics of questioning.[46] Evidence obtained under this procedure is not available to anyone other than the officeholder or other persons who could have applied for an order under s 236.[47]

39　See Marshall (1997).
40　Insolvency Act 1986, s 235(5).
41　See Insolvency Rules 1986, r 7.20; *Re Wallace Smith Trust Company Ltd* [1992] BCC 707.
42　*Morris v Murjani* [1996] 1 WLR 848.
43　Not of a creditor: *Re James McHale Automobiles Ltd* [1997] 1 BCLC 273.
44　A wider category of people than those subject to the obligations contained in s 235.
45　Including inspectors appointed by the Secretary of State to investigate the company: *Soden v Burns* [1996] 3 All ER 967, in which it was held that s 236 binds the Crown.
46　*Re Norton Warburg Holdings* (1983) 1 BCC 98,907.
47　Insolvency Rules 1986, r 9.5(4) and see section 3 of this chapter. In *Re Mid East Trading* [1997] 3 All ER 481, Evans-Lombe J observed that the results of the inquiry are confidential to the court and may not be used outside the winding up proceedings without the court's leave.

The House of Lords in *Re British & Commonwealth (Nos 1 and 2)*[48] described the s 236 procedure as 'an extraordinary and secret mode of obtaining information necessary for the proper conduct of the winding up' and held that, in deciding whether or not to make an order, the court had to balance the reasonable requirements of the officeholder in the carrying out of his or her functions with the need to avoid making an order which worked wholly unreasonably, unnecessarily or oppressively on the person concerned. It was not necessarily unreasonable to make the order simply because it was inconvenient to the addressee of the application or caused him or her a lot of work or might make him or her vulnerable to future claims or was addressed to a person who was not an officer or an employee or contractor of the company which was in insolvency.[49]

Applications under s 236 have to pass through two stages.[50] In the first stage, the officeholders have to satisfy the court that they reasonably require the information for the purpose of carrying out their task and must raise a *prima facie* case that the respondent is able to provide the information. Secondly, the court has to balance the requirements of the officeholder against the burden that the inquiry will impose on the respondent. The discretion of the court is unfettered, but it is possible to discern some general principles from the case law. It will be harder to obtain an order against a third party than against an officer or former officer of the company.[51] The production of documents is more likely to be ordered than an oral examination.[52] The question of whether the respondent has been charged with a criminal offence or whether or not the officeholder has reached a firm decision to sue the examinee are merely factors to be taken into account;[53] the courts have generally not permitted the use of s 236 once litigation has been commenced by the officeholder,[54] but in *Re RBG Resources Ltd, Shierson v Rastogi*,[55] the Court of Appeal recently did give such permission. This was a case in which there was evidence that there had been a 'shredding' operation immediately prior to the liquidation so that there was an absence of documentary and computer material which would normally have been expected to be available to the liquidators. This, together with the fact that the proposed examinees were officers of the company rather than third parties, outweighed the fact that litigation was already in progress. In *Re Arrows Ltd (No 2)*,[56] Vinelott J allowed a s 236 examination to go ahead in circumstances in which a criminal charge had actually been preferred, but where the criminal proceedings lay sufficiently far in the future for the examination not to be oppressive.

---

48 [1993] AC 426.

49 Lightman J in *Re Galileo Group Ltd* (1997) *The Times*, 10 December refused to make an order for disclosure in circumstances where he held that the liquidator had an insufficient need for the document in question to counterbalance the difficulty and potential oppression which would be involved in complying with the order.

50 *Re Mid East Trading* [1997] 3 All ER 481, upheld by the Court of Appeal at [1998] 1 BCLC 240.

51 See *Re PFTZM Ltd* [1995] BCC 280.

52 See *Re Westmead Consultants* [2002] 1 BCLC 384.

53 *Cloverbay Ltd v BCCI* [1990] Ch 90.

54 See discussion in *Re Bishopsgate Investment Management (No 2)* [1994] BCC 732; *Re Atlantic Computers plc* [1998] BCC 200. See *England v Smith* [2000] 2 BCLC 21 for a survey of the differences between English and Australian practice.

55 [2002] EWCA Civ 1624.

56 [1992] BCLC 1176.

5 PUBLIC EXAMINATION

(a) Bankruptcy

The public examination under s 290 of the Insolvency Act 1986 is a more draconian exercise than a court hearing under s 366. Public examination was first introduced by s 19 of the Bankruptcy Act 1869, which provided: 'the bankrupt ... shall produce a statement of his affairs to the first meeting of creditors and shall be publicly examined thereon on a day to be named by the court, and subject to such adjourned public examination as the court may direct.' This was re-enacted in the 1883 Act and carried into the 1914 Act with amendments which made it clear that the bankrupt could be examined as to 'his conduct, dealings and property'. A bankrupt was, until 1976, compelled to undergo a public examination into the circumstances surrounding the bankruptcy before he or she could be discharged; the requirement of public examination was probably one factor leading to a large number of bankrupts never seeking their discharge. The public examination is no longer compulsory and now requires an order of the court. Application for such an examination must come from the Official Receiver, but if half in value of the creditors request it, an application must be made. Robert Walker LJ in *Arora v Brewster & Johnson*[57] observed that such an examination is most commonly ordered when a bankrupt has declined to co-operate with the insolvency authorities.

Questions may be asked by the Official Receiver, the trustee in bankruptcy and creditors who have tendered proof of debts. The bankrupt must answer on oath all questions which the court allows to be put and may not refuse to answer questions on the grounds of self-incrimination, but if criminal proceedings have been commenced and the court thinks the examination may prejudice a fair trial, the examination may be adjourned. A written record of evidence may be used as evidence against the bankrupt in any proceedings.

The Cork Report considered[58] that a public examination was intended to serve three principal purposes. First, it would form the basis of reports which the Official Receiver might have to submit to the Department of Trade and Industry concerning the affairs of the bankrupt. Secondly, it would provide an opportunity to obtain material information for the administration of the estate which could not as well be obtained privately. Thirdly, it would give publicity, for the information of creditors and the community at large, to the salient facts and unusual features connected with the failure.

Failure by the bankrupt without reasonable excuse to comply with any of the obligations outlined above will amount to contempt of court and the bankrupt will be liable to be punished accordingly.[59]

---

57 (2000) unreported, 31 March.
58 At para 655.
59 In *Official Receiver v Cummings-John* [2000] BPIR 320, a bankrupt was imprisoned for 20 months.

(b) Public examination in the case of a liquidation

Where a company is in compulsory liquidation, the Official Receiver may at any time before the dissolution of the company apply to the court under s 133 of the Insolvency Act 1986 for a public examination.[60] The court may also order a public examination in a voluntary winding up by virtue of s 112 of the Insolvency Act 1986. There is no longer any need for the Official Receiver to allege fraud to justify the holding of a public examination.[61] The Official Receiver must make such a request, unless the court orders otherwise, where one-half in value of the company's creditors or three-quarters in value of the company's contributories so request. In *Re Casterbridge Properties, Jeeves v Official Receiver,*[62] Burton J held that the court would have a discretion on an application under r 7.47 of the Insolvency Rules 1986 to refuse a public examination, even where requested by the Official Receiver, but because the order would normally be mandatory, the onus of persuading the court to discharge it would rest on the applicant.

Those liable to public examination are those who are or have been officers of the company or have acted as liquidator, administrator, receiver or manager in relation to it or have otherwise been concerned, or taken part, in the promotion, formation or management of the company. They may be questioned on oath by the Official Receiver, liquidator, creditors and contributories as to the promotion, formation or management of the company or as to the conduct of its business and affairs or their conduct or dealings in relation to the company. The examinee must answer any question which the court allows to be put to him or her.[63] The court might refuse to allow questions to be asked if these were oppressive in terms of the time and effort involved or where the answers might prejudice the position of the examinee in other proceedings.[64] The court may order the arrest of anyone who fails to attend a public examination or looks likely to abscond in order to avoid it and may also order the seizure of books, papers, records, money or goods in that person's possession.[65]

---

60 Insolvency Rules 1986, rr 4.211–4.217 relate to public examination of company officers and others.

61 The position in relation to bankruptcies and liquidations is now the same in that public examination is not compulsory for either and can be requested in the same circumstances for both.

62 (2001) unreported, 21 November. Burton J held that the Insolvency Act 1986, s 133 has full extra-territorial effect.

63 *Bishopsgate Investment Management Ltd v Maxwell* [1992] 2 All ER 856 at 869–70.

64 *Richbell Strategic Holdings* [2000] 2 BCLC 794.

65 Insolvency Act 1986, s 133.

6   THE RIGHT TO SILENCE?[66]

One of the basic freedoms secured by English law, and now reinforced by the Human Rights Act 1998,[67] is that no one can be forced to answer questions or produce documents which may incriminate him or her in subsequent criminal proceedings. Lord Browne-Wilkinson explained in *Re Arrows (No 4)*[68] that the principle has evolved from the abhorrence felt for the procedures of the Star Chamber, under which the prisoner was forced, by the use of torture, to answer self-incriminating questions on the basis of which he or she was subsequently convicted. Balancing this freedom with the need in civil proceedings to discover what has happened to property obtained by fraud has proved problematic.

After considerable debate,[69] it is now settled that those subject to private or public examination may not invoke the privilege against self-incrimination as a ground for refusing to answer questions allowed by the court. The entire purpose of an examination under s 236 or 366 of the Insolvency Act 1986 would be likely to be frustrated if witnesses were able to rely on the privilege against self-incrimination, since the examination frequently happens because there is suspicion of fraud. It had been thought that a person examined under these provisions could refuse to answer self-incriminatory questions, but in *Re Bishopsgate Investment Management Ltd*,[70] the Court of Appeal held that the statutory provisions of the Insolvency Act impliedly overrode the privilege against self-incrimination.[71]

Section 433 makes statements made to an officeholder admissible against the examinee in subsequent proceedings. In order to ensure compliance with Art 6 of the European Convention on Human Rights, there are, however, now statutory restrictions[72] on the extent to which evidence obtained from a person under compulsion can be used in criminal proceedings in which that person is charged with an offence. No evidence relating to the answer may be adduced and no question relating to it may be asked by the prosecution unless evidence relating to it is adduced, or a question relating to it is asked, in the proceedings by or on behalf of that person. There is a distinction between an accused person's right to remain silent in order not to incriminate him or herself and the use of compulsory powers to locate pre-existing documents. The Court of Appeal (Criminal Division) held in *Attorney*

---

66   See Mitchell and Stockdale (2002) and, generally in relation to the impact of the Human Rights Act 1998 on insolvency law, Trower (2001).

67   Article 6 of the European Convention on Human Rights provides for the right to a fair trial. It has long been held that this includes the privilege against self-incrimination. See, for example, *Saunders v United Kingdom* (1997) 23 EHRR 313, in which the European Court of Human Rights held that the Convention was breached by the use in a trial for theft and false accounting by the prosecution of statements given by the defendant under legal compulsion to inspectors appointed under the companies legislation.

68   [1995] 2 AC 75.

69   Fletcher (1992) and (1994); McCormack (1993); Paulden (1994).

70   [1993] Ch 1.

71   The same position was reached in relation to inspections under the Companies Act 1985, s 432 by *Re London United Investments plc* [1992] BCC 202.

72   Insolvency Act 1986, s 433(2) (inserted by the Youth Justice and Criminal Evidence Act 1999) in relation to statements obtained by use of the coercive powers in the Insolvency Act 1986. Insolvency Act 1986, s 219(2A) (inserted by Insolvency Act 2000) in relation to evidence obtained under s 218(5) by use of the Companies Act 1985, s 431 or 432.

General's Reference (No 7 of 2000)[73] that the use in the prosecution of a bankrupt of documentary material obtained by the Official Receiver under compulsion pursuant to s 291(1) of the 1986 Act, but independently of the making of any statement by him or her did not violate his or her rights under Art 6 of the European Convention on Human Rights. The documents were admissible as a matter of English law subject to the trial judge's discretion to exclude them on grounds of fairness under s 78 of the Police and Criminal Evidence Act 1984. Prosecution for failure to comply with obligations imposed by the Insolvency Act to give information would not fall foul of the privilege against self-incrimination; in *R v Kearns*,[74] the Court of Appeal (Criminal Division) dismissed such an argument in relation to the prosecution of a bankrupt for failing to comply with the obligation imposed by s 354(3) of the Insolvency Act 1986 to account for loss of property in the year prior to the bankruptcy. The court held that the implied rights in Art 6 to remain silent and not to incriminate oneself were not rights of an absolute character, but could be qualified or restricted if there was proper justification and if the restriction was proportionate; that the public interest that the affairs of bankrupts should be investigated was ample justification for the limited restriction imposed by s 354(3)(a), the regime of which was a proportionate legislative response to the problem of administering and investigating bankrupt estates; and that, accordingly, the judge was right to conclude that s 354(3)(a) was compatible with Art 6.

The position in relation to civil proceedings[75] is different, since a party defending civil proceedings does not have a right of silence or a right not to incriminate himself or herself, but must give discovery of all relevant non-privileged documents, including documents of a confidential nature which may be seriously prejudicial to his or her case and which may result in its being decided against him or her. Nonetheless, there is still a right to a 'fair hearing' within Art 6(1) of the European Convention on Human Rights and it would be open to the court at the hearing to exclude the evidence if it thought it appropriate to do so.[76]

---

73 [2001] 1 WLR 1879. Barsby and Ormerod (2001).
74 [2002] 1 WLR 2815.
75 Including proceedings under the Company Directors Disqualification Act 1986: *Official Receiver v Stern* [2001] 1 All ER 633.
76 *Official Receiver v Stern* [2001] 1 All ER 633.

CHAPTER 22

SANCTIONS IN BANKRUPTCY

1 INTRODUCTION

As explained in Chapter 19, there has been a long-standing tension between the view that falling into a state of insolvency is necessarily culpable and the opposing view that the debtor has sometimes merely been unfortunate. Over time, the latter view has come to prevail but, as Cork recognised, there is still a requirement that the system should not favour the debtor to such an extent that there is no incentive for debtors to meet their obligations. In 1994, the Justice report suggested[1] that the combination of automatic discharge from bankruptcy and the infrequency with which income payments orders[2] are sought amounted to a relaxed regime which 'can only encourage debtors who started out as essentially honest people to repeat the process'. In April 2000, the Insolvency Service published a consultation paper (*Bankruptcy – A Fresh Start*) which proposed that there should be a distinction made between bankrupts on the basis of their culpability with a liberalisation of the approach taken towards non-culpable bankrupts and the introduction of a new restriction order to protect the public against dishonest and irresponsible debtors.

The 2001 White Paper, *Productivity and Enterprise – Insolvency: A Second Chance*, observed that responses to the consultation showed broad support for this provided that the reasons for a bankrupt's failures were tested with appropriate rigour. It pointed out, in support of the proposal for the introduction of restriction orders, that criminal sanctions were only being employed in about 3% of bankruptcy cases and that it would frequently be the case that the Official Receiver's enquiries would bring to light evidence of unacceptable behaviour which nonetheless fell short of the high evidential requirements of criminal proceedings. The White Paper did note the need to keep under review the machinery for dealing with individual indebtedness in the light of the increasing percentage of consumer bankruptcies over recent years; during the parliamentary debates on the Enterprise Bill, the issues of the increase in consumer bankruptcies in the United States following the relaxation of the bankruptcy laws there in the late 1970s was raised on several occasions. The Enterprise Act 2002 will implement the proposals of the White Paper for the reduction in the stigma of bankruptcy in most cases coupled with the introduction of the Bankruptcy Restriction Order which will have the effect of continuing bankruptcy restrictions for the financially irresponsible or downright dishonest bankrupts described in *Bankruptcy – A Fresh Start*[3] as 'in financial terms, the equivalent of dangerous drivers – in other words a menace to any credit-based economy'. It is expected that the personal insolvency provisions of the Enterprise Act 2002 will be implemented early in the 2004 financial year.

---

1 Justice, 1994, para 4.30.
2 See Chapter 27 for income payment orders.
3 At para 7.14.

This chapter considers first the personal disabilities automatically imposed on all bankrupts and then moves on to consider the potential criminal liability faced by a bankrupt and the new Bankruptcy Restriction Order.

2 PERSONAL DISABILITIES IMPOSED ON A BANKRUPT

An undischarged bankrupt is subject to a number of personal disabilities. Under s 11 of the Company Directors Disqualification Act 1986, it is an offence for an undischarged bankrupt to act as a director of, or directly or indirectly to take part in or be concerned in the promotion, formation or management of, a company without the leave of the court by which the bankruptcy order was made. The Official Receiver must be given notice of any intention to apply for such leave and will oppose it where he or she considers that it is contrary to the public interest.

A bankrupt is also barred from a number of public offices; in particular, s 427 of the Insolvency Act 1986 prevents an undischarged bankrupt from taking part in parliamentary proceedings or from being elected as an MP. An undischarged bankrupt cannot be a member of a local authority.[4] A number of other occupations are barred to undischarged bankrupts;[5] for example, it is not possible for an undischarged bankrupt to practice as a solicitor.[6] The Enterprise Act 2002 will repeal the provision which prevented a bankrupt from being a Justice of the Peace and has given[7] the power to the Secretary of State to repeal, revoke or amend by statutory instrument provisions disqualifying a bankrupt from acquiring a particular office or position or becoming or remaining a member of a body or a group. The White Paper observed[8] that this would provide an opportunity to review the relevance of apparently unnecessary or outdated restrictions. Section 268 of the Enterprise Act 2002 is drafted so as to allow for the possibility of restrictions being revoked on a selective basis depending on the culpability of the bankrupt.

The undischarged bankrupt will find it difficult to obtain credit.[9] Under s 360 of the Insolvency Act 1986, bankrupts will be guilty of an offence if they obtain credit of £250 or more without informing the creditor of their status as an undischarged bankrupt. Obtaining credit includes taking possession of goods under a hire-purchase or conditional sale agreement and being paid in advance for the supply of goods or services. It is also an offence for bankrupts to engage directly or indirectly in a business under a name other than that in which they were adjudged bankrupt without disclosing to all those with whom they enter into any business transaction the name in which they were made bankrupt.

---

4   Local Government Act 1972, s 80.
5   See the list set out in Annex B to *Bankruptcy – A Fresh Start*.
6   Solicitors Act 1974.
7   By the Enterprise Act 2002, s 268.
8   Paragraph 1.24.
9   Even after discharge his creditworthiness will not recover easily.

3 BANKRUPTCY OFFENCES

(a) General

Someone who is made bankrupt becomes vulnerable to the criminal offences set out in ss 350–62 of the Insolvency Act 1986. The offences are applicable even where the bankruptcy order has been annulled, but no proceedings will be instituted after an annulment.[10] Conduct by the bankrupt after discharge will not lead to liability under these provisions.[11] The offences are all subject to the defence of innocent intention.[12] The effect of R v Carass[13] is that if the bankrupt adduces evidence that he or she had no intent to defraud or conceal the state of his or her affairs, this will operate as a defence unless the prosecution can prove beyond reasonable doubt that there was no such intention. It is not a defence that anything relied on by the prosecution as constituting criminal activity took place abroad.[14] An undischarged bankrupt will also commit a criminal offence[15] by acting in the management of a company.

The existence of the offences will only assist in the maintenance of public confidence if they are perceived as material deterrents to malpractice. The Cork Committee observed[16] that 'we cannot stress too strongly our view that bankruptcy offences are serious matters, and need to be prosecuted more frequently, and with greater vigour, than is the case at present'. The 2001 White Paper observed that in the five years to 31 March 2001, there were a total of over 100,000 bankruptcies and that prosecution (or a warning letter) had followed in about 3% of these cases.

(b) Non-disclosure

Bankrupts will be guilty of an offence under s 353 of the Insolvency Act 1986 if they do not to the best of their knowledge and belief disclose all the property comprised in their estates[17] to the Official Receiver or the trustee or do not inform the Official Receiver or the trustee of any disposal of any property (other than a disposal in the ordinary course of business or by way of payment of the ordinary expenses of the bankrupt or his family) which would otherwise have fallen into the estate. There were 37 convictions under s 353 in 2000.

(c) Concealment of property

Under s 354 of the Insolvency Act 1986, bankrupts are guilty of an offence if they do not deliver up any property in their possession which the law requires them to deliver up to the Official Receiver or trustee. It is also an offence to conceal any debt due to or

---

10 Insolvency Act 1986, s 350(2).
11 Insolvency Act 1986, s 350(3).
12 Insolvency Act 1986, s 352.
13 [2002] 1 WLR 1714. The Court of Appeal (Criminal Division) reluctantly held in R v Daniel [2002] EWCA Crim 959 that they were bound by Carass and that it was impossible to distinguish the cases.
14 Insolvency Act 1986, s 350(4).
15 Under the Company Directors Disqualification Act 1986, s 11.
16 At para 1901.
17 As defined in the Insolvency Act 1986, s 351(a).

from them or to conceal property exceeding £500 in value which they are required to deliver up to the Official Receiver or trustee; conduct in the period of 12 months before the presentation of the petition and between the petition and order can also form the basis of this offence. Bankrupts will also be guilty of an offence if they remove, or removed between petition and order, property exceeding £500 which should have been handed over to the Official Receiver or trustee. The final offence under this section is that of failing, without reasonable excuse, to account for or explain when so required by the Official Receiver or the court the loss of any substantial part of their property in the 12 months before the presentation of the petition or between the petition and the order.[18] There were 53 convictions under s 354 of the Insolvency Act 1986 in 2000.

(d) Concealment or falsification of books and papers

Section 355 of the Insolvency Act 1986 provides that bankrupts will be guilty of an offence if they do not deliver up possession to the Official Receiver or the trustee all books, papers and other records of which they have possession or control and which relate to their estate or their affairs. It will also be an offence to prevent the production of such documents once a petition for bankruptcy has been presented. It will be an offence where, at any time after the 12 months before the petition, the bankrupt has concealed, disposed of, destroyed, altered, mutilated or falsified such documents (or has permitted such conduct) or has made, caused or permitted the making of any false entries in such documents. There were three convictions under this provision in 2000.

(e) False statements

The bankrupt will be guilty of any offence under s 356 of the Insolvency Act 1986 if he or she makes or has made any material omission in any statement made under the bankruptcy provisions of the Insolvency Act 1986 relating to his or her affairs. It will also be an offence for a bankrupt to fail to inform the trustee that he or she thinks a false debt has been proved in the bankruptcy or to attempt to account for any part of his or her property by fictitious losses or expenses. Section 356 of the Insolvency Act 1986 also provides that it will be an offence to attempt to account for property by fictitious losses or expenses at a meeting of the creditors from the 12 months before the petition or, at any time, to have been guilty of fraud in an attempt to obtain the consent of creditors to an agreement with reference to his or her affairs. There were 25 convictions under this provision in 2000.

(f) Fraudulent disposal of property

A bankrupt is guilty of an offence under s 357 of the Insolvency Act 1986 if he or she causes to be made any gift or transfer of, or charge over his or her property in the five years leading up to the bankruptcy. It is also an offence for the bankrupt to conceal or remove any part of his or her property after, or within two months before, the date on which a judgment or order for the payment of money has been obtained against him

---

18 Prosecution for failure to comply with this obligation to give information would not fall foul of the privilege against self-incrimination: *R v Kearns* [2002] 1 WLR 2815.

or her, being a judgment or order not satisfied before the commencement of the bankruptcy. There were 32 convictions under this provision in 2000. In *R v Mungro*,[19] a custodial sentence was imposed on a bankrupt of previously unblemished character who had failed to declare the receipt of a sum of money. Ognall J said that the conduct of those who sought to obtain their discharge and at the same time concealed assets attacked the whole basis on which the bankruptcy legislation was founded.

(g) Absconding

Absconding or preparing to abscond from England and Wales at any time after the date six months before presentation of the petition for bankruptcy with property to the value of more than £500 which the bankrupt is required to deliver up is an offence under s 358 of the Insolvency Act 1986. There were no convictions under this section in 2000 (the previous edition of this book noted that there was one conviction under this section in 1996).

(h) Fraudulent dealing with property obtained on credit

Disposing of (including pawning) property otherwise than in the ordinary course of business which was acquired on credit and has not yet been paid for will be an offence from a year prior to the petition under s 359 of the Insolvency Act 1986. This offence is also committed by anyone who acquires, other than in the ordinary course of the business of the bankrupt, property from the bankrupt knowing or believing that the bankrupt owed money in respect of the property which he or she did not intend, or was unlikely to be able, to pay. In determining for this section whether a transaction is in the ordinary course of the business of the bankrupt, it will be relevant to consider the price paid to the bankrupt for the property. There were three convictions under this section in 2000.

(i) Obtaining credit or engaging in business

Bankrupts are guilty of an offence under s 360 of the Insolvency Act 1986 if, either alone or jointly with any other person, they obtain credit of more than £250 without telling the creditor that they are an undischarged bankrupt. Obtaining credit involves the receipt of goods under a hire-purchase or conditional sale agreement and the payment in advance for goods or services to be provided by the bankrupt. The offence is absolute and does not depend on proof of dishonesty.[20] It is also an offence under this section for bankrupts to engage directly or indirectly in a business under a name other than that in which they were adjudged bankrupt without disclosing to everyone with whom they enter into any transaction the name under which they were made bankrupt. There were 143 convictions under this provision in 2000.

The Enterprise Act 2002[21] will repeal the previous offences of failure to keep proper accounts of business[22] and materially contributing to or increasing the extent

---

19   (1997) *The Times*, 3 July.

20   *R v Ramzan* [1998] 2 Cr App R 328.

21   Enterprise Act 2002, s 263.

22   Insolvency Act 1986, s 361. There were 52 convictions under this section in 2000.

of the insolvency by gambling or rash and hazardous speculations during the two years prior to the presentation of the petition.[23] These are matters which will now be relevant in considering whether a Bankruptcy Restriction Order should be imposed on the bankrupt.

4   BANKRUPTCY RESTRICTION ORDERS

The effect of s 257 of and Sched 20 to the Enterprise Act 2002 is to insert s 281A into the Insolvency Act 1986. Section 281A provides that 'Schedule 4A to this Act (bankruptcy restrictions order and bankruptcy restrictions undertaking) shall have effect'.

This procedure is intended to be broadly analogous to that operated under the Company Directors Disqualification Act 1986. An application for a Bankruptcy Restriction Order ('BRO') will be made where it appears expedient to the Secretary of State in the public interest, on the basis of a report by the Official Receiver, that such an order should be made. The application will be made, in practice by the Official Receiver, in the bankruptcy proceedings and must be made within a year of the commencement of the bankruptcy. The court may make an interim order if it thinks that there are *prima facie* grounds to suggest that the application will be successful and that it is in the public interest to do so.

The court will be required to make a BRO of between two and 15 years where it is satisfied that, having regard to the conduct of the bankrupt both before or during his bankruptcy, the public requires protection. The court will have regard to a statutory but non-exhaustive schedule of unfitted conduct set out in Sched 4A, para 2(2); this list includes references to failing to keep or produce records, entering into transactions of a type liable to be set aside by a trustee in bankruptcy, trading or incurring debts at a time when he or she knew or should have known of the unlikelihood of being able to pay, fraud, failure to co-operate, materially contributing to the bankruptcy by gambling, speculation or unreasonable extravagance or neglecting business affairs.

The consequences of a BRO will be that bankrupts cannot without the leave of the court be involved in the management of a limited company,[24] cannot obtain credit of more than £500 without disclosing that they are subject to a BRO and, if they trade in a name other than that in which they were made bankrupt, they must disclose that earlier name.[25]

Breach of the terms of an order will be a criminal offence punishable by a fine and/or imprisonment.

It will be possible for applications for a BRO to be settled by the bankrupt giving an undertaking to the Secretary of State which will have the same legal effect as a BRO. A public register of BROs and undertakings will be maintained.

---

23   Insolvency Act 1986, s 362. There were 15 convictions under this section in 2000.
24   Company Directors Disqualification Act 1986, s 11(1) as amended by the Enterprise Act 2002.
25   Insolvency Act 1986, s 360 as amended by the Enterprise Act 2002.

CHAPTER 23

PREVENTING ABUSE OF THE PRIVILEGE OF LIMITED LIABILITY

1 INTRODUCTION

There has long been recognition of the potential for abuse of the privilege of limited liability by those running their businesses through the medium of companies. The Cork Committee observed that both the Greene Committee in 1926 and the Jenkins Committee in 1962 had made recommendations which were never implemented. The Committee noted[1] considerable dissatisfaction with the perceived leniency of the law with regard to directors of insolvent companies and quoted[2] by way of example the evidence of a divisional consumer protection officer of the South Yorkshire County Council, who had said:

> The doctrine of limited liability may have its good points but it also leads to some indifference and lack of concern when company officials know that if the company goes down, they will not have any financial liability ... There are many fraudulent practices concerned with the formation and liquidation of companies. Companies are formed, debts run up, the assets milked and the company put into liquidation. Immediately a new company is formed and the process is repeated *ad infinitum*. Associated with the basic fraud is the practice of new companies buying the remaining stock of the old company at give-away prices, taking on the premises complete with fittings which are unpaid for, again at nominal prices.[3]

In 2000, the Company Law Review Steering Group described[4] an alternative form of phoenix in which, prior to the winding up of the original company, its controllers cause it to transfer its assets (probably on terms favourable to themselves, such as at an undervalue or for deferred consideration or in circumstances where no payment is made for goodwill) to a new company which they (or substantially the same managers) also control. They then permit the original company to go into liquidation and the liquidator is unable to take any effective action for lack of funds. Alternatively, the old company may simply be allowed to be struck off the register without any liquidation. The Steering Group observed that the phoenix syndrome creates problems for the creditors of both the old and the new companies, competitors of either and the general public. The old company's creditors are at risk of sale of its assets at an undervalue. The creditors of the new company may be duped into dealing with it, thinking it still to be the original business in a financially healthy state, or they may be unaware that the same incompetent or dishonest directors are managing the second company. Competitors suffer from the ability of the business to abandon its creditors and continue trading unburdened. The Group did also recognise that there were both 'good' and 'bad' phoenixes; there are occasions where honest individuals may, through misfortune or naïve good faith, find that they can no longer trade out of their difficulties and that the only way to continue an otherwise viable business may

---

1   In Chapter 45, which is entitled 'Delinquent directors and others'.
2   Paragraph 1741.
3   See *Re Keypak Homecare* [1987] BCLC 409 at 411 for a judicial description of this syndrome. The directors involved were subsequently disqualified for three years: see [1990] BCLC 440.
4   CLRSG, 2000, para 13.102.

be to do so in a new vehicle using the assets and trading style of the original company.[5]

The Cork Committee's recommendation[6] for dealing with phoenix companies was that anyone who had been a director or concerned in the management of a company in the two years prior to an insolvent liquidation should, unless the court ordered otherwise, be personally liable for the relevant liabilities of any company which started trading within a year of that insolvency which itself became insolvent within three years. An exception would be made where the second company had a paid up share capital of £50,000 or more or was a subsidiary of a company with such a share capital. This recommendation was not accepted and s 216 of the Insolvency Act 1986 was introduced at a late stage in the passage of the insolvency legislation through Parliament in 1985[7] instead; this attempts, as explained below, to prevent the phoenix company through restrictions on the subsequent use of a similar name. Additionally, the introduction of tighter controls on the conduct of voluntary liquidation[8] was prompted partly by a desire to prevent the mischief of the sale at an undervalue of the assets of the original company to those involved in its management.

The 1985 Insolvency Bill as presented to Parliament would have required that, on making a winding up order on grounds of the company's inability to pay its debts, the court should make a provisional order disqualifying all the directors, who would then have three months to apply for annulment of the order on grounds that they had 'acted in a manner which in the circumstances was in the best interests of the company's creditors'. This proposal provoked strong opposition on the grounds that the mandatory disqualification would catch the innocent, would cast an unfair burden on the director and would inhibit non-executive directors from accepting office and contributing their expertise on company boards.[9] The clause was defeated twice in the House of Lords and the requirement for a court order of disqualification was substituted. The provisions, considered in more detail later in this chapter, are contained in the Company Directors Disqualification Act 1986, as amended by the Insolvency Act 2000, which makes it possible for a director to be disqualified without court involvement.

The following quotation from the judgment of Henry LJ in *Re Grayan Services Ltd*[10] is typical of number of judicial observations on the mischief at which the disqualification legislation is directed:

> The concept of limited liability and the sophistication of our corporate law offer great privileges and great opportunities for those who wish to trade under that regime. But the corporate environment carries with it the discipline that those who avail themselves of those privileges must accept the standards laid down and abide by the regulatory rules and disciplines in place to protect creditors and shareholders. And,

---

5   See also Milman (2001c) on the difficult balance between suffocating entrepreneurship and protecting the public.

6   In para 1827.

7   See, generally, Milman (1997).

8   By introducing qualification requirements for liquidators (see Chapter 20) and removing the powers of the directors once a company is in voluntary liquidation (see Chapter 16).

9   The Singapore government enacted a provision for automatic disqualification on insolvent liquidation in 1984; after three years of criticism, it repealed the provision in 1987. See Hicks (1988).

10 [1995] 3 WLR 1. This was the first appeal to the Court of Appeal against a refusal to disqualify.

while some significant corporate failures will occur despite the directors exercising best managerial practice, in many, too many, cases there have been serious breaches of those rules and disciplines, in situations where the observance of them would or at least might have prevented or reduced the scale of the failure and consequent loss to creditors and investors. ... The parliamentary intention to improve managerial safeguards and standards for the long term good of employees, creditors and investors is clear.

The civil sanctions contained in ss 212–14 of the Insolvency Act 1986, considered in Chapter 31, also act as a sanction for malpractice on the part of directors. Their use, however, has depended on there being a willingness on the part of the liquidator to invoke them and the funding difficulties explained in Chapter 32 have acted as a deterrent. The Insolvency Service has sought to address this issue by the creation of the Forensic Insolvency Recovery Service to investigate and take action for civil recovery where there has been negligence, misconduct or misappropriation of assets and directors have been disqualified.

The next section of the chapter considers the criminal sanctions which are imposed by the Insolvency Act 1986 in relation to acts carried out both before the commencement of and during the insolvency. The chapter then goes on to explain the disqualification and the 'phoenix' provisions before finishing with an evaluation of their efficacy.

2   LIQUIDATION OFFENCES

(a) General

Sections 206–11 of the Insolvency Act 1986 set out a series of offences which may be committed by the officers of the company and, in some cases, others before or during a liquidation; many, but not all of the offences may be committed by shadow directors. In relation to many of these offences, the Act provides that it will be a defence to prove an absence of relevant intent; in *R v Carass*,[11] the Court of Appeal (Criminal Division) held that, in order to achieve compatibility with Art 6 of the European Convention on Human Rights by maintaining the presumption of innocence, these provisions must be read as providing that it will be a defence to raise evidence of an absence of intent unless the prosecution can then establish beyond reasonable doubt the existence of the intent.

It is frequently the case that those who have been involved in criminal activity in relation to a corporate insolvency will be charged with Theft Act offences. It should also be noted that under s 458 of the Companies Act 1985, any person knowingly a party to the carrying on of the business with intent to defraud creditors of the company or creditors of any other person or for any fraudulent purpose will be guilty of a criminal offence.[12] Criminal liability may also arise[13] in connection with any failure by the company to keep proper accounting records.

---

11   [2002] 1 WLR 1714.
12   Civil liability for fraudulent trading is considered in Chapter 31 below. The ingredients of fraudulent trading are the same for both civil and criminal purposes.
13   Under the Companies Act 1985, ss 221–23.

(b) Fraud in anticipation of winding up

Under s 206 of the Insolvency Act 1986, any past or present officer (including a shadow director) will have committed an offence if, within the 12 months leading up to the winding up or after the commencement of the winding up, he or she has done any of the following:

(a) concealed any part of the company's property to the value of £500 or more, or concealed any debt due to or from the company;

(b) fraudulently removed[14] any part of the company's property[15] to the value of £500 or more;

(c) concealed, destroyed, mutilated or falsified any book or paper affecting or relating to the company's property or affairs or been privy to the doing of this by others;

(d) made any false entry in any book or paper affecting or relating to the company's property or affairs or been privy to the doing of this by others;

(e) fraudulently parted with, altered or made any omission in any document affecting or relating to the company's property or affairs or been privy to the doing of this by others;

(f) pawned, pledged or disposed of any property of the company which has been obtained on credit and has not been paid for (unless the pawning, pledging or disposal was in the ordinary way of the company's business). Anyone who takes in pawn or pledge, or otherwise receives, property knowing of these circumstances will also commit an offence.

The accused will have a defence[16] in respect of (a) or (f) above if he or she can prove that he or she had no intent to defraud and under (c) or (d) if he or she can prove that they had no intent to conceal the state of affairs of the company or to defeat the law. There were three convictions under s 206 of the Insolvency Act 1986 in 2000.

(c) Transactions in fraud of creditors

An offence under s 207 of the Insolvency Act 1986 will be committed by anyone who was an officer of the company at the time and who either makes or causes to be made any gift or transfer of, or charge on, or causes or connives at the levying of any execution against, the company's property within the five years before the commencement of the winding up. It will also be an offence if such a person conceals or removes any part of the company's property since, or within two months before, the date of any unsatisfied judgment or order for the payment of money obtained against the company. In either event, it will be a defence for the accused to raise evidence that he or she had no intent to defraud the company's creditors unless the prosecution can then establish beyond reasonable doubt that he or she did. There was one conviction under this provision in 2000.

---

14   Or failed to return: *R v Robinson* [1990] BCC 656.
15   Including cheques in payment for property of the company: *R v McCredie* [2000] 2 BCLC 438.
16   Subject to *R v Carass* [2002] 1 WLR 1714; see above.

(d) Misconduct in the course of a winding up

Section 208 of the Insolvency Act 1986 provides that any past or present officer, including a shadow director, of a company in liquidation will commit an offence if he or she does any of the following:

(a) fails to give full discovery to the best of his or her knowledge and belief of the company's property and of its disposal other than in the ordinary way of the company's business;

(b) fails to deliver up company property in his or her custody and control which he or she is required to deliver up;

(c) fails to deliver up company books and papers in his or her custody or control which he or she is required to deliver up;[17]

(d) fails to inform the liquidator as soon as practicable of any false debts which he or she knows or believes to have been proved;

(e) after the start of the liquidation, prevents the production of any book or paper affecting or relating to the company's property or affairs unless he or she can prove that he or she had no intent to conceal the state of affairs of the company or to defeat the law;[18]

(f) attempts to account for any part of the company's property by fictitious losses or expenses within the 12 months preceding the winding up at a meeting of the company's creditors or after the start of the winding up.

In relation to (a) to (c), it will be a defence, subject to *R v Carass*,[19] for the accused to establish a lack of intent to defraud. There were seven convictions under s 208 in 2000.

(e) Falsification of company books

When a company is being wound up, any officer or contributory of the company commits an offence under s 209 of the Insolvency Act 1986 by destroying, mutilating, altering or falsifying any books, papers or securities, or making or being privy to the making of any false or fraudulent entry in any register, book of account or document belonging to the company with intent to defraud or deceive any person.

(f) Material omissions from statement of affairs

Past or present officers (including shadow directors) of a company in liquidation commit an offence under s 210 of the Insolvency Act 1986 by making, or having made prior to the commencement of the liquidation, a material omission in any statement relating to the company's affairs. It is a defence to prove there was no intent to defraud.[20]

---

17 *R v McCredie* [2000] BCLC 438: books and papers in this case included computer disks.
18 *R v Carass* [2002] 1 WLR 1714 will apply as above.
19 [2002] 1 WLR 1714.
20 *R v Carass* [2002] 1 WLR 1714 will apply as above.

(g) False representations to creditors

Under s 211 of the Insolvency Act 1986, any past or present officer, including a shadow director, of a company in liquidation will commit an offence if he or she makes, or has made prior to the winding up, any false representation or commits any other fraud for the purpose of obtaining the consent of the company's creditors to an agreement with reference to the company's affairs or to the winding up.

3   DISQUALIFICATION OF DIRECTORS[21]

(a) Introduction

Statutory disqualification of certain people from being company directors was first introduced by the Companies Act 1928, following the recommendations of the 1926 Greene Committee.[22] The provisions were re-enacted in the Companies Act 1948 and prevented undischarged bankrupts from acting as directors unless given leave by the court and made possible the disqualification of those convicted of fraudulent trading from being involved in the management of companies. In 1976, the disqualification provisions were extended to cover cases of misconduct in insolvency, the possible period of disqualification was increased to 15 years and the first proper provision was made for the registration of disqualification orders. Disqualification on the grounds of unfitness under the 1976 legislation required involvement with two companies which had become insolvent within five years of one another, a provision which was re-enacted in the Companies Act 1985.[23] The current provisions are contained within the Company Directors Disqualification Act 1986, as amended by the Insolvency Act 2000. There has been extensive case law relating to this legislation, in particular as to the kind of conduct which justifies disqualification and the length of disqualification, and the procedures under which it is operated.

(b) Disqualification

Section 1 of the Company Directors Disqualification Act 1986 defines a disqualification order as an order that a person shall not, without leave of the court, be a director, liquidator, administrator of a company or a receiver or manager of a company's property or be in any way, either directly or indirectly, concerned or take part in the promotion, formation or management of a company for a specified period. Section 1A, inserted by the Insolvency Act 2000, makes it possible in certain circumstances for the Secretary of State to accept an undertaking from a director which will have the same effect as a disqualification order. Anyone who acts in contravention of a disqualification order or undertaking commits a criminal offence[24] and will be personally liable for the debts of the company incurred whilst he or she

---

21   See generally Sealy, 2000; Walters and Davis-White, 1999; Griffin, 1999.
22   See Leigh (1986) on the history of disqualification.
23   Companies Act 1985, s 300. Cases on the concept of 'unfitness' under this section are still relevant under the current legislation.
24   Company Directors Disqualification Act 1986, ss 13, 14.

was so acting.[25] Anyone involved in the management of a company who acts or is willing to act on the instructions of someone he or she knows to be disqualified will also become personally liable for the debts of the company incurred at that time.[26] The effect of a disqualification order, therefore, may be to make the disqualified person almost unemployable in the corporate sector.[27]

The Secretary of State maintains a register of disqualification orders which is open to public inspection.[28]

(c) Grounds for disqualification[29]

The Companies Directors Disqualification Act 1986 provides for the disqualification from office of directors under various different sections[30] of the Act.

A person[31] convicted of an indictable offence in connection with the promotion, formation, management or liquidation of a company, or with the receivership or management of a company's property may also be disqualified for a maximum period of five years where the order is made by a court of summary jurisdiction and 15 years in other cases.[32] Persistent default in relation to the requirements of company legislation with regard to returns of information to the registrar of companies may result in disqualification for up to five years.[33] A person may be disqualified[34] for up to 15 years where it appears that he or she has been guilty, whether or not convicted, of knowingly being party to fraudulent trading or, while an officer[35] or liquidator of a company or receiver or manager of its property, of any fraud in relation to the company or breach of duty. An application in respect of any of the foregoing may be made by the Secretary of State or the Official Receiver, or by the liquidator or any past or present member or creditor of any company in relation to which that person has committed or is alleged to have committed an offence or other default.[36]

---

25 Company Directors Disqualification Act 1986, s 15.
26 Company Directors Disqualification Act 1986, s 15.
27 See Hicks (1987) at 244 for a discussion of what is 'management' and the suggestion that a disqualified person cannot be certain what employment he or she may take without committing a criminal offence.
28 Company Directors Disqualification Act 1986, s 18; Companies (Disqualification Orders) Regulations 1986 (SI 1986/2067).
29 See, *inter alia*, Leigh (1986); Hicks (1987); Drake (1989); Hoey (1997).
30 Including s 11 which automatically disqualifies undischarged bankrupts (see Chapter 15) and s 12 which provides for the possibility of an order where there has been a failure to pay under a county court administration order (see Chapter 8).
31 Whether or not a director.
32 Company Directors Disqualification Act 1986, s 2; see, for example, *R v Corbin* (1984) 6 Cr. App R 17; *R v Austen* (1985) 1 BCC 99, 528; *R v Goodman* [1992] BCC 625; *R v Georgiou* (1988) 4 BCC 322; *R v McCredie* [2000] BCLC 438 (CA, Criminal Division); *Secretary of State v Newstead* [2001] EWCA Civ 1083; *R v Early* [2002] EWCA Crim 1909. The making of a disqualification order under s 2 does not prevent the DTI from pursuing proceedings under s 6: *Secretary of State v Newstead* [2001] EWCA Civ 1083.
33 Company Directors Disqualification Act 1986, s 3.
34 Under the Company Directors Disqualification Act 1986, s 4.
35 Including a shadow director.
36 Company Directors Disqualification Act 1986, s 16(2).

If the court orders a person, on the application of the liquidator, to make a contribution to the company's assets under s 213[37] or 214[38] of the Insolvency Act 1986, it may also disqualify that person for up to 15 years.[39]

The Secretary of State may apply for a disqualification order[40] against any person who is or has been a director or shadow director of a company if, after investigation of a company under one of the relevant statutory provisions, it appears expedient in the public interest; the court may make a disqualification order of up to 15 years on such an application if it is satisfied that the conduct of the director in relation to the company makes him or her unfit to be concerned in the management of a company.

Section 6 of the Company Directors Disqualification Act 1986 is the central provision in this context. The majority of disqualifications are under s 6[41] which provides that it is the duty of the court to make a disqualification order of between two and 15 years against a person where two conditions are met. The conditions are, first, that the person is or has been a director or shadow director of a company which has at any time during or after his or her directorship become insolvent and, secondly, that the conduct of the director in connection with that company (either taken alone or taken together with his or her conduct as a director of any other company or companies) makes him or her unfit to be concerned with the management of the company.

A company becomes insolvent for these purposes if it goes into liquidation at a time when its assets are insufficient for the payment of its debts and other liabilities and the expenses of the winding up[42] or it goes into administration or administrative receivership. The director must be shown to have been unfit in relation to the company which has become insolvent; evidence of conduct in connection with the 'collateral' companies, which need not have become insolvent, should assist the court in reaching a conclusion of unfitness in connection with the 'lead' company, but need not be the same or similar as the conduct in relation to that company.[43] Where the court decides that the conduct had fallen below the appropriate standard (which is discussed at greater length below), it must make a disqualification order of at least two years and may not take into account that the director is unlikely to repeat the conduct in the future.[44]

A non-exhaustive list of matters relevant to the determination of unfitness is contained in s 9 of and Sched 1 to the Company Directors Disqualification Act 1986. Matters which the Schedule makes applicable in all cases include any misfeasance or breach of duty by the director in relation to the company, any misapplication or retention by the director of or conduct giving rise to an obligation to account for

---

37 Fraudulent trading: see Chapter 31 below.
38 Wrongful trading: see Chapter 31.
39 Company Directors Disqualification Act 1986, s 10. See, for example, *Re Brian D Pierson (Contractors) Ltd, Penn v Pierson and Another* [2000] 1 BCLC 275. See Griffin (2002).
40 Under the Company Directors Disqualification Act 1986, s 8.
41 For example, *Companies in 2001–2002*, Table D1 shows a total of 1,929 disqualifications, 1,761 related to s 6 unfitness, 16 under s 8 and 152 under ss 2–5.
42 Company Directors Disqualification Act 1986, s 6(2). *Re Gower Enterprises Ltd* [1995] BCC 293.
43 *Secretary of State for Trade and Industry v Ivens* [1997] 2 BCLC 334.
44 *Re Grayan Ltd* [1995] 3 WLR 1. Evidence of subsequent conduct may be relevant in deciding whether or not to give leave to act as a director under the Company Directors Disqualification Act 1986, s 17.

property of the company, the extent of the director's responsibility for the company entering into any transaction liable to be set aside under Part XVI of the Insolvency Act 1986 (transactions defrauding creditors)[45] and the extent of the director's responsibility for any failure of the company to comply with the accounting and notification requirements of the companies legislation.

Where the company has become insolvent, the court also has to take into account any failure by the director to provide specified information and assistance[46] in the insolvency and the extent of[47] the director's responsibility for the causes of the company becoming insolvent, the company entering into transactions liable to be set aside under s 127 or 238–40 of the Insolvency Act 1986,[48] the company's failure to supply goods or services which have been paid for and any failure by the directors to comply with the obligation to call a creditors' meeting in a creditors' voluntary winding up.[49]

(d) Who may be disqualified under s 6?

Under s 6 of the Company Directors Disqualification Act 1986, only those who have been directors or shadow directors of a company which has become insolvent may be disqualified.[50] *De facto* directors are those who hold themselves out as directors without having been properly appointed; it has been held that a *de facto* director can be disqualified.[51]

A disqualification order may be made against foreigners just as much as against British subjects and it is irrelevant whether or not they were present in the jurisdiction at the time the alleged activities took place.[52]

(e) Judicial interpretation of 'unfitness'

The courts have had to decide what conduct makes a director 'unfit' to be concerned in the management of a company and the cases contain various statements as to the sort of behaviour which justifies disqualification. In *Re Sevenoaks Stationers (Retail)*

---

45   See Chapter 30.

46   The failure of a director in *Secretary of State v McTighe* [1996] 2 BCLC 477 to co-operate with the officeholder and the Official Receiver led to an increase in the length of the disqualification order which would otherwise have been imposed. In *Secretary of State for Trade and Industry v Reynard* [2002] 2 BCLC 625, the Court of Appeal held that the conduct of the defendant during proceedings could be taken into account.

47   In *Secretary of State v Gash* [1997] 1 BCLC 341, the court pointed out that the legislation required it to consider not just whether the director was responsible, but also the extent of the responsibility.

48   See Chapter 30. See *Re Grayan Ltd* [1995] 3 WLR 1, in which the Court of Appeal overruled Arden J's view that the giving of preferences need not be taken into account because the liquidator had pursued other remedies in that respect.

49   Insolvency Act 1986, s 98; see Chapter 16 above.

50   Officers and members of partnerships are treated as directors by the Insolvent Partnerships Order 1994 (see Chapter 18). See Chapter 4 for an explanation of the term 'shadow director'.

51   *Re Lo-Line Electric Motors Ltd* [1988] BCLC 698; *Re Tasbian* [1992] BCC 358; *Re Moorgate Metals Ltd* [1995] BCC 143; *Re Richborough Furniture Ltd* [1996] 1 BCLC 507; *Secretary of State v Laing* [1996] 2 BCLC 324. See *Re Hydrodan (Corby) Ltd* [1994] 2 BCLC 180 for Millett J's discussion of the distinction between a *de facto* and a shadow director.

52   *Re Seagull Manufacturing Co Ltd (No 2)* [1994] 2 All ER 767.

Ltd,[53] which was the first case on the provision to reach them, the Court of Appeal held that whilst such judicial statements might be helpful, they should not be treated as judicial paraphrases of the words of the statute and that the question is one of fact in each case. Dillon LJ said:

> It is beyond dispute that the purpose of section 6 is to protect the public, and in particular potential creditors of companies, from losing money through companies becoming insolvent when the directors of those companies are people unfit to be concerned in the management of a company. The test laid down is ... whether the person's conduct as a director of the company or companies in question 'make him unfit to be concerned in the management of a company'. These are ordinary words of the English language and they should be simple to apply in most cases. It is important to hold to those words in each case.

Fraudulent and dishonest behaviour is obviously likely to lead to a finding of unfitness. Those who have been involved in 'phoenix' companies are also clearly at risk of disqualification.[54] *Re Ipcon Fashions Ltd*[55] was an early clear example of such a case. The court found that, although there was no personal dishonesty on the part of the director, there was a cynical exploitation of the privilege of limited liability, including a reckless disregard of all creditors' interests including in particular the Crown, which was the sort of behaviour from which the public clearly needed to be protected. Subsequently, the Court of Appeal in *Re Swift 736 Ltd*,[56] describing 'a deplorable pattern of six companies succeeding one another, carrying on the same business of shirt manufacturing from the same premises, as each became insolvent, one after the other', approved the comments of Hoffmann J at first instance in which he observed that this sort of behaviour was the very thing which the provisions for disqualification of directors were intended to prevent.

Directors will clearly be risking disqualification if they fail to comply with the statutory obligations in relation to maintaining proper books of account and filing information at Companies House.[57] In *Re Swift 736 Ltd*,[58] the Court of Appeal said that, in addition to conducting their companies with due regard to the ordinary standards of commercial morality, directors must be: 'punctilious in observing the safeguards laid down by Parliament for the benefit of others who have dealings with their companies ... Isolated lapses in filing documents are one thing and may be excusable. Not so persistent lapses which show overall a blatant disregard for this important aspect of accountability. Such lapses are serious and cannot be condoned even though, and it is right to have this firmly in mind, they need not involve any dishonest intent.' The failure to comply with filing obligations resulted in the difference between disqualification in *Re Swift 736 Ltd*[59] and non-disqualification in

---

53 [1990] BCC 765.

54 See, for example, *Re Travel Mondia (UK) Ltd* [1991] BCLC 120; *Re Linvale Ltd* [1993] BCLC 654; *Re Swift 736 Ltd* [1993] BCLC 1.

55 (1989) 5 BCC 773.

56 [1993] BCLC 896.

57 *Re Majestic Recording Studies Ltd* [1989] BCLC 1; *Re City Investment Centres Ltd* [1992] BCLC 956; *Re New Generation Engineers Ltd* [1993] BCLC 435; *Re Firedart* [1994] 2 BCLC 340; *Secretary of State v Van Hengel* [1995] 1 BCLC 545; *Re Continental Assurance Co of London plc* [1977] 1 BCLC 48.

58 [1993] BCLC 896 increasing the period of disqualification ordered by Hoffmann J, whose judgment is reported at [1993] BCLC 1.

59 [1997] 1 BCLC 34.

Secretary of State v Gash,[60] where the misconduct was otherwise similar. In *Re Hitco 2000 Ltd*,[61] the judge held that a failure on the part of a sole director to monitor and control the company's financial position or to ensure that he had the requisite professional guidance amounted to unfitness.

In the early days of this legislation,[62] there was considerable debate as to whether disqualification under s 6 demanded dishonesty or whether incompetence would suffice.[63] Many of the cases drew a clear distinction between commercial immorality and honest commercial misjudgment[64] and blameworthiness was clearly an issue. In *Re Lo-Line Electric Motors Ltd*,[65] Browne-Wilkinson VC said: 'Ordinary commercial misjudgment is in itself not sufficient to justify disqualification. In the normal case, the conduct complained of must display a lack of commercial probity, although I have no doubt in an extreme case of gross negligence or total incompetence disqualification could be appropriate.' Peter Gibson J in *Re Bath Glass Ltd*[66] stated a test requiring a lower degree of blameworthiness: 'To reach a finding of unfitness the court must be satisfied that the director has been guilty of a serious failure or serious failures, whether deliberately or through incompetence, to perform those duties of directors which are attendant on the privilege of trading through companies with limited liability.'

In *Re Sevenoaks Stationers (Retail) Ltd*,[67] which involved the disqualification of a director, a chartered accountant who had been extremely negligent in regard to the running of the business, the unfitness was established by reference to the incompetence of the director; there was no suggestion of dishonesty and, in fact, the director had lost significant quantities of his own money. Recent cases which have stressed the need for adequate levels of competence are *Re Continental Assurance Ltd*,[68] in which a senior employee of a bank who became a non-executive director of a client was disqualified despite his argument that he had no knowledge of the objectionable conduct since 'any competent director would have known' and *Secretary of State v Arif*,[69] in which the court observed: 'It is no answer ... to say "I did what I could". If a director finds that he is unable to do what he knows ought to be done, the only proper course is to resign.' In *Secretary of State v Gash*,[70] the court held that although a director whose advice was not being heeded would be prudent, in his or her own interests, to resign, failure to do so would not necessarily lead to disqualification. In that case, it was clear that some of the directors of the company should be disqualified; the director in question had advised the others that there was a risk of insolvency and had proposed improvements which were ignored and the judge held that the stage had not yet been reached when resignation was the only acceptable course of conduct. In

---

60   [1997] 1 BCLC 341.
61   [1995] BCC 161.
62   And its immediate predecessor, the Companies Act 1985, s 300.
63   Or, to put the issue another way, whether the measure was intended mainly to punish delinquent directors or to protect the public from inadequate (for whatever reason) directors. See Finch (1990).
64   See, for example, *Re CU Fittings Ltd* (1989) 5 BCC 210.
65   [1988] Ch 477.
66   (1988) 4 BCC 130.
67   [1990] BCC 765.
68   [1997] 1 BCLC 48.
69   [1997] 1 BCLC 34.
70   [1997] 1 BCLC 341.

Re Barings plc and Others (No 5),[71] Jonathan Parker J held that the court should assess the competence or otherwise of the director in the context of and by reference to the role in the management of the company which was in fact assigned to him or her or which he or she in fact assumed, and by reference to his or her duties and responsibilities in that role and it would be irrelevant to the question of disqualification that there might be other roles which he could in fact perform competently.

In *Re Westmid Packing Services Ltd; Secretary of State for Trade and Industry v Griffiths*,[72] the Court of Appeal held that whilst a proper degree of delegation and division of responsibility is permissible, and often necessary, total abrogation of responsibility is not acceptable. In that case, two of the three directors allowed the third to treat the assets of the company as if they were his own and had failed to exercise any degree of control over his activities. In *Secretary of State v Taylor*,[73] Chadwick J said: 'The duties of a director include, in my view, the duty to inform himself as to the company's affairs and the duty to make his views known to the other directors. If there comes a point at which his attendance at board meetings is purposeless because he must recognise that his co-directors take no account of his views and recommendations, then it may well be appropriate to ask why he continues to remain as a director.' Similarly, whilst it is reasonable to rely on professional advice, a director may not abrogate all responsibility in this respect and there will come a point where failure to ask questions will make the director 'unfit'.[74]

In *Secretary of State v Creegan*,[75] Nourse LJ observed that it was well established that causing a company to trade, first, while it is insolvent and, secondly, without a reasonable prospect of meeting creditors' claims is likely to constitute incompetence of sufficient seriousness to ground a disqualification order. He went on to emphasise that it will usually be necessary for both elements of that test to be satisfied. In general, it is not enough for the company to have been insolvent and for the director to have known it. It must also be shown that he or she knew or ought to have known that there was no reasonable prospect of meeting creditors' claims.

Another issue which originally gave rise to a certain amount of judicial disagreement was the question of whether failure to pay Crown debts was worse than failure to pay other types of creditor and, therefore, more likely to merit disqualification. Hoffmann J in *Re Dawson Print Group*[76] observed that failure to pay such debts was not to be regarded as a particularly immoral breach of duty; Vinelott J in *Re Stanford Services Ltd*[77] and Peter Gibson J in *Re Churchill Hotel (Plymouth) Ltd*[78] thought otherwise. The Court of Appeal, whilst recognising the particular difficulties that the Crown has in pressing for prompt payment, has held[79] that no distinction should be made between failure to pay Crown debts and failure to pay ordinary trade creditors. Directors who have failed to pay any of their creditors unless pressed to do

71   [1999] 1 BCLC 433.
72   [1998] 2 All ER 124.
73   [1997] 1 WLR 407.
74   *Re Bradcrown Ltd, Official Receiver v Ireland* [2001] 1 BCLC 547.
75   [2002] BCLC 99.
76   (1987) 3 BCC 322.
77   (1987) 3 BCC 326.
78   (1988) 4 BCC 112.
79   *Re Sevenoaks Stationers Ltd* [1991] BCLC 325; *Secretary of State v McTighe* [1996] 2 BCLC 477.

so are likely to be considered unfit particularly if continuing to pay themselves well at the same time.[80]

In *Re Grayan Ltd*,[81] the Court of Appeal held that it was not relevant that the director was unlikely to repeat the conduct which had made him 'unfit' in relation to the insolvent company. Hoffmann LJ said that the purpose of making disqualification mandatory was to ensure that everyone whose conduct had fallen below the appropriate standard was disqualified for at least two years: 'Parliament has decided that it is occasionally necessary to disqualify a company director to encourage the others.' The Court of Appeal also indicated in this case that it would usually be reluctant to overturn the decision of a first instance judge on unfitness, particularly where there is dispute on the primary findings of fact on which the trial judge will have had the advantage of seeing and hearing the witnesses. There would, however, be cases such as this where the trial judge reached an incorrect conclusion as to whether the conduct measured up to the standard of probity and competence fixed by the court when it would be appropriate for the appellate court to interfere.

(f) Disqualification procedures

An application for a disqualification order under s 6 may be made by the Secretary of State or the Official Receiver where it appears expedient in the public interest.[82] Disqualification is viewed as a public function which should be the concern of a neutral public body rather than being urged on the court by discontented creditors. The cost of the process, however, is to an extent funded by the creditors of insolvents rather than from the public purse, since the initial investigatory work is carried out by the officeholders who will be paid from the available assets. Officeholders under the Insolvency Act 1986 have a duty[83] to report to the Secretary of State if they form the opinion that someone should be disqualified under s 6 of the Company Directors Disqualification Act 1986. The Secretary of State or Official Receiver may require an insolvency practitioner to provide additional information about the conduct of any director of the company or to allow inspection of documentation relevant to the conduct of a director.[84]

Proceedings on an application for an order on the grounds of the director's unfitness are governed by the Insolvent Companies (Disqualification of Unfit Directors) Proceedings Rules 1987[85] and *Practice Direction*.[86] The claim form must be supported by affidavits which must set out the case against the person sought to be disqualified with sufficient clarity and identification of the evidence for the defendant

---

80   *Re Synthetic Technology Ltd* [1993] BCC 549; *Secretary of State v Van Hengel* [1995] 1 BCLC 545.

81   [1995] 3 WLR 1. See also *Re Pamstock Ltd* [1994] 1 BCLC 716.

82   Company Directors Disqualification Act 1986, s 7.

83   Company Directors Disqualification Act 1986, s 7(3) and the Insolvent Companies (Reports on Conduct of Directors) Rules 1996 (SI 1996/1909). The Rules (which strictly apply to voluntary liquidation but in practice are also followed by the Official Receiver in compulsory liquidations) require the making of a return in a prescribed form (referred to as a D form). A D3 return will state that the liquidator has not become aware of any information which would require him or her to make a report under s 7(3).

84   Company Directors Disqualification Act 1986, s 7(4).

85   SI 1987/2023.

86   [1996] 1 All ER 442.

to know where he or she stands.[87] The Court of Appeal[88] has said that it is on the basis of these allegations that the court must decide whether the conduct has 'fallen below the standards of probity and competence appropriate for persons fit to be directors of companies'. If the defendant wants evidence taken into account which is not contained in the affidavits, he or she must file an affidavit in opposition. The application for a disqualification order must be brought within two years from the day on which the company became insolvent, a time limit which the Insolvency Service often had difficulty meeting in the early days of the legislation and which led to a critical report by the National Audit Office in 1993 as to the paucity of disqualifications being achieved. The courts have had to consider applications for an extension of time on a number of occasions and have laid down guidelines as to the circumstances in which an extension will be granted;[89] amongst the factors which the court will consider are the length of the delay, the reasons for the delay, the strength and gravity of the case and the degree of prejudice caused by the delay. In *Secretary of State v Davies*,[90] the Court of Appeal held that the mere fact that there was no good reason for the delay was not necessarily enough by itself to justify a refusal to proceed out of time; there, the alleged conduct was particularly serious, there was an obvious public interest in having them determined and the delay had occasioned no prejudice to the directors.

Section 7(2A) of the Company Directors Disqualification Act 1986, inserted by Insolvency Act 2000, provides that if it appears to the Secretary of State that the conditions mentioned in s 6(1) are satisfied as respects any person who has offered to give him or her a disqualification undertaking, he or she may accept the undertaking if it appears to him or her that it is expedient in the public interest that he or she should do so.[91] The government supported this amendment on the basis that it would reduce the costs associated with disqualification of directors, save court resources and result in faster disqualification processes. The amendment was prompted by the development, in cases where there was no dispute between the two sides as to the facts of the case and the parties had reached broad agreement on the appropriate length of disqualification order, of the summary *Carecraft*[92] procedure to avoid a full-scale hearing. This involved placing before the court an agreed statement of facts which included some evidence of unfitness on which the court could act. The Court of Appeal took the opportunity to make some general observations on the *Carecraft* procedure in *Secretary of State for Trade and Industry v Rogers*[93] and said that where the parties invited the court to deal with the case on the basis of a statement in which the parties agree certain facts and agree not to pursue other disputed allegations, it was

---

87 Insolvent Companies (Disqualification of Unfit Directors) Proceedings Rules 1987 (SI 1987/2023), r 3(3) as amended. *Re Rex Williams Leisure Centre Ltd* [1993] 2 All ER 741 at 752. If the affidavit evidence is too vague or imprecise, the allegations (and possibly the entire application) may be struck out: *Re Sutton Glassworks* [1997] 1 BCLC 26.

88 In *Re Grayan Services Ltd* [1995] 3 WLR 1.

89 *Secretary of State for Trade and Industry v Langridge* [1991] 3 All ER 591; *Re Probe Data* [1992] BCLC 405 (CA); *Re Tasbian Ltd (No 3)* [1992] BCC 358; *Re Manlon Trading* [1995] BCC 579; *Secretary of State for Trade and Industry v McTighe* [1996] 2 BCLC 284; *Secretary of State v Davies* [1997] BCC 235.

90 [1996] 4 All ER 289.

91 Walters (2001b).

92 So called after the case of *Re Carecraft Construction Ltd* [1994] 1 WLR 172, in which the procedure was first used.

93 [1996] 2 BCLC 513.

not for the court to insist that other allegations be pursued or that cross-examination take place.[94] If the judge felt strongly that the course being taken by the Secretary of State was ill-advised, it would be possible to adjourn the case for a short time and invite the Secretary of State to reconsider, but that was all. Scott VC expressed the view[95] that it would be sensible in such cases if the disqualification could be imposed by a formal undertaking entered into by the director without the necessity for a court order; this would, however, require statutory amendment. The *Carecraft* procedure was not, however, to be seen as one in which the court was involved in a rubber-stamping exercise. This was emphasised by the Court of Appeal in *Re Blackspur Group plc, Secretary of State v Davies*,[96] in which it was held that the Secretary of State was entitled to refuse to accept an offer of an undertaking since the undertaking would not provide the public with the same level of protection as would a disqualification order.[97] Breach of the undertaking would merely be a breach of contract and there was no scope to enter an undertaking on the register of disqualification orders. Furthermore, there was no statutory procedure governing the grant of leave to act under an undertaking. The Court of Appeal in *Re Blackspur Group* also recommended legislative change.

Section 8A of the Company Directors Disqualification Act 1986 provides that the court may, on the application of a person who is subject to a disqualification undertaking, reduce the period for which the undertaking is to be in force or provide for it to cease to be in force. This provision seems to address the concern that the administrative nature of the new procedure might not comply with the European Convention on Human Rights.

In *Blackspur Group plc (No 3)*,[98] the issue arose of whether the Secretary of State can refuse to accept an undertaking unless it has a schedule of unfit conduct annexed to it. The defendant in this case was unwilling to agree to such a schedule for fear of the likely impact of any such admissions on his accountancy career and contended that the Secretary of State's refusal to accept a bare undertaking was unreasonable. The Court of Appeal held that it was not unreasonable to require such a schedule; it would provide a useful starting point on any subsequent application under s 8A or for leave to act under s 17. The statement would also be a useful basis for the Secretary of State to advertise the fact of the undertaking and the underlying reason for the disqualification.

---

94 In the *Rogers* case, the director was very concerned that there should be no finding of dishonesty against him and the Secretary of State was content not to pursue any such allegation. It was clear that if dishonesty had been alleged, the director would have refused to agree to the use of the *Carecraft* procedure. The Court of Appeal held that it was not, therefore, open to the judge to find that the director had been dishonest.

95 Previously expressed by him in *Practice Direction* [1996] 1 All ER 445.

96 [1998] 1 WLR 422.

97 A court might stay proceedings on the basis that an undertaking had been offered in circumstances where to pursue the proceedings would be an abuse of process; see *Re Homes Assured Corporation plc* [1996] BCC 297.

98 [2002] 2 BCLC 263. See Walters (2002) and Rajani (2002) for alternative views of the decision.

(g) The nature of disqualification proceedings

As has been observed on various occasions[99] and can be seen from the views expressed by the Court of Appeal in *Re Grayan Services Ltd*, there is a penal element to the disqualification provisions as well as an intention that the public should be protected from future failings. The guidelines laid down by the Court of Appeal in *Re Westmid Packing Services*[100] as to appropriate length of disqualification bear a resemblance to guidelines on sentencing. There is a question of the extent to which defendant directors should be accorded the same protections as are given to those who stand accused in criminal trials. There has been considerable discussion of whether the appropriate standard of proof in disqualification cases is the civil one of 'balance of probabilities' or whether it should be the more onerous criminal standard of proof beyond reasonable doubt.[101] The issue has also arisen as to the extent to which the rules against self-incrimination apply.

Browne Wilkinson VC in *Re Lo-Line Electric Motors Ltd*,[102] having said that the primary purpose of the disqualification provisions was 'not to punish the individual but to protect the public against the future conduct of companies by persons whose past records as directors of insolvent companies have shown them to be a danger to creditors and others', went on to hold that, since disqualification involves a substantial interference with the freedom of the individual, the rights of the individual should be fully protected. In that case, natural justice required that the director be given prior notice of a change in the case against him from an allegation of commercial dishonesty to one alleging gross commercial negligence.[103] In *Secretary of State for Trade and Industry v Baker, re Barings (No 5)*[104] it was held appropriate for the Secretary of State to disclose to a defendant a report which would have to be disclosed in criminal proceedings.

The expressed view of the court has tended to be that the unfitness must be proved on the balance of probabilities but in reality a much more conclusive weight of evidence seems to be required. In *Re Swift 736 Ltd*,[105] Hoffmann J said that the director should be allowed the benefit of any reasonable doubt, a view also expressed by Lindsay J in *Re Polly Peck International plc*,[106] who said that s 6 was 'plainly quasi-penal in effect'. In *Re Living Images Ltd*,[107] Laddie J said that criminal burden of proof was not appropriate and that the court should not allow the director the benefit of any reasonable doubt. He did say that, as disqualification proceedings were likely to introduce serious charges of moral condemnation, the courts should be wary of giving credence to allegations affecting a director's moral character without substantial evidence to confirm their validity. The judge also said that the court must be careful

---

99　By Professor Dine, in particular; see, for example, in Rajak, 1993, p 173; Dine (1988) and (1994). See also Finch (1993).

101　[1998] 2 All ER 124.

101　Griffin (1997).

102　[1988] BCLC 698 (on the Companies Act 1985, s 300).

103　This was cited with approval in *Langridge* [1991] BCLC 543; *Re Living Images Ltd* [1996] 1 BCLC 348.

104　[1999] 1 BCLC 262.

105　[1993] BCLC 1.

106　[1994] 1 BCLC 574.

107　[1996] 1 BCLC 348.

not to fall into the trap of being too wise after the event and that the evidence of unfitness must be overwhelming in terms of probability rather than marginally indicative. This seems at least to be approaching the criminal standard of proof.

In *Re Dawes and Henderson (Agencies) Ltd*,[108] the court held that disqualification proceedings are not criminal proceedings and therefore are subject to the usual rule in civil proceedings that evidence of the general reputation of the defendant is not admissible. Blackburne J adverted to the suggestion that the proceedings were akin to criminal proceedings and said[109] 'it is sufficient to say that disqualification proceedings are civil in nature and the fact that allegations of dishonesty are levelled against the respondents does not alter that fact'. In *DC v United Kingdom*,[110] the European Court of Human Rights was asked to hold that disqualification using the *Carecraft* procedure with evidence obtained under compulsion using s 235 of the Insolvency Act 1986 and with no opportunity to adduce character evidence was a breach of Art 6 of the European Convention on Human Rights. The Court held that disqualification proceedings were civil and regulatory rather than criminal so that the only part of Art 6 which was relevant was that requiring that there be a fair trial; exclusion of character evidence was not unfair as it had been excluded on the basis that it was not relevant to the matters in issue and the use of compulsorily obtained statements was not necessarily unfair either given the civil nature of the proceedings.

The Court of Appeal in *Re Westminster Property Management Ltd, Official Receiver v Stern*[111] followed *DC v United Kingdom* and held that it could not be declared in advance that the trial would necessarily be unfair, although it was possible that in particular circumstances the use of compelled evidence would be a breach of Art 6(1); it would be a matter for the trial judge in any particular case to ensure that there was no such breach. The court also conceded that, even in civil proceedings, a fair trial required 'equality of arms' with each party being afforded a reasonable opportunity to present his or her case under conditions which do not place him or her at a substantial disadvantage compared with his or her opponent. In relation to evidential questions, the court considered that this could be dealt with by the trial judge.

The nature of the proceedings also impacts on the issue of costs. Since disqualification proceedings have been characterised as civil, a director who loses will usually be ordered to pay the costs of the Secretary of State.[112] Sir Richard Scott VC, speaking extra-judicially,[113] expressed his unease at the heavy burden of costs often placed upon directors contesting disqualification proceedings[114] and suggested that the approach taken in criminal proceedings could be adopted so that the ability of the defendant to pay could be taken into account. In *Re Westminster Property Management Ltd, Official Receiver v Stern*,[115] in which he gave judgment shortly afterwards, the

---

108 [1997] 1 BCLC 329.
109 Referring to a similar statement by the Court of Appeal in *Re Southbourne Sheet Metal* [1993] BCLC 135.
110 [2000] BCC 710.
111 [2001] 1 All ER 633.
112 *Re Southbourne Sheet Metal* [1993] BCLC 135.
113 At a meeting of the Chancery Bar Association, 20 October 1999, reported at [2002] Co Lawyer 90.
114 Community Legal Service funding will not generally be available for disqualification proceedings.
115 [2001] 1 All ER 633.

issue of costs was raised in connection with an 'equality of arms' argument. He acknowledged that the potential costs burden on defendants to disqualification proceedings was a serious one, but held that the cost of litigation and an imbalance in the financial resources available to one party compared with the other is not, in civil cases at least, a ground for concluding that the less well-off party is deprived of a fair trial. He also observed that no attempt had been made by the defendant to demonstrate that he was prevented for financial reasons from contesting the disqualification proceedings.

The result of recent case law would appear to be that the focus of debate should shift from whether or not disqualification proceedings are criminal in nature to the issue of whether in any particular case the defendant has been afforded a fair trial within Art 6(1) of the European Convention on Human Rights.

(h) Length of disqualification

Although the intention of the legislation is said to be primarily the protection of the public, the length of the disqualification is calculated according to seriousness of the conduct by what seems to be a backward rather than forward looking approach.[116]

The Court of Appeal has held[117] that it has the power to interfere with the length of disqualification ordered by the judge in the usual limited circumstances in which it may intervene with the exercise by a judge of a discretion vested in him or her. In *Re Sevenoaks Stationers Ltd*,[118] the Court of Appeal issued guidance, of a sort, as to the appropriate length of a disqualification order. It held that periods of 10 years or more should be reserved for particularly serious cases,[119] including those where a director had previously had a disqualification order made against him or her, disqualification for between six and 10 years should apply for 'serious cases which do not merit the top bracket'[120] and the minimum bracket of two to five years should be applied where 'though disqualification is mandatory, the case is, relatively, not very serious'.

The Court of Appeal had another opportunity in *Re Westmid Packing Services Ltd; Secretary of State for Trade and Industry v Griffiths*[121] to consider the principles governing the determination of length of disqualification. The correct approach was to start with an assessment of the correct period to fit the gravity of the offence, bearing in mind that the period of disqualification had to contain deterrent elements, and then allow for mitigating factors. The fact that the court was minded to grant leave under s 17 to act as a director was no reason for deciding to impose the minimum period of disqualification. Relevant matters included the director's general reputation and conduct in discharge of the office of director, his or her age and state of health, the

---

116 See Davies, 1997, p 683.

117 *Secretary of State v Ettinger* [1993] BCLC 896.

118 [1990] BCC 765.

119 A subsequent Court of Appeal decision held that one of the directors in *Secretary of State v McTighe* [1996] 2 BCLC 477 should be disqualified for 12 years since his conduct was particularly serious, in that he had caused three companies successively to trade at the risk of their creditors, caused the assets of two of them to be removed from creditors and failed to co-operate with the liquidator or the Official Receiver. The other director in that case was equally responsible for the trading at the risk of creditors in three companies and for some misappropriation of property and was disqualified for six years. *Official Receiver v Stern (No 2)* [2002] 1 BCLC 119 is another recent example of a disqualification order in the top bracket.

120 See, for example, *Re Skyward Builders* [2002] All ER (D) 367 (Dec).

121 [1998] 2 All ER 124.

length of time he or she had been in jeopardy, whether he or she had admitted the offence, his or her general conduct before and after the offence and periods of disqualification of any co-directors that might have been ordered by other courts. The period of disqualification was a matter for the discretion of the judge and the Court of Appeal could not intervene and substitute its own view unless the judge had erred in principle. In the instant case, in imposing the minimum period of disqualification, the judge had not erred in principle or been plainly wrong to do so (although the Court of Appeal clearly felt that the directors should consider themselves lucky not to have been disqualified for longer) and therefore the appeal would be dismissed. Since these cases always ultimately rest on their own facts, detailed citation of previous cases was unlikely to be helpful.

The court has an inherent power to stay or suspend a disqualification order pending an appeal but this will only be exercised in exceptional circumstances.[122] In most cases, an interim order giving leave to act as a director would be more appropriate since the public interest may be protected by obtaining undertakings from the director and by limiting the permission to act to an identified company.

(i) Leave to act despite disqualification

A person who is subject to a disqualification order or undertaking may apply to the court for leave to act in a way otherwise forbidden as a result of the disqualification. Section 17(5) of the Company Directors Disqualification Act 1986 provides that the Secretary of State will appear on such an application and call the attention of the court to any matters which appear to be relevant and may him or herself give evidence or call witnesses. If the conditions attached by the court to leave are not complied with, the director is in breach of the disqualification order and so exposed to personal liability.[123] In *Secretary of State for Trade and Industry v Collins and Others*,[124] the Court of Appeal held that, wherever possible, applications for leave should be dealt with at the same time as disqualification since there was otherwise a risk that the judge hearing the application for leave would not be fully aware of the nature of the conduct leading to the disqualification; separate hearings would also lead to duplication and waste of resources. The application for leave should be supported by clear evidence as to the precise role which the applicant would play in the company or companies in question and up-to-date and adequate information about that company or those companies. The discretion should be exercised having regard to the purpose of the Act, which Peter Gibson LJ agreed was the protection of the public, including all relevant interest groups such as shareholders, employees, customers, lenders and other creditors. The case illustrates the difficulty of appealing successfully from a first instance decision on an application for leave to act.

The case law demonstrates that the major factors to be considered by the court are the risk to the public of giving leave and the need (particularly of the company or companies in respect of which the disqualified person seeks leave) for the leave to be given. Arden LJ in *Re Tech Textiles Ltd, Secretary of State for Trade and Industry v Vane*[125]

---

122 *Secretary of State v Bannister* [1996] 1 All ER 993.
123 *Re Brian Sheridan Cars Ltd* [1996] 1 BCLC 327.
124 (2000) *The Times*, 25 January.
125 [1998] 1 BCLC 259.

observed that there would be companies where the involvement of the applicant in the capacity sought is vital to customer or investor confidence, or for some other sufficient reason. *Re Majestic Recording Studios*[126] was an early example of a case in which such need was demonstrated; the director was regarded as the 'moving spirit' behind the company and was consequently given leave to act as a director during his five year disqualification period. This was because the business would otherwise cease and 55 employees would lose their jobs. The court imposed safeguards in the form of an independent chartered accountant approved by the court acting as a co-director and an assurance that the previous year's accounts were properly audited.

In *Re Barings plc and Others (No 3); Secretary of State for Trade and Industry v Baker and Others*,[127] Sir Richard Scott VC stressed that leave should not be granted in circumstances in which the effect of its grant would be to undermine the purpose of the disqualification order; the improprieties which have led to, and required the making of, a disqualification order should be kept clearly in mind when considering whether leave should be given. Where there was little risk to the public, correspondingly little emphasis needed to be placed on the issue of 'need'. This case concerned a director of Barings who had been disqualified on grounds of incompetence in performing his role rather than in connection with any dishonesty. He had since the events leading to his disqualification become involved with three other companies whose management wished to retain his services; this could most easily be done by his being a non-executive director of the companies in question but it would be possible for the same services to be provided simply as a consultant and there was, therefore, arguably no 'need' for him to be given leave to act as a director in relation to them. It was held that any risk to the public could be addressed by the conditions attached to the leave, which were intended to ensure that he did not assume any executive responsibilities, other than of a trivial nature, in that he was barred from entering into any director's employment contract with any of the companies and from accepting director's fees.

Hoffmann LJ in *Re Grayan Services Ltd*[128] said that the question of whether the director was likely to repeat the offending conduct would be highly material to whether he or she is granted leave or not. As demonstrated by *Re Britannia Homes Centres Ltd, Official Receiver v McCahill*[129] and *Secretary for Trade and Industry v Barnett*,[130] it is unlikely that leave will be given to a director who has been disqualified in connection with the running of a one-man business to be a director of another similar company. The risk to the public will be too great; if the individual wishes to continue to run the business or a similar business, he or she will have to do so without the benefit of limited liability.

---

126 [1989] BCLC 1.
127 [1999] 1 All ER 1017. See Walters (1999). See also *Re Dawes and Henderson* [1999] 3 BCLC 317.
128 [1995] 3 WLR 1.
129 [2001] 2 BCLC 63.
130 [1998] 2 BCLC 64.

4 PREVENTING DIRECTORS FROM RE-USING THE COMPANY NAME

(a) The basic provision

Section 216 applies to a person where a company has gone into insolvent liquidation[131] and the person was a director or shadow director at any time in the 12 months before the liquidation. It introduces the concept of a prohibited name as a name by which the insolvent company was known in that 12 months or which is so similar as to suggest an association with that company and restricts the ability of a person to whom s 216 of the Insolvency Act 1986 applies to be involved in a company or business under a prohibited name. Unless the court has given leave or the case falls in one of the three exceptions outlined below,[132] a person to whom the section applies may not for five years from the start of the liquidation be a director of or in any way involved in the promotion, formation or management of either a company or any other business known by a prohibited name. Breach is a criminal offence of strict liability.[133] In *R v Doring*,[134] the court held that it was irrelevant that the defendant had not intended to be in breach and did not consider that what she had done amounted to 'management', since it was sufficient that she had intended to do what she had done and that had as a matter of fact amounted to management. In *Re Migration Services International Ltd*,[135] Neuberger J held that breach of s 216 could be taken into account in considering a subsequent application for a disqualification order.

Section 217 of the Insolvency Act 1986 imposes personal liability for debts on those who contravene s 216.[136] A person will be personally responsible for all the 'relevant debts' of a company if he or she is either involved with the management of a company in contravention of s 216 of the Insolvency Act 1986 or, as a person involved in the management of a company, he or she acts or is willing to act on instructions given by a person whom he or she knows to be in contravention of s 216. A person who has at any time acted on instructions given by a person whom he or she knew to be in contravention of s 216 in relation to the company will be presumed to have been so willing at any time thereafter. Liability will be joint and several with the company and any other person so liable. 'Relevant debts' are those incurred by the company whilst

---

131 Section 216(7) defines this as going into liquidation at a time when its assets are insufficient for the payment of its debts and other liabilities and the expenses of the winding up. The provision only applies where a company is in liquidation and not to administrative receiverships or administrations.

132 Which, somewhat oddly, are tucked away in the Insolvency Rules 1986.

133 The penalties for breach are contained in the Insolvency Act 1986, s 430 and Sched 10. In *R v Cole* (1997) *The Times*, 17 July, the Court of Appeal held that *mens rea* was not necessary for liability under the Insolvency Act 1986, s 216.

134 [2002] EWCA Crim 1695.

135 [2000] 1 BCLC 666.

136 *Inland Revenue Commissioners v Nash* [2003] All ER (D) 373 (Mar) is an example. See also *Archer Structures Ltd v Griffiths* [2003] EWHC 957 (Ch). This is very similar to the personal liability imposed by the Company Directors Disqualification Act 1986, s 15 on a person acting in breach of a disqualification order.

the person was either involved in management in breach of s 216 or willing to act on the instructions of someone in breach of s 216.[137]

(b) Exceptions to the basic rule[138]

The first exception applies where a company (referred to in the rules as 'the successor company') acquires the whole, or substantially the whole, of the business of an insolvent company,[139] under arrangements made by a liquidator, administrator, administrative receiver or supervisor of a company voluntary arrangement. The successor company may give notice to the insolvent company's creditors within 28 days from the completion of the arrangements, telling them that the company has assumed or proposes to assume a name that is or will be prohibited under s 216 of the Insolvency Act 1986 and naming persons to whom the section applies as having been directors or shadow directors of the insolvent company whom it is proposed will be involved in the management of the successor company. If the successor company gives such a notice, any person named in the notice may act in relation to the successor company notwithstanding that he or she has not had leave of the court. It is therefore possible for a new company to be set up with a name otherwise prohibited and directors who would otherwise be prohibited, without the leave of the court, so long as notice is given to the creditors of the insolvent company. The creditors are not given the chance to challenge the notice or object. The only restriction on abuse is the integrity of the insolvency practitioner and the fact that where a sale to the original directors or management is contemplated, the liquidator must give notice to the creditors' committee and any creditor can apply to court in respect of the liquidator's actions.[140] This provision is intended to prevent the potential loss of value to creditors where the goodwill of a business depends on the involvement of particular managers and the continued use of an established name.

The second exception provides that where a person applies for leave of the court under s 216 of the Insolvency Act 1986 not later than seven days from the date on which the company went into liquidation he or she may act without leave for six weeks from the commencement of the liquidation unless the court disposes of the application for leave under s 216 earlier.[141] This exception is to deal with the situation in which the new business is already operating before the old one goes into liquidation and, in the absence of this grace period, the new business might be forced to close.

The third excepted case allows those subject to s 216 of the Insolvency Act 1986 to continue to act in relation to a company that has been known by a prohibited name for 12 months before the insolvency provided the company was not dormant during that time. The proviso is intended to prevent the incorporation of the phoenix company

---

137 In *Thorne v Silverleaf* [1994] BCC 109, the plaintiff obtained judgment under s 217 against a director who had been found guilty under s 216. The Court of Appeal held that he had not waived his rights to recovery under this section even though he had allegedly aided and abetted the director and was aware of the facts relating to the offence and that those facts constituted a breach of s 216.

138 Contained in the Insolvency Rules 1986, rr 4.228–4.230.

139 In *Re Bonus Breaks Ltd* [1991] BCC 546, Morritt J indicated that he would be surprised if there was a requirement that liabilities of the business be transferred as well as assets.

140 Under the Insolvency Act 1986, ss 165(6) and 167(2).

141 According to *dicta* in *Re Bonus Breaks* the court may extend the six week period.

well ahead of a possible liquidation. Were it not for this exception, s 216 of the Insolvency Act 1986 would give rise to problems in relation to groups of companies whose members bear similar names in the event of the insolvency of one member of the group.

(c) Leave to use prohibited name

There is little reported case law on the basis on which the court decides whether or not to grant leave under s 216. The first reported case was *Re Bonus Breaks Ltd*,[142] in which Morritt J. gave leave in return for undertakings that the new company's capital base was maintained and the company would not redeem any redeemable shares or purchase its own shares out of its profits for two years. It seems to have been assumed in this case that the court had to be satisfied with the prospects of the new company, thus treating applications for leave to use a prohibited name in the same way as applications for leave to act as a director whilst subject to a disqualification order.

In *Penrose v Official Receiver*,[143] Timothy Penrose and Ruth Penrose, who had been directors of Hudsons Coffee Houses Ltd, which had gone into insolvent liquidation, asked for the court's leave under s 216 of the Insolvency Act 1986 to act as directors of a new company, Hudsons Coffee Houses (Holdings) Ltd. The old company had run a successful coffee house in Birmingham but had failed in an attempt to expand the business to other towns. The directors bought out the original Birmingham business but needed to be able to use the Hudson name to keep the trade brought about by guidebook entries. The new name was clearly a prohibited name within s 216. The Official Receiver did not oppose the granting of leave, but the district judge in the county court took the view that he had to be satisfied with the capitalisation and management of the new company.

The appeal was heard by Chadwick J, who could only intervene if satisfied that an error of principle had occurred in the county court. In giving leave to act under s 216 of the Insolvency Act 1986, he laid down some principles for future use. He said that an application under s 216 was a different exercise from that carried out under the Company Directors Disqualification Act 1986 when a disqualified director sought leave to act. Section 216 was not intended to provide the public with general protection against the applicant acting as a company director. The mischiefs aimed at by the section were, first, the risk that the business of the insolvent company had been acquired at an undervalue and, secondly, that creditors of the old company might be misled into believing that the new company was the same as the old. In this case, there was no risk to the new company's creditors beyond that which was permitted under the law in relation to the incorporation of limited liability companies. It was possible that these applicants were inexperienced and that the company was undercapitalised, but that was a risk regarded as acceptable by the legislation. There were no other grounds on which to justify a refusal to grant leave and leave would therefore be given. If there had been evidence of unfitness such as would justify a disqualification order, then it would be appropriate to refuse consent.

---

142 [1991] BCC 546.
143 [1996] 2 All ER 96 and see Robinson (1996).

In *Re Lighting Electrical Contractors Ltd*,[144] the court followed this more relaxed attitude and gave permission to a director of a company which had gone into insolvent liquidation to use similar names in relation to one trading company and five other dormant companies. The lack of fault on the part of the applicant for the insolvency of the original company was emphasised, as was the support of its receiver and creditors. The court held that the legislation did not require the successor companies to be trading, but it did refuse leave in respect of future, unidentified companies.

5 EVALUATION OF THE PROVISIONS

The Cork Committee observed[145] that the dissatisfaction with the law relating to delinquent directors was due 'not to the absence of appropriate legislation but to a failure to make use of the existing legislation' and, in the early years of the 1986 legislation, it appeared that not much had changed. In October 1993, the National Audit Office produced a report[146] evaluating the extent to which the current arrangements for disqualification protect the public and improve the business practices of company directors. One of its conclusions was that up to half the cases where disqualification of the director could be said to be in the public interest were not pursued by the Insolvency Service. The report found that by March 1993, only 1,700 disqualification orders had been made in response to 2,900 applications made under the 1986 Act. It identified large variations between different Official Receiver offices in the approach to cases. The report also indicated a lack of awareness amongst directors of the provisions or the existence of the Act. Following the publication of this report, the Committee of Public Accounts also expressed concern.

The report appears to have had a salutary effect. A follow-up report by the National Audit Office[147] in 1999 found that the Insolvency Service had increased the resources devoted to disqualifications from £9 million in 1993–94 to £22 million in 1997–98 and was allocating more high grade and support staff to the caseload. The report found an improvement in the management of disqualification work and greater consistency between local offices. As a consequence of this improvement in resourcing and management, there had been a threefold increase in the number of unfit directors disqualified from 399 in 1993–94 to 1,267 in 1997–98.[148] The report recommended that the Insolvency Service should seek to reduce the time taken to achieve a disqualification and should ensure that it had contingency plans in place to deal with any sudden increase in workload; the introduction of the undertakings regime by the Insolvency Act 2000 will address the first point and the recommendations of the Quinquennial Review as to greater use of the private sector would meet the second. The report also recommended that there should be a continued focus on enforcing disqualification orders and, to facilitate this, that the telephone hotline set up in 1998

---

144 [1996] BCC 950.
145 Paragraph 1815.
146 National Audit Office, *The Insolvency Service Executive Agency: Company Director Disqualification*, HC 907 (1993).
147 HC 424 (1998–99). See Hicks (1999).
148 The numbers of disqualifications has continued to rise, with the assistance of the undertakings regime; 1,502 directors were disqualified in 2000 and 1,689 in 2001.

for the public to report suspected breaches should be made easier to use. The report did, however, comment on the need to increase directors' awareness of the disqualification arrangements and to build confidence in the effectiveness of the legislation. The National Audit Office survey for the 1993 report had showed that 58% of the directors surveyed were not even aware of the existence of the disqualification provisions. According to the survey for the follow-up report, an even lower percentage (44%) claimed to be aware of the legislation although, by way of contradiction, 61% claimed to be 'quite well or very well informed about the factors that could lead to their disqualification'. 61% of those surveyed thought the legislation was not successful in disqualifying those who should be disqualified and 65% thought it was unsuccessful in protecting the public. The National Audit Office postulated that the additional publicity given to government efforts to disqualify rogue directors might, in fact, have had an adverse effect on public perceptions of the situation.

There are arguably still problems with the operation of the current disqualification regime. One possible problem with the system is that it depends on the input of private sector insolvency practitioners whose main function is to maximise the assets for the creditors and who approach their public interest duties with varying levels of enthusiasm and commitment of time.[149] Research shows that there may still be a lack of consistency in the application of the legislation[150] due mainly to differences in approach as to when the obligation to report a director as unfit arises. Unfitness may mean different things to different insolvency practitioners and there are likely to be differences in the extent to which the insolvency practitioners are influenced by such, technically irrelevant, issues as the general character of the director. Another issue which may yet arise is the potential human rights aspects of the new undertakings regime, particularly in the light of the financial pressures on directors to agree to give undertakings rather than go to court.

Insolvency Service satisfaction with the increase in numbers of those disqualified begs the question of whether the current regime is the appropriate strategy for raising standards amongst those enjoying the privilege of limited liability. This revolves around the effectiveness of the legislation as a standard-setting mechanism and as a deterrent to those who might consider departing from the required standards. Research carried out by Andrew Hicks casts serious doubt on the efficacy of the current system[151] as being the appropriate strategy to bring about improvement in standards. According to his research,[152] insolvency practitioners have little confidence that the legislation makes directors behave better in running their companies. Hicks suggests that disqualification is probably least effective against the owners of small businesses who make up most of the disqualified and who might well consider that the risk of being apprehended is worth running particularly since, if disqualified, it will still be possible to trade on their own account. Even for those honest individuals who would adhere to required standards, it is not clear that the required standards are sufficiently clear and Hicks suggests that the introduction of a directors' code for

---

149 See Wheeler (1995) for an interesting account of research into the attitude of insolvency practitioners to unfit conduct of directors. Rajak (ed), 1993, Chapter 12 contains an account from an earlier stage of the research.

150 ACCA Research Report No 59, described in Hicks (1999b).

151 See Hicks (1999b).

152 Hicks (2001).

creditors might clarify matters. He also points to the Australian experience of educating the general public as to what is to be expected from directors. Other suggestions discussed by Hicks include the introduction of a minimum capitalisation requirement for companies,[153] limiting access to the availability of limited liability,[154] the introduction of civil penalties and the introduction of compensation orders.

The Company Law Review Steering Group was of the view that the phoenix problem continued to be a significant one[155] and recommended the strengthening of the provisions of s 320 of the Companies Act 1985, which requires general meeting approval for transactions with the directors and those connected with them, by requiring there to have been an independent valuation of the assets concerned where a resolution under the section has been passed by the votes of the directors within a year before an insolvent liquidation. It also suggested that an independent valuer who did not have reasonable cause for providing an inadequate valuation should be liable to the company. A further recommendation was that consideration should be given to amending the insolvency legislation by introducing a power to apply for an interim disqualification order. The White Paper *Modernising Company Law* has not taken up these suggestions, but restricts itself to suggesting[156] that there should be an extension in the information provided in plain language (and minority languages) to new directors about their obligations under company and insolvency law.

---

153 Viewed with favour by insolvency practitioners but likely to be considered anti-competitive and not recommended by the Company Law Review Steering Group.
154 See Chapter 19, note 4.
155 *Modern Company Law for a Competitive Economy*, Final Report 2001, para 15.59.
156 Paragraph 3.17.

PART V
THE CREDITORS' BATTLE
FOR THE ASSETS

CHAPTER 24

INTRODUCTION TO PART V

This Part of the text is concerned with the rights of the creditors of bankrupts and insolvent companies in liquidation. By definition, there will be insufficient funds available for all creditors to be paid in full. Chapter 25 explains the effect of bankruptcy and liquidation on the rights of the creditors; in particular, it will be seen that the individual rights of unsecured creditors to pursue the debtor are converted to a right to participate in the collective administration of the insolvent's assets. Secured creditors and those with other proprietary interests are relatively immune to the insolvency of the debtor; Chapter 29 deals with the circumstances in which the security may be challenged and it will be seen from Chapter 34 that floating charges are postponed to the preferential creditors. Chapter 33 explains some other sources of funds available to employees and those whose claims against the insolvent have been insured.

The insolvency practitioner will have to identify, collect and realise the assets of the insolvent for distribution to the creditors; Chapter 26 explains the general principles relating to the availability of assets. Where the insolvents are individuals, the question arises of the extent to which they should be divested of assets which are used domestically, particularly by dependants, or which may contribute to their rehabilitation; Chapter 27 considers the extent of the bankrupt's estate and, in particular, the issue of the bankrupt's home. The insolvency practitioner will only be entitled to those assets beneficially owned by the insolvent; Chapter 28 considers the grounds on which third parties may claim to be entitled to assets in the apparent ownership of the insolvent. The insolvency practitioner may find it possible to swell the assets by clawing back property with which the insolvent has previously parted; this is dealt with in Chapter 30. In the case of a liquidation, it may be possible to make claims against those responsible for the insolvency as explained in Chapter 31. The expense of indulging in the necessary litigation may, however, prevent such claims from being a practical proposition; this is considered in Chapter 32.

The insolvency practitioner is under a duty to distribute the proceeds of the realisations in accordance with statute; this is explained in Chapter 34. Although the theory of insolvency law is that the unsecured creditors should share equally in the shortfall, it will be seen that there are categories of creditor that are treated preferentially and it has been a matter for some debate as to whether and to what extent this should be so. Chapter 34 deals with the overtly distributional rules of insolvency law, but the entirety of Part V is, in reality, concerned with the distribution of the loss between the various interested parties. The protection given to proprietary rights acquired prior to the onset of an insolvency clearly has fundamental consequences for the distribution of the loss; Chapter 26 considers the rationale for this preferential treatment of proprietary rights as compared with personal rights. Discussion of the requisite ingredients of the various proprietary rights which protect those who might otherwise find themselves sharing in the loss caused by an insolvency has not tended traditionally to involve overt consideration of the policy issues involved. In many instances, the resolution of distributional issues is hidden by technical legal argument; for example, in a number of bankruptcy cases, the distributional issue as between bankrupt and creditors has been resolved by a decision as to whether or not assets fall within the definition of 'property' and questions of loss distribution in corporate insolvency have often revolved around the distinction between a fixed and a floating charge. It is probable that clarification of some of the less coherent areas of common law (defeasibility of interests on insolvency is an example) might be assisted by a sharper focus on the underlying policy issues. It will be seen that statute has intervened from time to time to adjust the distributional consequences of the common law rules. The all-embracing nature of the floating charge, for example, has been addressed by statute introducing, first, the notion of the preferential creditor and, most recently, the concept of ring-fencing part of the assets for the unsecured creditors. The consequences of the wide notion of the property to be acquired by the trustee in bankruptcy have led to statutory reform in relation to pension rights and, to a limited extent, in relation to the family home.

Other aspects of the battle for the assets in an insolvency are considered elsewhere in this text, notably in the consideration in Part II of the moratorium in a company administration and of the tension between employees and creditors in relation to attempted business rescue. The material in Part IV on the costs of the insolvency system is also of relevance in this context since the greater the costs, and the more of them that have to be borne by insolvent estates, the less there will be for the creditors.

CHAPTER 25

EFFECT OF LIQUIDATION OR BANKRUPTCY ON CREDITORS' RIGHTS

1 INTRODUCTION

This chapter explains the effect on a creditor's rights when a debtor becomes bankrupt or goes into liquidation; it will be seen that the individual right of the unsecured creditor to pursue the debtor will generally come to an end and will be replaced by a right to prove in the insolvency in accordance with the rules for quantification and set-off provided by the insolvency legislation. There are likely to be some pre-insolvency methods of enforcement in progress at the onset of the bankruptcy or liquidation; the consequences of the advent of the insolvency for these are explained. The rights of some potential creditors of the insolvent will be accelerated by the insolvency so that future and contingent claims can also be dealt with in the insolvency.

2 EFFECT OF ADVENT OF A LIQUIDATION OR BANKRUPTCY

(a) General principles

The debtor, once bankrupt or in liquidation, becomes subject to a collective regime in which the unsecured creditors share the available assets. This collective regime only applies to those with purely personal rights against the debtor. Where a creditor has taken security against the debtor, or otherwise obtained real rights over assets of the debtor before the insolvency, he or she will stand outside the collective insolvency regime to the extent of those rights.[1] The insolvency does not generally affect pre-existing rights and most vested property rights will be upheld,[2] although there are certain limited circumstances in which the insolvency practitioner will be able to reclaim assets for the benefit of the creditors.[3]

The right to bring or enforce individual unsecured claims against the debtor comes to an end with the onset of formal insolvency and is converted to a right to prove for the debt in the insolvency. The rationale for this was given in the early days of corporate insolvency law as maximisation of the limited assets of the insolvent through collective management of them, thus avoiding the costs involved in multiple individual actions.[4] It also has the effect of reducing harassment of the insolvent, which was one of the aims of insolvency law identified by the Cork Committee. There is some provision for the back-dating of the collectivisation to an earlier point by dint of the legislation on preferences.[5] The rules in relation to bankruptcy and the two types of liquidation are broadly the same but there are differences in detail.

---

1   In case of a floating charge the rights are limited to an extent: see Chapter 29. A claimant who has obtained security over monies paid into court will be allowed to proceed (but a freezing order does not provide such security): *Edwards v Flightline* [2003] EWCA Civ 63 (CA).
2   The various bases on which proprietary claims may be made are examined in Chapter 28.
3   These are examined in Chapter 30.
4   *Re David Lloyd* (1877) 6 Ch D 339.
5   See Chapter 30.

(b) Liquidation

The position in relation to liquidation differs somewhat depending upon whether the liquidation is voluntary or compulsory. Where a company has gone into compulsory liquidation or a provisional liquidator has been appointed, s 130(2) of the Insolvency Act 1986 provides that no action or proceeding shall be proceeded with or commenced against the company or its property except with the leave of the court. 'Action or proceeding' was held in *Re Memco Engineering Ltd*[6] to include any type of distress. In a voluntary winding up, or where a petition for compulsory liquidation has been presented but not yet adjudicated upon, there is no automatic stay, but the court may on application by an interested party restrain proceedings.[7] It was held in *Re Roundwood Colliery Co*[8] that the court would exercise its power to stay in a voluntary liquidation in those circumstances in which it would not give leave under s 130(2) in a compulsory liquidation.

Under s 128 of the Insolvency Act 1986, any attachment, sequestration, distress or execution put in force against the estate or effects of the company after the commencement of a compulsory liquidation is void.[9] Section 183(1) of the Insolvency Act 1986, which applies to both types of liquidation, provides that where a creditor has issued execution against the goods or land of a company or has attached any debt due to it, and the company is subsequently wound up, the creditor is not entitled to retain the benefit of the execution or attachment against the liquidator unless he or she has completed the execution or attachment before the commencement of the winding up or, where the creditor has had notice of a meeting being called to consider a voluntary liquidation, before the date of that notice. Section 183(2)(c) gives the court the power to set aside the rights conferred on the liquidator by s 183(1).

In order to understand the operation of s 183 of the Insolvency Act 1986, it is necessary to identify the point at which enforcement is complete and after which the creditor will be unaffected by a subsequent liquidation. Section 183(3) provides that execution against goods will be completed by seizure and sale or by the making of a charging order; execution against land is completed by seizure, the appointment of a receiver or the making of a charging order; and attachment of a debt is completed by receipt of the debt. A person who purchases in good faith under a sale by the sheriff any goods of a company on which execution has been levied in all cases acquires a good title to them against the liquidator.[10]

Section 184 of the Insolvency Act 1986 places various duties on a sheriff[11] who has taken goods in execution of judgment. Where the sheriff is given notice of the liquidation before completion of the execution, he or she must on request deliver to the liquidator the goods and any money seized or recovered but the costs of the execution are a first charge on the goods or money so delivered. Where goods are sold

---

6   [1986] Ch 86.
7   Insolvency Act 1986, s 126 in the case of a compulsory winding up. In a voluntary liquidation, the court has the power under the Insolvency Act 1986, s 112 to exercise any power which it has in a compulsory liquidation.
8   [1897] 1 Ch 373.
9   The liquidation will be deemed to have commenced on the date of the presentation of the petition on which the order was subsequently made.
10   Insolvency Act 1986, s 183(2)(b).
11   Under s 184(6), the term includes any officer charged with execution of process.

pursuant to execution of judgment in excess of £500,[12] the sheriff charged with the execution must retain the balance of the proceeds, after deducting costs, for the 14 day period beginning with the day of sale (or of payment to avoid such sale). If within that period, the sheriff is given notice of presentation of a petition for winding up or of a meeting to consider a resolution for winding up and a liquidation follows, the proceeds shall be paid to the liquidator in priority to the claim of the execution creditor.

Although the dominant principle is that the start of a liquidation brings individual rights of enforcement to an end, it can be seen from the above that there is a discretion to allow individual action to proceed. The courts have had to decide in what circumstances they should make an exception to the collective *pari passu* rule. An argument by creditors that they could have completed enforcement in time had they not given way to the pleas of the debtor is unlikely to persuade the court. In *Re Aro*,[13] however, the Court of Appeal held that s 183(2) gives the court the freedom to do 'what is right and fair in the circumstances' and gave leave for the plaintiff to pursue a maritime claim in respect of which all the necessary steps had been taken to give the plaintiff a real right against the ship Aro except the service of the writ on the ship. This step had not been taken because the ship had already been arrested by another claimant and the normal practice was for further claimants to protect their position by a caveat in the Admiralty register, which the plaintiff had done. The Court of Appeal held that there was a powerful argument for leaving undisturbed this long established practice rather than sending maritime claimants the message that all claimants should go through the process of arresting the ship.

In *Re BCCI*,[14] Parker J said that he considered that the paramount question was whether separate proceedings as opposed to the winding up process itself were the appropriate method for determining the claim. Where the proceedings have been in progress for some time and a hearing of an appeal from a refusal by the liquidator to admit the proof of debt would involve re-hearing the same issues, it may be felt appropriate to allow the case to proceed to judgment but not to allow execution of that judgment.[15] In *Bristol & West Building Society v Alexander and Malinek*,[16] the court was influenced by the fact that the defendants, who were solicitors facing claims of negligence and breach of contract, were insured by the Solicitors' Indemnity Fund against liability.[17] The judge referred to the principle set down in the Australian case of *Ex p Walker*[18] that leave is more likely to be granted where the defendant is insured, since the intention of the legislation was not to protect insurers.

---

12   The amount currently prescribed by the Insolvency Proceedings (Monetary Limits) Order 1986 (SI 1986/1996).

13   [1980] Ch 196. See also *New Cap Reinsurance Corporation v HIH Casualty & General Insurance* [2002] 2 BCLC 228, in which the Court of Appeal, following *Re Aro*, held that in deciding whether to lift a stay under s 130, the court had a broad and unfettered discretion to do what was fair and right.

14   [1994] 1 BCLC 419.

15   See, for example, *Buchler v Chiron Corporation* (1996) unreported, 21 August.

16   [1998] 1 BCLC 485.

17   In *Re Linkrealm* [1998] BCC 478, leave to proceed against a company in liquidation was given in an action by an employee for personal injury; the company was insured against liability.

18   [1982] ALR 423.

Where the creditor is claiming in respect of an obligation entered into after the start of the liquidation, permission is likely to be given to pursue the normal remedy since liquidation expenses are payable by the liquidator rather than provable in the liquidation.[19] A landlord will usually be given leave to distrain for rent due during a liquidation provided the liquidator is positively using the premises for the purposes of the liquidation. In *Re Oak Pitts Colliery Co*,[20] it was held that it is not sufficient for the landlord to show that the liquidator had taken no steps to surrender the lease; something more than passivity is required.

(c) Bankruptcy

In the case of bankruptcy, it is s 285 of the Insolvency Act 1986 which imposes restrictions on proceedings and remedies. At any time when proceedings on a bankruptcy petition are pending or an individual has been adjudged bankrupt, the court may stay any action, execution or other legal process against the property or person of the debtor or bankrupt. After the making of a bankruptcy order, no person who is a creditor of the bankrupt in respect of a debt provable in the bankruptcy shall have any remedy against the property or person of the bankrupt in respect of that debt or, before the discharge of the bankrupt, commence any action or other legal proceedings against the bankrupt except with the leave of the court. This is different from the position in liquidation in which all unsecured claims are subject to the same rule; in the case of a bankruptcy, any action may be stayed but only claims which are provable in bankruptcy[21] will automatically be stayed. In *Re Smith*,[22] the House of Lords (holding that 'legal process' included the issue of a warrant of committal for non-payment of rates) held that s 285 of the Insolvency Act 1986 was to be considered as new legislation and regard need not be had to previous authorities. In *Re Saunders*[23] it was held, refusing to follow *Re National Employees Mutual General Insurance Association*,[24] that the necessary leave may be given retrospectively. It was held that ss 130 and 285 of the Insolvency Act 1986 are sufficiently similar that case law under the one was likely to be applicable to the other.

Section 285(4) of the Insolvency Act 1986 provides that the section does not 'affect the right of a secured creditor of the bankrupt to enforce his security'. *Razzaq v Pala*[25] required Lightman J to consider whether s 285 prevented a landlord from relying on a right of re-entry. A landlord had forfeited a lease for non-payment of rent after a bankruptcy order had been made against the tenant and the court had to decide, first, whether forfeiture by re-entry was the enforcement of a security and, secondly, whether it constituted a remedy against the property of the tenant. Lightman J held that the right of re-entry was neither a security interest[26] nor a remedy, since it merely

---

19 See Chapter 34 for an explanation of liquidation expenses.
20 (1882) 21 Ch D 322.
21 See the next section of this chapter.
22 [1990] 2 AC 215.
23 [1997] 3 All ER 992.
24 [1995] 1 BCLC 232.
25 [1997] EGCS 75.
26 Lightman J relied on a Court of Appeal authority, *Ezekiel v Orakpo* [1977] 1 QB 260.

prevented the recurrence of breaches of covenant and removed a defaulting tenant from the premises. The forfeiture was therefore valid,[27] although the court granted the tenant relief from it, since the rent had been brought up to date.

Section 346 of the Insolvency Act 1986 provides that the creditor of a bankrupt is not entitled to retain the benefit of an execution or attachment, or sums paid to avoid it, unless the process has been completed or sums paid before the commencement of the bankruptcy.[28] This is a parallel provision to s 183 which was outlined above in relation to liquidation and contains a similar discretion for the court to set aside the rights conferred on the Official Receiver or trustee. Goods cannot be claimed from a person who has acquired them in good faith from an officer charged with an execution. Section 346(3) and (4) place the same obligations on a sheriff charged with execution as are imposed by s 184 in the case of a liquidation; s 346(8) provides that these obligations do not apply in relation to after acquired property[29] unless the sheriff had notice before the execution, completed that the property was being claimed by the trustee in bankruptcy under s 307 of the Insolvency Act 1986.

Section 347 of the Insolvency Act 1986 provides that the right to distrain for rent upon the goods and effects of an undischarged bankrupt is available against the bankrupt's estate,[30] but only for six months' rent accrued due before the commencement of the bankruptcy. Landlords may not subsequently distrain against property in the bankrupt's estate after the discharge of the bankrupt. If a landlord distrains after a petition for bankruptcy has been presented and an order is subsequently made, any amount in excess of the six months' rent will be held for the bankrupt as part of his or her estate. Any right to distrain other than for rent is not affected by the bankruptcy order even if the right is expressed by statute to be exercisable in like manner as a right to distrain for rent.

3 PROVING DEBTS

(a) Provable debts

On the commencement of a bankruptcy or liquidation the creditor's right to pursue the debtor to judgment in court is usually converted to a right to prove for a dividend in the distribution of the estate. The creditor will have to establish that he or she is claiming in respect of a debt or liability to which a company or bankrupt was subject at the start of the insolvency or which subsequently arose by reason of any obligation incurred before the insolvency.[31] 'Liability' is defined as a liability to pay money or money's worth, including any liability under an enactment, any liability for breach of

---

27 The judge also rejected a suggestion that the forfeiture was a knowing wrongful interference with the Official Receiver's performance of his or her duties as an officer of the court.

28 Insolvency Act 1986, s 346(5) makes the same provision for completion of process as outlined above in relation to liquidation.

29 See Chapter 27.

30 This contrasts with the position in liquidation, where leave of the court will have to be obtained by the landlord.

31 The definitions of debt and liability are contained in the Insolvency Rules 1986, r 13.12 in relation to liquidations (the debts are those to which the company is subject at the commencement of the liquidation) and the Insolvency Act 1986, s 382 in relation to bankruptcies (the debts are those to which the bankrupt is subject on the date of the order).

trust, any liability in contract, tort or bailment, and any liability arising out of an obligation to make restitution. All claims by creditors in an insolvency not specifically excluded are provable as debts against the company or bankrupt whether they are present or future, certain or contingent, ascertained or sounding only in damages.[32] Debts can therefore be proved which have arisen after the commencement of the insolvency under contracts entered into previously; for example, failure to meet rental obligations after the commencement of the insolvency gives rise to a provable debt since the obligation to pay was incurred before the insolvency even though the debt did not arise until subsequently. Damages for tort are only provable if the cause of action, which is what creates the obligation, accrued before the commencement of the insolvency. Liabilities which arise after the start of the insolvency will be expenses of the insolvency rather than provable debts.[33]

A secured creditor who is not relying solely on his or her security has a choice of three options. He or she may value the security in the proof and prove for the balance of the debt, realise the security and prove for any deficiency or surrender the security and prove for the entire debt.[34]

In the case of a liquidation, there are few debts which cannot be proved since, given that liquidation brings the company's existence to an end, there is no possibility of any debt surviving a liquidation. A bankrupt, however, will survive the bankruptcy and, although the bankrupt discharged from bankruptcy is released from most of the debts,[35] some debts do survive the bankruptcy. Some of these surviving debts may also be the subject of proof in the bankruptcy,[36] but some are not provable in the bankruptcy and the creditors will only be able to take action after the discharge of the bankrupt. Although within the definition of bankruptcy debts, claims for fines imposed for an offence and obligations arising under orders made in family proceedings[37] or under maintenance assessments under the Child Support Act 1991 are not provable and the bankrupt is not released from them on discharge. Pre-1986, the law was that arrears of maintenance in family proceedings were not provable in a bankruptcy but that an outstanding lump sum, although not released by discharge, was provable.[38]

The case of *Woodley v Woodley*[39] reflects the current law. In this case, the court ordered a divorced husband to pay a lump sum of £60,000 to the wife; no capital could be identified, but the judge was of the view that the husband had concealed the existence of assets. The husband did not pay and was made bankrupt on his own petition. The wife issued a judgment summons seeking the husband's committal to

---

32 Insolvency Rules 1986, r 12.3, which specifies some of the excluded debts. Rule 12.3(2A) provides for the possibility of postponed debts which are not provable until all other claims in the insolvency proceedings have been paid in full with interest.

33 See Chapter 34.

34 Insolvency Rules 1986, rr 4.75, 4.88 in a liquidation, rr 6.98, 6.109 in a bankruptcy.

35 The exceptions are set out in the Insolvency Act 1986, s 281; see Chapter 15 above.

36 Where the debt results from some fraud or fraudulent breach of trust to which the bankrupt was a party (fraudulent breach of trust in this context requires dishonesty, see discussion in *Woodland-Ferrari v UCL Group Retirements Benefit Scheme* [2002] 3 All ER 670) and, unless the court orders otherwise, damages in respect of personal injuries.

37 Including costs orders: *Levy v Legal Services Commission* [2001] 1 All ER 895.

38 See *Curtis v Curtis* [1969] 1 WLR 422.

39 [1993] 1 FCR 701 and *Woodley v Woodley (No 2)* [1993] Fam Law 471. See also *Re Mordant* [1995] BCC 209. Miller (1994) and (2002a).

prison for wilful refusal to pay. The husband argued that the bankruptcy made it impossible to pay. The court at first instance held that the bankruptcy was no bar because the lump sum order was not a debt provable in the bankruptcy. In the Court of Appeal, it was held that this view failed to take account of the fact that the assets had all vested in the trustee. The court pointed to the possible inconsistency between ss 382 and 281 of the Insolvency Act 1986, which described a lump sum order as a bankruptcy debt but one which survived the bankruptcy, and r 12(3) of the Insolvency Rules 1986, which provided that the debt was not provable in the bankruptcy. When a differently constituted Court of Appeal had occasion to consider the matter again subsequently it did not accept that r 12.3 might be open to challenge, but invited the attention of the Insolvency Rules Committee to consider restoring the former position under which a lump sum order could be proved but would not be released on the debtor's discharge. Balcombe LJ pointed out that there was no necessary or logical link between provability of a debt and its release on discharge; it is true that there are debts which are not provable and are not released, but equally liability to pay damages in respect of personal injuries is provable and is not released.[40] He said: 'It seems therefore that any link between provability and release on discharge is a matter of policy and I can see good policy grounds for saying that a lump sum order made in family proceedings should (like damages for personal injuries) be both provable in bankruptcy and yet not be released on discharge.' If this had been the state of the law, the wife in *Woodley* would have been in a position to get the trustee to investigate the disappearance of the husband's assets.[41]

It is understandable that periodical maintenance payments are not provable in the bankruptcy; the essence of such payments is that they are made out of current income and, in calculating the extent to which a bankrupt can be required to make over his or her income under an income payments order,[42] the court will not make an order which would reduce the income of the bankrupt below what appears to be necessary for meeting the reasonable domestic needs of the bankrupt and his or her family.

(b) The rule against double proof

The rule against double proof prevents more than one proof being submitted in respect of the same debt. The most common situation of potential double proof relates to contracts of suretyship or guarantee.[43] Sureties or guarantors of debts of the insolvent have contingent claims against the insolvent in that they may be called upon to pay the principal creditor of the insolvent. If both principal creditor and guarantor were permitted to claim, the same debt might be paid twice.[44] An attempt by a debtor of a company to set off potential liability under a guarantee was also defeated by this reasoning in *Re Glen Express Ltd*.[45]

---

40 See the Insolvency Act 1986, s 281(5)(a).

41 In 2001, a sub-committee of the Insolvency Court Users Committee, chaired by Evans Lombe J, proposed reforms under which lump sums, arrears of periodical payments and costs would be provable and not released but the government said that it could not find time in the current round of insolvency legislation: Brougham (2002).

42 See Chapter 27.

43 It may operate in other circumstances. See, for example, *The Liverpool (No 2)* [1963] P 64.

44 See Mellish LJ in *Re Oriental Commercial Bank* (1871) 7 Ch App 99; *Re Glen Express Ltd* [2000] BPIR 456.

45 [2000] BPIR 456.

The rule against double proof was considered by Robert Walker J in *Re Polly Peck International plc*,[46] a case brought by the administrators of Polly Peck International plc for directions in connection with a scheme of arrangement which was to provide for the collection, realisation and distribution of the assets of Polly Peck International in what the judge described as 'a sort of notional liquidation in advance of any actual liquidation, with a view to saving costs'. The scheme provided that claims should only be admitted which would be admissible in a compulsory liquidation commencing on the date the scheme took effect. Polly Peck International plc had raised money via its wholly owned subsidiary, PPIF, which had issued £400 million of bonds and then on-lent the money to Polly Peck International. Polly Peck International had guaranteed repayment of the bonds to the bondholders. PPIF had gone into liquidation and the liquidator was claiming repayment of the loan from Polly Peck International, which was also facing claims from the bondholders on the guarantees. Robert Walker J held[47] that the creditors (the bondholders) were entitled to proceed against both debtor (PPIF) and guarantor (Polly Peck), although not to receive more than was owed in total. He also observed that the guarantor could only prove in the debtor's liquidation if it had paid the creditors in full, in which case the creditors would drop out of the matter. The guarantor would not be able to claim in competition with the creditor, since the guarantor's contingent claim was not regarded as an independent, free-standing debt, but only as a reflection of the 'real' debt.

It has been held[48] that a distinction has to be drawn between the guarantee of part of a debt and the guarantee of a whole debt subject to a maximum limit on the liability of the guarantor which is less than the amount of the guaranteed debt. In the former case, payment of the amount guaranteed entitles the guarantor to prove, since he or she has discharged the entire liability to the creditor, whereas in the latter case only the creditor may prove. The guarantee of the whole of a fluctuating debt (such as an overdraft) with a limit on the liability of the guarantor will be construed as a guarantee of part of the debt unless the guarantee contract provides otherwise.

(c) Procedure for proving debts

The detailed provisions on proof of debts are contained in the Insolvency Rules.[49] In the case of a bankruptcy or compulsory liquidation, proof of debt forms requiring specified details will be sent out to every known creditor. In a voluntary liquidation debts may be proved more informally. The insolvency practitioner in any kind of insolvency may require affidavit support for the claim and if the claim is rejected in whole or in part, the insolvency practitioner must give reasons in writing to the creditor concerned. The creditor is then entitled to apply to the court within 21 days of the date of service of the rejection for the decision to be reversed. There is no time limit for the submission of proof of debt but a creditor who has not proved a debt cannot

---

46 [1996] BCC 486. See also *Re Parkfield Group plc* [1998] 1 BCLC 451.

47 Refusing to 'lift the corporate veil' and treat parent and subsidiaries companies as one entity, in which case the bondholders would have been bringing the same claim twice.

48 See *Ellis v Emmanuel* (1876) 1 Ex D 157; *Re Sass* [1896] 2 QB 12; *Barclays v TOSG* (1984) 1 BCC 99,017 in the Court of Appeal. The case went to the House of Lords [1984] 1 AC 626, where it was held that the debts in question were mutually exclusive and the rule against double proof did not have to be considered.

49 Insolvency Rules 1986, rr 4.73–4.94 in the case of a liquidation and rr 6.96–6.107 in the case of a bankruptcy.

benefit from any distribution of the assets nor vote at any meeting of creditors. Before declaring a dividend, notice must be given of the intention to do so to all known creditors who have not yet proved their debts.

(d) Quantification of claims

The insolvency practitioner will estimate the value of any debt which, because it is subject to a contingency or for some other reason, does not bear a certain value and this estimated amount will be the amount provable.[50] A debt incurred or payable in a currency other than sterling will be converted into sterling at the official exchange rate prevailing on the day of the bankruptcy order or when the company went into liquidation.[51] In case of rent and other payments of a periodical nature, the creditor may prove for any amounts due and unpaid up to the date when the liquidation began or the bankruptcy order was made.[52] A creditor may prove for a debt of which payment was not yet due on the date of going into liquidation or bankruptcy,[53] but the dividend payable will be adjusted for early payment.[54] Where a debt bears interest, interest in respect of the period before the start of the liquidation or bankruptcy will be provable as part of the debt. Interest up to the start of the insolvency may also be claimed in respect of a debt due by virtue of a written instrument which is payable at a certain time or where notice was served before the insolvency demanding payment and indicating an intention to charge interest from the date of the demand; in either case, the rate of interest will be that specified in s 17 of the Judgments Act 1838 on the date of the bankruptcy order or when the company went into liquidation.[55]

In quantifying the amount of the claim, the insolvency rules on set-off, which are considered in the next section, must be taken into account.

4   MUTUAL CREDIT AND SET-OFF[56]

(a) General

In quantifying the amount of the provable debts, the insolvency rules on set-off must be taken into account.[57] In the case of a bankruptcy, s 323 of the Insolvency Act 1986 provides as follows:

---

50   Insolvency Rules 1986, r 4.86 in a liquidation; Insolvency Act 1986, s 322(4) in the case of a bankruptcy.
51   Insolvency Rules 1986, rr 4.91(liquidation), 6.111 (bankruptcy).
52   Insolvency Rules 1986, rr 4.92 (liquidation), 6.112 (bankruptcy).
53   Insolvency Rules 1986, rr 4.94 (liquidation), 6.114 (bankruptcy).
54   In accordance with the formula provided in r 11.13.
55   The rules on interest are contained in the Insolvency Rules 1986, rr 4.93 (liquidation) and 6.113.
56   This account draws heavily on Derham, 2002. See also Goode, 1997, Chapter 8. In relation to employee creditors, see Pollard (1995). In relation to netting arrangements and cash collateral, see Turing (1996).
57   These are not the same as the equitable and statutory rules of set-off which apply where the parties are not insolvent. See Derham, 2002. Other forms of set-off which have taken effect before the start of the liquidation or bankruptcy may be relevant in the calculation of the indebtedness at that point.

(1) This section applies where before the commencement of the bankruptcy there have been mutual credits, mutual debts or other mutual dealings between the bankrupt and any creditor proving or claiming to prove for a bankruptcy debt.

(2) An account shall be taken of what is due from each party to the other in respect of the mutual dealings and the sums due from one party shall be set off against the sums due from the other.

(3) Sums due from the bankrupt to another party shall not be included in the account taken under subsection (2) if that other party had notice at the time they became due that a bankruptcy petition relating to the bankrupt was pending.

Similar provision is made in respect of a liquidation;[58] rather oddly, it is tucked away in the Insolvency Rules 1986 rather than being in the main body of the Act. Rule 4.90 is to the same effect as s 323; sums due to a creditor are to be excluded if at the time they became due the creditor had notice either of a petition for a compulsory winding up or of notice calling a meeting to put the company into voluntary liquidation.

These provisions will benefit a creditor of an insolvent[59] because he or she will get full credit for any amounts owed to the insolvent. Were it not for the set-off rules, the creditor of an insolvent would have to make full payment of any amounts owed whilst receiving only a dividend in respect of the amount owing from the insolvent; one explanation for the development of these rules is that this was perceived as an injustice.[60] It is true that, as between the insolvent and the individual creditor, the set-off rules appear fair, but the rules do have the effect of excluding some or all of the amount owing from the assets available to the creditors generally.[61]

By way of example, suppose that a bankrupt or company being wound up owed a creditor £100 as a result of one transaction, that the creditor owed the insolvent £60 as a result of another transaction (so that as a result of the two transactions the creditor would have expected to be £40 better off) and that a distribution of 10% would be all that the insolvency practitioner would be able to make to ordinary creditors. In the absence of set-off, the creditor would be under an obligation to pay £60 to the company and would receive £10 in the distribution; as a result of the two transactions, the creditor would be worse off by £50. The set-off provisions extinguish the claim against the creditor and leave him or her with a provable debt of £40 in respect of which he or she will be paid £4, a net gain of £4 on the two transactions.[62]

---

58 Insolvency set-off does not apply in other forms of corporate insolvency such as administration.

59 There is scope for terminological confusion in discussion of set-off since the parties involved will both be both debtor and creditor. In this discussion, the term 'creditor' is employed to describe the non-insolvent party unless the contrary is made clear.

60 In *Stein v Blake* [1995] 2 All ER 961, Lord Hoffmann said that where parties have been giving credit to each other in reliance on their ability to secure payment by withholding, it would be unjust to deprive the solvent party of this security. The origin of the rule is lost in history since, although the statutory provision only dates back to 1705, it reflects practice previous to this; it is likely that the explanation lies, at least in part, in a combination of the accounting practices of the Elizabethan commissioners in bankruptcy and the tendency of established practice to become embedded in English law.

61 It is not a rule of universal application. See *Re BCCI SA (No 10)* [1996] 4 All ER 796.

62 The dividend percentage would not, in fact, be the same in both situations since the effect of the set-off would reduce the total quantity of assets available to be divided amongst the creditors.

The insolvency set-off provisions have been held to be mandatory and creditors are not allowed to contract out of the right.[63] The Cork Committee recommended[64] that a creditor should be allowed to renounce the right, but the recommendation was not acted upon in the drafting of the legislation.

(b) Circumstances in which set-off applies

The legislation requires that the creditor and the insolvent have 'mutual credits, mutual debts or other mutual dealings'. It is necessary to consider, first, which claims and transactions fall into the categories of credits, debts or dealings and, secondly, what the requirement of mutuality imports.

Debts are claims which are both in existence and presently payable and credits, which would include debts payable at a future date, must be at least likely to result in debts.[65] Dealings,[66] a category introduced into the legislation in 1869, are wider and probably include all ordinary business transactions; for example, damages claims for breach of contract, transactions which are only debatably mutual credits and debts arising after the insolvency from prior transactions. This apparently goes beyond dealings arising out of contract; in *Re DH Curtis (Builders) Ltd,*[67] the cross-claims arose from the provisions of the tax legislation and it was held that the set-off provisions applied. It is necessary for a claim to be provable before set-off can apply, but the fact that a claim is provable will not necessarily be enough; it seems unlikely that a claim in tort not arising out of a prior dealing would fall within the provision.

Mutuality requires that the demands be between the same parties and that they be held in the same capacity, right or interest. Mutuality will be determined by reference to the beneficial, rather than the bare legal rights of the parties.[68] The courts have recently had to consider whether an insolvent bank can set off the amounts owed by borrowers against its liability to repay sums of money deposited with it by guarantors[69] of the borrowers' obligations. In *MS Fashions Ltd v BCCI,*[70] the guarantor had given both a personal guarantee and a deposit and it was held that since the guarantor had incurred personal liability to the bank, there was sufficient mutuality for set-off. In *Re BCCI (No 8),*[71] the depositors did not give a personal guarantee to the bank in addition to the deposit. The bank's liquidators wanted to know whether they should attempt to recover the whole of the loan from the principal debtors and leave the depositors to prove in the liquidation or whether they should set off the amount of the outstanding loan against the deposit and claim from the principal debtor only so much of any of the loan as exceeded the amount of the deposit. It was held that there was a lack of mutuality and set-off was not possible; there was no obligation due from

---

63 *National Westminster Bank v Halesowen Presswork and Assemblies* [1972] AC 785; *Stein v Blake* [1995] 2 All ER 961. See the discussion in Chapter 34 on the difficulties of contracting out of the statutory scheme of distribution.

64 Paragraph 1342. See Chapter 30 of the Cork Report generally on set-off.

65 *Palmer v Day & Sons* [1895] 2 QB 618, 621.

66 See *Peat v Jones & Co* (1881) 8 QBD 147; *Eberle's Hotels and Restaurant Co Ltd v E Jonas & Brothers* (1887) 18 QBD 459.

67 [1978] 1 Ch 162.

68 *BCCI v Prince Fahd Bin Salaman Abdul Aziz Al-Saud* [1997] BCC 63.

69 The guarantors were the beneficial owners of the borrowing companies.

70 [1993] Ch 425.

71 [1997] 4 All ER 568 (HL) affirming the Court of Appeal's decision at [1996] 2 All ER 121.

depositor to bank in respect of which the obligation to repay could be set off. The depositors would have to prove in the liquidation;[72] Lord Hoffmann observed that the sense of injustice felt by the depositors arose from the principle of separate legal personality (in that the depositors were only third parties in the eyes of the law and not in economic reality) rather than the rules of set-off.

The question has arisen as to whether there is mutuality where the cross-transactions involve different departments of the Crown. In *Re DH Curtis*,[73] it was held that tax due to one department of the Crown may be set off against a repayment due from a different department.[74] Both transactions were with the Crown and set-off can arise out of different transactions between the same parties. The Cork Committee[75] felt that this treatment of the Crown as one and indivisible conferred an unwarranted preference on it and recommended that government departments should be treated as separate entities for the purpose of set-off.[76] It also recommended that there should be no set-off between contractual and statutory obligations. These recommendations were not implemented.

Where a creditor is owned both preferential[77] and ordinary debts, the creditor would prefer to set off first against the non-preferred debt. In *Re Unit 2 Windows Ltd*,[78] Walton J said that equity required that the rights of set-off should be exercised proportionately against each class of debt.

Set off can only apply where the claims on each side are money demands. A proprietary claim may not be set off against a money claim.[79] A secured creditor may choose to rely entirely on the security, in which case the set-off provisions are irrelevant unless there is a balance owing after enforcement. Alternatively, the creditor may choose to surrender the security and prove for the debt, or value the security and prove for the balance. Where the creditor elects to prove on one of these bases, the provable debt can be the subject of a set-off.[80] Where the creditor has both secured and unsecured debt, he or she may choose to rely on the set-off as against the unsecured debt; the principle of *Re Unit 2 Windows Ltd* does not apply. Where the insolvent is holding a sum on trust for a creditor, the issue of the extent to which the amounts owing to the insolvent can be deducted from the trust moneys before these are returned to the creditor depends on the terms of the trust. In *Re ILG Travel Ltd*,[81] it

---

72 This produces the paradox that the bank was better off for not having taken a personal guarantee from the depositors. See Evans (1996) for a suggestion of how this paradox could be avoided. See also Chapter 29 and references cited therein.

73 [1978] 1 Ch 162. This was a case on the Bankruptcy Act 1914, but would be decided in the same way under the current legislation.

74 In *Secretary of State for Trade and Industry v Frid* [2002] All ER(D) 76, an attempt by the Crown to set off VAT due to the company against amounts paid out by the National Insurance Fund failed because the liability was only contingent at the date of the liquidation.

75 And the Blagden Committee before it.

76 Cork Report, paras 306–07, 309.

77 See Chapter 34.

78 [1985] 1 WLR 1383.

79 *Re Pollitt* [1893] 1 QB 455; *Re Mid-Kent Fruit Factory* [1896] 1 Ch 567. *Rolls Razor Ltd v Cox* [1967] 1 QB 552 appears to be an exception in that a salesman entrusted with the company's goods was entitled to keep them by way of set-off against sums owing to him by the company. The case may be justifiable on other bases, but is probably wrong on the law relating to set-off.

80 *Re Norman Holding Co Ltd* [1991] 1 WLR 10.

81 [1996] BCC 21.

was held that sums held by a travel agent on trust for the insolvent tour operator were required, as a matter of contract, to be handed over only after deduction of sums owed by the tour operator to the travel agent so that the set-off rules were not relevant.[82]

(c) Effect of set-off

The date which defines the accounts to be balanced is the date of the commencement of the bankruptcy[83] or of commencement of the liquidation.[84] This means, for example, that where the insolvency practitioner sells goods after the commencement of the insolvency, the purchaser will not be able to set off liability for the price against a provable debt owed to him.

The House of Lords in *Stein v Blake*[85] held that the balance will be struck automatically as at that date so that the separate debts cease to exist. In this case, the parties were involved in litigation in which each had a claim against the other. Before the action came to trial the plaintiff was adjudicated bankrupt and his trustee in bankruptcy assigned to him the trustee's claims in the action in return for a share of the net proceeds recovered in the action.[86] The defendant applied to have the action dismissed, claiming that after the plaintiff had become bankrupt, the plaintiff's claim and the defendant's counterclaim fell to be dealt with in the bankruptcy and until an account had been taken under s 323 of the Insolvency Act 1986, there was nothing to assign. The House of Lords held that the claims had been extinguished as separate choses in action by s 323 and replaced by a claim for the net balance. The trustee in bankruptcy could assign a claim to the net balance before that balance had been ascertained. The trustee had therefore been entitled to assign to the plaintiff his claim against the defendant.

A contingent liability owed by the insolvent may have a value put on it; in *Stein v Blake*, Lord Hoffmann said that 'due' means treated as having been owing at the relevant date with the benefit of hindsight and, if necessary, estimation prescribed by the insolvency law. The case of *Re Charge Card*[87] concerned a company which operated a charge card scheme and assigned its receivables to a factor under an agreement that if the company went into liquidation, it could be required to repurchase the debts at face value. The court had to decide whether, if a notice requiring repurchase was given after liquidation (so that at the start of the liquidation the liability to do so was merely contingent), the factor could set off the company's liability to pay the price against a debt owing by the factor to the company. Millet J held that provided the contingent liability is wholly referable to a prior agreement between the parties (as was the case here), set-off between them will be possible. There is, however, no machinery for quantifying contingent or unascertained claims of an insolvent against a creditor and such claims cannot be included in the insolvency set-off account.

---

82 See also *Obaray v Gateway (London) Ltd* (2000) unreported, 1 December, in which it was held that where the terms of the deed authorise the landlord to make deductions from the deposit to recover arrears of rent, the landlord may do so without claiming an insolvency set-off.

83 The date of the order.

84 The date of the resolution in a voluntary liquidation or of the court order; in a case involving both, it will be the earlier date.

85 [1995] 2 All ER 961.

86 See Chapter 32 on the problems faced by insolvency practitioners in funding litigation.

87 [1988] 3 WLR 764 (CA); affirming [1987] Ch 150.

(d) Limitations on application of set-off

The statutory provisions substitute an earlier date for striking a balance on the account between the insolvent and the other party where the other party had notice of a pending petition or of a meeting to consider a resolution for winding up. This does not deal with the situation where it is quite apparent to the creditor that the debtor is unable to pay his or her debts; the creditor will be able to assign the debt to someone indebted to the debtor who will thereby be able to obtain the full value of the assigned debt in the course of an insolvency. The Cork Committee recognised this problem[88] and recommended a change to the rules but this has not happened.

The principle precluding a person from relying on his or her own wrongful act to obtain a set-off extends to fraud, breach of trust and misfeasance amounting to breach of fiduciary duty, but probably not to breach of contract committed in order to benefit from set-off.

(e) Multiple bank accounts

Where a customer has several accounts with a bank, some in credit and some in debit, the bank may combine the accounts and proceed on the basis of the combined balance. The bank can thereby obtain the full benefit of the account in credit by setting it against the account in debit. This principle arises from the fact that there will be only one banker/customer relationship regardless of the number of accounts in existence.

---

88   Paragraphs 127, 307.

CHAPTER 26

ASSETS AVAILABLE TO THE CREDITORS: GENERAL PRINCIPLES

1   INTRODUCTION

The insolvent is likely to have a variety of assets which could be realised and the proceeds distributed to the creditors; most of these will become available to the creditors. In the case of a bankruptcy, the bankrupt's estate will fall into the custody and control of the Official Receiver on the making of the bankruptcy order[1] and will subsequently vest by operation of law without further formality in the trustee in bankruptcy when appointed,[2] with relation back to the start of the bankruptcy so that the trustee will be deemed to have owned the assets since the date of the bankruptcy order. There is an obligation on the bankrupt[3] to deliver up to the trustee possession of any property of which he or she has possession or control and of which the trustee is required to take possession. In contrast, the assets of a company in liquidation do not normally vest in the liquidator; the liquidator takes control of them[4] as agent for the company which remains the legal owner, holding the assets on trust for the creditors.[5] This distinction means that provision has to be made in a bankruptcy in respect of assets which materialise after the vesting of the estate in the trustee;[6] in the case of a liquidation, no such provision is necessary.

A bankruptcy also involves the additional complication that the bankrupt and any dependants will need to be left sufficient assets with which to maintain themselves.[7] An obviously difficult policy issue arises regarding the extent to which the creditors should suffer for the needs of the bankrupt's family and vice versa. The family home and the bankrupt's pension have given rise to particular problems. All the assets of a company will be distributed, but there are exceptions in the case of a bankruptcy;[8] in *Re Rae*,[9] Warner J said 'The specific exceptions exist either because the property is not appropriate for distribution among the bankrupt's creditors, such as property of which he or she is only a trustee, or because, unlike an insolvent company, the bankrupt is a human being whose life must continue during and after insolvency'.

As will be seen, the insolvency legislation has a very wide concept of the property which is available for distribution but, as indicated in the *dictum* of Warner J quoted in

---

1   Insolvency Act 1986, s 287.
2   Insolvency Act 1986, s 306.
3   Insolvency Act 1986, s 312.
4   Insolvency Act 1986, s 144. The court has the power under the Insolvency Act 1986, s 145 to vest property in the liquidator if necessary.
5   If necessary, the Insolvency Act 1986, s 234(2) gives the court the power to require any person to hand over to the liquidator property in his or her possession or control to which the company appears to be entitled.
6   See Chapter 27. There is an obligation on the bankrupt to notify the trustee of any property or increased income to which he or she becomes entitled during the course of the bankruptcy: s 333(2).
7   See Chapter 27.
8   See Chapter 27.
9   [1995] BCC 102.

the previous paragraph, the insolvency practitioner may only realise such beneficial interest as the insolvent holds in the assets.[10]

Some of the available assets may constitute a burden on the insolvent's estate rather than being capable of realising any distributable value. The insolvency practitioner may be able to disclaim assets which would otherwise have been available; this is considered in further detail below.

2 PROPERTY AVAILABLE

(a) Definition of property

The term 'property', as defined by s 436 of the Insolvency Act 1986, is of pivotal importance. Section 144 of the Insolvency Act 1986 provides that in a compulsory winding up, the liquidator takes into his or her custody or under his or her control all the property and things in action to which the company is entitled.[11] Section 107 of the Insolvency Act 1986 provides that the company's property in a voluntary winding up shall on the winding up be applied in satisfaction of the company's liabilities. In a bankruptcy, the bankrupt's estate, which vests in the trustee once appointed, comprises all property belonging to or vested in the bankrupt at the commencement of the bankruptcy and property which by virtue of the Act is treated as falling into that category.[12]

The construction of the term 'property' has also been central in a number of other contexts. Only 'property' is capable of being disclaimed under ss 178 and 315 of the Insolvency Act 1986. The moratorium in administration protects the 'property' of the company. The definition is the same in whatever context it is used. Section 436 of the Insolvency Act 1986 provides that, except in so far as the context requires, property 'includes money, goods, things in action, land and every description of property wherever situated and also obligations and every description of interest, whether present or future or vested or contingent, arising out of, or incidental to, property'. It is to be noted that the definition is self-referential in that it includes without definition the word 'property'; Warner J in Re Rae[13] said that in the insolvency context, the word connoted anything which is capable of being owned and of which the ownership can be asserted or defended in legal proceedings and he pointed out that 'property' as defined by s 436 is a wider concept than this. The Court of Appeal in Bristol Airport plc v Powdrill[14] observed of s 436 that it 'is hard to think of a wider definition of property'.

---

10 See below and see Chapter 28 for third party claims to beneficial interests in the assets.

11 Insolvency Act 1986, s 143 uses the term 'assets' rather than 'property' in obliging the liquidator in a court winding up to secure that the assets of the company are got in, realised and distributed to the company's creditors; it seems likely that assets and property would be considered synonymous.

12 Insolvency Act 1986, s 283. Chapter 27 explains the assets that are excluded from the bankrupt's estate.

13 [1995] BCC 102.

14 [1990] BCC 130.

This extensive but not exhaustive definition clearly encompasses interests in land (freeholds and leaseholds)[15] and personal property, both tangible and choses in action (including documentary intangibles). Intangible property will include goodwill of a business and intellectual property such as copyrights, patents and trademarks. Choses in action consist of personal rights to claim property rather than the actual physical property itself; included in this category are debts, negotiable instruments, shares, legacies and rights of action[16] arising from torts and breaches of contract.

The extent of the concept of property is illustrated by the case of *Re Rae*.[17] The bankrupt in this case had traded as the owner of four fishing vessels for which he held fishing licences under the Sea Fish (Conservation) Act 1967; the vessels vested in the trustee in bankruptcy but the licences did not. The effect of the bankruptcy order was to invalidate the licences, but the Ministry of Agriculture and Fisheries recognised what was referred to as an 'entitlement' (although this was completely at the discretion of the Ministry) in the holder, or in any person in whose favour the holder waived the entitlement, to be considered for the grant of fresh licences. That entitlement had a value, in that a practice had developed of the licence holder receiving a payment for the surrender of a licence which enabled the payer to receive a licence at the discretion of the Secretary of State; the issue in the case was whether the entitlement should enure for the benefit of the creditors or of the bankrupt himself. If the entitlement were property within the Insolvency Act 1986 and had therefore vested in the trustee, the court could order the bankrupt to sign the necessary waiver.[18] The judge concluded that to construe the Act as excluding the 'entitlement' from the property available to the creditors would be contrary to the purposes of the Act. He decided that the entitlement came within the category 'every description of interest', which was wide enough to include interests not enforceable in a court of law but nonetheless marketable and capable of being turned into money and that this interest was incidental to the property rights in the vessels and was therefore within the definition. Somewhat similar issues were considered by the Court of Appeal, and a similar conclusion reached, in relation to a waste management licence under the Environmental Protection Act 1990 in *Re Celtic Extraction*.[19]

In *Re Campbell*,[20] it was held that the prospect of receiving an award by the Criminal Injuries Compensation Board did not amount to an interest in property since the definition in s 436 could only encompass existing items (including existing contingent and future interests).[21]

---

15 And rights of pre-emption: *Dear v Reeves* (2001) unreported, 1 March (Southampton county court).

16 See Chapter 32 on selling causes of action.

17 [1995] BCC 102.

18 Under the power given to it by the Insolvency Act 1986, s 363 to direct the bankrupt to assist in the administration of the estate.

19 [1999] 4 All ER 684. The issue here was whether the licence was property which could be disclaimed.

20 [1996] 2 All ER 537.

21 It would appear that the trustee based his claim to the sum subsequently awarded on the grounds that it was property which had vested at the start of the bankruptcy. There would appear to have been no claim to it as after-acquired property.

(b) Defeasible interests

The insolvency practitioner will take property subject to any pre-existing equities or other rights over the assets; the insolvency practitioner will, for example, be bound by the right of a seller to rescind a contract which the seller had been induced to enter by the fraud of the buyer.[22]

The insolvent may have held the assets on terms that insolvency would bring the interest to an end. A transfer of property upon the condition that the asset will revest if the transferee becomes insolvent is void as contrary to insolvency law[23] and also for repugnancy, as such a provision is inconsistent with the outright transfer of ownership.[24] It is, however, often possible to achieve the same effect by conferring an interest which is expressed to be defeasible in the event of the transferee's insolvency.

It is common to find clauses in leases providing for re-entry on the lessee's insolvency;[25] the insolvency is treated as marking the limit of the lessee's interest rather than as imposing an invalid condition on it. The court will have jurisdiction to relieve against forfeiture under s 146 of the Law of Property Act 1925[26] within the year[27] after the commencement of the insolvency (and indefinitely if the lease is sold by the insolvency practitioner within that year) and will usually be willing to grant relief if the tenant pays the arrears and the landlord's expenses. In *Transag Haulage Ltd v DAF Finance plc*,[28] the courts recognised the validity of a clause providing that insolvency of the lessee would determine a chattel lease and held that there was an equitable jurisdiction to relieve against forfeiture in such a case. This was a case in which receivers had taken possession of vehicles supplied to the insolvent company under hire-purchase contracts which provided for termination and repossession of the vehicles in the event, *inter alia*, of the appointment of receivers. The vehicles were worth a total of about £70,000 and the remaining instalments to be paid amounted to about £14,000. The court agreed that the loss of the right to exercise the option to purchase at the end of the hire period was the loss of a proprietary right and held[29] that there was jurisdiction to relieve against forfeiture of an otherwise existing contingent proprietary right even where the property in question was personalty. Relief against forfeiture was granted on the condition that the outstanding instalments were paid within seven days.

Defeasibility in the event of insolvency is the basis of the protective trust. It was established by Lord Eldon in 1811 in *Brandon v Robinson*[30] that a condition restraining

---

22 *Gladstone v Hawden* (1813) 1 M&S 517; *Re Eastgate* [1905] 1 KB 465; *Tilley v Bourman Ltd* [1910] 1 KB 745; *Transag Haulage Ltd v DAF Finance plc* [1994] 2 BCLC 88.
23 In particular, the principle that a person is not allowed to agree with a creditor for a different distribution of his or her assets in an insolvency from that provided by law.
24 *Holroyd v Gwynne* (1809) 2 Taunt 176; *Ex p Mackay* (1873) 8 Ch App 643.
25 As early as *Roe d Hunter v Galliers* (1787) 2 TR 133, it was settled that a proviso for determination of a lease on bankruptcy would be valid. *Civil Service Co-operative Society Ltd v Trustee of McGrigor* [1923] 2 Ch 347 is a more recent example.
26 See *Milman and Davey* (1996) at p 546.
27 If the lease is not sold within the year, there is no subsequent jurisdiction to relieve from forfeiture since it has been held that the Law of Property Act 1925, s 146 ousts any non-statutory jurisdiction: *Official Custodian for Charities v Parway Estates Development Ltd* [1985] Ch 151.
28 [1994] 2 BCLC 88.
29 Referring to the judgment of Dillon LJ in *BICC plc v Burndy Corporation* [1985] Ch 232.
30 (1811) 18 Ves 429.

transfer to the then equivalent of a trustee in bankruptcy could not validly be imposed on an equitable life interest, but that a determinable interest was permissible: 'There is no doubt that property may be given to a man until he shall become bankrupt'. By the mid-19th century, the device had developed of adding a discretionary trust in favour of the beneficiary and his or her family to take effect on termination of the prior determinable interest.[31] Section 33 of the Trustee Act 1925 recognises the existence of such 'protective trusts'. Pension schemes use the device of the protective trust to prevent the rights of pension scheme members becoming available to their creditors on a bankruptcy. An attempt by a settlor to determine an interest by reference to his or her own bankruptcy will be void against the trustee in bankruptcy.

Neuberger J considered the law relating to defeasibility in insolvency in considerable detail in *Money Markets International Stockbrokers Ltd v London Stock Exchange*[32] and observed that it is clear from the authorities that there are occasions where a provision which appears to offend against the principles of insolvency law has been upheld and that is hard to discern a coherent set of principles. The intention of the parties in agreeing the deprivation provision is generally less important than its effect, but an intention to evade the insolvency rule might invalidate a provision which would otherwise be valid and the absence of such an intention will make it more likely that a provision will be upheld. Where the provision relates to a valueless asset or one which is incapable of transfer or which depends on the character or status of the owner, then it will normally be enforceable on insolvency. A deprivation provision which might otherwise be invalid in the light of insolvency principles may be held to be valid if the asset concerned is closely connected with or subsidiary to a right or other benefit in respect of which a deprivation provision is valid. In this particular case, the provision in question required the liquidator of a member firm of the London Stock Exchange to transfer back its share in the company running the exchange; since the Stock Exchange was about to demutualise and the shares carried rights of participation, the liquidator contended that the Stock Exchange was not entitled to deprive it of the disputed share to the detriment of its creditors. The court held that the share could not, at least in advance of demutualisation, be treated as a free-standing asset, but was merely ancillary to membership of the Stock Exchange; membership was a personal thing, incapable of uncontrolled transfer and expulsion from membership would normally follow insolvency.

(c) Recognition of pre-insolvency property rights

The onset of bankruptcy or liquidation will not generally affect property rights which have already been acquired by a third party.[33] Assets in the possession of the insolvent which are beneficially owned by third parties will not be available to the creditors and it will often transpire that the insolvent has far fewer assets than appeared to be the case. At one time, the doctrine of reputed ownership enabled creditors to claim some of the assets which appeared to belong to the insolvent; the doctrine never applied to companies and was abolished in relation to bankruptcy on the recommendation of the Cork Committee. Third party rights may arise by way of security, reservation of title

---

31   See Chesterman 'Family settlements on trust' in Rubin and Sugarman (eds), 1984.
32   [2001] 4 All ER 223.
33   Chapter 30 examines those situations in which transfers may be defeasible.

or on the basis of equitable interests in property whose legal title is vested in the insolvent.[34] The value to the insolvent estate of an asset subject to a security right in favour of a third party will be any extent to which the asset is worth more than the debt it secures. Much of the case law in this area is concerned with delineating the borders between personal and proprietary claim and with determining the circumstances in which assets which might have been thought to be available to the general body of creditors are in fact the property of someone else. It has been suggested[35] that, although creating proprietary rights has wider consequences than affording priority on insolvency, the law should only create proprietary rights if the claimant should be entitled to priority in the event of the defendant's insolvency.

It might be asked why creditors with rights *in rem* should be preferred in this way to those who hold merely personal rights against the insolvent.[36] One argument[37] is that the ability to give security allows borrowing by those with poor credit ratings which might otherwise be impossible or only possible at very high rates of interest.[38] The upholding of security rights has been justified[39] on the basis that, if debtors were not permitted to prefer some creditors over others by conferring security, the alternative would be a complicated contractual network of priority relationships arranged between the creditors themselves. The current system achieves the same result in a simpler and cheaper fashion. Professor Goode addressed this issue several years later[40] and concluded that the bargain element is widely accepted as a proper ground for giving the secured creditor priority so long as the grant of the security does not involve an unfair preference and other creditors have notice of the security interest, so that they are not misled into thinking that the assets comprising the security are the unencumbered property of the debtor. He concluded that those who choose to lend unsecured cannot complain of their subordinate position.[41] A number of proprietary rights could come under attack on this reasoning since the formalist distinction between sale credit with retention of title and loan credit and security means that much functional security is in fact hidden from view, although this will change if the recommendations of the Law Commission on registration of security interests become law.[42] The rights of creditors who can base their claims on an equitable proprietary basis are also hidden from view. Furthermore, many trade creditors are unlikely to be in a position to investigate their customers and discover the existence of the secured rights[43] and involuntary creditors will have to take their debtors as they find them.

---

34 See Chapters 28 and 29.
35 See Burrows (2001) at 425. See also Finch and Worthington in Rose (ed), 2000.
36 For recent debate on this side of the Atlantic, see Finch (1999a); Mokal (2001b); Mokal (2002).
37 See Oditah, 1991, pp 14–18.
38 It is not clear that the giving of security does necessarily result in a lower rate of interest (see, for example, Goode, 1997, p 41). It is also open to debate whether the system should encourage high risk borrowing at the potential expense of the borrower's unsecured creditors.
39 Most famously by Professors Jackson and Kronman in their much-cited article (1979).
40 Goode (1983–84).
41 See also Gough, 1996, Chapter 16.
42 See Law Commission Consultation Paper No 164, 2002.
43 It can be argued, though, that they are in a position to spread their risk amongst the totality of their customers and to reflect the risk in their prices.

The above arguments do not address the problem that it is possible for the entirety of the assets of a corporate debtor to be secured, leaving nothing for the unsecured creditors. This has caused dissatisfaction since the advent of the floating charge in the 19th century. In the infamous case of *Salomon v Salomon*,[44] Lord MacNaghten observed: 'I have long thought, and I believe some of your Lordships also think, that the ordinary trade creditors of a trading company ought to have a preferential claim on the assets in liquidation in respect of debts incurred within a certain limited time before the winding up. But that is not the law at present. Everybody knows that when there is a winding up debenture-holders generally step in and sweep off everything; and a great scandal it is.' Preferential creditors[45] were given priority over the holders of a floating charge in 1897, but this did nothing to assist the ordinary unsecured creditor. The Cork Committee recognised that this was a cause for justifiable dissatisfaction amongst unsecured creditors. They were also concerned at the disinterest displayed and, therefore, the lack of control exercised by most unsecured creditors in the insolvency proceedings, largely because of the unlikelihood of recovering much if any of what was owing. The suggested solution of the Cork Committee[46], which was not adopted, was that a fund equal to 10% of the net moneys which would otherwise be payable to a floating chargee from the realisation of assets would be set aside and distributed *pari passu* among the ordinary unsecured creditors, subject to the overriding limitation that they would not receive a greater percentage of their debts than the debentureholder. The Enterprise Act 2002 will finally be introducing something similar with the provision for 'ring-fencing' a proportion of the assets.[47]

3   DISCLAIMER BY INSOLVENCY PRACTITIONER

(a) Right to disclaim

A trustee in bankruptcy[48] or a liquidator[49] may, by the giving of the prescribed notice, disclaim any onerous property. Onerous property is defined as any unprofitable contract and any other property which is unsaleable or not readily saleable, or is such that it may give rise to a liability to pay money or perform any other onerous act. In *City of London v Brown*,[50] it was held that rights which are purely personal to a bankrupt and are not capable of being realised for the benefit of the creditors will not be included in the property which the insolvency practitioner is entitled to disclaim.

The case law on these provisions has been largely concerned with the disclaimer of leaseholds (which may contain onerous covenants and, if the state of the market makes the rent obligations unattractive, may be unsaleable), although there has

---

44   [1987] AC 22.
45   See Chapter 34.
46   In para 1539.
47   See Chapter 34.
48   Under the Insolvency Act 1986, s 315 *et seq*.
49   Under the Insolvency Act 1986, s 178 *et seq*. Until 1986, liquidators needed the leave of the court to disclaim property and this should be borne in mind when reading earlier cases.
50   (1990) 22 HLR 32. Insolvency Act 1986, s 283 as amended by the Housing Act 1988, s 117 now reflects this decision.

apparently also been a recent increase[51] in the disclaimer of freeholds.[52] There has been little case law relating to the disclaimer of personal property, but the statutory provisions are not restricted to interests in land. *Re Potters Oils Ltd*[53] was a case in which the liquidator sought to disclaim a quantity of chlorinated waste oil which would be expensive to have removed and was potentially hazardous; under the more restrictively worded statute then in force, it was held that the oil did not fall within the definition of property which could be disclaimed. If a similar case arose today, the insolvency practitioner would be able to disclaim the property. In a related context, the Court of Appeal held in *Re Celtic Extraction*[54] that a waste management licence under the Environmental Protection Act 1990 could be disclaimed, thus relieving the liquidator of the onerous obligations imposed by the licence. The insolvency practitioner is only entitled to disclaim 'property' within the definition provided by s 436 so that, for example, in *City of London Corporation v Brown*,[55] it was held that the trustee could not disclaim a statutory tenancy which was a mere personal right of irremoveability and not 'property'.[56]

(b) Loss of right to disclaim

The right to disclaim is not lost where the insolvency practitioner has exercised rights of ownership in relation to the property, but will be lost if a person interested in the property has written asking whether the insolvency practitioner will be disclaiming the property and notice of disclaimer is not given within the next 28 days.[57] Notice of disclaimer may only be served by a trustee in bankruptcy with the leave of the court in respect of after-acquired property[58] or exempt property within s 308[59] where either has been claimed for the estate by the trustee.

(c) Effect of disclaimer

A disclaimer will operate so as to determine the rights, interests and liabilities of the insolvent or the insolvency practitioner in or in respect of the disclaimed property as from the date of the disclaimer, except in the case of leaseholds.[60] Where an insolvency practitioner proposes to disclaim a lease, notice must be served on any underlessees or mortgagees claiming under the insolvent;[61] the disclaimer will not take effect until either the expiry of a 14 day period without an application being made for a vesting order or, if such an application is made, until the court directs that

---

51   In *Scmlla Properties v Gesso Properties (BVI) Ltd* [1995] BCC 793, the judge observed that he had been told that there were about 200 escheats per year.
52   *Re Nottingham General Cemetery Co* [1955] 1 Ch 683 was a case of a freehold subject to onerous obligations since it was used as a cemetery.
53   [1985] BCLC 203.
54   [2001] Ch 475.
55   (1990) 22 HLR 32.
56   Insolvency Act 1986, s 283(3A) inserted by the Housing Act 1988, s 117(1) makes it clear that such tenancies will not usually vest in the trustee.
57   Insolvency Act 1986, ss 178(5), 316.
58   See Chapter 27.
59   See Chapter 27.
60   Insolvency Act 1986, ss 178(4), 315(3).
61   Insolvency Act 1986, ss 179, 317.

the disclaimer shall take place. A similar provision[62] applies to the disclaimer by a trustee in bankruptcy of any property in a dwelling house; in this case, the notice has to be served on every person in occupation or claiming a right to occupy the house.

Third parties who either claim an interest in the disclaimed property or are under a liability in respect of it may apply for the vesting of the disclaimed property in, or for its delivery to, a person who is entitled to it or is under a liability in respect of it.[63] These provisions allow, for example, the vesting of a lease in an underlessee or of land in a mortgagee. The court will not make an order conferring the property on a person subject to a liability in respect of it unless it would be just to do so for the purpose of compensating that person; the guarantor of obligations under a disclaimed lease might be such a person. In *Hindcastle Ltd v Barbara Attenborough Associates Ltd*,[64] the House of Lords held that the disclaimer of a lease operated to determine the lease and accelerate the reversion but, overruling previous case law to the contrary, that the wording of the legislation required the obligations of a guarantor to be treated as though the lease had continued. Lord Nicholls of Birkenhead observed in the course of his judgment that it was essential to bear in mind that the fundamental purpose of an ordinary guarantee of another's debt is that the risk of the principal debtor's insolvency should fall on the guarantor and not the creditor and that it would defeat the object of the exercise if disclaimer released the guarantor.

Any person sustaining loss or damage in consequence of the operation of a disclaimer is deemed to be a creditor in the insolvency to the extent of the loss or damage;[65] the extent of the loss may be adjusted as a consequence of a vesting order. The rights and liabilities of others will not be affected by the disclaimer except in so far as is necessary to release the insolvent from any liability.

The question of what happens to disclaimed property has given rise to considerable conjecture. It now seems clear that, on disclaimer, a freehold interest determines and that the Crown automatically becomes owner of the land in question on an escheat.[66] A leasehold interest will also determine and the reversion will be accelerated;[67] any sub-lease carved out of the disclaimed lease also determines but the sub-tenant's interest is deemed to continue on the terms of the disclaimed headlease.[68] Harman J in *Re Potters Oils Ltd*[69] felt that disclaimed chattels would be *bona vacantia* and vest in the Crown. The Treasury Solicitor, invited to consider the prospect of the Crown becoming owner of such an unwelcome chattel, was of the opinion that it

---

62 Insolvency Act 1986, s 318.

63 Insolvency Act 1986, ss 181, 182, 321 contain provisions relating to the terms on which the court may vest leasehold property in an underlessee or mortgagee. See McCartney (2002). *Lloyds Bank SF Nominees v Aladdin Ltd* [1996] 1 BCLC 720 is authority that a person in occupation of premises of which he or she has agreed to take an assignment subject to the consent of the landlord does not have the necessary interest.

64 [1996] 2 BCLC 234.

65 See *Re Park Air Services Plc* [1999] 1 All ER 673 for a discussion of the quantification of damages payable to a landlord as a result of the disclaimer of a lease.

66 *Scmlla Properties v Gesso Properties (BVI) Ltd* [1995] BCC 793.

67 *Hindcastle Ltd v Barbara Attenborough Associates Ltd* [1996] 2 BCLC 234.

68 In *Hindcastle Ltd v Barbara Attenborough Associates Ltd,* the House of Lords thought it likely that any problems associated with sub-leases could be solved by a vesting order in favour of the sub-tenant. See Lowe (1996) for a discussion of the difficulties which may arise where the insolvent tenant has sub-let the property to more than one tenant.

69 [1985] BCLC 203.

would not automatically vest in the Crown, but the point did not in the event have to be decided. In a number of cases, the Crown has argued against the automatic vesting of onerous freeholds or chattels in it. It would seem likely, however, that the property would vest but that the Crown could argue that its rights and liabilities should not be affected by the disclaimer even if the disclaimer caused it to become the owner of the property.

CHAPTER 27

THE EXTENT OF A BANKRUPT'S ESTATE

1 INTRODUCTION

A bankrupt's estate includes all property belonging to or vested in the bankrupt at the commencement of the bankruptcy[1] unless specifically excluded by statute or at common law; these excluded assets are explained below. The bankrupt's house does not fall into the category of exempt asset, but the trustee in bankruptcy may need the leave of the court to sell it. Property falls into the bankrupt estate subject to the rights of any third parties[2] unless those rights have been released.[3] Property held by the bankrupt on trust does not fall into the bankrupt's estate.[4] Assets (including income) which the bankrupt acquires in the course of the bankruptcy may also be taken into the estate, as explained below.

2 ASSETS WHICH ARE NOT 'PROPERTY' AS A MATTER OF COMMON LAW

Despite the breadth of the definition of 'property' in s 436 of the Insolvency Act 1986, there are certain causes of action personal to the bankrupt which, as a matter of common law, do not vest in his or her trustee.[5] These include cases in which 'the damages are to be estimated by immediate reference to pain felt by the bankrupt in respect of his body, mind, or character, and without immediate reference to his rights of property'[6] such as actions for defamation and assault. Cozens-Hardy LJ in *Bailey v Thurston & Co Ltd*[7] held that, despite the generality of the language used in the Bankruptcy Acts, there were some contracts which could not vest in the trustee in bankruptcy. These included contracts for purely personal services, although sums due in respect of such services which had been rendered would vest in the trustee.[8] In *Ord v Upton*,[9] it was held that a cause of action would be part of the bankrupt's estate unless it consisted solely of a cause of action personal to the bankrupt. Where a cause of action for negligence gave rise to heads of damage for both loss of earnings and pain and suffering, that cause of action vested in the trustee; the right to recover personal damages, and the damages themselves, when actually recovered, were held

---

1 Insolvency Act 1986, s 283(1). The commencement of the bankruptcy will be the day on which the bankruptcy order is made: Insolvency Act 1986, s 278.
2 Insolvency Act 1986, s 283(5).
3 Pursuant to the Insolvency Act 1986, s 269 or the Insolvency Rules 1986.
4 Insolvency Act 1986, s 283(3).
5 See *Heath v Tang* [1993] 4 All ER 694.
6 *Beckham v Dale* (1849) 2 HL Cas 579, 604, *per* Erle J and *Wilson v United Counties Bank Ltd* [1920] AC 102.
7 [1903] 1 KB 137 at 145.
8 In *Grady v Prison Service* (2003) *The Times*, 18 April, the Court of Appeal held that a claim for unfair dismissal, both in its nature and in its remedies, was personal to the claimant and did not vest in the claimant's trustee in bankruptcy.
9 [2000] Ch 352.

on a constructive trust for the bankrupt by the trustee. In *Cork v Rawlins*,[10] the bankrupt attempted to stretch this principle to apply to benefits under insurance taken out to enable the repayment of loans in the event of disability or illness on the basis that the payments were conditional on pain and suffering. The Court of Appeal refused to do so, pointing out that that the policies had been purchased to discharge his liability to a particular creditor through the payment of premiums which would otherwise have formed part of his estate available for his creditors on bankruptcy, and that the policy moneys did not relate to or represent or compensate for loss or damage to the bankrupt personally and were not measured by such loss or damage. Chadwick LJ observed that: 'It is plainly in the general public interest that persons should be encouraged to make provision against the possibility that they will be unable to meet their commitments as a result of misfortune for which they are not responsible. But if public policy requires that they should be encouraged to do so by permitting them to shelter that provision from the claims of their creditors, then it is for Parliament to say so. It is not, in my view, for the courts to distort the bankruptcy code in order to achieve that result.'

In *Haig v Aitken*,[11] the common law principle was extended beyond purely personal choses in action to the bankrupt's correspondence. The bankrupt in this case was a former government minister and the trustee in bankruptcy had taken possession of his personal correspondence with parliamentary, ministerial and governmental colleagues which was estimated to have a substantial value. The trustee therefore sought a direction from the court that he was entitled to sell the correspondence for the benefit of the creditors. The court held that a bankrupt's personal correspondence was of a nature peculiarly personal to him or her and his or her life as a human being, and thus did not constitute part of his or her estate for the purposes of the 1986 Act. Rattee J said that it was also likely that any such sale would be a breach of Art 8 of the European Convention on Human Rights.

3 EXEMPT ASSETS

The Cork Committee made the point[12] that one aim of insolvency law is to enable the bankrupt to achieve rehabilitation as a useful and productive member of society. Certain assets necessary for this purpose are accordingly exempted from vesting in the trustee and are allowed to be retained by the bankrupt. Section 283(2) of the Insolvency Act 1986 provides that the following assets do not fall into the bankrupt's estate:

(a) such tools, books, vehicles and other items of equipment as are necessary to the bankrupt for use personally by him in his employment, business or vocation;

(b) such clothing, bedding, furniture, household equipment and provisions as are necessary for satisfying the basic domestic needs of the bankrupt and his family.

It will be noted that vehicles only fall within the first and not the second of these categories. It may be that other members of the family can establish an arguable claim

---

10   [2001] All ER 50.
11   [2001] Ch 110.
12   In para 1096.

to ownership of chattels used by the family. It will often be the case that the realisable value of the chattels is not worth incurring the costs of realisation and that the bankrupt will manage to keep many of these possessions.

Under s 308 of the Insolvency Act 1986, if it appears to the trustee that the realisable value of property exempted under s 283(2) of the Insolvency Act 1986 exceeds the cost of a reasonable replacement for that property, the trustee may by notice in writing within 42 days[13] of first learning of its existence claim the property for the estate. Upon the service of the notice, the property vests in the trustee as of the date of the commencement of the bankruptcy although any purchaser of the property in good faith, for value and without notice of the bankruptcy will be protected against the claim. The trustee must provide a reasonable replacement for the claimed asset out of the funds comprised in the estate. Property will be a reasonable replacement for other property if it is reasonably adequate for meeting the needs met by the other party. *Pike v Cork Gully*[14] is an example of this provision in operation. The trustee in bankruptcy had seized a horse box used by the bankrupt to earn about £1,000 a month. The horse box had been sold for £9,987.50. It was held that the horse box had been in the category of exempt assets and that the trustee had either to repay the net proceeds of the sale or, if less, the cost of a reasonable replacement. Another example is *Re Rayatt*[15] which involved the car needed by the bankrupt for use in his employment.

Under s 283(3A) of the Insolvency Act 1986, certain protected tenancies are also excluded from the bankrupt's estate unless the trustee claims them under s 308A of the Insolvency Act 1986. In *Rothschild v Bell*,[16] it was held that a continuation tenancy under Part I of the Landlord and Tenant Act 1954 was property which could be disclaimed by the trustee in bankruptcy; it was assignable, albeit probably valueless.

4 THE BANKRUPT'S HOME

(a) General

The Cork Committee made the point[17] that the bankrupt's home (or, more often, the residual value after repayment of the mortgage debt) is frequently the major asset of a consumer bankrupt and may also be the major asset of a sole or partnership trader and went on to say that eviction from the family home could be a disaster not only for the bankrupt but also for the bankrupt's dependants. The Committee wanted to see a wide discretion vested in the court to delay the sale of a family home, saying that this would be 'consonant with present social attitudes'.[18] The proposals of the Cork Committee were not accepted and the Insolvency Act 1986 contains provisions in

---

13   The time limit is contained in the Insolvency Act 1986, s 309.
14   (1995) unreported, 13 July.
15   [1998] 2 FLR 264.
16   [2000] QB 33; Davey (2000).
17   See Chapter 24, from para 1114.
18   A contrasting attitude had earlier been adopted by the Law Commission in its report on financial provision in matrimonial proceedings (Report No 25) which took the view that the claims of the spouse should be subordinated to those of the creditors since 'marriage is a form of partnership and, on normal partnership principles, neither partner should compete with the partner's creditors'.

relation to the bankrupt's home which are a continuation of the previous pro-creditor stance of the common law. Even without the restrictive interpretation which, as will be seen, the courts have given to the legislation, the legislation is tilted much more in favour of creditors than, for example, the homestead legislation of New Zealand and parts of Canada and the United States[19] which aims to give families security of occupation as against creditors.

One way of achieving a balance between the concern for the bankrupt's family and respect for the creditors' rights would have been to treat the bankrupt's home as an exempt asset within s 283(2) of the Insolvency Act 1986 so that the home would then have been subject to s 308 and the trustee in bankruptcy would have been entitled to claim it if the value of the property exceeded the cost of a reasonable replacement. Section 283 of the Insolvency Act 1986 does not, however, include the home of the bankrupt among the items exempted from the estate. The trustee will acquire such beneficial interest as the bankrupt had in the home. The trustee will need to establish the extent of that beneficial interest; frequently, there will be a mortgage and the bankrupt's interest will be limited to the equity of redemption. The trustee will often discover that the equity is owned jointly with a spouse or cohabitee.

In many cases, the interest of the trustee will be bought out either by a spouse or cohabitee remortgaging the property or a third party, such as a relative, producing funds. Alternatively, where there is negative equity or very low positive equity in the property, the trustee will usually give the bankrupt or someone else with an interest in the property the opportunity to acquire it for a nominal sum and minimal legal costs.[20] Where this is not possible, the trustee will only be able to realise the value of the property by rendering the bankrupt homeless which, if the bankrupt is occupying the property with family, is likely to involve an application to court.[21] The complexities of family property law[22] are such that the trustee in bankruptcy may find it difficult to establish who is entitled to share, and in what proportions, in the proceeds of any sale. Where the trustee cannot realise the value of a dwelling house occupied by the bankrupt, or by a spouse or former spouse, the trustee can apply to the court[23] for an order imposing a charge on the property for the benefit of the bankrupt's estate. The charge will vest in the trustee as part of the estate and the house itself will cease to form part of the estate. The Enterprise Act 2002[24] will amend s 313 of the Insolvency Act 1986 to fix the maximum value of the charge as the value of the bankrupt's interest in the property at the date of the court order together with interest on that amount so that the trustee will not be able to take advantage of any increase in value in the equity of redemption.

The Annual Report of the Insolvency Practices Council for 2000 identified widespread differences in practice in the attitudes of trustees in bankruptcy to the family house as a cause for concern. Although the government did not at first propose

---

19   See Gray, 2000, p 935.
20   Well advised bankrupts will ensure that they take advantage of this since, otherwise, they may face problems in the future should the equity in the house subsequently (perhaps years later) become positive.
21   Under the Insolvency Act 1986, s 335A, 336 or 337; see below.
22   Which this account can only begin to indicate. For a full explanation, see Gray, 2000 and Cretney and Masson, 2002.
23   Insolvency Act 1986, s 313.
24   Enterprise Act 2002, s 261.

to include provisions to meet this concern in the Enterprise Act, at a relatively late stage and in response to a clause proposed by a private member at committee stage, new ss 283A and 313A were introduced into the Insolvency Act 1986. Section 283A provides that the interest of a trustee in bankruptcy in the home of the bankrupt, the bankrupt's spouse or the bankrupt's former spouse will automatically re-vest in the bankrupt after three years[25] except in the circumstances set out in s 283A(3). These circumstances are that the trustee has already realised the interest or has agreed that the bankrupt will incur a specified liability to his or her estate in consideration of which the interest shall cease to form part of the estate or has applied to the court for an order for sale, possession or a charging order.[26] If an application for an order has been dismissed, the house will normally re-vest in the bankrupt at that point. Section 313A provides that where a trustee applies for such an order, the court shall dismiss the application if 'the value of the interest is below the amount prescribed for the purposes of this subsection'. These amendments contained in the Enterprise Act are designed to provide some certainty to all concerned as to the timescale for dealing with the family home.[27] The insertion of s 313A into the Insolvency Act 1986 is intended to address the practical problem for trustees in bankruptcy of cases where the bankrupt's share in the equity is such[28] that it is beyond the ability of the bankrupt or bankrupt's spouse to borrow the sum but that it is uneconomic for the trustee in terms of his or her own fees to pursue the matter through the courts. The government recognised that there would need to be wide consultation on the level of the 'amount prescribed' and that the differing values of property from one part of the country to another would need to be taken into account. The extent to which the amendments contained in s 261 of the Enterprise Act 2002 will ameliorate the position for bankrupts in relation to the family home will depend to a great extent on the level at which the 'amount prescribed' is pitched, but it would seem likely that the measure is seen more as a way of addressing a practical difficulty facing trustees in bankruptcy than a way of providing protection for the family.

The Insolvency Service, in its consultation document *Bankruptcy – A Fresh Start*, suggested that it might be possible to provide for a bankrupts to claim exemptions in relation to their interests in their homes on a pound for pound basis, up to a maximum limit, to the extent that they could demonstrate that they had introduced capital into their businesses. This was not a proposal which met with general support and was not carried through into the drafting of the Enterprise Act.

It should also be noted that, in many cases, where the bankrupt has little or no equity of redemption in the home, it will be the mortgagee of the property that will decide on the fate of the house which will be dealt with outside the ambit of insolvency law.

---

25 From the commencement of the bankruptcy or from any later date on which the trustee or Official Receiver becomes aware of the bankrupt's interest. The court may substitute a longer period and the rules may provide for a substitution of a shorter period.

26 Orders for sale are discussed below.

27 See comments of the minister, Melanie Johnson, introducing the clause to the House of Commons on 17 June 2002.

28 The minister suggested that this might apply to equity with a value between perhaps £2,500 and £10,000.

(b) Beneficial ownership of the home

The first issue for the trustee in bankruptcy to consider is that of who owns the property. The documentary evidence may show that the bankrupt is the sole owner of the property or it may show that the legal title to the property was conveyed to the bankrupt jointly with another, often a spouse or cohabitee. This joint ownership operates through the mechanism of a trust of land[29] and if one of the co-owners does not wish the property to be sold, a court order under s 14 of the Trusts of Land and Appointment of Trustees Act 1996[30] will be necessary before the property can be sold free of the dissentient owner's interest.

Even where the bankrupt appears to be the sole legal owner of the property, someone else may be able to establish an equitable interest in the property, in which case the bankrupt will hold the legal title to the property on trust for the person beneficially entitled; again, a court order under s 14 of the Trusts of Land and Appointment of Trustees Act 1996 would be necessary before the property could be sold free of the beneficial interest of the unwilling seller. There has been a series of cases in which a spouse or cohabitee[31] of a sole legal owner has claimed an equitable interest in the property on the basis of an implied, resulting or constructive trust.[32] Where two people provide the purchase money jointly but the house is conveyed into the name of one of them alone, there is a rebuttable presumption that the sole legal owner holds the property on trust for both of them.[33] In principle, a similar result may be achieved by one party making an indirect financial contribution to the purchase of a house which is conveyed into the name of another provided the court can find that this was the common intention of the parties. The courts are, however, reluctant to recognise that the necessary intention to share beneficial ownership can, in the absence of express words, be inferred from anything other than the making of a financial contribution to the purchase.[34]

(c) Sale where the home is not owned solely by the bankrupt

An application by a trustee in bankruptcy under s 14 of the Trusts of Land and Appointment of Trustees Act 1996 is now governed by s 335A of the Insolvency Act

---

29   Under the Trusts of Land and Appointment of Trustees Act 1996. Previously this would have been a trust for sale under the Law of Property Act 1925.

30   Previously the Law of Property Act 1925, s 30. The trustee in bankruptcy will be a person with 'an interest in property subject to a trust of land'. Where the dispute is between the original co-owners, the court will consider whether any collateral purpose of the trust is still subsisting.

31   Or other claimant; for example, in *Re Sharpe (a Bankrupt)* [1980] 1 WLR 219, it was the bankrupt's aunt who claimed an equitable interest in the house.

32   Proprietary estoppel, which in other circumstances may be relied on as establishing an interest in property, will be of no avail in a bankruptcy, since any interest established will only date from the court declaration and will not be back-dated to the commencement of the bankruptcy.

33   This was established in a line of cases which can be traced back to *Bull v Bull* [1955] 1 QB 234. More recent examples include *Williams and Glyn's Bank v Boland* [1980] 3 WLR 138; *City of London Building Society v Flegg* [1988] AC 54 and *Tinsley v Milligan* [1995] 1 AC 340.

34   *Gissing v Gissing* [1971] AC 886; *Pettitt v Pettitt* [1970] AC 777; *Lloyds Bank plc v Rosset* [1991] 1 AC 107. For a recent application in the insolvency context, see *Re Share (Lorraine)* [2002] 2 FLR 88.

1986. Section 335A[35] can be traced back to the Cork Committee, which concluded[36] that it would be consonant with modern social attitudes to alleviate the personal hardships of a bankrupt's dependants by allowing the court a discretion to postpone the sale of the family home. The Committee considered that primary consideration should be given to the needs of any children and that regard should be had to their age and other needs, avoiding emotional damage or interrupting their schooling and to the interests of the community in keeping the family together in suitable accommodation. The government response was that this was too heavily weighted against creditors and the proposal was not incorporated into the draft legislation. During the passage of the legislation through Parliament, strong pressure was brought to bear to include some measure and an inconclusive consultation process took place followed by the inclusion of provisions in the legislation at a late stage without much discussion.[37]

Section 335A provides that where a trustee makes an application under s 14 of the Trusts of Land and Appointment of Trustees Act 1996, the application is to be made to the court having jurisdiction in relation to the bankruptcy and the court shall make such order as it thinks just and reasonable having regard to:

(a) the interest of the bankrupt's creditors;

(b) where the application is in respect of land which includes a dwelling house which is or has been the home of the bankrupt or the bankrupt's spouse or former spouse:
  (i) the conduct of the spouse or former spouse, so far as contributing to the bankruptcy,
  (ii) the needs and financial resources of the spouse or former spouse, and
  (iii) the needs of any children, and

(c) all the circumstances of the case other than the needs of the bankrupt.

After a year from the vesting of the property in the trustee, the court shall assume, unless the circumstances of the case are exceptional, that the interests of the creditors outweigh all other considerations.

The attitude likely to be taken by the courts to s 335A of the Insolvency Act 1986 is illustrated by *Re Citro*,[38] a case which was decided on the basis of previous law[39] but after the enactment of the Insolvency Act 1986. The Court of Appeal made it clear that s 336 of the Insolvency Act 1986[40] merely enacted the previous test applied by the courts. The court pointed out that it was as well that that should be the case, since the legislation at that time only applied to spouses and not to cohabitees and it would be unfortunate if those two groups should be subject to different rules.[41]

---

35 Which was added to the Insolvency Act 1986 by the Trusts of Land and Appointment of Trustees Act 1996, Sched 3 and replaces those parts of the original s 336 which dealt with applications under the Law of Property Act 1925, s 30.

36 In para 1118.

37 See Cretney (1991).

38 [1991] Ch 142.

39 Because the bankruptcies in question commenced in 1985.

40 Now s 335A and s 336.

41 Section 335A applies regardless of the identity of the non-bankrupt co-owner rather than only, as previously, where the co-owner was a spouse or former spouse. The court can take into account the needs of the children, but it is not clear to what extent a court may feel able to extend its regard to 'all the circumstances of the case' to cover the financial needs and resources of the cohabitee where there has not been a marriage.

The facts of *Re Citro*[42] were that in 1985, Domenico Citro and his brother, Carmine, were made bankrupt. Their only substantial assets were their shares of the beneficial interests in their matrimonial homes. One of the brothers was judicially separated from his wife and the other was living with his family. Their debts exceeded the values of the interests. The trustee applied to court for declarations as to their beneficial interests and for orders for possession and sale. Hoffmann J held that they each had a beneficial interest in half the equity of redemption and made the requested orders; after considering the circumstances of the families and, in particular, the fact that it would not be possible to buy other accommodation in the area which would not lead to schooling problems, he imposed a provision for postponement of sale in each case until the youngest child reached the age of 16. In the Court of Appeal, a delay of six months was substituted. Lord Justice Nourse considered the previous case law[43] and held that, whether or not the collateral purpose of providing a family home continued,[44] the interests of the spouse could only prevail in exceptional circumstances, 'amounting to more than the ordinary consequences of debt and improvidence' which he found in these circumstances. Lord Justice Bingham regretfully agreed with this, expressing his view that a test of 'exceptional circumstances' was more stringent than was warranted, but conceding that Parliament 'appears expressly to have approved it'. Sir George Waller, the third member of the Court of Appeal, dissented; he felt that it was quite possible to argue, on the basis of the case law, that the educational difficulties which would be suffered by the children involved were sufficient to amount to the necessary exceptional circumstances.

Subsequent case-law has applied *Re Citro* and it would appear that the only situation in which the court may find exceptional circumstances is that involving serious health problems. For example, in *Claughton v Charalambous*,[45] the bankrupt's spouse was suffering from chronic renal failure and osteoarthritis and had a reduced life expectancy; the court suspended the order for sale for so long as the wife could live in the house. The Court of Appeal in *Jackson v Bell*[46] expressed the view that there might be an arguable point as to the compatibility of the interpretation of 'exceptional circumstances' with Art 8 of the European Convention on Human Rights; there have, however, been a number of cases[47] in which the courts have remarked upon the need to balance the interests of the creditors against the interference with the individual's rights. In *Re Karia*, Lightman J dismissed an appeal against an order under s 335A, saying that in his view, the case did not 'come within a mile of any unjustifiable interference' with any of the bankrupt's or his daughter's human rights.

Until 1996, the principles to be applied by the court were the same, regardless of whether the application for sale came from a trustee in bankruptcy or from a

---

42 [1991] Ch 142.
43 In particular, *Re Turner* [1974] 1 WLR 1556; *Re Densham* [1975] 1 WLR 1519; *Re Bailey* [1977] 1 WLR 278; *Re Holliday* [1981] Ch 405 (the only reported case in which a sale within a short period has not been ordered); *Re Lowrie* [1981] 3 All ER 353 and *Harman v Glencross* [1986] 2 WLR 637.
44 Which, in relation to the separated brother, it did not.
45 [1999] 1 FLR 740. See also *Re Raval* [1998] 2 FLR 718; *Re Bremner* [1999] 1 FLR 912; *Judd v Brown* [1998] 2 FLR 360. See [2000] Fam Law 184.
46 [2001] Fam Law 879.
47 Eg, *Re Karia* (2001) unreported, 12 November, ChD, *per* Lightman J (a s 335A application); *Pickering v Wells* [2002] 2 FLR 798 (an application under RSC Ord 88, r 5A in relation to a charging order); *Mountney v Treharne* at first instance.

mortgagee under the predecessor to s 14 of the Trusts of Land and Appointment of Trustees Act 1996.[48] In *Lloyds Bank v Byrne*,[49] which was an application by a creditor who had obtained a charging order for a sale, it was held that the same approach as that of the majority in *Re Citro* would be appropriate in balancing the interests of the debtor's family and the creditor. Parker LJ observed 'there is no difference in principle between the case of a trustee in bankruptcy and that of a chargee. All the circumstances must be weighed and the court must consider whose voice should in equity prevail.' In *Mortgage Corporation v Shaire*,[50] however, Neuberger J said that s 15 of the Trusts of Land and Appointment of Trustees Act 1996 has changed the law on the way in which the court will exercise its power to order a sale at the suit of a chargee of the interest of one of the owners of the beneficial interest in a property; also that the court now has greater flexibility as to how it exercises its jurisdiction in such cases on an application for an order for sale of land subject to a trust of land. In consequence, the cases decided under s 30 of the Law of Property Act 1925 should be approached with caution and will not necessarily be of much assistance. The Court of Appeal in *Bank of Ireland Home Mortgages Ltd v Bell and Another*[51] agreed that s 15 gave scope for a change in the practice of the court but said, ordering a sale of the property in that case, that a powerful consideration should be whether the chargee is being given adequate recompense for having to wait to recover the amounts owing to it.

(d) Rights of the family to remain in occupation

A spouse[52] who cannot establish either legal or equitable entitlement to the home will still have a right to remain in occupation (matrimonial home rights) under s 30 of the Family Law Act 1996. Section 336(2) of the Insolvency Act 1986 provides that where a spouse has matrimonial home rights under Part IV of the Family Law Act 1996, those rights continue to subsist notwithstanding the bankruptcy and will bind the trustee and persons deriving title from the trustee. Once a petition for bankruptcy has been presented, it will be too late to acquire matrimonial home rights. Where the spouse has rights of occupation, the trustee will have to apply under s 33 of the Family Law Act 1996 for termination of the rights. Section 336 of the Insolvency Act 1986 provides that where the non-bankrupt spouse has matrimonial home rights which bind the trustee in bankruptcy, any application for an order under s 33 of the Family Law Act 1996 shall be made to the court having jurisdiction in bankruptcy and the court shall make such order as it thinks just and reasonable taking into account the same factors as apply under s 335A of the Insolvency Act 1986 to an application in respect of a trust for land.

Section 337 of the Insolvency Act 1986 is designed to give some protection to children living with the bankrupt in the situation where neither s 335A nor s 336 applies; the most likely situation will be where the bankrupt is a single parent so that there is no family member with either an interest in the property or matrimonial home

---

48 Law of Property Act 1925, s 30.
49 [1933] Fam Law 183.
50 [2001] 4 All ER 364.
51 [2001] 2 FLR 809.
52 But not a cohabitee.

rights.[53] Section 337 applies where the bankrupt is entitled to occupy a dwelling house by virtue of a beneficial estate or interest and any persons under the age of 18 with whom the bankrupt had at some time occupied the dwelling house were living with the bankrupt at the time of presentation of the petition for bankruptcy and when the bankruptcy order was made. The bankrupt is given the right not to be evicted from the house without the leave of the court or, if appropriate, a right with the leave of the court to enter and occupy the house. These rights will be treated as a charge having the priority of an equitable interest created immediately before the commencement of the bankruptcy and will be treated as if they were matrimonial home rights under the Family Law Act 1996. On an application for an order under s 33 of the Family Law Act 1996 the court shall make such order as it thinks just and reasonable, having regard to the interests of the creditors, to the bankrupt's financial resources, to the needs of the children and to all the circumstances of the case other than the needs of the bankrupt. As with ss 335A and 336, after a year, the court will assume, unless the circumstances of the case are exceptional, that the interests of the bankrupt's creditors outweigh all other considerations.

(e) Division of the proceeds of sale

Once it has been established who has ownership rights to the property and that the property is to be sold, the proportions in which the co-owners are entitled to share the proceeds of sale may still have to be determined.[54] The beneficial interest in a house may have been co-owned by the bankrupt and another either as joint tenants[55] or as tenants in common;[56] the bankruptcy will have the effect of severing a joint tenancy[57] so that the co-owners become tenants in common and the bankrupt's share vests in the trustee in bankruptcy. The significance of this is that if the beneficial interest had been held under a joint tenancy, the shares will be equal, whereas if there had been a tenancy in common prior to the bankruptcy, it will be possible that the co-owners will hold the interest in unequal shares. Where the legal title is held jointly and the conveyance sets out the beneficial interests, that will usually be conclusive.[58] In the absence of such a declaration, the court will apply similar principles to those applicable where the bankrupt is the sole legal owner. Where the contributions to the purchase price are unequal, there is a presumption that the beneficial interest is held in proportionate shares.[59]

---

53 See Clarke (1991) for a discussion of the cases in which children will not fall within s 337.

54 The court may be asked to declare the beneficial interests under the Trusts of Land and Appointment of Trustees Act 1996, s 14.

55 Each co-owner is regarded as owning the whole interest jointly with the other co-owner so that if one of them dies the other automatically becomes sole owner of the whole.

56 Each holds a separate share of the property.

57 *Re Gorman (a Bankrupt)* [1990] 1 All ER 717; *Re Palmer (Deceased)* [1994] Ch 317.

58 *Goodman v Gallant* [1986] 1 FLR 513 (CA); *Re Gorman* [1990] 1 All ER 717; *Harwood v Harwood* [1991] 2 FLR 274 (CA); *Huntingford v Hobbs* [1992] Fam Law 437 (CA).

59 *Pettitt v Pettitt* [1970] AC 777. The application of this is often complicated by the existence of a mortgage – see, for example, *Spengette v Defoe* [1992] 2 FLR 388 and *Huntingford v Hobbs* [1993] 1 FLR 736. *Midland Bank v Cooke* [1995] 2 FLR 215, CA has also added to the difficulties in this area. If the bankrupt is permitted to occupy the premises on condition that he or she contributes to mortgage repayments or outgoings, the bankrupt will not by virtue of them acquire any interest in the premises: s 338. Where one co-owner is arguing for a greater share on the basis of contribution to the improvement of a matrimonial home, the provisions of the Matrimonial Proceedings and Property Act 1970, s 37 are declaratory of the law.

The division of the sale proceeds may also be affected by the equity of exoneration. If a charge is given over property by joint owners in order to secure a debt of one only of them, the other owner is entitled to have the secured indebtedness discharged so far as possible out of the debtor's share of the property provided that it can be inferred from the circumstances that this was their joint intention. *Re Pittortou (a Bankrupt)*[60] is an example of this principle in operation; the bankrupt's wife was entitled to require that debts incurred by her husband for his sole benefit should be treated as charged primarily on his half-share in the mortgaged property.

5 AFTER-ACQUIRED ASSETS

The trustee may, by serving a notice in writing, claim property acquired by or which devolves upon the bankrupt during the period of bankruptcy unless it is exempt property[61] or is property which may be the subject of an income payments order.[62] The notice must be served within 42 days of the day on which the acquisition by the bankrupt first came to the knowledge of the trustee. The property will vest in the trustee on service of the notice and the trustee's title will relate back to the time at which the bankrupt acquired the property. If, however, a person has acquired the property in good faith, for value and without notice of the bankruptcy or a banker has entered into a transaction in good faith and without such notice, the trustee will not have a remedy against that person or banker or anyone deriving title to property from them.

The bankrupt has a duty to inform the trustee whenever he or she acquires property during the period of the bankruptcy within 21 days of becoming aware of the relevant facts.[63] The bankrupt must then keep the property for 42 days unless he or she has the trustee's consent in writing to dispose of it.[64] A bankrupt who is running a business may provide the trustee with a half-yearly report instead.

6 BANKRUPT'S INCOME

The court may, on the application of the trustee before the discharge of the bankrupt, make an income payments order claiming for the bankrupt's estate so much of the income of the bankrupt during the period for which the order is in force as may be specified in the order.[65] The Enterprise Act 2002 amendments to s 310 of the Insolvency Act 1986 make it clear that the order may last longer than the period of bankruptcy, although not longer than three years from the date of the order; this is intended to align the potential length of an order with the pre-Enterprise Act standard length of a bankruptcy. Income is defined as comprising every payment in the nature of income which is from time to time made to the bankrupt or to which he or she from

---

60 [1985] 1 WLR 58.
61 Under the Insolvency Act 1986, s 283 or any other enactment.
62 Under the Insolvency Act 1986, s 310.
63 Insolvency Act 1986, s 333.
64 Insolvency Rules 1986, r 6.200.
65 Insolvency Act 1986, s 310 as amended by the Enterprise Act 2002, s 259. See Miller (2002b).

time to time becomes entitled, including any payment in respect of the carrying on of any business or in respect of any office or employment. The test of whether a payment is income is largely a matter of common sense.[66] It has been held to include payments received under a maintenance order made against the bankrupt's former spouse.[67] Section 310 of the Insolvency Act 1986 does not, unlike its predecessor provisions, apply to income whose source is property which has vested in the trustee in bankruptcy; the income is automatically that of the trustee.[68]

The court will not make an order which would have the effect of reducing the income of the bankrupt below what appears to the court to be necessary for meeting the reasonable domestic needs of the bankrupt and his or her family.[69] In *Re Rayatt*,[70] in which the bankrupt successfully argued that the costs of private education for his children fell within his reasonable domestic needs, it was held that the court ought to consider what was 'necessary for meeting the reasonable domestic needs of the bankrupt and his family', not what was 'necessary to enable the bankrupt to live'. The question was whether particular expenditure fell within the family's reasonable domestic needs, and it was not helpful to ask a general question whether expenditure on private education was a proper expenditure to take into account in bankruptcies. On the facts of this case,[71] the expenditure was a reasonable domestic need. The order may require payment by either the bankrupt or by the source of the income directly to the trustee. If there is already an attachment of earnings order in force against the bankrupt, the court may discharge or vary the order when making an order.

Section 310A of the Insolvency Act 1986, inserted by s 260 of the Enterprise Act 2002, provides for the making of an 'income payments agreement' between the bankrupt and the trustee or Official Receiver which may then be enforced as if it were an income payments order.

7 THE BANKRUPT'S PENSION

The bankrupt may already be in receipt of a pension or he or she may have a future right to pension and lump sum benefits on retirement or death, often with a right to call for early payment of the sums. *Re Landau*[72] established that contractual rights under a personal pension scheme would vest in the trustee in bankruptcy, whether or not the scheme contained a provision prohibiting assignment of the policy. The rights would remain vested in the trustee, even after discharge of the bankrupt, unless disclaimed by the trustee or, perhaps, re-assigned to the bankrupt in return for a suitable payment. Bankrupts whose pensions were provided by an occupational pension scheme set up by their employer were in a better position, since these

---

66   *Affleck v Hammond* [1912] 3 KB 162.
67   *Re Landau* [1934] 1 Ch 549; *Re Tennant's Application* [1956] 2 All ER 753.
68   *Re Landau* [1997] 3 All ER 322; *Performing Rights Society v Rowland* [1997] 3 All ER 336.
69   This would include maintenance payments.
70   [1998] 2 FLR 264. The principle was applied in *Re Scott (a Bankrupt)* [2003] All ER (D) 214. See also *R v Secretary of State for Education and Employment ex p Knight and Another* (2000) unreported, 17 March.
71   The likely effect on the eldest child of having to change schools.
72   [1997] 3 All ER 322. In *Krasner v Dennison* [2001] Ch 76, the Court of Appeal held that this did not infringe the European Convention on Human Rights.

schemes usually contained forfeiture clauses under which the bankruptcy of a member would cause his or her rights to be forfeited to the trustees who would then hold them on discretionary trusts for a class of beneficiaries, including the member and his or her dependants. This device was not available in the case of a personal contractual pension scheme since it would be tantamount to the member settling assets on protective trust in the event of bankruptcy which is not permissible.[73]

The *Re Landau* decision led to statutory reform and s 11 of the Welfare Reform and Pensions Act 1999 now provides that, in relation to bankruptcies where the petition was presented after 29 May 2000, any rights held by the bankrupt under an Inland Revenue approved occupational pension scheme, retirement annuity contract, personal pension scheme or relevant statutory scheme are excluded from the bankrupt's estate and do not pass to the trustee in bankruptcy.[74] Pension payments can continue to be taken into account when calculating a bankrupt's income for the purposes of an income payments order.[75] There are provisions within s 12 and associated Regulations allowing the court in certain circumstances to order that rights under an unapproved pension will remain with the bankrupt.

---

73 See Chapter 26. Welfare Reform and Pensions Act 1999, s 14 makes it impossible to forfeit pensions after 6 April 2002.

74 The Welfare Reform and Pensions Act 1999 does not have retrospective effect. In *Residuary Milk Marketing Board v Gunningham* (2000) unreported, 2 November, the Court of Appeal held that the fact that a delay in making a bankruptcy order until after 29 May 2000 would have protected the debtor's pension rights would not have been a good reason for refusing a bankruptcy order to which a creditor would otherwise be entitled.

75 Welfare Reform and Pensions Act 1999, s 18, Sched 2, paras 1, 2.

CHAPTER 28

ASSETS CLAIMED BY THIRD PARTIES

1 INTRODUCTION

The claim of third parties to be beneficially entitled to assets which appear to form part of the insolvent estate is the common theme of the material dealt with both by this chapter and the next. As has been seen, only those assets to which the insolvent has a beneficial entitlement are available to the creditors so each successful proprietary claim may reduce the amount available to those who merely have personal rights against the insolvent.[1] In many cases, however, the battle will be between competing proprietary claims and it will be clear that those who have purely personal rights will not, in any event, derive any benefit from the disputed assets.[2] This is particularly true of corporate insolvency, where in many cases the assets would anyway be caught by a floating charge and would be unavailable to the general creditors unless and until the debenture holder had been paid off. It has, for example, frequently been an administrative receiver rather than a liquidator disputing a claim to be entitled to assets on the basis of retention of title.

This chapter deals with claims to absolute beneficial title to assets in respect of which the insolvent has possession or legal title; Chapter 29 deals with claims to security rights over assets owned by the insolvent. Before looking in more detail at the common grounds for claims to be the beneficial owner of property, it is helpful to refer briefly to the following basic concepts of property law:[3]

(a) In order to claim a right over an asset, it is necessary to show a real right (a right 'in rem') to it as distinct to a personal right against someone in respect of it. As has been seen,[4] personal rights will not survive the insolvency of the defendant.

(b) The legal title to an asset may be split from the beneficial ownership of it; where this happens, the holder of the legal title will hold the property on trust for the beneficial, or equitable, owner. The historical explanation of this terminology is that the legal title is the right which would have been recognised by the courts of common law[5] (which refused to recognise divided ownership), whereas equity recognised the obligation of the legal owner to give effect to the beneficial rights which it had been intended should exist in relation to the property. Equity also treats as done that which should have been done and will give effect to an unexecuted agreement to transfer real property; this enables equity to recognise interests which cannot exist at law.[6] The general principle is that equitable rights attached to property bind future transferees of the property with the exception

---

1 See Belcher and Beglan (1997).
2 An insolvency practitioner will need funds for any litigation in which he or she seeks to dispute such proprietary claims. This question is considered in Chapter 32.
3 For a more detailed exposition in relation to personal property, see Goode, 1995, Chapter 2 and Lawson and Rudden, 2002.
4 In Chapter 25.
5 Until the Judicature Acts 1873–75, the rules of common law and the rules of equity were administered as separate systems by different courts.
6 Such as a right to future goods.

of the *bona fide* purchaser of the legal title without notice of the right.[7] Where competing claimants to property only claim equitable rights, the first in time will prevail provided the equities are equal. Where the legal and beneficial interest are vested in the same person, there will be no separate equitable interest and no scope for the application of equitable rules.

(c) Concurrent ownership of property is possible either as joint tenants (that is, each holding the same interest) or as tenants in common (where each has a distinct share in the property).[8]

(d) Acquisition of the legal title to property previously held by another happens by consensual transfer such as gift or sale or by operation of law on death or bankruptcy. The basic rule is that it is not possible to transfer a better title than one has,[9] but there are exceptions to this.[10]

(e) Transfer of title to property may be absolute or may be by way of security only, in which case the transferor will have the right to reclaim the property once the secured obligation has been met. Non-possessory security rights (that is, where the giver of the security remains in possession of the assets) may be granted by way of defeasible transfer of title to the property or by a charge which acts as an encumbrance over property. It will usually be necessary to register the security before the rights of the mortgagee or chargee will bind third parties.

(f) A proprietary claim will only succeed where the property is identifiable. If the claim fails because the property has been dissipated, destroyed or irrevocably commingled, the aggrieved party will probably have a personal claim in respect of the loss but this will not survive an insolvency. Where there has been substitution of the original assets, the so called tracing rules, explained in more detail below, will decide whether or not substitute property to which there is a proprietary claim can be identified. It can be difficult to decide whether a claim to money is a proprietary claim which will survive an insolvency or whether it is a personal claim which would, of course, be payable in money but which will not survive the insolvency; this is considered further below.

Third parties may be claiming that they own, both legally and beneficially, goods in the possession of the insolvent. This may be because they have expressly reserved title to the goods when giving possession to the insolvent or it may be that they originally had title to the goods and are claiming that the insolvent came into possession of the goods in circumstances which did not defeat that title.[11] Alternatively, the claim may be that the insolvent holds only the bare legal title to the asset and that the equitable interest is held on trust for the third party.

---

7   In relation to real property, general principles have been replaced by provisions of the land registration legislation.

8   See Chapter 27 above for further explanation of this in relation to land; the legal title to land can only be held jointly. In relation to chattels, it is possible to hold the legal title either jointly or in common.

9   Often expressed as the *nemo dat* rule: '*nemo dat quod non habet*' means that no one can give what he or she does not have.

10 See the Sale of Goods Act 1979, ss 21–26 and the Factors Act 1889. The anachronistic exception of the *bona fide* purchaser in market overt contained in the Sale of Goods Act 1979, s 22 has been repealed. See Goode, 1995, Chapter 16.

11 Ie, no exception to the *nemo dat* rule.

The claim may be to proprietary rights (either legal or equitable) by way of security over the assets of the insolvent; this is dealt with in the next chapter. Depending upon whether the value of the goods exceeds the amount owing, this may not be a claim to the assets in their entirety; the secured creditor will only retain the proceeds of realisation to the extent of the secured debt.

2   TRACING PROPERTY[12]

These rules on tracing property deal with the situation where the claimant has established that he or she originally owned property which can no longer be reclaimed but that the defendant is in possession of property which the claimant claims should be treated as a substitute. If the defendant is not in possession of such property, there may still be an equitable remedy for knowing receipt of trust property or assistance in a breach of trust, but this will be a personal remedy and will not survive the insolvency.[13] The issue generally arises in relation to attempts to trace money into and through bank accounts where it has been mixed with the money of others, but the same principles will apply where goods have been mixed or blended with other goods.[14]

This is one of the most complex areas of insolvency-related law, sitting as it does in that grey area of the law where property law and unjust enrichment law intersect. The debate[15] has been given fresh vigour recently by the House of Lords case of *Foskett v McKeown*.[16] This was not an insolvency case, but concerned the consequences of the traced property (the proceeds of an insurance policy) being higher in value than the original property (money used in breach of trust, together with money of the trustee, towards the purchase the policy); the House of Lords held that the claimants were entitled to a proportionate share of the proceeds. The judgments contain extensive consideration of the nature and history of tracing, particularly so far as mixed substitutions are concerned.

The holder of the legal title to property is entitled to follow it, even where it changes its form or passes through a number of hands, provided it remains possible to identify it as replacing the original property.[17] Someone who has parted with money will almost certainly have lost the title to that particular money, but where he or she can identify that money as having been through the hands of the defendant, there will be an action for money had and received unless the defendant has a defence; it seems[18] that this is a personal not a proprietary claim and therefore of no use against

---

12   See Goff and Jones, 2002; Smith, 1997.

13   *El Ajou v Dollar Land Holdings plc* [1993] 3 All ER 717; [1994] 2 All ER 688; *Royal Brunei Airlines v Tan* [1995] 3 All ER 97.

14   See, for example, *Glencore International AG v Metro Trading International Inc* [2001] 1 Lloyd's Rep 284.

15   See, for example, Burrows (2001); Stevens (2001); Grantham and Rickett (2000).

16   [2001] 1 AC 102.

17   *Lipkin Gorman (a Firm) v Karpnale Ltd* [1991] 2 AC 548.

18   This is a difficult issue because it is hard to differentiate between payment of a personal remedy in money and return of money to which the claimant had property rights. It is only of any consequence in an insolvency. See Millett (1991).

an insolvent defendant. Although the common law can follow money from one account to another where there has been physical transfer of cash or a document, it has been held unable to do so where the transfer has taken place by electronic means.[19] The common law has always had difficulty following assets if at some stage they have been mixed with other assets, since it becomes impossible to identify the property physically and the common law lacks the ability to subject the mixed fund to a charge in favour of the original owner of part of it. If the mixing is done by the defendant to the action, this is not an obstacle since the cause of action is complete when the property is received. If the mixing has happened somewhere between claimant and defendant, the claimant will have a problem: *Agip (Africa) Ltd v Jackson*.[20]

Since the common law did not recognise the rights of the equitable owner, such an owner would not be able to follow property at law and would have to trace on the basis of the equitable rules. The principle established by the Court of Appeal in *Re Diplock's Estate*[21] is that, provided there is an initial fiduciary relationship, the owner of the equitable interest in the property can trace it into the hands of anyone except a *bona fide* purchaser of the legal title for value and without notice.[22] Tracing will cease to be possible if the property is destroyed or dissipated or ceases to be identifiable. Equity, apparently unlike the common law, can trace in a mixed fund and, oddly, this has put the holder of an equitable interest in property into a stronger position than a legal owner since, given the absence of the necessary fiduciary relationship, a legal owner has not been able to rely on the equitable tracing rules.[23] There have been recent suggestions that this should no longer be the case.[24]

The rules on tracing into a mixed fund depend upon whether the property has been mixed with that of another innocent party or with that of the fiduciary. In the first case, the general rule is proportionate sharing, subject sometimes to 'first in, first out'.[25] In the second case, the general rule is proportionate sharing once any loss to the mixed fund has been borne by a fiduciary who mixed the assets in breach of trust.[26]

The exercise of a proprietary remedy depends upon the property being identifiable in the hands of the defendant. The rules applicable where a mixed fund becomes exhausted are an aspect of this; if the fund becomes exhausted at some point after the trust money has been paid into it, whether before or after the mixing, it will cease to be possible to trace the money.[27] *Bishopsgate Investment Management Ltd v Homan*[28] is an example of this in operation. Money from pension funds belonging to

---

19   Millett J in *Agip (Africa) Ltd v Jackson* [1989] 3 WLR 1367 followed in *Bank Tejarat v Hong Kong and Shanghai Banking Corp (CI) Ltd* [1995] 1 Lloyd's Rep 239.

20   [1989] 3 WLR 1367.

21   [1948] Ch 465.

22   See, for example, *Re Fleet Disposal Services Ltd* [1995] BCC 605.

23   In *Foskett v McKeown*, Lord Millett expressed the view that there is no justification for this distinction.

24   *Dicta* of Lord Millett in *Foskett v McKeown* [2000] 3 All ER 97 relied on in *Dick v Harper* (2001) unreported, 15 November, a decision of Leslie Kosmin QC sitting as a Deputy Judge of the Chancery Division.

25   *Re Diplock's Estate* [1948] Ch 465; *Barlow Clowes International Ltd (in Liquidation) v Vaughan* [1992] 4 All ER 22.

26   *Re Hallett's Estate* (1880) 13 Ch D 696; *Re Oatway* [1903] 2 Ch 356; *Re Tilley's Will Trusts* [1967] 1 Ch 1179.

27   *Re Goldcorp Exchange Ltd* [1995] 1 AC 74.

28   [1995] Ch 211. Breslin (1995).

the plaintiff had been wrongly transferred by Robert Maxwell into Maxwell Communication Corporation plc. The account into which the money was paid had either been or become overdrawn and it was held that this prevented the plaintiff from tracing the money.

3   CLAIM TO BE ENTITLED TO GOODS AS PURCHASER[29]

The third party may be claiming to be entitled, as a purchaser from the insolvent,[30] to goods still in the possession of the insolvent. A binding contract for the purchase of chattels does not, unlike a contract to sell land, confer title on the purchaser. The purchaser may already have become the owner of the goods despite the fact that they are still in the possession of the insolvent seller since possession of and property in goods do not necessarily pass to the purchaser at the same time. Where the property in the goods has passed to the purchaser, the purchaser will be entitled to take possession of them. If the property has not passed and the insolvency practitioner decides to repudiate the contract, the purchaser will only be able to prove in the insolvency either for damages for non-delivery or for return of the purchase price. A purchaser who has not yet paid for the goods at the time of the insolvency will only suffer a loss if he or she has incurred expenses in making the contract with the insolvent or has suffered loss due to the delay in delivery or can only obtain substitutes for more than the price asked by the insolvent seller. The purchaser who has paid for the goods in advance of their delivery and only has a personal claim will clearly lose as a result of the insolvency of the seller.

Section 17 of the Sale of Goods Act 1979 provides that property will pass when the parties intend it to and s 18 of the 1979 Act provides a number of presumptions as to the intention of the parties which will apply in the absence of any contrary indication. Contrary indication may be demonstrated by the terms of the contract, the conduct of the parties or other circumstances of the case. The basic proposition of the default rules provided by s 18 of the Sale of Goods Act 1979 is that property in goods will pass at the time the contract is made provided the contract is unconditional and the goods are both specified and in a deliverable state; provision for postponement of delivery or payment, or both, is immaterial. Where something is to be done to the goods by the seller to render them specific or deliverable or to ascertain the price, property will not pass until that has been done and the buyer has notice of it.

The goods must be ascertained before title can pass; until the goods have been ascertained and appropriated to the contract, the purchaser will not be able to acquire a proprietary right.[31] Goods may be unascertained because they are sold by description only and the seller has complete freedom as to how to source the order as in *Re Goldcorp Exchange Ltd*.[32] Customers of a New Zealand company which dealt in precious metals purchased bullion for future delivery on the basis that they were purchasing gold which would be physically stored for them by the company in safekeeping as an unallocated part of the company's total stock. The company became

---

29   See Goode, 1995, Chapter 8.
30   See Goode, 1995, Chapter 8 on the passing of property under a contract for sale.
31   Sale of Goods Act 1979, s 16.
32   [1994] 2 All ER 806.

insolvent and went into receivership under a debenture which secured by floating charge a debt exceeding the entire assets of the company. The only way in which the customers would retrieve anything from the insolvency was by demonstrating a proprietary claim to assets since there would be nothing left to meet personal claims after payment of the debenture holder. This was clearly a sale of generic goods on terms which preserved the seller's freedom to decide the source of the goods, and no title to the goods could pass as a result of the contract of sale[33] until the goods had been ascertained and appropriated to the particular contracts. Lord Mustill referred to the 'irresistible' reasoning of Atkin LJ in *Re Wait*[34] as pointing unequivocally to the conclusion that under a simple contract for the sale of unascertained goods, neither legal nor equitable title can pass merely by virtue of the sale.

Goods may also be unascertained because they form part of a bulk, only some of which is to be acquired by the purchaser. Where the bulk has been reduced to the amount the purchaser has contracted for, or less, title will pass provided he or she is the only buyer in respect of that bulk. This principle of 'ascertainment by exhaustion' was developed by the courts[35] and has been codified by the Sale of Goods (Amendment) Act 1995, which has added a third limb to rule 5 of s 18 of the Sale of Goods Act 1979.

There may be several purchasers whose orders are to be met from a specified bulk as in *Re Staplyton Fletcher Ltd*.[36] In this case, customers of a wine merchant in administrative receivership claimed ownership of wine which they had ordered and paid for but which was stored in the wine merchant's warehouse without individual bottles being appropriated to each contract. Wine which was being stored for customers in this way was physically removed from the trading stock. The court held that the wines in the company's warehouse had been ascertained by their segregation so that the customers were tenants in common of the segregated stock. It would now be possible to reach the same conclusion by relying on the new s 20A of the Sale of Goods Act 1979 introduced by the Sale of Goods (Amendment) Act 1995. This provides that in the absence of agreement to the contrary, a pre-paying buyer of goods forming part of a bulk, identified either in the contract or by subsequent agreement, becomes the owner of an undivided share in the bulk. If the buyer has paid in part only, he or she will receive a proportionate share and any delivery to him or her shall be ascribed first to the part for which he or she has paid. Where the aggregate of the undivided shares is more than the whole of the bulk, there will be proportionate reduction of each undivided share. This provision would not assist purchasers in the *Re Goldcorp Exchange* situation where the seller is not bound to provide the goods from an identifiable source.

Section 20B of the Sale of Goods Act 1979[37] provides that the co-owners of an undivided bulk shall be deemed to have consented to any dealing with the bulk

---

33 The Privy Council was chiefly concerned with arguments that equitable proprietary rights had arisen outside the contract by way of trust. These arguments also ran into the difficulty that the subject matter of any trust was insufficiently identified.

34 [1927] 1 Ch 606.

35 *The Elafi* [1982] 1 All ER 208.

36 [1994] 1 WLR 1181.

37 Also introduced by the Sale of Goods (Amendment) Act 1995.

including the delivery out of it to other co-owners. The Law Commissions[38] did consider whether there should be special rules applying in the case of insolvency since this deemed consent would have the effect of preferring earlier claimants. They considered the possibility of a *pro rata* apportionment scheme; this would, however, involve the insolvency practitioner in the exercise of apportionment despite the fact that the insolvent seller would have no interest in the outcome. It would have been unpopular with commodity traders who would be exposed to potential liability to unknown third parties even after taking delivery of the goods. The Law Commissions decided not to recommend a separate insolvency rule; those who did not act sufficiently quickly to claim their goods would lose out to those who had acted more speedily, but they would be no worse off than under the unamended law.

4 RETENTION OF TITLE BY SELLER[39]

(a) Introduction to the retention of title device

The third party may be claiming goods on the basis that they have been supplied to the insolvent under a contract containing a clause reserving title to the goods. This is clearly possible under the provisions of the Sale of Goods Act 1979 outlined above.

It has been commonplace since the 19th century for suppliers who provide goods on credit terms to provide that ownership of the goods will not pass until payment for the goods has been received; this form of transaction is described as a conditional sale. The hire-purchase agreement[40] was devised as a more sophisticated form of seller protection since, by structuring the transaction as a contract for hire coupled with an option to purchase at the end of the hire period,[41] the seller avoided the problem of the customer being a buyer in possession able to confer title to the goods to a third party[42] and could be sure of the right to repossess the goods in the event of default. During this century, the process has been taken a stage further with the development of the finance lease under which the customer takes a lease of equipment for the length of the anticipated useful life of the asset and pays rental which will amount to the cost of the asset and of the credit; the lessor of the equipment (usually a finance house) retains purely nominal ownership, but this is sufficient to allow repossession should the lessee become insolvent or otherwise default.

Retention of ownership, although designed to secure payment, has not been seen by English law as a form of security, since it does not involve the grant to another of rights over property. Registration as a company charge or as a bill of sale has not therefore been necessary for the device to be valid against third parties, who may be affected by rights whose existence there is no official means of discovering.[43] This

---

38 *Sale of Goods Forming Part of a Bulk*, 1993.
39 See Chapter 37 of the Cork Report (Cmnd 8558); McCormack, 1995.
40 *Helby v Matthews* [1895] AC 471.
41 By which time the rental payments would have amounted to the price together with a charge for the credit.
42 *Lee v Butler* [1893] 2 QB 318 was a leading case on the Factors Act 1889, s 9 which, with the Sale of Goods Act 1979, s 25(1) provide the 'sale by buyer in possession' exception to the *nemo dat* rule.
43 See the discussion of the distinction between sale and loan credit in Chapter 3.

very formalist distinction between sale credit and loan credit was abolished in the United States[44] some time ago and has been the subject of considerable criticism in this country.[45] If the proposals of the Law Commission in its Consultation Paper No 164 on *Registration of Security Interests: Company Charges and Property other than Land* are accepted, the situation in this regard will change dramatically; the supplier would need to file a notice that the terms of supply to the customer will be on the basis of retention of title. This would then put anyone dealing with the customer subsequently on notice of the possibility of retention of title.

Simple retention of title has been with us for a long time,[46] but the device has become more prominent and more complicated since the *Romalpa*[47] case, which appeared to open up the possibility of recovering not just the goods supplied but also products made with them and the proceeds of any sub-sales whenever any payment owed to the supplier was outstanding. Retention of title clauses have become more far-reaching although, as will be seen, in some cases those drafting them have been over-ambitious to counter-productive effect. Unwary draughtsmen have frequently been found to have created a registrable charge which is void for non-registration; once the buyer is conferring rights over his or her property on the seller, the thin dividing line between retention of title and charge will have been crossed.[48] If the Law Commission's proposals[49] are adopted, notice that the retention of title terms extend beyond simple retention of title would avoid the problems of the provisions being held subsequently to be void as a non-registered charge. In relation to any form of security other than straightforward purchase-money security, the protection conferred by the notice-filing would only extend to those dealing with the customer subsequently. A charge which had previously been protected would take precedence over a retention of title clause in relation to substitute assets and proceeds of sale.

(b) Claims to proceeds of sub-sales

The extended retention of title clauses devised recently are attempts to provide the seller of goods with protection against the buyer's insolvency in circumstances where the goods supplied are expected to be sold on or used before the time for payment arrives. In *Romalpa*, it was held that a seller who supplied on reservation of title terms but who authorised sub-sales on condition that the buyer accounted for the proceeds of the sub-sales had an equitable right to trace those proceeds and claim proprietary rights to them, thus giving the seller priority over the holder of a floating charge in respect of the proceeds. The decision has never been overruled, but in subsequent cases, the courts have distinguished it on every similar occasion. They have held that in the cases before them the parties must be assumed to have intended that the

---

44 Article 9 of the American Uniform Commercial Code
45 See Crowther, Cmnd 4596, 1971 and Diamond, 1989. The Cork Committee felt that some provision for the registration of retention of title clauses should be made.
46 See the comments of the Cork Committee at para 1599.
47 *Aluminium Industrie Vaassen BV v Romalpa Aluminium Ltd* [1976] 1 Lloyd's Rep 443.
48 For an account of a more flexible approach taken recently in Australia, see de Lacy (2001), noting *Associated Alloys Pty Ltd v Metropolitan Engineering & Fabrication Pty Ltd* (2000) 171 ALR 568.
49 Consultation Paper No 164.

interest in the proceeds should be by way of security only, rather than absolute, so that it amounted to an unregistered charge over the book debts arising from the sub-sales.

Mummery J in *Compaq Computer v Abercorn Group*[50] observed that once it was accepted that the seller's beneficial interest in the proceeds of sale was determinable on the payment of the debt, the seller was faced with the difficulty that the rights and obligations of the parties were in reality and in substance characteristic of those of the parties to a charge and not of the fiduciary relationship which would be required to give rise to the tracing rights. In *Re Weldtech Equipment Ltd*,[51] Hoffmann J considered a clause which provided:

> The goods remain our property until payment of the purchase price including any additional costs is effected in full and until all cheques and drafts have been cashed. This right is reserved for as long as we may have any claims against the purchaser resulting from other deliveries. With the exception of goods sold to a company for resale within the framework of their normal business operations, the customer is not entitled to sell or otherwise dispose of the goods before full payment of the purchase price. In the case of authorised resale of goods supplied by our company (in the original or a modified form or as an integral part of other deliveries) all rights to which the purchaser is entitled as a result of the contract with the third party, in particular for payment of the purchase price, are transferred to us automatically upon completion of the sale. The purchaser is obliged to advise us immediately of the resale or disposal of the equipment, stating the full address of the third party involved and the main content of the purchasing contract, in particular the terms of payment. This transfer takes place only for securing our claims against the purchaser and does not affect his payment obligations.

Hoffmann J held that the liquidator had been correct to regard the clause as effective to preserve the title of the vendor to the equipment which was physically in the company's possession. He went on to hold that the assignment of the debts was clearly only intended to be by way of charge.[52] Since the clause had not been registered under s 395 of the Companies Act 1985, it was void against the liquidator.

(c) Attempts to claim substitute goods

The courts have considered a number of cases in which sellers sought to rely on extended reservation of title clauses to claim ownership of goods made from or with the material supplied. The principle which can be derived from these cases is that the seller will succeed where the original material supplied remains identifiable provided that it was intended that the supplier should have absolute ownership of the substitute goods. Where the material has been mixed irrevocably with other goods, it will not be possible to identify it. *Re Andrabell Ltd*[53] was an example of the goods being mixed with others so that it was impossible to identify them. The retention of title clause in this case only reserved title until payment had been made for the particular consignment of goods; several consignments had been delivered, some paid for and some not, and it was not possible to identify the goods as coming from any

---

50 [1991] BCC 484.
51 [1991] BCC 16.
52 See also *Tatung (UK) Ltd v Galex Telesure Ltd and Others* (1989) 5 BCC 325.
53 [1984] 3 All ER 407.

particular consignment. Where goods change their identity in the course of manufacture, a new asset will have come into being to which the supplier could not have reserved title; any right claimed by the supplier over the new asset will have been granted by the purchaser and, unless it was intended to confer absolute ownership on the supplier, will be void as an unregistered security interest. In *Re Peachdart*,[54] for example, the title to leather which had been turned into handbags was lost and in *Borden (UK) Ltd v Scottish Timber Products Ltd*,[55] the supplier of resin which had been used to make chipboard could only claim a charge over the chipboard which, being unregistered, was void. *Hendy Lennox v Grahame Puttick*[56] was an example of revocable mixture; the goods in question were diesel engines which had been bolted into generating sets but, since they could be unbolted, it was held that the supplier could retain the right to repossess them. In *Chaigley Farms Ltd v Crawford, Kaye & Grayshire*,[57] it was held that a retention of title clause in respect of livestock sold to an abattoir was defeated by the slaughter of the animals.

(d) 'All moneys' clauses

The clause in *Romalpa* also provided that ownership in the material supplied would only transfer to the purchaser 'when he has met all that is owing to [the supplier], no matter on what grounds'. This type of so called 'all moneys' clause has become commonplace and was held by the House of Lords in *Armour v Thyssen Edelstahlweke AG*[58] to be valid. If there was a point after the supply of the material subject to the clause at which the purchaser had paid everything owing to the supplier, the material would have vested in the purchaser then and subsequent indebtedness would not, of course, have divested the purchaser of the title. There is a problem in relation to 'all moneys' clauses of a potential windfall for the supplier where the purchaser has made partial payment;[59] any attempt in the wording of the clause to prevent the supplier from taking advantage of this runs the risk of turning the provision into a charge. The question of the consequences of the supplied material being worth more than the indebtedness was considered, *obiter*, by the Court of Appeal in *Clough Mill v Martin*;[60] Sir John Donaldson MR said that the provision whereby the seller reserved 'the right to dispose of the material until payment in full for all the material has been received' meant that the sellers could re-sell the material until they had been paid in full, but that thereafter the material would be the property of the purchaser. Robert Goff LJ suggested that repossession by the seller would follow the seller's acceptance of the buyer's repudiatory breach of contract and that the buyer would be entitled to reclaim any part of the purchase price paid for the goods on the basis of total failure of consideration. The House of Lords in the *Armour* case observed that it did not have to consider what would happen where there had been part payment of the price before repossession of the goods.

---

54 [1984] Ch 131.
55 [1981] Ch 25.
56 [1984] 1 WLR 485.
57 [1996] BCC 957. The decision is queried in Whiteson (1997). The New Zealand High Court took a different view in *Re Weddel (NZ) Ltd* (1996) 5 NZBIC 104,055, discussed by de Lacy (1997).
58 [1991] 2 AC 339.
59 This is considered by Hicks (1992).
60 [1985] 1 WLR 111.

(e) Successive retention of title

In *Re Highway Foods International Ltd*,[61] the court had to consider the effect of a sale of meat on retention of title terms followed by a sub-sale also on retention of title terms. It was held that the sub-sale did not divest the original owner of title to the meat until the sub-purchaser either paid the purchaser or processed the meat.

(f) Incorporation of the clause into the contract

In addition to the debate in any particular case as to whether the agreement amounts to a charge, there will also be the question of whether there is indeed a reservation of title provision in the contract between supplier and the insolvent. The normal contractual principles apply; the term will only be part of the contract if the purchaser had been given reasonable notice of it before or at the time of making the contract.[62] In *John Snow & Co Ltd v DBG Woodcroft & Co Ltd*,[63] the defendant company went into voluntary liquidation at a time when it had not paid for timber supplied to it by the plaintiff company. The plaintiff claimed to be entitled to repossess the timber on the basis of a retention of title clause reserving the property in the timber to the plaintiff until the defendant had discharged the whole of its indebtedness. The defendant argued that the terms of sale did not contain any such provision[64] since the documentation used by the plaintiff did not bring the clause sufficiently to the defendant's attention. Boreham J held that sufficient notice had been given on the back of the plaintiff's quotation form and that retention of title clauses were not so unusual as to require 'red ink' treatment. Where both purchaser and supplier have their own standard terms, the 'battle of the forms' will usually be won by the last party to notify the terms before the contract is made, usually by the other party starting to perform.[65]

(g) Practical effect of retention of title claims

Although a valid retention of title clause will allow the supplier to repossess the goods, this will probably be something which the supplier will attempt to avoid having to do. In practice, the use of the clause is to give the supplier a bargaining lever to extract payment from an insolvency practitioner[66] who wants to be able to use the material. The strength of the bargaining lever will probably depend on the extent to which the insolvency practitioner needs the supplier to continue supplies. The case of *Leyland DAF Ltd v Automotive Products*[67] is an example of this; a supplier in a monopoly position was held to be entitled to refuse to continue to supply any more parts until they were paid in full for goods which had been supplied under retention

---

61 [1995] BCC 271.
62 See any standard contract textbook on the incorporation of unsigned standard terms into a contract. This issue, which used to arise and tends to be taught largely in connection with exclusion clauses, now frequently involves arguments about whether retention of title clauses form part of a contract.
63 [1985] BCLC 54.
64 They also argued unsuccessfully that the provision would be void as an unregistered charge.
65 *Butler Machine Tool Co Ltd v Ex-Cell-O-Corp (England) Ltd* [1979] 1 All ER 965.
66 Usually, in fact, an administrative receiver since a liquidator is not likely to carry on the business and a retention of title clause may not be enforced against an administrator.
67 [1993] BCC 389.

of title. *Lipe Ltd v Leyland DAF*[68] illustrates the normal practice of insolvency practitioners which is to give a personal undertaking promising to return goods or pay their value if the clause is upheld in court; in this case, the court refused to grant the supplier an injunction preventing the insolvency practitioner from dealing with the goods.

5   UNPAID SELLER'S RIGHTS

Section 39 of the Sale of Goods Act 1979 confers certain rights on an unpaid[69] seller of goods, notwithstanding that property may have passed to the buyer. An unpaid seller will have the right to reclaim goods which have not yet reached an insolvent purchaser despite the fact that title to the goods has passed.[70] If the seller is still in possession of the goods, he or she will have a lien over them in the circumstances specified in s 41 of the Sale of Goods Act 1979; the circumstances include the insolvency of the buyer.[71] The insolvency of the buyer does not bring the contract of sale to an end[72] and the seller must hold the goods available for the buyer against payment of the price unless and until the contract comes to an end. If the goods are perishable and the buyer does not pay within a reasonable time, the seller may resell the goods.[73] The seller may also resell the goods if the buyer, having been told of the seller's intention to resell, does not pay within a reasonable time.[74]

6   EQUITABLE INTERESTS UNDER A TRUST[75]

(a) General

Property held by the insolvent on trust for a third party will not be available to the general creditors. In the case of bankruptcy, there is a specific provision to this effect in s 283(3)(a) of the Insolvency Act 1986, whereas in the case of liquidation, it follows from the general principle that the creditors may only look to those assets in which the insolvent has a beneficial interest.

Readers are referred to general texts on equity, trusts and restitution for thorough discussion of this area. This text will restrict itself to a broad and somewhat simplistic indication of the circumstances in which a third party will be able to 'trump' the other creditors on the basis of being beneficially entitled to property under a trust together with more detailed consideration of several cases which have arisen in the insolvency context by way of illustration.

---

68   [1993] BCC 385.
69   Defined by the Sale of Goods Act 1979, s 38(1).
70   See Sale of Goods Act 1979, ss 44–46.
71   Sale of Goods Act 1979, ss 41–43 set out the unpaid seller's lien in greater detail.
72   Nor does the insolvency of the buyer since the contract may still be performed by the trustee in bankruptcy or liquidator.
73   Sale of Goods Act 1979, s 48.
74   Sale of Goods Act 1979, s 48 re-enacting the common law rule that the seller may make time of the essence of the contract so that failure to pay is a repudiatory breach.
75   See, generally, Hanbury and Martin, 2001; Hayton, 2001.

The essence of a trust is separation of the legal title in property, which is held by the trustee, from the equitable title which vests in the beneficiary. A beneficiary under a trust has a proprietary claim to the property (provided it can be identified) or to any substitute property into which it can be traced. There does have to be identifiable property subject to the trust; a contractual obligation to establish a trust fund will not suffice to give rise to proprietary remedies.[76]

Trusts are usually categorised as express, resulting or constructive; the term 'implied trust' is also used, but is probably a means of establishing one of categories of trust rather than a distinct category itself. The principles relating to express and resulting trusts are relatively clear, although there is always scope for difficulty in applying those principles to any particular set of facts. The law as to the circumstances in which a constructive trust will arise is less clear; the common thread is the split of equitable from legal title in circumstances where there is no express or resulting trust but there are a number of disparate circumstances in which this will happen. Further confusion arises from the use of the description 'constructive trustee' in respect of those who are personally liable for knowingly assisting in a breach of trust but against whom a proprietary claim is not necessarily possible.

Assets may be lost from a trust fund through authorised dealing by the trustee in which case the beneficiaries will have no right to reclaim them. For example, in *Space Investments Ltd v Canadian Imperial Bank of Commerce Trust Co (Bahamas) Ltd*,[77] a trustee bank was permitted by the rules of the trust to place money on deposit with any bank, including itself. It placed trust money on deposit with itself and subsequently went into insolvent liquidation; the Privy Council held that the money had become general money of the bank, whose obligations in relation to it were those of debtor and not of trustee. The beneficiaries were therefore ordinary creditors without any proprietary claim.

The vexed issue in this area is the extent to which a fiduciary relationship can co-exist with an ordinary contractual relationship. It can be argued that where a claimant has entered a transaction with the intention simply of becoming a creditor of the insolvent, there is no justification for affording him or her the priority of a trust interest on the basis that the debtor's behaviour has given rise to a fiduciary relationship. The Privy Council in *Re Goldcorp Exchange*[78] quoted with approval Atkin LJ in *Re Wait*[79] on the difficulties inherent in holding that a contract gives rise to obligations of a fiduciary nature. Lord Mustill said that the essence of a fiduciary relationship is that it creates obligations of a different character from those deriving from the contract itself and went on to say: 'It is possible without misuse of language to say that the customers put faith in the company, and that their trust has not been repaid. But the vocabulary is misleading; high expectations do not necessarily lead to equitable remedies.'

---

76 *Mac-Jordan Construction Ltd v Brookmount Erostin Ltd* [1991] BCLC 333. A court will usually grant a mandatory injunction to require the fund to be established provided the 'trustee' is not yet insolvent.
77 [1986] 3 All ER 75.
78 [1994] 3 WLR 199.
79 [1927] 1 Ch 606.

Equitable interests arising under a trust are not registrable and are not visible to the general creditors of the insolvent trustee. Discussions[80] of whether this makes the upholding of such interests unfair to the general creditors usually conclude that the general creditors should not be able to complain of the non-availability of assets which were never in the beneficial ownership of the insolvent in the first place and that possession without title should not be seen as misleading. More doubts tend to be expressed about conferring priority in respect of assets which the beneficiary could not have acquired for himself or where the trust device appears to be being used to confer a remedy for what is fundamentally a complaint of breach of contract.

(b) Express trusts

Where the insolvent is clearly a trustee under an express trust, the position will be unarguable; the property will not be available unless the insolvency practitioner can avoid the trust as a transaction intended to defeat creditors or at an undervalue.[81] Sometimes it is not clear whether or not an express trust has been created. The court will look for the so called 'three certainties' of words, subject and object. Informal language can give rise to a trust provided that the intention that the transferee of the property should not become unconditionally beneficially entitled to it is sufficiently clear.

Re Kayford Ltd[82] was an example of a case in which the court was prepared to construe the words used as having given rise to a trust. Kayford carried on a mail order business and its customers paid either fully or partially for goods when placing an order. Shortly before going into liquidation, Kayford opened a customers' trust deposit account and arranged that all money paid by customers in advance should be paid into the account and only released from it when the goods were delivered. Megarry J decided that the money in the account was held on trust for the customers who had paid it and should not be treated as part of the general assets of the company. The judge said that the general rule is that money sent to a company as advance payment for goods would usually give rise to a merely personal claim against the company, but that it was open to either sender or company to create a trust by using appropriate words, in which case the obligations would become contractual rather than proprietary.

In *Re Multi-Guarantee Co Ltd*,[83] a somewhat similar case, it was held that there was an insufficient manifestation of an intention to create a trust. In some cases, the argument for the existence of a trust has failed because the trust property could not be clearly identified. In *Re London Wine Co (Shippers) Ltd*,[84] in which a company sold wine to customers which it then stored for them, there was no appropriation of the wine until actual delivery.[85] The court, although apparently accepting that there had been

---

80 See Goode (1987); Goodhart and Jones (1980); Oakley (1995).
81 See Chapter 30.
82 [1975] 1 All ER 604. This case has been somewhat controversial; see, for example, Goodhart and Jones (1980), who argue strongly that the trust should be voidable as a preference. Professor Goode approves; see Goode, 1997, p 137 and the material cited therein at note 74.
83 [1987] BCLC 257.
84 (1975) 125 NLJ 977.
85 Contrast with the customers in *Re Staplyton Fletcher* considered in section 2 above, whose wine had been sufficiently segregated to give them legal title.

an intention to create a trust, held that the trust failed for uncertainty of subject matter. Even where the subject matter has been sufficiently clearly identified, if the property is dissipated in such a way as to prevent the beneficiary from being able to trace it, there will be no possible proprietary remedy. *Re Holiday Promotions (Europe) Ltd*[86] is an example of a unsuccessful attempt to claim rights under a *Re Kayford* trust.

(c) Resulting trusts

A resulting trust will arise where a person transfers, or purchases property and has it conveyed, into the name of another either as sole owner or jointly with himself. In the absence of evidence of intention to give the beneficial interest to the transferee, the beneficial interest will result to him. This has been described as a presumed resulting trust.[87] An automatic resulting trust will arise where there is a transfer of property which leaves some of the equitable interest undisposed of or where the disposition fails. Since 'equity abhors a beneficial vacuum',[88] the beneficial interest results back to the transferor.

This latter principle was applied in *Barclays Bank Ltd v Quistclose Investments Ltd*.[89] Quistclose lent money to a company for the purpose of paying a dividend which had been declared. The company sent the cheque to Barclays with a request that the bank pay it into a separate account and stating that the money would only be used to pay the dividend. The company went into liquidation before the dividend could be paid. Barclays claimed to be entitled to set off the money against the company's overdraft on its other accounts, but the House of Lords held that the money was impressed with a trust for repayment to Quistclose in the event of the failure of the primary trust for payment of the dividend and that Barclays had notice of this trust and was bound by it. It was held that existence of a contractual obligation to repay is not necessarily inconsistent with the existence of a trust. Lord Wilberforce looked as far back as 1819 to the case of *Toovey v Milne*[90] for authority that money advanced for a specific purpose would not become part of the insolvent's estate.

There were similar findings in the cases of *Carreras Rothmans Ltd v Freeman Matthews Treasure Ltd*,[91] in which payments were made to an advertising agency by a client for the specific purposes of discharging obligations to media creditors, and in *Re EVTR Ltd*,[92] in which a payment was made to a company specifically for the purchase of equipment. *Re Niagara Mechanical Services International Ltd (in Administration)*[93] was an example of such an arrangement in the context of an administration; administrators were put in funds specifically to pay a sub-contractor and when this became impossible they had to return the money on the basis that it was subject to a *Quistclose* trust.

---

86   [1996] 2 BCLC 618. The judge could find no intention that the moneys paid should be kept apart from the general assets of the company.
87   Refer back to section on the bankrupt's home in Chapter 27.
88   *Vandervell v IRC* [1966] Ch 261.
89   [1970] AC 567. See Millett (1985); Rickett (1991); Bridge (1992a); Ho and St J Smart (2001).
90   (1819) 2 B&A 683.
91   [1985] 1 All ER 155.
92   (1987) 3 BCC 389.
93   [2000] 2 BCLC 425.

The issue arises in relation to a *Quistclose* trust of who precisely the beneficiaries are and who would win in any contest between those identifiable people originally intended to benefit from the arrangement and the lender;[94] there have been suggestions that the arrangement amounts to a primary trust in favour of the intended beneficiaries followed, on the failure of the primary trust, by a secondary trust in favour of the lender. Lord Millett in his dissenting judgment in *Twinsectra v Yardley*[95] engaged in a thorough analysis of the *Quistclose* trust. In the course of his judgment, he observed that where money is advanced for a particular purpose, the lender acquires an equitable right to see that it is applied for the stated purpose and that this prevents the borrower from obtaining any beneficial interest in the money, at least whilst the purpose is still capable of being carried out. Once the purpose has been carried out, the lender has his or her normal remedy in debt. If for any reason the purpose cannot be carried out, the question arises whether the money falls within the borrower's general assets available to the general creditors or whether it is held on resulting trust for the lender. This will depend on the intention of the parties collected from the terms of the arrangement and the circumstances of the case. The mere fact that the money is paid with a particular purpose in mind is not sufficient to give rise to a trust; commercial life would be impossible if this were so. The question must be whether or not the parties intended the money to be at the free disposal of the recipient; an arrangement that the money will be used exclusively for the stated purpose will be determinative and, since it will be unconscionable for someone to disregard the specific terms on which it was received, will result in the imposition of a trust. Lord Millett in considering the true nature of the *Quistclose* trust said that the analysis must be that it is an orthodox resulting trust in that the money remains the property of the lender unless and until it is applied in accordance with his or her directions and that, in this sense, it is an arrangement akin to a retention of title clause.

(d) Constructive trusts[96]

Whilst it is not possible to list precisely all the circumstances in which a constructive trust may arise, there are certain recurrent situations which have been held to give rise to such a trust. There has been an increasing tendency for creditors to seek to obtain priority by claiming a proprietary interest under a constructive trust and the principles which apply in this area are far from clear. It would appear[97] that English law only recognises the 'institutional' constructive trust which comes into being at the time of receipt of the assets by the trustee and does not recognise the possibility of a 'remedial' constructive trust imposed by a court subsequently by way of equitable remedy. The following propositions can be made:

---

94 See, eg, *Re Northern Developments (Holdings) Ltd* (1978) unreported, 6 October.
95 [2002] 2 All ER 377. See Yeo and Tjio (2003), where the point is made that although this was a minority judgment, the reasoning is not logically inconsistent with the majority and is likely to be of significance in similar situations.
96 See Millett (1998).
97 *Re Polly Peck plc (No 2)* [1998] 3 All ER 812, CA.

(a) The vendor of property who has entered into a contract[98] to sell land holds the beneficial interest on constructive trust for the purchaser.[99]

(b) A person who has acquired title to another's property by fraud or some other unconscionable act may be required to hold the property on constructive trust for the person deprived.[100] *Dicta* of Lord Browne-Wilkinson in *Westdeutsche Landesbank Girozentrale v Islington BC*[101] suggest that this will always be the case but Ferris J in *Box v Barclays Bank plc*[102] said that it would not necessarily apply to a contract which was merely voidable, rather than void, because of fraud.

(c) In a large number of cases, a constructive trust has been imposed on property which has been received as a result of breach of a fiduciary relationship. An example is the rule in *Keech v Sandford*[103] under which a constructive trust will be imposed on property obtained by a trustee in his or her capacity as such, even if the beneficiary could not have obtained the property. This principle has been extended to agents,[104] company directors,[105] business partners[106] and others in a fiduciary relationship. The Privy Council have recently held in *Attorney General for Hong Kong v Reid*[107] that a fiduciary who receives a bribe holds it on constructive trust. The fiduciary was a Crown servant in Hong Kong who accepted bribes in breach of duty and used the proceeds to buy land in New Zealand. The Attorney General of Hong Kong claimed that the land belonged to the Crown. The New Zealand courts, following *Lister v Stubbs*,[108] held that although there was a personal claim against the fiduciary it was not possible to trace the money received by him into the land. The Privy Council, overruling the previous case law, held that the fiduciary held the bribe and any property acquired with it on constructive trust and that the Crown had an equitable interest in the land to the extent that the land had been purchased with the bribes.

(d) A person who receives property knowing[109] that the receipt is in breach of trust will hold it on constructive trust as will a person who, having received property, knowingly deals with it in breach of trust; if it is still in his or her possession or can be traced into substitute assets in his or her possession, the beneficiary will

---

98 Which complies with the formal requirements of the Law Reform (Miscellaneous Provisions) Act 1989.

99 *Walsh v Lonsdale* (1882) 21 Ch D 9.

100 *Bannister v Bannister* [1948] 2 All ER 133; *Binions v Evans* [1972] Ch 359.

101 [1996] 2 WLR 802.

102 [1998] All ER (D) 108.

103 (1726) Sel Cas Ch 61. This has been applied against directors in cases such as *Regal Hastings v Gulliver* [1967] 2 AC 134 and *IDC v Cooley* [1972] 2 All ER 162.

104 *Boardman v Phipps* [1967] 2 AC 46. The question of whether a principal will be a beneficiary of a trust in relation to money received by his or her agent depends on the construction of the agency agreement in the light of the circumstances at the time it was made: *Neste Oy v Lloyds Bank* [1983] 2 Lloyd's Rep 658; *Re Fleet Disposal* [1995] BCC 605.

105 *Cook v Deeks* [1916] 1 AC 554 is one of a number of examples.

106 *Featherstonhaugh v Fenwick* (1810) 17 Ves 298.

107 [1993] AC 713, overruling the earlier Court of Appeal decision in *Lister v Stubbs* (1890) 45 Ch D 1.

108 (1890) 45 Ch D 1.

109 See *Twinsectra v Yardley* [2002] 2 All ER 377 (House of Lords) for the question of the degree of dishonesty required in order to establish accessory liability for breach of trust.

be able to claim the assets. A person who knowingly assists in a breach of trust will incur personal liability,[110] but will not necessarily ever have been in possession of property to which a trust can attach.

It is less clear whether a constructive trust exists where there have been void, voidable or mistaken transactions.

Chase Manhattan Bank v Israel-British Bank (London)[111] is a controversial case on mistaken contracts. The plaintiff New York bank as a result of a clerical error made a payment twice to another New York bank for the credit of a third English bank which subsequently became insolvent. The plaintiff claimed to be entitled to trace the second payment in equity against the insolvent bank. The applicable law was that of New York where payment under mistake of fact will give rise to a constructive trust if the payee cannot in conscience retain the money. Goulding J observed that there would also be a constructive trust in this situation under English law. In *Westdeutsche Landesbank Girozentrale v Islington BC*,[112] Lord Browne-Wilkinson regarded this as incorrect although he thought the actual decision might be correct since the defendant knew of the mistake within two days of receiving payment; receipt of the money in ignorance of the mistake would not be sufficient to give rise to a constructive trust but retention after learning of the mistake might do so. Wide-ranging consideration was given to the law relating to mistaken payment recently by the High Court in *Papamichael v National Westminster Bank & Paprounis*.[113]

---

110 *Royal Brunei Airlines Sdn Bhd v Tan* [1995] 3 WLR 64 (PC). See Harpum (1995).
111 [1980] 2 WLR 202. Articles on the case include Tettenborn (1980).
112 [1996] 2 WLR 802.
113 [2003] All ER (D) 204 (Feb).

CHAPTER 29

SECURITY RIGHTS OVER ASSETS
OF THE INSOLVENT[1]

1 INTRODUCTION

A creditor's right to enforce security against assets of the debtor is usually unaffected by the liquidation or bankruptcy of the debtor;[2] the exceptions are, first, that questions of registration of company charges become of vital importance once the company is in liquidation; secondly, it may be possible to invalidate the security as a preference;[3] finally, s 245 of the Insolvency Act 1986 contains rules, explained in detail below, under which a floating charge may be invalidated by a liquidator or administrator. A floating chargee's rights are also postponed to those of certain other creditors.[4] The holder of a fixed charge is therefore in a more secure position in the event of the borrower's insolvency than is a floating chargee; there has therefore been a considerable amount of litigation on the issue of the distinction between the two types of charge which is considered below. Issues around the valid creation of the security, considered briefly in the next section, will be the same before and during a bankruptcy or liquidation.

2 VALID CREATION OF THE SECURITY

Entitlement to enforce a security depends first on the security having been validly created so that it has attached to the assets in question. In order for such attachment to occur, there are four requirements:[5] there must be an agreement between the debtor or surety and creditor that the interest shall attach, the asset must be identifiable as falling within the scope of the agreement, the debtor must have either a present interest in the asset or power to give the asset as security and there must be some current obligation which the asset is designed to secure.

Liquidators have sometimes argued that the security was invalid because the insolvent company lacked the capacity to enter into the security agreement or that those purporting to bind the company to the agreement lacked the authority to do so.[6] Sections 35–35A of the Companies Act 1985 now prevent the validity of the security from being challenged on the basis that it is beyond the capacity of the company and, in favour of those dealing with the company in good faith, the power of the board of directors to bind the company, or authorise others to do so, is deemed to be free of limitations under the company's constitution.[7]

---

1   See, generally, Goode, 1988; Gough, 1996; McCormack, 1994.
2   See Chapter 3 for an explanation of the categories of security interest and Chapter 5 for an explanation of how the security will be enforced.
3   See Chapter 30.
4   Explained in Chapter 34, which deals with the distributional rules of insolvency law.
5   See Goode, 1995, Chapter 23 on the creation and attachment of security interests.
6   *Re Introductions* [1970] Ch 199 was one of the few cases in which the argument has worked.
7   The directors will, however, remain liable to the company for exceeding their powers.

The validity of a security given jointly by two parties (typically, husband and wife in relation to the family home) or by one party by way of surety may be challenged on the grounds that the contract creating the security is voidable on the grounds of the undue influence or misrepresentation by the person whose debts are being secured; the stereotypical situation is that of a wife who has been persuaded by her husband to agree to a charge over the family home by way of security for a loan to his business. This is an issue which has gained in prominence in recent years with the growth both in home ownership and in joint ownership of those homes. A considerable amount of case law has been generated in recent years as the courts have attempted to establish a position which maintains the correct balance between protecting those in a weak position and ensuring that the rules are not so onerous as to prevent family homes being used to secure loans.[8]

The fundamental principles governing this area were established by the House of Lords in *Barclays Bank v O' Brien*[9] and the leading authority on this area is now the House of Lords decision in *Royal Bank of Scotland v Etridge (No 2)*.[10] There are two issues to be considered; whether or not there was undue influence or misrepresentation and, if so, whether that can be attributed to the lender so as to invalidate the security. A party alleging undue influence may give factual evidence supporting the actual existence of undue influence in relation to the particular transaction or may allege that the relationship raises the presumption of undue influence. A presumption of undue influence will arise if the nature of the relationship between two parties (either on the facts of the particular relationship or because of the category into which the relation ship falls),[11] coupled with the nature of the transaction between them, is such as to raise an inference that the transaction was procured by the undue influence of one party over the other. The nature of the transaction will be such that the alleged weaker party does not appear to derive any benefit from it so that the motivation for entering it needs explanation. The onus then shifts to the dominant party to rebut the presumption, usually by showing that the weaker party entered into the transaction on the basis of independent advice.[12]

In this situation, any undue influence will be operating between the joint chargers and the lender will only be affected if the actual or presumed undue influence can be attributed to it either because the dominant party is the agent of the lender or because the lender has constructive notice[13] of the undue influence. The lender will have constructive notice of possible undue influence whenever a wife offers to stand surety

---

8   See the comment of Lord Browne-Wilkinson in *Barclays Bank v O'Brien* [1994] 1 AC 180.

9   [1994] 1 AC 180.

10 [2001] 4 All ER 449, applied by the Court of Appeal in *Mortgage Agency Services Number Two Ltd v Chater and Another* [2003] EWCA Civ 490; [2003] All ER (D) 56 (Apr); *Lloyds TSB Bank v Holdgate* [2002] EWCA Civ 1543; *Governors and Company of the Bank of Scotland v Hill and Another* [2002] EWCA Civ 108; *Greene King plc v Stanley and Others* [2001] EWCA Civ 1966 (see Chapter 9) and *UCB Corporate Services Ltd v Williams and Others* [2002] 3 FCR 413. See also *National Westminster Bank plc v Amin* [2002] 1 FLR 735 (House of Lords) and Haley (2002).

11 The relationship of husband and wife does not automatically raise the presumption of undue influence, but a lender should be aware of the risk that there might be undue influence at work.

12 If in the course of the hearing it becomes clear that there was, in fact, no undue influence, then this will result in the charge being held to be valid.

13 Lord Nicholls in *Royal Bank of Scotland v Etridge (No 2)* recognised that this is an extended use of the traditional concept of constructive notice.

for her husband's debts, or the debts of a company,[14] since on its face, such a transaction is not to the financial advantage of the wife and there is a substantial risk in such transactions that the husband has committed a legal or equitable wrong that entitles the wife to set the transaction aside. In the case of a joint loan, the lender will only be put on inquiry if aware that the loan is being made for the husband's sole purposes.[15] Where such a rebuttable presumption of undue influence arises, the lender is required to take reasonable steps to satisfy itself that the wife has entered the transaction fully aware of the possible consequences and ordinarily it will be sufficient for the lender to rely on a statement from a solicitor acting for the wife[16] that she has been advised appropriately. The giving of appropriate advice will normally require a discussion of the financial circumstances of both husband and wife in the absence of the husband couched in suitably non-technical language. There is no responsibility on the solicitor to prevent the wife from making an unwise financial decision. The solicitor will not act as agent for the lender and any failure in giving appropriate advice will usually be a matter between the solicitor and the surety. In *Royal Bank of Scotland v Etridge (No 2)*, it was held that, since it was impossible to produce a comprehensive list of relationships in which there is a substantial risk of undue relationship, the *O'Brien* principles should be extended so that lenders would potentially be fixed with notice of undue influence or misrepresentation in any case where a joint chargee or surety had a non-commercial relationship with the main debtor. Lord Nicholls observed that 'in all conscience, it is a modest burden for banks and other lenders' to be obliged to take steps to bring home the risk being run by the surety.

As the Court of Appeal decision in *First National Bank plc v Achampong and Others*[17] demonstrates, a finding of invalidity in relation to the security in respect of one of the joint owners does not necessarily protect the property against the lender. Where the court holds that the charge is ineffective against one of the joint owners of the charged property, there will still be an equitable charge in the bank's favour over the beneficial share of any joint owner against whom the charge is valid to secure, so far as possible, the loan. Assuming that the property was not already held by way of a beneficial tenancy in common, this would effect a severance of the beneficial joint tenancy subsisting in relation to the property. The lender would then be able to apply for an order for sale and the court would have a discretion under s 14 of the Trusts of Land and Appointment of Trustees Act 1996[18] to enable the lender to realise its charge over the property.

---

14 Even is she is a director or secretary of the company or holds shares in it.
15 *CIBC Mortgages v Pitt* [1994] 1 AC 200.
16 Provided the conflict of interest problems are not too great, there is no reason why the solicitor should not also act for the husband.
17 [2003] All ER (D) 08 (Apr).
18 See Chapter 27.

3   REGISTRATION OF CHARGES

Entitlement to enforce security will also depend upon there having been compliance with any registration requirements;[19] nearly all consensual non-possessory[20] forms of security have registration requirements in order to perfect them against third parties.[21] Mortgages and charges given over land should be registered in accordance with the provisions of either the Land Charges Act 1925 or the Land Registration Act 1925. There are specialist registers for other specific types of property such as aircraft, ships and intellectual property rights. Mortgages given in writing by individuals over chattels should be registered in accordance with the Bills of Sale Acts 1878–82 and failure to do so will invalidate the charge against the debtor as well as against third parties. It is not possible to register a bill of sale over non-specific assets.

Section 396 of the Companies Act 1985 contains a list of charges created by companies which have to be registered; the list includes charges on land, on book debts, all floating charges and all charges created or evidenced by an instrument which, if executed by an individual, would require registration as a bill of sale. Section 395 of the Companies Act 1985 provides that a charge within the list which has not been registered within 21 days of its creation will be void against the liquidator, administrator and creditors[22] of the company; the liquidator will be able to realise the assets on the basis that they are unencumbered. The court may give permission for registration out of time in which case a condition will invariably be imposed that the registration is to be without prejudice to the rights of intervening creditors. Provided the interest is registered within 21 days of creation, registration does not constitute a priority point and the charge will have priority according to the date of creation; it will prevail over an interest created during the period between creation and registration, despite the fact that the subsequent interest had no means of discovering the prior interest from the register. Registration will constitute notice of all those particulars of the charge of which details have to be given during the registration process; it is not clear to what extent entering additional details on the register, such as information about negative pledges, will constitute notice. Registration of a charge is conclusive evidence that there was no defect in the registration, whether or not this was in fact the case.

The Companies Act 1989 contained a new registration regime to replace that contained in s 396 of the Companies Act 1985, including an updated list of registrable charges and a reduction in the effect of the certificate of registration, but this has never been brought into force. The Company Law Review Steering Group, which considered the issue of registration of company charges,[23] provisionally concluded[24] that the current system should be replaced with a system based on the 'notice-filing' model employed in various other jurisdictions, most notably in Art 9 of the US

---

19 See, generally, Goode, 1995, Chapter 24 and McCormack, 1994.
20 Possession gives sufficient notice to the world of the security interest.
21 In the case of a security interest over a debt, notice to the debtor will suffice.
22 Except in the context of an insolvency, this has been held to mean secured creditors only: *Re Ehrmann Bros Ltd* [1906] 2 Ch 697.
23 The consultation document *Registration of Company Charges* was published in October 2000 (URN 00/1213).
24 Chapter 12 of *Modern Company Law for a Competitive Economy*, Final Report 2001. See Tjio (2002).

Uniform Commercial Code,[25] and recommended that the Law Commission be requested to examine the system for registering company charges and security and 'quasi-security' generally over property other than land.[26] The Law Commission's Consultation Paper No 164, *Registration of Security Interests: Company Charges and Property other than Land*, published in July 2002, was the result.

The primary purpose of a notice-filing system is to determine the relative priority of registered charges; the registration also has the effect of ensuring that it is on the public record. Under a notice-filing system, a financing statement is registered rather than the charge itself. The statement gives notice that a charge has been taken or is intended to be taken; a would-be creditor should then undertake such enquiries as are necessary from the debtor and the already-secured creditors. Priority is determined by the date of the filing rather than the date of the transaction. The Law Commission has proposed that the filing should take place by a simple electronic process and that the financing statement would identify the parties, give a general description of the property to be charged (including identifying serial numbers where appropriate), confirm that the chargor consents to the filing and that the chargor either owns the asset beneficially or holds it in trust, indicate the duration of the security agreement and identify the charge as fixed or floating or both. Errors in the completion of the statement would only render it invalid if they were seriously misleading. Failure to file would allow priority to a subsequent secured creditor who files first and render the security invalid in the event of insolvency. The Law Commission invited views on whether voluntary registration of subordination agreements should be facilitated. The Law Commission proposed that, rather than attempting to update the list of registrable charges, all charges should be registrable unless they are specifically included on a list of those charges exempted from the system which should be capable of ministerial alteration. Amongst the list of charges which they suggested should be exempted were charges over bank accounts provided that the chargee has taken control of the account. The Commission recommended a function-based approach so that a number of quasi-security interests currently exempt from registration would be brought within the system. These would mean the inclusion of all retention of title clauses,[27] hire-purchase agreements, finance leases (as distinct from short term operational leases) and many types of factoring agreement.

The Law Commission raised several issues in relation to floating charges.[28] The current position is that a duly registered floating charge will rank after a duly registered fixed charge irrespective of the dates of creation of the two charges; this is because the floating charge permits the company to carry on business using the charged assets in the normal course of business and this will include giving fixed charges over the assets. If a floating charge contains a clause restricting the creation of subsequent security ranking equally with or ahead of the floating charge ('a negative pledge'), subsequent fixed charges will be postponed to the floating charge providing

---

25 See McCormack (2002a) for a comparison of the UK and US position.

26 The introduction of notice-filing had previously been recommended by both the Crowther Committee in 1971 and the Diamond Report, but had met with little enthusiasm; the response to the CLRSG consultation had been considerably more positive.

27 If the system were not extended to quasi-security, complex retention of title clauses should still be included since these are likely to amount to charges.

28 See Chapter 3 and the next section for an explanation of the floating charge. See McCormack (2003) on the Law Commission proposals and the floating charge.

the fixed charge holder has notice, which probably has to be actual, of the negative pledge. The Law Commission's view is that a debtor should not be able to create and give priority to a subsequent fixed charge on an asset of a class covered by a floating charge without the consent of the floating charge holder except in the case of a purchase money security interest (where the new chargee is taking security over an asset whose purchase it has funded). The Law Commission proposals envisage retaining a distinction between the fixed and floating charge,[29] but do not provide any assistance in distinguishing between the two forms of security.

4 DISTINCTION BETWEEN FIXED AND FLOATING CHARGES[30]

The classic description of the difference between these two types of charge is that given by Lord Macnaghten in *Illingworth v Houldsworth*:[31]

> A specific charge, I think, is one that without more fastens on ascertained and definite property or property capable of being ascertained and defined;[32] a floating charge, on the other hand, is ambulatory and shifting in its nature, hovering over and so to speak floating with the property which it is intended to affect until some event occurs or some act is done which causes it to settle and fasten on the subject of the charge within its reach and grasp.

The floating charge enables a borrower to appropriate a class of assets to repayment of the debt without specifically identifying the component elements of the class. The charge only attaches specifically to items of property when the charge crystallises into a fixed charge. Until that time, the borrower may use the assets within the class as if they were unencumbered; the assets comprising the class will change in the ordinary course of business. The essence of a floating charge is that the chargor can continue to deal with the assets as if they were unencumbered; this enables a company to give security over its circulating assets. The nature of the floating charge renders it a more vulnerable form of security than a fixed charge since the lender will not be able to predict with any certainty the value of the secured assets at the time of crystallisation of the charge. In addition to the ordinary vicissitudes of trade, the charge is vulnerable to subsequent fixed charges,[33] factoring of debts,[34] assignments of property, sales and lease-back arrangements, retention of title, execution completed[35] and rights of set-

---

29 Were this not to be the case, some considerable adjustments would need to be made to insolvency law in relation, particularly, to the rules relating to priority in distribution, the entitlement to instigate company administration and the powers of the administrator in relation to secured property.

30 For discussions of the theoretical basis of the floating charge see Pennington (1960); Gough, 1996, Chapter 13; Ferran (1988); Worthington (1994) and material cited therein.

31 [1904] AC 355 at 358.

32 It is possible to give a fixed charge over future property provided that it is sufficiently described to be identifiable when acquired: *Holroyd v Marshall* (1862) 10 HL Cas 191.

33 *Wheatley v Silkstone and Haigh Moor Coal Co* (1885) 29 Ch D 715; *Re Castell & Brown Ltd* [1898] 1 Ch 315.

34 In broad terms, factoring involves the sale by a company of debts (receivables) owing to it so that the company receives payment (less a discount) before the time when its customers are due to pay.

35 *Evans v Rival Granite Quarries* [1910] 2 KB 979; *Robson v Smith* [1895] 2 Ch 118.

off[36] arising before crystallisation. A lender who has taken a floating charge will need to monitor the borrower carefully to protect the value of the security.[37] Although the lender and borrower may agree to restrict the borrower's rights to confer rights over the assets ranking above the floating chargee, it is not possible to ensure that third parties have sufficient notice of such so called negative pledges to bind them to the chargee's rights.[38]

It is only possible for a company to grant a floating charge since if an individual attempts to do so, the charge will fall within the provisions of the Bills of Sale Acts (which do not apply to companies) and will be invalid unless specific details of the individual chattels subject to the charge are registered.[39] The floating charge may be over book debts, stock in trade or any other class of assets; frequently, it will be given over the undertaking as a whole. The fact that the security relates to both current and future assets of a company does not require it to be a floating charge. It is possible to have a specific equitable charge over future property[40] provided there is agreement that the charge will attach to the property immediately on its acquisition by the debtor.[41] Although it is usual for the class of assets subject to a floating charge to fluctuate both upwards and downwards in value, it is possible to have a floating charge over a class which can only diminish in value: *Re Bond Worth*[42] is an example.

In his classic description of the floating charge in *Re Yorkshire Woolcombers Association*,[43] Romer LJ suggested that a floating charge would be likely to be over existing and future assets of such a nature that they are likely to change in the ordinary course of events and with which the chargor retains freedom to deal in the ordinary course of business. This was understood for many years to mean that a charge over circulating assets would have to be floating. Then, in *Siebe Gorman & Co Ltd v Barclays Bank Ltd*,[44] Slade J held that it was possible for a fixed charge over future book debts to be granted such that the chargor was prevented from disposing of an unencumbered title to them; the essential element of a floating charge was not the nature of the assets subject to the security, but the freedom given to the debtor company to deal with the secured assets in the ordinary course of business.[45] The words used to describe the charge are not determinative; in *Re Armagh Shoes Ltd*[46] and

---

36   *Biggerstaff v Rowatt's Wharf* [1896] 2 Ch 93; *Rother Iron Works v Canterbury Precision Engineers Ltd* [1974] QB 1; *George Barker (Transport) Ltd v Eynon* [1974] 1 WLR 462.

37   See Gough, 1996 at p 440 on the policy issues relating to floating charges; he argues that the floating charge should be given greater protection.

38   Although details of the negative pledge may be registered at Companies House, registration is currently only notice to the world of the existence of the charge and not of its contents. See McCormack (2003) at p 3 for a discussion of the point.

39   The Cork Committee recommended (para 1569) that it should be possible for an individual to create a floating charge for business purposes. Law Commission Consultation Paper No 164 makes the same recommendation, but favours retaining the prohibition on floating charges for consumer debts.

40   *Holroyd v Marshall* (1862) 10 HL Cas 191; *Tailby v Official Receiver* (1888) 13 App Cas 523.

41   See *Re Reis* [1904] 2 KB 769; *Re Lind* [1915] 2 Ch 345; *Re Collins* [1925] Ch 556.

42   [1980] Ch 228.

43   [1903] 2 Ch 284 at 295.

44   [1979] 2 Lloyd's Rep 142.

45   The Cork Committee called for the *Siebe Gorman* decision to be reversed by statute, but this recommendation was not accepted.

46   [1984] BCLC 405.

in *Re Brightlife Ltd*[47] charges described as fixed were held to be floating in reality. In both cases, there was held to be insufficient restriction on the company's freedom to deal with the charged assets for the charge to be fixed. *Siebe Gorman* was distinguished as a case in which the lender controlled the account into which the proceeds of the book debts would be paid. In *Re Keenan Bros Ltd*,[48] in which the proceeds of the book debts were paid into a blocked account, the charge was held to be fixed.

The law in this area was taken a stage further by the Court of Appeal in *Re New Bullas Trading Ltd*[49] so that non-clearing bank lenders appeared to have almost the same access to the security as the clearing banks. The debenture in this case contained a provision described as a fixed charge over the company's present and future book debts. The agreement provided that the chargor would pay the proceeds of the book debts into a specified bank account, that the chargor would deal with the proceeds as directed by the chargee, but that in the absence of directions, the proceeds of the book debts were to be released from the fixed charge and be subjected to a floating charge. No directions were given by the chargee. The debenture holder stood to recover either all that it was owed or nothing, depending upon whether its charge was held to be fixed or floating, since the debts due to the preferential creditors exceeded the amounts which would be realised by the charged book debts. At first instance, it was held that this was a floating charge over the book debts, but the Court of Appeal reversed the decision and held that the book debts were subject to a fixed charge while uncollected and a floating charge on realisation. The judgment was based on the principle of freedom of contract and the clear agreement that the book debts and their proceeds were to be treated separately.

In *Agnew v Commissioners of Inland Revenue, Re Brumark Investments Ltd*,[50] on appeal from New Zealand, the Privy Council said that *Re New Bullas Trading* was incorrectly decided and held that a similarly drafted charge was a floating charge. The Privy Council held that the Court of Appeal in *Re New Bullas Trading* had been incorrect to treat the issue simply as one of construction of the contract. The question of what the parties had agreed was one of construction of contract, but the effect of that agreement was a matter of categorisation. For a charge to be fixed, the chargor must be prevented from dealing with the assets without the consent of the chargee. If the agreement which the parties had made was inconsistent with this essential element of a fixed charge, then the charge would be a floating charge however the parties had described it. It was inconsistent with the nature of a fixed charge to leave the company in control of the process by which the charged assets were extinguished and replaced by different assets which were at the free disposal of the company. The Privy Council said that there could be a fixed charge where the company collected the debts as agent for the chargeholder if the company were obliged to pay the proceeds into a blocked account in which they would not be available to the company. If the debenture provided for the existence of such a blocked account but it was not operated as such, the charge would be treated as a floating charge.[51] Decisions of the

---

47   [1987] Ch 22.
48   [1986] BCLC 242.
49   [1994] BCC 36.
50   [2001] 3 WLR 454.
51   This could give rise to difficulties of categorisation if the practice in relation to the operation of the account is not consistent: see Fennessy and Tamlyn (2002).

Privy Council are not strictly binding in English law, but there is clearly a strong likelihood that the decision would be followed in any future case on the point. Crown departments which may be in the position of proving for preferential debts in a liquidation[52] have said that they will not challenge any distribution made on the basis that a *New Bullas* charge was fixed where the distribution took place before the Privy Council decision, but that in relation to subsequent distributions, they reserve the right to challenge the status of any purported fixed charge where the charger has been allowed to draw freely on the proceeds of the book debts without the specific consent of the holder of the charge.

In the time since the Privy Council decision in *Re Brumark* was reported, there have already been several suggestions as to how it can be circumvented. The decision clearly does not prevent the creation of fixed charges over book debts, but to do so will require more cumbersome (and expensive) procedures; for example, it would be possible for a blocked account to be established and for the bank to consent at regular intervals to the transfer of some or all of the proceeds in the account to be transferred to the normal trading account of the company.[53] An alternative possibility[54] is that the documentation agreed between the company and the lending bank should make the book and other debts owed to the company subject to a fixed charge with no provision for the charge being converted into a floating charge over the proceeds of collection and that the lending bank should agree by a separate provision to lend to the company an equal amount to that credited to the bank account into which payment of the book debts is to be made as a separate and independent loan secured by a floating charge. It has been suggested that a consequence of *Re Brumark* will be a greater tendency to use factoring of book debts as a financing mechanism in place of a loan secured by a charge.[55] Lenders who take security over book debts but permit the proceeds of those debts to be paid into a third party bank account will have to ensure that the receiving account has the status of a trust account of which they are the beneficial owner.[56] *Re ASRS Establishment Ltd*[57] demonstrates that a clause in a debenture which purports to be a fixed charge over a variety of classes of assets will need to operate as a fixed charge over all of them or it will be treated as a floating charge in its entirety.

The principles expressed by the Privy Council in *Re Brumark* have subsequently been applied in determining the character of charges over assets over than book debts. In *Arthur D Little Ltd (in Administration) v Ableco Finance LLC*,[58] the question arose of the characterisation of a charge which had been given by a company in administration over its shares in a subsidiary.[59] *Smith (Administrator of Cosslet (Contractors) Ltd) v Bridgend CBC*[60] arose out of a contract for the renovation of a derelict site which

---

52 The Inland Revenue and Customs and Excise, until the provisions of the Enterprise Act 2002 come into force, and the Redundancy Service so far as subrogated to payments made to employees which the employees would have been able to claim as preferential.

53 See Fennessy and Tamlyn (2002).

54 Pennington (2003a).

55 See Rumley (2003); Leporte (2002).

56 Peterson (2002).

57 [2000] 1 BCLC 72.

58 [2002] EWHC 701.

59 The issue was one of the extent of the power of the administrator to deal with the shares as if they were unencumbered (see Chapter 10 for the powers of the administrator to deal with property subject to fixed or floating security).

60 [2002] 1 AC 336.

provided for the contractor to use equipment purchased with the assistance of a loan from Bridgend CBC. The contract provided for the equipment to be the property of the Council whilst on the site and prohibited its removal from the site without consent; on the insolvency of the contractor, the Council was to be entitled under clause 63(1) of the standard form of the Institute of Civil Engineers to give notice to expel the contractor from the site and to use the equipment to complete the work. The Council was also then entitled under the clause to sell the equipment and use the proceeds to meet any amounts due to it by the contractor under the contract. The contractor, on meeting financial difficulties, abandoned the site and subsequently went into administration. The administrator sought delivery up of the equipment on the basis that clause 63(1) was a floating charge void as against the company for want of registration. The House of Lords, citing *Re Brumark*, agreed with the Court of Appeal that the arrangement, being a right to sell an asset belonging to a debtor and appropriate the proceeds to payment of the debt, had to be a charge and that, since the property to which it attached consisted of assets which might be consumed or removed from the site in the ordinary course of the company's business, the charge must be floating.

The converse of the pre-*Siebe Gorman* assumption that a charge over circulating assets had to be floating was the assumption in *Re Atlantic Computer Systems plc*[61] and *Re Atlantic Medical*[62] that charges over specifically identified sub-lease agreements would be fixed despite the chargor's freedom to use the proceeds of the agreements. As Oditah observes,[63] these are odd decisions of questionable application since it is hard to see why a different rule should apply to lease receivables from that which applies to other contractual receivables.

The characterisation of a charge as fixed or floating may be of great significance for the liquidator and the preferential creditors. If the charge is fixed, then the assets will be unavailable to the liquidator, whereas if the charge is floating, then the liquidator's expenses and the preferential creditors will take precedence.[64] The diminution in the quantity of preferential debt as a result of the Enterprise Act 2002 may have the result that lenders are less concerned to achieve priority. The priority question will have no consequence for ordinary creditors who will come after the chargee and the preferential creditors whichever order they come in; if, however, the charge is floating rather than fixed, there is a possibility that it may be set aside under s 245 of the Insolvency Act 1986, in which case the assets subject to it will become available to the unsecured creditors.

5   VULNERABILITY OF FLOATING CHARGES UNDER SECTION 245

There are special rules in relation to the validity of floating charges granted by companies in the period immediately preceding a liquidation or administration which threaten the validity of floating charges granted gratuitously. These rules are designed

---

61   [1992] Ch 505.
62   [1993] BCLC 386.
63   Oditah (2001). See also Goode (1994).
64   See Chapter 34.

to prevent directors who realise that the company is in financial difficulty from securing indebtedness of the company to themselves or their associates.

When the provisions were originally enacted in 1908, the period of vulnerability was only three months, but it has been progressively lengthened to avoid it being possible to keep an insolvent company afloat just long enough to validate the charge. Re William C Leitch Brothers[65] is an example of a case in which a director was held guilty of fraudulent trading[66] on the basis of such behaviour.

Section 245 of the Insolvency Act 1986 now provides that a floating charge created within the 12 months before the commencement of a winding up[67] or the making of an administration order in favour of a person unconnected with the company will be invalid (except to the prescribed extent) if the company is unable to pay its debts[68] at the time of creation of the charge or becomes unable to do so in consequence of the transaction under which the charge is created. A charge caught by these provisions is valid only to the extent of any cash, goods or services supplied to[69] the company, or discharge of any debt[70] of the company 'at the same time as, or after, the creation of the charge'. Where the charge is invalidated, the lenders become ordinary unsecured creditors in respect of the loan and the assets which were alleged to be subject to the charge will become available to the unsecured creditors.[71]

Where the charge is in favour of a 'connected person', it is vulnerable for two years up to the petition and it is irrelevant whether or not the company was solvent immediately after its creation. 'Connected person'[72] includes directors and relatives and companies within a group.

There has been some debate as to the whether 'at the same time' is to be given a chronological or causal interpretation. In Power v Sharpe Investments Ltd,[73] the Court of Appeal decided that 'at the same time as' meant that the new consideration had to be supplied contemporaneously with the creation of the charge; there had previously been suggestions that the words imported a requirement of causal rather than temporal connection. Any delay in executing the charge after the new value is provided will render it invalid.

Where the consideration supplied is the continuation of an overdraft facility, it can be difficult to establish to what extent the consideration is new. This issue arose in Re Yeovil Glove,[74] in which a company went into liquidation with a bank overdraft of £67,000. The overdraft was secured by a floating charge given less than 12 months

---

65   [1932] 2 Ch 71.

66   See Chapter 31.

67   The date of the petition or resolution whichever is earlier.

68   Within the meaning of the Insolvency Act 1986, s 123.

69   In Re Fairway Magazine [1992] BCC 924 it was held that money paid straight into an overdrawn bank account was not 'paid to' the company within s 245(2)(a). Prentice (1993) suggests at that the payment could have come within s 245(2)(a) as a reduction of debt.

70   This provision is included despite the recommendation of the Cork Committee, which felt (see para 1564) that it would allow creditors to lend to discharge their earlier indebtedness and take a floating charge to secure the new loan, thus securing what was previously unsecured indebtedness.

71   Assuming there is no valid junior charge.

72   Which is defined by the Insolvency Act 1986, ss 249, 435.

73   [1994] 1 BCLC 111. At first instance, this case was reported as Re Shoe Lace.

74   [1965] Ch 148.

previously. Since the creation of the charge, the bank had met cheques drawn by the company for £110,000 and received a similar sum for payment into the company's account. The overdraft, therefore, was at a similar level to that at the time the charge was created. The unsecured creditors attacked the charge on the basis of the predecessor provision to s 245. The court held that the bank's acts of meeting the cheques drawn by the company supplied the necessary value. The rule in *Clayton's Case*[75] was to be applied so that the sums paid into the account were to be treated as discharging the earlier indebtedness first and, therefore, the overdraft at the commencement of the liquidation was entirely secured by the charge.

Section 245 of the Insolvency Act 1986 does not apply to fixed charges, which is a further reason why fixed charges are preferable to floating charges from the point of view of the lender.

6 'CHARGE-BACK' TO A BANK[76]

One issue which has given rise to considerable debate in this context is that of the so called 'charge' given to a bank over money deposited with it. This will arise where a bank provides financial accommodation to a customer and the customer deposits a sum of money with the bank by way of security; the deposit gives rise to a debt owing from the bank to the customer which the customer is said to charge in favour of the bank.

Re Charge Card Services[77] concerned a company, Charge Card Services Ltd, which entered into an agreement under which it factored its receivables to Commercial Credit Services Ltd (the factor). The agreement involved the company selling its debts to the factor at a discount and with a guarantee that all would be paid. The factor could require the company to repurchase the debts in certain circumstances (including the insolvent liquidation of the company). The factor had to maintain a current account which would be credited with amounts owing by the factor to the company and debited with amounts which the company owed the factor. The factor was also given the right to retain amounts as security for any claims against the company. The company went into liquidation and the liquidator disputed the factor's right to retain amounts standing to the credit of the company, arguing that it was void as an unregistered registrable charge on book debts. Millett J said: 'The sum due from Commercial Credit to the company under the agreement is, of course, a book debt of the company which the company can charge to a third party. In my judgment, however, it cannot be charged in favour of Commercial Credit itself, for the simple reason that a charge in favour of a debtor of his own indebtedness to the chargor is conceptually impossible.'[78] He explained this on the grounds that the benefit of a debt cannot be conveyed or assigned to or appropriated or made available to the debtor, since this would result in the release of the debt: 'The debtor cannot, and does not need to, resort to the creditor's claim against him in order to obtain the benefit of the security; his own liability to the creditor is automatically discharged or reduced.'

75 (1816) 1 Mer 572.
76 Calnan (1998); Goode (1998); McCormack (1998).
77 [1987] Ch 150.
78 A view supported by Goode, 1998, pp 124–29, but attacked by others (eg, Wood, 1989; Oditah (1992)).

Both the Court of Appeal and the House of Lords considered, *obiter*, in *Re BCCI (No 8)*[79] the question of whether this conclusion of Millett J was correct. In this case, the liquidators of Bank of Credit and Commerce International sought the directions of the court in relation to the situation where BCCI had lent money to a principal debtor and had taken a deposit from another party which was charged with repayment of the loan. The charge permitted BCCI to refuse to release the deposit until the entire outstanding liabilities of the principal debtor had been repaid in full and BCCI was given the express right to use the deposit in discharge of the outstanding liabilities of the principal debtor. BCCI went into liquidation before the loan was repaid. The case was decided on the basis of the rules relating to set-off,[80] but both the Court of Appeal and the House of Lords took the opportunity to express a reasoned view on the legal nature of a charge-back. In the Court of Appeal, the view was expressed that a charge-back cannot create and vest in the chargee a proprietary interest in the debt owed to the chargor, but that it takes effect as a matter of contract; the security of the 'chargee' in such a case depended on the rules relating to set-off and the extent to which the contractual prohibition on assignment of the 'charged' debt will bind third parties.[81] In the House of Lords, however, Lord Hoffmann differed and held that a debt was property over which its owner could confer security rights in the same way that security rights could be conferred over other property; it made no difference that the beneficiary of the charge is the debtor. Lord Hoffmann indicated his agreement with the view of the Court of Appeal that designating the arrangements as a charge probably added nothing to their protection, but observed 'that seems to me no reason for preventing banks and their customers from creating charges over deposits if, for reasons of their own, they want to do so. The submissions to the Legal Risk Review Committee[82] make it clear that they do'.

---

79   [1997] 4 All ER 568.
80   See Chapter 25 above. See *Linden Gardens Trust Ltd v Lenesta Sludge Disposals Ltd* [1994] AC 85.
81   As to which, see [1994] AC 85.
82   This was a committee set up in 1991 by the Bank of England to identify areas of obscurity and uncertainty in the law affecting financial markets.

CHAPTER 30

SWELLING THE ASSETS: CLAWING-BACK[1]

1 INTRODUCTION

The insolvency practitioner may be able to swell the value of the assets which were available to the creditors at the start of the insolvency by relying on claims arising from general law unrelated to the insolvency and also by bringing claims which are only available in a formal insolvency.

There may be claims which could have been brought by the insolvent, were it not for the insolvency, which can be brought by the insolvency practitioner[2] for the benefit of the creditors. These may include debts or other obligations owing to the insolvent and proprietary claims of the sort described in Chapter 28. There may also be claims arising from the circumstances leading to the insolvency. The insolvency practitioner will be looking for a defendant with 'deep pockets' (or an insurer) against whom it may be possible to bring action in respect of loss caused by the insolvency; accountants, for example, have been vulnerable to such claims[3] and banks have been very wary about the possibility of incurring liability in the course of dealing with businesses in financial difficulty. Cases in which personal liability has been imposed on constructive trustees for knowing assistance with breach of trust have often arisen where the principal wrongdoer has become insolvent and the trust property has been dissipated.

There are a number of provisions under which transactions prior to the insolvency can be unscrambled.[4] Transactions intended to defeat creditors are subject to challenge[5] by anyone who has suffered in consequence, whether or not a formal insolvency is in progress. There are also a number of provisions under which prior transactions may be re-opened which are only available on a liquidation or bankruptcy or, in some cases, a company administration; the ability to pursue such claims may be a reason for putting a debtor into a formal insolvency regime. The relevant provisions, which are all[6] considered in more detail later in the chapter, are the following:

(a) transfers after the presentation of a petition for bankruptcy or winding up;[7]

(b) legal process completed after the commencement of the insolvency;[8]

---

1   See generally Fletcher in Ziegel (ed), 1994, Chapter 12; Prentice, 'Effect of insolvency on pre-liquidation transactions' in Pettet (ed), 1987; Wheeler (1993).
2   With any necessary consent of the creditors.
3   *Caparo Industries plc v Dickman* [1990] 1 All ER 568 (HL) is a prominent example.
4   This untechnical term is used since the effect of the provisions on the transactions varies. Some transactions are rendered void but a number of them are rendered neither void nor strictly voidable but are subject to a wide discretionary power of the court to restore the previous position as far as possible.
5   Under the Insolvency Act 1986, s 423.
6   Except for legal process completed after the start of the insolvency, which has already been considered in Chapter 25.
7   Insolvency Act 1986, s 284 (bankruptcy); Insolvency Act 1986, s 127 (liquidation).
8   See Chapter 25.

(c) transactions intended to defeat creditors;[9]

(d) transfers at an undervalue immediately preceding the insolvency;[10]

(e) preferences in the lead up to the insolvency;[11]

(f) extortionate credit bargains;[12]

(g) recovery of excessive pension contributions;[13]

(h) general assignment of book debts in bankruptcy.[14]

These provisions have the effect of backdating the collective *pari passu* principle in order either to prevent creditors from jumping the queue or to prevent the insolvent from gaining from having transferred assets to associates or sheltered assets by excessive contributions to a pension scheme ahead of the insolvency. The Insolvency Act 1986 attempts in its definition of 'associate'[15] to give a comprehensive definition of those with whom the insolvent is likely to have been dealing at less than arm's length. In relation to a liquidation, the broader concept of 'connected person',[16] which includes the associates of the company, is used.

It is clear that the provisions of the insolvency legislation prevail over any property dispositions in the course of matrimonial proceedings.[17] In *Mullard v Mullard*,[18] the court ordering a transfer of property in favour of a wife recognised the possibility that it might be set aside in a subsequent bankruptcy of the husband and, in view of this, made a nominal order for maintenance payments which could be revisited at a later date.

In the case of a liquidation, it may also be possible to claim a contribution from shareholders, directors and others involved in running the company; this is considered in more detail in the next chapter.

A major factor to be taken into account by an insolvency practitioner will be the cost of any attempt to swell the assets with the inevitable risk that, if the attempt fails, the assets will have been diminished rather than increased. Consideration is given in Chapter 32 to the various means by which insolvency practitioners may seek financial assistance for an attempt to increase the assets but, in many cases, creditors may prefer not to gamble on increasing the assets. The willingness of any creditor to engage in an attempt to swell the assets will also depend on the extent to which any clawed-back assets will be subjected to a security from which the creditor will not benefit; as will be seen, the answer to the question of who will benefit from any recoveries may depend on the ground on which the claw-back claim is made.

---

9 Insolvency Act 1986, s 423.

10 Insolvency Act 1986, s 339 (bankruptcy); Insolvency Act 1986, s 238 (liquidation).

11 Insolvency Act 1986, s 340 (bankruptcy); Insolvency Act 1986, s 239 (liquidation).

12 Insolvency Act 1986, s 343 (bankruptcy); Insolvency Act 1986, s 244 (liquidation).

13 Insolvency Act 1986, ss 342A–342F inserted by the Welfare Reform and Pensions Act 1999.

14 Insolvency Act 1986, s 344.

15 Insolvency Act 1986, s 435.

16 Insolvency Act 1986, s 249.

17 Matrimonial Causes Act 1973, s 39 as amended makes this clear. See Miller (1994) for a discussion of the extent to which inter-spouse transfers should be attacked where there has been family breakdown.

18 [1982] 3 FLR 330. See also *Burton v Burton* [1986] 2 FLR 419; *Le Foe v Le Foe and Woolwich plc* [2001] 2 FLR 970.

2 DISPOSITIONS OF PROPERTY BETWEEN PETITION AND ORDER

(a) Circumstances in which such dispositions are void

Anyone dealing with a person or company against whom a petition for winding up or bankruptcy has been presented does so at their peril. If the court decides to make the requested bankruptcy or winding up order, any payments or dispositions of property[19] after the presentation of the petition will be void unless made with the consent of the court or subsequently ratified by the court. Section 127 of the Insolvency Act 1986 provides that any disposition of property or transfer of shares or alteration of the status of members will be void after the commencement of a winding up. The winding up will, once the order has been made, be deemed to have commenced with the presentation of the petition. Section 284 of the Insolvency Act 1986 provides for dispositions by the bankrupt to be void if made during the period beginning with the presentation of the petition and ending with the vesting of the estate in the trustee.[20] One major difference in the drafting of the two sections is that s 127 merely refers to dispositions without specifying any particular disponor; in *Re J Leslie Engineers*,[21] the court held that it was immaterial under s 127 whether the disposition was by the company or by a third party. Another difference is that s 127 makes no reference to the consequences of the voidness (leaving it to the general law), whereas s 284 is more specific. Guidance as to when consent will be given can be derived from the cases, most of which have arisen in the context of a compulsory liquidation[22] rather than bankruptcy.

In *Re Wiltshire Iron Co*,[23] Cairns LJ said:

> this is a wholesome and necessary provision to prevent during the period which must elapse before a petition can be heard, the improper alienation and dissipation of the property of a company *in extremis*. But where a company actually trading, which it is in the interests of everyone to preserve and ultimately to sell as a going concern is made the object of a winding-up petition which may fail or may succeed, if it were to be supposed that transactions in the ordinary course of its current trade, *bona fide* entered into and completed, would be avoided, and would not in the discretion given to the court, be maintained, the result would be that the presentation of a petition, groundless or well-founded, would, *ipso facto*, paralyse the trade of the company and great injury without any counter-balance of advantage, would be done to those interested in the assets of the company.

---

19 Including dispositions by a bankrupt of property which is not or would not form part of the bankrupt's estate (for example, equipment used by the bankrupt in his trade). A disposition is any act which transfers value from the insolvent to another person. The provisions have no effect on transactions which increase the liabilities of the insolvent.

20 There is little case law on this provision in the bankruptcy context, since it was only introduced into bankruptcy law in 1986; prior to 1986, much the same effect was achieved by relating the beginning of the bankruptcy back to the first available act of bankruptcy.

21 [1976] 2 All ER 85.

22 In the case of a voluntary liquidation, there is no 'twilight period' such as that between petition and order in the case of a compulsory liquidation. The commencement of the liquidation will be the passing of the resolution.

23 (1868) LR 3 Ch App 443.

In *Re Gray's Inn Construction*,[24] Buckley LJ said that the policy of the law was to procure so far as practicable rateable payments of the unsecured creditors' claims and it was clear that the court should not validate any transaction which might result in one or more pre-liquidation creditors being paid in full at the expense of the other creditors who would only receive a dividend unless there were special circumstances making such a course desirable in the interests of the unsecured creditors as a body. Buckley LJ observed that if it were in the interests of the creditors generally that the company's business should be carried on and this could only be achieved by paying for goods already supplied to the company when the petition was presented but not yet paid for, the court might think fit in the exercise of its discretion to validate payment for those goods. A disposition carried out in good faith in the ordinary course of business at a time when the parties were unaware that a petition had been presented would normally be validated by the court, unless there were any ground for thinking that the transaction might involve an attempt to prefer the disponee, in which case the transaction would probably not be validated. Post-liquidation dispositions for full value and transactions which increase or preserve the value of the assets could not harm the creditors.

There seem, therefore, to be two main factors to which the court will have regard: the *bona fides* of the transaction and whether it was in the ordinary course of business. In relation to the first issue, although ignorance of the petition will help to establish *bona fides*,[25] it is not necessarily fatal to the validity of the transaction that the person receiving the property or payment was aware of the presentation of the petition if he or she otherwise acted in good faith.[26] The transaction must also be in the ordinary course of business and, where the company has derived no benefit from it, this may be hard to establish. In *Re Clifton Place Garage Ltd*,[27] it was held that good faith and legitimacy of purpose are not sufficient if the disposition was not reasonable or the company did not benefit.

An application for the court's approval or confirmation of a disposition may be made by anyone with a particular interest in the matter[28] so that either party to a transaction or proposed transaction can seek consent or ratification. The court can approve a disposition in advance; in *AI Levy Ltd*,[29] the court permitted the company to dispose of a lease pending the hearing of the petition so that the provision contained in the lease for its forfeiture if the company were wound up should not take effect. This was followed in *Re Operator Control Cabs Ltd*,[30] in which permission was given to continue to trade in the ordinary way and to dispose of assets and pay debts without

24   [1980] 1 WLR 711. *Re S&D Wright* [1992] BCC 503 also contains a set of guidelines based partly on *Re Gray's Inn Construction*. See also the Court of Appeal decision, *Denney v John Hudson & Co Ltd* [1992] BCLC 901.

25   *Re J Leslie Engineers* [1976] 1 WLR 292, which demonstrates that ignorance will not necessarily lead to validation of a disposition.

26   *Re Park Ward & Co Ltd* [1926] Ch 828; *Re Steane's (Bournemouth) Ltd* [1950] 1 All ER 21.

27   [1970] Ch 477. Contrast *Re Civil Service and General Store Ltd* (1887) 57 LJ Ch 119, in which the creditor's knowledge of the petition led to court to think that the motive behind the transaction was to prefer the creditor.

28   *Re Argentum Reductions (UK) Ltd* [1975] 1 All ER 608.

29   [1964] Ch 19.

30   [1970] 3 All ER 657n.

needing to seek approval on each occasion; such permission is only likely to be given where it is probable that the business will be saleable in the liquidation.[31]

The case of *Re Flint*[32] is a relatively recent example of the operation of the provision in the bankruptcy context. A husband and wife married in 1969 and bought their matrimonial home as legal and beneficial joint tenants. They separated in 1986 and in 1988, the wife presented a divorce petition, giving notice of her intention to proceed with an application for ancillary relief in February 1989. In the same year, the husband started a business which failed and in May 1990, one of his creditors presented a bankruptcy petition against him. On 18 July 1990, the county court made a consent order that the husband should transfer all his estate and interest in the home to the wife within 28 days. Six days later before any steps were taken to comply with the order, a bankruptcy order was made in a different county court. In December 1991, the trustee in bankruptcy obtained a declaration from the court which had made the bankruptcy order that the order providing for the transfer of the home was void against the trustee in bankruptcy under s 284 of the Insolvency Act 1986 and that the home was held by the wife and trustee in equal shares. The wife appealed, arguing first that the order was a disposition by the court, not the husband and, secondly, that the court should have exercised a discretion to ratify it if the section did apply. It was held that the order was caught by the section[33] and that although there were no s 284 cases to provide guidance, the guidance should look at the liquidation cases under s 127 of the Insolvency Act 1986.[34] The cases showed that the court should consider what was just and fair in all the circumstances, having particular regard to good faith and honest intention. The county court had all the financial evidence and both husband and wife knew of the impending bankruptcy at the time of transfer; the decision not to exercise the discretion was not perverse or obviously wrong and there was no basis for interfering with it.

(b) Remedies available to the insolvency practitioner

Unless the court decides to validate a disposition between petition and order, the insolvency practitioner will be able to retrieve the property (or proceeds of its disposition) or payment from the transferee or payee. It will also be possible to retrieve the property (or its traceable substitute) from any subsequent transferee unless it is in or has passed through the hands of someone who received it before the commencement of the bankruptcy or liquidation in good faith, for value and without notice that the petition had been presented.

Section 284(4) of the Insolvency Act 1986 provides that there will be no remedy against a person in respect of property or payment received before the commencement of the bankruptcy in good faith, for value and without notice that the

---

31 *Re Gray's Inn Construction* [1980] 1 WLR 711; *Re McGuinness Bros (UK) Ltd* (1987) 3 BCC 571.

32 [1993] Ch 319.

33 In *Burton v Burton* [1986] 2 FLR 419, however, Butler-Sloss J expressed the view that a property transfer order was not itself a disposition of property and that the disposition occurs when the order is carried out. The Court of Appeal in *Mountney v Treharne* [2002] 3 WLR 1760, holding that it was bound by a previous Court of Appeal decision in *Maclurcan v Maclurcan* (1897) 77 LT 474, held that the order does operate to transfer the equitable interest.

34 It is not clear that this is correct, since the two provisions are not identical and the genesis of the Insolvency Act 1986, s 284 seems to lie in pre-1986 bankruptcy law.

petition had been presented. This re-enacts the pre-1986 bankruptcy law, but appears to conflict with a number of the cases on s 127 and its predecessors in the corporate context. In *Re J Leslie Engineers*,[35] a director of the insolvent company arranged matters so that a creditor of the company was paid after a petition for winding up had been presented. Part of the payment was made by a cheque drawn on the personal account of a director of the company; a cheque for the required amount had been drawn on the company's account in favour of the director. The money ceased to be the property of the company when it was mixed with other moneys in the directors' personal account and it could not thereafter be traced to the creditor. The rest of the payment was made by drawing a cheque for £250 cash on the company's account which was subsequently converted to money orders payable to the creditor of the company. The court held that there was throughout a clearly identifiable property of the company which passed to the creditor. The court held that the payment could not be allowed to stand, since it was clearly a preferential payment with the company's money and it was irrelevant that the creditor did not realise this.

In the case of an insolvent company, the liquidator may also recover the value of the property from directors or other persons who disposed of it in the company's name. There would clearly have been an action against the director in *Re J Leslie Engineers*[36] for the disposition of the company's property both on this ground and on the basis that he was in breach of his fiduciary duty as a director.

The court is not concerned to achieve anything more than the restoration of the value of the assets which have been lost to the general creditors.[37] It was held in *Mond v Hammond Suddards*[38] that, since the assets are being reclaimed on the basis that the transaction was void, they will fall into any charge over that class of asset.

(c) Operation of bank accounts in the 'twilight period'

The effect of s 127 of the Insolvency Act 1986 on the operation of a company's bank account[39] once a petition has been presented for the winding up of the company has been a contentious issue and given rise to a certain amount of case law. The normal practice of banks upon becoming aware of a winding up petition is to freeze the company's existing bank account and conduct all subsequent dealings through a new account in respect of which a validation order may be obtained. The Court of Appeal in *Re Gray's Inn Construction Co Ltd*[40] held that payments into and out of the company's account (which was overdrawn) were dispositions subject to s 127 which could be avoided as against the bank. In *Hollicourt (Contracts) Ltd v Bank of Ireland*,[41]

---

35   [1976] 2 All ER 85.
36   [1976] 2 All ER 85.
37   *Re Gray's Inn Construction* [1980] 1 All ER 814.
38   [1996] 2 BCLC 470.
39   The cases have arisen in the context of liquidation, but the same principles would apply in relation to s 284 in the bankruptcy context.
40   [1980] 1 WLR 711.
41   [2001] 1 All ER 289.

however, the Court of Appeal[42] held that cheques drawn on a company's bank account, whether in credit (as was the case here) or overdrawn, after the presentation of a winding up petition did not enable the company to recover the amounts paid from the bank. The purpose of s 127 enables the company to recover payment from the payee but does not extend to making the bank, which has merely obeyed as agent the order of its principal to pay out of the principal's money in the agent's hand, the guarantor of the payee's obligation to repay. *Re Gray's Inn Construction Co Ltd* was distinguished as being concerned with payments into an overdrawn account with any observations relating to payments out of the account not being considered *dicta* on argued points. *Gray's Inn* would appear still to be good authority for the proposition that payments into an overdraft (thereby reducing the liability to the bank) are caught by s 127.[42a] In *Re Barn Crown Ltd*,[43] it was held that payment into an account which is in credit is not a 'disposition' within s 127.

The withdrawal of money from the insolvent's account and the payment of money into the account of a third party will clearly be dispositions of the insolvent's property. It has been held that the further withdrawal from the account of the third party, where the money has been mixed, is not a disposal of the insolvent's property even if the insolvent could theoretically have obtained a declaration of a charge over the mixed fund.[44]

Section 284(5) of the Insolvency Act 1986 provides that where a bankrupt incurs a debt to a banker by making a payment which is void under this provision, the debt is deemed for bankruptcy purposes to have been incurred before the commencement of the bankruptcy (and, therefore, a bankruptcy debt) unless the banker had notice of the bankruptcy before the debt was incurred or it is not reasonably practicable for the amount of the payment to be recovered from the person to whom it was made. The consequence of deeming the debt to be a bankruptcy debt is that the bank will be able to prove for it in the bankruptcy.

3   TRANSACTIONS AT AN UNDERVALUE

(a) Relevant provisions

Transactions which the insolvent has entered into at an undervalue are vulnerable to attack under two provisions: s 423 of the Insolvency Act 1986, which applies to transactions entered into at any time with the intention of defeating creditors; and ss 238 and 339 of the Insolvency Act 1986, which apply to transactions entered into during a defined period immediately prior to the insolvency. The latter provisions avoid the need for an insolvency practitioner to prove a motive for the transfer; the more stringent rules in relation to bankruptcy reflect the fact that a company is less

---

42   Approving the judgment of Lightman J in *Coutts & Co v Stock* [2000] 2 All ER 56. This was a case in which the guarantor of the company's overdraft claimed that the increase in the overdraft during the post-petition period was void. Lightman J held that the bank had lent money to the company (a transaction not affected by s 127) and then, acting as agent of the company, had made payments which could only be recovered from the third party payees.

42a *Gray's Inn* was applied in *Re Tain Construction Ltd* [2003] All ER (D) 91.

43   [1994] 2 BCLC 186.

44   *Re Leslie J Engineers* [1976] 2 All ER 85.

likely than an individual to dispose of its property at an undervalue[45] and that, where it does so, there will often be a sound commercial motive. There are various presumptions designed to make it easier for the insolvency practitioner to attack transactions with persons associated with or connected to the insolvent; these are the cases in which it is likeliest that there has been a deliberate attempt to remove assets from the reach of creditors.

(b) Definition of a transaction at an undervalue

A transaction[46] will be at an undervalue for the purposes of ss 423, 238 and 339 of the Insolvency Act 1986 if the transferor receives no consideration or receives consideration the value of which in money or money's worth is significantly less than the value of the consideration provided by the debtor or receives only marriage consideration.[47]

In *Agricultural Mortgage Corp plc v Woodward*,[48] the plaintiff had been given a charge over the farm of the first defendant who granted the second defendant a tenancy at a full market rent. The tenancy was a protected agricultural tenancy and the intention was to give the second defendant security of tenure thus reducing the value of the mortgaged land. The Court of Appeal held that this was a transaction within s 423 of the Insolvency Act 1986, since the first defendant had suffered a substantial loss in the value of his land so that the true value received by the second defendant, which included the preservation of the farm business from the creditors, was much greater than the consideration received by the first defendant. The reality of the benefit received had to be considered, not merely the expressed consideration.[49] In *National Westminster Bank plc v Jones and Others*,[50] owners of a farm formed a company, granted an agricultural tenancy to it and sold the farming assets to the company at a proper value. The motive for this was to put the assets beyond the reach of their secured creditors. At first instance, it was held that the tenancy and the sale agreements were each transactions at an undervalue and were caught by s 423. The owners contended, citing *Agricultural Mortgage Corp plc v Woodward* as authority for the need to view the transactions as a whole, that when their overall asset position, including the value of their shares in the company, was considered as a whole, there was no transaction at an undervalue. The Court of Appeal dismissed the appeal, holding that the relevant transactions were the tenancy agreement and the sale agreement. The consideration for the tenancy agreement was the obligation to pay rent for possession of the farm land. The consideration for the sale agreement was a sum to be paid by 20 instalments. The issue of the shares in the company was not consideration for either transaction and the fact that the two transactions caused the shares in the company to increase in value was irrelevant to the question as to what was the relevant transaction and what was the relevant consideration.

---

45   Although members of a corporate group may act like members of a family of individuals.
46   Defined by the Insolvency Act 1986, s 436 as including 'a gift, agreement or arrangement'. A transaction other than a gift involves some element of dealing: *Re Taylor Sinclair (Capital) Ltd, Knights v Seymour Pierce Ellis Ltd* [2001] 2 BCLC 176.
47   Insolvency Act 1986, ss 423(1), 339(3), 238(4).
48   [1994] BCC 688, applied in *Walton v IRC* [1996] 21 EG 144.
49   See also *Barclays Bank plc v Eustice* [1995] BCC 978.
50   [2002] 1 BCLC 55.

The House of Lords had occasion to consider the definition of a transaction at an undervalue in the corporate context in *Phillips v Brewin Dolphin Bell Lowrie Ltd*,[51] which concerned the sale of shares in a business in return for the purchaser agreeing to take over the liabilities to the employees and the purchaser's parent company agreeing to make payments which were expressed to be rental for computer equipment. The House of Lords held that in determining the value of the consideration provided by the vendor company, the true value should be taken as that which would be paid by a purchaser acting on reasonably accurate information about the business. In determining whether or not the consideration given to the company was significantly less than the value provided by the company, all consideration in fact supplied had to be taken into account, including consideration provided under a collateral contract. In valuing uncertain consideration, reality should be given precedence over speculation so that the consideration could be held to be worthless where it was known as a fact that this had proved to be the case. The collateral consideration in this case was extremely precarious, depending as it did on the continued existence of a sub-lease of computer equipment by the company which was clearly in breach of the headlease. Lord Scott observed that in a case where the consideration is 'as speculative as is the case here', it was for the party relying on the consideration to establish its value. In *Re Thoars (Deceased); Reid v Ramlort Ltd*,[52] Morritt VC declared that the *ratio* of *Phillips* applied to a bankruptcy case under s 339 and said that he took that *ratio* to be that, first, the value of the consideration in money or money's worth is to be assessed as at the date of the transaction; secondly, if at that date value is dependent on the occurrence or non-occurrence of some event and that event occurs before the assessment of value has been completed, then the valuer may have regard to it, but, thirdly, the valuer is bound to take account of all other matters relevant to the determination of value as at the date of the transaction.

Trustees in bankruptcy have frequently attempted to have the transfer of property from one spouse to another set aside as a transfer at an undervalue; one issue that has arisen in these cases is that of whether an agreement to take over the mortgage repayments prevents the transfer of a house from being at an undervalue. Another is the extent to which a transfer in the context of a divorce settlement is saved from being at an undervalue by an agreement to give up all other claims against the transferor. In *Re Windle*,[53] the court held that where there is a substantial equity of redemption, a mere agreement to pay the mortgage cannot be valuable consideration. In *Re Abbott*,[54] which is the leading case under the old legislation,[55] a house was transferred to the wife by her husband, who was insolvent at the time although she did not know it, under a consent order as a result of a compromise of her claims for ancillary relief. The court held that relinquishing a claim to financial assistance could amount to valuable consideration. *Re Kumar*,[56] which was decided under the current provisions, concerned a transfer of a house in return for a agreement to pay the mortgage and to give up a claim to financial provision. The equity in the house was of

---

51 [2001] 1 All ER 673.
52 [2002] EWHC 2416. The case concerned the assignment of a life insurance policy by the insured who died intestate and insolvent several months later, shortly after a liver transplant.
53 [1975] 3 All ER 987.
54 [1983] Ch 45.
55 Which only caught transfers for no consideration, not those for less than commercial value.
56 [1993] 1 WLR 224.

considerable value and the consideration was clearly significantly less. The financial provision claim was worthless, since the husband had no other assets and she was earning more than he. The court held that *Re Abbott* remained authority that compromise of a claim to financial provision is capable of being consideration in money or money's worth, but the quantum of the value now arises for consideration and in *Re Kumar*, there was an imbalance which led to the transaction being at an undervalue.

(c) Transactions intended to defeat creditors: s 423

Section 423 of the Insolvency Act 1986 applies to individuals and companies and is of application whether or not there is a formal insolvency. The section allows the court to unscramble transactions entered into at an undervalue with the purpose of putting assets beyond the reach of creditors or of otherwise prejudicing the interests of such people. An application may be made by the insolvency practitioner in charge of insolvency or, with the leave of the court, by a victim of the transaction.[57]

A court faced with an application under s 423 of the Insolvency Act 1986 has to consider, first, whether the transaction was at an undervalue and, secondly, the purpose of the transaction. There is no restriction on the amount of time which may have elapsed since the transaction but the longer ago it was, the more difficult it will be to establish the necessary motive.[58]

Putting assets out of the reach of a creditor or creditors must have been the purpose[59] behind the transaction, not merely the result of it. In *Inland Revenue Commissioners v Hashmi*,[60] the Court of Appeal held that putting assets beyond the reach of a potential claimant did not have to be the dominant purpose of a transaction for it to be caught by s 423; it is sufficient that it is something which was positively intended rather than merely being the consequence of the transaction. The court observed that it will often be the case that more than one purpose is at hand between whose weight or influence it is on the evidence impossible to distinguish in practical terms. This was a case in which the Inland Revenue sought to attack a trust deed by which the taxpayer transferred in 1989 the beneficial interest in property to his son, then aged 16, in consideration of natural love and affection. The taxpayer subsequently admitted concealing profits of some £885,000 between 1983 and 1994 and agreed a settlement of his tax liabilities. The son accepted that the effect of the trust was to transfer the property to him at an undervalue, but argued that the primary purpose of the trust deed was to make provision for him and there was no evidence of intention to put the property beyond the reach of a claim by the Inland Revenue. The judge held[61] that the inescapable inference from the deceased's deliberate and dishonest concealment of substantial profits for which he would be liable to very substantial amounts of tax, interest and penalties if and when his

---

57 Insolvency Act 1986, s 424.
58 It is also likely to be more difficult for the court to find a remedy which does not prejudice innocent third parties.
59 But not necessarily the sole purpose: *Chohan v Saggar* [1992] BCC 750. See also *Royscot Spa Leasing Ltd v Lovett* [1995] BCC 502 (CA) and *Kubiangha v Ekpenyong* [2002] 2 BCLC 597.
60 [2002] 2 BCLC 489.
61 The Court of Appeal held that he was entitled to do so.

dishonesty was discovered was that an intention in executing the trust deed was to put the property beyond the reach of a claim by the Inland Revenue.

Moon v Franklin[62] is another example of a case in which an application under s 423 succeeded.[63] An accountant facing criminal charges and negligence actions decided to sell his accountancy practice. In anticipation of receiving around £68,000 for the practice, he agreed in June 1987 to pay £65,000 to his wife. She used the money to discharge the mortgage on their home, discharge a loan raised to help their son, pay £25,000 into an account in her sole name and buy a flat in the joint names of herself and her husband in August 1988. In August 1987, the matrimonial home was transferred into her sole name. The court found that the transfer of the £65,000 was a gift as was the transfer of the husband's interest in the house. As the wife's interest in the flat derived from the money originally owned by the husband, he had entered into a transaction at an undervalue with respect to the flat. The court was satisfied that the payment and the transfer were transactions entered into for the purpose of putting the assets out of the reach of those taking negligence proceedings against him. The key question was his intention and it was irrelevant that the wife thought the intention was to reward her loyalty and hard work. £5,000 of the amount in her account could be shown to come from the original £23,000 and should be preserved and, pending the outcome of the proceedings, she was to be restrained from dealing with the properties.

Arbuthnot Leasing International Ltd v Havelet Leasing Ltd[64] is an illustration of the provision in operation in the context of the corporate group. The first defendant company 'Leasing' fell into arrears in making payments under its financing agreements with Arbuthnot. In April 1990, Arbuthnot entered judgment against Leasing and obtained the appointment of receivers. The receivers discovered that between December 1989 and April 1990, the business and assets of Leasing had been transferred to Finance (incorporated in 1989 with two issued £1 shares). Arbuthnot sought to reverse the transfer of Leasing's business to Finance and the court ordered that the business and assets of Finance were to be held by it on trust for Leasing. The transfer was consistent with an intention to put Leasing's assets out of Arbuthnot's reach and was at an undervalue within the meaning of s 423 of the Insolvency Act 1986.

In *Midland Bank v Wyatt*,[65] the defendant had executed a trust deed in June 1987 giving his interest in the house he had purchased jointly with his wife to his wife and two daughters in order to shelter his assets from the risk of his business failing. The court held that s 423 of the Insolvency Act 1986 did not require proof of dishonesty, merely proof that the defendant intended to avoid his creditors.

62 (1990) *The Independent*, 22 June.
63 It was not brought in the context of an insolvency, but by plaintiffs bringing a claim who were concerned that assets were being transferred out of their reach.
64 [1990] BCC 306.
65 [1995] 1 FLR 697.

(d) Transactions at an undervalue within the relevant period

A trustee in bankruptcy, liquidator or administrator may apply to the court[66] for an order unscrambling transactions at an undervalue entered into during a period shortly before the insolvency, referred to as 'a relevant time'. Identification of whether the transaction was at the relevant time involves a combination of establishing how far before the commencement of the insolvency the transaction happened and, in some cases, the state of solvency of the eventual insolvent at the time. The rules are not the same for bankruptcy as for liquidation and administration.

In the case of a bankrupt, a transaction will have taken place at a relevant time if it happened in the five years before presentation of the petition on which the bankruptcy order was made provided that, if the transaction took place more than two years before the petition, it will only be at a relevant time if the bankrupt was unable to pay his debts[67] at the time or became so in consequence of the transaction.[68] Where the transaction is with an associate,[69] it will be rebuttably presumed that the bankrupt was insolvent at the time; in other cases, the burden of proof is on the insolvency practitioner and it may be difficult to reconstruct the financial affairs of the insolvent adequately.

In the case of a company, transactions at an undervalue are only vulnerable in the two years before the onset of the insolvency[70] and only if the company is unable to pay debts at the time or becomes so unable as a result of the transaction; a state of insolvency will be rebuttably presumed if the other party is connected with the company but in other cases the burden of proof will be on the insolvency practitioner. The court may not make an order in respect of a transaction at an undervalue entered into by a company where it is satisfied that the company entered into the transaction in good faith and for the purpose of carrying on its business, and that at the time, it did so there were reasonable grounds for believing that the transaction would benefit the company.[71]

(e) Remedies available in respect of transactions at an undervalue

The remedies available in respect of transactions subject to ss 423, 238 and 339 of the Insolvency Act 1986 are broadly identical. The court may make such order (against the insolvent or a third party) as it thinks fit for restoring the position to what it would have been if the transaction had not been entered into and for protecting the interests of persons who are victims of the transaction. There are specific examples of orders the court might make but these are without prejudice to the generality of the power

---

66　Under the Insolvency Act 1986, s 339 (bankruptcy) and the Insolvency Act 1986, s 238 (liquidation, administration). This provision has only been available in corporate insolvency since 1986. Prior to its introduction, liquidators had to use ordinary company law doctrines of *ultra vires* and directors' duties to challenge transactions at an undervalue.

67　Within the meaning of the Insolvency Act 1986, s 123.

68　Insolvency Act 1986, s 240.

69　Defined in the Insolvency Act 1986, s 435.

70　The date of presentation of a petition for administration in the case of a company in administration or which goes into liquidation immediately upon the discharge of an administration order or, in other cases, the date of the commencement of the winding up (petition or resolution, whichever is earlier).

71　See *Re Rosshill Properties Ltd* [2003] All ER (D) 88 (Apr).

given to the court. Amongst the possibilities are the vesting in the applicant of property, or the proceeds of property, transferred as part of the transaction, the release of security or the payment to the applicant of benefits received from the transaction. The only limitation[72] on the order the court can make is that it cannot prejudice any interest in property which was acquired from a person other than the insolvent in good faith for value and without notice of the relevant circumstances, or prejudice any interest deriving from such an interest and shall not require a person who received a benefit from the transaction in good faith, for value and without notice of the relevant circumstances to pay any sum unless he or she was a party to the transaction. In cases to which ss 238 and 339 of the Insolvency Act 1986 apply, there is a presumption of lack of good faith in respect of someone who has acquired an interest in property other than from the insolvent or who has received a benefit and who had notice of the relevant circumstances and the relevant proceedings or was connected with or associated with the insolvent or the person with whom the insolvent entered the transaction.

In *Chohan v Saggar*,[73] a Mr Bhambra (who was facing an action for damages for libel) transferred a house, which was subject to a legal charge in favour of Anglia Building Society, to Mrs Saggar for £50,000. On the same day, the charge in favour of Anglia Building Society was discharged and a charge in favour of Chelsea Building Society was executed to secure a loan to Mrs Saggar. About a month later, Mrs Saggar executed a trust deed to the effect that she held the property on trust for Mr Mallard, a business associate of Mr Bhambra. The judge, on the application of the plaintiff in the libel action, made an order under s 423(2) of the Insolvency Act 1986 setting aside the trust deed and declaring that Mrs Saggar held the property, subject to the charge in favour of the Chelsea Building Society, on trust for Mr Bhambra and herself. On appeal, it was held that the judge had been right to set aside the trust deed rather than the transfer, since to have set aside the transfer to Mrs Saggar would have prejudiced the interests of the Chelsea Building Society. An order under s 423 of the Insolvency Act 1986 must seek so far as practicable both to restore the position to what it would have been if the transaction had not been entered into and to protect the interests of the victims of the transaction. The court held that the charge in favour of the Chelsea Building Society should be debited wholly against the interest of Mrs Saggar and this would restore to the estate what had been lost by the transaction at an undervalue.

In the case of a company whose assets are subject to a crystallised floating charge, the issue arises of whether the general creditors or the debenture holder should benefit from the restored property under this provision and the provision on preference considered next. The case law has arisen in relation to preference claims and is considered in that context.

---

72 Contained in the Insolvency Act 1986, s 425(2). It was established in *Chohan v Sagger* [1992] BCC 750 that this provision overrides the generality of the Insolvency Act 1986, s 423.
73 [1993] BCLC 661.

4 PREFERENCES[74]

(a) Background

Where a company in administration or liquidation or a bankrupt has given a preference at a 'relevant time' to any person, the insolvency practitioner may apply[75] to the court for an order. These provisions are designed to prevent the insolvent enabling some of the creditors to jump the queue and obtain full repayment at a time when the collective principle of *pari passu* ought to be in operation. Where the court is persuaded that such a preference has been given, it will make such order as it thinks fit for restoring the position to what it would have been if the preference had not been given. The orders which may be made are identical to those which may be made in respect of a transaction at an undervalue.

The Cork Committee were not of one mind as to the basis of the doctrine of voidable preferences. A minority proposed that the doctrine should rest purely on the consequences of the transaction[76] rather than on the intention of the debtor, but the majority felt that creditors should be allowed to obtain payment by applying pressure on the debtor even where this meant that they did better than other creditors in a subsequent liquidation or bankruptcy.

(b) Definition of a preference

An insolvent will have given a preference to a person if that person was one of the insolvent's creditors or a surety or a guarantor for any liability of the insolvent and the insolvent does anything or suffers anything to be done which has the effect of putting that person into a position which, in the event of the insolvency, will be better than the position he or she would have been in if that thing had not been done. Typical examples of preference are the payment or part-payment of a debt, which may prefer the creditor himself or herself[77] or a party such as a director who has guaranteed the debt,[78] and the provision of security or extra security for an existing debt.

The court will only make an order if the insolvent giving the preference was influenced in deciding to give it by a desire[79] to produce the effect mentioned in the section. Such influence is presumed[80] where the preference was given to a connected person (in the case of a company) or an associate (in the case of a bankrupt) other than an employee. The fact that something was done in pursuance of a court order does not without more prevent the doing or suffering of that thing from constituting the giving of a preference. It can be seen that there are two elements constituting a preference; these can be referred to as 'preference in fact', which is to be determined objectively,

---

74 See Prentice 'Some observations on the law relating to preferences' in Cranston (ed), 1997. Keay (1998a); Keay (2000a); Keay (1998b); Hemsworth (2000).

75 Under the Insolvency Act 1986, s 239 (liquidation); Insolvency Act 1986, s 340 (bankruptcy).

76 As is the case, for example, in Australia and the United States.

77 Eg, *Re Brian D Pierson (Contractors) Ltd* [2000] 1 BCLC 275; *Wills v Corfe Joinery Ltd* [1998] 2 BCLC 75.

78 Eg, *Re Agriplant Services Ltd* [1997] 2 BCLC 598.

79 At the date when the preference is conferred: *Wills v Corfe Joinery Ltd* [1998] 2 BCLC 75.

80 See *Weisgard v Pilkington* [1995] BCC 1, 108 and *Re Exchange Travel (Holdings) Ltd* [1996] BCC 933 for examples of a case where the directors were unable to rebut the presumption.

and 'preference in law', which is to be determined subjectively with presumptions establishing where the burden of proof lies.

Millett J in *Re MC Bacon*[81] stressed that the Insolvency Act 1986 had introduced new law on preferences and that previous case law on the old 'fraudulent preference' was no longer relevant. This case concerned the attempt of a liquidator to set aside a floating charge created to secure the company's previously unsecured overdraft three months before the company went into liquidation. The bank had threatened to withdraw the overdraft facility in the absence of such security, which would have forced the company to stop trading. He held that the word 'desire' was to be interpreted subjectively so that the liquidator had to establish that the debtor 'positively wished' to improve the bank's position in the event of the company's insolvent liquidation. Since the reason for giving the security was the wish to enable the company to continue trading rather than any wish to prefer the bank, the floating charge was not a voidable preference. A similar conclusion was reached in *Re Fairway Magazine Ltd*,[82] in which a company created a charge to secure a loan by a person who had guaranteed the company's overdraft. However, it was held not to be a preference even though part of the loan was to be used to discharge the overdraft, since the purpose of the loan was to enable to company to continue trading and the lender was not willing to make the loan without the security. It has been suggested[83] that this commercially sensible result of retaining the possibility of bank lending to ailing companies could be better achieved by an effect-based test of preference coupled with a defence of the transaction being entered into in good faith and for the purpose of carrying on its business in circumstances when there were reasonable grounds for believing that the transaction would benefit the company and its unpaid creditors.

The case of *Re Ledingham-Smith*[84] is an example of a case brought by a trustee in bankruptcy. The trustee was attacking payments made to the bankrupt's accountants, who had made it clear that they would not continue to act unless their outstanding fees were met. It had been agreed that the partnership would pay a weekly sum of £5,000, firstly to satisfy any fees incurred in that week with the balance being used to reduce outstanding fees. Before this agreement, payment had been made by a standing order of £1,000 a month. Three months later, the partnership was declared bankrupt. The judge held that original standing orders were not a preference, but that the arrangements for paying at £5,000 a week were and should be repaid. Morritt J, on appeal, held that there was no preference in fact and that it was not possible to infer on the facts a desire to prefer on the part of the bankrupts. The burden was on the trustee to show that a preference had been conferred.

(c) Relevant time

The court can only make an order in respect of a preference which was given at a 'relevant time'. If the preference is also a transaction at an undervalue, the rules about

---

81   [1990] BCLC 324. Fletcher (1991).
82   [1993] BCLC 643.
83   By Fletcher in Ziegel (ed), 1994, Chapter 12.
84   [1993] BCLC 635.

time periods for transactions at an undervalue will prevail.[85] If the preference is not also a transaction given at an undervalue, it will only be given at a relevant time if the insolvent was at that time unable to pay its debts or became so as a result of the preference; where the preference is given to a connected or associated person, there will be a rebuttable presumption that the necessary state of insolvency existed. Where the preference has been given to a connected or associated person, then the relevant period is the two years before the administration, liquidation or bankruptcy. A preference given to anyone else will only be vulnerable in the six months before the insolvency.

(d) Remedies

The remedies available to the court are very similar to those in relation to transactions at an undervalue.

(e) Who benefits from recoveries?

Where the undertaking of a company in liquidation is subject to a floating charge and the liquidator recovers amounts paid away as transactions at an undervalue or preferences, the question arises of whether the charge bites on the recoveries or whether the recoveries are available for the unsecured creditors. In *Re Yagerphone*,[86] it was held that the money in question was paid away before the crystallisation of the charge and was therefore not within the scope of the charge. It has also been argued that title to sue is vested in the liquidator on behalf of the general creditors.[87]

5 EXTORTIONATE CREDIT BARGAINS

Section 244 of the Insolvency Act 1986 applies where a company in liquidation or administration is, or has been, a party to a transaction for, or involving, the provision of credit to the company within the three years before the insolvency which the court decides is extortionate. A transaction will be extortionate if, having regard to the risk accepted by the person providing the credit, the terms of it required grossly exorbitant payments to be made or it otherwise grossly contravenes ordinary principles of fair dealing. The burden of proof is on those seeking to establish that a transaction was not extortionate. The court may make an order setting aside or varying such a transaction and requiring repayment or the retransfer of property. Section 343 of the Insolvency Act 1986 contains a similar provision in relation to bankruptcy.

---

85 In the case of a company, two years provided the company was insolvent at the time. In the case of an individual, five years if the individual was insolvent, but two years if the individual was not insolvent at the time.
86 [1935] 1 Ch 392, discussed in Hemsworth (1997).
87 See Parry (2002) for a suggestion that the position under the provisions of the Insolvency Act 1986 may be different. See Walters (2003) for a consideration of the Australian position.

6 EXCESSIVE PENSION CONTRIBUTIONS

Section 15 of the Welfare Reform and Pensions Act 1999 has inserted ss 342A–342C into the Insolvency Act 1986. Section 342A enables the trustee in bankruptcy to apply to the court on the basis that the bankrupt's rights under any pension arrangement are the fruits of excessive contributions, the making of which has unfairly prejudiced the interests of creditors.[88] The court has the power to make such order as it thinks fit for restoring the position to what it would have been if the excessive contributions had not been made. In determining whether or not to make an order, the court shall consider in particular whether any of the contributions were made for the purpose of putting assets beyond the reach of creditors and whether the total amount of any contributions made by or on behalf of the individual is excessive in view of the individual's circumstances when those contributions were made. Sections 342D–342F of the Insolvency Act 1986[89] provide for contributions in certain circumstances to be recovered under s 339 or 340 of the Insolvency Act 1986 from a pension share which has been awarded to a former spouse.

7 GENERAL ASSIGNMENT OF BOOK DEBTS BY A BANKRUPT

A general assignment, whether or not by way of security, of existing or future book debts by a person engaged in any business who is subsequently adjudged bankrupt will be void under s 344 of the Insolvency Act 1986 against the trustee of the bankrupt's estate as regards book debts which were not paid before the presentation of the petition unless the assignment was registered under the Bills of Sale Act 1878.

8 LIMITED LIABILITY PARTNERSHIP CLAW-BACK[90]

Section 214A of the Insolvency Act 1986 will have effect in relation to those who are or have been a member of a limited liability partnership where, in the course of the winding up of that partnership, it appears that within the two years before the winding up, there had been withdrawals of the property[91] of the partnership and the liquidator proves that at the time of the withdrawal, the partner knew or had reasonable grounds for believing that the partnership was insolvent on a balance sheet basis or would become so as a result of the withdrawal (and any other contemporaneous or contemplated withdrawals by other partners). The court may require the partner to make a contribution to the assets up to the amount of the withdrawal. The partner's state of knowledge is to be assessed in the same way as for s 214 of the Insolvency Act 1986.[92]

---

88 It is not clear whether these provisions apply to bankruptcies commenced or contributions made before the coming into force of the sections on 6 April 2002.

89 Inserted by the Welfare Reform and Pensions Act 1999, Sched 12, para 71.

90 See Cross (2003).

91 Whether in the form of a share of profits, salary, repayment of or payment of interest on a loan to the limited liability partnership or any other withdrawal of property.

92 See Chapter 31.

CHAPTER 31

SWELLING THE ASSETS: THIRD PARTY LIABILITY[1]

1 INTRODUCTION

The previous chapter considered the ability of the officeholder to swell the assets available to the creditors by clawing back into the estate assets previously transferred by the insolvent. This chapter considers the ability of the liquidator of an insolvent company to impose liability to contribute to the assets of the insolvent on those controlling the company whose actions have contributed to the loss of the creditors. The shareholders of a company with limited liability will only be liable to contribute to the assets available for the repayment of creditors up to the amount which they have agreed to pay for their shares. The insolvency legislation contains provisions intended to prevent those controlling businesses from unjustifiably sheltering behind the protection of limited liability. The insolvency legislation provides the liquidator with an easier method of bringing claims which were already vested in the company at the start of the liquidation where the defendants have been responsible for the management of the company.[2] The legislation also provides grounds for action against those guilty of allowing the company to continue incurring credit at a time when it should have stopped trading.[3]

There will only be any point in the liquidator bringing such an action against a defendant who has the assets to meet a successful claim. Directors who are insured against breach of duty would fall into this category. The liquidator may use the inquisitorial powers[4] to seek disclosure of existence and scope of such insurance, despite the fact that the policy will usually require the policy holder and the assured not to disclose its existence.[5]

One entity which may well have sufficient funds to meet the claims of the creditors is a solvent parent company. The doctrine of separate legal personality means that the parent company will ordinarily bear no responsibility[6] for the debts of its subsidiaries; this is seen by many as an unsatisfactory state of affairs. The situations in which the liquidator may be able to look to the parent company are considered together with some of the suggestions for reform.

The liquidator will face the same funding problems in relation to the claims discussed in this chapter as in relation to claims to claw back assets. It also has to be considered whether any sums recovered will fall into a floating charge.

---

1   See generally Finch, 'Directors duties: insolvency and the unsecured creditor' in Clarke (ed), 1991; Cheffins, 1997, p 537 *et seq*; Sealy in Ziegel (ed), 1994, Chapter 20.
2   Insolvency Act 1986, s 212.
3   Insolvency Act 1986, ss 213, 214.
4   See Chapter 21.
5   See Finch (1994). Companies Act 1985, s 310 as amended by the Companies Act 1989 allows companies to fund such policies for directors.
6   Unless it has given a guarantee.

2 PAYMENTS BY CONTRIBUTORIES

Contributories are[7] those who are liable to contribute to the assets of a company in the event of its being wound up except for those liable on the basis of fraudulent or wrongful trading.

Section 74 of the Insolvency Act 1986 provides that when a company is wound up, every present and past member is liable to contribute to its assets to any amount sufficient for payment of its debts and liabilities and the expenses of the winding up, and for the adjustment of the rights of the contributories themselves. This is subject to the major limitation that, in the case of a company limited by shares, no contribution is required from any member exceeding the amount (if any) unpaid on the shares in respect of which he or she is liable as a present or past member.

A past member is not liable if he or she has not been a member for at least a year before the liquidation or in respect of any debts or liabilities contracted after ceasing to be a member or unless the existing members are unable to satisfy the contributions required to be made by them.

A sum due to any member of the company (in his or her character of a member)[8] by way of dividends, profits or otherwise is not deemed to be a debt of the company payable to that member in a case of competition between himself and any other creditor not a member of the company, but any such sum may be taken into account for the purpose of the final adjustment of the rights of the contributories among themselves.[9] This means that a contributory may not set off a debt owed to him by the company against a call made on him by the liquidator.

If a company has created a floating charge over its assets including uncalled capital, any capital called up by the liquidator will be applied to the debt secured by the floating charge in priority to the company's ordinary unsecured debts.[10]

It is rare for shares to be issued unpaid these days and these provisions are unlikely to swell the assets of the insolvent company to any extent.[11] In a compulsory liquidation the Insolvency Rules 1986[12] require the liquidator to settle a list of contributories as soon as possible after his or her appointment, unless the court dispenses with such a list, which it will where the company is a limited one whose shares are fully paid. The liquidator must notify those who will be included on the list and they are given an opportunity to object,[13] after which the list will be conclusive against them. The liquidator will then, with the sanction of either the liquidation committee or the court, be able to make calls against the contributories. In the case of a voluntary liquidation,[14] the contributories do not have to be given notice of their inclusion on the list, but have the opportunity to object when a call is made on them.

---

7   Insolvency Act 1986, s 79.
8   *Soden v British and Commonwealth Holdings plc* [1997] 4 All ER 353.
9   Insolvency Act 1986, s 74(2)(f).
10   *Re Anglo-Austrian Printing and Publishing Union* [1895] 2 Ch 891.
11   It is notable that nearly all the case law on this area dates from the Victorian period. *Re Apex Film Distributors Ltd* [1960] Ch 378 is one of the few exceptions.
12   Insolvency Rules 1986, r 4.198.
13   Insolvency Rules 1986, r 4.198.
14   Insolvency Rules 1986, rr 4.202–4.205.

Under s 76 of the Insolvency Act 1986, the liquidator may be able to seek repayment of sums paid to a person to purchase or redeem his or her shares out of capital within the year before the liquidation. The directors who had signed the requisite statutory declaration of the company as to the solvency of the company under s 173(3) of the Companies Act 1985 would also be liable, joint and severally with the ex-shareholder, for the repayment unless they had reasonable grounds for forming the opinion set out in the declaration.

3 MISFEASANCE APPLICATIONS

(a) Section 212

Section 212 of the Insolvency Act 1986 applies where, in the course of winding up, it appears that a person in the designated categories has misapplied, retained or become accountable for money or property of the company or has been guilty of any misfeasance or breach of any fiduciary or other duty in relation to the company. The designated categories are those who are or have been an officer of the company or have acted as liquidator, administrator or administrative receiver of the company or have been otherwise involved in the promotion, formation or management of the company. The court may on the application of the Official Receiver, liquidator, creditor or (with the leave of the court) contributory examine the conduct of the person and compel him or her to repay, restore or account for the money or property or any part of it, with interest at such rate as the court thinks just, or to contribute such sum to the company's assets by way of compensation in respect of the misfeasance or breach of fiduciary or other duty as the court thinks just.

This section provides a summary procedure for enforcing rights possessed by the company at the commencement of the liquidation; it does not provide for any new substantive rights. Defendants to a s 212 application have, in addition to any substantive defence, a possible defence under s 727 of the Companies Act 1985, which provides that an officer of the company may be relieved from liability where he or she has acted fairly, honestly and ought reasonably to be excused.

The duties owed by directors to their companies[15] are the duty to act with reasonable care and skill, the duty to act within their powers and the fiduciary duty to exercise those powers in good faith in the interests of the company as a whole. Whilst the company is solvent,[16] it is open to members to ratify what would otherwise have been a breach of duty by the directors, thus depriving a future liquidator of a cause of action, provided that the ratification does not amount to a fraud on the minority.

---

15 Which can only be enforced by the company or by the liquidator and not by individual shareholders or creditors. See Pasban (2001) for a comparison of the duties owed by directors of insolvent companies in the UK and the US. See Keay (2000b).

16 But probably not when it reaches a state of near or actual insolvency, since the members have an obligation to exercise their powers *bona fide* in the interests of the company as a whole, a concept which probably includes the creditors once the company is insolvent; see (d) below.

(b) Directors' common law duty of care

The scope of the misfeasance application was extended in 1986 so that it now includes negligence actions; company directors[17] are under an obligation to carry out their duties with reasonable care and skill. Historically, a low standard of care has been imposed on directors. In *Re City Equitable Fire and Insurance Co Ltd*,[18] it was held that the standard was a subjective one and that a director need not exhibit in performance of his or her duties a greater degree of skill than might reasonably be expected from a person of his or her knowledge and experience. It was also held that a director is not bound to give continuous attention to the affairs of the company. Where duties may properly be left to some other official, a director is justified in trusting the official in the absence of grounds for suspicion.[19]

A director who also has a service contract with the company will be under stricter obligations, since he or she will be expected to show the skill and care appropriate to the holding of that position and the contract is likely to impose a requirement of full time involvement in the affairs of the company. There has also been some movement recently towards imposing a stricter standard on directors *per se*; in *Re D'Jan of London Ltd*,[20] Hoffmann LJ[21] accepted that the duty of care is the objective one contained in s 214 of the Insolvency Act 1986, which is considered later in this chapter.[22] *Re D'Jan of London Ltd* was a summons by a liquidator under s 212 against a former officer of the company whom the liquidator alleged had been negligent in completing and signing a proposal form for fire insurance, with the result that the company was uninsured when a fire destroyed stock worth £174,000. It was held that the defendant was liable to compensate the company for the loss caused by his breach of duty in an amount not exceeding any unpaid dividends to which he would otherwise be entitled as an unsecured creditor. Hoffmann LJ went on to hold that the economic reality of his 99% shareholding in the company could be taken into account in exercising the discretionary power under s 727 of the Companies Act 1985 in limiting his liability to preventing his participating any further in the distribution to creditors rather than requiring him make a contribution to the assets of the company. This was not a gross breach of duty and at the time, the company was solvent, so the only persons whose interests he was foreseeably putting at risk were himself and his wife.

(c) Directors' breach of fiduciary duty

Directors are in a fiduciary relationship to the company. They must act in good faith in what they believe to be the best interests of the company. They must exercise their powers for the purposes for which they were given. They must not fetter their discretion as to how they act. They must not, without the consent of the company,

---

17 There is no difference between the duties owed by executive and non-executive directors: *Dorchester Finance Co Ltd v Stebbing* [1989] BCLC 498.
18 [1925] Ch 407.
19 *Dovey v Cory* [1910] AC 477.
20 [1993] BCC 649; Hicks (1994).
21 Sitting as an additional judge of the Chancery Division in the Companies Court.
22 See also the discussion in *Cohen v Selby* [2000] 1 BCLC 176 (CA) and *Re Westlowe Storage and Distribution Ltd (in Liquidation)* [2000] 2 BCLC 590.

place themselves in a position in which their personal interests or duties to others are liable to conflict with their duties to the company.[23]

(d) Directors' duty to consider interests of creditors[24]

Directors owe their duties of care and skill and their fiduciary duties to the company. It has been suggested that once the company is no longer solvent, the interests of the company include those of the creditors. Street CJ in the Australian case of *Kinsela v Russell Kinsela Pty Ltd*[25] observed that once a company is insolvent, in a practical sense the assets under the management of the directors are those of the creditors and the directors' duty to the company will extend to not prejudicing their interests. Dillon LJ endorsed these comments in *obiter dicta* in *West Mercia Safetywear Ltd v Dodd*[26] and Lord Templeman in *Winkworth v Edward Baron Development Co Ltd*[27] said that a duty was owed 'by the directors to the company and to the creditors of the company to ensure that the affairs of the company are properly administered and that its property is not dissipated or exploited for the benefit of the directors themselves to the prejudice of the creditors'. It seems unlikely that the suggestion that the directors might owe a duty directly to the creditors could be correct.[28] The introduction of liability for wrongful trading seems likely[29] to destroy any impetus for the further development of the line of cases suggesting that common law liability for breach of duty to the company might be imposed on the directors for failing to take the interests of the creditors into account.

(e) Who is entitled to the proceeds of a s 212 application?

It seems that any sums recovered by the liquidator for breach of duty will fall into the general assets subject to any floating charge or charge over future property.[30]

---

23   There are a vast number of cases on this area. From the recent insolvency context, see, for example, *Re Welfab Engineers Ltd* [1990] BCC 600 where, on the facts, the court held that there was no breach of duty and that, if there had been, the Companies Act 1985, s 727 defence would apply. See also *Re Purpoint* [1991] BCC 121 and *Re DKG Contractors Ltd* [1990] BCC 903, both of which are dealt with in greater detail in the context of wrongful trading, below.
24   See Finch (1989); Grantham (1991); Keay (2002b).
25   (1986) 10 ACLR 395, 401. Other Antipodean cases in which similar statements have been made are *Walker v Wimborne* (1976) 50 ALJR 446 and *Nicholson v Permacraft (NZ) Ltd* [1985] 1 NZLR 242. See Hiley (1989).
26   [1988] BCLC 250. The case actually involved fraudulent preference and misfeasance.
27   [1986] 1 WLR 1512.
28   Toulson J in *Yukong Lines Ltd v Rendsburg Investments Corporation* [1998] 2 BCLC 485 held that there was no duty to an individual creditor.
29   Although it has been suggested (see, eg, Keay (2002b)) that the section might still be used by administrators and administrative receivers to whom s 214 is not available. Some of the funding difficulties can be avoided by liquidators using s 212 rather than s 214 but this will cease to be relevant once the Enterprise Act 2002, s 253 is in force.
30   *Re Anglo-Austrian Printing and Publishing Union* [1895] 2 Ch 891.

4 FRAUDULENT TRADING

Section 213 of the Insolvency Act 1986 provides that if in the course of liquidation it appears that the business of the company has been carried on with intent to defraud creditors[31] of the company or of any other person or for any fraudulent purpose, the court may order anyone knowingly[32] party to carrying on that business in that manner to make such contribution to the company's assets[33] as the court thinks proper. The court may also direct that any debt owed by the company to someone guilty of fraudulent trading will be deferred until all other debts and interest thereon has been paid by the company.[34]

Dishonesty is a necessary element of fraudulent trading.[35] In *Re William C Leitch*,[36] it was held that if a company continues to carry on business and to incur debts at a time when there is to the knowledge of the directors no reasonable prospect of the creditors ever receiving payment of those debts, it is in general a proper inference that the company is carrying on business with intent to defraud. In *Re White & Osmond (Parkstone) Ltd*,[37] the court held that directors who genuinely believe that 'clouds will roll away and the sunshine of prosperity shine upon them' are entitled to credit to help them over the bad time. In *R v Grantham*,[38] however, the Court of Appeal said the question was not whether the directors thought the company would be able to pay its way at some indeterminate time in the future, but whether they thought the company in incurring further credit could pay its debts as they fell due or shortly thereafter. If they realised there was no prospect of the company being able to do this, they were guilty of fraudulent trading even if they had some expectation that ultimately all debts would be paid. Liability requires active participation in the management of the company.[39] Anyone who knowingly participates in fraudulent trading may be held liable; in *Re Gerald Cooper Chemicals Ltd*,[40] it was held that a creditor of a company who accepts payment of his debt out of money which he knows its directors to have obtained by fraud may be compelled personally to repay the amount. Preferring one

---

31 *R v Smith* [1996] 2 BCLC 109 (a criminal case under the Companies Act 1985, s 458) established that creditors may be potential or contingent, not merely those who could currently sue the company.

32 This includes wilful blindness and reckless indifference: *Morris v Bank of America* [2001] 1 BCLC 771 (CA).

33 Not to particular creditors. There were *dicta* in *Re Cyona Distributors Ltd* [1967] Ch 889 that payment to particular creditors was possible under the previous provision, but these were disapproved by Lindsay J in *Re Esal (Commodities) Ltd* [1993] BCLC 872. *Re Cyona Distributors Ltd* held that the order could include a punitive as well as a compensatory element but this was doubted by the Court of Appeal in *Morphites v Bernasconi* [2003] All ER (D) 33 (Mar).

34 Insolvency Act 1986, s 215, which also provides that the court may give such other directions as it thinks proper for giving effect to the order to pay compensation. Fraudulent trading may also lead to disqualification from being concerned in the management of any company. It is also a criminal offence under the Companies Act 1985, s 458.

35 *Re Patrick & Lyon* [1933] Ch 786; *Morphites v Bernasconi* [2003] All ER (D) 33 (Mar). This requirement for dishonesty means that s 213 cannot apply to cases of mismanagement or undercapitalisation of subsidiaries: *Re Augustus Barnett & Son Ltd* [1986] BCLC 170 (and see (1987) 103 LQR 11).

36 [1932] 2 Ch 71.

37 Referred to in *R v Grantham* [1984] 2 All ER 166. See Wheeler (1993) at p 263.

38 [1984] QB 675.

39 *Re Maidstone Building Provisions Ltd* [1971] 3 All ER 363.

40 [1978] Ch 262.

creditor does not necessarily amount to fraudulent trading.[41] In *Morphites v Bernasconi*,[42] Chadwick LJ said that it was not the case that whenever a fraud on a creditor was perpetrated in the course of carrying on business, it necessarily followed that the business was being carried on with intent to defraud creditors.

There is a scarcity of reported cases and it was recognised by the Cork Committee as being of little assistance in swelling the assets of a company for distribution to creditors, although it may well be that it assisted liquidators in achieving out-of-court settlements. The Cork Committee considered that it was unnecessary to continue to require the establishment of dishonesty, which the courts required to be established beyond reasonable doubt, before civil liability could be imposed. They recommended the imposition of liability for irresponsible trading for which a test of unreasonable conduct should apply and which they suggested should be called 'wrongful trading' and they proposed abolishing civil liability for fraudulent trading. In fact, the Insolvency Act 1986 adds the provision on wrongful trading, but retains civil liability for fraudulent trading. It is unlikely that liquidators will choose to bring actions for fraudulent trading against directors since a successful wrongful trading action will be easier to achieve[43] and will have the same consequences, discussed below in the context of wrongful trading.

5 WRONGFUL TRADING

(a) The statutory provisions

Section 214 of the Insolvency Act 1986 introduces the concept of wrongful trading,[44] which imposes an objective standard of reasonable conduct, in contrast to the subjective test for fraudulent trading. Wrongful trading is a purely civil matter and has no criminal aspect. Liability is imposed on directors[45] and shadow directors[46] who knew or should have realised that there was no reasonable prospect of avoiding an insolvent liquidation and failed to take every step which should have been taken to minimise loss to creditors. Liability may result either from continuing to incur liability or by dissipating assets. Insolvent liquidation in this context means a liquidation at a time when the company's assets are insufficient for the payment of its liabilities and the expenses of the winding up. A director or shadow director guilty of wrongful trading may be ordered, on the application of the liquidator, to make such contribution to the assets of the company as the court thinks fit.[47]

For the purposes of deciding what a director should have known or done, a combined objective and subjective test is to be applied. The facts which should have

---

41 *Re Sarflax Ltd* [1979] Ch 592.

42 [2003] All ER (D) 33 (Mar).

43 See, for example, *Official Receiver v Doshi* [2001] 2 BCLC 235, in which a successful action for wrongful trading was based on fraudulent activity.

44 It is only referred to as such in the marginal note; the section itself does not use the phrase.

45 Including *de facto* directors: *Re Hydrodan (Corby) Ltd* [1994] BCC 161.

46 See below.

47 Insolvency Act 1986, s 215 provides that the court may make such further directions as it thinks proper for giving effect to the order. It may also direct that debts owed by the company to the director will be deferred to other debts owed by the company.

been known, the conclusions which should have been reached and the steps which ought to have been taken are those which would be known, reached or taken by a reasonably diligent person having both the general knowledge, skill and experience that may reasonably be expected of a person carrying out the same functions as are carried out by that director in relation to the company and the general knowledge, skill and experience that the director does have.[48] It has been held[49] that the defence provided by s 727 of the Companies Act 1985[50] is not available in wrongful trading proceedings.[51]

(b) Judicial interpretation of s 214 of the Insolvency Act 1986

For reasons which will be considered below, there has been a paucity of case law relating to s 214. The main issues considered by the cases which have been heard are whether and, if so, when directors should have realised that insolvent liquidation was inevitable. This has involved the courts in considering what information the directors should have had available to them and what conclusions they should have drawn from that information. It is clear that liquidators must identify a particular date at which to establish that the directors should have realised the inevitability.[52]

It is apparent from the cases that the directors will at least be expected to have provided themselves in a timely fashion with the accounting information which the Companies Acts require them to have. In each of *Re Produce Marketing Consortium*,[53] *Re DKG Contractors Ltd*[54] and *Re Purpoint Ltd*,[55] the accounting information was inadequate. They will be deemed to have the factual information which should have been available and acquiescing in the delay of their auditors will not be an excuse.[56] They are not, except perhaps in the case of a finance director of a plc,[57] expected to have the technical accounting expertise of professional accountants, but will be expected to ensure that the management accounts provide a reasonably accurate picture of the company's financial position.[58] The factual information which they should have sought may vary according to whether or not there were warning signs, such as pressure from creditors, indicating a particular need to monitor the solvency of the company. In *Re DKG Contractors Ltd*,[59] the warning signs were such that they should have introduced some kind of financial control.

In considering what conclusions the directors should have drawn, assuming them to have considered the relevant information, the standard to be applied is that of the reasonably prudent businessman and, whilst it is recognised that this is 'a breed

---

48 This was applied in *Re DKG Contractors Ltd* [1990] BCC 903.
49 *Re Produce Marketing Consortium Ltd* (1989) 5 BCC 399.
50 Discussed in the context of misfeasance applications, above.
51 For a comparison of the various actions which can be brought against directors, see Wheeler (1993).
52 See *Re Continental Assurance* [2001] BPIR 733 and *Re Brian D Pierson* [2000] 1 BCLC 275.
53 [1989] BCLC 520.
54 [1990] BCC 903.
55 [1991] BCC 121.
56 *Re Produce Marketing Consortium* [1989] BCLC 520.
57 *Re Continental Assurance Co of London plc* [2001] BPIR 733.
58 *Re Brian D Pierson* [2000] 1 BCLC 275.
59 [1990] BCC 903.

which is likely to be less temperamentally cautious than lawyers and accountants',[60] unwarranted optimism with no realistic factual basis will not be acceptable. In *Re Brian D Pierson*,[61] the director had refused 'to face facts' and had persistently ignored negative aspects, such as the expenses which would be incurred in obtaining expected income. Whilst it will be reasonable to rely on the advice, or on the absence of any warning, from experts such as banks and auditors provided that they have had the position fully disclosed to them, in that case the director had not actually asked for advice and had been presenting the auditors and the bank with the best possible interpretation of the facts. Advice which is given and ignored will count against them.[62] Where the directors' own knowledge, skill and experience are inadequate for the task in hand, they will be under an obligation to seek appropriate advice.[63] It has been held that some of the directors may rely to an extent on the greater expertise and knowledge of one of their number. In *Re Sherborne Associates*,[64] it was accepted that two non-executive directors, recruited for reasons quite different from financial expertise, were entitled to rely on an active chairman, who had far greater involvement with the company and its figures. In *Re Continental Assurance Co of London plc*,[65] it was held to be reasonable for the other directors to rely on the figures presented to them by the finance director, provided that they did not simply accept the figures in a blind and unquestioning way but probed and discussed them at as much length and in as much depth as they thought was needed.

The standard required will vary as between different types of company and as between directors fulfilling different functions in the same company. The general knowledge, skill and experience expected will be much less extensive in a small company in a modest way of business, with simple accounting procedures and equipment, than it will be in a large company with sophisticated procedures.[66] There is, however, a minimum standard to be expected of all directors and there is no concept of 'the sleeping director'. In *Re Brian D Pierson*,[67] the two directors were husband and wife and the wife, who was also the company secretary, took no active part in the management decisions of the company. She signed documents on the advice of her husband and the company's professional advisers. She was held to have acted honestly and reasonably for the purposes of a s 727 of the Companies Act 1985 defence to a misfeasance action, but was nonetheless held to be liable under s 214.

The courts have distinguished between those cases where the directors, being clearly aware of the possibility and consequences of insolvent trading, had considered the position carefully before deciding to trade on and those cases where the directors had made no real attempt to address the issue. The courts have stressed the need to avoid hindsight;[68] the fact that a decision to trade on, taken after careful consideration, turned out to be wrong should not in itself give rise to liability. In *Re*

60 *Re Brian D Pierson* [2000] 1 BCLC 275.
61 [2000] 1 BCLC 275.
62 *Re DKG Contractors Ltd* [1990] BCC 903.
63 *Re DKG Contractors Ltd* [1990] BCC 903.
64 [1995] BCC 40.
65 [2001] BPIR 733.
66 *Re Produce Marketing Consortium Ltd* [1989] BCLC 520.
67 [2000] 1 BCLC 275.
68 *Re Sherborne Associates Ltd* [1995] BCC 40; *Re Brian D Pierson* [2000] 1 BCLC 275; *Re Continental Assurance Co of London plc* [2001] BPIR 733.

Continental Assurance,[69] Park J commented that if he had had to find the directors liable for wrongful trading in the circumstances of the case, it would be 'hard to imagine any well-advised person ever agreeing to accept appointment as a non-executive director of any company'. The liquidators' initial argument was that the accounting information available was inadequate to enable the directors to form a view as to the solvency of the company; by the end of the trial this argument had fallen away and the liquidators were left to argue that appropriate accounting policies had not been applied to the raw data in the accounts and that, if they had been, the company would have been seen to be insolvent and the directors ought to have realised that. After detailed consideration of the adjustments which the liquidators argued should have been made to the accounts, the judge concluded that even if he had accepted all the adjustments so that the accounts should have shown the company to be in a state of insolvency, he would not have held that the directors should have been aware of the position. This would have required an understanding of accounting concepts of a particularly specialised and sophisticated nature which should not be expected even of the directors of such a specialised business.

Section 214(3) of the 1986 Act requires the director, on actual or imputed foresight of insolvent liquidation, to take 'every step... with a view to minimising the potential loss to the company's creditors as ... he ought' to take, the only limitation being that he or she is liable only for failure to take steps which a reasonably diligent person in his or her position would have taken. The director is, subject to that qualification, expected to follow the course of conduct which will reduce as far as possible the potential loss. Resignation from the board is not such a course, and it has been assumed in all the cases to date that the only realistic option is some form of insolvency proceeding. The director is still, however, required to decide what form of proceedings will in fact minimise the creditors' losses, and for this purpose the preliminary step of seeking advice may be not only permissible but necessary. There is a risk that s 214 could actually precipitate insolvency proceedings, which in some cases may have been avoidable, particularly as directors face possible disqualification if held liable under the section.

(c) Who can be made liable for wrongful trading?

Directors and shadow directors[70] may be made liable for wrongful trading. The definition of shadow director[71] provides that a shadow director is a person in accordance with whose directions or instructions the directors of the company are accustomed to act, but that a person will not be a shadow director by reason only that the directors act on advice given by him or her in a professional capacity. In *Secretary of State v Deverell*,[72] the Court of Appeal held that the concept was intended to identify those, other than professional advisers, with real influence in the affairs of the company;[73] although a shadow director will frequently 'lurk in the shadows', this is

---

69　[2001] BPIR 733.

70　By the Insolvency Act 1986, s 214(7).

71　Insolvency Act 1986, s 251.

72　[2001] Ch 340. This was apparently the first case in which the interpretation of the definition was crucial to the outcome of the case. It has since been applied in *Secretary of State for Trade and Industry v Becker* [2002] EWHC 2200.

73　See Godfrey (2002) on the risks for the turnaround practitioner.

not essential. Those who are in a position to dictate how at least some part of the affairs of a company will be managed are, therefore, at risk of liability for wrongful trading if they allow it to continue trading once they should realise that it is insolvent. Liquidators have sought on occasion to argue that banks and parent companies are capable of being shadow directors.

There were early suggestions that banks could incur liability where they provide credit on stringent conditions to financially troubled companies which permits them to continue trading. In *Re a Company (No 005009 of 1987)*,[74] it was argued that where a company took steps to implement recommendations in a report submitted after an investigation by the bank, the bank had become a shadow director. The court held that the argument was not obviously unsustainable and refused to strike it out. Millett J writing extra-judicially[75] suggested that it would be reasonable for a bank to impose conditions upon its continuing support and as long as the company is allowed to make up its own mind as to whether to continue trading or go into liquidation, the bank would not be a shadow director even though company in reality had no choice but to accept the conditions. In *Re PFTZM Ltd (in Liquidation)*,[76] a company informed its bankers that it was unable to meet its commitments under a loan from them; it was then agreed that weekly management meetings would be attended by officers of the bank. This happened for almost two years until the company went into liquidation. The liquidators claimed that there was a *prima facie* case that the officers of the bank who had attended these meetings were shadow directors of the company. The court did not agree; the bank's officers were merely acting in defence of the bank's interests and the company did not have to accept the bank's suggestions.

There may be circumstances in which a parent company may become a shadow director of its subsidiaries. In *Re Hydrodan (Corby) Ltd*,[77] which was an application to have a s 214 application against directors of the parent company struck out, Millett J's judgment indicated that the courts were likely to take a restrictive view of the idea of shadow directorship and wrongful trading unless there was very clear evidence to the contrary. A parent would not be taken to be a director of its subsidiary merely because it controlled the composition of the board of directors of the subsidiary or because members of the parent board were also directors of the subsidiary or because the parent imposed budgetary or operational rules on the subsidiary or required certain decisions taken by subsidiary directors to be approved by the parent. Some direct assumption of the day-to-day running of the business would be necessary. He held that even if the parent company was a shadow director, that did not automatically make its directors shadow directors if all they had done was act as directors of the parent company by passing resolutions at meetings of its board. If the directors of the parent company, or some of them, had individually and personally given directions to the directors of the subsidiary, they could thereby have caused themselves to be shadow directors.

---

74 [1989] BCLC 13.
75 Millett (1991b).
76 [1995] BCC 280 (see Bhattacharyya (1995)).
77 [1994] BCC 161.

(d) Consequences of liability for wrongful trading

In *Re Produce Marketing Consortium Ltd*,[78] Knox J considered the approach the court should adopt in deciding on the level of contribution a director should be ordered to pay. He held that s 214 of the Insolvency Act 1986 is primarily a compensatory provision and directors should be ordered to make good the loss caused without regard to their culpability, although it would be wrong to exclude entirely from consideration the degree of a director's culpability.

There is no express requirement in the statute for a causal link between the wrongful trading and the loss to the creditors. In *Cohen v Selby*,[79] there was a suggestion that it might not be necessary to establish such a connection. In *Re Continental Assurance*,[80] however, Park J made it clear that issues of causation would be relevant in calculating the amount of the contribution whether or not causation formed part of the substantive structure of s 214. In that case, even if a finding of wrongful trading had been made, no loss was caused to the creditors by the delay in going into liquidation, since the insolvency was largely the result of events earlier in the trading life of the company and no further net loss had been caused by the alleged delay. In *Re Brian D Pierson*,[81] it was held that issues of remoteness of causation entered into the contribution calculation and the contribution ordered was reduced to take account of the fact that the worsening of the company's position was increased by factors outside the directors' control or reasonable anticipation.

Section 215 of the Insolvency Act 1986 gives further powers to a court which has made a declaration of fraudulent or wrongful trading. In particular, the court may provide for the liability to pay a contribution to be a charge on any debt or obligation due from the company to the person liable or anyone claiming through him or her as an assignee, unless the assignee was a *bona fide* purchaser for value. Amounts owing by the company to a person declared to be liable for fraudulent or wrongful trading may be subordinated in ranking to debts owing to all other creditors. Further penalty may also be imposed[82] in the form of a disqualification order for up to 15 years.[83]

Although Knox J held in *Re Produce Marketing Consortium Ltd*[84] that the compensation fell into the assets subject to the bank's floating charge, the better view is that it increases the amount available for the general creditors, since the cases draw a very clear distinction between claims which could have been brought before the liquidation to recover the company's property and claims such as those under s 214 which are only available to the liquidator.[85]

---

78 [1989] BCLC 520.
79 [2000] 1 BCLC 176.
80 [2001] BPIR 733.
81 [2000] 1 BCLC 275.
82 Under the Company Directors Disqualification Act 1986, s 10.
83 In *Official Receiver v Doshi* [2001] 2 BCLC 235, the procedural device was used of hearing together a claim under s 214 and an application for disqualification under the Company Directors Disqualification Act 1986, s 6.
84 [1989] BCLC 520.
85 *Re MC Bacon (No 2)* [1990] BCLC 607; *Re Oasis Merchandising Services Ltd* [1995] 2 BCLC 493; *Re Ayala Holdings Ltd (No 2)* [1996] 1 BCLC 467.

(e) How effective is s 214 of the Insolvency Act 1986?

There have been very few successful claims for wrong trading. Andrew Hicks discovered in an informal survey[86] in the relatively early days of s 214's existence that liquidators often managed to achieve an out-of-court settlement of actual or potential wrongful trading claims. It has been suggested that the provision is having an effect on the practice of company management[87] in that those advising directors are very aware of the need to warn their clients of the consequences of wrongful trading and banks are likely to require an accountant's certificate that continued trading will not be wrongful where the company's financial situation appears fragile. The increasingly apparent lack of successful cases has, however, fuelled the growing perception of recent years that s 214 has not achieved its purpose.[88]

A major problem has been that of funding proceedings for wrongful trading given the decision in *Re MC Bacon (No 2)*[89] that a liquidator would incur personal liability for costs in an unsuccessful action; recent amendments, discussed in Chapter 32 below, may ease this problem. In many cases, the directors in question will, of course, have insufficient assets to make them worth suing.

6 LIABILITY FOR INSOLVENT SUBSIDIARIES[90]

Each member of a group of companies is a separate person in the eyes of the law and therefore, in the absence of a guarantee,[91] a parent company will not ordinarily be liable for the debts of its insolvent subsidiary.

Lord Justice Templeman in *Re Southard*[92] made the trenchant observation that 'A parent company may spawn a number of subsidiary companies, all controlled directly or indirectly by the shareholders of the parent company. If one of the subsidiary companies, to change the metaphor, turns out to be the runt of the litter and declines into insolvency to the dismay of its creditors, the parent company and the other subsidiary companies may prosper to the joy of the shareholders without any liability for the debts of the insolvent subsidiary.' As Hugh Collins says: 'the costs of mismanagement, the risks of undercapitalisation, or liability for hazards such as tort claims by third parties are thrown onto the creditors of the subsidiary firm, rather than being born by the economic organisation which effectively controls the productive operation.'[93]

There are sound policy reasons for upholding the principle of separate legal personality in this context since, without the ability to ring-fence potential liability, a successful enterprise might be reluctant, to the detriment of the general economy, to

---

86 Hicks (1993).
87 See Sealy in Ziegel (ed), 1994, Chapter 20.
88 See, eg, Cook (1999); Godfrey and Nield (1995); Schulte (1999).
89 [1990] BCLC 607.
90 See, generally, Prentice, 'Group indebtedness' in Schmittoff and Wooldridge (eds), 1991; Schulte (1997).
91 Banks will frequently seek cross-guarantees when lending to a member of a group.
92 [1979] 1 WLR 1198.
93 (1990) 53 MLR 731.

expand its activities into financially risky areas. Equally, there are situations in which creditors of the insolvent subsidiary may feel justifiably aggrieved at being unable to look to the solvent parent company.[94] In some instances, the business of the subsidiary will have been run as an integral part of the business of the parent company, with the interests of the group given priority over the interests of the subsidiary.[95] The subsidiary may have been undercapitalised from the start or the parent may have contributed capital by way of debt rather than share capital so that the parent competes with the creditors in the insolvency. The group may have projected an image which gave the creditors of the subsidiary the false impression that they could look to the parent company for payment.

The Cork Committee recognised the potential for the abuse of the corporate group and observed that, even with the introduction of wrongful trading, the law would remain in an unsatisfactory state.[96] It felt unable to make definite recommendations because of the consequential effects on company law, but expressed the need for reform to be considered. It identified two principal questions which arise in insolvency in relation to corporate groups: first, whether or not one or more of the companies in the group should be made liable for the external debts of the insolvent company and, secondly, how the claims of other companies in the group against the insolvent company should be treated.

The *pari passu* rule currently prevents the subordination of claims by other members of same group other than claims made by shareholders of the insolvent company in their capacity as such. In the United States, the courts have an equitable jurisdiction to subordinate the claims of parent companies or other controlling shareholders against an insolvent company until the claims of the other creditors have been met.[97] The jurisdiction is discretionary and can be invoked where the conduct of the parent has been in some way unconscionable. The view of the Cork Committee[98] was that the existence of the jurisdiction had not created undue uncertainty, nor had it discouraged group activity of an entrepreneurial character.

It may be possible to employ some of the provisions already discussed in this chapter and the previous chapter to impose liability on other members of the corporate group to contribute to the assets of the insolvent company. The member companies of a group are likely to be 'connected persons'[99] in relation to each other, thus making it easier to establish the existence of invalid floating charges, preferences and transactions at an undervalue between them.

In the event of fraudulent use of the concept of separate legal personality, the courts will 'pierce the veil of incorporation' and impose liability on the parent company, but the Court of Appeal in *Adams v Cape Industries*[100] made it clear that it is

---

94 The refusal of the then apparently solvent Pentos to meet the obligations of its insolvent subsidiary Athena in January 1995 led to a rash of adverse press comment. Parent companies may decide to meet the obligations for reasons of public relations.

95 Directors of a subsidiary who have given priority to the interests of other members of the corporate group will have committed a breach of their duties to the subsidiary, but in many instances the parent company will be able to ratify the breach.

96 Chapter 51 of the Cork Report.

97 This 'Deep Rock' doctrine is now contained in the Bankruptcy Code, s 510(c), USCA Title 11.

98 Paragraph 1937.

99 Under the Insolvency Act 1986, ss 249, 435.

100 [1991] 1 All ER 929.

not fraudulent to organise the corporate group so as to isolate the liabilities of one area of operation from another.

Section 214 of the Insolvency Act 1986 would permit a statutory 'lifting of the veil' if it could be established that the parent company had been actively involved in the management of a subsidiary (and therefore a shadow director) and had been negligent with regard to the solvency of that company; there has yet to be a case in which a parent company has been held to be a shadow director.

There have been suggestions that the normal rules of vicarious liability might lead to the imposition of liability on parent companies but the case law is not encouraging.[101]

Other jurisdictions with the same basic approach to company law have taken bolder steps to deal with this problem. Australia, for example, introduced provisions into the Australian Corporations Law[102] by the Corporate Law Reform Act 1992 which impose liability on a holding company for the unsecured debts of its subsidiary incurred at a time when the subsidiary was insolvent and there were reasonable grounds for the holding company or one or more of its directors to suspect that to be the case. The liquidator of the subsidiary will be able to bring proceedings against the holding company to recover compensation for the benefit of the subsidiary's unsecured creditors. Two presumptions of insolvency are provided to assist in proving insolvency at the relevant time. If it can be proved that the company was insolvent at any time during the 12 months before the start of the liquidation, it will be presumed that it was insolvent continuously thereafter. If there has been a failure to comply with the accounting records requirements, it must be presumed that the company was insolvent during the period of contravention. In New Zealand, company law[103] allows the consolidation of a group's assets in circumstances where the court considers it 'just and equitable' to do so.

At one stage, it appeared that the UK might be prompted by Europe to consider reform. The EC draft 9th Directive on groups was based on the German model which draws a distinction between contractual groups and *de facto* groups. In the former, the controlling enterprise is bound to make good the losses of subsidiaries, but is allowed to induce a subsidiary to act against its own interest. In the *de facto* group, the controlling enterprise may not cause the subsidiary to act against its own interests. The draft Directive is, however, unlikely to make any further progress.

---

101 Grantham (1997); *New Zealand Guardian Trust Co Ltd v Brooks* [1995] 2 BCLC 242 at 245–46; *Kuwait Asia Bank EC v National Mutual Life Nominees Ltd* [1991] AC 187.
102 See Stapledon (1995). Herzberg, in Ziegel (ed), 1994, Chapter 21.
103 New Zealand Companies Act 1955, s 245 (as amended).

CHAPTER 32

FUNDING LITIGATION BY THE INSOLVENCY PRACTITIONER

1 INTRODUCTION

A major problem faced by a liquidator or trustee in bankruptcy in trying to swell the assets or, indeed, fight off claims which will deplete the assets is that of funding any necessary litigation. Costs of all proceedings will now[1] be a first charge on the assets of the insolvent,[2] thus reducing the amount available for distribution, but until recently the insolvency practitioner would become personally liable in some cases unless she or he could obtain an indemnity from elsewhere. It may be that, in any event, the assets provide the insolvency practitioner with insufficient resources to embark on litigation unless an additional sources of finance can be found. It may be possible to persuade some of the creditors to finance the litigation or to indemnify the insolvency practitioner against the costs on the basis that they will be indemnified out of the net recoveries of the action before any distribution of the recoveries is made. Where creditors might be prepared to provide funds, they may be deterred by the prospect of any proceeds of the litigation being shared with creditors who are not prepared to take the same risk.[3] The issue of whether any recovered assets will be subject to any floating charge[4] may also influence their views.

Creditors who are unwilling to risk losing more money may well refuse to provide support and may often be in a position to prevent an insolvency practitioner who could use assets in the insolvent estate from pursuing the litigation at all. A liquidator has the power to bring or defend any action or other legal proceeding in the name and on behalf of the company, but will need consent to exercise the power in the case of a compulsory winding up.[5] A trustee in bankruptcy will also need the sanction of the creditors to bring, institute or defend any action or legal proceedings relating to the property comprised in the bankrupt's estate.[6] The Enterprise Act 2002 has amended the Insolvency Act 1986 to require the insolvency practitioner to obtain consent before bringing actions for wrongful or fraudulent trading or under the various claw-back provisions.[7]

---

1   Since amendments to the Insolvency Rules 1986 which came into force on 1 January 2003; see below.
2   See Chapter 34.
3   See Pugh (1996) for the suggestion that we should adopt the example set by Australian Supreme Court in *Household Financial Services Pty Ltd v Chase Medical Centre Pty Ltd*, in which proceeds of the action were paid to the creditor who had funded the litigation on the basis that the recoveries were less than total of the creditor's claim and the costs of litigation. The liquidator had warned the other creditors when he was trying to obtain funding that he proposed to seek such an order. See now the Australian Corporations Act 2001, s 564 (see Keay (2002a)).
4   Recoveries under actions only available to the liquidator have been held not to fall into the assets subject to charge, unlike the proceeds of claims brought under the Insolvency Act 1986, s 212 or 127. See Parry (2002).
5   See the Insolvency Act 1986, s 165, 167, Sched 4, as amended by the Enterprise Act 2002, s 253.
6   Insolvency Act 1986, Sched 5, Part I.
7   Enterprise Act 2002, ss 253 and 262 amending the first parts of the Insolvency Act 1986, Scheds 4 and 5.

An additional problem for officeholders in relation to insolvent companies is that if they attempt to bring an action in the name of the company, they may be faced with an order for security under s 726 of the Companies Act 1985, which allows such an order to be made against a limited company which appears to be unable to pay the costs of the other side if it loses.[8] There is no equivalent provision in bankruptcy, but a defendant will be entitled to seek security for costs from any claimant acting as a nominal claimant whom there is reason to believe will be unable to pay the defendant's costs if ordered to do so.[9]

Obtaining outside financial support for litigation may involve obstacles presented by the doctrines of champerty and maintenance although insolvency practitioners are exempted to a large extent from the operation of these doctrines. Non-parties to the litigation who have influence over it may also be at risk of an order for costs being made against them in the event that they are unsuccessful.[10] Conditional fee arrangements coupled with insurance against the costs of losing the action avoid these difficulties.

2 FUNDING FROM THE ASSETS UNDER THE CONTROL OF THE INSOLVENCY PRACTITIONER

The normal position is that the expenses of the insolvency will be met out of the assets[11] ahead of other claims.[12] In the case of liquidation, the 'expenses of the winding up' will be payable out of assets subject to a floating charge where there are insufficient 'free' assets.[13] The question arises as to the extent to which of the costs of litigation instigated by the liquidator or trustee in bankruptcy will be treated as expenses of the insolvency. The courts have had to work out for themselves what falls within the category of expenses of the insolvency; the terms 'expenses of winding up' and 'expenses of bankruptcy' are used in various sections of the Insolvency Act 1986 without further definition. In particular, s 175[14] of the Insolvency Act 1986, which provides for the priority of preferential debts over other debts, says that preferential debts 'rank equally among themselves after the expenses of the winding up'; s 115,

---

8 See *Northampton Coal, Iron and Waggon Co v Midland Waggon Co* (1878) 7 Ch D 500; *Pure Spirit Company v Fowler* (1890) 25 QBD 235; *Aquila Design (GRB) Products Ltd v Cornhill Insurance plc* [1988] BCLC 134 (in which the court refused to make a security order which would have forced the plaintiff company to abandon a claim with a reasonable prospect of success) and RSC Ord 23. Millett LJ in *Abraham v Thompson* [1997] 4 All ER 362 observed that the power had often not been exercised where it would have had the effect of stifling *bona fide* proceedings. Section 726 was considered in the context of a provisional liquidation in *Smith v UIC Insurance Company* (2000) unreported, 19 January, QBD (Commercial Court), in which the court refused to make an order for security.

9 CPR, r 25.13(2)(f). See *Ramsey v Hartley* [1977] 1 WLR 686; *Semler v Murphy* [1967] 2 All ER 185; *Farmer v Moseley (Holdings) Ltd* [2001] 2 BCLC 572 (in which Neuberger J expressed the view that previous case law on RSC Ord 23, r 1(1)(b) was still authoritative in this area).

10 Supreme Court Act 1981, s 51 and CPR, r 48.2.

11 In *Re MC Bacon (No 2)* Millet J held, relying on *Re Silver Valley Mines* (1882) 21 Ch D 381 and *Re Wilson Lovatt & Sons Ltd* [1977] 1 All ER 274, that this was a common law rather than a statutory right and that the statutory provisions merely dealt with matters of priority.

12 See Chapter 34.

13 Insolvency Act 1986, s 175(2)(b). *Re Barleycorn Enterprises Ltd* [1970] Ch 465; *Re Portbase Clothing Ltd* [1993] Ch 388, 407–09.

14 Insolvency Act 1986, s 328 makes equivalent provision in the case of a bankruptcy.

which applies to voluntary winding up, provides that 'all expenses properly incurred in the winding up ... are payable out of the company's assets in priority to all other claims', again without providing further definition of 'all expenses'; and s 156, which applies to all types of liquidation, provides that 'the court may, in the event of the assets being insufficient to satisfy the liabilities, make an order as to the payment out of the assets of the expenses incurred in the winding up in such order of priority as the court thinks just'. The Insolvency Rules 1986 originally provided[15] that expenses properly chargeable or incurred by the officeholder in preserving, realising or getting in any of the assets of the company or of the bankrupt are first in the general order of priority of costs. There has been considerable controversy as to whether the expenses of claims under the claw-back provisions or for fraudulent or wrongful trading fall within the category of expenses incurred in preserving, realising or getting in the assets. In *Re MC Bacon Ltd (No 2)*,[16] Millett J decided that the costs of proceedings instituted by a liquidator to challenge the validity of a charge as a voidable preference and to make the company's bank liable for wrongful trading were not expenses in realising or getting in the assets of the company. The liquidator was not, therefore, entitled to look to the assets of the company for reimbursement in priority[17] to the claims of the bank as floating chargee. Millett J said that the proceedings were not brought by or on behalf of the company[18] nor were they brought in order to recover assets belonging to the company at the date of the winding up. This decision, which is thought to be one of the main reasons for the paucity of wrongful trading actions by liquidators,[19] was criticised, *obiter*, by the Court of Appeal in *Katz v McNally*,[20] but subsequently upheld by two differently constituted Courts of Appeal in *Mond v Hammond Suddards*[21] and *Lewis v IRC*.[22] In *Lewis v IRC*,[23] the Court of Appeal confirmed that the expenses of claims under ss 214 and 239 of the Insolvency Act 1986 did not fall within r 4.218(1) and that it was not possible, as argued by the liquidator, to read either s 115 or s 175(2) as giving the liquidator a more general right to recoup litigation costs out of the assets of the company. These are merely concerned with priority of expenses, whereas r 4.218 sets out the expenses which are to be treated as the expenses of a liquidation and the priority which the expenses bear amongst themselves.

A further reason why the courts in *Re MC Bacon* and *Mond v Hammond Suddards* were not prepared to hold that the litigation expenses were 'expenses of the winding up' within r 4.218 was that the litigation had been unsuccessful. Millett J in *Re MC Bacon* said that the expenses of getting in the assets do not include unsuccessful attempts; he was not prepared to accept that the costs of unsuccessful litigation were

---

15 Insolvency Rules 1986, r 4.218 (liquidation), r 6.224 (bankruptcy). See below for the current position.
16 [1990] BCLC 607.
17 Insolvency Rules 1986, r 4.218(1)(a).
18 The Insolvency Act 1986 provides that they are actions to be brought by the liquidator.
19 See Milman and Parry (1998).
20 [1997] 2 WLR 764.
21 [2000] Ch 40; the court was not referred to *Katz v McNally* [1997] 2 WLR 764. *Mond v Hammond Suddards* was factually similar to *MC Bacon* in that the liquidator was seeking to claim the expenses of unsuccessful litigation against the holder of a floating charge from the assets subject to the floating charge.
22 [2001] 3 All ER 499 (CA). See Walters (2001a).
23 [2001] 3 All ER 499 (CA).

'expenses of the winding up' within either s 175(2) of the Act or r 4.218(1) as then drafted. Chadwick LJ in *Mond v Hammond Suddards* said that ss 115 and 156 both recognise that there will be expenses properly incurred in the winding up which do not fall within the more restricted expressions used in s 175(2) and r 4.218(1)(a), but which are nevertheless payable out of the assets of the company (although not in priority to a floating chargee) and that[24] those expenses may include the costs of unsuccessful litigation. In *Lewis v IRC*, the Court of Appeal thought it possible that they might have 'an entirely desirable and beneficial' discretionary power to permit recovery of the costs of proposed litigation from the assets of the company, although it was not at all clear what the source of such authority might be and it would be surprising to have to rely on the inherent jurisdiction of the court in a 'field so overlaid with statutory provisions'. In any event, the court was certainly not prepared to exercise it in the absence of sufficient information of the kind which would be provided on a trustee's *Beddoe* application.[25] Subsequently, in *Re Demaglass Ltd*,[26] it was held that 'expenses which are properly chargeable or incurred' in r 4.218 refers solely to sums of money which have already been expended and does not confer on the liquidator a power to require the payment of sums out of floating charge assets held by an administrative receiver in advance of expenditure actually being incurred, but that, in an appropriate case, it should in principle be possible for a liquidator to seek reassurance that proposed expenditure was something in respect of which he or she was going to be able to claim recoupment.[27]

There have been cases in which the courts have been prepared to order that expenses could be met from assets which transpire not to be beneficially owned by the insolvent. *Re Berkeley Applegate (Investment Consultants) Ltd (Nos 2 and 3)*[28] concerned a company in voluntary liquidation whose business was making investments on behalf of clients on the security of first mortgages of freehold property which were taken in the company's name. Client money awaiting investment and the benefit of the mortgages were held on trust by the company for the investors. The expenses and remuneration of the liquidator were considerable and likely to exceed greatly the extent of the company's non-trust assets. The court held that, since it had jurisdiction to enforce the investors' equitable interests in the property, it would have a discretion to require an allowance to be made for costs incurred and skill and labour expended in the administration of the property. In this case, the work had been of substantial benefit to the trust property and if it had not been carried out by the liquidator, it would have had to have been carried out by someone else at the expense of those equitably entitled to the property. The possibility of the insolvency practitioner obtaining authority in advance of incurring the cost was postulated. In *Re Biddencare Ltd*,[29] Hartford Fire Insurance Company had brought proceedings against Biddencare Ltd in order to determine whether moneys held in three bank accounts belonged to it or to the company which was in liquidation. The liquidators sought an order in

---

24 Citing *Re Silver Valley Mines* (1882) 21 ChD 381 and *Re Wilson Lovatt & Sons Ltd* [1977] 1 All ER 274, referred to by Millett J in *Re MC Bacon Ltd (No 2)* [1991] Ch 127, 140.
25 See *Weth and Others v HM Attorney General and Others* (1997) unreported, 21 November at section g for a clear explanation of orders on a *Beddoe* application and pre-emptive costs orders.
26 (2002) unreported, 10 July (ChD).
27 See Walters (2003b).
28 [1989] Ch 32 and (1989) 5 BCC 803.
29 [1994] 2 BCLC 160.

advance that they would be entitled to their costs and expenses in dealing with a proprietary claim by a third party. It was held that such a pre-emptive costs order should not be made in hostile proceedings where there was no evidence that it would not be feasible to raise a 'fighting fund' from other creditors with an interest in challenging the applicant's claim. The insolvent company in *Re Telesure Ltd*[30] sold insurance policies and paid all moneys received from the sale of policies into a designated insurance broker's bank account. It went into administrative receivership and subsequently into creditors' voluntary liquidation. A number of insurers claimed a proprietary interest in the insurance broker's account. The liquidators applied for an order that the remuneration and costs incurred by them in investigating the entitlement to the insurers brokers account moneys be paid out of the assets of Telesure Ltd whether or not those assets belonged beneficially to the company or were held as trustees. Jacob J held that the work of sorting out the insurance companies' claims had to be done by somebody and that even were the receivers to do it (and they were not willing at this stage to do so), the liquidators would have had to vet that operation in order to fulfil their own duties. Recourse to the funds concerned would be permitted for the purpose of investigation and at this stage there was no need for a liquidator to show that there was no prospect of obtaining a fighting fund from the creditors. The liquidators would have to return to court once their investigations were complete to obtain further directions as to the cost of any court proceedings.

There has now been statutory amendment to this area of the law in that s 253 of the Enterprise Act 2002 will confer on liquidators the power, with sanction, to bring legal proceedings under s 213, 214, 238, 239, 242, 243 or 423 of the Insolvency Act 1986.[31] Amendments have been made to Insolvency Rules 1986[32] to amend the provisions of rr 4.218(1)(a) and 6.224(1)(a). Rule 4.218(1)(a)(i) now refers to expenses or costs 'which are properly chargeable or incurred by the Official Receiver or the liquidator in preserving, realising or getting in any of the assets of the company or otherwise relating to the conduct of any legal proceedings which he or she has the power to bring or defend whether in his or her own name or the name of the company'. Rule 6.224(1)(a)(i) similarly refers to expenses or costs which 'are properly chargeable or incurred by the Official Receiver or the trustee in preserving, realising or getting in any of the assets of the bankrupt or otherwise relating to the conduct of any legal proceedings which he or she has the power to bring (whether the claim on which the proceedings are based forms part of the estate or otherwise) or defend'.

The new wording of rr 4.218 and 6.224 appears to extend to the costs of unsuccessful proceedings provided the insolvency practitioner had the power to bring them and the costs are 'properly chargeable or incurred'. An insolvency practitioner may be held personally liable for the expenses if he or she fails to obtain any necessary consent to pursue the litigation, but retrospective authorisation for payment out of the assets may be given.[33] A trustee in bankruptcy will need the consent of the court or the creditor's committee[34] to bring or defend any legal action relating to the bankrupt's estate. A liquidator in a compulsory liquidation will similarly always need

---

30   [1997] BCC 580.
31   Insolvency Act 1986, s 262 confers a similar power on a trustee in bankruptcy.
32   By the Insolvency (Amendment) (No 2) Rules 2002 (SI 2002/2712).
33   *Re Associated Travel Leisure and Services Ltd* [1978] 1 WLR 547.
34   The Secretary of State where the Official Receiver is the trustee.

consent whether bringing an action in his or her own name or in the name of the company. A liquidator in a voluntary liquidation will need consent to bring actions in his or her own name (that is, under the claw-back provisions and for fraudulent or wrongful trading) but not for actions brought in the name of the company.

The issue arises[34a] as to whether, if the second limb of rr 4.218(1)(a)(i) and 6.224(1)(a)(i) as now drafted does extend to the costs of unsuccessful litigation, this overrides the previous interpretation of the first limb as only applying to successful actions or whether the courts will still be able to exercise the sort of discretion demonstrated in *Re Biddencare Ltd*[35]and similar cases. If a discretion is still available, it is unlikely that it would be exercised to allow liquidators to claim the expenses of an unsuccessful challenge to a floating chargee from the assets subject to the floating charge.[36]

3   THIRD PARTY FUNDING FOR LITIGATION[37]

(a) Introduction

Insolvency practitioners may be able to get a third party to provide funding for the litigation in return for a share in any recoveries from the litigation. This may be done either by selling the cause of action (which includes assigning a disputed debt for consideration) or by selling the right to share in the recoveries if the action is successful, a course which is often referred to as selling the 'fruits of the action'. Sale of the cause of action, usually in return for an immediate lump sum together with a percentage of any recoveries, is likely to provide a quicker and more certain return for the creditors. In some cases, the assignee may have personal reasons for wishing to pursue the litigation which will make it more valuable to him or her than to the officeholder, particularly where the officeholder feels that the litigation is very speculative.[38] The ancient doctrine of champerty which prohibits trafficking in litigation may place obstacles in the way of this form of funding.

(b) Champerty and maintenance[39]

It is no longer possible to trace the origins of the doctrines of maintenance and champerty,[40] but they appear to have developed to deal with weaknesses in the early court system, at a time when an independent judiciary had not yet emerged, which allowed the assignment of claims whose prospects were poor to those in a stronger

---

34a See Tolmie (2003).

35   [1994] 2 BCLC 160.

36   See, in particular, the comments of Millett J in *Re MC Bacon*.

37   See Fennell (1997); Walters (2000b); Winterborne (2001).

38   The officeholder should not encourage vexatious litigation: see *Khan v Official Receiver* (1996) unreported, 18 June. See also *Re Papaloizou* [1999] BPIR 106; *Cummings v Official Receiver* (2002) unreported, 29 July. In *Official Receiver v Davis* [1998] BPIR 771, the court held that where the potential defendant offered the highest sum for assignment of the cause of action, this should be accepted.

39   See Walters (1996).

40   See Lord Mustill in *Giles v Thompson* [1994] 1 AC 142. The judgment of Steyn LJ in the Court of Appeal in *Giles v Thompson* contains a thorough consideration of the history of the doctrine together with further references.

position to influence the courts. In the Law Commission Report[41] which recommended its abolition as a crime, maintenance was defined as 'the procurement by direct or indirect financial assistance of any person to institute or carry on or defend civil proceedings without lawful justification'. Champerty is an aggravated form of maintenance under which the assistance is provided in return for a share of the recoveries from the action. The interest of the third party will amount to lawful justification if it amounts to a proprietary or genuine commercial interest, actual or contingent, in the subject matter of the litigation.[42] Although champerty and maintenance are no longer either crimes or torts, they can still be raised as grounds for invalidating an arrangement on public policy grounds.

Where a party assigns a right of action outright to a stranger in consideration for a share of any recoveries, the stranger will usually be substituted as claimant. If the assignment is illegal, the defendant will have a complete defence. Where the assignment is of a contingent future right to share in any recoveries in consideration for funding, the original claimant retains the right to sue and the assignee will usually require some say in the conduct of proceedings. A champertous agreement will be unenforceable and a successful litigant funded by such an arrangement may therefore have difficulty recovering costs from the other side. It was held by Lightman J in *Grovewood Holdings plc v James Capel*[43] that if the assignment is champertous, the defendant can apply for the proceedings to be stayed on the grounds that they are an abuse of process. More recently, in *Stocznia Gdanska SA v Latvian Shipping Co (No 2)*,[44] Toulson J refused to stay an action which the defendants alleged was being funded by a champertous agreement on the basis that, even if the agreement was champertous, it would not necessarily be an abuse of process to continue the proceedings.[45]

(c) General exceptions to the doctrine of champerty

It is clear that a third party with an interest in the outcome of the action may provide funding. There is, therefore, nothing objectionable in some or all of the creditors providing the insolvency practitioner with a 'fighting fund' in respect of litigation which may swell the assets available for distribution.

There is also nothing objectionable in the legal or equitable assignment of a debt by its owner even where it was apparent at the time of the assignment that litigation would be necessary to recover it; this has quite clearly been the case since the Supreme Court of Judicature Act 1873[46] made assignable in law any debt or other legal chose in

---

41 Law Com No 7, 1966.

42 See *Trendtex Trading Corporation v Credit Suisse* [1980] QB 629; *Advanced Technology Structures Ltd v Cray Valley Products Ltd* [1993] BCLC 723; *Stocznia SA v Latvian Shipping* [1999] 3 All ER 822. The mere possibility of a funder making some profit beyond the amount of the funder's preceding loss does not necessarily mean that the agreement will be champertous.

43 [1994] 4 All ER 417, distinguishing *Martell v Consett Iron Co Ltd* [1955] 1 All ER 481, in which it had been held that a stay should not be granted, on the grounds that that was a case in which maintenance rather than champerty had been alleged and that since then, maintenance and champerty had ceased to be crimes. Potter LJ in *Abraham v Thompson* [1997] 4 All ER 362 indicated that he preferred the reasoning in *Martell*.

44 [1999] 3 All ER ER 822.

45 See Walters (2001a).

46 The current provision is the Law of Property Act 1925, s 136.

action by the insolvency practitioner extends to the sale of a share of the fruits of the litigation.

It was held by Lightman J in *Grovewood Holdings plc v Capel & Co Ltd*[64] that the exemption from the doctrine of champerty which applies to the outright sale of the cause of action, on the grounds that otherwise the statutory power of sale would have no purpose since the sale would of necessity be champertous, does not apply to an assignment of an interest in the recoveries, since the statutory immunity is unnecessary. This case involved the liquidator entering into a 'sponsorship arrangement' with backers under which the sponsor agreed to continue the action in the name of the company[65] with the assistance of the liquidator. It was envisaged by the agreement that the sponsors might sell on part of their rights under the agreement in return for a contribution to the funding. The liquidator's solicitors agreed to defer charging costs to the sponsor until the outcome of the litigation. It was agreed that if the litigation was successful, the recoveries would be applied first in meeting costs and that the balance would be shared equally between the sponsor and the company in liquidation. The sponsors agreed to meet the costs if the recoveries were insufficient. The liquidation committee approved the arrangement. Lightman J held that if the assignment of the potential recoveries was unobjectionable, as in *Glegg v Bromley*,[66] the insolvency practitioner would need no immunity and, if the assignment was objectionable as including a provision for the financing of litigation, he could see no reason for extending the statutory immunity to cover it. The agreement appeared to be objectionable on two particular grounds. In the first place, it was improper for the liquidator to surrender his fiduciary power to control proceedings commenced in the name of the company. Secondly, the fact that the agreement envisaged the sponsor selling part of its rights was objectionable. The agreement was clearly champertous and Lightman J granted a stay of the proceedings on the basis that they constituted an abuse of process.

There have been conflicting Court of Appeal *dicta* as to whether the approach of Lightman J was correct. Simon Brown LJ in *Circuit Systems Ltd v Zuken-Redac Ltd*[67] observed, *obiter*, of the *Grovewood* case: 'the decision was that the necessity for the statutory exemption applicable in the case of sales of bare causes of action does not extend to sales of the fruits of litigation; these remain subject to the full force and effect of the law of maintenance.' Robert Walker J, at first instance in *Re Oasis Merchandising*,[68] said that, although he did not have to decide the point, he was inclined to think that the statutory power of sale conferred on a liquidator to sell a cause of action should extend to the power to sell the fruits of a cause of action even where the transferee was to play some part in the control of the litigation. In *Farmer v Moseley (Holdings) Ltd*, Neuberger J also said that if he had to decide the point, which on the facts of the case he did not, he would prefer the views of Robert Walker J in *Re Oasis Merchandising* to those of Lightman J in *Grovewood*.

---

64 [1994] 4 All ER 417.
65 The sponsors were extremely concerned to remain anonymous, which probably explains why an outright sale of the cause of action which would then proceed in their name was not possible.
66 [1912] 3 KB 474.
67 [1997] 1 WLR 721.
68 [1995] 2 BCLC 493. See also the comments of Robert Walker LJ, again not having to decide the point, in *ANC Ltd v Clark Goldring & Page Ltd* [2001] BPIR 568.

Re Oasis Merchandising,[69] which was a case in which a liquidator wished to pursue the directors of the company for wrongful trading, involved consideration of both the assignment of fruits of the action and the extent of the statutory power of the liquidator. The liquidator entered into an agreement which provided that the proceedings would be in the name of the liquidator but that the assignee, an organisation specialising in the funding of litigation, would be in control of the proceedings and would be reimbursed for any expenditure from any recoveries with any balance being divided. Peter Gibson J in the Court of Appeal said that the question of loss of control over the proceedings was relevant to the propriety of the liquidator's act in entering into the agreement: 'As a matter of policy we think there is much to be said for allowing a liquidator to sell the fruits of an action provided that it does not give the purchaser the right to influence the course of, or interfere with the liquidator's conduct of, the proceedings.' The actual basis of the Court of Appeal decision was that the liquidator had no power under Sched 4, para 6 to assign the fruits of a s 214 action, since property assignable under that paragraph did not include property which arose in the future and which was recoverable only by the liquidator and then held by him on the statutory trust for distribution. It was also held that since s 214 of the Insolvency Act 1986 had a public or penal element, the court was entitled to expect to have the assistance of the liquidator so that even a partial loss of control by the liquidator of the litigation was objectionable. The Court of Appeal also dismissed an argument that the liquidator could rely on the statutory power in Sched 4, para 13 'to do all such other things as may be necessary for winding up the company's affairs and distributing its assets', holding that the power was limited to what was necessary and that it was a general power which did not authorise the carrying out of illegal acts. Furthermore, given that the liquidator had now managed to negotiate a conditional fee arrangement[70] with a firm of solicitors, it could not be said that the champertous agreement was the only way of funding the action.

It would appear, therefore, to be impossible for a liquidator to assign the cause of action in respect of claims for fraudulent or wrongful trading or to set aside a transfer at an undervalue or a preference. Although the officeholder could, as a matter of common law, assign the fruits of such an action, it is possible that an agreement giving the funder any degree of control over the litigation will be found to be champertous; it is not likely that potential funders will be interested in arrangements under which they have no power to influence the conduct of proceedings.

(e) Community Legal Service funding

In a number of cases, the object of the assignment of the cause of action to an individual has been to enable the individual to pursue the action with the benefit of legal aid which would not be available to the company or the trustee in bankruptcy. The assignment to an individual by a liquidator also avoids the problem of the company being ordered to give security for costs.

In *Norglen Ltd v Reeds Rains Prudential Ltd*,[71] a cause of action had been assigned to directors of the company. At first instance, it had been held that this was a sham to

---

69   [1995] 2 BCLC 493 (Robert Walker J); [1997] 1 All ER 1009 (CA).
70   See below.
71   [1996] BCC 532.

enable the action to be continued by individuals at the expense of the Legal Aid Board and to avoid security for cost being imposed. The Court of Appeal held[72] that the legal aid aspect should not invalidate the assignment, since it was something the liquidator had the power to do. This was followed by the Court of Appeal in *Circuit Systems Ltd v Zuken-Redac Ltd*.[73] The House of Lords has upheld the Court of Appeal decisions in both cases,[74] holding that the question of whether an assignment was an abuse of legal aid was a matter for the Legal Aid Board.

The House of Lords in *Stein v Blake*[75] had previously upheld the assignment by a trustee in bankruptcy of a cause of action back to the bankrupt in return for a share in the realisations in a situation where it was anticipated that the bankrupt would get legal aid. Lord Hoffmann referred to the suggestion that there were policy reasons for taking a restrictive view of assignments of causes of action by insolvency practitioners to individuals, but observed that 'the problems can be said to arise not so much from the law of insolvency as from the insoluble difficulties of operating a system of legal aid and costs which is fair to both plaintiffs and defendants. Mr Blake is in no worse position now than he was before the bankruptcy when Mr Stein was suing him with legal aid (although this would not have been the case if the plaintiff had been a company). Mr Blake's complaint is that the bankruptcy has brought him no relief. But whether it should seems to me a matter for Parliament to decide.'

Parliament subsequently intervened to an extent to limit the practice of assigning causes of action to those likely to obtain a legal aid certificate which would guarantee both funding and probably immunity from liability for the other side's costs. The legal aid authorities were given the power to refuse a certificate to a person who is an assignee where the assignment was entered into 'with a view' to allowing the action to be commenced or continued with the benefit of legal aid.[76]

The Access to Justice Act 1999 introduced the Community Legal Service Fund, administered by the Legal Services Commission to replace legal aid. Schedule 2 to the Act provides that services which may not be funded include matters of company or partnership law or other matters arising out of the carrying on of a business. The Guidance Notes issued by the Lord Chancellor under s 23 of the Act explain that: 'It is not thought justified to spend public money helping businessmen who fail to insure against the risk of facing legal costs.' Legal services may only be funded for an individual, not for a company, and funding may be withdrawn from an individual who has had a bankruptcy order made against him or her.[77] Personal insolvency proceedings are within the scope of provision whether or not connected with business.[78] The Guidance Notes provide[79] that 'when a person is declared bankrupt and the trustee in bankruptcy assigns the cause of action back to the client, funding

---

72　Following *Eurocross Sales Ltd v Cornhill Insurance plc* [1995] 1 WLR 1517 and distinguishing *Advanced Technology Ltd v Cray Valley Products Ltd* [1993] BCLC 723.

73　[1997] 1 WLR 721.

74　(1997) *The Times*, 1 December.

75　[1995] 2 All ER 961.

76　Civil Legal Aid (General) Regulations 1996 (SI 1996/1257) inserting reg 33A into the 1989 Regulations.

77　See the Funding Code.

78　Guidance Notes.

79　Paragraph 3.10.

may not be granted to the client if that cause of action arose out of the client's business'.

(f) Third party costs order

The court has jurisdiction to make an order for costs against a non party to the litigation where the interests of justice so require.[80] There is a risk that an insolvency practitioner who retains control over litigation or a funder who acquires control might be liable to such an order. A number of costs applications have also been made in relation to directors of insolvent companies who have caused the companies to bring unsuccessful actions. The Court of Appeal indicated in *Taylor v Pace Developments Ltd*[81] that, although such orders were not impossible, in the absence of bad faith on the part of the director, such an order would usually be an impermissible breach of the principle of limited liability.

It would appear, from *Metalloy Supplies Ltd v MA (UK) Ltd*[82] that similar principles will apply to liquidators. The defendants applied for an order that the liquidator personally pay the cost of the action, which had been discontinued when the company was ordered to make a payment of security for costs. The defendants argued that the liquidator had known that the plaintiff had insufficient funds to cover the cost of the trial. At first instance, it was held that the liquidator was liable for the costs from the date on which the defendants had served a defence. The Court of Appeal, allowing the appeal, held that the jurisdiction to order a liquidator as a non-party to proceedings brought by the insolvent company to pay costs personally would only be exercised in exceptional circumstances where there had been impropriety on the part of the liquidator. In most such cases, the court observed, the defendant would be protected by the ability to apply for security for costs.[83]

Third party funders of litigation might be at greater risk of an order for costs, although in *Condliffe v Hislop*,[84] the Court of Appeal held that the mere fact of lending money to a plaintiff to fund litigation ought not to lead to a risk of liability. In *Cooper v Maxwell*,[85] a mother who funded her bankrupt son's unsuccessful appeal to the Court of Appeal was held not to be personally liable for the costs. This case appears to reflect the general view, although in *Thistleton v Hendricks*,[86] a similar case, the mother was ordered to contribute towards the successful defendant's costs. The judge was influenced to make the order by the fact that the son was the plaintiff (in the *Maxwell*

80　CPR, rr 25.14 and 48.2 and *Farmer v Moseley*. There is no power to make an order for security of costs in advance against a defendant: *CT Bowring & Co (Insurance) Ltd v Corsi Partners* [1994] 2 Lloyd's Rep 567. In *Abraham v Thompson* [1997] 4 All ER 362, the Court of Appeal refused to stay an action on the grounds that it was being maintained by a third party which would not accept liability for costs; the proper course was to seek a costs order after the event.

81　[1991] BCC 406.

82　[1997] 1 All ER 418.

83　See *Eastglen Ltd v Grafton* [1996] 2 BCLC 279.

84　[1996] 1 WLR 753.

85　(1992) unreported, 20 March, CA, quoted in *Murphy v Young & Co's Brewery* [1997] 1 All ER 518.

86　(1992) 32 Con LR 123.

declarations on the debtor's liability to him and the insurer's potential liability to him or her under the insurance contract. It would not be necessary for the third party to proceed against the debtor at all, so problems would no longer arise where a company has already been dissolved. The proposed Order would allow third parties to obtain information about any rights transferred to them in order to enable a decision to be taken on whether to continue litigation or not. The view of the Lord Chancellor's Department is that the number of successful claims by third parties is likely to rise as a result of the Law Commission's recommendations and that there will be savings from the reduction in litigation on worthless claims and the new streamlined procedures.

2   CLAIMS OF EMPLOYEES AGAINST THE NATIONAL INSURANCE FUND

(a) Background

Certain payments owing to the employees of an insolvent employer are guaranteed by the state and will be met out of the National Insurance Fund by the Redundancy Payments Offices. This is a requirement of the EC Insolvency Directive.[6] Where an employer has several places of establishment in different Member States, the competent guarantee institution for meeting claims under the directive is that of the state within whose territory the claimants were employed.[7]

The Redundancy Payments Offices handle around 110,000 redundancy and other insolvency claims from redundant workers every year, and pay more than £180 million from the National Insurance Fund.[8] If payment is made to an employee, the Department of Employment becomes subrogated to his or her rights against the employer.[9] In 1996, the National Audit Office[10] concluded that if the Redundancy Payments Service were to be a more active creditor it could recover a higher proportion of the payments of then around £240 million each year that it made to employees who have become redundant on the insolvency of their employers.

---

6   EEC 80/987. It is not entirely clear that this Directive has been correctly implemented: see Hepple and Byre (1989). It was the failure of the Italian government properly to implement this directive which led to the landmark decision of *Francovich v Italian Republic* [1992] IRLR 84, in which the European Court of Justice held that a claim could in some circumstances be brought against a government by an individual who has suffered as a result of the failure in implementation. See Clarke and Rajak (2000). For an account of the introduction of a similar scheme in Australia, see Keay (2000c).

7   *Everson and Another v Secretary of State for Trade and Industry and Another* [2000] IRLR 202. In this case, the applicants were working in the UK for a branch of a company incorporated and being wound up in the Republic of Ireland. The employees' guaranteed claims should be met by the UK.

8   Information on the Insolvency website in early 2003.

9   See Chapter 34 for discussion of the view of the Cork Committee on this.

10 Published on 17 October 1996.

(b) Categories of guaranteed payments

(i) Redundancy payments.[11] These are guaranteed[12] both where the employer is formally insolvent and where the employee has taken all reasonable steps (other than legal proceedings to enforce an employment tribunal decision) to recover the payment, and the employer has refused or failed to pay. This will include the situation where the employer has so few assets that no one has thought it worth incurring the expense of a formal insolvency.

(ii) Other payments guaranteed on a formal insolvency are set out in s 184 of the Employment Rights Act 1996. The requirements for these payments are more complicated than for redundancy and maternity payments and are considered below.

(c) Payments guaranteed under s 184 of the Employment Rights Act 1996

Before a payment will be made out of the Fund, the Department of Employment must be satisfied of the following four elements:

(i) The debt claimed is within the categories specified by s 184 of the Employment Rights Act 1996. These are, broadly: remuneration[13] due during the eight weeks prior to the commencement of the insolvency; notice moneys for the statutory periods of notice;[14] holiday pay; and unfair dismissal basic awards. The calculation of the gross amount[15] of any periodic payment guaranteed by the Fund is subject to a statutory maximum currently[16] set at £260 per week. If the employee owes money to the employer, the set-off provisions will apply.[17]

(ii) The employer is formally insolvent, as defined in s 183. This requires bankruptcy, liquidation, administration, administrative receivership or a voluntary arrangement; this is a wider definition of insolvency than is required by Directive 80/987. The list is exhaustive and if the situation does not fall within it, the employees may have to seek a winding up or bankruptcy themselves in order to take advantage of the guarantee provision.[18] The

---

11 Under the Employment Rights Act 1996, s 135.

12 By the Employment Rights Act 1996, s 166.

13 Defined to include protective awards (see Chapter 12).

14 Set out in the Employment Rights Act 1996, s 86.

15 Which will be subject to deduction for mitigation: *Westwood v Secretary of State for Employment* [1984] IRLR 209. In *Secretary of State for Employment v Cooper* [1987] ICR 766, the Employment Appeal Tribunal held that the payment made from the Fund should be reduced by an amount equivalent to the basic rate of income tax. See *Secretary of State for Employment v Wilson* [1996] IRLR 334 in the context of unemployment benefit.

16 Employment Rights (Increase of Limits) (No 2) Order 2002 (SI 2002/2927).

17 *Secretary of State v Wilson* [1996] IRLR 330. In *Secretary of State for Trade and Industry v Frid* [2002] All ER (D) 76, it was held that insolvency set-off could not apply to the subrogated claims of the Secretary of State since these were only contingent at the start of the liquidation.

18 *Pollard v Teako* [1967] 2 ITR 357; *Re Eloc Electro-Optieck and Communicatie BV* [1981] 2 All ER 1111; *Secretary of State for Trade and Industry v Walden* [2000] IRLR 168.

employer will not be insolvent for these purposes on the basis that a receiver has been appointed pursuant to a fixed charge.[19] Where the employer is a partnership, the section has been construed as requiring that all the partners be individually bankrupt before the employer will be treated as insolvent.[20]

(iii) The employment of the employee has been terminated.

(iv) The debt was due on the appropriate date. The appropriate date[21] is, in relation to arrears of pay and holiday pay, the date on which the employer became insolvent, as defined by s 183 of the Employment Rights Act 1996. In relation to protective awards under s 189 of the Trade Union and Labour Relations (Consolidation) Act 1992 and basic awards of compensation for unfair dismissal, the appropriate date is the latest of the date on which the employer became insolvent, the date of the termination of the employee's employment, and the date on which the award was made. In relation to any other guaranteed payment, it is the later of the date on which the employer became insolvent and the date of termination of the employee's employment.

(d) Validity of the statutory ceiling and other limits

In *Potter v Secretary of State for Employment*,[22] the Court of Appeal left open the question of whether the statutory weekly ceiling on the amount to be claimed by any employee is in accordance with the social objective of the Insolvency Directive. In the Employment Appeal Tribunal, it had been held that the ceiling could be justified as avoiding the payment of sums going beyond the protection aimed at by the Insolvency Directive, which expressly permitted a ceiling provided it was consistent with the social objective of the Directive. In the Court of Appeal, it was decided that protective awards, the subject matter of the claim, did not fall within the Insolvency Directive so it did not have to decide the point. It did, however, point out that attention had been drawn to the increasing disparity between the average level of earnings in the UK and the ceiling; it said that in other circumstances it might have thought it right to refer a question to the European Court of Justice for guidance as to the circumstances to be taken into account in considering the validity of a ceiling. The case went to the House of Lords as *Mann v Secretary of State for Employment*[23] where Lord Hoffmann considered the argument that the statutory ceiling was set at too low a level, since it might be of relevance in cases which were subject to the Directive,[24] and said that, although he did not find it an easily justiciable question,[25] he did not think the limit 'unreasonably low', even though it was lower than average earnings.[26]

---

19   *Secretary of State v Stone* [1994] ICR 761 (fixed charge over book debts).

20   *Secretary of State v Forde* [1997] IRLR 387.

21   Employment Rights Act 1996, s 185.

22   [1997] IRLR 2.

23   [1999] ICR 898. See Clarke and Rajak (2000).

24   This case was not since it arose out of an administrative receivership and administrative receiverships do not fall within the Insolvency Directive.

25   He noted that in a footnote to his opinion in *Regeling v Bestuur van de Bedrijfsvereniging voor de Metaalnijverheid* [1999] IRLR 566, Mr Advocate General Cosmas had said that the European Court of Justice had the right and duty, to ascertain whether the conditions for the application of Art 4, para 3 of Directive 80/987 had been satisfied.

26   Employment Relations Act 1999, s 34 subsequently introduced indexation of the guaranteed payments; the decline in the real value of the payments since redundancy payments were first introduced in 1965 has not, however, been reversed. If it had been, the statutory weekly ceiling would now be over £400.

There was also an issue in *Mann* as to which weeks were the relevant eight weeks and the House of Lords held that s 184(1)(a) of the Employment Rights Act 1996, which restricts the guarantee period to a maximum of eight weeks, must be read on the basis that it was passed in order to give effect to the Insolvency Directive, even though the Directive had no effect in this particular case. The limit was a permitted derogation under the Insolvency Directive and, accordingly, must be interpreted restrictively so as to afford maximum benefit to the employee. In *Titchener and Others v Secretary of State for Trade and Industry*,[27] it was argued that a similar approach should be taken to the statutory ceiling so that the appropriate deductions should be made from the gross figure before applying the statutory cap since that approach was more advantageous to employees and would have resulted in an increased sum being paid to each applicant. The Employment Appeal Tribunal held that it was bound by the decision in *Morris v Secretary of State for Employment*,[28] which it held had not been implicitly overruled by *Mann*, that the cap should be applied before the deductions were calculated.

(e) Complaints against the Fund

An employee may complain to an employment tribunal that the Fund has paid too little.[29] Such application must be presented within three months of the Department's decision; there is no right to complain of an unreasonable delay in the Department reaching a decision. If the complaint is proved, the tribunal will make a declaration as to the amount due, but will not actually order payment.

(f) Who is an employee?

Payments will only be made out of the National Insurance Fund to those who are employees as distinct from those who are independent contractors.[30]

It has been necessary to consider on a number of occasions whether a controlling shareholder can be an employee of a company for these purposes.[31] The leading case on the subject is the Court of Appeal decision in *Secretary of State for Trade and Industry v Bottrill*,[32] in which it was held that the question of whether a relationship of employment existed could only be determined by having regard to all the relevant facts. The fact of a controlling shareholding would probably be significant in all situations and might be decisive in some but could not by itself be determinative of the issue. The Court of Appeal said that a tribunal should first consider whether there had been a genuine contract between the company and the shareholder. If it concluded that the contract was not a sham, it would probably wish to consider

---

27   [2002] ICR 225.

28   [1985] IRLR 297.

29   Employment Rights Act 1996, s 188.

30   See *McMeechan v Secretary of State for Employment* [1997] IRLR 353 for an example of a case in which it was necessary to decide whether a claimant against the National Insurance Fund was an employee or an independent contractor.

31   *Eaton v Robert Eaton Ltd and the Secretary of State for Employment* [1988] ICR 302. The EAT came to conflicting decisions in *Buchan v Secretary of State for Employment* [1997] IRLR 80 and *Fleming v Secretary of State for Trade and Industry* [1997] IRLR 682.

32   [2000] 1 All ER 915. See Jefferson (1998).

whether the contract actually gave rise to an employer/employee relationship and the degree of control exercised by the company over the shareholder employee would be important in this context. The actual conduct of the parties pursuant to the contract was also likely to be important. On the facts of the particular case, the tribunal had been entitled to conclude that Mr Bottrill was an employee of the company. The *Bottrill* decision was applied in *Hauxwell and Another v Secretary of State for Trade and Industry and Another;*[33] on the facts of this case, it was held that the controlling shareholders were not employees.[34]

---

33 EAT/386/01 (unreported).

34 The Employment Appeal Tribunal observed in the course of its judgment that there was considerable moral force in the argument that they had for years been contributing to the State by way of National Insurance contributions and had foregone the advantages of Schedule D taxation to be taxed as employees under Schedule E; it would undoubtedly have been just for them to have received redundancy payments from the Secretary of State.

CHAPTER 34

DISTRIBUTION OF THE AVAILABLE ASSETS

1 INTRODUCTION

Once the liquidator or trustee in bankruptcy has identified and realised the assets which are available to the creditors of the insolvent, the question arises as to the manner and order of distribution. As has been seen, a basic principle of insolvency law since Tudor times is that of rateable or *pari passu* distribution of the assets.[1] In reality, the recognition of pre-existing proprietary rights explained in the foregoing chapters is likely to mean that in many cases, the unsecured creditors are participating rateably in very little.[2] Although the ordinary creditors share the available assets equally, the expenses of the insolvency and the preferential creditors must be paid before any assets become available to them.[3] The ordinary creditors are a residual class comprising all creditors not specifically designated as preferential or deferred. Post-insolvency interest on preferential and ordinary debts will only be paid if there are funds left after payment of the ordinary creditors. Finally, there is a category of deferred or postponed debts. Each category of debts has to be paid in full before the next category of creditors is entitled to receive anything and where there is insufficient to pay all members of a category fully, the amounts paid will be reduced rateably.

Secured creditors will often alter the order of priority amongst themselves by mutual agreement and this has led to some conundrums of priority where floating charges and preferential creditors are involved. Those who will be unsecured creditors in the event of an insolvency may also wish to agree amongst themselves that distribution will be other than *pari passu*. They will face the same difficulty as those who wish to contract out of the statutory set-off scheme in that the court is likely to hold that such an agreement is of no effect, although recently, the courts have showed some relaxation of the rule in this context.

This chapter considers each category of creditor in turn, starting at the top of the order of priority. It concludes by considering the extent to which unsecured creditors may contract out of the statutory scheme.

2 MANNER OF DISTRIBUTION

The statutory provisions about the manner of distribution to the creditors are identical in bankruptcy and liquidation. In relation to bankruptcy the rules are contained in the Insolvency Act 1986;[4] identical provisions relating to liquidation are to be found in the

---

1   For recent discussion of the *pari passu* principle and suggestions of alternative bases of distribution (eg, ranking of debts on the basis of chronology, ethics, size, policy), see Finch (2000) (developed further in Finch, 2002, p 483 *et seq*); Mokal (2001a).

2   See Oditah (1992) on the impact of proprietary claims.

3   The provisions on priority of payment are found in the Insolvency Act 1986, s 328 (bankruptcy), s 107 (voluntary winding up) and the Insolvency Rules 1986, r 4.181 (compulsory winding up). The rules on set-off considered in Chapter 25 above also have the effect of bestowing a preference on those creditors able to take advantage of them.

4   Insolvency Act 1986, ss 324, 325, 326, 330.

Insolvency Rules.[5] Part 11 of the Insolvency Rules contains additional provisions about the declaration and payment of dividends which apply to both winding up and bankruptcy.

Whenever the officeholder has sufficient funds in hand, he or she shall,[6] subject to the retention of sums necessary to meet the expenses of the insolvency, declare and distribute dividends amongst the creditors in respect of the debts which they have proved. Notice of the intention to declare and distribute a dividend must be given to all creditors whose addresses are known to the officeholder and who have not proved their debts; unless the creditors have already been invited by public advertisement to prove their debts, there must be a public advertisement of the intention to declare a dividend. The notices will specify a last date for proving, which must not be less than 21 days from the notice; the dividend will usually be declared within four months from that date. Where a dividend has been declared, details of it shall be given to those who have proved their debts.

In the calculation and distribution of a dividend, the officeholder shall make provision for any debts which appear to him or her to be due to persons who live at a distance and have not yet been able to establish a proof. He or she must also provide for any debts which are the subject of claims which have not yet been determined and for disputed proofs and claims. Creditors who have not proved their debts before the declaration of a dividend are not entitled to disturb that dividend but, when their debts have been proved, will be entitled to be paid any dividend which they have failed to receive, out of any money for the time being available for the payment of any further dividend, before further dividends are paid to other creditors. No action lies against the officeholder for a dividend but, if he or she refuses to pay a dividend, the court may, if it thinks fit, order it to be paid and also to pay, out of the officeholder's own money, interest on the dividend and the costs of the proceedings in which the order to pay is made.

If there is property which cannot be readily or advantageously sold, the officeholder may obtain the permission of the creditors' committee to distribute the property itself according to its value.[7] Permission must relate to a particular proposed exercise of the power in question. If the officeholder has acted in a case of urgency to distribute the property *in specie*, the court or the creditors' committee may ratify his or her act for the purpose of enabling him or her to recoup his or her expenses provided he or she seeks ratification without undue delay.

Where the officeholder has realised all the estate or so much of it as he or she thinks can be realised without needlessly protracting the insolvency, notice shall be given of his or her intention to declare a final dividend or that no dividend, or further dividend, will be declared.[8] The notice shall require claims to be established by the final date specified in the notice. After the final date, which may be delayed by the court on the application of any person, the officeholder shall defray any outstanding expenses out of the estate and declare and distribute any final dividend without regard to any claims which have not already been proved.

---

5   Insolvency Rules 1986, rr 4.180, 4.182, 4.183, 4.184, 4.186.
6   Insolvency Act 1986, s 324; Insolvency Rules 1986, r 4.180.
7   Insolvency Act 1986, s 326; Insolvency Rules 1986, r 4.183.
8   Insolvency Act 1986, s 330; Insolvency Rules 1986, r 4.186.

Sections 334 and 335 of the Insolvency Act 1986 make provision for the situation where a bankruptcy order is made against an undischarged bankrupt. Once the trustee in the first bankruptcy has notice of the petition for the second bankruptcy, any subsequent distribution out of property acquired as after-acquired property or by virtue of an income payments order in the first bankruptcy will be void unless made with the consent of the court or subsequently ratified by the court. After-acquired property (and its proceeds) and the proceeds of income payments orders held by the first trustee at the commencement of the second bankruptcy will fall into the estate for the purposes of that bankruptcy. The expenses of the first trustee in relation to property which has fallen into the estate in the second bankruptcy will be a first charge on that estate. The creditors of the earlier bankruptcy will not be creditors in respect of the same debts in the later bankruptcy, but the first trustee may prove in the later bankruptcy for the unsatisfied balance of the debts, interest payable on that balance and any unpaid expenses of the earlier bankruptcy; the claims will be deferred to the debts and interest provable in the later bankruptcy.

3 EXPENSES AND POST-INSOLVENCY CREDITORS[9]

As explained above, the officeholder will retain sums to meet the expenses of the insolvency before making distributions to the creditors. Expenses are payable in full by the officeholder out of the available assets rather than provable in the insolvency. The court will usually permit a post-insolvency creditor to take individual action against the insolvent.[10] In relation to a corporate insolvency, the liquidator can look to assets subject to a floating charge[11] even if the floating charge crystallised before the commencement of the winding up.[12]

Section 328 of the Insolvency Act 1986, which sets out the order of priority of debts in a bankruptcy, provides that the preferential debts will be postponed to the expenses of the bankruptcy but will be paid in priority to other debts. This has the effect of placing the expenses of the bankruptcy at the top of the order of distribution. The Insolvency Rules 1986[13] set out the order of priority of the expenses. The issue of the expenses of a bankruptcy does not seem to have generated the same volume of litigation as has been the case in the context of liquidation.

The provisions of the Insolvency Act 1986 relevant to liquidations date back to provisions of the Companies Act 1862, which themselves reflected previous case law on the subject.[14] Section 115 of the Insolvency Act 1986 provides that all expenses properly incurred in the winding up, including the remuneration of the liquidator, are payable out of the company's assets in priority to all other claims.[15] Section 156 of the

---

9   Insolvency Act 1986, s 115 (voluntary winding up); Insolvency Rules 1986, r 4.180(1) (compulsory winding up); Insolvency Act 1986, s 324 (bankruptcy). For more specific discussion of the expenses of litigation undertaken by the officeholder, see Chapter 32.

10 See Chapter 25.

11 *Re Barleycorn* [1970] Ch 465.

12 *Re Leyland DAF* [2002] 1 BCLC 571. This is being appealed to the House of Lords. See Pennington [2003b] Co Lawyer 119.

13 Insolvency Rules 1986, r 6.224.

14 See, generally, Moss and Segal (1997) on the history of the liquidation expenses principle.

15 In *Re Dermaglass* [2002] BPIR 1093, it was held that the liquidator could only look to the assets for expenses already incurred, not to establish a fighting fund for future expenses.

Insolvency Act 1986 provides that the court may, in the event of the assets being insufficient to satisfy the liabilities, make an order as to the payment out of the assets of the expenses incurred in the winding up in such order of priority as the court thinks just. The Insolvency Rules 1986[16] set out the general order of priority of payment of the expenses of liquidation; it is to be noted that each category is to be paid in full before anything is paid to the next and that the remuneration of the liquidator comes towards the bottom of the list.[17] First in the order of priority are the expenses properly incurred in preserving, realising or getting in any of the assets of the company which reflects the common law view that the other expenses could only be paid out of the assets net of the costs of realisation.[18] The Insolvency Rules 1986 expressly provide[19] that this order of priority is subject to the power of the court under s 156 of the Insolvency Act 1986 to order how the expenses are to be met where the assets are insufficient to satisfy the liabilities. It is also provided[20] that nothing in the Rules affects the power of any court in proceedings by or against the company to order costs to be paid by the company or the liquidator. It will be seen that the statutory provisions do not confer an absolute right of priority on the expenses of the liquidation, since the court is given an ultimate discretion. Millett J in Re MC Bacon[21] observed that s 115 of the Insolvency Act 1986 was concerned with priority of payment out of the assets; it assumed that the expenses would be payable out of the assets, but did not so provide. Lord Hoffmann in Re Toshoku Finance UK plc[22] said that r 4.218, together with r 4.220, was intended to be a definitive statement of liquidation expenses and there was no scope for putting a gloss on the provisions by requiring that the expenses be incurred for the benefit of the estate.[23]

Debts and liabilities arising in the course of the liquidation as a result of contracts entered into by the liquidator on behalf of the company clearly fall within the category of liquidation expenses; the position with regard to contracts and leases which the liquidator has continued has given rise to more difficulty. Where the leased property has been used or contractual performance accepted for the purposes or convenience of the winding up, it has been held that the rent or payment should be treated as an expense of the winding up.[24] The expansion of the concept of a liability incurred as an expense of the liquidation to include liabilities incurred before the liquidation in respect of property afterwards retained by the liquidator for the benefit of the

---

16   Insolvency Rules 1986, rr 4.218, 4.219. An order of priority was first provided in 1890.
17   Items ahead of the liquidator's own remuneration include the fees of the Official Receiver, the costs of the petition, costs in connection with any provisional liquidation, certain costs in connection with the preparation of the statement of affairs and disbursements, including the allowable expenses of the liquidation committee. Necessary disbursements were held in Re Mesco Properties Ltd [1980] 1 WLR 96 to include tax on any post-liquidation profits. See also Re Toshoku Finance UK plc [2002] 1 WLR 671.
18   Re London Metallurgical [1895] 1 Ch 758.
19   Insolvency Rules 1986, r 4.220.
20   Insolvency Rules 1986, r 4.220(2).
21   [1990] BCLC 607.
22   [2002] 1 WLR 671.
23   See Chapter 32 in relation to the whole issue of the place of the costs of litigation undertaken by the officeholder in the hierarchy of distribution.
24   See Re Lundy Granite Co (1871) LR 6 Ch App 462; Re Oak Pitts Colliery Co (1882) 21 Ch D 322; Re ABC Coupler & Engineering Co [1970] 1 WLR 702; Re Downer [1974] 1 WLR 1460; Nolton Business Centres Ltd v The Common Council of the City of London [1996] 1 BCLC 400 (on apportionment as between pre and post-liquidation rates).

insolvent estate was considered by Lord Hoffmann in *Re Toshoku Finance UK plc*.[25] He observed that, although it was originally based upon a statutory discretion to allow a distress or execution against the company's assets, the courts had quickly recognised that its effect could be to promote a creditor from merely having a claim in the liquidation to having a right to payment in full. In *Re ABC Coupler & Engineering Co*,[26] Plowman J observed that 'it appears that, apart from the question of some special equity ... the test of liability for payment in full of rent accrued since the winding up is whether the liquidator has retained possession "for the convenience of the winding up" and that whether he has done so or not, depends upon his purpose in retaining possession'. A distinction has to be drawn between active 'preservation' of property and mere retention as a result of inaction.[27]

Preservation of the assets may require payment by the insolvency practitioner of a pre-insolvency debt, for example, to avoid forfeiture of a lease or distress; in this case, payment will be an expense of the insolvency. Public utility suppliers are no longer permitted to make payment of amounts owing in respect of pre-insolvency services a condition of continuing to supply;[28] the suppliers would have to prove as ordinary creditors for such payments. Such suppliers may, however, require a personal guarantee from the insolvency practitioner in respect of payment for services supplied during the insolvency; the insolvency practitioner would be entitled to an indemnity from the assets.

One question which has yet to be answered is the status of liability under the environment protection legislation;[29] it is not clear whether post-insolvency remedial work would be an expense of the insolvency. *Dicta* of Neuberger J in *Re Mineral Resources Ltd*[30] suggest that it would be.

In some cases, there may be successive insolvency practitioners. The Insolvency Rules 1986[31] provide that where a compulsory winding up follows immediately on a voluntary winding up, the remuneration of the voluntary liquidator and the costs and expenses of the voluntary liquidation allowed by the court will rank with the first category of expenses in the compulsory liquidation. In *Re Tony Rowse NMC Ltd*,[32] the court said that it would usually allow costs unless there was a good reason otherwise. In that case, the liquidator appointed in the voluntary liquidation had speedily given work which was not really necessary to an associate despite the fact that he knew the creditors were likely to seek a compulsory liquidation; the costs of the work were disallowed. In *Merrygold v Horton*,[33] the court held that where there were insufficient

---

25 [2002] 1 WLR 671. This case decided that corporation tax liabilities arising after the commencement of a liquidation are to be treated as an expense of the liquidation. See Milman (2000a).

26 [1970] 1 WLR 702.

27 *Re Linda Marie* [1989] BCLC 46.

28 Insolvency Act 1986, s 233, enacted in response to criticism by the Cork Committee (Chapter 33).

29 Environmental Protection Act 1990; Environment Act 1995. See the discussion in Goode, 1997, p 162.

30 [1999] 1 All ER 746. The Court of Appeal in *Re Celtic Extraction* [1999] 4 All ER 684 in partially overruling the case, on the basis that a waste management licence is capable of disclaimer, did not have to consider the status of expenses incurred under a licence which was not disclaimed. See Armour (2000).

31 Insolvency Rules 1986, r 4.129.

32 [1996] 2 BCLC 225.

33 [1998] 1 BCLC 401.

assets to meet the expenses of successive liquidators of a company in creditors' voluntary liquidation, their claims should abate rateably.

The Insolvency Rules 1986[34] also provide for the priority of expenses where there are successive bankruptcies.

4 PRE-PREFERENTIAL BANKRUPTCY DEBTS

Under s 348 of the Insolvency Act 1986, apprentices or articled clerks articled to the bankrupt may recover, ahead of the distribution of the estate, such part of any premium which was paid as the trustee thinks fit if their articles are discharged.[35] If the bankrupt was an officer of a Friendly Society, the trustees have a first right against his or her estate in respect of any money or property in his or her possession at the time of being adjudicated bankrupt.[36] The funeral expenses of a deceased insolvent are also pre-preferential.[37]

5 PREFERENTIAL CREDITORS

(a) Background history[38]

Employees have had a statutory preferential claim to payment of certain sums owing to them since the Bankruptcy Act 1825 and, before this, it is likely that they were treated as expenses of the insolvency as a matter of practice. Crown preference at common law is also of great antiquity. It was first given statutory expression in the insolvency legislation in the Bankruptcy Act 1849 in relation to assessed taxes; local rates were also given statutory preferential status at the same time. It was held in *Food Controller v Clark*[39] that the statutory provisions were exhaustive of Crown preference in the distribution of an insolvent's assets.

By the time of the Cork Report, the categories of Crown preferential debt had expanded greatly.[40] The Cork Committee received a considerable amount of critical comment on the existence of preferential debts and recommended major changes.[41] The Insolvency Act 1986 incorporated their recommendation that Crown preference should only be retained for taxes collected by insolvents rather than for those assessed on them; the rationale for retaining the preference for collected taxes was that it would be wrong for statutory provisions enacted for the more convenient collection of revenue to enure to the benefit of private creditors. The Insolvency Service in *A Review of Company Rescue and Business Reconstruction Mechanisms*[42] rehearsed the arguments

---

34 Insolvency Rules 1986, rr 6.225–6.228.
35 This is also guaranteed out of the National Insurance Fund.
36 Friendly Societies Act 1974, s 59.
37 Administration of Insolvent Estates of Deceased Persons Order 1986, Art 4(2).
38 See Keay and Walton (1998).
39 [1923] AC 647.
40 See the list at para 1402.
41 See Chapter 32.
42 Consultation document published in 1999 and final report of the Review Group in 2000. See also Keay and Walton (1999).

for the preferential status of the Crown. The two principal arguments in favour were that the Crown is an involuntary creditor and that Crown debts are debts due to the public purse. Little merit was seen in these arguments by either the Review Group or those who responded to the consultation. It was pointed out that the Crown is far from unique in being an involuntary creditor,[43] that it has remedies available to it (such as distress and the imposition of penalties) which are not available to other creditors and that it is in a much better position to absorb bad debts than the average trade creditor. The Review Group observed in the final report that resolution of the issue of principle regarding Crown preference in insolvency was ultimately a political choice and that abolition of preferential status would cost the Crown £60–90 million a year. The government decided that it would be equitable to remove Crown preference;[44] recognising that, without further change, this would mainly benefit holders of floating charges rather than ordinary creditors in a liquidation, it was also decided to ring-fence a proportion of the funds which would otherwise be available to a floating chargee. Section 251 of the Enterprise Act 2002 brings to an end the preferential status of any debt due to the Inland Revenue, Customs and Excise or in respect of social security contributions. Section 252 of the Enterprise Act 2002 inserts a new s 176A into the Insolvency Act 1986 which is intended to pass on to unsecured creditors the, approximately, 10% of all distributions which had been going preferentially to the Crown; this is considered in greater detail later in this chapter.

The provisions of the Insolvency Act 1986 conferring preferential status on the categories of debt set out in s 386 of and Sched 6 to the Insolvency Act 1986 are s 328 in relation to bankruptcy and s 175 in relation to liquidation. These categories are now restricted to contributions to occupational pension schemes, certain sums owing to employees and levies on coal and steel production.

(b) 'Relevant date'

The preferential debts are all defined by reference to 'the relevant date'. This is itself defined[45] as follows:

(i) In relation to a compulsory winding up, the earliest of the date of an administration order[46] immediately preceding the winding up, a resolution for voluntary liquidation, the appointment of a provisional liquidator or the making of the winding up order.

(ii) In relation to a voluntary winding up, the date of the resolution for winding up.

(iii) In relation to a bankruptcy, the date of the bankruptcy order unless an interim receiver was appointed between the presentation of the petition and the making of the order, in which case the relevant date will be the date of that appointment.

(iv) In relation to a company in receivership, the date of the appointment of the receiver.

---

43 Anyone with a claim arising from a tortious act of the insolvent is also an involuntary creditor.
44 White Paper, 2001, para 2.19.
45 By the Insolvency Act 1986, s 387.
46 There is no parallel provision in relation to an administration preceding a voluntary liquidation.

(v) In relation to an individual voluntary arrangement, the date of the interim order.

(vi) In relation to a company voluntary arrangement, the date of approval of the arrangement or, if the company is in administration, the date of the making of the administration order.

(c) Categories of preferential debt abolished by Enterprise Act 2002

The following categories of preferential debt will cease to have preferential status once s 251 of the Enterprise Act 2002 comes into force:

(i) Sums due to the Inland Revenue on account of deductions of income tax from emoluments paid during the 12 months before the relevant date. These deductions are those which the debtor was liable to make under the pay as you earn (PAYE) provisions of the Income and Corporation Taxes Act 1988 less the amount of the repayments of income tax which the debtor was liable to make during that period.

(ii) Debts due to Customs and Excise in respect of value added tax, insurance premium tax, landfill tax and climate change levy referable to the period of the six months before the relevant date, car tax and various gaming taxes which became due during the 12 months before the relevant date and excise duty on beer which became due during the six months before the relevant date.

(iii) Class 1 and Class 2 social security contributions which became due from the debtor in the 12 months before the relevant date and up to one year's Class 4 contributions due to the Inland Revenue.

(d) Remaining categories of preferential debt

As a result of the Enterprise Act 2002, there are now three categories of preferential debt, which all rank *pari passu* amongst themselves so that, if there is insufficient to pay all the preferential claims, each preferential creditor will receive the same proportion of what is owing as the others. The categories of preferential debt are as follows:

(i) Contributions to occupational pension schemes and state scheme premiums owed by the debtor to which Sched 4 to the Pension Schemes Act 1993 applies.

(ii) Remuneration[47] owed to current or past employees in respect of the four months before the relevant date up to the limit prescribed by the Secretary of State which is currently £800 per claimant. Accrued holiday remuneration in respect of any period of employment before the relevant date to a person whose employment by the debtor has been terminated, whether before, on or after that date. Amounts due under the Reserve Force (Safeguard of Employment) Act 1985 in respect of a default before the relevant date in obligations under that Act.

(iii) Sums due at the relevant date in respect of levies on the production of coal and steel referred to in the ECSC Treaty.

---

47   As defined in the Insolvency Act 1986, Sched 6, para 13. This includes wages or salary whether for time or for piecework or by way of commission. It also includes a number of other payments to which employees may be entitled under the employment protection and collective labour law legislation.

(e) Subrogation[48]

Where sums have been advanced to pay remuneration or holiday pay which would otherwise have been preferential payments, that loan becomes a preferential debt.[49] The Cork Committee observed[50] that the subrogated and preferential claims of banks and others who had advanced money for the purpose of paying wages were of far greater significance than the claims by the employees. Prior to 1986, this right of subrogation only existed in relation to corporate insolvency. The Committee was satisfied that the difference in treatment as between bankruptcy and liquidation could not be supported, but was divided as to whether this right of subrogation should be retained at all, acknowledging the argument that it sometimes encouraged banks to continue to support non-viable businesses. The majority of the Committee were persuaded by the argument that the banks might refuse to make the necessary loans were they to be denied this preferential status and that this might lead to the closure of viable businesses which might otherwise have continued trading. It did suggest that any repayments by the insolvent during the four month period should be set against the money advanced to pay the wages rather than against earlier advances; this suggestion was not accepted.

Where employees are owed amounts which both carry preferential status and are guaranteed, they will generally recover more of what is owed (since the monetary limit on guaranteed payments is higher) more quickly by claiming against the National Insurance Fund than from proving in the insolvency proceedings. The only circumstances in which an employee is likely to prove for preferential debts will be where the claim is for sums due for periods outside the Fund limits (eight weeks) or where the employee is still employed by the insolvent employer. If the employees have made claims on the National Insurance Fund, the Secretary of State will be subrogated to their claims including any priority in respect of preferential debts. The Cork Committee suggested, in a recommendation which was not accepted, that employees' claims should be dealt with through the state guarantee system and removed from the category of preferential debt so that the subrogated claim of the Department of Employment would be as an ordinary creditor. The Committee said[51] that 'we would emphasise that the priority accorded to employees in an insolvency is a social measure, intended to alleviate special financial hardship, and that in modern times the cost of meeting such social needs ought properly to be borne by the community'.

(f) Preferential debts and distress for rent

Where a landlord or other person has distrained on the goods of an insolvent within the three months before a compulsory liquidation or bankruptcy, preferential debts are charged on the goods distrained and the proceeds of selling them if the company's

---

48   Milman (2000c).
49   Insolvency Act 1986, Sched 6, para 11. *Re Primrose (Builders) Ltd* [1950] Ch 561; *Re Rampgill Mill Ltd* [1967] Ch 1138; *Re EJ Morel (1934) Ltd* [1962] Ch 21; *Re James R Rutherford & Sons Ltd* [1964] 3 All ER 137.
50   At para 1436.
51   At para 1435.

unencumbered assets are insufficient to satisfy the preferential debts in full.[52] In the case of a bankruptcy, the charge is over distrained goods recovered in respect of the six months' rent due before the bankruptcy rather than over goods in respect of an earlier period which will already have fallen in the bankrupt's estate under s 347(2) of the Insolvency Act 1986. The distrainor is subrogated to the rights of the company's preferential creditors to the extent that their claims are satisfied out of the distrained goods or the proceeds of sale.

This does not apply in a voluntary liquidation[53] in respect of which the only limitation is that the court may order that distress shall not be levied or completed after the passing of the winding up resolution.[54] The court will usually interfere where the landlord tries to distrain after the liquidation has commenced in respect of arrears which have arisen before the commencement of the liquidation.

6 PREFERENTIAL DEBTS AND FLOATING CHARGES

The holders of floating charges have been postponed to preferential creditors since 1897. The current provision is s 175(2)(b) of the Insolvency Act 1986, which provides that preferential debts, so far as the assets of the company available for payment of general creditors are insufficient to meet them, have priority over the claims of holders of debentures secured by, or holders of, any floating charge[55] created by the company, and shall be paid out of property subject to that charge.

Creditors secured by a floating charge are entitled to an indemnity from the general assets of the company; this will have no relevance where the floating charge is over the entire undertaking. If a floating charge crystallises before the company goes into liquidation as a result of the appointment of a receiver, claimants in respect of debts which would be preferential on a liquidation at that date have priority for payment out of the assets subject to the charge.[56] If the company then goes into liquidation, another set of preferential claims will arise in respect of that later relevant date. Where a liquidation precedes a receivership, the only set of preferential claims will be that arising at the start of the liquidation.

As has already been seen, the postponement of the floating charge to the preferential creditors also has the effect of giving priority to the expenses of the liquidation.[57] Once s 176A of the Insolvency Act 1986 comes into force, the ring-fenced proportion of the assets will also have to be distributed to the unsecured creditors before a distribution can be made to any post-commencement floating charge-holder.[58]

---

52 Insolvency Act 1986, s 176 (liquidation); s 347(3) (bankruptcy).

53 *Herbert Berry Associates Ltd v IRC* [1978] 1 All ER 161.

54 *Re Roundwood Colliery Co* [1897] 1 Ch 373. The liquidator has the power to apply to the court for such an order under the Insolvency Act 1986, s 112.

55 Defined by the Insolvency Act 1986, s 251 as a charge which, as created, was a floating charge. The question of whether and, if so, when the charge crystallised is not, therefore, relevant.

56 Insolvency Act 1986, s 40. See Chapter 6 above.

57 *Re Barleycorn* [1970] Ch 465; *Re Leyland DAF* [2002] 1 BCLC 571.

58 See below.

In certain circumstances, problems of circularity of priority can give rise to difficulty in deciding the order of payment. This happens where a floating charge has priority over a subsequent fixed charge, which in turn has priority over the preferential debts. In *Re Woodroffes (Musical Instruments) Ltd*,[59] it was held that the floating chargee should be treated as subrogated to the rights of the fixed chargee to the extent of the sum secured by the floating charge, so that the floating chargee obtained priority over preferential creditors in right of the fixed charge. In *Re Portbase Clothing Ltd*,[60] Chadwick J disputed the correctness of this analysis and preferred instead to follow the Australian case of *Waters v Widdows*[61] in which it was held that, as a matter of statutory policy, the fixed chargee by subordinating his claim to that of the floating chargee also subordinated them to the preferential creditors.

The question of what happens when a receiver is appointed under a floating charge which is subordinate to another floating charge has been considered above.[62]

7 ORDINARY CREDITORS

Section 252 of the Enterprise Act 2002 provides for a new s 176A to be inserted into the Insolvency Act 1986. This section applies where a floating charge, created after this provision first comes into force (expected to be during September 2003), relates to property of a company in liquidation, administration or receivership. Section 176A(2) provides that a prescribed part of the company's net property (defined in sub-s (6) as the property which would, but for this section, be available for satisfaction of claims of floating chargeholders)[63] will be made available for the satisfaction of unsecured debts and will not be distributed to the holder of the floating charge unless it exceeds the amount required for satisfaction of the unsecured debts. Section 176A(2) will not apply if the net property of the company is less than the prescribed minimum (the draft Insolvency Act 1986 (Prescribed Part) Order 2003 sets this at £10,000) and the officeholder thinks that the cost of making a distribution to unsecured creditors would be disproportionate to the benefits. Where the net property is above the prescribed minimum, s 176A(5) will allow the officeholder to ask the consent of the court to disapply s 176A(2) where the cost of making a distribution would be disproportionate to the benefits; this might be the case if there were a very large number of unsecured creditors.

The rules for calculating the prescribed part of the net property will be contained in secondary legislation and the government has promised wide consultation. During the passage of the legislation through Parliament, it was suggested that the prescribed minimum might be in the region of £5,000 and that the ring fence would be set on a sliding scale. For example, it might be provided that the ring fence is 50% of the first £10,000 available for distribution to the floating chargeholder; then 10% until the net property reaches the value of £1,000,000; and thereafter the figure should be reduced

---

59 [1986] Ch 366.

60 [1993] Ch 388.

61 [1984] VR 503.

62 See Chapter 6.

63 Ie, having taken account of the expenses of the liquidation, the preferential debts and any pre-commencement floating chargeholders.

to 5%. Section 176A of the Insolvency Act 1986 has, however, been drafted in sufficiently wide terms to allow other methods of calculation to be prescribed.[63a]

Section 176A of the Insolvency Act 1986 will finally implement a version of the 'Ten Percent Fund' recommended by the Cork Committee.[64] The suggestion met fierce opposition from the banks at the time and the suggestion was not carried through into the government's Green or White Papers, nor into the Insolvency Bill introduced into Parliament.[65] Attempts were made to insert the measure into the legislation as it went through Parliament but these failed. The banks successfully claimed that, if it was implemented, they would be forced to raise interest rates and refuse to lend to riskier businesses and that, therefore, the measure would damage the very creditors it was designed to benefit.

The ordinary creditors are a residual category of creditors in that they encompass all those who have not been specifically allocated to some other category of creditor.

8 POST-INSOLVENCY INTEREST[66]

Interest will be payable on debts proved in the insolvency at the official rate of interest.[67] Interest on both preferential and ordinary debts will be paid out of any surplus remaining after payment of the ordinary creditors. Interest will rank equally irrespective of the status of the debt on which it is payable.

9 DEFERRED CREDITORS[68]

A number of provisions have the effect of deferring the claims of those who have been involved in an insolvent business at less than arms' length. If money is advanced in return for payments contingent on or varying with the profits of the business by a lender who does not thereby become a partner in the business, that lender is postponed to all the other creditors in the event of the borrower's insolvency.[69] If a company is under an obligation to repurchase or redeem shares at the start of a liquidation, those claims are postponed to all other debts and liabilities of the company except those due to members in their character as such.[70] Sums due to a member in his or her character as member may not be claimed in competition with any other creditor who is not a member of the company.[71] The House of Lords has

---

63a The draft Order provides that the prescribed part will be 50% of the net property not exceeding £10,000 and 20% of the excess subject to a maximum of £600,000.

64 See paras 1538–49. See Milman (2000d); Milman (1999).

65 Described graphically by Carruthers and Halliday, 1998, pp 339–46.

66 Insolvency Act 1986, s 189 (liquidation); s 328 (bankruptcy).

67 The greater of the rate specified in the Judgments Act 1838, s 17 on the day on which the insolvency regime started and the rate applicable to the debt apart from the insolvency.

68 Insolvency Rules 1986, r 12.3(2A).

69 Partnership Act 1890, ss 2(3), 3.

70 Companies Act 1985, s 178.

71 Insolvency Act 1986, s 74.

held[72] that sums due to a member in his or her character as a member are restricted to those sums falling due under and by virtue of the statutory contract contained in s 14 of the Companies Act 1985; a member having a cause of action independent of the statutory contract will be in the same position as other creditors. Sums owed to those found liable for fraudulent or wrongful trading may also be deferred to other claims against the company.[73] As noted above,[74] English law has not developed a doctrine of equitable subordination as has happened in the United States.

A similar principle of deferring the claims of those closely associated with the insolvent can be seen in the provision of bankruptcy law which defers loans by spouses. Section 329 of the Insolvency Act 1986 provides that bankruptcy debts[75] owed in respect of credit provided by a person who was the bankrupt's spouse at the commencement of the bankruptcy[76] will rank in priority after the ordinary debts and interest on the preferential and ordinary debts.

10 ATTEMPTS TO CONTRACT OUT OF THE STATUTORY SCHEME[77]

The *pari passu* principle is mandatory and strikes down agreements which have as their effect on an insolvency an unequal distribution (except as provided for by the law) amongst the ordinary creditors.[78] Agreements may seek to achieve this effect by excluding or altering the set-off rules which would otherwise apply or by subordinating the right of a debtor or debtors to be paid *pari passu* with the other ordinary creditors. There has been more success with the latter category of agreement than the former.[79]

National Westminster Bank Ltd v Halesowen Presswork & Assemblies Ltd[80] is a leading case on this area. This was a case in which it had been agreed during attempts to rescue an ailing company that the company's overdrawn account would be frozen and that a new account would be opened which would remain in credit; the bank would not set the two accounts off against each other. The company subsequently went into liquidation and the House of Lords held that an agreement of this sort could not operate to exclude the rules on set-off contained in the insolvency legislation. These were rules of public policy for the orderly administration of the assets of an insolvent rather than private rights which creditors would be free to alter. The only way to have achieved the desired result would have been to open the second account with a different bank.

---

72 *Soden v British Commonwealth Holdings* [1997] 4 All ER 353. The shareholder was claiming damages for negligent misrepresentation which had induced the purchase of the shares; this was held not to be owed in its character as a member.

73 Insolvency Act 1986, s 215(4).

74 Chapter 31.

75 And interest on them since the start of the bankruptcy.

76 Their status at the time the credit was provided is irrelevant.

77 See Wood in Gough, 1996, Chapter 40; Oditah (1992); Nolan (1995); Ferran, 1999, Chapter 16.

78 *Ex p Mackay* (1873) 8 Ch App 643.

79 See *Hamilton v Law Debenture Trustees Ltd* [2001] 2 BCLC 159 for the treatment of subordinated claims for voting purposes in creditors' meetings.

80 [1972] AC 785.

A set-off agreement which provides for set-off in circumstances not provided for by the insolvency legislation will be equally ineffective; those with claims against the company must be paid *pari passu* and the quantum of the claim is to be established in accordance with the legislation. An example was the case of *British Eagle International Air Lines Ltd v Compagnie Nationale Air France*.[81] The International Air Transport Association ('IATA') had set up a clearing house system for the monthly settlement of debits and credits arising as between members. A balance would be struck between the total sum owing to a particular member in respect of services supplied by it for all other members and the total owing by that member in respect of services supplied by all other members. The House of Lords said that debits and credits cleared through the system before the commencement of a liquidation would bind the liquidator of a member, but that the liquidator could recover uncleared credits owing to the company and that members with uncleared debits against the company would each have to prove for them. Each member could set off the sums owing to it individually by the company against its individual indebtedness to the company.

The Cork Committee recommended that a creditor should be permitted to agree in advance to waive his or her right to invoke set-off, but the recommendation was not accepted. It has, however, been held in *Re Maxwell Communications Corp (No 2)*[82] that a subordination agreement, in which a creditor agrees to subordinate his or her claim to that of others, will be effective. Vinelott J held that the principle for which the *Halesowen* case is authority only prevented one creditor from gaining an advantage over another and that a subordination agreement does not have that effect. It has also been pointed out[83] that creditors are expressly permitted[84] to assign a right of dividend in a liquidation to other creditors; it would be strange if the agreement pursuant to which such an assignment were made were to be held void.

---

81   [1975] 1 WLR 758.
82   [1994] 1 BCLC 1.
83   Goode, 1997, p 146.
84   By the Insolvency Rules 1986, r 11.11(1).

PART VI
AN INTRODUCTION TO ISSUES OF
CROSS-BORDER INSOLVENCY

CHAPTER 35

AN INTRODUCTION TO CROSS-BORDER ISSUES

1 INTRODUCTION

Many insolvencies (particularly, and increasingly, corporate insolvencies) have international aspects to them in that either the assets or the creditors, or both, are in more than one jurisdiction. Whilst the most efficient and, therefore, asset-maximising approach would be for the insolvency to be dealt with in one set of proceedings with universal effect, there are tremendous problems in achieving such an outcome. Jurisdictions adopt different approaches to the question of what sort of connection with the jurisdiction the parties to litigation there should have. It can be difficult to achieve a genuinely collective outcome as between all the creditors where the assets are widely dispersed between jurisdictions in which insolvency proceedings take effect at differing times, if at all, so that creditors in some jurisdictions are able to continue individual actions. The insolvency laws of the various jurisdictions differ considerably both in matters of principle and matters of detail so that the outcome for any particular creditor may be significantly different depending upon which set of rules determines his or her claim. There can be huge difficulties in deciding who should control the proceedings and what rules should be applied. A couple of examples from recent global insolvencies serve to demonstrate the nature of the issues which may arise.

Re BCCI (No 10)[1] is an example of the how two systems may have fundamentally different distributional rules. Liquidations were being conducted in England and in Luxembourg, with the English liquidation ancillary to the main one. The English liquidators wished to transfer the funds at their disposal to the foreign liquidators to facilitate worldwide distribution. Luxembourg law does not recognise the right to set-off provided by insolvency law in the UK. The court held that the liquidators would have to retain sufficient funds to satisfy those creditors in the English liquidation who would have benefited from rights of set-off.

The simultaneous administration and Chapter 11 bankruptcy in the United States of Maxwell Communication Corp plc threw into sharp relief the many differences between the two systems, both of principle and of detail. The agreement arrived at with creditors in both jurisdictions had to cope with numerous differences of detail between the requirements of the English scheme of arrangement and the US plan of reorganisation. For example, Chapter 11 debars new creditors from coming forward and claiming in an insolvency after a fixed date, whereas English law allows creditors to catch up with distributions which they have missed. Chapter 11 converts claims into dollars at the time of filing, whereas English law converts claims into sterling at the start of the scheme. United States priority and English preferential creditors are defined differently. Under Chapter 11, creditors can vote by post and approval needs a two-thirds majority, whereas in England, they must vote at the meeting and the required majority is three-quarters. A major difference in principle was encountered by the administrators in their attempt to set aside various payments made to creditors

---

1   [1996] BCC 980. See Fletcher (1997a).

immediately prior to the administration which had the effect of putting those creditors in a better position than the other unsecured creditors.[2] As has been seen,[3] English law requires that the insolvency practitioner establish that the company was influenced by the desire to prefer in making the payments, whereas under the United States Bankruptcy Code, the question of intention is irrelevant.

This chapter will consider briefly[4] the issues of English jurisdiction over insolvencies with a foreign aspect to them, English recognition of overseas insolvencies and attempts at achieving international co-operation.

2   THE JURISDICTION OF ENGLISH COURTS[5]

(a) Insolvent foreign individual

A bankruptcy petition may not be presented to the court[6] unless the debtor is domiciled[7] in England and Wales or is personally present in the jurisdiction on the day when the petition is presented or has at any time in the three years ending on that day been ordinarily resident,[8] has had a place of residence or has carried on business[9] in the jurisdiction.[10] Where the debtor is normally absent from the jurisdiction, it may prove difficult to serve a statutory demand.

An individual can only be adjudicated bankrupt if he or she owes debts recognised by English law. If he or she has been discharged from the debts as a result of proceedings in another jurisdiction and that discharge is recognised by English law, he or she will not be a debtor. English courts will only recognise the discharge if it was granted in the country whose law is the proper law of the obligation or is recognised by that law. In *Gibbs v La Société Industrielle*,[11] for example, the English courts refused to recognise discharge of a debt granted by the French courts where they considered that the proper law of the obligation was English. The individual will also not be a debtor for the purposes of being made bankrupt if the debt is based on a foreign judgment not recognised in this country.

---

2   *Barclays Bank Plc v Homan* [1992] BCC 757 (CA). See Fletcher (1997b).

3   See Chapter 30.

4   For greater detail on this area, see Fletcher, 2002, Part III; Fletcher, 1997; Smart, 1998; Ziegel (ed), 1994; Rajak, 1993, Part IV. Useful articles include Fletcher (2000b); Fletcher (1999), pp 20–22; Fletcher (2000c) pp 57, 68.

5   The Brussels Convention on the Jurisdiction and Enforcement of Judgments (implemented by the Civil Jurisdiction and Judgments Act 1982) does not apply to insolvencies.

6   Insolvency Act 1986, s 265. See *North v Skipton BS* (2002) unreported, 7 June for a case in which a bankruptcy order was annulled after the court decided that the debtor was not within s 265.

7   See Dicey and Morris, 2000. *Udny v Udny* (1869) LR 1 Sc & D 441.

8   *Re Bright* (1903) 19 TLR 203.

9   See *Theophile v Solicitor General* [1950] AC 186; *Re Bird* [1962] 2 All ER 406; *Re Brauch* [1978] Ch 316; *Re a Debtor* [1992] Ch 554.

10 For a recent case in which a bankruptcy order was annulled on the basis that the debtor was neither domiciled, resident nor carrying on a business in the jurisdiction, see *North v Skipton Building Society* (2002) unreported, 7 June (ChD).

11 (1890) 25 QBD 399.

The court's jurisdiction to make a bankruptcy order is discretionary, so even where the above requirements are met, the court may still decide that it would be more appropriate for insolvency proceedings to take place elsewhere. In practice, the courts will refuse to make an order if the debtor has no assets in the jurisdiction.[12] It is no obstacle[13] to the making of an order that concurrent proceedings are pending abroad or that the debtor has already been adjudicated bankrupt abroad.

(b) Insolvent foreign company

Any company incorporated in England and Wales will be treated as a domestic company subject to liquidation under Part IV of the Insolvency Act 1986 regardless of where its business is carried out. This is because the English courts use the 'state of incorporation' doctrine to decide questions of domicile and nationality rather than 'real seat' doctrine used by some jurisdictions.

A company which was incorporated abroad may be wound up under Part V of the Insolvency Act 1986 as an unregistered company[14] on the basis that it is dissolved, or has ceased to carry on business, or is carrying on business only for the purpose of winding up its affairs, or is unable to pay its debts, or where the court is of the opinion that it is just and equitable that it should be wound up. Given that English law recognises the dissolution of a company under the laws of its country of incorporation, this means that, in the case of a company which has been dissolved, strictly there is nothing left to be wound up and that the English assets of the dissolved company will have passed to the Crown as *bona vacantia*. The courts have adopted the approach that in such a case, the dissolved foreign company is deemed to be revived in order to undergo winding up in this country;[15] the Crown's title to the goods is treated as defeasible on such a revival.[16]

Section 225 of the Insolvency Act 1986 provides specifically that an overseas company carrying on business in Great Britain may be wound up here even though it has been dissolved under the laws of its country of incorporation.[17]

There is no statutory explanation of when the courts should exercise their wide jurisdiction and order a winding up; the relevant principles have to be extracted from the case law. There will have to be some connection with this jurisdiction before the court will agree to make an order.[18] The company need not have a place of business here,[19] but there has usually needed to be either assets of the company within the

---

12 Smart (1989).

13 Subject to what is said below about the effect of the EU Insolvency Regulation.

14 Insolvency Act 1986, s 221(5).

15 *Russian and English Bank v Baring Bros* [1936] AC 405.

16 *Russian and English Bank v Baring Bros* [1936] AC 405; also *Re Azoff-Don Commercial Bank* [1954] 1 Ch 315; *Re Banque Industrielle de Moscou* [1952] 1 Ch 919.

17 This was added to the legislation in 1929 but in fact adds little to the common law position which the courts have arrived at in relation to the predecessors of the Insolvency Act 1986, s 221(5).

18 *Re Real Estate Development Co* [1991] BCLC 210 is an example of a case in which the court refused to make an order on the basis that there was insufficient connection with the jurisdiction. *Banco Nacional de Cuba v Cosmos* [2000] 1 BCLC 813 is another.

19 *Banque des Marchands de Moscou v Kindersley* [1951] 1 Ch 112 (CA).

jurisdiction or one or more persons concerned with the distribution of the assets over whom jurisdiction is exercisable.[20] The assets may be of any nature so that a claim against an insurer[21] or some right of action maintainable here with a reasonable possibility of success[22] will suffice. The assets need not be distributable by the liquidator to the creditors; it will suffice that a claim may be made against a third party such as an insurer under the Third Parties (Rights Against Insurers) Act 1930 or, by an employee, against the National Insurance Fund. The Court of Appeal in *Stocznia Gdanska SA v Latreefers Inc (No 2)*[23] held[24] that there were three basic requirements before the court would make a winding up order. There had to be a sufficient connection with England and Wales which might, but not necessarily had to, consist of assets within the jurisdiction; there had to be the reasonable possibility, if a winding up order was made, of benefit to those applying for the winding up order; and one or more persons interested in the distribution of assets of the company had to be persons over whom the court could exercise jurisdiction. The existence of potential claims for misfeasance and fraudulent and wrongful trading sufficed to demonstrate a sufficient connection.

The court may decide to stay proceedings in this country on the basis that foreign proceedings constitute a more appropriate forum. It may also make a winding up order with the object of conducting an ancillary winding up.[25] An ancillary liquidation involves the application of the rules of English insolvency law[26] to the realisation of the English assets and the assembling of a list of the creditors who prove in the English insolvency.

(c) Entitlement of foreign claimants

The English court will give equal effect to claims by foreign creditors with the exception of claims by foreign states to enforce tax debts.[27]

(d) Assets of the insolvent abroad

English adjudication purports to have universal application regardless of the location of the property. In relation to property outside the jurisdiction, the insolvency practitioner will have to submit a claim under local law and will be dependent on the local courts recognising the English ruling and his or her authority.[28] Under a general

---

20 *Re Compania Merabello San Nicholas SA* [1973] 1 Ch 75.
21 *Re Compania Merabello San Nicholas SA* [1973] 1 Ch 75.
22 *Re Eloc Electro-Optieck and Communicatie BV* [1981] 2 All ER 1111.
23 [2001] 2 BCLC 116.
24 Observing that there had been some permissible reformulation of the law over the last 40 years and approving the approach adopted in *International Westminster Bank v Okeanos* [1988] Ch 210 and *Re Real Estate Development Co* [1991] BCLC 210.
25 See the discussion of the history of ancillary liquidation in *Re BCCI (SA) (No 10)* [1996] 4 All ER 796.
26 In *Re BCCI (SA) (No 10)* [1996] 4 All ER 796, it was held that there was no discretion to disapply provisions of English law in an ancillary liquidation.
27 *Taylor v Government of India* [1955] AC 491.
28 *Re Maudslay, Sons and Field* [1900] 1 Ch 602. The Polly Peck International plc insolvency was an example of a case in which English administrators were unable to take control of the many assets of the company which were in Northern Cyprus. See, eg, *Polly Peck International plc v Nadir (No 2)* [1992] 4 All ER 769 (CA).

rule of private international law, the courts of one country will not enforce a foreign judgment or order which is in substance an order for the payment of foreign taxes. Courts tend to be readier to allow access to the debtor's movable property than to the immovable property. The insolvent will be under a duty to assist in the recovery of the property.

(e) Creditor pursuing insolvent in another jurisdiction

Where an insolvent has assets in another jurisdiction, it would be possible for a creditor to seek redress there in a way which could obtain a greater percentage of what was owing than would be obtained by other creditors who were only able to claim in the English insolvency.[29] This would be contrary to the *pari passu* rule and the courts will do what they can to prevent this happening. There is no objection to creditors enforcing overseas security rights against the insolvent.[30]

The English courts have no power to compel a foreign court to abandon proceedings,[31] although it may agree to do so.[32] However, a creditor who is subject to the jurisdiction of the English courts can be restrained from bringing or continuing any proceedings abroad in the courts' inherent power to restrain foreign proceedings.[33] If the creditor is not subject to the *'in personam'* jurisdiction of the English courts nothing can be done unless and until the creditor seeks to prove in the English insolvency. A creditor seeking to prove in the English insolvency can be compelled to bring sums recovered abroad into the common fund for the benefit of creditors generally under the hotchpot rule.[34] In *Banco de Portugal v Waddell*,[35] the appellants, who had received a dividend in Portugal, sought to prove in the English bankruptcy. The House of Lords held that they could only receive a dividend after all the other creditors had received an amount equal to the dividend they had received in the Portuguese proceedings.

3   RECOGNITION OF FOREIGN PROCEEDINGS BY ENGLISH COURTS

Representatives of a foreign insolvency may seek to take action through the English courts in an attempt to preserve or realise assets subject to English jurisdiction. During the time that it takes the foreign representative to establish entitlement to the action sought, irrevocable individual action can continue to be taken against the assets of the

---

29 See, for example, the factual background to *Re Buckingham International plc* (1997) *The Times*, 20 November, in which judgment creditors of an English company noticed that assets of the debtor included debts due in the US, obtained an order in Florida recognising the English debt and sought to garnishee the debts. In this case, the US court granted the English liquidator a stay and, in effect, referred the case to the English court for decision.

30 *Re Oriental Inland Steam Co* (1874) LR 9 Ch App 557.

31 *Re Vocalion (Foreign) Ltd* [1932] 2 Ch 196.

32 *Re BCCI (No 10)* [1996] 4 All ER 796.

33 *Bank of Tokyo v Karoon* [1987] 1 AC 45; *SN Industrielle Aerospatiale v Lee Kui Jak* [1987] AC 871; *Re Maxwell Communications Corporation plc (No 2)* [1992] BCC 757.

34 See the Privy Council discussion of the hotchpot rule in *Cleaver v Delta American Reinsurance Co* [2001] 2 WLR 1202.

35 (1880) 5 App Cas 161.

debtor to the detriment of the creditors in the insolvency. The risk of this happening and the costs involved in pursuing action in the English courts will frequently be sufficient to deter the foreign representative from attempting to pursue action of this sort and, if possible, to proceed by opening insolvency proceedings in England.

As a matter of common law, the English courts will recognise bankruptcy proceedings in the country of domicile of a bankrupt and also in other situations where the bankrupt was properly subject to the jurisdiction of the courts of the country in which he or she was made bankrupt. Where the bankruptcy is recognised, the trustee will acquire title to moveable property in England and court may allow the sale of immovable property for the benefit of creditors.

The court will recognise liquidations where they are conducted or recognised by the country of incorporation of the insolvent company where the company has submitted to the jurisdiction of the foreign court[36] or where the company has carried on business within the foreign jurisdiction. There is no automatic vesting of title to the corporate assets in a foreign liquidator (since there is no automatic transfer of assets in an English liquidation), but the court has a discretion to give the liquidator the power to deal with the assets unless there is an ancillary English winding up taking place.

Claims to assets in England will still be subject to any existing rights of creditors under English law. In *Galbraith v Grimshaw*,[37] the House of Lords held that a judgment creditor who had commenced garnishee proceedings in England in order to satisfy a judgment obtained against his debtor in Scotland was not to be deprived of the fruits of this attachment by reason of the judgment debtor's subsequently becoming subject to sequestration in Scotland.

Insolvency proceedings will not be recognised where they are offensive to English public policy or are in breach of natural justice. Insolvency proceedings which amount to nothing more than an attempt to enforce the criminal or taxation laws of another country will not be recognised.[38] The courts will refuse to assist a foreign court where the English creditors will be unfairly discriminated against in the foreign proceedings; this was demonstrated in *Felixstowe Dock and Railway Co v USL Inc*.[39] USL, which was a United States shipping company incorporated in Delaware which carried on business in many countries including England, was in Chapter 11 bankruptcy.[40] The New York court had issued an order purporting to be a worldwide restraint on legal action against USL. The plaintiffs proceeded to seek, and obtain, Mareva injunctions in England preventing USL from removing its assets from the jurisdiction. Hirst J refused USL's application to have the injunctions set aside and the assets repatriated to the US on a number of bases. Amongst the factors contributing to his decision was the intention of USL to withdraw from the European market so that it was unlikely that the English creditors would benefit from the worldwide reorganisation. In the course of his judgment, he observed that the usual practice was to regard the courts of the place of incorporation as the principal forum for controlling a winding up of a company but that, in so far as the company had assets in England, it would be normal

---

36   *Re International Power Industries NV* [1985] BCLC 128.

37   [1910] AC 508.

38   See *Government of India v Taylor* [1955] AC 491; *Peter Buchanan v McVey* [1955] AC 516; *Re State of Norway's Application (Nos 1 and 2)* [1989] 1 All ER 745.

39   [1989] QB 360.

40   This is not a liquidation, but similar recognition issues arise.

to carry out an ancillary winding up in England in accordance with English rules. He held that the assets should remain in England pending distribution in an ancillary winding up.[41]

4 INTERNATIONAL CO-OPERATION

(a) Introduction

Attempts at obtaining international agreement about the method of dealing with cross-border insolvency go back to the 19th century,[42] but it is only relatively recently, with the increasing recognition that an agreed jurisdictional framework is the way forward rather than an attempt to harmonise the substantive law, that progress has been made in putting formal co-operation structures in place. At the same time, there has been evidence of a willingness of English courts to consider co-operation with the courts and officeholders of other jurisdictions on an *ad hoc* basis. The simultaneous administration order proceedings in England and Chapter 11 bankruptcy in the United States of Maxwell Communications Corp plc are much cited as an example of what can be achieved by judicial co-operation.[43] *Barclays Bank v Homan*,[44] which was heard in the course of this saga and evidences this co-operation, involved an application by the plaintiff for the court to prevent the administrator from taking proceedings in the US to set aside certain payments.[45] Hoffmann J refused to grant an injunction, observing that it could serve no purpose except to antagonise the US court and prejudice co-operation. He said that if the US judge did not think there was sufficient connection with the US jurisdiction, she would dismiss the action and, if she thought otherwise, the action would be allowed to go ahead despite any injunction.

There are now two formal co-operation mechanisms which form part of English insolvency law. Section 426 of the Insolvency Act 1986 provides for English courts to assist with insolvency processes in other parts of the UK and in a number of other, mainly Commonwealth, designated jurisdictions. The European Council Regulation on Insolvency Proceedings, which came into force on 31 May 2002, provides a jurisdictional framework for dealing with cross-border insolvency within the European Union. In addition, the UNCITRAL Model Law has the potential to provide a similar framework of wider application.

---

41 Professor Ian Fletcher argues in [1993] Insolv Intelligence 10 that the *Felixstowe* case was a low point in judicial comity and that in subsequent cases, particularly those connected with the Maxwell case, a greater spirit of co-operation has been apparent.

42 See Graham (1989). See Prior in Rajak (ed), 1993, Chapter 14 for a survey of the insolvency treaties in existence at the beginning of the 1990s. He identified three main multilateral treaties between the Nordic countries, a group of South American countries and a group of Central American countries.

43 See Ziegel (ed), 1994, Chapter 25. See Homan (2002) for the view that it is better to avoid the need for such co-operation by endeavouring to have a primary insolvency proceeding in one jurisdiction only.

44 [1992] BCC 757.

45 See above in the introductory section of this chapter.

(b) Section 426 of the Insolvency Act 1986

Section 426(4) of the Insolvency Act 1986[46] provides that the courts having jurisdiction in relation to insolvency law in any part of the UK 'shall' assist the courts (not the officeholder) having the corresponding jurisdiction in any other part of the UK or any relevant country or territory. This latter category is defined[47] to denote the Channel Islands, the Isle of Man and any country or territory designated for the purposes of this section by the Secretary of State by order made by statutory instrument.[48]

Early examples of co-operation under the provision were *Re Dallhold Estates (UK) Pty Ltd*,[49] in which Chadwick J made an administration order pursuant to a letter of request from the Australian Federal Court, and *Re BCCI (No 2)*,[50] in which declarations under ss 213, 214 and 238 of the Insolvency Act 1986 were made at the request of the Grand Court of the Cayman Islands. In *Re Focus Insurance Co Ltd*,[51] however, the court refused to make an order for the assistance of foreign liquidators where the relief sought (examination of a former director of the company in liquidation in relation to the existence of English assets) could be obtained by the English trustee in bankruptcy, since this would potentially subject the defendant to having to go through the same process of investigation twice.

The Court of Appeal had its first opportunity to consider the operation of s 426 of the Insolvency Act 1986 in *Hughes v Hannover Ruckversicherungs-Aktiengesellschaft*,[52] in which it had to consider a request by the Bermudan court for worldwide injunctive relief. It confirmed that the wording of s 426(5), which empowers the court to apply the insolvency law 'applicable by either court in relation to comparable matters falling within its jurisdiction', gives the court a discretion to exercise a jurisdiction that it might not otherwise have had.[53] The English court may use all its general powers and jurisdiction whether or not conferred on it by virtue of 'insolvency law' as defined in s 426(10) of the Insolvency Act 1986. The court considered the operation of the word 'shall' in s 426(4) and held that the English court did still have a discretion to refuse to assist, but that where it was being asked to apply a measure of 'insolvency law', it should grant the assistance requested provided it could properly do so. Where the assistance requested was a measure not having its source in insolvency law as defined within the section (as was the case here), the court had a greater degree of discretion.

---

46   Which is the successor to the Bankruptcy Act 1914, s 122 (itself the last in a series of provisions dating back to 1869) which applied identical provisions to 'British courts' in relation to individual insolvency. Section 426 was enacted to meet the Cork Committee's recommendation (in Chapter 49) that the provision should be modernised and remodelled and extended to corporate insolvency.

47   By the Insolvency Act 1986, s 426(10).

48   SI 1986/2123, SI 1996/253. The vast majority of countries designated are Commonwealth members. The US is not designated despite the fact that s 304 of its bankruptcy code allows assistance in the other direction.

49   [1992] BCC 394.

50   [1994] 2 BCLC 636.

51   [1996] BCC 659.

52   [1997] 1 BCLC 497. See Fletcher (1997b); Moss (1999).

53   Such as the ability of the court in *Re Dallhold* to make an administration order in respect of a foreign company. In *Re Television Trade Rentals Ltd* (2002) unreported, 19 February (ChD), the court enabled an Isle of Man company to make a proposal for a CVA which might not have been possible without relying on s 426.

The Court of Appeal had a further opportunity to consider s 426(5) in *England v Smith*.[54] This concerned a request by the Supreme Court of South Australia that the liquidator of an Australian company sent a letter of request for the examination of an English accountant who had been involved in the audits of its accounts. The judge at first instance, having heard expert evidence, found that a judge in Australia, applying the relevant Australian legislation, would have exercised his or her discretion so as to order examination, but held that on a comparable application under s 236 of the 1986 Act, an examination would have been held to be oppressive and would not have been ordered. He therefore refused the application. The Court of Appeal allowed the liquidator's appeal,[55] on the basis that once the judge had chosen to apply the law of Australia, he should have directed himself by reference to the principles and practice of the Australian court, in accordance with which it was the judicial duty of the person conducting the examination to avoid any oppression of the examinee. Since the requesting court had exercised its discretion to seek the examination, it was not for the English court to perform that task again unless it was shown that the requesting court had been ignorant of some material fact or that subsequent events had undermined the justification for the request. Morritt LJ observed that there was an issue of comity involved and that it was plain that one object of the section was to provide for some form of reciprocal assistance for insolvencies with an international dimension, confined to countries or territories with insolvency laws corresponding to the Insolvency Act 1986 which the Secretary of State has determined in his or her discretion to designate. Morritt LJ said that it would be inconsistent with such a framework that the Companies Court, having elected to apply the insolvency law of the requesting court, should then stigmatise either the substantive law or the exercise by the requesting court of the jurisdiction thereby conferred as oppressive.[56]

(c) The European Council Regulation on Insolvency Proceedings[57]

This Regulation, which came into force on 31 May 2002, is intended to simplify the position in relation to reciprocal recognition and enforcement of insolvency proceedings within the EU. It lays down rules to determine the state in which insolvency proceedings should be opened, provides for the mutual recognition and enforcement of judgments given in those insolvency proceedings, creates certain uniform conflict of laws rules for insolvency proceedings and guarantees information for creditors and their right to lodge claims. There is no attempt to harmonise the substantive laws of the individual Member States. As a Regulation, it has direct effect in the Member States without the need for specific implementation. It applies to both corporate and individual proceedings of a collective nature, whether intended for

---

54 [2001] Ch 419. See Editorial 'International insolvency' [2000] Co Lawyer 69. The decision was applied in *Duke Group Ltd v Carver* [2001] BPIR 459.

55 Overruling the decision of Evans-Lombe J in *Re JN Taylor Finance Pty Ltd* [1999] 2 BCLC 256. See also *Re Trading Partners* [2002] 1 BCLC 655 (allowing the liquidators of a British Virgin Islands company which mainly operated in England access to the investigatory powers available to liquidators under the Insolvency Act 1986).

56 Laws LJ simply agreed with Morritt LJ. Jonathan Parker LJ did consider whether granting the request would be oppressive under English law and concluded that it would not be, an approach which seems at variance with that of the majority.

57 [2000] OJ L160/1.

rehabilitation or for liquidation.[58] It will not apply to administrative receivership and will only apply to a creditors' voluntary liquidation if confirmed by the court.[59] In *BRAC Rent-A-Car International Inc*,[60] Lloyd J held that the Regulation did not only apply to entities incorporated in a Member State, but gave jurisdiction to the courts of a Member State to open insolvency proceedings in relation to a company incorporated elsewhere if the centre of the company's main interests was in that Member State. This enabled him to make an administration order in respect of a company incorporated in Delaware, but which was based entirely in the UK.

The Regulation distinguishes between 'main' and other proceedings. Main proceedings are those opened in the Member State where the centre of the debtor's main interests is situated.[61] In the case of a company, it will be presumed that this is the state which contains the registered office unless the contrary is proved. Territorial proceedings may be opened in any other state where the debtor has an 'establishment', defined[62] as 'any place of operations where the debtor carries out a non-transitory economic activity with human means and goods'.[63] This provision will restrict the ability of the English courts to make winding up orders against companies whose main centre of interests is in another EU Member State. Where proceedings have not been opened in the state of the debtor's main interests, territorial proceedings can only be opened in another state if proceedings cannot be opened under the law of the state of the main interests or if the territorial proceedings are requested by a creditor domiciled, resident or with a registered office in the state where the establishment is situated, or whose claim arises from the operation of that establishment.[64] The opening of main proceedings does not prevent the opening of territorial proceedings elsewhere; in this case, they will be secondary proceedings (which must be winding up rather than rehabilitative in nature) subject to the provisions of Chapter III of the Regulation. If the opening of territorial proceedings precedes the opening of main proceedings, the territorial proceedings then become secondary proceedings. Secondary proceedings may also be requested by the officeholder in the main proceedings. Where territorial rehabilitative proceedings have been opened before the opening of the main proceedings, the officeholder in the main proceedings may request that they be converted to winding up proceedings if this is in the interest of the creditors in the main proceedings.[65] The Preamble to the Regulation observes that secondary proceedings may serve purposes in addition to the protection of local interests; the estate may be too complex to administer as one unit or the differences between the legal systems concerned may be so great as to make separate proceedings desirable. Officeholders in main proceedings may request a stay of the secondary proceedings, for up to three months in the first instance.

---

58   The proceedings to which the Regulation applies are set out in Arts 1 and 2 and the annexes to the Regulation.
59   The procedure is contained in the new Chapter 10 which has been added to Part 7 of the Insolvency Rules 1986.
60   [2003] 2 All ER 201.
61   Article 3.1.
62   In Art 2(h).
63   Article 3.2.
64   Article 3.4.
65   A new Chapter 7 has been added to both Parts 1 and 2 of the Insolvency Rules 1986 to deal with the procedure for this in the UK.

Main proceedings will normally be effective throughout all other Member States with the same effect as under the domestic law of the state of the proceedings.[66] Territorial and secondary proceedings will have more restricted effect than main proceedings and will only apply to the assets of the debtor in the state where the proceedings were opened. The theoretical universal application of an English insolvency will be amended in a case where there are territorial or secondary proceedings against an insolvent in another state, in that the assets in the latter proceedings will be ring-fenced and recognised as beyond the reach of the English officeholders.[67] The Regulation obliges officeholders in concurrent proceedings to co-operate and communicate with each other.[68]

Whatever the nature of the proceedings (main, territorial or secondary), the law applicable will be that of the state where the proceedings are opened.[69] The officeholder appointed in the main proceedings may exercise all the powers conferred on him or her by the law of the state of the opening of proceedings in any other state provided no insolvency proceedings have been opened there.[70] He or she must comply with the law of the state in which he or she is taking action, particularly in the realisation of assets. An officeholder appointed in territorial or secondary proceedings may reclaim movable property which has been removed from the territory of the state where the proceedings were opened. Articles 5 to 15 lay down conflict of law rules for dealing with situations where parties to a transaction affected by the insolvency are in different Member States. Amongst these are provisions to the effect that the opening of proceedings will have no affect on the rights *in rem* of creditors or third parties over assets belonging to the debtor which are situated in another Member State. Reservation of title rights are similarly preserved. Whether or not set-off is permitted will be determined by the law applicable to the insolvent debtor's claim. The effect of insolvency proceedings on contracts relating to immovable property will be governed by the law in which the property is situated. The effect of insolvency proceedings on contracts of employment will be governed by the law of the contract. Anti-avoidance provisions cannot be employed in relation to an act which is subject to the law of a Member State other than that of the proceedings and that law does not permit the act to be challenged. The effect on pending lawsuits of the insolvency proceedings will be governed by the law of the state in which the lawsuit is pending.

Chapter IV of the Regulation provides for the provision of information to creditors and their entitlement to lodge claims in the proceedings. Any EU creditor will have the right to lodge a claim. Officeholders in one set of proceedings will be entitled to be treated as creditors in proceedings against the debtor in another state.

---

66   The provisions on recognition of insolvency proceedings are to be found in Chapter II of the Regulation.
67   The definition of property in the Insolvency Act 1986, s 436 has been amended by a new s 436A to make it clear that where there are insolvency proceedings both in the UK and another member state, 'property' only includes property which may be dealt with in the UK proceedings.
68   Article 31.
69   Article 4.
70   Article 18.

(d) The UNCITRAL Model Law on Cross-border Insolvency[71]

The United Nations Commission on International Trade Law (UNCITRAL) was established in 1966 as the organ through which the UN can attempt to reduce or remove obstacles to international commerce. The final text of the Model Law on Cross-Border Insolvency was adopted by UNCITRAL in May 1997. It was approved by the General Assembly in December 1997 with a recommendation that Member States review their insolvency legislation and give favourable consideration to enacting the Model Law. The Model Law consists of 32 articles drafted as model provisions capable of being enacted into the existing laws of any state. States can decide to use as much or as little of the Model Law as they see fit and have complete freedom as to how the provisions should be incorporated.

The Model Law is along similar lines to the European Regulation. Chapter II contains provisions enabling access to the courts for representatives of foreign insolvency proceedings (broadly, collective insolvency proceedings subject to court control). On application for recognition, provisional relief may be available (for example, a stay on proceedings). Chapter III provides for recognition of foreign proceedings. These may be recognised as either 'main', if taking place in the state where the debtor has the centre of its main interests, or 'non-main', if taking place in a state where the debtor has an establishment. Article 20 provides for certain automatic consequences of recognition as a main proceeding (for example, a stay over any type of execution against the debtor's rights) and Article 21 contains certain other discretionary powers which apply to all recognised proceedings. Recognition of a foreign proceeding enables the foreign representative to initiate proceedings to avoid acts detrimental to the interests of creditors of the sort available to officeholders in local insolvency proceedings. Chapter IV contains provisions designed to promote cross-border co-operation between courts and officeholders and Chapter V deals with the co-ordination of concurrent proceedings. Creditors are also given rights of access and participation by Chapter II.

Success for the Model Law will depend upon its adoption by a significant number of countries. Reciprocity is not a requirement for the operation of the Model Law, although the extent to which a foreign jurisdiction has enacted the Model Law might be a relevant consideration in exercising a discretion as to whether to provide assistance in relation to an insolvency in that jurisdiction. It is thought that, provided a critical mass of countries were to adopt it, a 'snowballing effect' would then take place.[72] So far the Model Law has only been adopted by Eritrea, Mexico, South Africa and Montenegro. A number of other countries are considering adopting it; these include Australia, Canada, New Zealand and the US. In England, s 14 of the Insolvency Act 2000 provides for the Model Law to be brought into operation by statutory instrument and this forms part of the Insolvency Service Strategic Plan for 2002–05.

---

71   See Fletcher (2000b); Omar (2002).
72   See Fletcher (2000b) at p 174.

BIBLIOGRAPHY

JOURNAL ARTICLES

Note: journal articles have been indicated in the footnotes by the year of publication appearing in brackets after the author's surname.

Abbott — 'Expanding environmental accountability' [2001] Insolv Law 114

Aghion, Hart and Moore 'Insolvency reform in the UK: a revised proposal' (1995) 11 IL&P 67

Armour — 'Who pays when polluters go bust?' (2000) 116 LQR 200

Armour and Deakin — 'Bargaining in the shadow of TUPE' [2000] ILJ 395

Armour and Frisby — 'Rethinking receivership' (2001) 21 OJLS 73

Armstrong and Cerfontaine — 'The rhetoric of inclusion? Corporate governance in insolvency law' [2000] Insolv Law 38

Baird — 'Loss distribution, forum shopping and bankruptcy: a reply to Warren' 54 Univ of Chicago L Rev 815 (1987)

Baird and Jackson — 'Corporate re-organisations and the treatment of diverse ownership interests' 51 Univ of Chicago L Rev 97 (1984)

Baird and Jackson — 'Bargaining after the fall and the contours of the absolute priority rule' 55 Univ of Chicago Law Rev 738 (1988)

Barsby and Ormerod — 'Case comment' [2001] Crim LR 736

Belcher and Beglan — 'Jumping the queue' [1997] JBL 1

Berg — 'Duties of a mortgagee and receiver' [1993] JBL 213

Berg — 'Recharacterisation after Enron' [2003] JBL 205

Bhattacharyya — 'Shadow directors and wrongful trading revisited' (1995) 16 Co Lawyer 313

Breslin — 'Tracing into an overdrawn bank account: when does money cease to exist?' (1995) 16 Co Lawyer 307

Bridge — 'The Quistclose trust in a world of secured transactions' (1992a) 12 OJLS 358

Bridge — 'Form, substance and innovation in personal property security law' [1992b] JBL 1

Brougham — 'Letters: bankruptcy as a means of enforcement' [2002] Fam LJ 396

Brown — 'Administration as liquidation' [1998] JBL 75

Bulman and Fitzsimmons 'To run or not to run ... (the borrower's business)?' [1999] Insolv Law 306

Burger and Schelberg 'The "insolvency plan" in the new German insolvency law' (1995) 11 IL&P 8

Burrows 'Proprietary restitution: unmasking unjust enrichment' (2001) 117 LQR 412

Calnan 'Fashioning the law to suit the practicalities of life' (1998) 114 LQR 174

Campbell 'Investigation by insolvency practitioners: powers and restraints' (2000) 16 IL&P 182 (Part I), 211 (Part II)

Campbell 'Protection by elimination: winding up of companies on public interest grounds' (2001) 17 IL&P 129

Campbell 'The equity for debt proposal: the way forward' (1996) 12 IL&P 14

Clarke 'Children of bankrupts' (1991) Child Law 116

Clarke 'Distress for rent' (1992) 45 CLP 81

Clarke and Rajak 'Case comment on Secretary of State v Mann' (2000) 63 MLR 895

Cohen 'History of imprisonment for debt and its relation to the development of discharge in bankruptcy' (1982) 3(2) Journal of Legal History 153

Collins 'Transfer of undertakings and insolvency' (1989) 18 ILJ 144

Collins 'Ascription of legal responsibility in complex patterns of economic integration' (1990) 53 MLR 731

Cook 'Wrongful trading – is it a real threat to directors or a paper tiger?' [1999] Insolv Law 99

Cooke and Hicks 'Wrongful trading – predicting insolvency' [1993] JBL 338

Cretney 'Women and children last?' (1991) 107 LQR 177

Cross 'Limited Liability Partnerships Act 2000: problems ahead' [2003] JBL 268

Davey 'Insolvency and the family home' [2000] Insolv Law 46

Davies 'Acquired rights, creditors rights, freedom of contract and industrial democracy' (1989) 9 Yearbook of European Law 21

Dawson 'The administrator, morality and the court' [1996] JBL 437

Day and Taylor 'Financial distress in small firms: the role played by debt covenants and other monitoring devices' [2001] Insolv Law 97

De Lacy 'Retention of title and claims against processed goods' (1997) 13 IL&P 163

De Lacy 'Corporate insolvency and retention of title clauses: developments in Australia' [2001] Insolv Law 64

Diamond	'The reform of the law of security interests' (1989) 42 CLP 231
Dine	'Punishing directors' [1994] JBL 325
Dine	'The disqualification of company directors' (1988) 9 Co Lawyer 213
Drake	'Disqualification of directors – the "red card"' [1989] JBL 474
Evans	'Decision in the Court of Appeal in Morris v Agriculturals Ltd' (1996) 17 Co Lawyer 102
Evans and Pond	'Debtor non-co-operation in IVAs' (1995) 11 IL&P 95
Fennell	'Selling litigation – assignment of causes of action by insolvency office-holders' (1997) 13 IL&P 106
Fennessy and Tamlyn	'Case comment on Re Brumark' [2002] Insolv Law 56
Ferran	'Floating charges – the nature of the security' [1988] CLJ 213
Finch	'Directors' duties towards creditors' (1989) 10 Co Lawyer 23
Finch	'Disqualification of directors: a plea for competence' (1990) 53 MLR 385
Finch	'Company directors: who cares about skill and care?' (1992) 55 MLR 179
Finch	'Disqualifying directors: issues of rights, privileges and employment' (1993) 22 ILJ 35
Finch	'Personal accountability and corporate control' (1994) 57 MLR 880
Finch	'The measures of insolvency law' (1997) 17 OJLS 227
Finch	'Insolvency practitioners: regulation and reform' [1998] JBL 334
Finch	'Security, insolvency and risk: who pays the price?' (1999a) 62 MLR 633
Finch	'Controlling the insolvency professionals' [1999b] Insolv Law 228
Finch	'Is pari passu passé?' [2000] Insolv Law 194
Finch	'Public interest liquidation: PIL or placebo?' [2002] Insolv Law 157
Finch and Freedman	'The Limited Liability Partnership: pick & mix or mix up?' [2002] JBL 475
Fletcher	'The genesis of modern insolvency law' [1989] JBL 385
Fletcher	'"Voidable preference" judicially explained' [1991] JBL 71
Fletcher	'The silence of the wolves: confidentiality and self-incrimination' [1992] JBL 442
Fletcher	'The ascendence of Comity from the ashes of Felixstowe Dock' [1993] 6 Insolv Intelligence 10

Fletcher	'Subordination agreements and the *pari passu* rule' [1994] JBL 282
Fletcher	'Adoption of contracts of employment' [1995] JBL 596
Fletcher	'International insolvency issues: recent cases' [1997a] JBL 471
Fletcher	'Cross border assistance under s 426' [1997b] JBL 480
Fletcher	'Making a better world – current international initiatives in cross-border insolvency' (1999) 12 Insolv Intelligence 4 and 20
Fletcher	'A new age of international insolvency – the countdown has begun' (2000a) 13 Insolv Intelligence 57 and 68
Fletcher	'Insolvency bridges to the future' [2000b] CFiLR 161
Fletcher	'S426 assistance restated and expanded' (2000c) 13 Insolv Intelligence 38
Floyd	'Changes in the channel' (1989) 5 IL&P 177
Floyd	'Corporate recovery: the London approach' (1995) 11 IL&P 82
Floyd	'The dinosaur must go – do we need the Insolvency Service?' (1999) 15 IL&P 85
Frisby	'Making a silk purse out of a pig's ear' (2000a) 63 MLR 413
Frisby	'TUPE or not TUPE? Employee protection, corporate rescue and "one unholy mess"' [2000b] CFiLR 249
Godfrey	'The turnaround practitioner – adviser or director?' (2002) 18 IL&P 3
Godfrey and Nield	'The wrongful trading provisions – all bark and no bite?' (1995) 11 IL&P 139
Goode	'Is the law too favourable to secured creditors?' (1983–84) 8 Can Bus LJ 53
Goode	'The modernization of personal property security law' (1984) 100 LQR 234
Goode	'Charge backs and legal fictions' (1998) 114 LQR 178
Goode	'Ownership and obligation in commercial transactions' (1987) 103 LQR 433
Goode	'Charges over book debts: a missed opportunity' (1994) 110 LQR 592
Goodhart and Jones	'The infiltration of equitable doctrines into English commercial law' (1980) 43 MLR 489
Graham	'Cross-border insolvency' (1989) 42 CLP 217
Grantham	'Directors' duties and insolvent companies' (1991) 54 MLR 576
Grantham	'Liability of parent companies for the actions of the directors of their subsidiaries' (1997) 18 Co Lawyer 138

Grantham and Rickett	'Tracing and property rights: the categorical truth' (2000) 63 MLR 905
Griffin	'*De facto* directors' [2000] CFiLR 126
Griffin	'Accelerating disqualification under s 10 CDDA' [2002] Insolv Law 32
Griffin	'Standard of proof applicable to s 6 of the Company Directors Disqualification Act 1986' (1997) 18 Co Lawyer 24
Haley	'The *O'Brien* defence – a compromise reworked?' [2002] Child & Family Law Quarterly 93
Hamilton *et al*	'Back from the dead: survival potential in administrative receiverships' (1997) 13 IL&P 78
Hardy	'Some TUPE implications for insolvency lawyers' [2003] Insolv Law 24
Harper	'Mortgagees and county court administration orders' (1997) 13 IL&P 43
Harpum	'Accessory liability for procuring or assisting a breach of trust' (1995) 111 LQR 545
Harrison	'The Insolvency Practices Council' [2002] Insolv Law 175
Hemsworth	'Voidable preference: desire and effect' (2000) 16 IL&P 54
Hemsworth	'Mortgagees and county court administration orders' (1997) 13 IL&P 48
Hepple and Byre	'EEC labour law in the UK: a new approach' (1989) 18 ILJ 129
Hicks	'Company law reform in Singapore' (1987) 8 Co Lawyer 243
Hicks	'Disqualification of directors – forty years on' [1988] JBL 27
Hicks	'Retention of title – latest developments' [1992] JBL 398
Hicks	'Wrongful trading – has it been a failure?' (1993) 9 IL&P 134
Hicks	'Corporate form: questioning the unsung hero' [1997] JBL 306
Hicks	'Director disqualification – the National Audit Office follows up' (1999a) 15 IL&P 112
Hicks	'Director disqualification – is it a lottery?' (1999b) 15 IL&P 73
Hicks	'Director disqualification: can it deliver?' [2001] JBL 433
Hicks	'Directors' liability for management errors' 110 LQR 390
Hiley	'Directors' duties and the interests of creditors' (1989) 10 Co Lawyer 87
Ho and St J Smart	'Re-interpreting the *Quistclose* trust' (2001) OJLS 267
Hoey	'Disqualifying delinquent directors' (1997) 18 Co Lawyer 130

Hoffmann	'The fourth Annual Leonard Sainer Lecture' (1997) 18 Co Lawyer 194
Homan	'Cross-border insolvency in fifteen minutes' [2002] Insolv Intelligence 60
Hunter	'The nature and functions of a rescue culture' [1999] JBL 491
Ingram	'TUPE reforms and pensions – how far will the government go?' [2002] Employment Law Bulletin 5
Jackson	'Translating assets and liabilities to the bankruptcy forum' (1985) 14 Journal of Legal Studies 73
Jackson	'Bankruptcy, non-bankruptcy entitlements and the creditors' bargain' (1982) 92 Yale LJ 857
Jackson and Kronman	'Secured financing and priorities among creditors' (1979) 88 Yale LJ 1143
Jefferson	'Directors, controlling shareholders, employees and rights on insolvency' (1998) 19 Co Lawyer 307
Katz and Mumford	'Should Investigating Accountants be allowed to become administrative receivers?' ICAEW Discussion Paper, September 1999
Keay	'Public interest petitions' (1999) 20 Co Lawyer 296
Keay	'Preferences in liquidation law: time for a change' [1998a] 2 CFiLR 198
Keay	'The avoidance of pre-liquidation transactions: an Anglo-Australian comparison' [1998b] JBL 515
Keay	'The recovery of voidable preferences: aspects of restoration' [2000a] 1 CFiLR 1
Keay	'Supervision and control of liquidators' [2000b] Conveyancer 295
Keay	'The advent of a national scheme to protect entitlements of employees in Australia' [2000c] Insolv Law 137
Keay	'Balancing interests in insolvency law' [2001a] CLWR 30
Keay	'Claims for malicious presentation' [2001b] Insolv Law 136
Keay	'Funding litigation' [2002a] Insolv Law 90
Keay	'The duty of directors to take account of creditors' interests: has it any role to play?' [2002b] JBL 379
Keay and Walton	'The preferential debts regime' [1998] CFiLR 84
Keay and Walton	'Preferential debts: an empirical study' [1999] Insolv Law 112
Lawson	'The reform of the law relating to security interests in property' [1989] JBL 287

Leigh	'Disqualification orders in company and insolvency law' (1986) 7 Co Lawyer 179
Leporte	'Security interests over receivables: divergent trends in the US and the UK' [2002] JBL 220
Lightman	'The challenges ahead' [1996] JBL 113
Lightman	'Office-holders' charges' [1998] Insolv Intelligence 1
Lowe	'Disclaimer: a bitter pill for guarantors' (1996) 12 IL&P 148
Marks and Emmet	'Administrative receivers' [1994] JBL 1
Marshall	'Office-holders' inquisitorial powers' (1997) 13 IL&P 66 and 118
McCartney	'Disclaimer of leases and its impact: the "pecking order"' (2002) 18 IL&P 79
McCormack	'Self-incrimination in the corporate context' [1993] JBL 425
McCormack	'Charge backs and commercial certainty in the House of Lords' [1998] CFiLR 111
McCormack	'Receiverships and the rescue culture' [2000] 2 CFiLR 229
McCormack	'Notice filing versus transaction filing' [2002a] Insolv Law 166
McCormack	'Security interest in deposit accounts: an Anglo-American perspective' [2002b] Insolv Law 7
McCormack	'The floating charge and the Law Commission consultation paper' [2003] Insolv Law 2
Miller	'The effect of insolvency on financial provision and property adjustment on divorce' (1994) 10 IL&P 66
Miller	'Bankruptcy as a means of enforcement in family proceedings' [2002a] Fam LJ 21
Miller	'Income Payments Order' (2002b) 18 IL&P 43
Millett	'The *Quistclose* Trust' (1985) 101 LQR 271
Millett	'Tracing the proceeds of fraud' (1991a) 107 LQR 71
Millett	'Restitution and constructive trusts' (1998) 114 LQR 399
Milman	'Curbing the phoenix syndrome' [1997] JBL 224
Milman	'Ten per cent fund' [1999] Insolv Law 47
Milman	'Post liquidation tax as a winding-up expense' [2000a] Insolv Law 169
Milman	'Fresh light on shadow directors' [2000b] Insolv Law 171
Milman	'Subrogation claims on insolvency' [2000c] Insolv Law 130
Milman	'Clawback and limited liability partnerships' [2001a] Insolv Law 7

Milman	'Schemes of arrangement: their continuing role' [2001b] Insolv Law 135
Milman	'The "phoenix" syndrome' [2001c] Insolv Law 199
Milman	'A new deal for companies and unsecured creditors' (2000d) 21 Co Lawyer 59
Milman and Davey	'Debtor rehabilitation' [1996] JBL 541
Milman and Parry	'A study of the operation of transactional avoidance mechanisms in corporate insolvency practice' ILA Research Report, 1997
Milman and Parry	'Transaction avoidance provisions in corporate insolvency' (1998) 14 IL&P 280
Mitchell and Stockdale	'Your answers may not be used in evidence against you' (2002) 23 Co Lawyer 32
Mokal	'Priority as pathology: the *pari passu* myth' [2001a] CLJ 581
Mokal	'The authentic consent model' [2001b] Legal Studies 400
Mokal	'The search for someone to save: a defensive case for the priority of secured credit' [2002] OJLS 22
Moss	'Cross-frontier co-operation in insolvency' [1999] Insolv Law 146
Moss and Segal	'The expenses doctrine in liquidation, administration and receivership' [1997] CFiLR 1
Mujih	'Legitimising charge-backs' [2001] Insolv Law 3
Nolan	'Less equal than others' [1995] JBL 485
Oakley	'Proprietary claims and their priority in insolvency' [1995] CLJ 377
Oditah	'Legal aspects of receivables financing' [1991] JBL 49
Oditah	'Case comment on Welsh Development Agency' [1992] JBL 541
Oditah	'Fixed charges over book debts after *Brumark*' [2001] Insolv Intelligence 49
Ogilvie	'Rehabilitation, equity and efficiency: the new bankruptcy law in Canada' [1994] JBL 304
Omar	'The UNCITRAL insolvency initiative: a five-year review' [2002] Insolv Law 228
Parry	'The destination of proceeds of insolvency litigation' [2002] Co Lawyer 49
Pasban	'Directors' liabilities of an insolvent company in the US and England' [2001] JBL 33
Paulden	'Corporate fraud: civil disclosures in criminal proceedings' (1994) 57 MLR 280

Pearson	'Asset tracing and recovery' (2002) 18 IL&P 90
Pennington	'The interchangeability of fixed and floating charges' [2003a] Company Law 60
Pennington	'Should debentureholders be required to meet the costs of winding up the company?' [2003b] Company Law 119
Pennington	'The genesis of the floating charge' (1960) 23 MLR 630
Petersen	'The end of New Bullas' [2002] Company Law 1
Phillips	'The administration procedure and creditors' voluntary arrangements: the case for radical reform' (1996) Insolv Law 14
Pickin	'Getting rid of waste management licences' [1999] Insolv Intelligence 79
Pollard	'Adopted employees in insolvency' (1995) 24 ILJ 141
Pollard	'Insolvent companies and TUPE' (1996) 25 ILJ 191
Pollard	'Insolvency set off and employees' (1995) 11 IL&P 46
Pond	'The Individual Voluntary Arrangement experience' [1995] JBL 118
Pond	'New rules and new roles for the Individual Voluntary Arrangement' (2002) 18 IL&P 9
Pond	'An alternative to bankruptcy - an empirical study of Individual Voluntary Arrangements' (1989) Loughborough University Banking Centre Research Monograph
Pond	'Do Individual Voluntary Arrangements really work?' (1993) Loughborough University Banking Centre Research Monograph
Prentice	'Preferences and defective floating charges' (1993) 109 LQR 373
Pugh	'Overcoming the handicap of a lack of funding in pursuing recoveries by insolvency practitioners' (1996) 12 IL&P 167
Rajani	'Director disqualification undertakings and the *Blackspur* case' (2002) 18 IL&P 14
Rickett	'Different views on the scope of the *Quistclose* analysis' (1991) 107 LQR 608
Robinson	'By the time I get to Phoenix ...' (1996) 12 IL&P 160
Rumley	'Brumark: where are we now?' [2003] Insolv Intelligence 19
Ryder	'Banking on credit unions in the new millennium' [2001a] Insolv Law 164 and [2001b] JBL 510
Sargeant	'An amended acquired rights directive' [1998] JBL 577
Sargeant	'Transferring liability for employee claims' [2000] JBL 188
Sargeant	New transfer regulations' [2002a] ILJ 35

Sargeant	'Proposed transfer regulations and insolvency' [2002b] JBL 108
Schulte	'Enforcing wrongful trading' (1999) 20 Co Lawyer 80
Schulte	'Corporate groups and the equitable subordination of claims on insolvency' (1997) 18 Co Lawyer 2
Schumacher	'Business transfers and insolvency: case law of the German Federal Labour Court' (1994) 23 ILJ 101
Sealy	'Directors' duties revisited' (2001) 22 Co Lawyer 79
Sealy	'Mortgagees and receivers – a duty of care resurrected and extended' [2000] CLJ 31
Simmons	'What proceedings are barred by an administration order?' (2003) 16 Insolv Intelligence 9
Singleton	'Interest on unpaid bills – the new rules' [2002] Consumer Law Today 8
Smart	'*Forum non conveniens* in bankruptcy proceedings' [1989] JBL 126
Stapledon	'A parent company's liability for the debts of an insolvent subsidiary' (1995) 16 Co Lawyer 152
Stevens	'Vindicating the proprietary nature of tracing' [2001] Conveyancer 94
Tettenborn	'Remedies for recovery of money paid by mistake' [1980] CLJ 272
Tjio	'The future for company charges' [2002] JBL 457
Tolmie	'Funding litigation by liquidators: a consideration of the amendment to rule 4.218' [2003] Insolv Law 153
Trower	'Human rights: Article 6 – the reality and the myth' [2001] Insolv Law 48
Turing	'Set-off and cash collateral: three important cases of 1995' [1996] JBL 170
Unwin	'Lien over title deeds' (2003) Insolv Intelligence 4
Villiers	'Employees as creditors: a challenge for justice in insolvency law' (1999) 20 Co Lawyer 222
Walters	'Leave to act as a company director following disqualification' (1999) Co Lawyer 239
Walters	'Directors' disqualification: the Vice Chancellor's address' (2000a) Co Lawyer 90
Walters	'Staying proceedings on the grounds of champerty' [2000b] Insolv Law 16
Walters	'Case comment on *Re Floor Fourteen*' (2001a) 22 Co Lawyer

Walters	'Directors' disqualification after the Insolvency Act 2000: the new regime' [2001b] Insolv Law 86
Walters	'Bare undertakings in disqualification proceedings' (2002) 23 Co Lawyer 123
Walters	'Unlawful preferences and proprietary rights' (2003a) 119 LQR 28
Walters	'Recovery costs of litigation as a liquidation expense' (2003b) Co Lawyer 84
Walters	'A modern doctrine of champerty' (1996) 112 LQR 560
Warren	'Bankruptcy policy' 54 Univ of Chicago L Rev 775 (1987)
Wheeler	'Swelling the assets for distribution in corporate insolvency' [1993] JBL 256
Wheeler	'Directors' disqualification: insolvency practitioners and the decision making process' (1995) Legal Studies 283
Whiteson	'Retention of title over cows and sheep' (1997) 13 IL&P 25
Winterborne	'The second hand cause of action market' (2001) Insolv Intelligence 65
Worthington	'Floating charges – an alternative theory' [1994] CLJ 81
Yeo and Tjio	'The Quistclose Trust' (2003) 119 LQR 8
Ziegel	'Set-off and cash collateral: three important cases of 1995' [1995] CLJ 430

BOOKS

Argenti	*Corporate Collapse*, 1976, McGraw Hill
Belcher	*Corporate Rescue*, 1997, Sweet & Maxwell
Berthoud and Kempson	*Credit and Debt: The PSI Report*, 1992, Policy Studies Institute
Bhandari and Weiss	*Corporate Bankruptcy: Economic and Legal Perspectives*, 1996, CUP
Carruthers and Halliday	*Rescuing Business; The Making of Corporate Bankruptcy Law in England and the US*, 1998, Clarendon
Cheffins	*Theory, Structure and Operation of Companies*, 1997, OUP
Clarke (ed)	*Current Issues in Insolvency Law*, 1991, Sweet & Maxwell
Cornish and Clark	*Law and Society in England 1750–1950*, 1989, Sweet & Maxwell
Cranston (ed)	*Making Commercial Law*, 1997, Clarendon
Davies	*Gower's Principles of Modern Company Law*, 6th edn, 1997, Sweet & Maxwell
Derham	*Set Off*, 3rd edn, 2002, Clarendon
Dicey and Morris	*The Conflict of Laws*, 13th edn, 2000, Sweet & Maxwell

Farrar and Hannigan	*Farrar's Company Law*, 4th edn, 1998, Butterworths
Ferran	*Company Law and Corporate Finance*, 1999, OUP
Finch	*Corporate Insolvency Law: Perspectives and Principles*, 2002, CUP
Fletcher	*Law of Insolvency*, 3rd edn, 2002, Sweet & Maxwell
Fletcher	*Insolvency in Private International Law*, 1997, OUP
Ford	*Consuming Credit: Debt and Poverty in the UK*, 1991, CPAG
Franks and Sussman	*The Cycle of Corporate Distress, Rescue and Dissolution: A Study of Small and Medium Size UK Companies*, April 2000, Institute of Finance and Accounts
Goff and Jones	*Law of Restitution*, 6th edn, 2002, Sweet & Maxwell
Goode	*Principles of Corporate Insolvency*, 2nd edn, 1997, Sweet & Maxwell
Goode	*Commercial Law*, 2nd edn, 1995, Penguin
Goode	*Legal Problems of Credit and Security*, 2nd edn, 1998, Sweet & Maxwell
Gough	*Company Charges*, 2nd edn, 1996, Butterworths
Gray	*Elements of Land Law*, 3rd edn, 2000, Butterworths
Griffin	*Personal Liability and Disqualification of Company Directors*, 1999, Hart
Hanbury and Martin	*Modern Equity*, 16th edn, 2001, Sweet & Maxwell
Hayton	*Cases and Commentary on the Law of Trusts and Equitable Remedies*, 11th edn, 2001, Sweet & Maxwell
Holdsworth	*A History of English Law*, Vol 8, 2nd edn, 1937, Methuen
Howell *et al*	*Aspects of Credit and Debt*, 1993, Sweet & Maxwell
Jackson	*The Logic and Limits of Bankruptcy Law*, 1986, Harvard UP
Justice	*Insolvency Law: An Agenda for Reform*, 1994, Justice
Kempson	*Money Advice and Debt Counselling*, 1995, Policy Studies Institute
Lawson and Rudden	*The Law of Property*, 3rd edn, 2002, OUP
Lightman and Moss	*The Law of Receivers and Administrators of Companies*, 3rd edn, 2000, Sweet & Maxwell
Lingard	*Corporate Rescue and Insolvencies*, 2nd edn, 1989, Butterworths
Markham Lester	*Victorian Insolvency*, 1995, Clarendon
McCormack	*Registration of Company Charges*, 1994, Sweet & Maxwell
McCormack	*Reservation of Title*, 2nd edn, 1995, Sweet & Maxwell
Morse	*Partnership Law*, 5th edn, 2001, Blackstone

Muscat	*The Liability of the Holding Company for the Debts of its Insolvent Subsidiaries*, 1996, Dartmouth
Oditah	*Legal Aspects of Receivables Financing*, 1991, Sweet & Maxwell
Prentice	'Effect of insolvency on pre-liquidation transactions', in Pettet (ed), *Company Law in Change*, 1987, Stevens
Rajak (ed)	*Insolvency Law: Theory and Practice*, 1993, Sweet & Maxwell
Ramsey (ed)	*Debtors and Creditors: A Socio-Legal Perspective*, 1986, Professional Books
Rose (ed)	*Restitution and Insolvency*, 2000, Mansfield
Rubin and Sugarman	*Law, Economy and Society*, 1984, Abingdon,
Schmittoff and Wooldridge (eds)	*Groups of Companies*, 1991, Sweet & Maxwell
Sealy	*Disqualification and Personal Liability of Directors*, 5th edn, 2000, CCH
Simpson	*A History of the Common Law of Contract*, 1975, Clarendon
Smart	*Cross Border Insolvency*, 1998, Butterworths
Smith	*Law of Tracing*, 1997, Clarendon
Walters and Davis-White	*Directors' Disqualification: Law and Practice*, 1999, Sweet & Maxwell
Wood	*English and International Set-off*, 1989, Sweet & Maxwell
Ziegel (ed)	*Current Developments in International and Comparative Corporate Insolvency Law*, 1994, Clarendon

GOVERNMENT PUBLICATIONS

Baldwin	*Evaluating the Effectiveness of Enforcement Procedures in Undefended Claims in the Civil Courts*, 2003, LCD
Beatson	*Independent Review of Bailiff Law*, July 2000
CLRSG	*Final Report*, July 2001
CLRSG	*Completing The Structure*, November 2000
Crowther	*Report of the Crowther Committee on Consumer Credit*, 1971, Cmnd 4596
Diamond	*Review of Security Interests in Property*, 1988, DTI
Dominy and Kempson	*Can't Pay or Won't Pay*, 2003, LCD Research
DTI	*Quinquennial Review of the Insolvency Service*, 2000
DTI	*Opportunity for All in a World of Change*, 2001, White Paper
HM Treasury	*Taskforce Report Credit Unions of the Future*, 1999, HMSO

Insolvency Service	*Bankruptcy – A Fresh Start*, 2000
Insolvency Service	*Review of Company Rescue and Business Reconstruction Mechanisms*, 2000
Kempson	*Household Survey on Cause, Extent and Effects of Overindebtedness*, November 2002
Law Commission	*Registration of Security Interests: Company Charges and Property other than Land*, July 2002
Law Commission	*Sale of Goods Forming Part of a Bulk*, 1993, Law Com No 215, Scot Law Com No 145, HC 807
LCD	*Effective Enforcement: Improved Methods of Recovery*, March 2003, White Paper
LCD	*Distress for Rent*, May 2001, Consultation Paper
LCD	*Towards Effective Enforcement: A Single Piece of Bailiff Law*, May 2002a, Green Paper
LCD	*National Standards for Enforcement Agents*, May 2002b
White Paper	*Productivity and Enterprise – Insolvency: A Second Chance*, 2001, Cm 5234, DTI
White Paper	*Revised Framework on Insolvency Law*, 1984, Cmnd 9175, DTI: HMSO

OTHER

| British Bankers' Association | *Banks and Businesses: Working Together When You Borrow. A Statement of Principles*, March 2001, British Banking Association |

WEBSITES

Association of British Credit Unions	http://www.abcul.org
Bank of England	http://www.bankofengland.co.uk
British Bankers' Association	http://www.bba.org.uk
Consumer Credit Association	http://www.ccauk.org
Consumer Credit Counselling Service	http://www.ccss.co.uk
Council of Mortgage Lenders	http://www.cml.org.uk
Credit Services Association	http://www.csa-uk.com
ESRC Centre for Business Research, Cambridge	http://www.cr.cam.ac.uk
Finance and Leasing Association	http://www.fla.org.uk

INDEX